Note to the Student

The *Study Guide,* prepared by the authors, will help you master the text material by providing a summary of essential points in each chapter and testing your knowledge with a series of objective questions and exercises. Each chapter contains highlights from each text chapter, True/False Questions, Completion, Multiple Choice, and Test Yourself Exercises. Have your bookstore or instructor order one for you today.

Software

Sanfield, Incorporated: A Computerized Audit Case by Arsan & Satterfield, both of West Georgia College, lets students analyze company status through Lotus templates. Transactions are described in the accompanying manual. The package contains two diskettes for use with an IBM PC and any version of Lotus®1-2-3®.

We at Irwin sincerely hope that this text package will assist you in reaching your goals both now and in the future.

Principles of Auditing

The Robert N. Anthony/Willard J. Graham Series in Accounting

Principles of Auditing

Walter B. Meigs
University of Southern California

O. Ray Whittington
School of Accountancy
San Diego State University

Kurt Pany
School of Accountancy
Arizona State University

Robert F. Meigs
School of Accountancy
San Diego State University

1989 Ninth Edition

Homewood, IL   60430
Boston, MA   02116

Material from Uniform CPA Examination Questions and Unofficial Answers, copyright ©
1977, 1978, 1979, 1980, 1981, 1982, 1983, 1984, 1985, 1986, 1987, 1988 by the American
Institute of Certified Public Accountants, Inc., is reprinted (or adapted) with permission.

Sponsoring editor: Ron M. Regis
Project editor: Waivah Clement
Production manager: Irene H. Sotiroff
Compositor: Bi-Comp, Incorporated
Typeface: 10/12 Times Roman
Printer: R. R. Donnelley & Sons Company

LIBRARY OF CONGRESS
Library of Congress Cataloging-in-Publication Data

Principles of auditing/Walter B. Meigs . . . [et al.].—9th ed.
    p.   cm.
    Rev. ed. of: Principals of auditing/Walter B. Meigs, O. Ray
Whittington, Robert F. Meigs. 8th ed. 1985.
    Includes bibliographies and index.
    ISBN 0-256-06803-8
    1. Auditing. I. Meigs, Walter B. II. Meigs, Walter B.
Principles of auditing.
HF5667.M43 1989   88–19834
657'.45—dc19   CIP

Printed in the United States of America
    3 4 5 6 7 8 9 0 DO 5 4 3 2 1 0 9

Preface

In an attempt to close a gap between the way in which users perceive auditors' report, and made an unprecedented one-time change in pro- the profession has adopted a new code of professional conduct, made changes in the generally accepted auditing standards, revised the standard auditors' report, and made an unprecedented one-time change in professional standards. These developments make the introductory auditing course both more interesting and more challenging. We have comprehensively revised the ninth edition of *Principles of Auditing* to provide complete coverage of these important new professional developments.

The first 10 chapters emphasize the philosophy and environment of the auditing profession, with special attention paid to the nature and economic purpose of auditing, auditing standards, professional conduct, legal liability of auditors, the auditors' consideration of internal control, audit sampling, and the nature of audit evidence. Subsequent chapters deal with the various internal control cycles and auditing techniques in an organized and understandable manner. In the final two chapters, we discuss the auditors' reporting responsibilities and other attestation and accounting services, such as compilations and reviews of financial statements and reports on prospective financial statements.

FEATURES OF THIS EDITION

This edition of our textbook contains a host of learning and instructional aids. Among the major features of this edition are the following:

Study objectives for each chapter provide the students with a concise summary of the important concepts that should be mastered.

Research and Discussion Cases, provocative case-study situations often based upon actual auditing dilemmas. These cases are designed to acquaint students with the process of researching auditing problems and to illustrate the inescapable need for exercising personal professional judgment. These cases, which are labeled as "Group IV" problem material, are provided for a majority of our chapters.

An increased number of *illustrations, tables, and flow charts.* These graphic displays have been designed to visually summarize key points.

For example, the procedural chapters of the text contain new tables that clearly relate audit procedures to their objectives. Also increased in number are the *Illustrative Cases,* using actual business examples to illustrate important concepts.

A *Study Guide,* written by the textbook authors, enables your students to review textbook material and to test their understanding. The guide includes a summary of the highlights of each chapter and an abundance of objective questions and exercises. Answers to the questions and exercises are included at the back of the guide to provide students with immediate feedback.

Our *Instructors' Lecture Guide* includes topical outlines of each chapter, the authors' personal comments on each chapter, and numerous instructional aids, such as transparency masters and topics to supplement classroom discussions. A *Manual of Tests* is available which includes many original questions and problems as well as questions adapted from various professional examinations.

The chapter on the audit of electronic data processing systems includes control and audit considerations relating to advanced computer systems and to minicomputers. Throughout the textbook, we have increased the emphasis upon auditing in an EDP environment.

Our discussion of professional conduct covers emerging, controversial issues which illustrate the need for judgment in evaluating situations that might impair independence.

Our easy to understand chapter on audit sampling places emphasis on the basic concepts of importance to every auditor. For those who want to place more emphasis on statistical techniques, two appendixes have been added to the chapter to describe in detail the computational aspects of the audit risk model and probability-proportional-to-size sampling.

An extensively revised last chapter distinguishes between the responsibilities of a CPA when performing attestation services and those of a CPA performing accounting services. Emphasis is placed on the responsibilities assumed by the CPA in issuing special reports, reports on internal control, reports on prospective financial statements, and performing accounting and review services.

Both text discussion and problem material have been updated to reflect the latest pronouncements of the Auditing Standards Board, the Accounting and Review Services Committee, the SEC, the GASB, and the FASB. This material is integrated into text and problem material to assure coverage of all topical areas included in recent CPA examinations. In addition, both the text and problem material have been expanded to include coverage of topics that are simply too controversial to be taken up by the professional standard-setting committees.

END-OF-CHAPTER PROBLEM MATERIAL

The questions, problems, and case materials at the end of each chapter are divided as follows: Group I—Review Questions; Group II—Questions Requiring Analysis; Group III—Problems; and Group IV—Research and Discussion Cases.

The review questions are closely related to the material in the chapter and provide a convenient means of determining whether the student has grasped the major ideas and implications which are contained in that chapter.

The questions requiring analysis call for thoughtful appraisal of realistic auditing situations and the application of generally accepted auditing standards. Many of these Group II questions are taken from CPA examinations, others from actual audit engagements. These thought-provoking questions requiring analysis differ from the Group III problems in that they are generally shorter and tend to stress value judgments and conflicting opinions.

Many of the Group III problems have been drawn from CPA examinations; in the selection of these problems, consideration was given to all auditing problems that have appeared in CPA examinations in recent years. Other problems reflect actual audit situations from the experience of practicing accountants. Many of the problems are new, but problems appearing in the previous editions have been retained (usually with some modification) if they were superior to other available problems. In response to the recent shift in content of the auditing section of the CPA examination, problems requiring extensive working papers and quantitative applications have been minimized, and short case-type questions have been emphasized. Also, the number of multiple choice questions has been increased by fifty percent over that included in the eighth edition.

RESEARCH AND DISCUSSION CASES

A pedagogical feature that began with the eighth edition is the inclusion of Research and Discussion Cases in the end-of-chapter problem material. These cases involve controversial situations that do not lend themselves to clear-cut answers. Students are asked to research the appropriate auditing and accounting literature and then to formulate and justify their personal positions on the issue. The cases are designed to acquaint students with the professional literature, to develop research and communications skills, and to demonstrate that several diverse yet defensible positions may be argued persuasively in a given situation. Research and Discussion Cases appear as Group IV problem material at the ends of Chapters 2, 3, 4, 5, 7, 10, 12, 14, 18, and 19.

REFERENCES TO AUTHORITATIVE SOURCES

Numerous references are made to the pronouncements of the Auditing Standards Boards, the Accounting and Review Services Committee, the American Institute of Certified Public Accountants, the Financial Accounting Standards Board, and the Securities and Exchange Commission. Special attention is given to the *Code of Professional Conduct,* to *Statements on Standards for Accounting and Review Services,* and to *Statements on Auditing Standards.* The cooperation of the AICPA in permitting the use of its published materials and of questions from the Uniform CPA Examination brings to an auditing text an element of authority not otherwise available.

CONTRIBUTIONS BY OTHERS

We want to express our sincere thanks to the many users of the preceding editions who offered helpful suggestions for this edition. Especially helpful were the advice and suggestions of the following reviewers: Louis Braiotta, State University of New York; Kurt E. Chaloupecky, Southwest Missouri State University; Wai P. Lam, University of Windsor; Don Loster, University of California, Santa Barbara; and Sharon Robinson, Frostburg State College.

Walter B. Meigs
O. Ray Whittington
Kurt Pany
Robert F. Meigs

Contents

tions. Lawsuits by clients. Third-party beneficiaries enjoy the same rights as clients. AUDITORS' LIABILITY TO OTHER THIRD PARTIES. Liability to third parties under common law. Liability to third parties under statutory law. Securities Act of 1933. Securities Exchange Act of 1934. Comparison of the 1933 and 1934 Acts. The Racketeer Influenced and Corrupt Organizations Act. Auditors' civil liability: a summary. Auditors' criminal liability under the Securities Acts. The SEC's regulation of accountants. Accountants' liability for accounting and review services. The CPAs' posture in the age of litigation.

THE AUDITORS' CONSIDERATION OF INTERNAL CONTROL IN AN EDP SYSTEM. Obtain an understanding of internal control sufficient to plan the audit. Assess control risk and design additional tests of controls. Conduct additional tests of controls. Computer service centers. Reassess control risk and design substantive tests.

DEPRECIATION. The auditors' perspective toward depreciation. Accelerated Cost Recovery System (ACRS). The auditors' objectives in auditing depreciation. Audit program—depreciation expense and accumulated depreciation. Testing the client's provision for depreciation. Verification of natural resources. Verification of intangible assets. Examination of plant and equipment in advance of the balance sheet date. Unaudited replacement cost information.

ACCOUNTS PAYABLE. Sources and nature of accounts payable. The auditors' approach in examination of accounts payable. Internal control over accounts payable. Internal control and the computer. Audit working papers for accounts payable. AUDIT PROGRAM. OTHER LIABILITIES. Amounts withheld from employees' pay. Sales taxes payable. Unclaimed wages. Customers' deposits. Accrued liabilities. Balance sheet presentation. Time of examination.

INTEREST-BEARING DEBT. Sources and nature of interest-bearing debt. The auditors' approach in examination of interest-bearing debt. Internal control over interest-bearing debt. Audit working papers. AUDIT PROGRAM FOR INTEREST-BEARING DEBT. Time of examination—interest-bearing debt. EQUITY CAPITAL. Sources and nature of owners' equity. The auditors' approach in examination of owners' equity. Internal control for owners' equity. Control of capital stock transactions by the board of directors. Independent registrar and stock transfer agent. The stock certificate book. The stockholders ledger. Internal control over dividends. Audit working papers for owners' equity. AUDIT PROGRAM—CAPITAL STOCK. RETAINED EARNINGS AND DIVIDENDS. Time of examination—stockholders' equity. Financial statement presentation of stockholders' equity. AUDIT OF SOLE PROPRIETORSHIPS AND PARTNERSHIPS. DISCLOSURE OF CONTINGENCIES. Commitments. General risk contingencies. Audit procedures for loss contingencies. Liability representations. Financial presentation of loss contingencies.

Nature of revenue and expenses. The auditors' approach in examination of revenues and expenses. REVENUE. Relationship of revenue to balance sheet accounts. Miscellaneous revenue. EXPENSES. Relationship of expenses to balance sheet accounts. Audit program for selling, general, and administrative expenses. THE AUDIT OF PAYROLL. Internal control. Methods of achieving internal control. The employment function. Timekeeping. Payroll records and payroll preparation. Distributing paychecks or cash to employees. Description of internal control for payroll. Audit program for payrolls. INCOME STATEMENT PRESENTATION.

How much detail in the income statement? Reporting earnings per share. Reporting by diversified companies. Examination of the statement of cash flows. COMPLETING THE AUDIT. Audit procedures. Evaluating audit findings. Communication with the audit committee. Responsibilities for other information in the financial report.

Principles of Auditing

The role of the auditor in the American economy

Chapter 1 study objectives

After studying this chapter, you should be able to:
— Describe the nature of an audit of financial statements.
— Explain why audits are demanded by society.
— Describe the various types of audits and types of auditors.
— Describe the major organizations that have an effect on the public accounting profession.
— Describe the 10 generally accepted auditing standards.
— Explain the key elements of the auditors' standard report.
— Discuss the other types of reports that are issued by auditors.

Dependable financial information is essential to the very existence of our society. The investor making a decision to buy or sell securities, the banker deciding whether to approve a loan, the government in obtaining revenue based on income tax returns, all are relying upon information provided by others. In many of these situations, the goals of the providers of information run directly counter to those of the users of the information. Implicit in this line of reasoning is recognition of the social need for independent auditors—individuals of professional competence and integrity who can tell us whether the financial information on which we rely constitutes a fair and complete picture of what is really going on.

Our purpose in this chapter is to make clear the nature of an independent audit and to show how essential the work of the independent auditor is to the efficient working of our economy. Another goal is to emphasize the significance of generally accepted auditing standards and to summarize the influence exerted on the public accounting profession by the American Institute of Certified Public Accountants (AICPA), by the Financial Accounting Standards Board (FASB), by the Governmental Accounting Standards Board (GASB), and by the Securities and Exchange Commission (SEC). Also in this chapter, we will explore types of auditing other than the examination of financial statements and note the impact of the Institute of Internal Auditors and of the General Accounting Office.

Finally, we will consider the nature of the independent auditors' report—that brief but all important document that emerges as the end product of an audit engagement. It is this report by the independent auditors that gives credibility to a set of financial statements and makes them acceptable to investors, bankers, government, and other users.

What is an audit?

The type of audit we are primarily concerned with throughout this textbook is an examination of a company's financial statements by a firm of independent public accountants. The audit consists of a searching investigation of the accounting records and other evidence supporting those financial statements. By obtaining an understanding of the company's internal control and by inspecting documents, observing assets, making inquiries within and outside the company, and performing other auditing procedures, the auditors will gather the evidence necessary to determine whether the financial statements provide a fair and reasonably complete picture of the company's financial position and its activities during the period being audited. The flowchart in Figure 1–1 illustrates the audit of financial statements.

In every audit, it is important to state clearly the boundaries of the examination. These boundaries identify the economic entity to be examined and the time period to be covered. Thus, the boundaries serve to define and to limit the auditors' responsibilities. The economic entity to be audited may be a sole proprietorship, a partnership, a corporation and its subsidiaries, a school district, or other organization. The time period is usually one year, although some audits cover shorter periods.

The examination conducted by the independent auditors provides the basis for the audit report. *Never do auditors express an opinion on the fairness of financial statements without first performing an audit.* Personal

Figure 1–1 Audit of financial statements

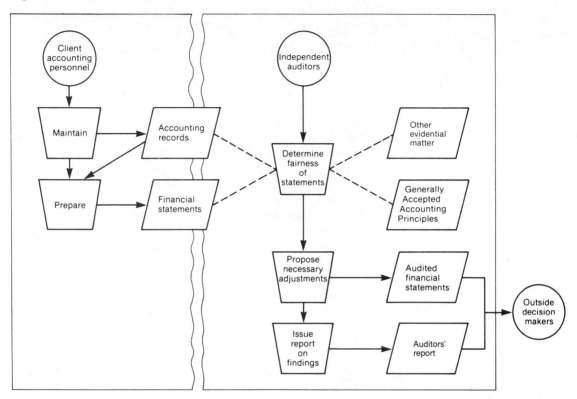

experience with the business, audits made in prior years, belief in the integrity of the owners and managers—none of these factors is sufficient to warrant an expression of opinion on the financial statements by the independent public accountants. Either they make an audit of the current year's financial statements or they do not. If they do not perform an audit, they do not express an opinion on the fairness of the financial statements.

The evidence gathered by the auditors during an examination will support the assertions that the assets listed in the balance sheet really exist, that the company has title to these assets, and that the valuations assigned to these assets have been established in conformity with generally accepted accounting principles. Evidence will be gathered to show that the balance sheet contains *all the liabilities* of the company; otherwise the balance sheet might be grossly misleading because certain important liabilities had been deliberately or accidentally omitted. Similarly, the auditors will gather evidence about the income statement. They will demand evidence that the reported sales really occurred, evidence that the goods were actually shipped to customers, and evidence that the recorded costs and expenses are applicable to the current period and that all expenses have been recognized.

The audit procedures comprising an examination will vary considerably from one engagement to the next. Many of the procedures appropriate to the audit of a small retail store would not be appropriate for the audit of a giant manufacturing corporation such as General Motors. Auditors make examinations of all types of business enterprise, and of not-for-profit organizations as well. Banks and breweries, factories and stores, colleges and churches, airlines and labor unions—all of these are regularly visited by auditors. The selection of the audit procedures best suited to each engagement requires the exercise of professional skill and judgment.

Economic decision making requires dependable information

A decision by a bank to make a loan to a business is usually based on careful study of the company's financial statements along with other information. The bank's purpose in making the loan is to earn interest and to collect the principal of the loan at maturity. But what if the financial statements submitted by the company along with its loan application are not dependable? Assume, for example, that the financial statements overstate current assets and annual earnings, and omit major liabilities. Assume also that the bank, acting on the basis of such misleading information, makes the loan. The end result is likely to be that the bank does not receive the expected interest income and may have to write the loan off as a loss.

Our economy today is characterized by large corporate organizations that have gathered capital from millions of investors and that control economic resources spread throughout the country or even throughout the world. Top management in the corporate headquarters is remote from the operations of company plants and branches and must rely on financial statements and other reports to control the company's resources. In brief, the decision makers in a large organization cannot get much information on a firsthand basis. They must rely on information provided by others, and this fact increases the risk of receiving undependable information.

The millions of individuals who have entrusted their savings to corporations by investing in securities rely upon annual and quarterly financial statements for assurance that their invested funds are being used honestly and efficiently. Even greater numbers of people entrust their savings to banks, insurance companies, and pension funds, which in turn invest the money in corporate securities. Thus, directly or indirectly, almost everyone has a financial stake in corporate enterprise, and the public interest demands prompt, *dependable* financial reporting on the operations and the financial health of publicly owned corporations.

The revenue of the federal government is derived in large part from income taxes based on the reported incomes of individuals and corporations. The information on tax returns is provided by taxpayers and may be biased because of the self-interest of the providers. The government attempts to compensate for this inherent weakness through verification by audits carried out by agents of the Internal Revenue Service.

Good accounting and financial reporting aid society in allocating its resources in the most efficient manner. The goal is to allocate our limited capital resources to the production of those goods and services for which demand is greatest. Economic resources tend to be attracted to the industries, the areas, and the organizational entities that are shown by accounting measurements to be capable of using more resources to the best advantage. Inadequate accounting and inaccurate reporting, on the other hand, conceal waste and inefficiency and thereby prevent our economic resources from being allocated in a rational manner.

The attest function

The principal reason for the existence of a public accounting profession is to perform the attest function. Performing this function places public accountants in a unique and vital role in society. It is not surprising that the attest function has expanded beyond attesting to financial statements. Public accountants currently attest to a wide range of other types of information. This expansion of the attest function and the professional standards that apply to those services are discussed in Chapter 19. At this point, we will focus on the attest function as it applies to financial statements.

To *attest* to financial statements means to provide assurance as to their fairness and dependability. The attest function includes two distinct steps or stages, as shown in Figure 1–2. First, the independent public accountants must carry out an examination (or audit); this examination provides the objective evidence that enables the auditors to express an informed opinion on the financial statements. The second stage of the attest function is the issuance of the auditors' report, which conveys to users of the financial statements the auditors' opinion as to the fairness and dependability of the financial statements.

It may be helpful to pose the question: Who is qualified to perform the attest function? As a brief answer, we can say that the persons who attest to financial statements must be both *technically competent* to conduct an

Figure 1–2 The attest function

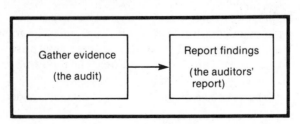

audit and *independent* of the company being audited so that the public will have confidence in their objectivity and impartiality.

Regular audits by independent public accountants offer the most important kind of protection to the public. Although every investment involves some degree of risk, investors will incur unnecessary risks if they invest in companies that do not have regular audits of their financial statements by independent public accountants.

Recognition of the responsibility of independent accountants to third parties led to the organization of Institutes of Chartered Accountants in Scotland and England more than a century ago. The technical competence of persons desiring to become chartered accountants was tested by examinations. Independence, integrity, and professional responsibility were recognized as qualities as important in chartered accountants as technical skill. Through the Institutes of Chartered Accountants, ethical principles were evolved to encourage auditors to follow professional standards in performing the attest function of auditing. In the United States, the American Institute of Certified Public Accountants (AICPA) has played a similar role in establishing professional standards for public accountants.

Credibility—the contribution of the independent auditor to financial reporting

The contribution of the independent auditor is to give credibility to financial statements. *Credibility,* in this usage, means that the financial statements can be *believed;* that is, they can be relied upon by outsiders, such as stockholders, creditors, government, and other interested third parties.

Audited financial statements are now the accepted means by which business corporations report their operating results and financial position. The word *audited* when applied to financial statements means that the balance sheet, statements of income and retained earnings, and statement of cash flows are accompanied by an audit report prepared by independent public accountants, expressing their professional opinion as to the fairness of the company's financial statements.

Financial statements prepared by management and transmitted to outsiders without first being audited by independent accountants leave a credibility gap. In reporting on its own administration of the business, management can hardly be expected to be entirely impartial and unbiased, any more than a football coach could be expected to serve as both coach and official referee in the same game.

Unaudited financial statements may have been honestly but carelessly prepared. Liabilities may have been overlooked and omitted from the balance sheet. Assets may have been overstated as a result of arithmetical errors or through violation of generally accepted accounting principles. Net income may have been exaggerated because revenue expenditures were capitalized or because sales transactions were recorded in advance of delivery dates.

Finally, there is the possibility that unaudited financial statements have been deliberately falsified in order to conceal theft and fraud or as a means of inducing the reader to invest in the business or to extend credit. Although deliberate falsification in financial statements is not common, it does occur and can cause disastrous losses to persons who rely upon such misleading statements.

For all these reasons (accidental errors, deviation from accounting principles, unintentional bias, and deliberate falsification), unaudited annual financial statements are much less reliable than statements which have been examined by independent auditors.

Major auditing developments of the 20th century

Although the objectives and concepts that guide present-day audits were almost unknown in the early years of the 20th century, audits of one type or another have been made throughout the recorded history of commerce and of government finance. The original meaning of the word *auditor* was "one who hears" and was appropriate to the era during which governmental accounting records were approved only after a public hearing in which the accounts were read aloud. From medieval times on through the Industrial Revolution, audits were made to determine whether persons in positions of fiscal responsibility in government and commerce were acting and reporting in an honest manner.

During the Industrial Revolution, as manufacturing concerns grew in size, their owners began to use the services of hired managers. With this separation of the ownership and management groups, the absentee owners turned increasingly to auditors to protect themselves against the danger of fraud by both managers and employees. Before 1900, auditing was concerned principally with the detection of fraud. In the first half of the 20th century, the direction of audit work tended to move away from fraud detection toward the new goal of determining whether financial statements gave a fair picture of financial position, operating results, and changes in financial position. This shift in emphasis was a response to the needs of the millions of new investors in corporate securities. No longer were bankers the only important outside users of audited financial data. Consequently, auditors no longer concentrated their attention on the balance sheet. The fairness of reported earnings became of prime importance.

In recent years, the detection of large-scale management fraud has assumed a larger role in audit philosophy. This latest shift of emphasis is a result of the dramatic increase in the number of lawsuits charging that management fraud has gone undetected by independent auditors. This issue is considered more fully in Chapter 3.

Development of sampling techniques   In the early days of the auditing profession, a normal audit was one that included a *complete review of all transactions.* However, about 1900, as large-scale business enterprise developed rapidly in both Great Britain and the United States, auditors adopted a *sampling technique.* This new auditing technique transformed the audit process into the making of tests of selected transactions rather than the verification of all transactions. Auditors and business managers gradually came to accept the proposition that careful examination of relatively few transactions selected at random would give a reliable indication of the accuracy of other similar transactions.

Internal control as a basis for testing and sampling   As auditors gained experience with the technique of sampling, they became aware of the importance of effective internal control. The meaning of internal control and the methods by which auditors obtain an understanding of a company's internal control are thoroughly explored in Chapter 5 and illustrated throughout this textbook. At this point a concise definition will serve to explain why good internal control makes it possible for auditors to rely greatly upon sampling techniques. A company's internal control consists of the policies and procedures established to provide reasonable assurance that specific objectives of the company will be achieved, including the objective of preparing accurate financial statements.

One example of internal control is an organization plan that separates the custody of assets from the function of record keeping. Thus, a person handling cash should not also maintain accounting records. Another example is the subdivision of duties so that no one person handles a transaction in its entirety, and the work of one employee serves to prove the accuracy of the work of another.

Evaluation of internal control became recognized as a prerequisite to successful use of sampling techniques. Auditors found that by studying the client's accounting system and by considering the flow of accounting work and the methods provided for automatic proof of recorded data, they could determine the extent and direction of the tests needed for a satisfactory audit of the financial statements. *The stronger the internal control, the less testing required by the auditors.* For any section of the accounts or any phase of financial operations in which controls were weak, the auditors learned that they must expand the scope and intensity of their tests.

The increasing use of computers has not lessened the importance of internal control to the auditors. However, the changes in clients' organization structures caused by reliance on computers have led auditors to develop new approaches to studying internal control.

Many of the ideas mentioned in this brief historical sketch of the development of auditing will be analyzed in detail in later sections of this book. Our purpose at this point is merely to orient ourselves with a quick overall look at some of the major auditing developments of the 20th century:

1. A shift in emphasis to the determination of fairness in financial statements.
2. Increased responsibility of the auditor to third parties, such as governmental agencies, stock exchanges, and an investing public numbered in the millions.
3. A change in auditing method from detailed examination of individual transactions to use of sampling techniques, including statistical sampling.
4. Recognition of the need to consider the effectiveness of internal control as a guide to the direction and amount of testing and sampling to be performed.
5. Development of new auditing procedures applicable to electronic data processing systems, and use of the computer as an auditing tool.
6. Recognition of the need for auditors to find means of protecting themselves from the current wave of litigation.
7. An increase in demand for prompt disclosure of both favorable and unfavorable information concerning any publicly owned company.

Types of audits

Audits are often viewed as falling into three major types: (1) audits of financial statements, (2) compliance audits, and (3) operational audits.

Audits of financial statements The audit of financial statements (which is our primary concern) ordinarily covers the balance sheet and the related statements of income, retained earnings, and cash flows. The goal is to determine whether these statements have been prepared in conformity with generally accepted accounting principles. Financial statement audits are normally performed by firms of certified public accountants; the user groups include management, investors, bankers, creditors, financial analysts, and government agencies.

Compliance audits The performance of a compliance audit is dependent upon the existence of verifiable data and of recognized criteria or standards established by an authoritative body. A familiar example is the audit of an income tax return by an auditor of the Internal Revenue Service (IRS). Such audits seek to determine whether a tax return is in compliance with tax laws and IRS regulations. The findings of the IRS auditors are transmitted to the taxpayer by means of the IRS auditor's report.

Another example of a compliance audit is the periodic bank examination conducted on a surprise basis by bank examiners employed by the Federal Reserve System, the Federal Deposit Insurance Corporation, and the state banking departments. These audits measure compliance with banking laws and regulations and with traditional standards of sound banking practice.

In recent years, many state and local governmental entities have arranged for compliance audits under the requirements of the Single Audit Act of 1984. This federal act requires any state or local government unit, such as a school district, that obtains more than $100,000 in federal assistance to have an annual financial and compliance audit. In performing these audits, the auditors consider federal program results, compliance with laws and regulations that may have an effect on each major federal assistance program, and the economy and efficiency of the programs. The results of the compliance audits are reported to the federal government.

Operational audits An operational audit is a study of some specific unit of an organization for the purpose of measuring its performance. The operations of the receiving department of a manufacturing company, for example, may be evaluated in terms of its *effectiveness,* that is, its success in meeting its stated goals and responsibilities. Performance is also judged in terms of *efficiency,* that is, success in using to best advantage the resources available to the department.

The boundaries of an operational audit often are drawn from an organization chart. If the activities under review are grouped under a single administrative authority, the task of communicating the audit findings and implementing the auditors' recommendations are more easily carried out. The broad scope of operational auditing often makes it necessary for the audit team to include a variety of experts, such as engineers, accountants, lawyers, and computer specialists. The operations to be reviewed may be lodged in the accounting department, the legal department, the manufacturing plant, the marketing department, or any other unit of the organization.

Because the criteria for effectiveness and efficiency are not as clearly established as are generally accepted accounting principles or tax regulations, an operational audit tends to require more subjective judgments than do audits of financial statements or compliance audits. The end product of an operational audit is usually a report to management containing recommendations for improvements in operations.

CPAs and other types of auditors

Although our interest is primarily in the audit of financial statements by certified public accountants, other professional groups carry on large-scale auditing programs. Among these other well-known types of auditors are internal auditors, auditors of the General Accounting Office, and internal revenue agents.

Certified public accountants In recognition of the public trust imposed upon independent public accountants, each state recognizes public accountancy as a profession and issues the certificate of Certified Public Accountant. The CPA certificate is not only a license to practice but also a symbol of technical competence. This official recognition by the state is comparable to that accorded to the legal, medical, and other professions. A CPA certificate is issued by state and territorial governments to those individuals who have demonstrated, through written examinations and the satisfaction of educational and experience requirements, their qualifications for entry to the public accounting profession.

The licensing of CPAs by the states reflects a belief that the public interest will be protected by an official identification of competent, professional accountants who offer their services to the public. The opinion of an independent public accountant concerning the fairness of a set of financial statements is the factor that causes these statements to be generally accepted by bankers, investors, and government agencies. To sustain such confidence, the independent public accountant must be a professional person of the highest integrity and competence.

In addition to passing an examination and meeting certain educational requirements, the candidate for a CPA certificate in many states must also complete from one to three years of professional experience. The requirements as to amount of education and public accounting experience differ considerably among the various states.

Internal auditing   Nearly every large corporation maintains an internal auditing staff. A principal goal of the internal auditors is to investigate and appraise the effectiveness with which the various organizational units of the company are carrying out their assigned functions. Much attention is also given to the study and evaluation of both accounting and administrative controls.

The internal auditing staff usually reports to an audit committee of the board of directors, or to the president or other high executive. This strategic placement high in the corporate structure helps assure that the internal auditors will have ready access to all units of the business, and that their recommendations will be given prompt attention by department heads. It is imperative that the internal auditors be independent of the department heads and other line executives whose work they review. Thus, it would not be satisfactory for the internal auditing staff to be under the authority of the chief accountant. However, the internal auditors are not independent in the same sense as the CPA. The internal auditors are employees of the company in which they work, subject to the restraints inherent in the employer-employee relationship.

A large part of the work of the internal auditors consists of operational audits; in addition, however, they may conduct numerous compliance audits. The number and kind of investigative projects varies from year to year. Unlike the CPAs who are committed to verify each significant item in the annual financial statements, the internal auditors are not obligated to repeat their audits on an annual basis. Internal auditing is considered more fully in Chapter 5.

General Accounting Office Congress has long had its own auditing staff, headed by the controller general and known as the General Accounting Office, or GAO. The work of GAO auditors includes both compliance audits and operational audits. These assignments include audits of government agencies to determine that spending programs follow the intent of Congress and operational audits to evaluate the effectiveness and efficiency of selected government programs. GAO auditors also conduct examinations of corporations holding government contracts to verify that contract payments by government have been proper.

The enormous size of many of the federal agencies has caused the GAO to stress the development of computer auditing techniques and statistical sampling plans. Its pioneering in these areas has led to the recognition of the GAO as a sophisticated professional auditing staff. Experience as a GAO auditor is accepted by many states as meeting the experience requirements for the CPA certificate.

Internal revenue agents The Internal Revenue Service is responsible for enforcement of the federal tax laws. Its agents conduct compliance audits of the income tax returns of individuals and corporations to determine that income has been computed and taxes paid as required by federal law. Although IRS audits include some simple individual tax returns that can be completed in an hour or so in an IRS office, they also include field audits of the nation's largest corporations and involve highly complex tax issues.

The CPA examination

The CPA examination is a uniform national examination prepared and graded by the American Institute of Certified Public Accountants. It is given twice each year, in May and November. Although the preparation and grading of the examination are in the hands of the AICPA, the issuance of CPA certificates is a function of each state or territory. Passing the CPA examination does not, in itself, entitle the candidate to a CPA certificate; most states require from one to three years of professional experience before a certificate will be awarded. Each state also determines the educational qualifications and other criteria to be met by its citizens who wish to take the examination. Some states require a separate additional examination on professional ethics or other topics. Students interested in taking the examination may obtain helpful information from the AICPA publication, *Information for CPA Candidates,* available from the AICPA, 1211 Avenue of the Americas, New York, N.Y. 10036. Also available from the AICPA are past CPA examinations and unofficial solutions.

The CPA examination is essentially an academic one; in most states, candidates are not required to have any work experience to sit for the examination. In the opinion of the authors, the ideal time to take the examination is immediately after the completion of a comprehensive program of accounting courses in a college or university. The examination extends over two and a half days and covers four fields: auditing, accounting theory, accounting practice, and business law. Although the subject of federal income taxes is not presented as a separate field, this topic is usually emphasized in several parts of the examination.

Over the years only about 10 percent of the candidates taking the examination have passed all four parts on their first attempt. However, of the candidates who hold a university degree with a major in accounting, the percentage passing two or more parts on the first attempt is somewhat higher. In other words, admission to the examination is relatively easy, but passing the examination is relatively difficult.

The compilation of the questions and problems included in this textbook involved a review of all CPA examinations of the past 10 years and the selection of representative questions and problems. Use of this material is with the consent of the American Institute of Certified Public Accountants. Many other problems and questions (not from CPA examinations) are included with each chapter.

CPA firms

CPA firms range in size from one person to several thousand on the professional staff. In terms of size, CPA firms are often grouped into the following four categories:

Local firms   Local firms typically have one or two offices, include only one or a few CPAs as partners, and serve clients in a single city or area. The services provided emphasize income tax returns, management advisory services, and accounting services. Auditing is usually only a small part of the practice. Audit clients tend to be small business concerns that find need for audited financial statements to support applications for bank loans.

Regional firms   Many local firms have become regional firms by opening additional offices in neighboring cities or states and increasing the number of professional staff. Merger with other local firms is often a route to regional status. This growth is often accompanied by an increase in the amount of auditing as compared to other services.

National firms   CPA firms with offices in most major cities in the United States are called national firms. These firms operate in other countries as well, either with their own offices or through affiliations with firms in other countries.

Big Eight firms Often in the news are the eight largest CPA firms in the United States, known as the Big Eight. All of these firms maintain offices in major cities throughout the world. Since only a very large CPA firm has sufficient staff and resources to audit a giant corporation, these Big Eight firms audit nearly all of the largest American corporations. Although these firms offer a wide range of services, auditing represents the largest share of their work. Annual revenue of a Big Eight firm is in the hundreds of millions of dollars. In alphabetical order, these eight firms are Arthur Andersen & Co.; Arthur Young & Co.; Coopers & Lybrand; Deloitte Haskins & Sells; Ernst & Whinney; Peat Marwick, Main & Co.; Price Waterhouse & Co.; and Touche Ross & Co.

American Institute of Certified Public Accountants

At the very heart of the public accounting profession is the AICPA, a voluntary national organization of more than 200,000 CPAs. Three of the major areas of the AICPA's work are of particular interest to students of auditing. These are:

1. Establishing standards and rules to guide CPAs in their conduct of audits, accounting and review services, tax work, and management advisory services.
2. Carrying on a continuous program of research and publication which has been a key factor in the growth and increasing stature of the profession.
3. Contributing to the profession's system of self-regulation.

Among other important activities of the AICPA is the continuing education program sponsored for CPAs. For CPAs to remain knowledgable with respect to today's unending stream of changes in accounting, tax laws, auditing, computers, and management advisory services, attendance at seminars conducted by the AICPA, state societies of CPAs, or large CPA firms is virtually a necessity. State laws generally require CPAs to participate in continuing education programs as a condition for license renewal.

Establishing standards The AICPA has assigned to its Auditing Standards Board (ASB) responsibility for issuing official pronouncements on auditing matters. A most important series of pronouncements on auditing by the ASB and its predecessors is entitled *Statements on Auditing Standards* (SASs). Later in this chapter we will consider how CPA firms utilize SASs in every audit engagement.

Another unit of the AICPA establishes standards for reporting on financial statements when the CPA's role has been to compile or review the statements rather than to perform an independent audit. Responsibility for setting such standards rests with the Accounting and Review Services Committee. The series of pronouncements by this group is called *Statements on Standards for Accounting and Review Services* (SSARS). These SSARS provide guidance for the many sensitive situations in which a CPA firm is in some way associated with a set of financial statements and therefore needs to make clear whether or not it assumes responsibility for their fairness. SSARSs are discussed more fully in Chapter 19.

Research and publication   The AICPA maintains a research staff and also commissions research studies by others. Many accounting students are familiar with the *Journal of Accountancy,* published monthly by the AICPA. Another AICPA monthly journal is *The Tax Adviser.*

Publications by the AICPA that bear directly on auditing include the following:

Statements on Auditing Standards (SASs).

Industry Audit Guides. (Several different fields, including, for example, *Audits of Casinos.*)

Auditing Procedure Studies. This new series is intended to keep auditors informed of new developments and advances in auditing procedures.

A few of the many AICPA publications primarily concerned with accounting issues are:

Accounting Research Bulletins. These 51 bulletins issued over a period of 15 years were one of the earliest efforts to develop greater uniformity of accounting practice.

Opinions of the Accounting Principles Board.

Accounting Research Studies.

Statements of Position of the Accounting Standards Division.

Accounting Trends & Techniques. (An annual study of current reporting practices of a large number of corporations.)

Uniform CPA Examinations. Questions and Unofficial Answers. (Published for each semiannual examination.)

Self-regulation   A hallmark of the public accounting profession is an effective system of self-regulation to enforce its professional standards. The AICPA has contributed significantly to this regulatory process by developing regulatory mechanisms that apply to both CPA firms and individual CPAs.

Regulation of CPA firms   In 1977, the AICPA organized a division in which the members are CPA firms, rather than individual CPAs. The *Division for CPA Firms* was created for the purpose of improving the quality of practice in CPA firms of all sizes. The division actually has two sections: the Private Companies Practice Section and the SEC Practice

Section. Membership is voluntary; a CPA firm may join either, or both, sections. Once a CPA firm joins one of the sections, it is subject to the membership requirements of that section, which include mandatory peer review.

A *peer review* occurs when a CPA firm arranges for a critical review of its practices by another CPA firm. Such an external review clearly offers a more objective evaluation of the quality of performance than could be made by self-review. The purpose of this concept is to encourage rigorous adherence to the AICPA's quality control standards. Quality control standards and the peer review process are discussed in detail in Chapter 9.

Regulation of individual CPAs It is a tribute to the profession's system of self-regulation that Congress has not elected to enact legislation to regulate the profession. The profession has not been free from criticism, however. Over the years, various congressional committees have threatened to intercede, usually as a result of some highly publicized financial failure. The profession's system of self-regulation has had to be responsive to changes in the legislative, economic, and legal environment. In 1988 the membership of the AICPA adopted significant changes in the ethical rules for CPAs and the requirements for AICPA membership. These changes were prompted by the recommendations of the Special Committee on Standards of Professional Conduct for CPAs (the Anderson Committee).

At the core of the new requirements is a new goal-oriented *Code of Professional Conduct*. This new ethical code differs from previous codes in that it sets forth positively stated principles on which CPAs can make decisions about appropriate conduct. The AICPA *Code of Professional Conduct* is described completely in Chapter 2.

A desire for effective self-regulation also is apparent in the new requirements for membership in the AICPA, which include the following:

1. Members in public practice must practice with a firm enrolled in an approved practice (peer) review program.
2. Members must obtain continuing education; 120 hours every three years for members in public practice, and 60 hours every three years for other members.

In addition to these new membership requirements that apply currently, after the year 2000, applicants for AICPA membership must have 150 semester hours of college education, including a bachelor's degree from an accredited college or university.

The AICPA—in perspective Throughout its existence, the AICPA has contributed enormously to the evolution of generally accepted accounting principles as well as to development of professional standards. The many technical divisions and committees of the Institute (such as the Auditing Standards Board) provide a means of focusing the collective experience and ability of the profession on current problems. Such governmental agencies as the Securities and Exchange Commission and the Internal Revenue Service continually seek the advice and cooperation of the Institute in improving laws and regulations relating to accounting matters.

Financial Accounting Standards Board

Auditors must determine whether financial statements are prepared in conformity with generally accepted accounting principles. The AICPA has designated the Financial Accounting Standards Board as the body with power to set forth these principles. Thus, *FASB Statements,* exposure drafts, public hearings, and research projects are all of major concern to the public accounting profession.

The structure, history, and pronouncements of the FASB (and its predecessor, the Accounting Principles Board) are appropriately covered in introductory and intermediate accounting courses.

Governmental Accounting Standards Board

The Governmental Accounting Standards Board (GASB) was established in 1984 to establish and improve standards of financial accounting for state and local government. The operational structure of the GASB is similar to that of the FASB. Auditors of state and local government entities, such as cities and school districts, look to the GASB pronouncements for the appropriate accounting principles.

Securities and Exchange Commission

The SEC is an agency of the U.S. government. It administers the Securities Act of 1933, the Securities Exchange Act of 1934, and other legislation concerning securities and financial matters. The function of the SEC is to protect investors and the public by requiring full disclosure of financial information by companies offering securities for sale to the public. A second objective is to prevent misrepresentation, deceit, or other fraud in the sale of securities.

The term *registration statement* is an important one in any discussion of the impact of the SEC on accounting practice. To *register* securities means to qualify them for sale to the public by filing with the SEC financial statements and other data in a form acceptable to the Commission. A registration statement contains *audited financial statements,* including balance sheets for a two-year period and income statements and statements of cash flows for a three-year period.

The legislation creating the SEC made the Commission responsible for determining whether the financial statements presented to it reflected proper application of accounting principles. To aid the Commission in discharging this responsibility, the Securities Acts provided for an examination and report by an *independent* public accountant. Thus, from its beginning, the Securities and Exchange Commission has been a major user of audited financial statements and has exercised great influence upon the development of accounting principles, the strengthening of auditing standards, and especially upon the concept of independence.

Protection of investors, of course, requires that the public have available the information contained in a registration statement concerning a proposed issue of securities. The issuing company is therefore required to deliver to prospective buyers of securities a *prospectus,* or selling circular, based on the registration statement. The registration of securities does not insure investors against loss; the SEC definitely does not pass on the merit of securities. There is in fact only one purpose of registration: That purpose is to provide disclosure of the important facts so that the investor has available all pertinent information on which to base an intelligent decision on whether to buy a given security. If the SEC believes that a given registration statement does not meet its standards of disclosure, it may require amendment of the statement or may issue a stop order preventing sale of the securities.

To improve the quality of the financial statements filed with it and the professional standards of the independent accountants who report on these statements, the SEC has adopted a basic accounting regulation known as *Regulation S-X* and entitled *Form and Content of Financial Statements.* Between 1937 and 1982, the SEC issued 307 *Accounting Series Releases* (ASRs) addressing various accounting and auditing issues. In 1982 the series was replaced by two series—*Financial Reporting Releases* and *Accounting and Auditing Enforcement Releases. Financial Reporting Releases,* in addition to codifying the ASRs still considered relevant to financial reporting, present the SEC's current views on financial reporting issues. *Accounting and Auditing Enforcement Releases* summarize enforcement activities against auditors when the SEC has found deficiencies in the auditors' work.

Generally accepted auditing standards (GAAS)

Standards are authoritative rules for measuring the *quality* of performance. The existence of generally accepted auditing standards is evidence that auditors are much concerned with the maintenance of a uniformly high quality of audit work by all independent public accountants. If every certified public accountant has adequate technical training and performs audits with skill, care, and professional judgment, the prestige of the profession will rise, and the public will attribute more and more significance to the auditor's opinion attached to financial statements.

What are the standards developed by the public accounting profession? The AICPA has set forth the following basic framework:

General standards
1. The examination is to be performed by a person or persons having adequate *technical training* and *proficiency* as an auditor.
2. In all matters relating to the assignment, an *independence in mental attitude* is to be maintained by the auditor or auditors.
3. *Due professional care* is to be exercised in the performance of the examination and the preparation of the report.

Standards of field work
1. The work is to be *adequately planned* and assistants, if any, are to be *properly supervised.*
2. A *sufficient understanding of the internal control structure* is to be obtained to plan the audit and to determine the nature, timing, and extent of tests to be performed.
3. *Sufficient competent evidential matter* is to be obtained through inspection, observation, inquiries, and confirmations to afford a reasonable basis for an opinion regarding the financial statements under examination.

Standards of reporting
1. The report shall state *whether* the financial statements are presented in accordance with *generally accepted accounting principles.*
2. The report shall identify those circumstances in which such principles have *not* been *consistently observed* in the current period in relation to the preceding period.
3. *Informative disclosures* in the financial statements are to be regarded as reasonably adequate *unless otherwise stated in the report.*
4. The report shall either contain an *expression of opinion* regarding the financial statements, taken as a whole, or an assertion to the effect that an opinion cannot be expressed. When an overall opinion cannot be expressed, the reasons therefore should be stated. In all cases where an auditor's name is associated with financial statements, the report should contain a clear-cut indication of the *character of the auditor's examination,* if any, and the *degree of responsibility* he is taking. [Emphasis added.]

Application of auditing standards

The 10 standards set forth by the American Institute of Certified Public Accountants include such intangible and subjective terms of measurement as "*adequate* planning," "*sufficient* understanding of the internal control structure," "*sufficient competent* evidential matter," and "*adequate* disclosure." To decide under the circumstances of each audit engagement what is adequate, sufficient, and competent requires the exercise of professional judgment. Auditing cannot be reduced to rote; the exercise of judgment by the auditor is vital at numerous points in every examination. However, the formulation and publication of carefully worded auditing standards are of immense aid in raising the quality of audit work, even though these standards require professional judgment in their application.

Training and proficiency

How does the independent auditor achieve the "adequate technical training and proficiency" required by the first general standard? This requirement is usually interpreted to mean college or university education in accounting and auditing, substantial public accounting experience, ability to use procedures suitable for computer-based systems, and participation in continuing education programs. A technical knowledge of the industry in which the client operates is also part of the personal qualifications of the auditor. It follows that a CPA firm must not accept an audit engagement without first determining that members of its staff have the technical training and proficiency needed to function effectively in the particular industry.

Independence—the most important auditing standard

An opinion by an independent public accountant as to the fairness of a company's financial statement is of no value unless the accountant is truly independent. Consequently, the auditing standard that "in all matters relating to the assignment an independence in mental attitude is to be maintained by the auditor" is perhaps the most essential factor in the existence of a public accounting profession.

If auditors owned shares of stock in a company that they audited, or if they served as members of the board of directors, they might subconsciously be biased in the performance of auditing duties. A CPA should therefore avoid any relationship with a client that would cause an outsider who had knowledge of all the facts to doubt the CPA's independence. It is not enough that CPAs be independent; they must conduct themselves in such a manner that informed members of the public will have no reason to doubt their independence.

Due professional care

The third general standard requires due professional care in the conduct of the audit and in the preparation of the audit report. This standard requires the auditors to carry out every step of the audit engagement in an alert and diligent manner. Full compliance with this standard would rule out any negligent acts or material omissions by the auditors. Of course, auditors, as well as members of other professions, inevitably make occasional errors in judgment, but this human element does not justify indifference or inattention to professional responsibilities.

Standards of field work—accumulating evidence

The three standards of field work relate to accumulating and evaluating evidence sufficient for the auditors to express an opinion on the financial statements. One major type of evidence is the client's internal control. By obtaining an understanding of the internal control structure, the auditors can assess whether the structure offers assurance that the financial statements will be free from material errors and irregularities. A second major type of evidence consists of information that substantiates the amounts on the financial statements being audited. Examples of such evidence include written confirmations from outsiders and firsthand observation of assets by the auditors. The gathering and evaluating of evidence lies at the very heart of the audit process and is a continuing theme throughout this textbook.

Adequate planning and supervision

Adequate planning is essential to a satisfactory audit. Some portions of the examination can be performed prior to the end of the year under audit; some information may be compiled by the client's staff and made available for the auditors' review. The appropriate number of audit staff of various levels of skill and the time required of each need to be determined in advance of field work. These are but a few of the elements of planning the audit.

Most of the field work of an audit is carried out by staff members with limited experience. The key to successful use of relatively new staff members is close supervision at every level. This concept extends from providing specific written instructions to staff members all the way to an overall review by the partner in charge of the engagement.

Sufficient understanding of internal control

An excellent internal control structure provides strong assurance that the client's records are dependable and that its assets are protected. When the auditors find this type of strong internal control, the quantity of other evidence required is much less than if controls were weak. Thus, the auditors' assessment of internal control has great impact on the length and nature of the audit process.

Sufficient competent evidential matter

The third standard of field work requires that the auditors gather sufficient competent evidence to have a basis for expressing an opinion on the financial statements. The term **competent** refers to the quality of the evidence; some forms of evidence are stronger and more convincing than others. In Chapter 7, we shall explore at length the meaning of this standard.

The reporting standards

The four reporting standards establish some specific directives for preparation of the auditors' report. The report must specifically state whether the financial statements are in conformity with generally accepted accounting principles. The report must contain an opinion on the financial statements as a whole, or must disclaim an opinion. Consistency in the application of generally accepted accounting principles and adequate informative disclosure in the financial statements is to be assumed unless the audit report states otherwise. These basic reporting standards are considered more fully in Chapters 18 and 19.

Statements on Auditing Standards (SASs)

Statements on Auditing Standards are serially numbered pronouncements issued by the Auditing Standards Board. The first in the series, *SAS 1,* is a codification of 54 *Statements* previously issued over many years by the Committee on Auditing Procedure, a predecessor of the ASB. Since *SAS 1* was released in 1972, many additional statements on specific topics have been issued to provide more detailed guidance than was available from the 10 generally accepted auditing standards.

The SASs are considered to be *interpretations* of the 10 generally accepted auditing standards discussed earlier in this chapter. They are the most authoritative references that auditors can utilize to resolve problems encountered during an audit. The term *auditing standards* is often used in practice to refer to the SASs, to the 10 generally accepted auditing standards, or to both.

The authoritative status of the SASs is derived from the AICPA *Code of Professional Conduct* (Rule 202). The Code recognizes the SASs as interpretations of generally accepted auditing standards and requires auditors to adhere to these pronouncements. A CPA firm must be prepared to justify any departure from the SASs, a task not to be taken lightly.

The SASs, although more detailed and specific than GAAS, do not usually prescribe specific auditing procedures to be followed. For more detailed, but less authoritative guidelines on specific audit problems, auditors can refer to *Industry Audit Guides* and *Audit Procedure Studies,* various technical studies published by the AICPA, auditing textbooks, and articles in the *Journal of Accountancy* and in *The Accounting Review*.

The 10 basic concepts embodied in generally accepted auditing standards and the role of the SASs are summarized in Figure 1–3. Keep in

Figure 1–3   Summary of ten generally accepted auditing standards

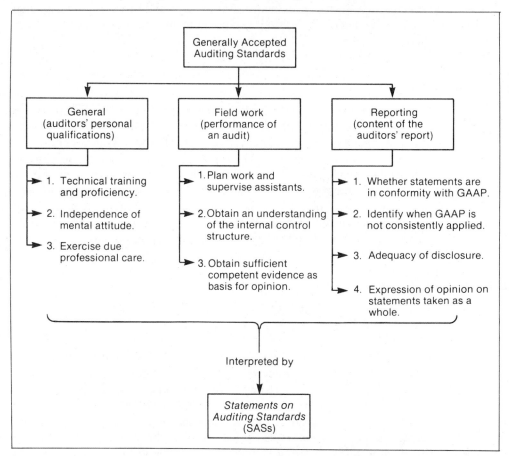

mind, however, that compliance with the SASs does not represent an ideal of audit performance, but rather a ***minimum standard*** for all audit engagements.

Throughout this textbook, we will be making references to individual SASs. Each SAS is identified under two numbering systems: the original SAS number and the AU number. The SAS numbering system organizes the SASs by date of issue, whereas the AU numbering system organizes them by topic. Thus, *Statement on Auditing Standards 11*, "Using the Work of a Specialist," is identified as *SAS 11* and AU 336. The AU numbering system is used in the AICPA *Codification of Statements on Auditing Standards* and also in the AICPA *Professional Standards, Volume A,* published annually by Commerce Clearing House.

The auditors' report

The end product of an audit of a business entity is a report expressing the auditors' opinion on the client's financial statements. In 1988 the Auditing Standards Board made a number of changes in the profession's reporting standards. The auditors' *standard unqualified report* (also called a standard report) that resulted from these changes consists of three paragraphs. The first paragraph clarifies the responsibilities of management and the auditors and is referred to as the *introductory paragraph.* The second paragraph, which describes the nature of the audit, is called the *scope paragraph;* the final paragraph, the *opinion paragraph,* is a concise statement of the auditor's opinion based on the audit.

Independent Auditors' Report

To the Board of Directors and Stockholders
XYZ Company:

We have audited the accompanying balance sheet of XYZ Company as of December 31, 19—, and the related statements of income, retained earnings, and cash flows for the year then ended. These financial statements are the responsibility of the Company's management. Our responsibility is to express an opinion on these financial statements based on our audit.

We conducted our audit in accordance with generally accepted auditing standards. Those standards require that we plan and perform the audit to obtain reasonable assurance about whether the financial statements are free of material misstatement. An audit includes examining, on a test basis, evidence supporting the amounts and disclosures in the financial statements. An audit also includes assessing the accounting principles used and significant estimates made by management, as well as evaluating the overall financial statement presentation. We believe that our audit provides a reasonable basis for our opinion.

In our opinion, the financial statements referred to above present fairly, in all material respects, the financial position of XYZ Company as of December 31, 19—, and the results of its operations and its cash flows for the year then ended in conformity with generally accepted accounting principles.

Blue, Gray + Company

Los Angeles, Calif.

Certified Public Accountants
February 26, 19XX

The auditors' report is addressed to the person or persons who retained the auditors; in the case of corporations, the selection of an auditing firm is usually made by the board of directors and ratified by the stockholders.

Importance of the auditors' report

The writing of the auditors' report is the *final* step in completing an examination. Why, then, should we study the auditors' report at the *beginning* of a course in auditing? The answer is that if we appreciate the significance of the auditors' report, and understand why it is prepared and how it is used as a basis for financial decisions, we are then in an excellent position to understand the purpose of the various audit procedures that comprise an examination. Every step in the auditing process is taken to enable the auditors to express an informed opinion on the fairness of the client's financial statements. Later chapters of this textbook present the auditors' work in verification of cash, inventories, and other financial statement topics. In these chapters, students may appropriately ask themselves at each step: How does this verification work relate to the preparation of the auditors' report?

Since the auditors' report is so very briefly and concisely worded, a full understanding of its meaning requires that we consider the significance of each of its key phrases. Phrases such as "generally accepted auditing standards" and "generally accepted accounting principles" mean very different things, and a clear understanding of each is essential to an appreciation of the purpose and nature of auditing. In the following sections of this chapter, we shall, therefore, give careful consideration to each of the main ideas in the auditors' report.

The introductory paragraph of the auditors' report

To gain a full understanding of the introductory paragraph of the auditors' report we need to emphasize the following two points:

1.   The client company is primarily responsible for the financial statements.

The management of a company has the responsibility of maintaining adequate accounting records and of preparing proper financial statements for the use of stockholders and creditors. Even though the financial statements are sometimes constructed and typed in the auditors' office, primary responsibility for the statements remains with management.

The auditors' product is their report. It is a separate document from the client's financial statements, although the two are closely related and transmitted together to stockholders and to creditors.

Once we recognize that the financial statements are the statements of the company and not of the auditors, we realize that the auditors have no right to make changes in the financial statements. What action then should the auditors take if they do not agree with the presentation of a material item in the balance sheet or income statement? Assume, for example, that the allowance for doubtful accounts is not sufficient (in the auditors' opinion) to cover the probable collection losses in the accounts receivable.

The auditors will first discuss the problem with management and point out why they believe the valuation allowance to be inadequate. If management agrees to increase the allowance for doubtful accounts, an adjusting entry will be made for that purpose, and the problem is solved. If management is not convinced by the auditors' arguments and declines to increase the doubtful accounts allowance, the auditors will probably *qualify* their opinion by stating in the report that the financial statements reflect fairly the company's financial position and operating results, *except for the effects of not providing an adequate provision for doubtful account losses.* Usually such issues are satisfactorily disposed of in discussions between the auditors and the client, and a qualification of the auditors' opinion is avoided. A full consideration of the use of qualifications in the auditors' report is presented in Chapter 18.

2.   The auditors render a report on the financial statements, not on the accounting records.

The primary purpose of an audit is to provide assurance to the users of the financial statements that these statements are reliable. Auditors do not express an opinion on the client's accounting records. The auditors' investigation of financial statement items includes reference to the client's accounting records, but is not limited to these records. The auditors' examination includes observation of tangible assets, inspection of such documents as purchase orders and contracts, and the gathering of evidence from outsiders (such as banks, customers, and suppliers), as well as analysis of the client's accounting records.

It is true that a principal means of establishing the validity of a balance sheet and income statement is to trace the statement figures to the accounting records and back through the records to the original evidence of transactions. However, the auditors' use of the accounting records is only a means to an end—and merely a part of the audit. It is, therefore, appropriate for the auditors to state in their report that they have made an audit of the *financial statements* rather than to say that they have made an audit of the accounting records.

The scope paragraph of the auditors' report

The scope paragraph describes the nature of the CPAs' audit. It states that the audit was conducted in accordance with generally accepted auditing standards and points out that while an audit is meant to provide *reasonable assurance* that the financial statements are free of material misstatement, the procedures are applied on a test basis. Thus, an audit cannot provide *absolute assurance* that the financial statements are free from material misstatement; the auditors do, however, believe the procedures provide a reasonable basis for their opinion.

The opinion paragraph of the auditors' report

The opinion paragraph consists of only one sentence, which is restated here with certain significant phrases shown in italics:

> *In our opinion,* the financial statements referred to above *present fairly, in all material respects,* the financial position of XYZ Company as of December 31, 19X1, and the results of its operations and its cash flows for the year ended in conformity with *generally accepted accounting principles.*

Each of the italicized phrases has a special significance. The first phrase, "in our opinion," makes clear that the auditors are expressing nothing more than an informed opinion; they are not guaranteeing or certifying that the statements are accurate, correct, or true. In an earlier period of public accounting, the wording of the audit report contained the phrase "We certify that . . . ," but this expression was discontinued on the grounds that it was misleading. To "certify" implies a positive assurance of accuracy, which an audit simply does not provide.

The auditors cannot guarantee the correctness of the financial statements because the statements themselves are largely matters of opinion rather than of absolute fact. Furthermore, the auditors do not make a complete and detailed examination of all transactions. Their examination is limited to a program of tests that leaves the possibility of some errors going undetected. Because of limitations inherent in the accounting process and because of practical limitations of time and cost in performing an audit, the auditors' work culminates in the expression of an opinion and not in the issuance of a guarantee of accuracy. The growth of public accounting and the increased confidence placed in audited statements by all sectors of the economy indicate that the auditors' opinion is usually sufficient assurance that the statements may be relied upon.

The financial statements "present fairly, in all material respects . . ."

Since many of the items in financial statements cannot be measured exactly, the auditors cannot say that the statements present exactly or correctly the financial position or operating results. The meaning of "present fairly" as used in the context of the auditors' report has been much discussed in court cases and in auditing literature. Some accountants believed that financial statements were fair if they conformed to GAAP; others insisted that fairness was a distinct concept, broader than mere compliance with GAAP. This discussion led to the issuance by the AICPA of *SAS 5* (AU 411), "The Meaning of 'Present Fairly in Conformity with Generally Accepted Accounting Principles' in the Independent

Auditor's Report.''[1] In the opinion of the authors, the essence of *SAS 5* is to equate the quality of *presenting fairly* with that of *not being misleading*. Financial statements must not be so presented as to lead users to forecasts or conclusions that a company and its independent auditors know are unsound or unlikely.

What is "material"?   Auditors cannot issue an unqualified opinion on financial statements that contain *material* deficiencies. The term *material* may be defined as "sufficiently important to influence decisions made by reasonable users of financial statements." In the audit of a small client—such as a condominium property owners' association—$1,000 might be considered material. On the other hand, in the audit of an IBM or a General Motors an amount of $1 million might be considered to be immaterial.

In practice, one of the most significant elements of professional judgment is the ability to draw the line between material and immaterial departures from good accounting practices. The auditor who raises objections over immaterial items will soon lose the respect of both clients and associates. On the other hand, the auditor who fails to identify and disclose material deficiencies in financial statements may be liable for the losses of those who rely upon the audited statements. In short, applying the concept of materiality is one of the most complex problems faced by auditors.

Materiality depends upon both the *dollar amount* and the *nature of the item*. For example, a $500,000 error in the balance of the Cash account is far more important than a $500,000 error in the balance of Accumulated Depreciation. If a corporation sells assets to a member of top management and then buys the assets back at a higher price, this *related party transaction* warrants disclosure even though the dollar amounts are not large in relation to the financial statements as a whole. The reason for requiring disclosure of such a transaction—that is, the risk of management impropriety—is based more on the nature of the transaction than upon the dollar amount.

Adequate informative disclosure   If financial statements are to present fairly, in all material respects, the financial position and operating results of a company, there must be adequate disclosure of all essential information. A financial statement may be misleading if it does not give a complete picture. For example, if an extraordinary item arising from an uninsured flood loss of plant and equipment were combined with operating income and not clearly identified, the reader might be misled as to the earning power of the company.

---

[1] AICPA, *Statement on Auditing Standards 5,* "The Meaning of 'Present Fairly in Conformity with Generally Accepted Accounting Principles' in the Independent Auditor's Report" (New York, 1975), par. 3, AU 411.03.

Generally accepted accounting principles (GAAP)

In our study of the main ideas contained in the auditors' report, the next key phrase to be considered is "generally accepted accounting principles." The wording of the audit report implies that generally accepted accounting principles represent a concept well known to CPAs and sophisticated users of financial statements. However, no official list of accounting principles exists, and a satisfactory concise definition is yet to be developed.

When evaluating whether a particular accounting principle used by a client is generally accepted, the auditors may refer to a variety of sources, from *Statements of the FASB* to articles in accounting journals. The auditors look to these references to determine whether or not there is **substantial authoritative support** for the principle. Figure 1-4 illustrates the relative authority of sources of generally accepted accounting principles from the category with highest authority to that with the least.

In situations in which there is a conflict between the accounting treatment suggested by pronouncements from two different categories, the pronouncement from the higher category prevails. For example, authoritative body pronouncements prevail over pronouncements of other experts and widely recognized pronouncements and practices. When there

Figure 1–4 Sources of generally accepted accounting principles

	Category	Pronouncement
a.	Authoritative Body Pronouncements	Financial Accounting Standards Board (FASB) *Statements* and *Interpretations* Governmental Accounting Standards Board (GASB) *Statements* and *Interpretations* Accounting Principles Board (APB) *Opinions* (not superceded)
b. (1)	Other Expert Pronouncements	AICPA Industry Audit Guides and Accounting Guides AICPA Statements of Position FASB and GASB Technical Bulletins
(2)	Widely Recognized Pronouncements and Practices	AICPA Accounting Interpretations Widely accepted industry practice
c.	Other Accounting Literature	APB Statements AICPA Issues Papers Accounting Standard Executive Committee Practice Bulletins Minutes of the FASB Emerging Issues Task Force FASB Concepts Statements International Accounting Standards Other Professional Association and Regulatory Pronouncements Accounting textbooks and articles

is a conflict within a category, the auditors should select the accounting principle that most clearly reflects the *economic substance* of the particular transaction.

Other types of auditors' reports

The form of auditors' report discussed in this chapter is called a *standard unqualified opinion.* Such a report may be regarded as a "clean bill of health" issued by the auditors. An unqualified opinion denotes that the examination was adequate in scope and that the financial statements present fairly the financial position and results of operations in conformity with generally accepted accounting principles. Under these circumstances, the auditors are taking *no exceptions* and inserting *no qualifications* in the report.

An unqualified opinion is the type of report the client wants and also the type auditors prefer to issue. In some audits, however, the circumstances do not permit the auditors to give their unqualified opinion on the financial statements. As alternatives to an unqualified opinion, auditors may issue a *qualified opinion,* an *adverse opinion,* or a *disclaimer of opinion.* In some situations, the auditors also include additional *"explanatory language"* in the report.

The auditors issue a *qualified opinion* on financial statements when there is some limitation on their examination, or when one or more items in the financial statements are not presented in accordance with generally accepted accounting principles. The limitation or exception must be significant but not so material as to overshadow an overall opinion on the financial statements.

An *adverse opinion* states that the financial statements are not fairly presented. In practice an adverse opinion is rare, because it would be of little use to the client. If the financial statements are so deficient as to warrant an adverse opinion by the auditors, this situation will be discussed between the auditors and the client's management. The management probably will agree to make the changes necessary to avoid an adverse opinion or will decide to terminate the audit engagement and thus avoid paying additional audit fees.

The auditors will issue a *disclaimer of opinion* if they are unable to determine the overall fairness of the financial statements. This type of report results from very significant limitations in the scope of the auditors' examination or limitations that are imposed by the client.

It is important for users of financial statements to be informed of certain matters, such as material uncertainties that may affect the financial statements, changes in accounting principles in relation to the prior year, or the fact that another audit firm is responsible for a significant aspect of the audit. The auditors direct the users' attention to such matters by adding *explanatory language* to their report. This additional language does not affect the auditors' opinion on the financial statements; it may be included in any of the four types of reports described above.

The cost of an audit

Audits are expensive. Even for a small business, the cost of an audit will run into the thousands of dollars; for the largest corporations, the cost may exceed a million dollars. Is an audit worth the price?

For most business entities, the answer is definitely yes. The audited financial statements of many companies go to a wide variety of users: bankers, other creditors, investors, labor unions, government agencies, and others. If these financial statements were not audited, they would not meet the needs of these many decision-making users. Presumably each decision maker would then have to conduct its own investigation to provide assurance of acting on the basis of reliable information. These multiple investigations would be far more costly than having a competent CPA firm establish the reliability of the financial statements for the benefit of all the many users.

For a small business, an independent audit may or may not represent a justifiable cost. The most common reason for a small business to incur the cost of an audit is the influence exerted by a bank that insists upon audited financial statements as a condition for granting a bank loan. If a small business is not in need of bank credit, it may see little need for an independent audit.

One alternative is to retain a CPA firm to perform other services, such as the *compilation* or *review* of financial statements. To compile financial statements means to prepare them; this service is often rendered by a CPA firm when the client does not have accounting personnel capable of preparing statements. A *review* of financial statements by a CPA is substantially less in scope than an audit and is designed to lend a limited degree of credibility to the statements. It stresses inquiries by the CPA and comparison of amounts in the statements with prior year amounts. These types of analytical procedures are useful in bringing to light any unreasonable relationships among financial statement amounts. Compilations and reviews will be discussed in Chapter 19.

KEY TERMS INTRODUCED OR EMPHASIZED IN CHAPTER 1

Adverse opinion An opinion issued by the auditors that the financial statements they have examined *do not present fairly* the financial position, results of operation, or cash flows in conformity with generally accepted accounting principles.

American Institute of Certified Public Accountants (AICPA) The national professional organization of CPAs engaged in promoting high professional standards and improving the quality of financial reporting.

Attest function The primary function of the independent public accountant—to attest to information (usually financial statements); that is, to bear witness as to its reliability and fairness. The independent opinion of the CPA lends credibility to audited financial information.

Audit   An examination or investigation by independent public accountants of a set of financial statements, and the accounting records and other supporting evidence both within and outside the client's business.

Auditors' standard report   A very precise document designed to communicate exactly the character and limitations of the responsibility being assumed by the auditors; in standard form, the report consists of an introductory paragraph, a scope paragraph, and an opinion paragraph, which cover the basic financial statements.

Certified public accountant   A person licensed by the state to practice public accounting as a profession, based on having passed the Uniform CPA Examination and having met certain educational and experience requirements.

Compliance audit   An audit to determine whether verifiable data such as income tax returns or other financial reports are in compliance with established criteria.

Consistency   The concept of using the same accounting principles from year to year so that the successive financial statements issued by a business entity will be comparable.

CPA examination   A uniform examination administered twice a year by the American Institute of Certified Public Accountants for state boards of accountancy to enable them to issue CPA licenses. The examination covers the topics of auditing, accounting theory, accounting practice, and business law.

Disclaimer of opinion   A form of report in which the auditors state that they do not express an opinion on the financial statements; it should include a separate paragraph stating the auditors' reasons for disclaiming an opinion and also disclosing any reservations they may have concerning the financial statements.

Disclosure   Making public all material information about financial affairs.

Fraud   Misrepresentation by a person of a material fact, known by that person to be untrue or made with reckless indifference as to whether the fact is true, with intent to deceive and with the result that another party is injured.

Generally accepted accounting principles (GAAP)   Concepts or standards established by such authoritative bodies as the Accounting Principles Board (APB), the FASB, and the GASB and accepted by the accounting profession as essential to proper financial reporting.

Generally accepted auditing standards (GAAS)   A set of 10 standards adopted by the AICPA and binding on its members—designed to ensure the quality of the auditors' work.

Independence   A most important auditing standard, which prohibits CPAs from expressing an opinion on financial statements of an enterprise unless they are independent with respect to such enterprise; independence is impaired by a material financial interest, service as an officer or trustee, loans to or from the enterprise, and various other relationships.

Internal control structure   A company's control environment, accounting system, and control policies and procedures that are established to provide reasonable assurance that the company's objectives will be achieved. Such objectives include: (1) safeguarding its resources from waste, fraud, and inefficiency; (2) promoting accuracy and reliability in accounting and operating data; (3) encouraging compliance with company policy; and (4) judging the efficiency of operations in all divisions of the business.

Operational audit   A review of a department or other unit of a business or governmental organization to measure the efficiency of operations.

Qualified opinion   The appropriate form of audit report when there is a limitation in the scope of the audit or the financial statements depart from GAAP significantly enough to require mention in the auditors' report, but not so materially as to necessitate the expression of an adverse opinion or the disclaiming of an opinion.

Securities and Exchange Commission (SEC)   A government agency authorized to review financial statements of companies seeking approval to issue securities for sale to the public.

Statements on Auditing Standards (SASs)   A series of statements issued by the Auditing Standards Board of the AICPA. Considered to be interpretations of generally accepted auditing standards.

Unqualified opinion   The form of audit report issued when the examination was adequate in scope and the auditors believe that the financial statements present fairly the financial position and operating results in conformity with generally accepted accounting principles.

GROUP 1: REVIEW QUESTIONS

1-1.   What is the principal use and significance of an audit report to a large corporation with securities listed on a stock exchange? To a small family-owned enterprise?

1-2.   When a CPA firm completes an audit of a business and issues a report, does it express an opinion on the client's accounting records, financial statements, or both? Give reasons.

1-3.   Is an *independent status* possible or desirable for internal auditors as compared with the independence of a CPA firm? Explain.

1-4.   What is the difference between generally accepted accounting principles (GAAP) and generally accepted auditing standards (GAAS)? Give an example of a generally accepted accounting principle and an example of a generally accepted auditing standard falling under the subhead of *general standards*.

1-5.   The generally accepted auditing standards established by the AICPA list first the requirement that "the examination is to be performed by a person or persons having adequate technical training and proficiency as an auditor." What would be the usual avenues for an individual to meet these personal qualifications?

1-6.   What relationship exists between generally accepted auditing standards (GAAS) and the Statements on Auditing Standards (SASs)?

1-7.   The first SAS issued was substantially larger and different in coverage from all the following ones. What explains this difference?

1-8.   What does an operational audit try to measure? Does an operational audit involve more or fewer subjective judgments than a compliance audit or an audit of financial statements? (Explain.) To whom is the report directed after completion of an operational audit?

1–9. The attest function is said to be the principal reason for the existence of a public accounting profession. What is meant by attesting to a client's financial statements, and what two steps are required?

1–10. Identify the two principal qualifications that should be possessed by a person who is to perform the attest function for a company's financial statements.

1–11. You are to evaluate the following quotation:

"If a CPA firm completes an examination of Adam Company's financial statements following generally accepted auditing standards and is satisfied with the results of the audit, an ***unqualified*** audit report may be issued. On the other hand, if no audit is performed of the current year's financial statements, but the CPA firm has performed satisfactory audits in prior years, has confidence in the management of the company, and makes a quick review of the current year's financial statements, a qualified report may be issued."

Do you agree? Give reasons to support your answer.

1–12. Distinguish between a compliance audit and an operational audit.

1–13. CPA firms are sometimes grouped into the categories of local firms, regional firms, and national firms. Explain briefly the characteristics of each. Include in your answer the types of services stressed in each group.

1–14. Contrast the objectives of auditing at the beginning of this century with the objectives of auditing today.

1–15. How does the role of the Securities and Exchange Commission differ from that of the AICPA?

1–16. Describe briefly the function of the General Accounting Office.

1–17. Pike Company has had an annual audit performed by the same firm of certified public accountants for many years. The financial statements and copies of the audit report are distributed to stockholders each year shortly after completion of the audit. Who is primarily responsible for the fairness of these financial statements? Explain.

1–18. List two of the more important contributions to auditing literature by the American Institute of Certified Public Accountants.

1–19. Draft the standard form of audit report commonly issued after a satisfactory examination of a client's financial statements.

1–20. Apart from auditing, what other professional services are offered by CPA firms?

1–21. Davis & Co., Certified Public Accountants, after completing an audit of Samson Company decided that it would be unable to issue an unqualified opinion. What circumstances might explain this decision?

1–22. State four principal assertions made by the auditors in the opinion paragraph of the auditors' standard report.

1–23. Alan Weston, CPA, completed an examination of Kirsten Manufacturing Company and issued an unqualified audit report. What does this tell us about the extent of the auditing procedures included in the examination?

1–24. A CPA firm does not guarantee the financial soundness of a client when it renders an opinion on financial statements, nor does the CPA firm guarantee the absolute accuracy of the statements. Yet the CPA firm's opinion is respected and accepted. What is expected of the CPA firm in order to merit such confidence?   (AICPA, adapted)

1–25. Criticize the following statement: "Throughout this audit, for all purposes, we will define a 'material amount' as $500,000."

1–26. The AICPA has made significant contributions to improving the quality of practice by CPAs. Describe the AICPA membership requirements that are designed to achieve that purpose.

1–27. What were some of the factors that caused auditors to adopt a sampling technique rather than make a complete review of all transactions?

1–28. Describe several business situations that would create a need for a report by an independent public accountant concerning the fairness of a company's financial statements.

1–29. Spacecraft, Inc. is a large corporation audited regularly by a CPA firm and also maintaining an internal auditing staff. Explain briefly how the relationship of the CPA firm to Spacecraft differs from the relationship of the internal auditing staff to Spacecraft.

1–30. If a CPA firm has made a thorough professional examination of a client's financial statements, should it not be able to issue a report dealing with facts rather than the mere expression of an opinion? Explain.

1–31. What is the meaning of *quality control* and *peer review* as these terms relate to the operation of a CPA firm? Is peer review mandatory? Explain.

GROUP II: QUESTIONS REQUIRING ANALYSIS

1–32. The self-interest of the provider of financial information (whether an individual or a business entity) often runs directly counter to the interests of the user of the information.
  a. Give an example of such opposing interests.
  b. What may be done to compensate for the possible bias existing because of the self-interest of the individual or business entity providing the financial information?

1–33. Evaluate the following quotation: "Every business, large or small, should have an annual audit by a CPA firm. To forgo an audit because of its cost is false economy."

1–34. An attitude of independence is a most essential element of an audit by a firm of certified public accountants. Describe several situations in which the CPA firm might find it somewhat difficult to maintain this independent point of view.

1–35. Jane Lee, a director of a large corporation with large numbers of stockholders and lines of credit with several banks, suggested that the corporation appoint as controller John Madison, a certified public accountant on the staff of the auditing firm that had made annual audits of the corporation for many years. Lee expressed the opinion that this move would effect a considerable saving in professional fees because annual audits would no longer be needed. She proposed to give the controller, if appointed, an internal auditing staff to carry on such continuing investigations of accounting data as appeared necessary. Evaluate this proposal.

1–36. "The auditors' work is essentially complete when they have determined that the dollar amounts in the financial statements are in agreement with the amounts in the client company's ledger accounts." Do you agree with this quotation? Explain.

1–37. During a political campaign, a candidate for public office made the following statement: "If a large corporation breaks any federal law or takes any action that violates moral standards, it is the responsibility of that corporation's independent auditors to make full and prompt disclosure of such action. By strict enforcement of this concept, we can deter criminal acts and reduce the congestion in our courts." Evaluate this quotation. In your answer, consider separately the question of illegal acts by the large corporate client and violation of moral standards.

1–38. The role of the auditor in the American economy has changed over the years in response to changes in our economic and political institutions. Consequently, the nature of an audit today is quite different from that of an audit performed in the year 1900. Classify the following phrases into two groups: (1) phrases more applicable to an audit performed in 1900 and (2) phrases more applicable to an audit performed today.

    a. Complete review of all transactions.
    b. Assessment of internal control.
    c. Auditors' attention concentrated on balance sheet.
    d. Emphasis upon use of sampling techniques.
    e. Determination of fairness of financial statements.
    f. Audit procedures to prevent or detect fraud on the part of all employees and managers.
    g. Registration statement.
    h. Fairness of reported earnings per share.
    i. Influence of stock exchanges and the investing public upon use of independent auditors.
    j. Generally accepted auditing standards.
    k. Bankers and short-term creditors as principal users of audit reports.
    l. Pressure for more disclosure.
    m. **Certification** by the auditors.

1–39. Select the best answer for each of the following items and give reasons for your choice.

    a. Which of the following is responsible for the fairness of the representations made in financial statements?
        (1) Client's management
        (2) Independent auditor
        (3) Audit committee
        (4) AICPA
    b. The most important reason for having an annual audit by a CPA firm is to—
        (1) Provide assurance to investors and other outsiders that the financial statements are dependable.
        (2) Enable officers and directors to avoid personal responsibility for any deficiencies in the financial statements.
        (3) Meet the requirements of government agencies.
        (4) Provide assurance that fraud, if any exists, will be brought to light.

   c. The nature and content of the three generally accepted auditing stan-
      dards classified as standards of field work are best summarized as—
      (1) The need to maintain an independence in mental attitude in all
          matters relating to the audit.
      (2) The criteria of audit planning and evidence-gathering.
      (3) The criteria for the content of the auditors' report on financial
          statements and related footnote disclosure.
      (4) The competence, independence, and professional care of per-
          sons performing the audit.
   d. Which of the following ultimately determines the specific audit proce-
      dures necessary to provide an independent auditor with a reasonable
      basis for expression of an opinion?
      (1) The audit program.
      (2) The auditor's judgment.
      (3) Generally accepted auditing standards.
      (4) The auditor's working papers.
   e. An unqualified standard audit report by a CPA normally does not
      explicitly state—
      (1) The CPA's opinion that the financial statements comply with
          generally accepted accounting principles.
      (2) That generally accepted auditing standards were followed in the
          conduct of the audit.
      (3) That the internal control structure of the client was found to be
          satisfactory.
      (4) The subjects of the audit examination.
   f. The general group of the generally accepted auditing standards in-
      cludes a requirement that—
      (1) The auditor maintain an independent mental attitude.
      (2) The audit be conducted in conformity with general accepted ac-
          counting principles.
      (3) Assistants, if any, be properly supervised.
      (4) The auditor obtain an understanding of internal control.

                                                      (AICPA, adapted)

**GROUP III:
PROBLEMS**

1–40. For the purposes of this problem, you are to assume the existence of five
       types of auditors: CPA, GAO, IRS, bank examiner, and internal auditor.
       Also assume that the work of these various auditors can be grouped into
       five classifications: audits of financial statements, compliance audits, op-
       erational audits, accounting services, and management advisory services.

       For each of the following topics, you are to state the type of auditor
       most probably involved. Also identify the topic with one of the above
       classes of work.

       You should organize your answer in a three-column format as follows:
       Column 1, list the number of the topic; Column 2, list the type of auditor
       involved; and Column 3, list the class of work.

       1. Financial statements of a small business to be submitted to a bank in
          support of a loan application.
       2. Financial statements of a large bank listed on the New York Stock
          Exchange to be distributed to stockholders.

3. Review of the management directive stating the goals and responsibilities of a corporation's mail-handling department.

4. Review of costs and accomplishments of a military research program carried on within the Air Force to determine whether the program was cost-effective.

5. Examination on a surprise basis of Midtown State Bank. Emphasis placed on verification of cash, marketable securities, and loans receivable and on consistent observation of banking code.

6. Analysis of the accounting system of a small business with the objective of making recommendations concerning installation of a computer-based system.

7. Determination of fairness of financial statements for public distribution by a corporation that has a professional-level internal auditing staff.

8. Review of the activities of the receiving department of a large manufacturing company, with special attention to efficiency of materials inspection and promptness of reports issued.

9. Review of tax return of corporate president to determine whether charitable contributions are adequately substantiated.

10. Review of daily attendance during spring term at Blue Ridge Consolidated School District to ascertain whether payments received from state were substantiated by pupil-day data. Also to determine whether disbursements by District were within authorized limits.

11. Review of transactions of government agency to determine whether disbursements under Payment-In-Kind program of U.S. Department of Agriculture followed the intent of Congress.

12. Compilation of quarterly financial statements for a small business that does not have any accounting personnel capable of preparing financial statements.

1–41. *a.* Listed below are 10 publications in the fields of auditing and accounting.
1. The *Accounting Review*.
2. *Statements on Auditing Standards* (SASs).
3. The *Journal of Accountancy*.
4. *Regulation S-X. Form and Content of Financial Statements*.
5. *Statements on Standards for Accounting and Review Services* (SSARSs).
6. *Financial Reporting Releases* (FRR).
7. Accounting and Reporting Standards for Corporate Financial Statements.
8. Accounting and Reporting Standards for Governmental Entities.
9. *Industry Audit Guides*.
10. *Auditing Procedure Studies*.

The list of organizations shown below includes the sponsors or publishers of the above 10 publications.
(*a*) Accounting Principles Board (APB).
(*b*) Securities and Exchange Commission (SEC).
(*c*) American Accounting Association (AAA).

(d)   American Institute of Certified Public Accountants (AICPA).
(e)   Financial Accounting Standards Board (FASB).
(f)   Internal Revenue Service (IRS).
(g)   General Accounting Office (GAO).
(h)   Federal Reserve Board (FRB).
(i)   Governmental Accounting Standards Board (GASB).

Required:
You are to identify the sponsoring organization for each of the 10 publications. (Some of the organizations may not have a publication in this list.) Organize your answer in a two-column format. In the left-hand column, list the number and name of each publication in the order shown above. In the right-hand column, list the identifying letter and name of the sponsoring organization. For example, on line 1, list (1) *The Accounting Review* in the left column and (2) American Accounting Association in the right column.

b.   Each auditing term (or organizational name) in Column One below bears a close relationship to a term in Column Two.

Column one	**Column two**
1. Quality control.	a. Compliance audit.
2. Operational audit.	b. Attest function.
3. Internal control.	c. Material information.
4. General Accounting Office.	d. Credibility.
5. Disclosure.	e. Peer review.
6. Major reason for existence of public accounting profession.	f. Registration statement.
7. Internal Revenue Service.	g. Measurement of effectiveness and efficiency of a unit of an organization.
8. Securities and Exchange Commission.	h. Basis for sampling and testing.
9. Audited financial statements.	i. Auditing staff reporting to Congress.
10. Auditors' unqualified report.	j. Due professional care.
11. General standards group of generally accepted auditing standards.	k. Sufficient, competent evidential matter.
12. Standards of field work.	l. Introductory paragraph, scope paragraph, and opinion paragraph.

Required:
You are to identify the most closely related terms in Columns One and Two. Organize your answer in a two-column format by copying the numbers and terms in Column One as given. Then, rearrange the sequence of terms in Column Two so that each line of your schedule will contain two closely related terms.

1–42.   Joe Rezzo, a college student majoring in accounting, helped finance his education with a part-time job maintaining all accounting records for a small business, White Company, located near the campus. Upon graduation, Rezzo passed the CPA examination and joined the audit staff of a national CPA firm. However, he continued to perform all accounting work for White Company during his "leisure time." Two years later, Rezzo received his CPA certificate and decided to give up his part-time work with White Company. He notified White that he would no longer be available after preparing the year-end financial statements.

On January 7, Rezzo delivered the annual financial statements as his final act for White Company. The owner then made the following request: "Joe, I am applying for a substantial bank loan, and the bank loan officer insists upon getting audited financial statements to support my loan application. You are now a CPA, and you know everything that's happened in this company and everything that's included in these financial statements, and you know they give a fair picture. I would appreciate it if you would write out the standard audit report and attach it to the financial statements. Then I'll be able to get some fast action on my loan application."

Required:
a. Would Rezzo be justified in complying with White's request for an auditor's opinion? Explain.
b. If you think Rezzo should issue the audit report, do you think he should first perform an audit of the company despite his detailed knowledge of the company's affairs? Explain.
c. If White had requested an audit by the national CPA firm for which Rezzo worked, would it have been reasonable for that firm to accept and to assign Rezzo to perform the audit? Explain.

1–43. The following audit report is deficient in several respects.

> To Whom It May Concern:
>
> We have examined the accounting records of Garland Corporation for the year ended June 30, 19—. We counted the cash and marketable securities, studied the accounting methods in use (which were consistently followed throughout the year), and made tests of the ledger accounts for assets and liabilities. The internal control structure contained no weaknesses.
>
> In our opinion the accompanying balance sheet and related income statement present correctly the financial condition of the Corporation at June 30, 19—.
>
> The accounting records of Garland Corporation are maintained in accordance with accounting principles generally observed throughout the industry. Our examination was made in accordance with generally accepted auditing standards, and we certify the records and financial statements without qualification.

Required:
You are to criticize the report systematically from beginning to end, considering each sentence in turn. Use a separate paragraph with identifying heading for each point, as for example, Paragraph 1, Sentence 1. You may also wish to make comments on the overall contents of each paragraph and upon any omissions. Give reasons to support your views. After completing this critical review of the report, draft a revised report, on the

assumption that your examination was adequate in all respects and disclosed no significant deficiencies.

1–44. Bart James, a partner in the CPA firm of James and Day, received the following memorandum from John Gray, president of Gray Manufacturing Corporation, an audit client of many years.

Dear Bart:

   I have a new type of engagement for you. You are familiar with how much time and money we have been spending in installing equipment to eliminate the air and water pollution caused by our manufacturing plant. We have changed our production process to reduce discharge of gases; we have changed to more expensive fuel sources with less pollution potential; and we have discontinued some products because we couldn't produce them without causing considerable pollution.

   I don't think the stockholders and the public are aware of the efforts we have made, and I want to inform them of our accomplishments in avoiding danger to the environment. We will devote a major part of our annual report to this topic, stressing that our company is the leader of the entire industry in combating pollution. To make this publicity more convincing, I would like to retain your firm to study what we have done and to attest as independent accountants that our operations are the best in the industry as far as preventing pollution is concerned.

   To justify your statement, you are welcome to investigate every aspect of our operations as fully as you wish. We will pay for your services at your regular audit rates and will publish your "pollution opinion" in our annual report to stockholders immediately following some pictures and discussion of our special equipment and processes for preventing industrial pollution. We may put this section of the annual report in a separate cover and distribute it free to the public. Please let me know at once if this engagement is acceptable to you.

Required:

Put yourself in Bart James's position and write a reply to this client's request. Indicate clearly whether you are willing to accept the engagement and explain your attitude toward this proposed extension of the auditor's attest function. (In drafting your letter, keep in mind that Gray is a valued audit client whose goodwill you want to maintain.)

1–45. John Clinton, owner of Clinton Company, applied for a bank loan and was informed by the banker that audited financial statements of the business must be submitted before the bank could consider the loan application. Clinton then retained Arthur Jones, CPA, to perform an audit. Clinton informed Jones that audited financial statements were required by the bank and that the audit must be completed within three weeks. Clinton also promised to pay Jones a fixed fee plus a bonus if the bank approved the loan. Jones agreed and accepted the engagement.

   The first step taken by Jones was to hire two accounting students to conduct the audit. He spent several hours telling them exactly what to do. Jones told the students not to spend time reviewing internal controls but instead to concentrate on proving the mathematical accuracy of the ledger accounts and summarizing the data in the accounting records that support Clinton Company's financial statements. The students followed Jones's instructions and after two weeks gave Jones the financial statements that did not include any footnotes. Jones reviewed the statements and prepared an unqualified audit report. The report, however, did not refer to generally accepted accounting principles.

Required:

List on the left side of the sheet of paper the generally accepted auditing standards that were violated by Jones, and indicate how the actions of Jones resulted in a failure to comply with each standard. Organize your answer as follows:

Generally accepted auditing standards	Actions by Jones resulting in failure to comply with generally accepted auditing standards
General standards (1) The examination is to be performed by a person or persons having adequate technical training and proficiency as an auditor.	(1)

1–46. The business activities of Casa Royale, Inc. consist of the administration and maintenance of approximately 400 condominiums and common property owned by individuals in a suburban residential development. Revenue consists of monthly fees collected from each condominium owner, plus some miscellaneous revenue. The principal expenses are property taxes and maintenance of all the buildings, shrubbery, swimming pools, lakes, parking lots, and other facilities. The furniture, fixtures, and equipment owned by the corporation and used to perform its maintenance functions represent about 25 percent of its total assets of $400,000.

The corporation retained Howard Smith, CPA, to perform an audit of its financial statements for the current year and received from him the following audit report.

Independent Auditors' Report

Board of Governors
Casa Royale, Inc.

I have audited the accompanying balance sheet of Casa Royale, Inc. as of December 31, 19X1, and the related statements of income, retained earnings, and cash flows for the year then ended. These financial statements are the responsibility of the Company's management. My responsibility is to express an opinion on these financial statements based on my audit.

I conducted my audit in accordance with generally accepted auditing standards. Those standards require that I plan and perform the audit to

(Continued)

obtain reasonable assurance about whether the financial statements are free of material misstatement. An audit includes examining, on a test basis, evidence supporting the amounts and disclosures in the financial statements. An audit also includes assessing the accounting principles used and significant estimates made by management, as well as evaluating the overall financial statement presentation. I believe that my audit provides a reasonable basis for my opinion.

As further amplified in Note 3 to the financial statements, my engagement did not include an examination of records relating to furniture, fixtures, equipment, or other assets indicated on the balance sheet.

In my opinion, except for the effects of such adjustments, if any, as might have been determined to be necessary had I been able to examine evidence regarding plant assets, the financial statements referred to above present fairly, in all material respects, the financial position of Casa Royale, Inc. as of December 31, 19X1, and the results of its operations and its cash flows for the year then ended in conformity with generally accepted accounting principles.

Howard Smith, CPA

The note to the financial statements referred to in the audit report read as follows: "The equipment necessary for administration and maintenance was acquired in various years going back as far as the origin of the Corporation 10 years ago. Therefore, the records do not lend themselves readily to application of standard auditing procedures and are not included in our engagement of independent auditors. The equipment is being depreciated using the straight-line method over various estimated useful lives."

Required:
a. What type of audit report did the CPA issue? Was this the appropriate type of report under the circumstances? Explain.
b. What contradiction, if any, exists between the scope paragraph of the audit report and the note to the financial statements? Do you consider the note to be a reasonable statement? Why or why not?
c. Did the omission of the examination of plant assets from the audit engagement have any bearing on the evidence needed by the auditor in order to express an opinion on the income statement? Explain fully.

Professional ethics

Chapter 2 study objectives

After studying this chapter, you should be able to:
— Describe the reasons that professions establish professional ethics.
— Identify the two parts of the AICPA *Code of Professional Conduct.*
— Discuss the Principles section of the AICPA Code.
— Describe each of the Rules contained in the AICPA Code.
— Explain the concept of independence and identify circumstances in which independence is impaired.
— Describe *The Institute of Internal Auditors, Inc., Code of Ethics.*

The need for professional ethics

All recognized professions have developed codes of professional ethics. The fundamental purpose of such codes is to provide members with guidelines for maintaining a professional attitude and conducting themselves in a manner that will enhance the professional stature of their discipline.

To understand the importance of a code of ethics to public accountants and other professionals, one must understand the nature of a profession as opposed to other vocations. Unfortunately, there is no universally accepted definition of what constitutes a profession; yet, for generations, certain types of activities have been recognized as professions while others have not. Medicine, law, engineering, architecture, and theology are examples of disciplines long accorded professional status. Public accounting is a relative newcomer to the ranks of the professions, but it has achieved widespread recognition in recent decades.

All of the recognized professions have several common characteristics.

The most important of these characteristics are (*a*) a responsibility to serve the public, (*b*) a complex body of knowledge, (*c*) standards of admission to the profession, and (*d*) a need for public confidence. Let us briefly discuss these characteristics as they apply to public accounting.

Responsibility to serve the public   The certified public accountant is the representative of the public—creditors, stockholders, consumers, employees, and others—in the financial reporting process. The role of the independent auditor is to assure that financial statements are *fair to all parties* and not biased to benefit one group at the expense of another. This responsibility to serve the public interest must be a basic motivation for the professional. If a CPA firm's only concern were maximizing its income, the firm would presumably work for the benefit of creditors, investors, management, or whichever group offered the highest fee.

There is a saying in public accounting that "the public is our only client." This expression is an oversimplification, since the entity being audited pays the auditor's fee and is, in fact, the client. Yet the saying conveys an ideal that is essential to the long-run professional status of public accounting. Public accountants must maintain a high degree of independence from their client (the company) if they are to be of service to the larger community. Independence is perhaps the most important concept embodied in public accounting's code of professional ethics.

Complex body of knowledge   Any practitioner or student of accounting has only to look at the abundance of authoritative pronouncements governing financial reports to realize that accounting is a complex body of knowledge. One reason why such pronouncements continue to proliferate is that accounting must reflect what is taking place in an increasingly complex environment. As the environment changes—such as the trend toward business combinations in the 1960s and the increase in litigation and government intervention in more recent years—accounting principles and auditing practices must adapt. The continual growth in the "common body of knowledge" for practicing accountants has led the AICPA to enact continuing education requirements for CPAs. The need for technical competence and familiarity with current standards of practice is embodied in the *Code of Professional Conduct*.

Standards of admission to the profession   Attaining a license to practice as a certified public accountant requires an individual to meet minimum standards for education and experience. The individual must also pass the uniform CPA examination showing mastery of the body of knowledge described above. Once licensed, certified public accountants must adhere to the ethics of the profession or risk disciplinary action.

Need for public confidence   Physicians, lawyers, certified public accountants, and all other professionals must have the confidence of the public to be successful. To the CPA, however, public confidence is of special significance. The CPA's product is credibility. Without public confidence in the attestor, the attest function serves no useful purpose.

Professional ethics in public accounting as in other professions have developed gradually and are still in a process of change as the practice of accounting itself changes. Often new concepts are added as a result of unfortunate incidents that reflect unfavorably upon the profession, although not specific violations of existing standards.

Professional ethics in public accounting

A principal factor in maintaining high professional standards of practice has been the development of a code of professional ethics under the leadership of the American Institute of Certified Public Accountants. Careless work or lack of integrity on the part of any CPA is a reflection upon the entire profession. Consequently, the members of the profession have acted in unison through their national organization to devise a code of conduct. This code provides practical guidance to the individual member in maintaining a professional attitude. In addition, this code gives assurance to clients and to the public that the profession intends to maintain high standards and to enforce compliance by individual members.

Evidence that public accounting has achieved the status of a profession is found in the willingness of its members to accept voluntarily standards of conduct more rigorous than those imposed by law. These standards of conduct set forth the basic responsibilities of CPAs to the public, clients, and fellow practitioners. To be effective, a body of professional ethics must be attainable and enforceable; it must consist not merely of abstract ideals but of attainable goals and practical working rules that can be enforced.

In the short run, the restraints imposed on the individual CPA by a body of professional ethics may sometimes appear to constitute a hardship. From a long-run point of view, however, it is clear that the individual practitioner, the profession as a whole, and the public all benefit from the existence of a well-defined body of professional ethics.

The AICPA *Code of Professional Conduct* was restructured by vote of its membership in November 1987. Developing the new Code represents a positive response by the profession to the rapidly changing environment of public accounting. It is designed to provide a framework for expanding professional services and responding to other changes in the profession, such as the increasingly competitive environment.

The restructured *Code of Professional Conduct* consists of two sections. The first section, the Principles, is a goal-oriented, positively stated discussion of the profession's responsibilities to the public, clients, and fellow practitioners. The Principles provide the framework for the Rules, the second section of the Code. The Rules are enforceable applications of the Principles. They define acceptable behavior and identify sources of authority for performance standards.

To provide guidelines for the scope and application of the Rules, the AICPA issues ***interpretations.*** Senior Technical Committees of the AICPA, such as the Auditing Standards Board, interpret the Rules applying to their area of responsibility; the Professional Ethics Division Executive Committee issues interpretations that apply to all professional activities. The AICPA also issues ***ethics rulings*** which explain the application of the Rules and Interpretations to specific factual circumstances involving professional ethics.

A portion of the Principles section of the *Code of Professional Conduct* is quoted below, followed by a presentation and analysis of the section of the Code that includes the Rules.

SECTION I—PRINCIPLES[1]

Preamble

Membership in the American Institute of Certified Public Accountants is voluntary. By accepting membership, a certified public accountant assumes an obligation of self-discipline above and beyond the requirements of laws and regulations.

These Principles of the *Code of Professional Conduct* of the American Institute of Certified Public Accountants express the profession's recognition of its responsibilities to the public, to clients, and to colleagues. They guide members in the performance of their professional responsibilities and express the basic tenets of ethical and professional conduct. The Principles call for an unswerving commitment to honorable behavior, even at the sacrifice of personal advantage.

---

[1] Copyright © 1988 by the American Institute of Certified Public Accountants, Inc.

Article I
Responsibilities

In carrying out their responsibilities as professionals, members should exercise sensitive professional and moral judgments in all their activities.

As professionals, certified public accountants perform an essential role in society. Consistent with that role, members of the American Institute of Certified Public Accountants have responsibilities to all those who use their professional services. Members also have a continuing responsibility to cooperate with each other to improve the art of accounting, maintain the public's confidence, and carry out the profession's special responsibilities for self-governance. The collective efforts of all members are required to maintain and enhance the traditions of the profession.

Article II
The Public Interest

Members should accept the obligation to act in a way that will serve the public interest, honor the public trust, and demonstrate commitment to professionalism.

A distinguishing mark of a profession is acceptance of its responsibility to the public. The accounting profession's public consists of clients, credit grantors, governments, employers, investors, the business and financial community, and others who rely on the objectivity and integrity of certified public accountants to maintain the orderly functioning of commerce. This reliance imposes a public interest responsibility on certified public accountants. The public interest is defined as the collective well-being of the community of people and institutions the profession serves.

In discharging their professional responsibilities, members may encounter conflicting pressures from among each of those groups. In resolving those conflicts, members should act with integrity, guided by the precept that when members fulfill their responsibility to the public, clients' and employers' interests are best served.

Those who rely on certified public accountants expect them to discharge their responsibilities with integrity, objectivity, due professional care, and a genuine interest in serving the public. They are expected to provide quality services, enter into fee arrangements, and offer a range of services—all in a manner that demonstrates a level of professionalism consistent with these Principles of the *Code of Professional Conduct.*

All who accept membership in the American Institute of Certified Public Accountants commit themselves to honor the public trust. In return for the faith that the public reposes in them, members should seek continually to demonstrate their dedication to professional excellence.

Article III
Integrity

To maintain and broaden public confidence, members should perform all professional responsibilities with the highest sense of integrity.

Article IV
Objectivity and Independence

A member should maintain objectivity and be free of conflicts of interest in discharging professional responsibilities. A member in public practice should be independent in fact and appearance when providing auditing and other attestation services.

Article V
Due Care

A member should observe the profession's technical and ethical standards, strive continually to improve competence and the quality of services, and discharge professional responsibility to the best of the member's ability.

Article VI
Scope and Nature of Services

A member in public practice should observe the Principles of the Code of Professional Conduct in determining the scope and nature of services to be provided.

Each of these Principles should be considered by members in determining whether or not to provide specific services in individual circumstances. In some instances, they may represent an overall constraint on the nonaudit services that might be offered to a specific client. No hard-and-fast rules can be developed to help members reach these judgments, but they must be satisfied that they are meeting the spirit of the Principles in this regard.

In order to accomplish this, members should—

• Practice in firms that have in place internal quality-control procedures to ensure that services are competently delivered and adequately supervised.
• Determine, in their individual judgments, whether the scope and nature of other services provided to an audit client would create a conflict of interest in the performance of the audit function for that client.

- Assess, in their individual judgments, whether an activity is consistent with their role as professionals (for example, is such activity a reasonable extension or variation of existing services offered by the member or others in the profession?).

SECTION II—RULES

Applicability

The bylaws of the American Institute of Certified Public Accountants require that members adhere to the Rules of the Code of Professional Conduct. Members must be prepared to justify departures from these Rules.

Figure 2–1 is a complete listing of the Rules, which are presented and analyzed below.

Figure 2–1 The rules of the AICPA *Code of Professional Conduct*

Rule	Title
101	Independence
102	Integrity and Objectivity
201	General Standards
202	Compliance with Standards
203	Accounting Principles
301	Confidential Client Information
302	Contingent Fees
501	Acts Discreditable
502	Advertising and Other Forms of Solicitation
503	Incompatible Occupations
505	Form of Practice and Name

Independence

Rule 101   A member in public practice shall be independent in the performance of professional services as required by standards promulgated by bodies designated by Council.

Examples of independence problems   Interpretation 101–1 of the Code contains examples of transactions, interests, and relationships which result in a lack of independence in appearance. Specifically, the interpretation states that independence will be considered impaired if:

A. During the period of a professional engagement or at the time of expressing an opinion, a member or a member's firm:
   1. Had or was committed to acquire any direct or material indirect financial interest in the enterprise.

2. Was a trustee of any trust or executor or administrator of any estate if such trust or estate had or was committed to acquire any direct or material indirect financial interest in the enterprise.
3. Had any joint, closely held business investment with the enterprise or with any officer, director, or principal stockholders thereof that was material in relation to the member's net worth or to the net worth of the member's firm.
4. Had any loan to or from the enterprise or any officer, director, or principal stockholder of the enterprise. This proscription does not apply to the following loans from a financial institution when made under normal lending procedures, terms, and requirements:
   a. Loans obtained by a member or a member's firm that are not material in relation to the net worth of such borrower.
   b. Home mortgages.
   c. Other secured loans, except loans guaranteed by a member's firm which are otherwise unsecured.

B. During the period covered by the financial statements, during the period of the professional engagement, or at the time of expressing an opinion, a member or a member's firm:
   1. Was connected with the enterprise as a promoter, underwriter, or voting trustee, a director or officer or in any capacity equivalent to that of a member of management or of an employee.
   2. Was a trustee for any pension or profit-sharing trust of the enterprise.

The above examples are not intended to be all-inclusive.

Analysis of independence

The first Rule of Conduct is concerned with the vital issue of the auditors' independence. Two distinct ideas are involved in the concept of independence. First, the CPAs must in fact be independent of any enterprises they audit. *Independence in fact* refers to the CPAs' ability to maintain an objective and impartial mental attitude throughout the engagement. Second, the relationships between the CPAs and their clients must be such that the accountants will *appear independent* to third parties.

If the attest function is to lend credibility to financial statements, it is essential that readers of those statements *perceive* the CPAs as being objective and impartial. Thus, public accountants must not only *be* independent; they must also *appear* independent to outsiders who are given all relevant information about the relationships between the CPAs and their client.

Applicability of the independence rule   The independence rule does not apply to all services performed by public accountants. CPAs perform a host of services in which the client is the only beneficiary, such as management consulting, tax, and accounting services. In performing these services, the CPAs are not attesting to information for third parties, *and observance of the independence rule is not required.* Of course, the independence rule applies to auditing, but it also applies to all other attestation services, such as reviews of financial statements, examinations of financial forecasts, and the application of agreed-upon procedures to financial information. Our comments below regarding independence when performing audits apply equally to CPAs when they are performing any service that involves lending credibility to information in reports to third parties.

Independence of partners and staff   Does Rule 101 apply to all employees of a CPA firm? The term *a member or a member's firm* as used in Interpretation 101–1 applies to (1) *all* partners (or stockholders) in the firm, (2) all managerial employees[2] *assigned to an office* that significantly participates in the engagement, and (3) all professional staff *personally participating* in the engagement. Thus, the independence of a large CPA firm is not necessarily impaired merely because one employee of the firm is not independent of the client. If the employee does not have managerial responsibilities, the problem easily can be resolved by assigning the employee to other engagements. If the employee does have managerial responsibilities, it will be necessary to transfer the employee to an office of the firm that is not involved with this audit engagement.

Financial interests in audit clients   Naturally, outsiders will question the auditors' impartiality if the auditors have a financial interest in the client's business. When a CPA firm acquires a new audit client, the firm will notify its partners and staff that they must dispose of any stockholdings in the company before the audit engagement begins. By disposing of any such investments, the auditors avoid a challenge to their independence in dealing with the new client company.

Direct and indirect financial interests   Interpretation 101–1 makes a distinction between direct and indirect financial interests. Any *direct* financial interest in an audit client, such as the ownership of the client's stock, impairs independence; materiality is not an issue. However, an auditor may have an *indirect* interest in an audit client if the investment is not material to the CPA's net worth. This distinction enables auditors to

---

[2] Loosely translated, the term *managerial employee* refers to professional staff at the rank of "manager" or above. Staff auditors, often called "assistants" and "seniors," are not "managerial employees."

invest in companies or in mutual funds, which in turn may hold minor interests in audit clients.

Illustrative case

John Bates, a partner in the CPA firm Reynolds and Co., owns shares in a regulated mutual investment fund, which in turn holds shares of stock in audit clients of Reynolds and Co. The CPA firm inquired of the AICPA Professional Ethics Division whether this financial interest by Bates affected the firm's independence.

The response was that this indirect interest would not normally impair the independence of the CPA firm, because investment decisions are made only by the mutual fund's management. However, if the portfolio of the mutual fund were heavily invested in securities of a client of Reynolds and Co., the indirect interest could become material to Bates and thereby impair the independence of the CPA firm.

Past employment with the client Independence problems from financial interests, which are described in the first part of Interpretation 101–1, can be remedied simply by disposing of the financial interest before the engagement commences. This is not true of relationships described in part B of that Interpretation. CPAs can never issue an audit report covering any period which the auditors were employed in a management capacity with the client. To do so would violate the basic concept that individuals cannot act independently in evaluating the results of their own decisions.

Interests of a CPA's relatives Another question that often arises in discussions of independence may be stated as follows: How is independence affected by a financial interest or business position held by a relative of a CPA? The answer depends on the *closeness* of the family relationship and on whether the CPA works in a firm office that participates in the audit. The financial interests and business positions of a CPA's spouse, dependent children, or relatives supported by the CPA are attributed *directly to the CPA.* Accordingly, if the CPA's spouse owns even one share of a client's stock, the situation is evaluated as if the CPA owned the stock. Independence is impaired.

A problem of independence also may result from financial interests or business activities of other close relatives, such as parents, brothers, sisters, and nondependent children. However, the financial interests of these relatives are not attributed directly to the CPA, and independence is impaired only by investments that are material to the relative's net worth. Independence problems concerning close relatives may be mitigated if the CPA is geographically separated from the relatives and the CPA is not assigned to an office that participates in the engagement. To avoid an impairment of independence, it sometimes is necessary for a CPA firm to transfer a partner or staff member to an office that does not participate in a particular engagement.

Impairment of independence does not result from an investment or business relationship by distant relatives of a CPA, unless there are close financial ties between the CPA and the relative.

Other problems of independence   It is impossible to describe all the situations that impair the appearance of independence. Interpretations and Ethics Rulings are issued regularly describing the application of Rule 101 to new situations. For example, rulings have been issued regarding past-due audit fees, gifts from clients, and client-auditor litigation.

If fees owed by a client to a CPA firm become long overdue, it may appear that the CPAs' prospects for collection depend upon the nature of the auditors' report on the current financial statements. Thus, independence is considered impaired if fees for professional services rendered in prior years have not been collected before issuance of the auditors' report for the current year.

An outsider may question the independence of a CPA firm in situations in which a partner or employee accepts an expensive gift from a client. It would appear that special considerations might be tied to the acceptance of the gift, and the auditor might not act with complete impartiality. To avoid this implication of lack of independence, auditors should decline all but token gifts from audit clients.

Litigation may also affect the independence of auditors if the litigation involves the client and the auditors. The relationship between the auditors and client management must be characterized by complete candor and full disclosure. A relationship with these characteristics may not exist when litigation places the auditors and client management in an adversary position. Auditors in litigation, or potential litigation, with a client must evaluate the situation to determine whether the significance of the litigation affects the client's confidence in the auditors or the auditors' objectivity.

Independence as defined by the SEC   A discussion of professional ethics would be incomplete without considering the important role played by the Securities and Exchange Commission. A principal aim of the Commission throughout its existence has been the improvement of auditing standards and the establishment of high levels of professional conduct by the independent public accountants practicing before the Commission.

The laws administered by the SEC require that financial statements be examined by certified public accountants. The Commission therefore faces the task of deciding upon the meaning of *independence* on the part of accountants. The following was adopted as part of Rule 2–01 of *Regulation S-X:*

> The Commission will not recognize any certified public accountant . . . as independent who is not in fact independent. For example, an accountant will be considered not independent with respect to any person . . . (1) in which, during the period of his professional engagement to examine the financial statements being reported on or at the date of his report, he or his firm or a member thereof had, or was committed to acquire, any direct financial interest or any material indirect financial interest; or (2) with which, during the period of his professional engagement to examine the financial statements being reported on, at the date of his report or during the period covered by the financial statements, he or his firm or a member thereof was connected as a promoter, underwriter, voting trustee, director, officer, or employee . . . . For the purposes of Rule 2–01 the term "member" means all partners in the firm and all professional employees participating in the audit or located in an office of the firm participating in a significant portion of the audit.

In applying this rule to specific cases, the SEC has held that the public accountant was not independent in the following situations, among others:

1. A partner in an accounting firm also acted as legal counsel for the audit client.
2. An accounting firm performed the month-end accounting work of the audit client, including the making of adjusting and closing entries for the general ledger.
3. A partner of an accounting firm that audited a wholly owned subsidiary company invested in a nominal amount of stock of the subsidiary's nonclient parent company.

Independence when the auditors perform accounting services One difference between the concept of independence required by the SEC and that set forth in the AICPA *Code of Professional Conduct* relates to auditors who perform accounting services for a client. Can the auditors who post the general ledger, make closing entries, and maintain subsidiary records also serve as independent auditors for the company? The SEC answer is no; the CPA is not independent under these circumstances. The auditor should be an outsider who reviews the work performed by the client's accounting employees. If independent auditors perform the original accounting work, they cannot maintain the posture of an outside critic. In *Financial Reporting Releases, Sec. 602,* the SEC states: "The Commission is of the opinion that an accountant cannot objectively audit books and records which he has maintained for a client."

Illustrative case

The SEC found in one famous case (In the Matter of Interstate Hosiery Mills, Inc., 4 SEC 706, 717 [1939]) that a staff member of the CPA firm had been maintaining the accounting records of a client; the financial statements had been falsified, and the audit staff member was responsible for the falsification. Clearly the dual role of internal accountant and independent auditor played by this individual had resulted in defeating the purpose of the audit.

The AICPA, on the other hand, has often considered the propriety of combining the performance of manual or automated accounting services with the conduct of an independent audit for a client but has not opposed the practice as damaging to the auditor's independence. As long as the client takes responsibility for the financial statements and the auditors perform their engagement in accordance with generally accepted auditing standards, the AICPA indicates that independence is not impaired. Of course, the accounting services cannot include executing transactions or performance of any other management function.

If the AICPA ruled that independence is impaired whenever the auditors perform accounting services, such a ruling would no doubt be a blow to many small public accounting firms with practices including considerable write-up work and occasional audits for write-up clients. Despite this attitude of the AICPA, the SEC position denying the independence of a CPA who maintains a client's accounting records appears much sounder in terms of basic auditing philosophy.

Does rendering of management advisory services threaten the auditors' independence? A problem to be considered in rendering management advisory services is the possible threat to the auditors' independence when auditing and a variety of consulting services are performed for the same client. Can a public accounting firm that renders extensive *management advisory services* for a client still maintain the independent status so essential in an audit and in the expression of an opinion on the client's financial statements?

A CPA who becomes a part-time controller for a client and assumes a *decision-making* role in the client's affairs is not in a position to make an independent audit of the financial statements. On the other hand, public accounting firms have long been rendering certain purely *advisory* services to management while continuing to perform audits in an independent manner that serves the public interest. Advisory services can generally be distinguished from management proper; the work of the consultant or adviser consists of such functions as conducting special studies and investigations, making suggestions to management, pointing out the existence of weaknesses, outlining various alternative corrective measures, and making recommendations.

To provide guidelines for CPAs engaged in rendering advisory services, the AICPA issues a series of *Statements on Standards for Management Advisory Services*.

Independence—a matter of degree The concept of independence is not absolute; no auditors can claim **complete** independence of a client. Rather, independence is relative—a matter of degree. As long as the auditors work closely with client management and are paid fees by their clients, complete independence can be considered merely an ideal. Auditors must strive for the greatest degree of independence consistent with their environment.

Recent developments have served to increase the auditor's independence in dealings with management. One of these developments is the widespread adoption of audit committees by corporations. Members of these audit committees are selected from the company's board of directors. Ideally, audit committee members are outside directors, that is, board members who are not also officers of the company. The functions of the audit committee include appointing and discharging the independent auditors, determining the scope of the auditors' services, reviewing audit findings, and resolving conflicts between the auditors and management.

Another development that has strengthened the CPA's independence is an SEC requirement applying to public companies that change auditors. These companies must file an informative disclosure (Form 8-K) describing the reason for the change in auditors. The discharged auditors may also respond if they disagree with management's analysis. This requirement and the widespread establishment of audit committees restrict management from **shopping for accounting principles.** Shopping for accounting principles occurs when a company changes auditors to a CPA firm that is more likely to sanction a disputed accounting principle. A company's management might search for auditors, for example, who would accept a questionable inventory valuation method as being in accordance with generally accepted accounting principles. Concern about this problem also led to the issuance of *SAS 50* (AU 625),[3] which provides guidance to public accountants when they get a request from a company for a **written or oral** report on the accounting treatment of a prospective or completed transaction.

Before providing the report, the accountants should take steps to make sure they have a complete understanding of the form and substance of the transaction, including consulting with the company's current accountants. They should also review existing accounting principles, and consult

---

[3] *SAS 50,* "Reports on the Application of Accounting Principles" (New York, 1987), AU 625.

appropriate references and experts to provide an adequate basis for their conclusions. Although cases in which management actually shops for accounting principles are not common, it is clear that if management can change auditors casually, undue pressure is placed on auditors' independence.

Integrity and Objectivity

Rule 102 In the performance of any professional service, a member shall maintain objectivity and integrity, shall be free of conflicts of interest, and shall not knowingly misrepresent facts or subordinate his or her judgment to others.

Analysis of integrity and objectivity

Rule 102 applies to all members of the AICPA and all services provided by CPAs. It recognizes that clients, employers, or others may at times attempt to influence the judgment of CPAs on professional matters. To maintain the confidence and respect of the public, CPAs must never subordinate their professional judgments to others.

It is often difficult to determine if an individual has "knowingly misrepresented facts." Thus in evaluating whether a CPA has violated that part of Rule 102, we must look to whether or not, based on the circumstances, the CPA *should have known* of the misrepresentation. A ruling that a CPA violated Rule 102 is most commonly based upon evidence that the auditors should have been knowledgeable of the facts.

General Standards

Rule 201 A member shall comply with the following standards and with any interpretations thereof by bodies designated by Council.
A. Professional Competence. Undertake only those professional services that the member or the member's firm can reasonably expect to be completed with professional competence.
B. Due Professional Care. Exercise due professional care in the performance of professional services.
C. Planning and Supervision. Adequately plan and supervise the performance of professional services.
D. Sufficient Relevant Data. Obtain sufficient relevant data to afford a reasonable basis for conclusions or recommendations in relation to any professional services performed.

Analysis of general standards

In addition to performing audits, CPAs also provide accounting, review, tax, and management advisory services. Clients and the general public expect these services to be performed with competence and professional care. Therefore, ethical standards have been established under the category of general standards that apply to **all CPA services.**

Compliance with Standards

> *Rule 202   A member who performs auditing, review, compilation, management advisory, tax, or other professional services shall comply with standards promulgated by bodies designated by Council.*

Analysis of compliance with standards

Rule 202 requires CPAs to adhere to professional standards issued by other technical bodies. To date, the Council of the AICPA has recognized four bodies and given them authority for the following performance standards:

Technical body	Authority	Performance standards
Auditing Standards Board	Prescribe standards for accountants' association with financial statements, and supplementary information required by the FASB	*Statements on Auditing Standards*
Management Advisory Services Executive Committee	Prescribe standards for management advisory services	*Statements on Standards for Management Advisory Services*
Accounting and Review Services Committee	Prescribe standards for unaudited financial information services for nonpublic companies	*Statements on Standards for Accounting and Review Services*
Financial Accounting Standards Board	Prescribe disclosure standards for supplementary information outside the financial statements	*Statements of Financial Accounting Standards* and related *Interpretations*

CPAs must become familiar with such statements and apply them to their engagements. To violate standards prescribed by these bodies is to violate Rule 202 of the Code.

Accounting Principles

> *Rule 203   A member shall not (1) express an opinion or state affirmatively that the financial statements or other financial data of*

any entity are presented in conformity with generally accepted ac-counting principles or (2) state that he or she is not aware of any material modifications that should be made to such statements or data in order for them to be in conformity with generally accepted accounting principles, if such statements or data contain any depar-ture from an accounting principle promulgated by bodies desig-nated by Council to establish such principles that has a material effect on the statements or data taken as a whole. If, however, the statements or data contain such a departure and the member can demonstrate that due to unusual circumstances the financial state-ments or data would otherwise have been misleading, the member can comply with the rule by describing the departure, its approxi-mate effects, if practicable, and the reasons why compliance with the principle would result in a misleading statement.

Analysis of accounting principles

Rule 203 recognizes the authority of certain designated bodies to issue accounting principles. Under this rule, the AICPA has designated the pronouncements of the Financial Accounting Standards Board and its predecessor, the Accounting Principles Board, and the Governmental Accounting Standards Board as primary sources of generally accepted accounting principles. CPAs should not issue an unqualified opinion on a set of financial statements that materially depart from one of these pro-nouncements, except in the *rare* situation in which application of the pronouncement would result in misleading financial statements.

Confidential Client Information

Rule 301   A member in public practice shall not disclose any confidential client information without the specific consent of the client.

This rule shall not be construed (1) to relieve a member of the member's professional obligations under rules 202 and 203, (2) to affect in any way the member's obligation to comply with a validly issued and enforceable subpoena or summons, (3) to prohibit review of a member's professional practice under AICPA or state CPA society authorization, or (4) to preclude a member from initiating a complaint with or responding to any inquiry made by a recognized investigative or disciplinary body.

Members of a recognized investigative or disciplinary body and professional practice reviewers shall not use to their own advantage or disclose any member's confidential client information that comes to their attention in carrying out their official responsibilities. How-ever, this prohibition shall not restrict the exchange of information with a recognized investigative or disciplinary body or affect, in any way, compliance with a validly issued and enforceable subpoena or summons.

Analysis of confidential client information

Rule 301 stresses the confidential nature of information obtained by CPAs from their clients. The nature of accountants' work makes it necessary for them to have access to their clients' most confidential financial affairs. Independent accountants may thus gain knowledge of impending business combinations, proposed financing, prospective stock splits or dividend changes, contracts being negotiated, and other confidential information that, if disclosed or otherwise improperly used, could bring the accountants quick monetary profits. Of course, the client would be financially injured, as well as embarrassed, if the CPAs were to "leak" such information. Accountants must not only keep quiet as to their clients' business plans, but they rarely even mention in public the names of their clients. Any loose talk by independent public accountants concerning the affairs of their clients would immediately brand them as lacking in professional ethics. On the other hand, the confidential relationship between the CPA and the client is *never* a justification for the CPA to cooperate in any deceitful act. The personal integrity of the CPA is essential to the performance of the attest function.

Confidentiality versus privileged communications The communications between CPAs and their clients are confidential, but they are not *privileged* under common law, as are communications with attorneys, clergymen, or physicians. The difference is that disclosure of legally privileged communications cannot be required by a subpoena or court order. Thus, auditors may be compelled to disclose their communications with clients in certain types of court proceedings. Some individual states, however, have adopted statutes providing that public accountants cannot be required by the state courts to give evidence gained in confidence from clients. Such state laws, however, do not apply to federal courts.

Contingent Fees

Rule 302 Professional services shall not be offered or rendered under an arrangement whereby no fee will be charged unless a specified finding or result is attained, or where the fee is otherwise contingent upon the finding or results of such services. However, a member's fees may vary depending, for example, on the complexity of services rendered.

Fees are not regarded as being contingent if fixed by courts or other public authorities, or, in tax matters, if determined based on the results of judicial proceedings or the findings of governmental agencies.

Analysis of contingent fees   An accountant is prohibited by Rule 302 from performing services on a contingent fee basis. For example, a company in need of an auditor's report to support its application for a bank loan might offer to make the auditor's fee contingent upon approval of the loan by the bank. Such an arrangement would create an undesirable temptation for the auditor to abandon an independent viewpoint and to lend support to the statements prepared by management.

As of the publication of this book, the AICPA has entered into a consent decree with the Federal Trade Commission that would allow contingent fees from clients that are not receiving certain compilation and attestation services from the CPA.

Acts Discreditable

Rule 501   *A member shall not commit an act discreditable to the profession.*

Analysis of acts discreditable

Rule 501 permits the disciplining of those members who act in a manner damaging to the reputation of the profession. The rule is not specific as to what constitutes a discreditable act; it is subject to interpretation. In the past, such acts as signing a false or misleading opinion or statement, committing a felony, and engaging in discriminatory employment practices have been interpreted to be violations of Rule 501.

One interesting practice that has been interpreted to be discreditable is failure to return client records. These situations generally arise when the CPAs have been discharged and not paid for their services. To refuse to return a client's ledger is clearly wrong, but what if the CPA retains working papers needed by the client? To enforce collection of a fee, some CPAs have refused to allow the client or the successor CPAs access to their working papers. Since the working papers are the CPAs' property, this is a legitimate business practice, not a violation of Rule 501. However, a problem sometimes arises in the definition of working papers. Documents that provide the only support or analysis for entries in client records are considered part of the client's records, even if the papers were prepared by the CPAs. Failure to provide the client with access to such documents constitutes a violation of Rule 501.

Advertising and Other Forms of Solicitation

Rule 502   *A member in public practice shall not seek to obtain clients by advertising or other forms of solicitation in a manner that is false, misleading, or deceptive. Solicitation by the use of coercion, overreaching, or harassing conduct is prohibited.*

Analysis of advertising and other forms of solicitation

Until 1978, advertising by CPAs was strictly forbidden by the Rules of Professional Ethics. Most certified public accountants considered advertising in any form to be unprofessional. However, this prohibition was dropped because it was deemed a possible violation of the federal antitrust laws. Members of the public accounting profession may now advertise their services so long as the advertising is not false, misleading, or deceptive. Unethical advertising includes advertising that creates unjustified expectations of favorable results, makes incomplete comparisons with other CPAs, or indicates an ability to influence a court or other official body.

Acceptable advertising is that which is informative and based upon verifiable fact. Indications of the types of services offered, certificates and degrees of members of the firm, and fees for services are all acceptable forms of advertising.

Commissions

Rule 503   The acceptance by a member in public practice'of a payment for the referral of products or services of others to a client is prohibited. Such action is considered to create a conflict of interest that results in a loss of objectivity and independence.

A member shall not make a payment to obtain a client. This rule shall not prohibit payments for the purchase of an accounting practice or retirement payments to individuals formerly engaged in the practice of public accounting or payments to their heirs or estates.

Analysis of commissions

Clients look to their CPAs for advice on the purchase of products and services. For example, CPAs often perform studies and make recommendations regarding the computer hardware and software that best meets the computing needs of their clients. The first paragraph of Rule 503 recognizes that public accountants cannot maintain an appearance of objectivity and independence when they are receiving commissions from the vendors of these products and services.

As of the publication of this book, the AICPA has entered into a consent decree with the Federal Trade Commission that would allow a CPA to accept a commission from referring goods or services to clients that do not receive certain compilation and attestation services from the CPA. However the CPA would be required to disclose to the client that a commission was involved in the referral.

Rule 504 (Deleted)

Form of Practice and Name

Rule 505   *A member may practice public accounting only in the form of a proprietorship, a partnership, or a professional corporation whose characteristics conform to resolutions of Council.*

A member shall not practice public accounting under a firm name that is misleading. Names of one or more past partners or shareholders may be included in the firm name of a successor partnership or corporation. Also, a partner or shareholder surviving the death or withdrawal of all other partners or shareholders may continue to practice under such name which includes the name of past partners or shareholders for up to two years after becoming a sole practitioner.

A firm may not designate itself as "Members of the American Institute of Certified Public Accountants" unless all of its partners or shareholders are members of the Institute.

Analysis of form of practice and name

Corporations have certain tax advantages not available to partnerships, such as tax deductibility of pension and profit-sharing plans. Therefore, many state laws as well as the AICPA Rules of the *Code of Professional Conduct* allow CPAs to form professional corporations. However, the AICPA did not wish to allow the corporate form to be used to limit CPAs' liability or to allow them to undertake unethical activities. For this reason, the requirements for professional incorporation are very specific. In addition to providing for financial liability, all corporate stock must be owned and control over professional matters must rest with individuals authorized to practice public accounting.

Previous versions of Rule 505 prohibited public accountants from practicing under a name that was fictitious or indicated a specialization. Because this prohibition was sensitive to antitrust attack, the revised Rule 505 allows fictitious names so long as they are not false, misleading, or deceptive. An example of a misleading firm name is where a partner surviving the withdrawal of all other partners continues to practice under the partnership name for longer than a two-year period. It is misleading for a sole practitioner to practice in a partnership name.

The CPA as tax adviser—ethical problems

What is the responsibility of the CPA in serving as tax adviser? The CPA has a primary responsibility to the client: that is, to see that the client pays the proper amount of tax and no more. In the role of tax adviser, the certified public accountant may properly resolve questionable issues in favor of the client; the CPA is not obliged to maintain the posture of independence required in audit work. When CPAs express an opinion on financial statements, they must be unbiased; freedom from bias is not required in serving as a tax adviser. On the other hand, CPAs must adhere to the same standards of truth and personal integrity in tax work as in all other professional activities. Any departure from these standards on a tax engagement would surely destroy the reputation of certified public accountants in performing their work as independent auditors.

A second responsibility of CPAs on tax engagements is to the public, whose interests are represented by the government—more specifically by the Internal Revenue Service. To meet this responsibility, CPAs must observe the preparer's declaration on the tax returns they prepare. The declaration requires the preparer to state that the return is "true, correct, and complete . . . based on all information of which the preparer has any knowledge." To comply with this declaration, what steps must the CPA firm take to acquire knowledge relating to the tax return? The firm is not required to make an audit; knowledge of the return may be limited to information supplied to the firm by the client. However, if this information appears unreasonable or contradictory, the CPAs are obligated to make sufficient investigation to resolve these issues. Information that appears plausible to a layman might appear unreasonable to CPAs, since they are experts in evaluating financial data. CPAs are not obligated to investigate any and all information provided by the taxpayer, but they cannot ignore clues that cast doubt on the accuracy of these data.

In addition to being guided by the declaration on the tax return, CPAs should look to a series of pronouncements issued by the AICPA, entitled *Statements on Responsibilities in Tax Practice*. These statements address such questions as: Under what circumstances should a CPA sign the preparer's declaration on a tax return? What is the CPA's responsibility for errors in previously filed returns? Should CPAs disclose the taking of positions that differ from IRS interpretations of the tax code? The purpose of this series is educational and the statements are not directly enforceable under the *Code of Professional Conduct*.

Enforcement of professional ethics

The AICPA and the state societies of CPAs have established a joint ethics enforcement plan. Under the plan, complaints about a CPA's conduct are first referred to the Professional Ethics Division of the AICPA for investigation. If the Professional Ethics Division finds the complaint to be valid, it may take several courses of action. For minor violations, the Division may take direct remedial action, such as requiring the member to get additional continuing education. More serious violations are turned over to the joint trial board for a hearing. If found guilty, the offending member may be censured, suspended from membership for up to two years, or expelled permanently from the AICPA. Although expulsion from the AICPA would not in itself cause the loss of a CPA's license, the damage to the CPA's professional reputation would be very substantial.

The provisions of the AICPA Rules have been used as a model by the boards of accountancy throughout the country to develop the ethical standards in their states. Thus, revocation of the CPA's license to practice also is a possible consequence of violation of the AICPA ethical standards.

ETHICS FOR INTERNAL AUDITORS

Internal auditors, acting through their national organization, the Institute of Internal Auditors, have developed their own code of professional ethics. *The Institute of Internal Auditors, Inc., Code of Ethics* is organized with an Introduction, an Interpretation of Principles, and eight Articles. The Articles primarily address internal auditors' obligations to their employers, but they also include provisions that prescribe honesty, objectivity, competence, and morality in the practice of the internal auditing profession. Although not stated in the Code, it is generally understood that violation of the articles could result in revocation of the auditor's membership in the Institute of Internal Auditors. *The Institute of Internal Auditors, Inc., Code of Ethics* is reproduced below.

THE INSTITUTE OF INTERNAL AUDITORS, INC., CODE OF ETHICS

Introduction

Recognizing that ethics are an important consideration in the practice of internal auditing and that the moral principles followed by members of The Institute of Internal Auditors, Inc., should be formalized, the Board of Directors at its regular meeting in New Orleans on December 13, 1968, received and adopted the following resolution:

Whereas the members of The Institute of Internal Auditors, Inc., represent the profession of internal auditing; and

Whereas managements rely on the profession of internal auditing to assist in the fulfillment of their management stewardship; and

Whereas said members must maintain high standards of conduct, honor and character in order to carry on proper and meaningful internal auditing practice;

Therefore be it resolved that a Code of Ethics be now set forth, outlining the standards of professional behavior for the guidance of each member of The Institute of Internal Auditors, Inc.

In accordance with this resolution, the Board of Directors further approves of the principles set forth.

Interpretation of principles

The provisions of this Code of Ethics cover basic principles in the various disciplines of internal auditing practice. Members shall realize that individual judgment is required in the application of these principles. They have a responsibility to conduct themselves so that their good faith and integrity should not be open to question. While having due regard for the limit of their technical skills, they will promote the highest possible internal auditing standards to the end of advancing the interest of their company or organization.

Articles

I. Members shall have an obligation to exercise honesty, objectivity, and diligence in the performance of their duties and responsibilities.

II. Members, in holding the trust of their employers, shall exhibit loyalty in all matters pertaining to the affairs of the employer or to whomever they may be rendering a service. However, members shall not knowingly be a party to any illegal or improper activity.

III. Members shall refrain from entering into any activity which may be in conflict with the interest of their employers or which could prejudice their ability to carry out objectively their duties and responsibilities.

IV. Members shall not accept a fee or a gift from an employee, a client, a customer, or a business associate of their employer without the knowledge and consent of their senior management.

V. Members shall be prudent in the use of information acquired in the course of their duties. They shall not use confidential information for any personal gain nor in a manner which would be detrimental to the welfare of their employer.

VI. Members, in expressing an opinion, shall use all reasonable care to obtain sufficient factual evidence to warrant such expression. In their reporting, members shall reveal such material facts known to them, which, if not revealed, could either distort the report of the results of operations under review or conceal unlawful practice.

VII. Members shall continually strive for improvement in the proficiency and effectiveness of their service.

VIII. Members shall abide by the bylaws and uphold the objectives of The Institute of Internal Auditors, Inc. In the practice of their profession, they shall be ever mindful of their obligation to maintain the high standard of competence, morality, and dignity which The Institute of Internal Auditors, Inc. and its members have established.

Audit committee   A committee of a corporation's board of directors that engages independent auditors, reviews audit findings, monitors activities of the internal auditing staff, and intervenes in any disputes between management and the independent auditors. Preferably, members of the audit committee are outside directors, that is, members of the board of directors who do not also serve as corporate officers.

Direct financial interests   A personal investment under the direct control of the investor. The *Code of Professional Conduct* prohibits CPAs from having any direct financial interests in their audit clients. Investments made by a CPA's spouse or dependent child also are regarded as direct financial interests of the CPA.

Ethics Rulings   Pronouncements of the AICPA that explain the application of Rules and Interpretations of the *Code of Professional Conduct* to specific factual circumstances involving professional ethics.

Independence   A most important Rule of Conduct that prohibits CPAs from expressing an opinion on financial statements of an enterprise unless they are independent with respect to such enterprise; independence is impaired by a financial interest, service as an officer or trustee, loans to or from the enterprise, and various other relationships.

Indirect financial interests   An investment in which the specific investment decisions are not under the direct control of the investor. An example is an investment in a professionally managed mutual fund. The *Code of Professional Conduct* allows CPAs to have indirect financial interests in audit clients, as long as the investment is not material in relation to the CPA's net worth.

Interpretations of Rules   Guidelines issued by the AICPA for the scope and applications of the Rules of Conduct.

Principles of the Code   The part of the AICPA *Code of Professional Conduct* that expresses the profession's responsibilities to the public, clients, and colleagues, and provides a framework for the Rules.

Profession   An activity that involves a responsibility to serve the public, has a complex body of knowledge, has standards for admission, and has a need for public confidence.

Rules   A group of enforceable ethical standards included in the AICPA *Code of Professional Conduct*.

Shopping for principles   Conduct by some enterprises that discharge one independent auditing firm after seeking out another firm that will sanction a disputed financial statement principle or presentation.

2–1.   What is the basic purpose of a code of ethics for a profession?

2–2.   Briefly describe the two parts of the AICPA *Code of Professional Conduct*.

2–3.   Three months ago, a national CPA firm hired Greg Scott to work as a staff auditor in its New York office. Yesterday Scott's father was hired to be the chief financial officer of one of the CPA firm's New York clients. Has the independence of the CPA firm with respect to this client been impaired?

2–4. In Chapter 1, the 10 generally accepted auditing standards were discussed. How does the AICPA *Code of Professional Conduct* relate, if at all, to these 10 generally accepted auditing standards?

2–5. Explain how a CPA might have an indirect financial interest in an audit client. Does the AICPA *Code of Professional Conduct* prohibit such interests?

2–6. Wallace Company is indebted to John Greer, a CPA, for unpaid fees and has offered to issue to him unsecured interest-bearing notes. Would the CPA's acceptance of these notes have any bearing upon his independence in his relations with Wallace Company? Discuss.   (AICPA, adapted)

2–7. Sara Kole, CPA, has been requested by the president of Noyes Company, a closely held corporation and audit client, to cosign Noyes Company checks with the Noyes treasurer when the president is away on business trips. Would Kole violate the AICPA *Code of Professional Conduct* if she accepted this request? Explain.

2–8. How do the positions of the SEC and the AICPA differ with respect to the independence of a CPA who performs routine accounting services for a client?

2–9. What bodies are given authority to issue performance standards under Rule 202 of the AICPA *Code of Professional Conduct?* What authoritative standards does each body issue?

2–10. Arthur Brown is a CPA who often serves as an expert witness in court cases. Is it proper for Brown to receive compensation in a damage suit based on the amount awarded to the plaintiff? Discuss.

(AICPA, adapted)

2–11. Laura Clark, wife of Jon Clark, CPA, is a life insurance agent. May Jon Clark refer audit clients needing officer life insurance to Laura Clark or to another life insurance agent who will share a commission with Laura Clark? Explain.

2–12. Must a CPA maintain independence and an impartial mental attitude when preparing a client's income tax return? Explain.

2–13. In preparing a client's income tax return, a CPA feels that certain expenses are unreasonably high and probably are overstated. Explain the CPA's responsibilities in this situation.

2–14. "Since internal auditors are employees, they have no ethical responsibilities to others beyond their employers." Comment on this statement.

GROUP II: QUESTIONS REQUIRING ANALYSIS

2–15. Sally Adams, CPA, is an auditor with a large CPA firm. Her husband, Steve Adams, plans to accept a position as controller of Coast Corporation, an audit client of Sally's firm. Comment upon whether the CPA firm's independence will be impaired assuming that Sally Adams is:
a. A partner in the CPA firm.
b. A managerial employee of the CPA firm.

2–16. Tracy Smith, CPA, is in charge of the audit of Olympic Fashions, Inc. Seven young members of the CPA firm's professional staff are working with Smith on this engagement, and several of the young auditors are avid skiers. Olympic Fashions owns two condominiums in Aspen, Colorado, which it uses primarily to entertain clients. The controller of Olympic Fashions has told Smith that she and any of her audit staff are welcome to use the condominiums at no charge any time that they are not already in use. How should Smith respond to this offer? Explain.

2–17. Harris Fell, CPA and member of the AICPA, was engaged to audit the financial statements of Wilson Corporation. Fell had half-completed the audit when he had a dispute with the management of Wilson Corporation and was discharged. Hal Compton, CPA, was promptly engaged to replace Fell. Wilson Corporation did not compensate Fell for his work to date; therefore, Fell refused to allow Wilson Corporation's management to examine his working papers. Certain of the working papers consisted of adjusting journal entries and supporting analysis. Wilson Corporation's management had no other source of this information. Did Fell violate the AICPA *Code of Professional Conduct?* Explain fully.

2–18. With the approval of its board of directors, Thames Corporation made a sizable payment for advertising during the year being audited by Leslie Wade, CPA. The corporation deducted the full amount in its federal and state income tax returns. The controller, John Warren, acknowledges that this deduction probably will be disallowed because it related to political matters. He has not provided for this disallowance in his income taxes provision and refuses to do so because he fears that this will cause the federal and state revenue agents to believe that the deduction is not valid. What is the CPA's responsibility in this situation? Explain.

(AICPA, adapted)

2–19. Select the best answer for each of the following. Explain the reasons for your selection.
  a. In which of the following situations would a CPA firm be in violation of the AICPA *Code of Professional Conduct* in determining its fee?
     (1) A fee based on whether or not the CPA firm's report leads to the approval of the client's application for a bank loan.
     (2) A fee to be established at a later date by the Bankruptcy Court.
     (3) A fee based upon the nature of the engagement rather than upon the actual time spent on the engagement.
     (4) A fee based on the fee charged by the client's former auditors.
  b. The ultimate decision as to whether or not CPAs maintain an appearance of independence from their audit clients must be made by the—
     (1) Auditors.
     (2) Client.
     (3) Audit committee.
     (4) Public.
  c. Which of the following is implied when a CPA signs the preparer's declaration on a federal income tax return?
     (1) The return is not misleading based on all information of which the CPA has knowledge.
     (2) The return is prepared in accordance with generally accepted accounting principles.
     (3) The CPA has audited the return.
     (4) The CPA maintained an impartial mental attitude while preparing the return.

    d. The AICPA *Code of Professional Conduct* states that a CPA shall not disclose any confidential information obtained in the course of a professional engagement except with the consent of the client. This rule should be understood to preclude a CPA from responding to an inquiry made by

      (1) An investigative body of a state CPA society.

      (2) The trial board of the AICPA.

      (3) A CPA-shareholder of the client corporation.

      (4) An AICPA voluntary quality review body.

    e. Pursuant to the AICPA rules of conduct, if a partner in a two-member partnership dies, the surviving partner may continue to practice as an individual under the existing firm title which includes the deceased partner's name

      (1) For a period of time **not** to exceed five years.

      (2) For a period of time **not** to exceed two years.

      (3) Indefinitely.

      (4) Until the partnership pay-out to the deceased partner's estate is terminated.

    f. Glen Page, CPA, accepted the audit engagement of Todd Company. During the audit, Page became aware of his lack of competence required for the engagement. What should Page do?

      (1) Disclaim an opinion.

      (2) Issue a qualified opinion.

      (3) Suggest that Todd Company engage another CPA to perform the audit.

      (4) Rely on the competence of client personnel. (AICPA, adapted)

GROUP III: PROBLEMS

2–20. The firm of Bell & Greer, CPAs, has been asked to audit Trek Corporation for the year ended December 31, Year 5. Bell & Greer has two offices: one in Los Angeles and the other in Newport Beach. Trek Corporation would be audited by the Los Angeles office. For each of the following independent cases, indicate whether Bell & Greer would be independent with respect to Trek Corporation and explain why.

    a. A partner in the Los Angeles office of Bell & Greer has been a long-time personal friend of the chief executive officer of Trek Corporation.

    b. The former controller of Trek Corporation became a partner in the Newport Beach office of Bell & Greer on March 15, Year 5, resigning from Trek Corporation on that date.

    c. A managerial employee in the Newport Beach office of Bell & Greer is the son of the treasurer of Trek Corporation.

    d. A partner in the Newport office of Bell & Greer jointly owns a cattle ranch in Montana with one of the directors of Trek Corporation. The value of the investment is material to both parties.

    e. Trek Corporation has not yet paid Bell & Greer for professional services rendered in Year 4. This fee is substantial in amount and is now 15 months past due.

2–21. Roland Company, a retail store, has utilized your services as independent auditor for several years. During the current year, the company opened a new store; in the course of your annual audit, you verify the cost of the fixtures installed in the new store by examining purchase orders, invoices, and other documents. This review brings to light an understated invoice nearly a year old in which a clerical error by the supplier, Western Showcase, Inc. caused the total of the invoice to read $28,893.62 when it should have read $82,893.62. The invoice was paid immediately upon receipt without any notice of the error, and subsequent statements and correspondence from Western Showcase, Inc. showed that the account with Roland Company had been paid in full. Assume that the amount in question is material in relation to the financial position of both companies.

Required:

a. What action should you take in this situation?

b. If the client should decline to take any action in the matter, would you insist that the unpaid amount of $54,000 be included in the liabilities shown on the balance sheet as a condition necessary to your issuance of an unqualified audit report?

c. Assuming that you were later retained to make an audit of Western Showcase, Inc., would you utilize the information gained in your examination of Roland Company to initiate a reopening of the account with that company?

2–22. Auditors must not only appear to be independent; they must also be independent in fact.

Required:

a. Explain the concept of an "auditor's independence" as it applies to third-party reliance upon financial statements.

b. (1) What determines whether or not an auditor is independent in fact?

(2) What determines whether or not an auditor appears to be independent?

c. Explain how an auditor may be independent in fact but not appear to be independent.

d. Would Joe Marks, a CPA, be considered independent for an examination of the financial statements of a—

(1) Church for which he is serving as treasurer without compensation? Explain.

(2) Women's club for which his wife is serving as treasurer-accountant if he is not to receive a fee for the examination? Explain.

(AICPA, adapted)

2–23. An audit client, March Corporation, requested that John Day, CPA, conduct a feasibility study to advise management of the best way the corporation can use electronic data processing equipment and which computer, if any, best meets the corporation's requirements. Day is technically competent in this area and accepts the engagement. Upon completion of Day's study the corporation accepts his suggestions and installs the computer and related equipment that he recommended.

Required:

a. Discuss the effect that acceptance of this management advisory services engagement would have upon John Day's independence in expressing an opinion on the financial statements of March Corporation.

    b. A local company printing data processing forms customarily offers a commission for recommending it as supplier. The client is aware of the commission offer and suggests that Day accept it. Would it be proper for Day to accept the commission with the client's approval? Discuss. (AICPA, adapted)

2–24. Lauren Brown, CPA, has been requested by the management of Walker Corporation, an audit client, to perform a nonrecurring engagement involving the implementation of an information and control system. Walker's management requests that in setting up the new system and during the period before conversion to the new system Brown:

    (1) Counsel on potential expansion of business activity plans.

    (2) Search for and interview new personnel.

    (3) Hire new personnel.

    (4) Train personnel.

In addition, Walker's management requests that during the three months subsequent to the conversion Brown:

    (1) Supervise the operation of the new system.

    (2) Monitor client-prepared source documents and make changes in basic data generated by the system as Brown may deem necessary without concurrence of the client.

Required:

    a. If Brown completes the engagement for implementation of the system as outlined before she begins the audit of Walker Corporation, is her independence impaired? Explain.

    b. Which of the services may Brown perform and remain independent with respect to Walker Corporation?

    c. If Walker Corporation was Brown's tax client and not her audit client, could Brown implement the system as outlined and continue to perform tax services for the client? Discuss. (AICPA, adapted)

2–25. Thomas Gilbert and Susan Bradley formed a professional corporation called "Financial Services Inc.—A Professional Corporation," each taking 50 percent of the authorized common stock. Gilbert is a CPA and a member of the AICPA. Bradley is a CPCU (Chartered Property Casualty Underwriter). The corporation performs auditing and tax services under Gilbert's direction and insurance services under Bradley's supervision.

    One of the corporation's first audit clients was Grandtime Company. Grandtime had total assets of $600,000 and total liabilities of $270,000. In the course of his examination, Gilbert found that Grandtime's building with a carrying value of $240,000 was pledged as collateral for a 10-year-term note in the amount of $200,000. The client's financial statements did not mention that the building was pledged as collateral for the 10-year-term note. However, as the failure to disclose the lien did not affect either the value of the assets or the amount of the liabilities, and his examination was satisfactory in all other respects, Gilbert rendered an unqualified opinion on Grandtime's financial statements. About two months after the date of his opinion, Gilbert learned that an insurance company was planning to loan Grandtime $150,000 in the form of a first-mortgage note on the building. Realizing that the insurance company was unaware of the existing lien on the building, Gilbert had Bradley notify the insurance company of the fact that Grandtime's building was pledged as collateral for a term note.

Shortly after the events described above, Gilbert was charged with a violation of professional ethics.

Required:

Identify and discuss at least five ethical implications of those acts by Gilbert that were in violation of the AICPA *Code of Professional Conduct.*   (AICPA, adapted)

**GROUP IV:
RESEARCH AND
DISCUSSION CASE**

2-26. You are the Partner-In-Charge of a large metropolitan office of a regional CPA firm. Two members of your professional staff have come to you to discuss problems that may affect the firm's independence. Neither of these situations has been specifically addressed by the AICPA Professional Ethics Division. Therefore, you must reach your own conclusions as to what to advise your staff members, and what actions, if any, are to be taken by the firm.

Case 1: Don Moore, a partner in the firm, has recently moved into a condominium which he shares with his girlfriend, Joan Scott. Moore owns the condominium and pays all of the expenses relating to its maintenance. Otherwise, the two are self-supporting. Scott is a stockbroker, and recently she has started acquiring shares in one of the audit clients of this office. The shares are held in Scott's name. At present, the shares are not material in relation to her net worth.

Case 2: Mary Reed, a new staff auditor with no managerial responsibilities in the firm, has recently separated from her husband. Mary has filed for divorce, but the divorce cannot become final for at least five months. The property settlement is being bitterly contested. Mary's husband has always resented her professional career and has just used community property to acquire one share of common stock in each of the publicly owned companies audited by the office in which Mary works.

Required:

For each case, you are to:

a. Set forth arguments indicating that the firm's independence has ***not*** been impaired.

b. Set forth arguments indicating that the firm's independence has been impaired.

c. Express your personal opinion. Identify those arguments from parts (*a*) or (*b*) that you found most persuasive. If you believe that the firm's independence has been impaired, make suggestions as to how the problem might be resolved.

Suggested references:

AICPA, *Professional Standards, Volume B,* Commerce Clearing House. See Section 101.

Legal liability
of auditors

Chapter 3 study objectives

After studying this chapter, you should be able to:
— Define the major legal concepts that relate to auditors' liability.
— Distinguish between auditors' liability under common law and their liability under statutory law.
— Explain the factors that must be proven by clients and third parties to be successful in actions against the auditors under common law and the auditors' defenses.
— Contrast liability under the Securities Act of 1933 and the Securities Exchange Act of 1934.
— Describe the auditors' responsibility for detecting material errors and irregularities.
— Describe accountants' liability for accounting and review services.

We live in an era of litigation, in which persons with real or fancied grievances are likely to take their grievances to court. In this environment, investors and creditors who suffer financial reversals find auditors, as well as attorneys and corporate directors, tempting targets for lawsuits alleging professional "malpractice." Auditors must approach every engagement with the prospect that they may be required to defend their work in court. Even if the court finds in favor of the auditors, the costs of defending a legal action can be astronomical. As a result, the cost of professional liability insurance has escalated at an alarming rate.

Costs are not the only concern in this area; lawsuits can be extremely damaging to a professional's reputation. In extreme cases, the auditors may even be tried criminally for malpractice. Every man and woman considering a career in public accounting should be aware of the legal liability inherent in the practice of this profession.

Before we begin our technical discussion, we should warn the reader that laws and court interpretations vary from one jurisdiction to another. Thus, a CPA firm's liability in the state courts of New Jersey may differ from its liability as viewed by the state courts of New York.

Unique vulnerability of accountants to lawsuits

The potential liability of CPAs to persons who might be injured as a result of improper professional practice greatly exceeds that of physicians or any other group of professionals. One reason for this is the large potential number of injured parties. If a physician or an attorney is negligent, the injured party usually consists only of the professional's patient or client. If a CPA is negligent in expressing an opinion on financial statements, literally millions of investors may sustain losses.

Illustrative case

A vice president of a major insurance company was recently quoted in *The Wall Street Journal* as saying, "We dropped out of the business of insuring accounting firms for liability. . . . We couldn't get the premiums needed for the kinds of losses we were suffering." The company continues to insure engineers, architects, attorneys, physicians, and surgeons. "The risks aren't as great," the vice president observed.

Judgments of as much as $80 million have been awarded against CPA firms. If the amount of a judgment exceeds the limits of the firm's professional liability insurance, the firm's partners are personally liable for any uninsured loss.

Definition of terms

Discussion of auditors' liability is best prefaced by a definition of some of the common terms of business law. Among these are the following:

Ordinary negligence is violation of a legal duty to exercise a degree of care that an ordinarily prudent person would exercise under similar circumstances with resultant damages to another party. For the CPA, ordinary negligence is failure to perform a duty in accordance with applicable professional standards. For practical purposes, ordinary negligence may be viewed as "failure to exercise due professional care."

Gross negligence is the lack of even slight care, indicative of a *reckless disregard* for one's professional responsibilities. Substantial failures on the part of an auditor to comply with generally accepted auditing standards might be interpreted as gross negligence.

Fraud is defined as misrepresentation by a person of a material fact, known by that person to be untrue or made with reckless indifference as to whether the fact is true, with the intention of deceiving the other party and with the result that the other party is injured. Rule 102 of the AICPA's *Code of Professional Conduct* (discussed in Chapter 2) states that a member of the AICPA shall not knowingly misrepresent facts. A CPA found to have violated this provision of Rule 102 might be sued for fraud by the client or another injured party.

Constructive fraud differs from fraud as defined above in that constructive fraud does not involve a misrepresentation with intent to deceive. Gross negligence on the part of an auditor has been interpreted by the courts as constructive fraud.

Privity is the relationship between parties to a contract. A CPA firm is in privity with the client it is serving, as well as with any *third-party beneficiary*.

A *third-party beneficiary* is a person—not the promisor or promisee—who is named in a contract or intended by the contracting parties to have definite rights and benefits under the contract. For example, if Warren & Co., CPAs, is engaged to examine the financial statements of Arthur Company and to send a copy of its audit report to Third National Bank as support for a loan, the bank is a third-party beneficiary under the contract between Warren & Co. and Arthur Company.

Engagement letter is the written contract summarizing the contractual relationships between auditor and client. The engagement letter typically specifies the scope of professional services to be rendered, expected completion dates, and the basis for determination of the CPA's fee. Engagement letters will be discussed more fully in Chapter 4.

Breach of contract is failure of one or both parties to a contract to perform in accordance with the contract's provisions. A CPA firm might be sued for breach of contract, for example, if the firm failed to deliver its audit report to the client by the date specified in the engagement letter. Negligence on the part of the CPAs also constitutes breach of contract.

Proximate cause exists when damage to another is directly attributable to a wrongdoer's act. The issue of proximate cause may be raised as a defense in litigation. Even though a CPA firm might have been negligent in rendering services, it will not be liable if its negligence was not the proximate cause of the *plaintiff's* loss.

Plaintiff is the party claiming damages and bringing suit agains₁ the *defendant*.

Contributory negligence is negligence on the part of the plaintiff that has contributed to his or her having incurred a loss. Contributory negligence may be used as a defense, because the court may limit or bar recovery by a plaintiff whose own negligence contributed to the loss.

Comparative negligence is a concept used by certain courts to allocate damages between negligent parties based on the degree to which each party is at fault.

Common law is unwritten law that has developed through court decisions; it represents judicial interpretation of a society's concept of fairness. For example, the right to sue a person for fraud is a common law right.

Statutory law is law that has been adopted by a governmental unit, such as the federal government. CPAs must concern themselves particularly with the federal securities acts and state blue-sky laws. These laws regulate the issuance and trading of securities.

Litigation placed in perspective

As we discuss auditors' liability for negligence, gross negligence, and fraud, there may be a tendency to conclude that CPAs are often careless in rendering professional services. This is simply not the case. The overwhelming majority of engagements are completed successfully by CPAs without any allegations of improper conduct. However, in any endeavor as complex as auditing, it is inevitable that some mistakes will be made. Any large CPA firm that performs thousands of audits will, at one time or another, find that it has issued an unqualified auditor's report on financial statements that were, in some respect, misleading. Also, investors who have sustained large losses become desperate to recover their losses by any means possible. Thus, if bringing suit against a company's CPAs offers even the most remote chance of recovery, the injured parties are likely to initiate legal action.

CPAs must recognize occasional allegations of misconduct as a fact of life. Some of the lawsuits brought against CPAs will be frivolous—desperate attempts by plaintiffs to recover their losses. Others will have some basis in fact—judgmental errors made by the CPAs during the engagement. No matter how careful CPAs are, any CPA firm may occasionally find itself as a defendant in litigation.

Notice in our definitions of terms that *negligence, gross negligence,* and *fraud* each represent different *degrees of improper performance* by the CPA. The extent to which the CPAs' services are found to be improper determines the parties to whom the CPAs are liable for losses proximately caused by their improper actions. Liability may arise from improper performance on any type of engagement—an audit, tax services, accounting services, or management advisory services. However, CPAs are *never liable to any party* if they perform their services with *due professional care.* Having exercised due professional care (sometimes called "due diligence") is a *complete defense* against any charge of improper conduct.

AUDITORS' LIABILITY TO THEIR CLIENTS

When CPAs take on any type of engagement, they are obliged to render due professional care. This obligation exists whether or not it is specifically set forth in the written contract with the client. Thus, CPAs are liable to their clients under common law for any losses proximately caused by the CPAs' *failure to render due professional care.* In short, *ordinary negligence* is a sufficient degree of misconduct to make CPAs liable for damages caused to their clients.

CPAs' responsibilities for the detection of errors and irregularities

CPAs' liability to clients most often arises from the CPAs' failure to uncover an embezzlement or defalcation being perpetrated against the client by client employees. A client who has sustained such losses may allege that the auditors were negligent in not uncovering the scheme and sue the auditors for the amount of the loss. The key factor in determining whether the auditors are liable is *not* just whether the auditors failed to uncover the fraud. Rather, the issue is whether this failure *stems from the auditors' negligence.*

SAS 53 (AU 316) defines the term *errors* as unintentional mistakes or omissions in financial statements, including mistakes in the application of accounting principles.[1] *Irregularities,* on the other hand, is a term used to describe intentional misstatements of financial statements (management fraud) and theft of assets (employee fraud). *SAS 53* (AU 316) requires that auditors (1) design their audit to provide *reasonable assurance* of detecting errors and irregularities that are material to the financial statements, (2) exercise due care and professional skepticism in planning and conducting their examination, and (3) communicate irregularities of any consequence and proposed audit adjustments to the audit committee of the client's board of directors.

These requirements *do not imply* that auditors were negligent whenever errors or irregularities are later found to exist in audited financial statements. An audit has certain limitations; it does not involve a complete and detailed examination of all records and transactions. To do so would entail an almost prohibitive cost, which would certainly not be warranted under ordinary business conditions. There can never be absolute assurance that errors or irregularities do not exist among the transactions not included in the auditors' tests. Also, the possibility exists that documents have been so skillfully forged or other irregularities so ex-

---

[1] AICPA, *Statement on Auditing Standards No. 53,* "The Auditor's Responsibility to Detect and Report Errors and Irregularities" (New York, 1988), AU 316.

pertly concealed that the application of normal auditing techniques would not reveal the irregularities. When a CPA firm's examination *has been made in accordance with generally accepted auditing standards,* the firm *should not be held liable* for failure to detect the existence of errors or irregularities.

Lawsuits by clients

To obtain a judgment against its auditors, an injured client must prove that it sustained a loss as a result of the auditors' negligence. As defendants, the auditors can refute this claim by showing that either (1) they were not negligent in the performance of their duties, or (2) their negligence was not the proximate cause of the client's loss. Demonstrating *contributory negligence* by the client is one means of showing that the auditors' negligence was not the cause (or sole cause) of the client's loss. In some jurisdictions, a defense of contributory negligence will entirely eliminate the auditors' liability to their client. In others, the concept of *comparative negligence* is used to allocate damages between the client and the auditors based on the extent to which each is at fault.

Illustrative case

Calvert Roth, CPA, has audited the financial statements of Metro Bank for the last five years. At the conclusion of each audit, Roth has suggested improvements in Metro Bank's internal controls over consumer loans. However, Metro's management failed to make the recommended improvements in internal controls. Recently, it was discovered that Harold Kay, a loan officer, had embezzled funds through the creation of fictitious consumer loans. Metro Bank filed suit against Roth for negligence in the performance of his audits. By means of expert testimony by other CPAs, it was established that Roth had been negligent in the performance of the last two audits. The court concluded that if Roth had performed his audit work adequately, there was a reasonable chance that the defalcations would have been detected. However, the court also concluded that Metro Bank's management was negligent in not carrying out the suggested improvements in internal control. Following the principle of *comparative negligence,* management of the bank was found to be 80 percent at fault, and Roth was found to be 20 percent at fault. Thus, Roth was held liable for only 20 percent of the losses of Metro Bank.

Third-party beneficiaries enjoy the same rights as clients

The client's right to recover damages caused by auditors' ordinary negligence stems from common-law precedents concerning contracts. Third-party beneficiaries also have rights under the contracts between auditors and clients and also may recover any losses caused by the auditors' ordinary negligence.

In some jurisdictions, third-party beneficiaries are limited to those parties *identified by name* to the auditors. In other jurisdictions, however, any "reasonably limited class of third parties who could be foreseen to rely on the auditors' report" are considered third-party beneficiaries, even though the names of these parties are not known to the auditors. This principle of auditor liability for ordinary negligence to a limited class of foreseen third parties is supported by the American Law Institute's *Second Restatement of the Law of Torts,* which guides many courts in common-law rulings. Several courts have followed this principle, including a court in Rhode Island in the leading case of *Rusch Factors, Inc.* v. *Levin* (1968).

Illustrative case

Dianne Holiday, CPA, performed the audit of Lyman Corporation for the year ended December 31. Holiday was aware that Lyman intended to use the audit report to obtain bank loans. However, no specific banks were identified to Holiday. After the report was issued, Lyman obtained loans from First National Bank and Dime Box State Bank. Also, Wallace Manufacturing Co. relied on Holiday's opinion in providing trade credit to Lyman. If the court applied the principles contained in the *Second Restatement of the Law of Torts,* Holiday could be held liable to First National and Dime Box if she were found guilty of ordinary negligence in the performance of her examination. The banks form a limited class of third parties who could be foreseen to rely on the audit report. On the other hand, a strict application of the primary beneficiary principle by the court would not give First National and Dime Box the same rights as the client under common law because the parties were not specifically identified at the time the examination was performed. Under either set of principles, Wallace Manufacturing Co. would not have rights under the contract. The audit was not performed for the use of trade creditors; therefore, Wallace would not be considered a part of a limited class of foreseen parties.

**AUDITORS'
LIABILITY TO
OTHER THIRD
PARTIES**

Clients and third-party beneficiaries have recourse against an auditor for damages caused by an improper audit because these parties have rights under a contract with the auditor. But what about the many other third parties who rely upon audited financial statements but who do not have specific contractual rights? May these parties recover their losses from an auditor who has performed an improper audit?

Liability to third parties under common law

Unfortunately, auditors' liability to third parties under common law varies from one jurisdiction to another. The most widely cited common-law precedent stems from the landmark case, *Ultramares* v. *Touche & Co.* (1931). In this case, the defendant CPAs issued an unqualified opinion on the balance sheet of a company engaged in the importation and sale of rubber. On the basis of the CPAs' opinion, Ultramares, a factor, made several loans to the company. Shortly thereafter, the company was declared bankrupt, and Ultramares sued the CPAs for negligence. The New York Court of Appeals (the state's highest court) found that auditors could *not* be held liable to unidentified third parties for *ordinary negligence.* However, the court also ruled that auditors could be held liable to unidentified third parties for *gross negligence or fraud.* (The Ultramares case eventually was settled out of court, with no determination as to whether the auditors had been grossly negligent.)

The *Ultramares* precedent has been reaffirmed in many subsequent cases. Recently, the New York Court of Appeals upheld the rule in the case of *Credit Alliance Corp.* v. *Arthur Andersen & Co.* (1985). The court stated that before the auditors may be held liable for ordinary negligence to a third party (1) the auditors must have knowledge of reliance on the financial statements by that party for a particular purpose, and (2) some action by the auditors must indicate that knowledge.

The *Ultramares* rule, however, has not been embraced by the courts in all states. In 1983, the Supreme Court of New Jersey established a very different standard in the case of *Rosenblum* v. *Adler*. In this case, the defendant CPAs issued an unqualified report on the financial statements of Giant Stores Corporation, which showed the corporation to be profitable. In reliance upon these statements, Rosenblum sold a catalog showroom business to Giant in exchange for shares of Giant's stock. Shortly afterwards, Giant filed for bankruptcy and the stock became worthless. Rosenblum sued Giant's CPAs, alleging ordinary negligence. The case was dismissed by the trial court, on the premise that the CPAs were not liable to third parties for ordinary negligence. However, the state supreme court reversed the lower court, finding that CPAs *can* be held liable for ordinary negligence to any third party the auditors could "reasonably foresee" as recipients of the statements for routine business purposes.

Common-law cases are decided, in large part, by reference to established precedents—that is, past decisions in similar cases. The decisions in the *Ultramares* and *Credit Alliance* cases, on one hand, and the *Rosenblum* case on the other, create conflicting precedents as to whether auditors are liable to other third parties for ordinary negligence. Each of these landmark cases was decided by a prestigious and influential state high court. Presumably, courts within New York and New Jersey will adhere to the standard established by their respective highest courts. The standard likely to be applied in other jurisdictions, however, is less certain. The *Rosenblum* v. *Adler* precedent, which has subsequently been embraced by courts in other states, has certainly opened the door to auditors being held liable under common law to all "foreseeable" third parties for ordinary negligence.

The burden of proof   Legal actions under the common law require the plaintiffs to bear most of the burden of affirmative proof. Thus, the plaintiffs seeking damages from a CPA firm must prove that they sustained losses, that they relied upon audited financial statements that were misleading, that this reliance was the proximate cause of their losses, and that the auditors were guilty of a certain degree of negligence. The auditors named as defendants in a common-law action are in the position of having to refute the charges brought by the plaintiffs.

As indicated in the following section, legal actions brought against auditors under the Securities Act of 1933 tend to shift much of the burden of proof to the auditors. The plaintiffs must prove only that they sustained losses and that the financial statements were misleading. The auditors must then bear the burden of proof to show that they were not negligent or that the misleading financial statements were not the proximate cause of the plaintiffs' losses. For these and other reasons, it is important in considering specific cases involving auditors' liability to third parties to determine whether the legal action is being brought under common law or statutory law.

Liability to third parties under statutory law

Statutory law is written law, created by state or federal legislative bodies. Most states have "blue-sky" laws, which regulate the issuance and trading of securities within the state. The two most important federal laws relating to auditors' liability are the Securities Act of 1933 (1933 Act) and the Securities Exchange Act of 1934 (1934 Act). Surprisingly, CPAs must also be concerned with the application of the Racketeer Influenced and Corrupt Organizations Act (RICO). Even though our discussion of statutory law will be limited to these three federal acts, the auditors should be familiar with the other laws administered by the SEC, and the "blue-sky" laws in those states in which their clients sell securities.

Courts have much less discretion in deciding statutory cases than common-law cases. Common law is unwritten and evolves from court decisions. In deciding a common-law case, a court may even depart from past decisions and create a new legal precedent, as was done in *Rosenblum* v. *Adler*. In deciding a statutory case, however, the court interprets the law exactly as it is written.

An injured party may elect to bring suit against auditors under either common law or, if applicable statutes exist, under statutory law. The plaintiff will select the form of suit that has the best prospects for recovery. Since the federal Securities Acts allow class-action lawsuits, in which an entire class of investors becomes the plaintiff in a single legal action, and hold auditors to very strict standards, most lawsuits against auditors by stockholders or bondholders in a publicly owned corporation are brought under these statutes.

Securities Act of 1933

The 1933 Act requires a company intending to offer its securities for sale to the public to first file a *registration statement* with the Securities and Exchange Commission (SEC).[2] The 1933 Act states that both the company filing the registration statement and its auditors may be held liable to the initial purchasers of the securities in the event that the registration statement is found to contain material misstatements or omissions.[3] The wording of Section 11(a) of the Act on this point is as follows:

> In case any part of the registration statement, when such part became effective, contained an untrue statement of a material fact or omitted to state a material fact required to be stated therein or necessary to make the statements therein not misleading, any person acquiring such security (unless it is proved that at the time of such acquisition he knew of such untruth or omission) may . . . sue. . . .

Plaintiffs' rights under the 1933 Act The 1933 Act offers protection only to a limited group of investors—those who initially purchase a security (stock or bond) offered for sale to the public. However, the Act gives these initial investors the right to recover losses caused by the auditors' *ordinary negligence* as well as gross negligence or fraud.

Furthermore, the 1933 Act shifts much of the burden of proof from the plaintiff to the defendant. The plaintiffs (security purchasers) need only prove that (1) they sustained a loss and (2) the registration statement was misleading. They *need not* prove that they relied upon the registration statement or that the auditors were negligent. *The burden of proof in these areas is shifted to the defendants.*

Auditors' defenses under the 1933 Act If auditors are to avoid liability for the plaintiffs' losses, they must affirmatively prove that either (1) they were not negligent (the *due diligence* defense) or (2) their negligence was not the proximate cause of the plaintiffs' losses. Thus, the 1933 Act establishes the highest level of auditor liability. Not only are the auditors liable for losses caused by acts of ordinary negligence, but they must *prove their innocence,* rather than merely refuting the accusations of the plaintiffs.

---

[2] The 1933 Act requires registration statements to be filed by any company that will offer securities for sale to the public through the mails or interstate commerce. There are certain exceptions, however, for charitable institutions and other not-for-profit organizations.

[3] The auditors are liable for misstatements or omissions in only those portions of the registration statement covered by their examination and report.

Escott* v. *BarChris Construction Corporation   A significant case involving auditors' liability under the Securities Act of 1933 was the *BarChris* case. *Escott* v. *BarChris Construction Corporation,* 283 F. Supp. 643 (1968), was an action under Section 11 of the Securities Act of 1933 undertaken by purchasers of BarChris's registered debentures against the directors, underwriters, and independent auditors of BarChris. Subsequent to issuance of the debentures, BarChris, a builder of bowling alleys, became bankrupt. The plaintiffs claimed that the registration statement for the debentures contained materially false statements and material omissions; the defendants all countered with due diligence defense. The court found that the registration statement (Form S-1) was false and misleading and that with a few exceptions none of the defendants had established their due diligence defense. The court also found that the CPA firm had failed to comply with generally accepted auditing standards. The court was especially critical of the CPA firm's conduct of the S-1 review, so-called because it is an investigation carried out by a CPA firm some time after completion of the audit, but just prior to the effective date of the registration statement filed with the SEC. In an S-1 review, the CPAs look for any evidence arising since their audit that indicates that the registration statement is misleading as filed. The court criticized the CPA firm's excessive reliance on questioning of client management during the review, with no substantiation of management's answers.

Securities Exchange Act of 1934

The 1934 Act requires all companies under SEC jurisdiction to file audited annual financial statements with the SEC.[4] The Act also creates potential liability for the filing company and its auditors to anyone who buys or sells the company's securities in the event that these annual statements are found to be misleading. Remember that the 1933 Act created liability only to those investors who originally purchased the security at a public offering. Thus, the 1934 Act offers recourse against the auditors to a far greater number of investors than does the 1933 Act.

Section 18(a) of the 1934 Act provides the following liability for misleading statements:

> Any person who shall make or cause to be made any statement in any application, report, or document filed pursuant to this . . . (Act) or any rule or regulation thereunder . . . , which statement was at the time and in the
>
> *(Continued)*

---

[4] Companies with total assets exceeding $3 million and 500 or more stockholders are under SEC jurisdiction. Almost all publicly owned corporations fall into this category.

light of the circumstances under which it was made false or misleading with respect to any material fact, shall be liable to any person (not knowing that such statement was false or misleading) who, in reliance upon such statement, shall have purchased or sold a security at a price which was affected by such statement, for damages caused by such reliance, **unless the person sued shall prove that he acted in good faith** and had no knowledge that such statement was false or misleading. [Emphasis added.]

In addition, Rule 10b-5 promulgated by the SEC under Section 10(b) of the Act reads as follows:

It shall be unlawful for any person, directly or indirectly, . . .
(1) to employ any device, scheme, or artifice to defraud,
(2) to make any untrue statement of a material fact or to omit to state a material fact necessary in order to make the statements made . . . not misleading, or
(3) to engage in any act, practice, or course of business which operates or would operate as a fraud or deceit upon any person, in connection with the purchase or sale of any security.

Most lawsuits against certified public accountants have been filed under Section 18(a) and Rule 10b-5. Section 18(a) states that defendants may be liable unless they prove that they "acted in good faith," which means that they were not *grossly* negligent. Thus, Section 18(a) establishes liability for gross negligence or fraud, but *not for ordinary negligence.* The wording of Rule 10b-5 appears to create liability only for fraudulent misrepresentations. In some court decisions, however, the rule was interpreted more broadly and auditors have been held liable for losses caused by ordinary negligence even when fraudulent intent was not established. In 1976, however, the U.S. Supreme Court clarified auditors' liability under Rule 10b-5 in the *Hochfelder* v. *Ernst* case.

Hochfelder **v.** *Ernst* This landmark case is one of the few court decisions that has served to reduce, rather than expand, auditors' liability to third parties. The suit was brought by a group of investors against the CPA firm that for 21 years had audited the financial statements of First Securities Company of Chicago, a small brokerage firm. The president of First Securities, who was also its majority stockholder, committed suicide, leaving a note stating that the firm was insolvent and disclosing a fraud that he had perpetrated upon several investors. The president had persuaded the investors to mail him their personal checks, the funds from which he was to invest in escrow accounts yielding high returns to the investors. There were no such escrow accounts in the accounting records of First Securities Company; instead, the president converted the investors' checks to his own use immediately upon receipt.

The investors filed suit under SEC Rule 10b-5 (and the related Securities Exchange Act of 1934 Section 10[b]) against the CPA firm, charging it with **ordinary negligence,** and thus with responsibility for the investors' losses in the fraud. The plaintiffs did **not accuse the CPA firm of fraud or intentional misconduct.**

The basis for the plaintiffs' charge of negligence was that the CPA firm failed to discover a weakness in First Securities Company's internal control that enabled the company's president to carry on the fraud. The control weakness, called the "mail rule," was the president's policy that **only he** could open mail addressed to him at First Securities, or addressed to First Securities to his attention. (It is common practice at financial institutions for **all** incoming mail to be opened in the mailroom, in part to avoid the possibility of employees' perpetrating some type of fraud.)

The U.S. district court which heard the case dismissed it, holding that there was no issue of material fact as to whether the CPA firm had conducted its audits of First Securities in accordance with generally accepted auditing standards. The U.S. Court of Appeals reversed the district court and ruled that the CPA firm was liable for damages for aiding and abetting the First Securities president's fraud because the CPA firm had breached its duty of inquiry and disclosure regarding the First Securities internal control weakness.

The U.S. Supreme Court reversed the court of appeals, deciding that an action for damages under Section 10(b) of the 1934 Act and the related SEC Rule 10b-5 was not warranted in the absence of **scienter (intent to deceive, manipulate, or defraud)** on the auditors' part. In the Court's opinion, Mr. Justice Powell wrote:

> The words "manipulative or deceptive" used in conjunction with "device or contrivance" strongly suggest that (Section) 10(b) was intended to proscribe knowing or intentional misconduct.
>
> * * * * *
>
> When a statute speaks so specifically in terms of manipulation and deception, and of implementing devices and contrivances—the commonly understood terminology of intentional wrongdoing—and when its history reflects no more expansive intent, we are quite unwilling to extend the scope of the statute to negligent conduct.

Based upon this ruling, auditors can no longer be held liable for ordinary negligence under Section 10(b) and Rule 10b-5 of the 1934 Act. On the surface, the decision seems to imply that Rule 10b-5 creates liability only for acts of fraud. However, several lower federal courts subsequently have held auditors liable for **gross negligence,** on the premise that gross negligence constitutes intent to deceive.

Comparison of the 1933 and 1934 Acts

The 1933 Act holds the auditors to a higher standard of performance than does the 1934 Act, but its protection is offered to fewer third parties. The 1933 Act offers recourse only to the **initial** purchasers of securities, whereas the 1934 Act offers recourse to **any** person buying or selling the securities at a later date.

The 1933 Act holds the auditors liable for acts of **ordinary negligence.** Following the *Hochfelder* decision, the 1934 Act creates liability for gross negligence and fraud, but not for ordinary negligence.

In comparison to common law, both of the federal Securities Acts shift significant burdens of proof from the plaintiffs to the defendants. However, some differences exist between the defendant's burden under the 1933 and 1934 Acts. Under the 1933 Act, plaintiffs **need not prove reliance** upon the audited financial statements; it is left to the defendant to show that misstatements in the financial statements were not the proximate cause of the plaintiffs' losses. The 1934 Act, however, generally requires plaintiffs to prove that they relied upon the misleading statements.

Next, both Acts place the burden of proving adequate performance on the defendants. The 1933 Act requires the auditors to prove "due diligence"—that is, that they were **not negligent.** The 1934 Act is more lenient in that the CPAs must only prove that they "acted in good faith," meaning that they were **not grossly negligent.** The "good faith" defense is considerably easier to establish than is "due diligence."

The Racketeer Influenced and Corrupt Organizations Act

In 1970, Congress enacted the Racketeer Influenced and Corrupt Organizations Act (RICO) to be a potent weapon against mobsters and racketeers who were influencing legitimate business. A discussion of RICO would appear to be out of place in a discussion of legal liability of auditors. However, the act broadly defines the term **racketeering activities** to include crimes such as mail fraud and fraud in the sale of securities. These provisions have been used successfully in a small number of cases against CPAs in which it could be shown that the CPAs knew, or perhaps should have known, of material misstatements of financial statements when the problems were indicative of a pattern of improper activity.

A primary concern with the RICO act is the provision that allows triple damages in civil cases brought under the act. Thus investors might be awarded three times their losses, if they can prove racketeering activities on the part of the CPAs. This creates a potential liability of overwhelming proportions for CPAs that are auditors of large public companies.

Auditors' civil liability: a summary

The auditors' civil liability under common law and under the federal Securities Acts is summarized in Figure 3–1. Notice that under certain circumstances auditors may be held liable to any third party—not just to clients—for losses attributable to acts of ordinary negligence. In common-law cases brought by third parties, the extent of the auditors' liability may vary depending upon the state (jurisdiction) in which the suit is filed. Thus, the only safe policy for a CPA firm is to perform every engagement with a degree of care that no court could interpret as negligent.

Auditors' criminal liability under the Securities Acts

Both the Securities Act of 1933 and the Securities Exchange Act of 1934 include provisions for *criminal charges* against persons violating provisions of the Acts. These provisions are found in Section 17(a) of the Securities Act of 1933 and Section 32(a) of the Securities Exchange Act of 1934. In addition, in extreme cases CPAs can be prosecuted under the criminal provisions of the Racketeer Influenced and Corrupt Organizations Act.

The *Continental Vending Machine Corporation* case was accompanied by a celebrated criminal case involving three members of the CPA firm that audited Continental's financial statements. The criminal charges rocked the profession, because there was no intent to defraud on the part of the CPAs; they were convicted of criminal fraud on the basis of gross negligence. The verdict of guilty was affirmed by a U.S. Court of Appeals, and the U.S. Supreme Court refused to review the case. The three CPAs were later pardoned by the President of the United States.

The principal facts of the *Continental Vending* case (*United States* v. *Simon,* 425 F.2d 796 [1969]) are as follows. The U.S. government's case of fraud against the three CPAs hinged upon a footnote to Continental's audited financial statements, which read:

> The amount receivable from Valley Commercial Corp. (an affiliated company of which . . . [Continental's president] is an officer, director, and stockholder) bears interest at 12 percent a year. Such amount, less the balance of the notes payable to that company, is secured by the assignment to the Company of Valley's equity in certain marketable securities. As of . . . [the date of the auditors' report] . . . the amount of such equity at current market quotations exceeded the net amount receivable.

Figure 3–1 Summary of auditors' civil liability

Plaintiff (injured party)	Suit brought under:	Burden of proof for:	
		Plaintiff	Defendant auditor
Client	Common law	Loss Auditor negligence Proximate cause	None* (unless defense is based on proving contributory negligence on the part of the plaintiff)
Third-party beneficiary	Common law	Loss Auditor negligence Proximate cause	None* (unless defense is based on proving other causes for the plaintiffs' losses)
Other third parties	Common law	Loss Auditor gross negligence (ordinary negligence in certain jurisdictions) Proximate cause	None* (unless defense is based on proving other causes for the plaintiffs' losses)
Initial purchaser of security in a public company	Securities Act of 1933	Loss Financial statements were misleading	Due diligence or Not proximate cause (loss caused by other factors)
Any security owner in a public company	Securities Exchange Act of 1934	Loss Financial statements were misleading Reliance on statements Scienter by auditor	Acted in good faith or Not proximate cause (loss caused by other factors)

* Under common law, the entire burden of proof is borne by the plaintiff, as the defendant is presumed innocent until proven guilty. The defendant may actively participate in the case, however, by introducing evidence to refute the plaintiff's allegations.

The U.S. government charged the CPAs should have insisted that the note be worded as follows:

> The amount receivable from Valley Commercial Corp. (an affiliated company of which . . . [Continental's president] is an officer, director and stockholder), which bears interest at 12 percent a year, was uncollectible at . . . [the balance sheet date], since Valley had loaned approximately the same amount to . . . [Continental's president] who was unable to pay. Since that date . . . [Continental's president] and others have pledged as security for the repayment of his obligation to Valley and its obligation to Continental (now $3,900,000, against which Continental's liability to Valley cannot be offset) securities, which, as of . . . (the date of the auditors' report) . . . , had a market value of $2,978,000. Approximately 80 percent of such securities are stock and convertible debentures of the Company.

The auditors' defense in this case was that the footnote complied with existing generally accepted accounting principles. However, the judge rejected this argument and instructed the jury to evaluate whether the financial statements were "fairly presented" without reference to generally accepted accounting principles. The finding by the jury that the balance sheet did not "present fairly" Continental's financial position led to conviction of the three CPAs.

The *Continental Vending* case has significant implications for the public accounting profession. Not only is civil liability an ever-present hazard for public accountants, but criminal charges may also be involved.

The SEC's regulation of accountants

The SEC has issued rules for the appearance and practice of CPAs, attorneys, and others before the Commission under the statutes it administers. Rule of Practice 2(e), giving the SEC the power of suspension and disbarment, has the following wording:

> The Commission may deny, temporarily or permanently, the privilege of appearing or practicing before it in any way to any person who is found by the Commission . . . (1) not to possess the requisite qualifications to represent others, or (2) to be lacking in character or integrity or to have engaged in unethical or improper professional conduct.

On occasions, the Commission has taken punitive action against public accounting firms when it has found the audit work deficient with regard to financial statements filed with the Commission. These actions against public accounting firms usually arise when a listed corporation encounters financial difficulties and it later appears that misleading financial statements had served to conceal for a time the losses being incurred by the company. In recent years, the SEC has taken action against CPA firms by the use of consent decrees in which the CPAs have agreed to certain penalties or restrictions. For example, a CPA firm may agree under pressure from the SEC not to accept new clients during a specified period and to permit a review of its practice.

Accountants' liability for accounting and review services

Up to this point, we have emphasized the liability of CPA firms when they are associated with audited financial statements. In addition, CPAs may perform many accounting services, such as income tax work and *compilations* or *reviews* of unaudited financial statements. These services differ from audits in that the CPAs neither perform the investigative procedures involved in an audit nor do they issue an auditors' opinion as to the fairness of the financial information.

The term *compilation* refers to the *preparation* of financial statements based upon information provided to the CPA by the client (or the client's representatives). A compilation is *not intended to lend any assurance* to any party that the CPA has determined the information to be reliable. A *review* consists of *limited* investigative procedures, *substantially less in scope than an audit,* designed to provide users of the unaudited financial statements with a *limited* degree of assurance as to the statements' reliability. Compilations and reviews will be discussed in Chapter 19.

Do CPAs associated with unaudited financial statements have any potential legal liability? The answer is *yes.* The CPAs, acting as *accountants* rather than as *auditors,* still have a liability to their client to exercise due professional care. In addition, they still may be liable under common law for losses to third parties attributable to the accountants' ordinary or gross negligence.

Accountants or auditors? When CPAs are associated with unaudited financial statements, a possibility exists that the client or third parties may misinterpret the extent of the CPAs' services and believe that the accountants actually are acting as auditors.

The risks to CPA firms engaged in the preparation of unaudited financial statements were brought sharply into focus by the *1136 Tenants' Corporation* v. *Rothenberg* case. In this common-law case, an incorporated apartment cooperative, which was owned by its shareholder-tenants and managed by a separate realty agent, orally retained a CPA firm for a period of 17 months to perform services leading to the preparation of financial statements for the cooperative, and also including letters containing tax information to the shareholders. The CPA firm's fee was to be only $600 per year.

The CPA firm submitted financial statements of the corporation for one full year and the first six months of the following year. The financial statements bore the notation "subject to comments in letter of transmittal." The referenced letter of transmittal read in part:

> Pursuant to our engagement, we have reviewed and summarized the statements of your managing agent and other data submitted to us by . . . [the agent], pertaining to 1136 Tenants' Corporation. . . .
> The following statements were prepared from the books and records of the Corporation. No independent verifications were undertaken thereon. . . .

The client corporation later sued the CPA firm for damages totaling $174,000 for the CPAs' alleged failure to discover defalcations of the corporation's funds committed by the managing agent. The client contended that the CPAs had been retained to render all necessary accounting *and auditing* services for it. The CPAs maintained they had been engaged to do write-up work only, although a working paper they had prepared supporting accrued expenses payable in the balance sheet included an entry for "audit expense."

The New York state trial court ruled in favor of the plaintiff in this common-law case, as did the Appellate Court of New York. The latter found that the CPAs' working papers indicated that the CPAs had examined the client's bank statements, invoices and bills, and had made notations in their working papers concerning "missing invoices." The New York Court of Appeals affirmed the decision.

In summary, the court held the CPAs liable because it found that they had led their client to believe that they were performing an audit. Consequently, the courts held the CPAs responsible for performing their work in accordance with generally accepted auditing standards, which they clearly had not done. More importantly, however, the court also concluded that the CPAs had a duty to follow up on significant problems (the missing invoices) uncovered during their engagement. Thus, it is probable that the CPA firm would have been held liable to its client *even if the court had recognized that the firm was not performing an audit.* Whenever CPAs encounter evidence that their client may be sustaining a loss through embezzlement or other irregularities, they should warn the client immediately.

There are many lessons for CPA firms in the *1136 Tenants' Corporation* case:

1. CPAs who prepare unaudited financial statements should adhere closely to Rules of Conduct 102 and 202 of the AICPA's *Code of Professional Conduct.* Rule 102 states that a CPA shall not knowingly

misrepresent facts, and Rule 202 requires a CPA firm to comply with professional standards, including standards for accounting and review services. The actions of the CPA firm described in the preceding paragraph might be construed as violating both rules.

2. Engagement letters are as essential for accounting and review services as they are for independent audits. Oral arrangements for accounting and review services are of scant assistance when there is a dispute as to the nature of the services to be rendered by the CPA firm to the client.

3. A CPA engaged to perform **accounting or review** services should be alert for, and follow up on, such unusual items as missing invoices. As professionals, CPAs are bound to exercise **due professional care,** even though their engagements do not include independent audits of the client's financial statements.

4. CPAs should report on financial statements clearly and concisely, using as far as possible the standardized language set forth in *Statements on Auditing Standards* and *Statements on Standards for Accounting and Review Services*. Reports should indicate the nature of the services rendered and the degree of responsibility being assumed by the CPA firm.

The CPAs' posture in the age of litigation

In addition to the preceding court cases, several other actions against CPAs, under both common law and the Securities Acts, are pending trial. It is apparent that lawsuits will continue to plague the public accounting profession, as they have the legal and medical professions. The question thus is: What should be the CPAs' reaction to this age of litigation?

In the opinion of the authors, positive actions helpful to CPAs in withstanding threats of possible lawsuits include the following:

1. Greater emphasis upon compliance with the public accounting profession's generally accepted auditing standards and *Code of Professional Conduct*. Close analysis of the court cases and other actions described in this chapter discloses numerous instances in which the auditors appear not to have complied fully with one or more auditing standards and Rules of Conduct.

2. Retain legal counsel that is familiar with CPAs' legal liability. The CPAs should thoroughly discuss all potentially dangerous situations with their legal counsel and should carefully consider their counsel's advice.

3. Maintenance of adequate liability insurance coverage. Although liability insurance coverage should not be considered a substitute for the CPAs' compliance with the preceding recommendations, public accountants must protect themselves against possible financial losses from lawsuits. Adequate liability insurance is essential.

4. Thorough investigation of prospective clients. As indicated in preceding sections of this chapter, many court cases involving CPAs have been accompanied by criminal charges against top management of the CPAs' clients. CPAs should use great care in screening prospective clients to avoid the risks involved in professional relationships with the criminally inclined.

5. Obtain a thorough knowledge of the client's business. One of the major causes of audit failures has been a lack of understanding by auditors of the client's business and of industry practices.

6. Use of engagement letters for all professional services. Controversies over what services are to be rendered by a CPA can be minimized by a clearly written contract describing the agreed-upon services. Engagement letters are discussed in Chapter 4.

7. In planning engagements, carefully assess the probability of errors and irregularities in the client's financial statements. Exercise special care when the client has material weaknesses in internal control.

8. Exercise extreme care in audits of clients in financial difficulties. Creditors and shareholders of companies that are insolvent or in bankruptcy are likely to seek scapegoats to blame for their losses. As the court cases described in this chapter demonstrate, litigation involving CPAs tends to center around auditing of clients who later become bankrupt.

KEY TERMS INTRODUCED OR EMPHASIZED IN CHAPTER 3

Common law   Unwritten legal principles developed through court decisions.

Compilation of financial statements   The preparation of financial statements by CPAs based on representations of management, with the expression of no assurance concerning the statements' compliance with generally accepted accounting principles.

Constructive fraud   Performing duties that require exceptional care with such recklessness that persons believing the duties to have been completed carefully are being misled. Differs from fraud in that constructive fraud does not involve knowledge of misrepresentations within the financial statements.

Credit Alliance Corp. v. Arthur Andersen & Co.   A recent common-law decision by the New York Court of Appeals (New York's highest court) stating that auditors must demonstrate knowledge of reliance on the financial statements by a third party for a particular purpose to be held liable for ordinary negligence to that party. Basically, upheld the *Ultramares* v. *Touche* rule.

Due diligence   A CPA firm's contention that its audit work was adequate to support its opinion on financial statements included in a registration statement filed with the SEC under the Securities Act of 1933.

Errors   Unintentional mistakes in financial statements and accounting records, including mistakes in the application of accounting principles.

Fraud   Misrepresentation by a person of a material fact, known by that person to be untrue or made with reckless indifference as to whether the fact is true, with intent to deceive and with the result that another party is injured.

Gross negligence   Reckless disregard for responsibilities.

Hochfelder v. Ernst A landmark case in which the U.S. Supreme Court decided that auditors could not be held liable under the Securities Exchange Act of 1934 for ordinary negligence.

Irregularities Intentional distortions in financial statements, often accompanied by falsifications in the accounting records.

Negligence Violation of a legal duty to exercise a degree of care that an ordinarily prudent person would exercise under similar circumstances, with resultant damages to another party.

Precedent A legal principle that evolves from a common-law court decision and then serves as a standard for future decisions in similar cases.

Registration statement A document including audited financial statements that must be filed with the SEC by any company intending to sell its securities to the public through the mails or interstate commerce. The Securities Act of 1933 provides liability to security purchasers for material misrepresentations in registration statements.

Review of financial statements The performance of limited investigative procedures that are substantially less in scope than an audit made in accordance with generally accepted auditing standards. The procedures provide the CPAs with a basis to provide *limited* assurance that the financial statements are in accordance with generally accepted accounting principles.

Rosenblum v. Adler A common-law decision by the New Jersey Supreme Court that holds CPAs liable for acts of ordinary negligence to ''reasonably foreseeable third parties'' not in privity of contract. Conflicts with the precedent established in the *Ultramares* and *Credit Alliance* decisions.

Scienter Intent to deceive, manipulate, or defraud. The U.S. Supreme Court held in the *Hochfelder* case that scienter must be proved for the auditors to be held liable under Securities Exchange Act of 1934.

Securities Act of 1933 A federal securities statute covering registration statements for securities to be sold to the public. The Act requires auditors to exercise ''due diligence,'' and creates both civil and criminal penalties for misrepresentation.

Securities Exchange Act of 1934 A federal securities statute requiring large companies to file annual audited financial statements with the SEC. The Act requires auditors to ''act in good faith,'' and creates civil and criminal penalties for misrepresentation.

Statutory law Written law created by state or federal legislative bodies.

Third-party beneficiary A person—not the auditors or their client—who is named in a contract (or known to the contracting parties) with the intention that such person should have definite rights and benefits under the contract.

Ultramares v. Touche & Co. A common-law decision by the New York Court of Appeals (New York's highest court) stating that auditors are liable to third parties not in privity of contract for acts of fraud or gross negligence, but not for ordinary negligence. Conflicts with New Jersey Supreme Court's finding in *Rosenblum* v. *Adler*.

GROUP I: REVIEW QUESTIONS

3–1. Assume that a large CPA firm exercises due professional care on every engagement. Can the firm reasonably expect that it will never face a lawsuit accusing the firm of professional misconduct? Explain.

3–2. Explain why the potential liability of CPAs for professional "malpractice" exceeds that of physicians or other professionals.

3–3. Distinguish between common law and statutory law.

3–4. Distinguish between ordinary negligence and gross negligence within the context of a CPA's work.

3–5. What is meant by the term *privity?* How does privity affect the auditor's liability under common law?

3–6. Define the term *third-party beneficiary*.

3–7. Describe the auditors' responsibility for detecting errors and irregularities in financial statements.

3–8. Briefly describe the different common-law precedents set by the *Ultramares* v. *Touche* case and the *Rosenblum* v. *Adler* case.

3–9. What landmark case was embraced by the court in the case of *Credit Alliance Corp.* v. *Arthur Andersen & Co.?* Identify the two factors that the court stated must be proved for the auditors to be held liable to ordinary third parties.

3–10. Why did Congress enact the Racketeer Influenced and Corrupt Organizations Act? Why is it of concern to CPAs?

3–11. Compare auditors' common-law liability to clients and third-party beneficiaries with their common-law liability to other third parties.

3–12. Compare the rights of plaintiffs under common law with the rights of persons who purchase securities registered under the Securities Act of 1933 and sustain losses. In your answer emphasize the issue of who must bear the burden of proof.

3–13. State briefly a major distinction between the Securities Act of 1933 and the Securities Exchange Act of 1934 with respect to the type of transactions regulated.

3–14. Why was the *Hochfelder* v. *Ernst* decision considered a "victory" for the accounting profession?

3–15. How was the *Continental Vending* case unusual with respect to penalties levied against auditors?

3–16. How does the SEC regulate CPAs who appear and practice before the commission?

3–17. In the *1136 Tenants'* case, what was the essential difference in the way the client and the auditors viewed the work to be done in the engagement?

3–18. Are engagement letters needed both for audits and for accounting and review services performed by CPAs? Explain.

3–19. Assume that in a particular audit the CPAs were negligent but not grossly negligent. Indicate whether they would be "Liable" or "Not liable" for the following losses proximately caused by their negligence:
   a. Loss sustained by client; suit brought under common law.
   b. Loss sustained by trade creditor, not in privity of contract; suits brought in state courts that adhere to the *Ultramares* v. *Touche* precedent.
   c. Loss sustained by a bank known to the auditors to be relying on the financial statements for a loan; suits brought in state courts that adhere to the *Credit Alliance* v. *Arthur Andersen* precedent.

d. Losses to stockholders purchasing shares at a public offering; suit brought under Securities Act of 1933.

e. Loss sustained by a bank named as a third-party beneficiary in the engagement letter; suit brought under common law.

f. Loss sustained by a lender not in privity of contract; suit brought in state courts which adhere to the *Rosenblum* v. *Adler* precedent.

g. Losses sustained by stockholders; suit brought under Sections 18(a) and 10(b) of the Securities Exchange Act of 1934.

GROUP II: QUESTIONS REQUIRING ANALYSIS

3–20. Rogers and Green, CPAs, admit they failed substantially to follow generally accepted auditing standards in their audit of Martin Corporation. "We were overworked and understaffed and never should have accepted the engagement," said Rogers. Does this situation constitute fraud on the part of the CPA firm? Explain.

3–21. The partnership of Porter, Potts & Farr, CPAs, was engaged by Revolutionary Products, Inc., a closely held corporation, to perform an audit of the company's financial statements. The engagement letter said nothing about the CPA firm's responsibility for defalcations. Porter, Potts & Farr performed its examination in a careful and competent manner, following generally accepted auditing standards and using appropriate auditing procedures and tests under the circumstances.

Subsequently, it was discovered that the client's chief accountant was engaged in major defalcations. However, only an investigation specifically designed to discover possible defalcations would have revealed the fraud. Revolutionary Products asserts that Porter, Potts & Farr is liable for the defalcations.

Required:
Is Porter, Potts & Farr liable? Explain.   (AICPA, adapted)

3–22. Jensen, Inc. filed suit against a CPA firm, alleging that the auditors' negligence was responsible for failure to disclose a large defalcation that had been in process for several years. The CPA firm responded that it may have been negligent, but that Jensen, Inc. was really to blame because it had completely ignored the CPA firm's repeated recommendations for improvements in the internal control structure.

If the CPA firm was negligent, is it responsible for the loss sustained by the client? Does the failure by Jensen, Inc. to follow the CPAs' recommendation for better internal controls have any bearing on the question of liability? Explain.

3–23. Susan Harris is a new assistant auditor with the CPA firm of Sparks, Watts, and Wilcox. On her third audit assignment, Harris examined the documentation underlying 60 disbursements as a test of controls over purchasing, receiving, vouchers payable, and cash disbursement procedures. In the process, she found five disbursements for the purchase of materials with no receiving reports in the documentation. She noted the exceptions in her working papers and called them to the attention of the senior auditor. Relying on prior experience with the client, the senior auditor disregarded Harris' comments, and nothing further was done about the exceptions.

Subsequently, it was learned that one of the client's purchasing agents and a member of its accounting department were engaged in a fraudulent scheme whereby they diverted the receipt of materials to a public warehouse while sending the invoices to the client. When the client discovered the fraud, the conspirators had obtained approximately $700,000, of which $500,000 was after the completion of the audit.

Required:
Discuss the legal implications and liabilities to Spark, Watts, and Wilcox as a result of the above facts.   (AICPA, adapted)

3–24. The CPA firm of Hanson and Brown was expanding very rapidly. Consequently, it hired several staff assistants, including James Small. Subsequently, the partners of the firm became dissatisfied with Small's production and warned him that they would be forced to discharge him unless his output increased significantly.

At that time Small was engaged in audits of several clients. He decided that to avoid being fired, he would reduce or omit entirely some of the required auditing procedures listed in audit programs prepared by the partners. One of the CPA firm's non-SEC clients, Newell Corporation, was in serious financial difficulty and had adjusted several of its accounts being examined by Small to appear financially sound. Small prepared fictitious working papers in his home at night to support purported completion of auditing procedures assigned to him, although he in fact did not examine the Newell adjusting entries. The CPA firm rendered an unqualified opinion on Newell's financial statements, which were grossly misstated. Several creditors, relying upon the audited financial statements, subsequently extended large sums of money to Newell Corporation.

Required:
Would the CPA firm be liable to the creditors who extended the money in reliance on the erroneous financial statements if Newell Corporation should fail to pay the creditors? Explain.   (AICPA, adapted)

3–25. Match these important cases with the appropriate legal precedent or implication.

Case

_____ a.   *Hochfelder* v. *Ernest*
_____ b.   *Escott* v. *BarChris Construction Corp.*
_____ c.   *Credit Alliance* v. *Arthur Andersen & Co.*
_____ d.   *Ultramares* v. *Touche & Co.*
_____ e.   *Rosenblum* v. *Adler*
_____ f.   *Rusch Factors, Inc.* v. *Levin*
_____ g.   *United States* v. *Simon (Continental Vending)*

Legal Precedent or Implication

1. A landmark case establishing that auditors should be held liable to third parties not in privity of contract for gross negligence, but not for ordinary negligence.
2. A case in which the court used the guidance of the *Second Restatement of the Law of Torts* to decide the auditors' liability to third parties under common law.
3. A landmark case in which the auditors were held liable under Section 11 of the Securities Act of 1933.

4. A case in which auditors were held liable for criminal negligence.
5. A case that established that auditors should not be held liable under the Securities Exchange Act of 1934 unless there was intent to deceive.
6. A case that established the precedent that auditors should be held liable under common law for ordinary negligence to all foreseen third parties.
7. A recent common-law case in which the court held that auditors should be held liable for ordinary negligence only to third parties they know will use the financial statements for a particular purpose.

3–26. For several years, the CPA firm of Carter, Reed, & Co. has audited Cobra Corporation, a closely held manufacturing company that is not under SEC jurisdiction. Cobra is now planning to "go public," issuing common shares to the public and using the proceeds to finance growth. The planned stock offering would put the company under the jurisdiction of the SEC.

Required:
Discuss the reasons why the CPA firm's potential legal liability with respect to this client will increase substantially if the company "goes public."

3–27. Dandy Container Corporation engaged the accounting firm of Adams and Adams to examine financial statements to be used in connection with an interstate public offering of securities. The audit was completed, and an unqualified opinion was expressed on the financial statements that were submitted to the Securities and Exchange Commission along with the registration statement. Two hundred thousand shares of Dandy Container common stock were offered to the public at $11 a share. Eight months later the stock fell to $2 a share when it was disclosed that several large loans to two "paper" corporations owned by one of the directors were worthless. The loans were secured by the stock of the borrowing corporations, which was owned by the director. These facts were not disclosed in the financial statements. The director involved and the two corporations are insolvent.

Required:
State whether each of the following statements is true or false, and explain why.
a. The Securities Act of 1933 applies to the above-described public offering of securities.
b. The accounting firm has potential liability to any person who acquired the stock.
c. An insider who had knowledge of all the facts regarding the loans to the two paper corporations could nevertheless recover from the accounting firm.
d. In court, investors who bought shares in Dandy Container need only show that they sustained a loss and that failure to explain the nature of the loans in question constituted a false statement or misleading omission in the financial statements.
e. The accountants could avoid liability if they could show they were not negligent.

    f. The accountants could avoid or reduce the damages asserted against them if they could establish that the drop in the stock's market price was due in whole or in part to other causes.

    g. The Securities and Exchange Commission would defend any action brought against the accountants in that the SEC examined and approved the registration statement.   (AICPA, adapted)

3–28. Gordon & Moore, CPAs, were the auditors of Fox & Company, a brokerage firm. Gordon & Moore examined and reported on the financial statements of Fox, which were filed with the Securities and Exchange Commission.

Several of Fox's customers were swindled by a fraudulent scheme perpetrated by two key officers of the company. The facts establish that Gordon & Moore were negligent, but not reckless or grossly negligent, in the conduct of the audit, and neither participated in the fraudulent scheme nor knew of its existence.

The customers are suing Gordon & Moore under the antifraud provisions of Section 10(b) and Rule 10b-5 of the Securities Exchange Act of 1934 for aiding and abetting the fraudulent scheme of the officers. The customers' suit for fraud is predicated exclusively on the negligence of the auditors in failing to conduct a proper audit, thereby failing to discover the fraudulent scheme.

Required:
Answer the following, setting forth reasons for any conclusions stated.
a. What is the probable outcome of the lawsuit? Explain.
b. What other theory of liability might the customers have asserted?
        (AICPA, adapted)

3–29. Wanda Young, doing business as Wanda Young Fashions, engaged the CPA partnership of Scott & Green to examine her financial statements. During the examination, Scott & Green discovered certain irregularities that would have indicated to a reasonably prudent auditor that James Smith, the chief accountant, might be engaged in a fraud. However, Scott & Green, not having been engaged to discover defalcations, submitted an unqualified opinion in its report and did not mention the potential defalcation problem.

Required:
What are the legal implications of the above facts as they relate to the relationship between Scott & Green and Wanda Young? Explain.
        (AICPA, adapted)

3–30. Select the best answer for each of the following questions and explain the reasons for your choice.
    a. With respect to errors and irregularities, the auditors should—
        (1) Design their examination to provide reasonable assurance of detecting errors and irregularities that would have a material effect on the financial statements.
        (2) Plan to search for errors and irregularities that would have a material effect on the financial statements.
        (3) Design their examination to provide reasonable assurance of detecting errors that would have a material effect and irregularities

that would have either a material or immaterial effect on the financial statements.

(4) Design their examination to provide reasonable assurance of detecting irregularities that would have a material effect and errors that would have either a material or immaterial effect on the financial statements.

b. An independent auditor has the responsibility to design the audit to provide reasonable assurance of detecting errors and irregularities that have a material effect on the financial statements. Which of the following, if material, would be an *irregularity* as defined in Statements on Auditing Standards?

(1) Misappropriation of an asset or groups of assets.

(2) Clerical mistakes in the accounting data underlying the financial statements.

(3) Mistakes in the application of accounting principles.

(4) Misinterpretation of facts that existed when the financial statements were prepared.

c. Which of the following statements best expresses the factors that purchasers of securities registered under the Securities Act of 1933 need prove to recover losses from the auditors?

(1) The purchasers of securities must prove negligence by the auditors and reliance on the audited financial statements.

(2) The purchasers of securities must prove that the financial statements were misleading and that they relied on them to purchase the securities.

(3) The purchasers of securities must prove that the financial statements were misleading; then, the burden of proof is shifted to the auditors to show that the audit was performed with "due diligence."

(4) The purchasers of securities must prove that the financial statements were misleading and the auditors were negligent.

d. The most significant aspect of the *Continental Vending* case was that it—

(1) Created a more general awareness of the auditor's exposure to criminal prosecution.

(2) Extended the auditor's responsibility to all information included in registration statements.

(3) Defined the CPA's responsibilities for unaudited financial statements.

(4) Established a precedent for auditors being held liable to third parties under common law for ordinary negligence.

e. The *1136 Tenants'* case was chiefly important because of its emphasis upon the legal liability of the CPA when associated with—

(1) A review of interim statements.

(2) Unaudited financial statements.

(3) An audit resulting in a disclaimer of opinion.

(4) Letters for underwriters.

f. A CPA is subject to *criminal* liability if the CPA—

(1) Refuses to turn over the working papers to the client.

(2) Performs an audit in a negligent manner.

(3) Willfully omits a material fact required to be stated in a registration statement.

(4) Willfully breaches the contract with the client.   (AICPA)

GROUP III: PROBLEMS

3–31. Austin & Co. is the auditor of Silex Products. During the past three audits, Austin & Co. has repeatedly warned Silex's top management of serious weaknesses in the company's internal control over cash disbursements. Management has not, however, taken any corrective action.

During the current year's audit, the CPAs were negligent in failing to test inventory for obsolescence. Certain items were in fact obsolete; and as a result, inventory was overstated by a material amount in the company's audited financial statements for the year.

Shortly after the audit, Silex learned that two employees in its accounting department had been embezzling money for the last two years. The scheme involved authorizing cash disbursements to fictitious people, recording these disbursements in various expense accounts, and then arranging to have the checks cashed. Each of the improper disbursements was for a relatively small amount, but the cumulative effects of the fraud were material in each of the last two years. Silex has brought suit against Austin & Co. for the amount of its losses in this cash fraud.

Required:

a. Without regard to the above case, briefly describe the auditors' responsibility for the detection of errors and irregularities within the accounting records and financial statements of a client.

b. Suggest two arguments that the auditors might make in court that might lessen or eliminate their liability for the client's losses in the embezzlement scheme.

c. What argument might Silex advance to indicate that the auditors were negligent in failing to discover the embezzlement scheme?

3–32. Risk Capital Limited, a publicly held Delaware corporation, was considering the purchase of a substantial amount of the treasury stock held by Florida Sunshine Corporation, a closely held corporation. Initial discussions with the Florida Sunshine Corporation began late in 198X.

Wilson and Wyatt, CPAs, Florida Sunshine's public accountants, regularly prepared quarterly and annual unaudited financial statements. The most recently prepared unaudited financial statements were for the fiscal year ended September 30, 198X.

On November 15, 198X, after protracted negotiations, Risk Capital agreed to purchase 100,000 shares of no-par, Class A treasury stock of Florida Sunshine at $12.50 per share. However, Risk Capital insisted upon audited statements for the calendar year 198X. The contract specifically provided: "Risk Capital shall have the right to rescind the purchase of said stock if the audited financial statements of Florida Sunshine for calendar year 198X show a material adverse change in the financial position of the Corporation."

At the request of Florida Sunshine, Wilson and Wyatt audited the company's financial statements for the year ended December 31, 198X. The December 31, 198X, audited financial statements furnished to Florida Sunshine by Wilson and Wyatt showed no material adverse change from the September 30, 198X, unaudited statements. Risk Capital relied upon the audited statements and purchased the treasury stock of Florida Sunshine. It was subsequently discovered that as of the balance sheet date, the audited statements contained several misstatements and that in fact there had been a material adverse change in the financial position of the corporation. Florida Sunshine has become insolvent, and Risk Capital will lose virtually its entire investment.

Risk Capital seeks recovery against Wilson and Wyatt.

Required:

a. Discuss each of the theories of liability that Risk Capital will probably assert as its basis for recovery.

b. Assuming that only ordinary negligence by Wilson and Wyatt is proven, will Risk Capital prevail? State yes or no and explain.

(AICPA, adapted)

3–33. Meglow Corporation, a closely held manufacturer of dresses and blouses, sought a loan from Busch Factors. Busch had previously extended $50,000 credit to Meglow but refused to lend any additional money without obtaining copies of Meglow's audited financial statements.

Meglow contacted the CPA firm of Seavers & Dean to perform the audit. In arranging for the examination, Meglow clearly indicated that its purpose was to satisfy Busch Factors as to the corporation's sound financial condition and to obtain an additional loan of $100,000. Seavers & Dean accepted the engagement, performed the examination in a negligent manner, and rendered an unqualified opinion. If an adequate examination had been performed, the financial statements would have been found to be misleading.

Meglow submitted the audited financial statements to Busch Factors and obtained an additional loan of $70,000. Busch refused to lend more than that amount. After several other factors also refused, Meglow finally was able to persuade Maxwell Department Stores, one of its customers, to lend the additional $30,000. Maxwell relied upon the financial statements examined by Seavers & Dean.

Meglow is now in bankruptcy, and Busch seeks to collect from Seavers & Dean the $120,000 it loaned Meglow. Maxwell seeks to recover from Seavers & Dean the $30,000 it loaned Meglow.

Required:

a. Will Busch recover? Explain.

b. Will Maxwell recover? Explain.   (AICPA, adapted)

3–34. Mark Williams, CPA, was engaged by Jackson Financial Development Company to audit the financial statements of Apex Construction Company, a small closely held corporation. Williams was told when he was engaged that Jackson Financial needed reliable financial statements that would be used to determine whether or not to purchase a substantial amount of Apex Construction's convertible debentures at the price asked by the estate of one of Apex's former directors.

Williams performed his examination in a negligent manner. As a result of his negligence, he failed to discover substantial defalcations by Carl Brown, the Apex controller. Jackson Financial purchased the debentures, but it would not have done so if the defalcations had been discovered.

After discovery of the fraud, Jackson Financial promptly sold them for the highest price offered in the market at a $70,000 loss.

Required:
a. What liability does Williams have to Jackson Financial? Explain.
b. If Apex Construction also sues Williams for negligence, what are the probable legal defenses Williams's attorney would raise? Explain.
c. Will the negligence of Mark Williams, CPA, as described above prevent him from recovering on a liability insurance policy covering the practice of his profession? Explain.   (AICPA, adapted)

3–35. Cragsmore & Company, a medium-size partnership of CPAs, was engaged by Marlowe Manufacturing, Inc., a closely held corporation, to examine its financial statements for the year ended December 31, 198X.

Before preparing the audit report, William Cragsmore, a partner, and Joan Willmore, a staff senior, reviewed the disclosures necessary in the notes to the financial statements. One note involved the terms, costs, and obligations of a lease between Marlowe and Acme Leasing Company.

Willmore suggested that the note disclose the following: "The Acme Leasing Company is owned by persons who have a 35 percent interest in the capital stock and who are officers of Marlowe Manufacturing, Inc."

On Cragsmore's recommendation, this was revised by substituting "minority shareholders" for "persons who have a 35 percent interest in the capital stock and who are officers."

The audit report and financial statements were forwarded to Marlowe Manufacturing for review. The officer-shareholders of Marlowe who also owned Acme Leasing objected to the revised wording and insisted that the note be changed to describe the relationship between Acme and Marlowe as merely one of affiliation. Cragsmore acceded to this request.

The audit report was issued on this basis with an unqualified opinion. But the working papers included the drafts that showed the changes in the wording of the note.

Subsequent to delivery of the audit report, Marlowe suffered a substantial uninsured fire loss and was forced into bankruptcy. The failure of Marlowe to carry any fire insurance coverage was not noted in the financial statements.

Required:
What legal problems for Cragsmore & Company are suggested by these facts? Discuss.   (AICPA, adapted)

3–36. After Commuter Airlines was forced into bankruptcy, the company's stockholders brought suit against Thomas & Ross, the company's independent auditors. Three independent assumptions concerning this litigation are listed below:

Independent assumptions:
a. Commuter Airlines is not under SEC jurisdiction. The plaintiff's suit is brought under common law in a state court that adheres to the *Ultramares* doctrine of auditors' liability.
b. Commuter Airlines had recently issued its publicly held securities. The stockholders' suit is brought in federal court under the Securities Act of 1933.

c. Commuter Airlines is under SEC jurisdiction. The stockholders' suit is brought in federal court alleging violations of Sections 18(a) and 10(b) of the Securities Exchange Act of 1934.

Required:
Under each of the independent assumptions, separately explain (1) the allegations that must be proven in court by the plaintiffs, and (2) any defenses for which the auditors must bear the burden of proof if they are to avoid or reduce their liability.

3–37. Charles Worthington, the founding and senior partner of a successful and respected CPA firm, was a highly competent practitioner who always emphasized high professional standards. One of the policies of the firm was that all reports by members or staff be submitted to Worthington for review.

Recently, Arthur Craft, a junior partner in the firm, received a phone call from Herbert Flack, a close personal friend. Flack informed Craft that he, his family, and some friends were planning to create a corporation to engage in various land development ventures; that various members of the family are presently in a partnership (Flack Ventures), which holds some land and other assets; and that the partnership would contribute all of its assets to the new corporation and the corporation would assume the liabilities of the partnership.

Flack asked Craft to prepare a balance sheet of the partnership that he could show to members of his family, who were in the partnership, and to friends, to determine whether they might have an interest in joining in the formation and financing of the new corporation. Flack said he had the partnership general ledger in front of him and proceeded to read to Craft the names of the accounts and their balances at the end of the latest month. Craft took the notes he made during the telephone conversation with Flack, classified and organized the data into a conventional balance sheet, and had his secretary type the balance sheet and an accompanying letter on firm stationery. He did not consult Worthington on this matter or submit this work to him for review.

The transmittal letter stated: "We have reviewed the books and records of Flack Ventures, a partnership, and have prepared the attached balance sheet at March 31, 198X. We did not perform an examination in conformity with generally accepted auditing standards, and therefore do not express an opinion on the accompanying balance sheet." The balance sheet was prominently marked "unaudited." Craft signed the letter and instructed his secretary to send it to Flack.

Required:
What legal problems are suggested by these facts? Explain.

(AICPA, adapted)

3–38. The limitations on professional responsibilities of CPAs when they are associated with unaudited financial statements are often misunderstood. These misunderstandings can be reduced substantially if CPAs carefully follow professional pronouncements in the course of their work and take other appropriate measures.

Required:
The following list describes four situations CPAs may encounter in their association with and preparation of unaudited financial statements. Briefly discuss the extent of the CPAs' responsibilities and, if appropriate, the actions to be taken to minimize misunderstandings. Identify your answers to correspond with the letters in the following list.

a. A CPA was engaged by telephone to perform accounting work including the compilation of financial statements. His client believes that the CPA has been engaged to audit the financial statements and examine the records accordingly.

b. A group of business executives who own a farm managed by an independent agent engage Linda Lopez, a CPA, to compile quarterly unaudited financial statements for them. The CPA compiles the financial statements from information given to her by the independent agent. Subsequently, the business executives find the statements were inaccurate because their independent agent was embezzling funds. The executives refuse to pay the CPA's fee and blame her for allowing the situation to go undetected, contending that she should not have relied on representations from the independent agent.

c. In comparing the trial balance with the general ledger, a CPA finds an account labeled Audit Fees in which the client has accumulated the CPA's quarterly billings for accounting services including the compilation of quarterly unaudited financial statements.

d. To determine appropriate account classification, John Day, CPA, reviewed a number of the client's invoices. He noted in his working papers that some invoices were missing but did nothing further because he thought they did not affect the unaudited financial statements he was compiling. When the client subsequently discovered that invoices were missing, he contended that the CPA should not have ignored the missing invoices when compiling the financial statements and had a responsibility to at least inform him that they were missing.   (AICPA, adapted)

**GROUP IV:
RESEARCH AND
DISCUSSION CASE**

3–39. You are a partner in the Denver office of a national CPA firm. During the audit of Mountain Resources, you learn that this audit client is negotiating to sell some of its unproved oil and gas properties to SuperFund, a large investment company. SuperFund is an audit client of your New York office.

Mountain Resources acquired these properties several years ago at a cost of $15 million. The company drilled several exploratory wells but found no developable resources. Last year, you and Mountain Resources agreed that the value of these unproved properties had been "impaired" as defined in paragraph 28 of *FASB 19*. The company wrote the carrying value of the properties down to an estimated realizable value of $9 million and recognized a $6 million loss. You concurred with this treatment and issued an unqualified auditors' report on the company's financial statements.

You are now amazed to learn that the sales price for these properties being discussed by Mountain Resources and SuperFund is $42 million. You cannot understand why SuperFund would pay such a high price and you wonder what representations Mountain Resources may have made to SuperFund concerning these properties. The management of Mountain Resources declines to discuss the details of the negotiations with you, calling them "quite delicate" and correctly pointing out that the future sale of these properties will not affect the financial statements currently under audit.

Required:

a. Summarize the arguments for advising SuperFund (through your New York office) that you consider the properties grossly overpriced at $42 million.

b. Summarize the arguments for remaining silent and not offering any advice to SuperFund on this matter.

c. Express your personal opinion as to the course of action you should take. Indicate which arguments from parts (a) or (b) most influenced your decision.

Suggested references:

FASB Statement No. 19, "Financial Accounting and Reporting by Oil and Gas Producing Companies," pars. 15, 28, and 208.

AICPA, Professional Standards, Volume B, "Code of Professional Ethics," Section 301, Commerce Clearing House.

AICPA, Statement on Auditing Standards No. 53, "The Auditor's Responsibility to Detect and Report Errors and Irregularities" (New York, 1988), AU 316.

AICPA, Statement on Auditing Standards No. 54, "Illegal Acts by Clients" (New York, 1988), AU 317.

The public accounting profession: Planning the audit

Chapter 4 study objectives

After studying this chapter, you should be able to:

— Describe how CPA firms are typically organized and the responsibilities of auditors at the various levels in the organization.

— Explain a CPA's responsibilities when planning an audit.

— Describe the manner in which an audit is affected by the auditors' assessment of audit risk and materiality.

— Identify and explain the components of audit risk.

— Describe the major steps in the audit process.

Most public accounting practices are organized as partnerships, although a CPA may also practice as a sole practitioner or as a member of a professional corporation. In comparison with a sole proprietorship, the partnership form of organization offers several advantages. When two or more CPAs join forces, the opportunity for specialization is increased, and the scope of services offered to clients may be expanded to include such areas as tax planning and management-advisory services. Also, qualified members of the audit staff may be rewarded by admission to the partnership. Providing an opportunity to become a part owner of the business is an important factor in a CPA firm's ability to attract and retain competent personnel. A partnership also provides opportunities for professional growth through the exchange of ideas and frequent discussions among partners concerning audit problems and the issues confronting the profession.

CPA firms organized as partnerships vary in size from local offices with as few as two partners to international organizations with 1,000 or more partners. Only a very large public accounting firm can perform an audit of a business such as Sears, Roebuck or IBM, with plants and branches in many different countries. At present, there are eight large international public accounting firms, often called the Big Eight.[1] Each of the Big Eight firms has hundreds of partners, thousands of employees, and hundreds of offices located in cities all over the world. Most large corporations are audited by these eight firms. In addition to the Big Eight, there are a few smaller national firms and more than 10,000 regional and local public accounting firms that offer a wide variety of auditing, tax planning, and management-advisory services.

In past decades, state laws generally prohibited professionals from organizing their practices as corporations. This prohibition was founded on the premise that professionals should not be able to "hide behind the corporate veil" and avoid taking personal responsibility for their professional acts. Now, however, most states recognize the ***professional corporation*** as a permissible form of organization for professional practices. Professional corporations differ from traditional corporations in a number of respects. For example, all shareholders and directors of a professional corporation must be engaged in the practice of public accounting. In addition, shareholders and directors of the professional corporation are still legally liable for the corporation's actions, although they may choose to carry liability insurance to cover damages caused by negligent actions.

Responsibilities of the professional staff

Human resources—the competence, judgment, and integrity of personnel—represent the greatest asset of any public accounting firm. The professional staff of a typical public accounting firm includes partners, managers, senior accountants, and staff assistants.

---

[1] The Big Eight includes Arthur Andersen & Co.; Arthur Young & Co.; Coopers & Lybrand; Deloitte Haskins & Sells; Ernst & Whinney; Peat Marwick, Main & Co.; Price Waterhouse & Co.; and Touche Ross & Co.

Partners   The principal responsibility of the partner is to maintain contacts with clients. These contacts include discussing with clients the objectives and scope of the audit work, resolving controversies that may arise as to how items are to be presented in the financial statements, and attending the client's stockholders' meetings to answer any questions regarding the financial statements or the auditors' report. Other responsibilities of the partner include recruiting new staff members, general supervision of the professional staff, reviewing audit working papers, and signing the audit reports.

Specialization by each partner in a different area of the firm's practice is often advantageous. One partner, for example, may become expert in tax matters and head the firm's tax department; another may specialize in SEC registrations; and a third may devote full time to design and installation of data processing systems.

The partnership level in a public accounting firm is comparable to that of top management in an industrial organization. Executives at this level are concerned with the long-run well-being of the organization and of the community it serves. They should and do contribute important amounts of time to civic, professional, and educational activities in the community. Participation in the state society of certified public accountants and in the AICPA is, of course, a requisite if the partners are to do their share in building the profession. Contribution of their specialized skills and professional judgment to leadership of civic organizations is equally necessary in developing the economic and social environment in which business and professional accomplishment is possible.

An important aspect of partners' active participation in various business and civic organizations is the prestige and recognition that may come to their firms. Many clients select a particular public accounting firm because they have come to know and respect one of the firm's partners. Thus, partners who are widely known and highly regarded within the community may be a significant factor in attracting business to the firm.

Managers   In large public accounting firms, managers or supervisors perform many of the duties that would be discharged by partners in smaller firms. A manager may be responsible for supervising two or more concurrent audit engagements. This supervisory work includes reviewing the audit working papers and discussing with the audit staff and with the client any accounting problems that may arise during the engagement. The manager is responsible for determining the audit procedures applicable to specific audits and for maintaining uniform standards of field work. Often, managers have the administrative duties of compiling and collecting the firm's billings to clients.

Familiarity with tax laws and with SEC regulations, as well as a broad and current knowledge of accounting theory and practice, are essential qualifications for a successful manager. Like the partner, the audit manager may specialize in specific industries or other areas of the firm's practice.

Senior auditors   The senior auditor is an individual qualified to assume responsibility for the planning and conducting of an audit and the writing of the audit report, subject to review and approval by the manager and partner. In conducting the audit, the senior will delegate most audit tasks to assistants based on an appraisal of each assistant's ability to perform particular phases of the work. A well-qualified university graduate with a formal education in accounting may progress from staff assistant to senior auditor within two or three years, or even less.

One of the major responsibilities of the senior is on-the-job staff training. When assigning work to staff assistants, the senior should make clear the end objectives of the particular audit operation. By assigning assistants a wide variety of audit tasks and by providing constructive criticism of the assistants' work, the senior should try to make each audit a significant learning experience for the staff assistants.

The review of working papers as rapidly as they are completed is another duty of the senior in charge of an audit. This enables the senior to control the progress of the work and to ascertain that each phase of the engagement is adequately covered. At the conclusion of the field work, the senior will make a final review, tracing all items from individual working papers to the financial statements.

The senior will also maintain a continuous record of the hours devoted by all members of the staff to the various phases of the examination. In addition to maintaining uniform professional standards of field work, the senior is responsible for preventing the accumulation of excessive staff-hours on inconsequential matters and for completing the entire engagement within the budgeted time, if possible.

Staff assistants   The first position of a college graduate entering the public accounting profession is that of a staff assistant. Staff assistants usually encounter a variety of assignments that fully utilize their capacity for analysis and growth. Of course some routine work must be done in every audit engagement, but college graduates with thorough training in accounting need have no fear of being assigned for long to extensive routine procedures when they enter the field of public accounting. Most firms are anxious to assign more and more responsibility to younger staff members as rapidly as they are able to assume it. In recent years, the demand for accounting services has been so high as to create a situation in which every incentive has existed for rapid development of promising assistants.

The audit staff members of all public accounting firms attend training programs that are either developed "in house" or sponsored by professional organizations. One of the most attractive features of the public accounting profession is the richness and variety of experience acquired even by the beginning staff member. Because of the high quality of the experience gained by certified public accountants as they move from one audit engagement to another, many business concerns select individuals from the public accounting field to fill such executive positions as controller or treasurer.

Professional development for CPA firm personnel

A major problem in public accounting is keeping abreast of current developments within the profession. New business practices; new pronouncements by the Auditing Standards Board, the SEC, and the FASB; and changes in the tax laws are only a few of the factors that require members of the profession continually to update their technical knowledge.

A CPA firm's system of quality control should provide assurance that the professional staff remains continuously up to date on technical issues. To assist in this updating process, most large public accounting firms maintain a separate professional development section.

Professional development sections offer a wide range of seminars and educational programs to personnel of the firm. The curriculum of each program is especially designed to suit the needs and responsibilities of participants. Partners may attend programs focusing on the firm's policies on audit quality control or means of minimizing exposure to lawsuits; on the other hand, programs designed for staff assistants may cover audit procedures or use of the firm's microcomputers. In addition to offering educational programs, the professional development section usually publishes a weekly newsletter or monthly journal for distribution to personnel of the CPA firm and other interested persons.

Many public accounting firms that are too small to maintain their own professional development departments have banded together into associations of CPA firms. These associations organize educational programs, distribute information on technical issues, and engage in other professional activities that are designed to meet the needs of their members. Since the cost of the association's professional activities are shared by all members, the firms are provided with many of the benefits of having their own professional development department at a fraction of the cost.

Continuing education—the CPA's response to change

The need for CPAs to expand their knowledge and improve their skills continues throughout their professional careers. Many states have recognized this need by adopting continuing education legislation. Such legislation requires all licensed practitioners within the state to devote at least a specified number of hours each year (or every two or three years) to acceptable professional development programs. In addition, 120 hours of continuing education is required every three years for all members of the AICPA who are in public practice, as well as for the entire professional staff of a firm in the AICPA Division for CPA Firms. Members not in public practice currently are required to obtain 60 hours of job related Continuing Professional Education (CPE) over a three-year period. Professional development sections of CPA firms, associations of CPA firms, various state societies of certified public accountants, the AICPA, and many universities provide programs that meet the needs of CPAs for continuing education. Home study materials providing continuing education credit are also available through the AICPA.

Seasonal fluctuations in public accounting work

One of the traditional disadvantages of the public accounting profession has been the concentration of work during the "busy season" from December through April, followed by a period of slack demand during the summer months. This seasonal trend is caused by the fact that many companies keep their records on a calendar-year basis and desire auditing services immediately after the December 31 closing of the accounts. Another important factor is the spring deadline for filing of federal income tax returns.

Auditors often work a considerable number of hours of overtime during the busy season. Some public accounting firms pay their staff a premium for overtime hours. Other firms allow their staff to accumulate the overtime in an "overtime bank" and to "withdraw" these hours in the form of additional vacation time during the less busy times of the year.

Relationships with clients

The wide-ranging scope of public accountants' activities today demands that CPAs be interested and well informed on economic trends, political developments, sports events, and the many other topics that play a significant part in business and social contacts. Although an in-depth knowledge of accounting is a most important qualification of the CPA, an ability to meet people easily and to gain their confidence and goodwill may be no less important in achieving success in the profession of public accounting. The ability to work effectively with clients will be enhanced by a sincere interest in their problems and by a relaxed and cordial manner.

The question of the auditors' independence inevitably arises in considering the advisability of social activities with clients. The partner in today's public accounting firm may play golf or tennis with the executives of client companies and other business associates. These relationships actually may make it easier to resolve differences of opinions that arise during the audit, if the client has learned to know and respect the CPA partner. This mutual understanding need not prevent the CPA from standing firm on matters of accounting principle. This is perhaps the "moment of truth" for the practitioners of a profession.

However, the CPA must always remember that the concept of independence embodies an *appearance* of independence. This appearance of independence may be impaired if an auditor becomes excessively involved in social activities with clients. For example, if a CPA frequently attends lavish parties held by a client or dates an officer or employee of a client corporation, the question might be raised as to whether the CPA will appear independent to outsiders. This dilemma is but one illustration of the continual need for judgment and perspective on the part of an auditor.

PLANNING THE AUDIT

Auditors do not merely accept a new audit client and then arrive at the client's premises to "start auditing." The first standard of field work states:

> The work is to be *adequately planned* and assistants, if any, are to be *properly supervised.* [Emphasis added.]

In addition, the Auditing Standards Board has issued *SAS 22* (AU 311), "Planning and Supervision," to provide CPAs with guidance for adequate planning of each audit engagement.

The concept of adequate planning includes investigating a prospective client before deciding whether to accept the engagement, obtaining an understanding of the client's business operations, and developing an overall strategy to organize, coordinate, and schedule the activities of the audit staff. Although much planning is done before beginning the actual audit field work, the planning process continues throughout the engagement. Whenever a problem is encountered during the audit, the auditors must plan their response to the situation. For example, if weaknesses are discovered in the client's internal control, the auditors must plan audit procedures to satisfy themselves that these weaknesses have not resulted in material errors in the financial statements. In short, the planning process begins with the auditor's decision on accepting a prospective audit client and continues until the audit report is signed and delivered.

Accepting new audit clients

Public accounting is a competitive profession, and most CPA firms are anxious to obtain new clients. However, a CPA firm's principal product is its reputation for credibility. No auditor can afford to be associated with clients who are engaging in management fraud or other misleading reporting practices.

The recent wave of litigation involving auditors underscores the need for CPA firms to develop quality control policies for investigating prospective clients *before accepting an engagement.* The CPAs should investigate the history of the prospective client, including such matters as the identities and reputations of the directors, officers, and major stockholders. The incentive for management to overstate operating results is increased when the client company is in a weak financial position or is greatly in need of capital. Therefore, auditors should consider the financial strength and credit rating of a prospective client as factors in the overall risk of an association with that business entity. When an audit client goes bankrupt, the auditors often are named as defendants in lengthy and costly lawsuits. For that reason, many CPAs choose to avoid engagements entailing a relatively high risk of overstated operating results or of subsequent litigation; others may accept such engagements, recognizing the need to expand audit procedures to compensate for the unusual levels of risk.

Audit committees Many companies organize an audit committee within the board of directors to take an active role in overseeing an entity's accounting and financial reporting policies and practices. Audit committees maintain contact with both the company's internal auditors and its CPAs.

An audit committee usually is composed of three to five *outside directors*—that is, directors who are neither officers nor employees of the client organization. The exclusion of officer-directors from the audit committee allows the CPAs to discuss more openly various information regarding the scope and results of the audit. This information includes weaknesses in internal control, disagreements with management as to accounting principles, and possible indications of management fraud or other illegal acts by corporate officers. These discussions assist the committee in its oversight of the financial reporting and disclosure process for which management is responsible. The communications between the audit committee and the CPAs provide the board of directors with up-to-date information about the financial position of the business, as well as with information useful in evaluating the ability and integrity of the company's management.

Not all audit clients, however, have audit committees. For example, the concept of an audit committee is not applicable to clients organized as sole proprietorships, partnerships, or small, closely held corporations. Arrangements for an audit of a small or medium-size business often are made with the owners, a partner, or an executive, such as the president, treasurer, or controller.

Communication with predecessor auditors An excellent source of information about a prospective client who previously has been audited is the predecessor auditor. The *successor auditors'* examination may be greatly facilitated by consulting with the *predecessor auditors* and reviewing the predecessors' working papers. Communication with the predecessor auditors can provide the successor CPAs with background information about the client, details about the client's internal control structure, and evidence as to the account balances at the beginning of the year under audit.

On occasion, a client may seek to change auditors because of disagreements with the predecessor auditors over accounting principles or audit procedures. For this reason, *SAS 7* (AU 315) requires the successor auditors to make certain inquiries of the predecessor auditors ***before accepting the engagement***.[2] These inquiries should include questions regarding disagreements with management over accounting principles, the integrity of management, the predecessor's understanding of the reason for the change in auditors, and other matters that will assist the successor auditors in deciding whether to accept the engagement. This communication with the predecessor is extremely important. A review of cases involving management fraud reveals that a significant number of the companies involved had recently changed their auditors, often because of disagreement over accounting principles. Regulations of the SEC require companies subject to its jurisdiction to file a Form 8-K reporting changes in independent auditors, and the reasons therefore.

Auditors are ethically prohibited from disclosing confidential information obtained in the course of an audit without the consent of the client. The successor auditors should therefore obtain the prospective client's consent before making inquiries of the predecessor auditors. In addition, they should ask the client to authorize the predecessor auditors to respond fully. If a prospective client is reluctant to authorize communications with the predecessor auditors, the successor CPAs should consider the implications in deciding whether or not to accept the engagement.

The auditors may also make inquiries of other third parties in obtaining background information about a prospective audit client. For example, the client's bankers can provide information regarding the client's financial history and credit rating. The client's legal counsel can provide information about the client's legal environment, including such matters as pending litigation and regulatory requirements.

Obtaining a knowledge of the client's business

When should a racquetball club recognize its revenue from the sale of lifetime memberships? Is a company organized to produce a motion picture a going concern? Is it appropriate for a real estate developer to use the percentage-of-completion method of revenue recognition? What is a reasonable useful life for today's most advanced computer system? We will not attempt to answer these questions in this textbook; we raise

---

[2] AICPA, *Statement on Auditing Standards 7,* ''Communications between Predecessor and Successor Auditors'' (New York, 1975), AU 315.

them simply to demonstrate that the auditors must have a good working knowledge of an audit client's business and business environment if they are to express an opinion on the fairness of the client's financial statements.

The auditor's knowledge of the client's business should include an understanding of such factors as the client's organizational structure, accounting policies and procedures, capital structure, product lines, and methods of production and distribution. In addition, the CPA should be familiar with matters affecting the industry within which the client operates, including economic conditions and financial trends, inherent types of business risk, governmental regulations, changes in technology, and widely used accounting methods. Without such a knowledge of the client's business environment, the auditor would not be in a position to evaluate the appropriateness of the accounting principles in use or the reasonableness of the many estimates and assumptions embodied in the client's financial statements.

Numerous sources of information on prospective clients are available to the auditors. AICPA audit and accounting guides, trade publications, and governmental agency publications are useful in obtaining an orientation in the client's industry. Previous audit reports, annual reports to stockholders, SEC filings, and prior years' tax returns are excellent sources of financial background information. Informal discussions between the auditor-in-charge and key officers of the prospective client can provide information about the history, size, operations, accounting records, and internal controls of the enterprise.

Analytical procedures Analytical procedures are comparisons of financial statement balances and ratios for the year under audit with comparable information from sources such as the client's prior years' financial statements, published industry statistics, and budgets. When used for planning purposes, analytical procedures assist the auditors in obtaining an understanding of the financial characteristics of the client's business. Also, significant fluctuations revealed by the comparisons identify accounts that might contain material errors or other problems that might affect the fairness of the financial statements. The auditors will then plan a more thorough investigation of these potential problem areas, and perform a more effective audit. Therefore, *SAS 56* (AU 329) requires the auditors to perform analytical procedures as a part of the planning process for *every* audit.[3]

An example of the use of an analytical procedure for planning purposes is the comparison of the client's inventory turnover for the current year with comparable statistics from prior years. A significant decrease in

---

[3] AICPA, *Statement on Auditing Standards No. 56,* "Analytical Procedures" (New York, 1988), AU 329.

inventory turnover might lead the auditors to consider the possibility that the client has excessive amounts of inventory. As a result, the auditors would plan a more extensive search for inventory items that may be obsolete. Analytical procedures are discussed in detail in Chapter 7.

Tour of plant and offices   Another useful preliminary step for the auditors is to arrange an inspection tour of the plant and offices of a prospective client. This tour will give the auditors some understanding of the plant layout, manufacturing process, principal products, and physical safeguards surrounding inventories. During the tour, the auditors should be alert for signs of potential problems. Rust on equipment may indicate that plant assets have been idle; excessive dust on raw materials or finished goods may indicate a problem of obsolescence. A knowledge of the physical facilities will assist the auditors in planning how many audit staff members will be needed to participate in observing the physical inventory.

The tour affords the auditors an opportunity to observe firsthand what types of internal documentation are used to record such activity as receiving raw materials, transferring materials into production, and shipping finished goods to customers. This documentation is essential to the auditors' consideration of internal control.

In going through the offices, the auditors will learn the location of various accounting records. The auditors can ascertain how much subdivision of duties is practical within the client organization by observing the number of office employees. In addition, the tour will afford an opportunity to meet the key personnel whose names appear on the organization chart. The auditors will record the background information about the client in a ***permanent file*** available for reference in future engagements.

Preliminary arrangements with clients

The auditors' approach to an engagement is not that of detectives looking for evidence of fraud; instead, the approach is a positive, constructive one of gathering evidence to prove the fairness and validity of the client's financial statements.

A conference with the client before beginning the engagement is a useful step in avoiding misunderstandings. The conference should include a discussion of the nature, purpose, and scope of the audit and any matters that could conceivably produce friction. Since the fee is usually in the mind of both client and auditors, it should be frankly discussed, but without creating the impression that the auditors' chief interest is in the earning of a fee.

A clear understanding between the client and the auditors concerning the scope of the examination and the condition of the accounting records at the starting date is an essential step in planning an audit. Otherwise, the auditors may arrive to begin an examination only to find that transactions for the period to be examined have not yet been fully recorded. It is not the auditors' job to draft routine adjusting entries or to balance the subsidiary ledgers with the control accounts.

A new client should be informed as to the extent of investigation of the beginning balances of such accounts as plant and equipment and inventories. To determine the propriety of depreciation expense for the current year and the proper balances in plant and equipment accounts at the balance sheet date, the auditors must investigate the validity of the property accounts at the beginning of the current period. If the auditors are unable to obtain satisfactory evidence as to the balance of *beginning inventory,* it may be necessary to disclaim an opinion on the income statement in the first audit of a new client.

In some cases, satisfactory audits of the business in preceding years by other reputable auditing firms may enable the auditors to accept the opening balances of the current year with a minimum of verification work; in other cases, in which no satisfactory recent audit has been made, an extensive analysis of transactions of prior years will be necessary to establish account balances as of the beginning of the current year. In these latter situations, the client should be made to understand that the scope and cost of the initial audit may exceed that of repeat engagements, which will not require analysis of past years' transactions.

Fee arrangements When a business engages the services of independent public accountants, it will usually ask for an estimate of the cost of the audit. In supplying this estimate, the accountants will give first consideration to the time probably required for the audit. Staff time is the basic unit of measurement for audit fees. Each public accounting firm develops a per hour or per diem fee schedule for each category of audit staff, based on direct salaries and such related costs as payroll taxes and insurance. The direct rate is then increased for allocated overhead costs and a profit element.

In addition to basic per diem or per hour fees, clients are charged for direct costs incurred by the public accounting firm for staff travel, report processing, and other out-of-pocket expenditures.

Estimating a fee for an audit thus usually involves the application of the CPA firm's daily or hourly rates to the estimated time required. Since the exact number of days cannot be determined in advance, the auditors may merely give a rough estimate of the fee. Or they may multiply the rates by the estimated time, add an amount for unforeseen problems, and quote a range or bracket of amounts within which the total fee will fall. Once the auditors have given an estimate of the fee to a client, they naturally feel some compulsion to keep the charges within this limit.

Per diem rates for audit work vary considerably in different sections of the country, and even within a given community, in accordance with the reputation and experience of the accounting firm. Of course, the salaries paid to audit staff members are much less than the rates at which audit time is billed to clients. In many firms, salaries represent about 40 percent of billing rates; the remainder is required to cover the cost of nonbillable time when auditors are not assigned, overhead expenses of the office, and a profit to the partners.

Use of the client's staff   Another issue to be discussed in the preliminary conference is what the client's staff can do to prepare for the audit. As previously mentioned, the client's staff should have the accounting records up to date when the auditors arrive. In addition, many audit working papers can be prepared for the auditors by the client's staff, thus reducing the cost of the audit and freeing the auditors from routine work. The auditors may set up the columnar headings for such working papers and give instructions to the client's staff as to the information to be gathered. These working papers should bear the label *Prepared By Client* or *PBC,* and also the initials of the auditor who verifies the work performed by the client's staff. Working papers prepared by the client should never be accepted at face value; such papers must be reviewed and tested by the auditors in order that the CPA firm maintain its independent status.

Among the tasks that may be assigned to the client's employees are the preparation of a trial balance of the general ledger, preparation of an aged trial balance of accounts receivable, analyses of accounts receivable written off, lists of property additions and retirements during the year, and analyses of various revenue and expense accounts. Many of these working papers may be in the form of computer printouts.

Engagement letters

These preliminary understandings with the client should be summarized by the auditors in an *engagement letter,* making clear the nature of the engagement, any limitations on the scope of the audit, work to be performed by the client's staff, scheduled dates for performance and completion of the examination, and the basis for computing the auditors' fee. When the engagement letter is accepted by the authorized client official, it represents an *executory contract* between the auditor and the client. Engagement letters do not follow any standard form; an example of such a letter is presented in Figure 4–1.

The use of engagement letters is not limited to audit engagements. Professional standards for accounting and review services also require that the accountant have an understanding with the client as to the nature of the services to be performed. *This "understanding" preferably should be in writing and signed by the client and the CPA.*

Figure 4–1   Engagement letter

Adams, Barnes and Company

CERTIFIED PUBLIC ACCOUNTANTS

July 17, 19X5

Mr. J. B. Wilson
Chairman of the Audit Committee
Board of Directors
Barker Tool Company
1825 LeMay Street
Chicago, Illinois 60642

Dear Mr. Wilson:

This letter is to confirm our arrangements for our audit of the financial statements of Barker Tool Company for the year ended December 31, 19X5.

Our examination will be performed in accordance with generally accepted auditing standards and will include all procedures which we consider necessary to provide a basis for expression of our opinion as to the fairness of the financial statements. Our examination will include procedures to obtain an understanding of the company's internal control, and we will prepare a letter with our recommendations for correcting weaknesses brought to light by this study.

An examination performed in accordance with generally accepted auditing standards is designed to provide reasonable assurance of defecting errors and irregularities which would have a material effect upon the financial statements. However, such an examination cannot be relied upon to disclose all errors and cases of fraud or defalcation.

Our examination is scheduled for performance and completion as follows:

Begin field work	September 10, 19X5
Delivery of internal control letter	November 15, 19X5
Completion of field work	February 20, 19X6
Delivery of audit report	March 1, 19X6

Our fees for this examination will be based on the time spent by various members of our staff at our regular rates, plus direct expenses. We will notify you immediately of any circumstances we encounter that could significantly affect our initial fee estimate of $35,000.

In order for us to work as efficiently as possible, it is understood that your accounting staff will provide us with a year-end trial balance by January 15, 19X6, and also with the schedules and account analyses described on the separate attachment.

If these arrangements are in accordance with your understanding, please sign this letter in the space provided and return a copy to us at your earliest convenience.

Very truly yours,

Charles Adams, CPA

Accepted by: _____

Date: _____

Illustrative case

In the *1136 Tenants' Corporation* v. *Rothenberg* case, an incorporated apartment cooperative sued its CPAs for failing to detect embezzlement losses caused by a managing agent. The CPAs maintained they had been engaged only to do write-up work and not to perform any audit procedures. The court found that the CPAs had not made it sufficiently clear to the client that the engagement did not include audit procedures and held the CPAs liable for damages totaling $174,000. (The CPAs' fee for the engagement had been only $600.) Had the CPAs clearly set forth the scope of the engagement in an engagement letter, the case might never have been brought to court.

Developing an overall audit strategy

After obtaining a knowledge of the client's business, the auditor-in-charge should formulate an overall audit strategy for the upcoming engagement. The best audit strategy is the approach that results in the most *efficient* audit—that is, an effective audit performed at the least possible cost to the client. In formulating this audit strategy, the CPA should consider whether statistical sampling or EDP audit techniques might be used to advantage. They should also decide the appropriate experience levels of the audit staff to be assigned to the engagement, and whether another CPA firm should be engaged to audit any branch locations rather than having audit staff members travel to a distant city.

SAS 47 (AU 312) states that in planning an audit, the auditors must consider carefully the appropriate levels of *materiality* and *audit risk*.[4] Although it is not required, many auditors develop quantitative measures of materiality that are used to assist them in planning the nature and extent of their audit procedures.

Materiality, for planning purposes, is the auditor's preliminary estimate of the smallest amount of misstatement that would probably influence the judgment of a reasonable person relying upon the financial statements. As such, materiality may differ between the various financial statements. The auditors may, for example, estimate that a $100,000 misstatement of the income statement is material, while a $200,000 misstatement of the balance sheet is material. Since most misstatements affect equally the balance sheet and the income statement, the auditors would have to design their audit to detect misstatements that would be material to any one of the financial statements, in this case $100,000.

The term *audit risk* refers to the possibility that the auditors may unknowingly fail to appropriately modify their opinion on financial state-

---

[4] AICPA, *Statement on Auditing Standards 47,* "Audit Risk and Materiality in Conducting an Audit" (New York, 1983), AU 312.

ments that are materially misstated. At the overall financial statement level, audit risk is the chance that a material misstatement exists in the financial statements, and the auditors do not detect the misstatement with their audit procedures.

In developing an audit plan, the auditors must consider factors that affect audit risk. An essential concept here is that the risk of misstated statements is higher for some audits than for others. Auditors are aware that very few audits involve material misstatements of financial statements, but when such misstatements do exist, they can result in millions of dollars of potential liability to the auditors. Experience has shown that many undetected misstatements of financial statements are intentional irregularities, rather than unintentional errors.

Illustrative note

An analysis of 456 court cases filed against CPAs indicates that management fraud was present approximately 44 percent of the time. Other employee defalcations were believed to be present 2 percent of the time. An assortment of accounting and auditing errors was alleged in the remaining cases.

Figure 4–2 presents a list of risk factors, or "red flags" which may indicate a higher than normal risk of misstated financial statements. While none of these risk factors in and of itself would normally indicate the existence of a misstatement with certainty, each one should be considered by the auditors in planning the audit.

Figure 4–2 Financial Statement Audit Risk Factors[5]

Management characteristics

— Management operating and financing decisions are dominated by a single person.

— Management attitude toward financial reporting is unduly aggressive.

— Management turnover (particularly senior accounting personnel) is high.

— Management places undue emphasis on meeting earnings projections.

— Management's reputation in the business community is poor.

Operating characteristics

— Profitability of entity relative to its industry is inadequate or inconsistent.

— Sensitivity of operating results to economic factors (inflation, interest rates, unemployment, etc.) is high.

(Continued)

---

[5] AICPA, *Statement on Auditing Standards 53,* "The Auditor's Responsibility to Detect and Report Errors and Irregularities" (New York, 1988), AU 316.

— Rate of change in entity's industry is rapid.

— Direction of change in entity's industry is declining with many business failures.

— Organization is decentralized without adequate monitoring.

— Internal or external matters that bring into question the entity's ability to continue in existence are present.

Engagement characteristics

— Many contentious or difficult accounting issues are present.

— Significant difficult-to-audit transactions or balances.

— Significant and unusual related party transactions not in the ordinary course of business.

— Nature, cause (if known), or the amount of known and likely misstatements detected in the audit of prior period's financial statements is significant.

— New client with no prior audit history or sufficient information is not available from the predecessor auditor.

Considering the possibility of misstatement of account balances   At the individual account balance level, audit risk may be disaggregated into three components—inherent risk, control risk, and detection risk. *Inherent risk* refers to the possibility of a material misstatement occurring in an account, assuming no related internal controls. *Control risk* is the risk that a material misstatement will not be prevented or detected on a timely basis by the company's internal control, and *detection risk* is the risk that the auditors' procedures will lead them to conclude that a material misstatement does *not* exist in an account balance, when in fact the account is materially misstated.

Note that while detection risk relates directly to the effectiveness of the auditor's procedures, inherent and control risk are functions of the client and its environment. In planning the audit, the auditors must assess the extent of inherent and control risks for each material financial statement account, and then plan sufficient audit procedures to reduce detection risk to the appropriate level. In this way, the overall audit risk will be sufficiently low to justify the auditors' opinion that the financial statements are not materially misstated. For example, if the auditors believe that the client's internal controls over accounts receivable are poor, resulting in a high level of control risk for receivables, the auditors may compensate by increasing their substantive procedures for receivables and, thereby, reducing detection risk.

The auditors must be especially careful in considering financial statement accounts that are affected by estimates made by management (often referred to as accounting estimates), especially those in which a wide range of accounting methods are considered acceptable. Examples of accounting estimates include allowances for loan losses and obsolete inventory, and estimates of warranty liabilities. Making accounting estimates is management's responsibility, and such estimates are generally more susceptible to material misstatement than accounts which are more certain in amount. *SAS 57* (AU 342) requires the auditors to determine that (a) all necessary estimates have been developed, (b) the accounting estimates are reasonable, and (c) the accounting estimates are properly accounted for and disclosed.[6]

Determining whether all necessary estimates have been developed and accounted for properly (steps [a] and [c]) requires a knowledge of the client's business and the applicable generally accepted accounting principles. When evaluating the reasonableness of accounting estimates (Step [b]), one or a combination of the following three basic approaches may be taken:

1. Reviewing and testing management's process of developing the estimates—this will often involve reviewing the steps performed by management and considering their reasonableness.
2. Independently developing an estimate of the amount to compare to management's estimate.
3. Reviewing subsequent events or transactions bearing on the estimate, such as examining actual payments made subsequent to year-end.

The wide range of potential accounting methods complicates transactions involving accounting estimates. Pensions, leases, and long-term construction contracts are just a few examples of transactions with complex accounting methods that vary depending on the nature of the agreements and the specific circumstances. It is the auditors' responsibility to evaluate whether the accounting rules followed are appropriate in the circumstances. While it sounds so basic as to almost be trivial, it is essential that the auditors understand the transactions in which their clients are involved. In practice, this requirement is onerous since the auditors may be involved in a variety of audits, requiring knowledge of a host of different accounting methods.

Illustrative case

Volkswagen AG reported that "criminal manipulation" of its foreign-exchange positions has cost the firm as much as 259 million dollars. The fraud prompted the resignation of the company's chief financial officer and the ouster of its foreign-exchange manager. The auditors did not detect the irregularities until fraudulent contracts came due and were rejected by banks. An insider suggested that auditors often don't know enough about complicated currency instruments to detect such problems.

---

[6] AICPA, *Statement on Auditing Standards 57,* "Auditing Accounting Estimates" (New York, 1988), AU 342.

Developing an efficient and effective audit strategy requires considerable audit experience as well as a familiarity with the client's business operations. For a large audit client, the audit strategy would be developed by a partner or manager; for smaller clients, the strategy might be formulated by a senior, subject to review by the manager.

Audit plans

The planning process is documented in the audit working papers through the preparation of *audit plans, audit programs,* and *time budgets.* These "planning and supervision" working papers serve a dual purpose. First, they provide documentary evidence of the CPA firm's compliance with the "adequate planning" requirement of the first standard of field work. Second, these working papers provide the auditor-in-charge with a means of coordinating, scheduling, and supervising the activities of the audit staff members involved in the engagement.

An audit plan is an overview of the engagement, outlining the nature and characteristics of the client's business operations and the overall audit strategy. Although audit plans differ in form and content among public accounting firms, a typical plan includes details on the following:

1. Description of the client company—its structure, business, and organization.
2. Objectives of the audit (e.g., audit for stockholders, special-purpose audit, SEC filings).
3. Nature and extent of other services, such as preparation of tax returns, to be performed for the client.
4. Timing and scheduling of the audit work, including determining which procedures may be performed before the balance sheet date, what must be done on or after the balance sheet date, and setting dates for such critical procedures as cash counts, accounts receivable confirmations, and inventory observation.
5. Work to be done by the client's staff.
6. Staffing requirements during the engagement.
7. Target dates for completing major segments of the engagement, such as the consideration of internal control, tax returns, the audit report, and SEC filings.
8. Any special problems to be resolved in the course of the engagement, such as those revealed by analytical procedures.
9. Preliminary judgments about materiality levels for the engagement.

The audit plan is normally drafted before starting work at the client's offices. However, the plan may be modified throughout the engagement as special problems are encountered and as the auditors' study and evaluation of internal control lead to identification of areas requiring more or less audit work.

Audit programs

An audit program is a detailed outline of the auditing work to be performed, specifying the procedures to be followed in verification of each item in the financial statements and giving the estimated time required. As each step in the audit program is completed, the date, the auditor's initials, and the actual time consumed may be entered opposite the item. An audit program thus serves as a useful tool both in scheduling and in controlling audit work. It indicates the number of persons required and the relative proportions of senior and staff assistant hours needed, and it enables supervisors to keep currently informed on the progress being made.

The inclusion of detailed audit instructions in the program gives assurance that essential steps in verification will not be overlooked. These written instructions enable inexperienced auditors to work effectively with less personal supervision than would otherwise be required, and thus permit seniors and managers to concentrate upon those features of the examination that demand a high degree of analytical ability and the discriminating exercise of professional judgment.

Audit programs are considerably more detailed than audit plans. The audit plan outlines the objectives of the engagement; the audit program lists the specific procedures that must be performed to accomplish these objectives.

Illustrative audit program A typical example of the detailed audit procedures set forth in an audit program is the following partial list of procedures for the audit of investments in marketable securities:

X COMPANY
Partial Audit Program—Securities
December 31, 19—

Working paper reference	Date and initials		Time	
			Estimated	Actual
		1. Inspection of securities:		
		a. Obtain or prepare list of securities owned as of balance sheet date.		
		b. Compare list of securities with corresponding ledger account.		
		(Continued)		

> c. Inspect securities on hand at or near date of balance sheet and compare with list of securities at balance sheet date. Reconcile securities to date of balance sheet and vouch transactions for intervening period. Maintain control of securities during this period.
> d. Compare serial numbers of securities inspected with serial numbers listed for these securities in prior year's audit.

Tailor-made audit programs The conditions and problems encountered differ with every audit engagement; hence it is necessary for the auditor-in-charge of each examination to determine what procedures are appropriate under the circumstances. In the advance planning of an engagement, only a *tentative* audit program can be prepared. The auditor should expect this first draft of the program to be modified during the audit as strengths and weaknesses in the client's internal control and other special considerations are encountered.

Weak internal control, as manifested by poor accounting records, incompetent personnel, or lack of internal auditing, necessitates much more extensive auditing than would be necessary for a well-staffed concern with strong internal controls, good accounting records, and an effective internal auditing department. Internal control is sometimes adequate for certain operations of the company but weak or absent in other areas. The amount of testing by the auditors should be increased in areas of operations for which internal controls are deficient and may properly be minimized in areas subject to strong internal controls. The great variation in quality of internal controls encountered, coupled with the variety of accounting methods and special problems peculiar to individual business concerns, requires that the audit program be modified as the auditors learn more about the circumstances of the individual audit engagement.

The value of the audit program as a means of giving coherence, order, and logical sequence to the investigation is beyond dispute. The audit program must not, however, be considered a substitute for an alert, resourceful attitude on the part of the audit staff. Staff members should be encouraged to explore fully any unusual transactions or questionable practices that come to their attention from any source and cautioned not to restrict themselves to the investigative routines set forth in a prearranged audit program.

Time budgets for audit engagements

Public accounting firms usually charge clients on a time basis, and detailed time records must therefore be maintained on every audit engagement. A time budget for an audit is constructed by estimating the time required for each step in the audit program for each of the various grades of auditors and totaling these estimated amounts. Time budgets serve other functions in addition to providing a basis for estimating fees. The time budget communicates to the audit staff those areas the manager or partner feel are critical and require more time. It also is an important tool of the audit senior—it is used to measure the efficiency of staff assistants and to determine at each stage of the engagement whether the work is progressing at a satisfactory rate.

There is always pressure to complete an audit within the estimated time. The staff assistant who takes more than the normal time for a task is not likely to be popular with supervisors or to win rapid advancement. Ability to do satisfactory work when given abundant time is not a sufficient qualification, *for time is never abundant in public accounting*.

The development of time budgets is facilitated in repeat engagements by reference to the preceding year's detailed time records. Sometimes time budgets prove quite unattainable because the client's records are not in satisfactory condition, or because of other special circumstances that arise. Even when time estimates are exceeded, there can be no compromise with qualitative standards in the performance of the field work. The CPA firm's professional reputation and its legal liability to clients and third parties do not permit any shortcutting or omission of audit procedures to meet a predetermined time estimate.

The audit trail

In developing audit procedures, the auditors are assisted by the organized manner in which accounting systems record, classify, and summarize data. The flow of accounting data begins with the recording of thousands of individual transactions on such documents as invoices and checks. The information recorded on these original documents is summarized in journals; and at the end of each month, the amounts in the journals are posted to ledger accounts. At the end of the year, the balances in the ledger accounts are arranged in the form of financial statements.

In thinking of the accounting records as a whole, we may say that a continuous trail of evidence exists—a trail of evidence that links the thousands of individual transactions comprising a year's business activity with the summary figures in the financial statements. In a manual accounting system, this *audit trail* consists of source documents, journal entries, and ledger entries. An audit trail also exists within a computer-based accounting system, although it may have a substantially different form; this will be discussed in Chapter 6.

Just as a hiker may walk in either direction along a mountain path, an auditor may follow the audit trail in either of two directions. For example, the auditor may follow specific transactions from their origin forward to their inclusion in the financial statement summary figures. This approach provides the auditor with assurance that all transactions have been properly interpreted and processed.

On the other hand, the auditors may follow the stream of evidence back to its sources. This type of verification consists of tracing the various items in the statements (such as cash, receivables, sales, and expenses) back to the ledger accounts, and from the ledgers on back through the journals to original documents, evidencing transactions. This process of working backward from the financial statement figures to the detailed evidence of individual transactions provides assurance that financial statement figures are based upon valid transactions.

Although the technique of working along the audit trail is a useful one, bear in mind that the auditors must acquire other types of evidence obtained from sources other than the client's accounting records.

Planning a recurring engagement

Planning a repeat engagement is far easier than planning for a first audit of a new client. The auditor-in-charge of a repeat engagement generally was involved in the previous year's audit and has a good working knowledge of the client's business. Also, the previous year's audit working papers contain a wealth of information useful in planning the recurring engagement. For example, the audit plan provides background information about the client and explains the overall strategy employed in the last audit. The prior year's audit program shows in detail the procedures performed and the length of time required to perform them. In addition, last year's working papers substantiate the beginning balances for the current year's audit.

While the prior year's working papers are extremely useful in planning the new engagement, the auditor-in-charge should not merely duplicate last year's audit program. Each audit should be a learning experience for the auditors, enabling them to design a more efficient audit in the following year. Also, the auditors may need to modify their approach to the audit for any changes in the client's operations or business environment.

THE AUDIT PROCESS

Although specific audit procedures vary from one engagement to the next, the fundamental steps which follow planning of the audit process are essentially the same in almost every engagement:

1. Obtain an understanding of internal control sufficient to plan the audit.
2. Assess control risk and design additional tests of controls.
3. Perform additional tests of controls.

4. Reassess control risk and design substantive tests.
5. Perform substantive tests and complete the audit.
6. Form an opinion and issue the audit report.

1. Obtain an understanding of internal control sufficient to plan the audit. The second standard of field work states:

> A sufficient understanding of the internal control structure is to be obtained to plan the audit and to determine the nature, timing, and extent of tests to be performed.

The nature and extent of the audit work to be performed on a particular engagement depends largely upon the effectiveness of the client's internal control in preventing material misstatements in the financial statements. Before auditors can evaluate the effectiveness of the structure (system), they need a knowledge and understanding of how it works: what procedures are performed and who performs them, what controls are in effect, how various types of transactions are processed and recorded, and what accounting records and supporting documentation exist. Thus, an assessment of the client's internal control structure is a logical first step in every audit engagement.

Sources of information about the client's structure include interviews with client personnel, audit working papers from prior years' engagements, plant tours, and the client's manuals. In gathering information about a structure, it is often useful to study the sequence of procedures used in processing major categories of transactions. The sequence of procedures used for processing such major types of transactions is often termed a *transaction cycle.* In a manufacturing business, for example, the major transaction cycles might include: (*a*) *sales cycle,* involving sales, accounts receivable, and cash receipts; (*b*) *purchase cycle,* involving various assets and expenses, accounts payable, and cash disbursements; (*c*) *production cycle,* involving production costs, inventories, and the cost of goods sold; (*d*) *payroll cycle,* involving payroll expense, payroll taxes, and cash disbursements; and (*e*) *financing cycle,* involving long-term debt, capital stock, and cash receipts and disbursements.

To illustrate one of these transaction groups, let us consider sales transactions. The procedures used in processing sales transactions might include receiving a customer's purchase order, credit approval, shipment of merchandise, preparation of sales invoices, recording the sale, recording the account receivable, billing, and handling and recording the cash received from the customer.

A working knowledge of the client's internal control is needed throughout the audit; consequently, the auditors usually prepare working papers fully describing their understanding of the system. Frequent reference to these working papers will be made to aid in designing audit procedures, ascertaining where documents are filed, familiarizing new audit staff with the system, and as a refresher in beginning next year's engagement.

The description of internal control is usually prepared in the form of systems flowcharts. As an alternative to flowcharts, parts of the system may be described by written narratives or by the completion of specially designed questionnaires. All of these systems description working papers are illustrated and discussed in Chapter 5.

2. Assess control risk and design additional tests of controls.

After analyzing the design of the internal control structure, the auditors must decide whether the structure, as designed, seems strong enough to prevent or to detect and correct material misstatements. In terms of the audit risk model, the auditors make an assessment of control risk. If they assess internal control to be weak (control risk is high), they will rely primarily on substantive tests to reduce audit risk to an acceptable level. On the other hand, if the system seems capable of preventing or detecting and correcting material misstatements, the auditor must decide which additional controls, if any, can efficiently be tested.

3. Perform additional tests of controls.

Audit tests may be performed to determine whether key internal control procedures have been ***properly designed and are operating effectively.*** To illustrate a ***test of a control,*** consider the control procedure in which the accounting department accounts for the serial sequence of all shipping documents before preparing the related journal entries. The purpose of this control is to provide assurance that each shipment of merchandise is recorded in the accounting records. As a test of the control procedure, the auditors might select a sample of shipping documents prepared at various times throughout the year and inspect the related journal entries.

Notice that a test of an internal control measures the effectiveness of a particular ***control procedure;*** it ***does not*** substantiate the dollar amount of an account balance. Actually, a particular control procedure may affect several financial statement amounts. If, for example, the test described above indicates that the accounting department does not effectively account for the serial sequence of shipping documents, the auditors should be alert to the possibility of material misstatements in sales revenue, accounts receivable, cost of goods sold, and inventories.

4. Reassess control risk and design substantive tests.

After completing their tests of controls, the auditors are in a position to reassess control risk based on the results of the tests, and determine the ***nature, timing,*** and **extent** of the substantive tests necessary to complete the audit. **Substantive tests** are procedures designed to substantiate the fairness of specific financial statement items. Examples of substantive tests include confirmation of accounts receivable and observation of how the client takes physical inventory. A major objective of internal control is to produce accurate and reliable accounting data. Thus, auditors should make an intensive investigation of account balances in areas for which internal control is weak; however, they are justified in performing less extensive testing of account balances in areas for which they have determined that controls are operating effectively. This process of deciding upon the matters to be emphasized during the audit, based upon the assessment of internal control, means that the auditors will modify their audit program by expanding substantive tests in some areas and by reducing them in others.

Not all weaknesses in internal control require action by the auditors. For example, poor internal control over a small petty cash fund is not likely to have a material impact upon the fairness of the financial statements. On the other hand, if one employee is responsible for initiating cash disbursements and also for signing checks, this combination of duties might result in material error in the financial statements and substantial defalcations. In each instance, the auditors must exercise professional judgment in determining whether to modify the nature and extent of their audit procedures and whether to make recommendations to the client for improving internal control.

When significant deficiencies in internal control are discovered, the auditors should communicate the details to the client. In general, significant weaknesses (reportable conditions) must be communicated to top management and to the audit committee of the board of directors. In addition, a *management letter* is often issued in which the auditors discuss the deficiencies in greater detail and provide management with workable suggestions for improvements in the system. If the assessment of internal control is completed before the balance sheet date, the auditors' recommendations may be implemented quickly enough to contribute to the reliability of the financial statements for the year under audit.

5. Perform substantive tests and complete the audit.

Some procedures for verifying account balances may be performed early in the audit. However, only after having completed the assessment of internal control are the auditors in a position to complete the procedures necessary to substantiate account balances.

6. Form an opinion and issue the audit report.

The date upon which the last audit procedures are completed is termed the *last day of field work*. Although the audit report is dated as of the last day of field work, it is not actually issued on that date. Since the audit report represents an acceptance of considerable responsibility by the CPA firm, a partner must first review the working papers from the engagement to ascertain that a thorough examination has been completed, and decide the type of report that is appropriate. If the auditors are to issue anything other than an unqualified opinion of standard form, considerable care must go into the precise wording of the audit report. Consequently, the audit report is usually issued a week or more after the last day of field work.

Relationship between tests of controls and substantive tests

Tests of controls provide auditors with evidence as to whether prescribed internal control procedures are in use and operating effectively. The results of these tests assist the auditors in evaluating the *likelihood* of material misstatements having occurred. Substantive tests, on the other hand, are designed to *detect* material errors if they exist in the financial statements. The amount of substantive testing done by the auditors is greatly influenced by their assessment of the likelihood that material errors exist.

To illustrate, assume that a client's procedures manual indicates that the finished goods warehouse is to be locked at all times and accessible only to authorized personnel. Through tests of controls consisting of inquiry and observation, the auditors learn that the warehouse often is unlocked and that several employees who are not authorized to be in the warehouse regularly eat lunch there. As the client's internal control procedure is not operating properly, the auditors should recognize that the *risk* of inventory shortages is increased. However, the tests of controls have *not* determined that an inventory shortage does, in fact, exist.

The principal substantive test to detect shortages of inventories is the auditors' observation of a physical inventory taken by the client. As part of this observation, the auditors make test counts of various items. In our case of the unlocked warehouse, the auditors' test has shown that internal control cannot be relied upon to prevent shortages. Therefore, the auditors should increase the number of test counts in an effort to detect any shortage that might exist.

Timing of audit work

The value of audited financial statements is enhanced if the statements are available on a timely basis after the year-end. To facilitate an early release of the audit report, auditors normally begin the audit well before the balance sheet date. The period before the balance sheet date is termed the *interim period*. Audit work that can always be performed during the interim period includes the consideration of internal control, issuance of the management letter, and substantive tests of transactions that have occurred to the interim date.

Interim tests of certain financial statement balances, such as accounts receivable, may also be performed, but this results in additional risk that must be controlled by the auditors. Significant errors or irregularities could arise in these accounts during the *remaining period* between the time that the interim test was performed and the balance sheet date. Thus, to rely on the interim test of a significant account balance, the auditors must be confident regarding the effectiveness of the client's internal controls over that account, or perform additional tests of the account during the remaining period.

Performing audit work during the interim period has numerous advantages in addition to facilitating the timely release of the audited financial statements. The independent auditors may be able to assess internal control more effectively by observing and testing controls at various times throughout the year. Also, they can give early consideration to accounting problems. Another advantage is that interim auditing creates a more uniform workload for CPA firms. With a large client, such as General Motors, the auditors may have office space within the client's buildings and carry on auditing procedures throughout the entire year.

Auditing terminology

The terms used to describe the various phases of audit work need to be precisely defined in order that audit programs, other working papers, and reports may be clearly understood. The following terms are among those most commonly employed; others will be defined as they are introduced in later chapters.

Analyze—the process of identifying and classifying for further study all the debit and credit entries contained in a ledger account. Accounts are analyzed in order to ascertain the nature of all the transactions that gave rise to the balance. An account such as Miscellaneous Expense, for example, requires analysis before any real understanding of its contents is possible.

Compare—the process of observing the similarity or variations of particular items in financial statements from one period to the next. If the comparison of a given type of revenue or expense for two successive years shows substantial change, further investigation to ascertain the cause of the change is necessary. The term may also be used by the auditor to mean ascertaining the agreement or lack of agreement between a journal entry and the corresponding entry in a ledger account, or between such related documents as a purchase order and an invoice.

Confirm—the process of proving the authenticity and accuracy of an account balance or entry by direct written communication with the debtor, creditor, or other party to the transaction. Obtaining proof from a source outside the client's records is thus a basic element of confirmation. It is standard practice to confirm bank balances by direct correspondence with the bank, and to confirm accounts receivable by direct correspondence with customers. The letters or forms sent to outsiders for this purpose are called *confirmation requests*.

Examine—to review critically or to investigate. An "examination of the financial statements" has the same meaning as an "audit of the financial statements."

Extend—to compute by multiplication. To extend the client's physical inventory listing is to multiply the quantity in units by the cost per unit. The resultant product is the extension.

Foot (or *down-foot*)—the process of proving the totals of vertical columns of figures; *cross-foot* means the proving of totals of figures appearing in horizontal rows. By footing and cross-footing schedules and records, the auditor derives positive assurance of their arithmetical accuracy.

Inspect—a careful reading or point-by-point review of a document or record. Other terms frequently used by the auditor to convey the same or a similar meaning are *scrutinize* and *examine.*

Reconcile—to establish agreement between two sets of independently maintained but related records. Thus, the ledger account for Cash in Bank is reconciled with the bank statement, and the home office record of shipments to a branch office is reconciled with the record of receipts maintained by the branch.

Test—to select and examine a representative sample from a population of similar items. If the sample is properly chosen, the results of this limited test should reveal the same characteristics as would be disclosed by an examination of the entire lot of items.

Trace—the process of following a transaction from one accounting record to another. The purchase of machinery, for example, might be verified by tracing the transaction from the voucher register to the check register.

Verify—to prove the validity and accuracy of records or to establish the existence and ownership of assets. Verification of plant and equipment, for example, might include analysis of ledger accounts, proof of footings, tracing of postings from journals, examination of documents authorizing acquisitions and retirements, and physical observation of the assets.

Voucher—a term used to describe any document supporting a transaction. Examples are petty cash receipts, receiving memoranda, and paid checks.

Vouching—establishing the accuracy and authenticity of entries in ledger accounts or other records by examining such supporting evidence of the transactions as invoices, paid checks, and other original papers.

KEY TERMS INTRODUCED OR EMPHASIZED IN CHAPTER 4

(Note: The preceding section of this chapter contains definitions of terms describing specific steps in the audit process. These terms are not repeated in this glossary.)

Analytical procedures   Substantive tests that involve comparisons of financial data for the current year to that of prior years, budgets, nonfinancial data, or industry averages. From a planning standpoint, analytical procedures help the auditors obtain an understanding of the client's business, and identify financial statement amounts that appear to be affected by errors or irregularities, or other potential problems.

Audit committee   A committee composed of outside directors (members of the board of directors who are neither officers nor employees) charged with responsibility for maintaining contact with the company's internal and independent auditors.

Audit plan A broad overview of an audit engagement prepared in the planning stages of the engagement. Audit plans usually include such matters as the objectives of the engagement, nature of the work to be done, a time schedule for major audit work and completion of the engagement, and staffing requirements.

Audit program A detailed listing and explanation of the specific audit procedures to be performed in the course of an audit engagement. Audit programs provide a basis for assigning and scheduling audit work and for determining what work remains to be done. Audit programs are specially tailored to each engagement.

Audit risk The risk that the auditors may unknowingly fail to appropriately modify their opinion on financial statements that are materially misstated.

Control risk The risk of a material misstatement occurring in an account and not being detected on a timely basis by internal control.

Detection risk The risk that the auditors' procedures will lead them to conclude that an account is not materially misstated, when in fact such misstatement does exist.

Engagement letter A formal letter sent by the auditors to the client at the beginning of an engagement summarizing the nature of the engagement, any limitations on the scope of audit work, work to be done by the client's staff, and the basis for the audit fee. The purpose of engagement letters is to avoid misunderstandings, and they are essential on nonaudit engagements as well as audits.

Inherent risk The risk of material misstatement of an account, assuming there were no related internal controls.

Interim period The time interval from the beginning of audit work to the balance sheet date. Many audit procedures can be performed during the interim period to facilitate early issuance of the audit report.

Management letter A report to management containing the auditors' recommendations for correcting any deficiencies disclosed by the auditors' consideration of internal control. In addition to providing management with useful information, a management letter may also help limit the auditors' liability in the event a control weakness subsequently results in a loss sustained by the client.

Predecessor auditor The CPA firm that formerly served as auditor but has resigned from the engagement or has been notified that its services have been terminated.

Professional corporation A form of organization for professional practices that is now permitted in most states. Professional corporations enable practitioners to limit their exposure to legal liability and to obtain the tax benefits of incorporation. All shareholders and directors of a professional corporation must be licensed practitioners of the profession.

Substantive tests Tests of account balances and transactions designed to detect any material errors in the financial statements. The nature, timing, and extent of substantive testing is determined by the auditors' consideration of the client's internal control.

Successor auditor An auditor who has accepted an engagement or who has been invited to make a proposal for an engagement to replace the CPA firm that formerly served as auditors.

Time budget An estimate of the time required to perform each step in the audit program.

GROUP I: REVIEW QUESTIONS

4-1. What are the advantages of organizing a CPA firm as a partnership rather than a sole proprietorship?

4-2. How does a professional corporation differ from the traditional corporation?

4-3. Describe the various levels or grades of accounting personnel in a large public accounting firm.

4-4. Distinguish between the responsibilities of a senior auditor and a staff assistant.

4-5. List three of the more important responsibilities of a partner in a public accounting firm.

4-6. What are analytical procedures? How are such procedures useful to auditors in planning an audit?

4-7. What information should a CPA firm seek in its investigation of a prospective client?

4-8. Describe the preferred composition and role of the audit committee of a board of directors.

4-9. What topics should be discussed in a preliminary meeting with a prospective audit client?

4-10. Are auditors justified in relying upon the accuracy of working papers prepared for them by employees of the client?

4-11. In planning an audit the auditors must consider those factors that affect the risk of the particular engagement. List three risk factors relating to each of the following: management characteristics, operating characteristics, engagement characteristics.

4-12. List and briefly describe three approaches to auditing accounting estimates that are included in the financial statements.

4-13. State the purpose and nature of an engagement letter.

4-14. Define and differentiate between an *audit plan* and an *audit program.*

4-15. Should a separate audit program be prepared for each audit engagement, or can a standard program be used for most engagements?

4-16. "An audit program is desirable when new staff members are assigned to an engagement, but an experienced auditor should be able to conduct an examination without reference to an audit program." Do you agree? Discuss.

4-17. Suggest some factors that might cause an audit engagement to exceed the original time estimate. Would the extra time be charged to the client?

4-18. The following statements illustrate incorrect use of auditing terms. You are to substitute the proper terms for the italicized words.
a. We *checked* the cash on hand.

      b. We *analyzed* the bank statement with the ledger balance for Cash in Bank.

      c. We *confirmed* the ledger account for Miscellaneous Expense by classifying and reviewing the various kinds of debit and credit entries in the account.

      d. We *vouched* the accounts receivable by direct written communication with customers.

      e. We *reconciled* the minutes of directors' meetings for the entire period under audit.

4–19. Define and differentiate between a test of a control and a substantive test.

GROUP II: QUESTIONS REQUIRING ANALYSIS

4–20. When planning an audit, the auditors must assess the levels of risk and materiality for the engagement. Explain how the auditors' judgments about these two factors affect the auditors' planned audit procedures.

4–21. Morgan, CPA, is approached by a prospective audit client who wants to engage Morgan to perform an audit for the current year. In prior years, this prospective client was audited by another CPA. Identify the specific procedures that Morgan should follow in deciding whether or not to accept this client. (AICPA, adapted)

4–22. How does a knowledge of the client's business help the auditors in planning and performing an examination in accordance with generally accepted auditing standards? (AICPA, adapted)

4–23. Arthur Samuels, CPA, agreed to perform an audit of a new client engaged in the manufacture of power tools. After some preliminary discussion of the purposes of the audit and the basis for determination of the audit fee, Samuels asked to be taken on a comprehensive guided tour of the client's plant facilities. Explain specific ways that the knowledge gained by Samuels during the plant tour may help in planning and conducting the audit.

4–24. A CPA has been asked to audit the financial statements of a publicly held company for the first time. All preliminary discussions have been completed between the CPA, the company, the predecessor auditor, and all other necessary parties. The CPA is now preparing an engagement letter. List the items that should be included in the engagement letter.

(AICPA, adapted)

4–25. The audit plan, the audit program, and the time budget are three important working papers prepared early in an audit. What functions do these working papers serve in the auditor's compliance with generally accepted auditing standards? Discuss.

4–26. The first standard of field work requires, in part, that "the work is to be adequately planned." An effective tool that aids the auditor in adequately planning the work is an audit program. What is an audit program and what purposes does it serve? (AICPA, adapted)

4–27. How can a CPA make use of the preceding year's audit working papers in a recurring examination? (AICPA, adapted)

4–28. Ann Knox, president of Knox Corporation, is a close friend of a client of yours. In response to a strong recommendation of your audit work by her friend, Ann Knox has retained you to make an audit of Knox Corporation's financial statements. Although you have had extensive auditing experience, you have not previously audited a company in the same line of business as Knox Corporation.

Ann Knox informs you that she would like to have an estimate of the cost of the audit. List all the steps you would take in order to have an adequate basis for providing an estimate of the audit fee for the Knox Corporation engagement.   (AICPA, adapted)

4–29. Select the best answer for each of the following. Explain the reasons for your selection.

    a. As generally conceived, the audit committee of a company should be made up of—

        (1) Representatives from the client's management, investors, suppliers, and customers.

        (2) The audit partner, the chief financial officer, the legal counsel, and at least one outsider.

        (3) Representatives of the major equity interests, such as preferred and common stockholders.

        (4) Members of the board of directors who are not officers or employees.

    b. When a CPA is approached to perform an audit for the first time, the CPA should make inquiries of the predecessor auditor. This is a necessary procedure because the predecessor auditor may be able to provide information that will assist the successor auditor in determining whether—

        (1) The predecessor's work should be utilized.

        (2) The company follows a policy of rotating its auditors.

        (3) The predecessor is aware of any weaknesses in internal control.

        (4) The engagement should be accepted.

    c. Early appointment of the independent auditors will enable—

        (1) A more thorough examination to be performed.

        (2) A sufficient understanding of internal control to be obtained.

        (3) Sufficient competent evidential matter to be obtained.

        (4) A more efficient examination to be planned.

    d. Which of the following portions of an audit may **not** be completed before the balance sheet date?

        (1) Tests of controls.

        (2) Issuance of a management letter.

        (3) Substantive testing.

        (4) Assessment of control risk.

    e. Which of the following should the auditors obtain from the predecessor auditor prior to accepting an audit engagement?

        (1) Analysis of balance sheet accounts.

        (2) Analysis of income statement accounts.

        (3) All matters of continuing accounting significance.

        (4) Facts that might bear on the integrity of management.

    f. A CPA, while performing an audit, strives to achieve independence in appearance in order to:

        (1) Eliminate risk and liability.

        (2) Become independent in fact.

(3) Maintain public confidence in the profession.

(4) Comply with the generally accepted standards of field work.

(AICPA, adapted)

GROUP III:
PROBLEMS

4–30. For many years, the financial and accounting community has recognized the importance and use of audit committees and has endorsed their formation.

At this time, the use of audit committees has become widespread. Independent auditors have become increasingly involved with audit committees and consequently have become familiar with their nature and function.

Required:

a. Describe what an audit committee is.

b. Identify the reasons audit committees have been formed and are currently in operation.

c. What are the functions of an audit committee?   (AICPA, adapted)

4–31. In a discussion between Peters and Ferrel, two auditing students, Peters made the following statement:

"A CPA is a professional person who is licensed by the state for the purpose of providing an independent expert opinion on the fairness of financial statements. To maintain an attitude of mental independence and objectivity in all phases of audit work, it is advisable that the CPA not fraternize with client personnel. The CPA should be courteous but reserved and dignified at all times. Indulging in social contacts with clients outside of business hours will make it more difficult to be firm and objective if the CPA finds evidence of fraud or of unsound accounting practices."

Ferrel replied as follows:

"You are 50 years behind the times, Peters. An auditor and a client are both human beings. The auditor needs the cooperation of the client to do a good job; you're much more likely to get cooperation if you're relaxed and friendly rather than being cold and impersonal. Having a few beers or going to a football game with a client won't keep the CPA from being independent. It will make the working relationship a lot more comfortable, and will probably cause the client to recommend the CPA to other business people who need auditing services. In other words, the approach you're recommending should be called 'How to Avoid Friends and Alienate Clients.' I will admit, though, that with so many women entering public accounting and other women holding executive positions in business, a few complications may arise when auditor-client relations get pretty relaxed."

Evaluate the opposing views expressed by Peters and Ferrel.

4–32. Valley Finance Company opened four personal loan offices in neighboring cities on January 2. Small cash loans are made to borrowers who repay the principal with interest in monthly installments over a period not exceeding two years. Ralph Norris, president of the company, uses one of the offices as a central office and visits the other offices periodically for supervision and internal auditing purposes.

Required:

Assume that you agreed to examine Valley Finance Company's financial statements for the year ended December 31. No scope limitations were imposed.

a. How would you determine the scope necessary to complete your examination satisfactorily? Discuss.

b. Would you be responsible for the discovery of fraud in this examination? Discuss.   (AICPA, adapted)

4–33. You are invited by John Bray, the president of Cheviot Corporation, to discuss with him the possibility of your conducting an audit of the company. The corporation is a small, closely held manufacturing organization that appears to be expanding. No previous audit has been made by independent certified public accountants. Your discussions with Bray include a review of the recent monthly financial statements, inspection of the accounting records, and review of policies with the chief accountant. You also are taken on a guided tour of the plant by the president. He then makes the following statement:

"Before making definite arrangements for an audit, I would like to know about how long it will take and about how much it will cost. I want quality work and expect to pay a fair price, but since this is our first experience with independent auditors, I would like a full explanation as to how the cost of the audit is determined. Will you please send me a memorandum covering these points?"

Write the memorandum requested by John Bray.

GROUP IV: RESEARCH AND DISCUSSION CASE

4–34. Tammy Potter, a new partner with the regional CPA firm of Tower & Tower, was recently appointed to the board of directors of a local civic organization. The chairman of the board of the civic organization is Lewis Edmond, who is also the owner of a real estate development firm, Tierra Corporation.

Potter was quite excited when Edmond indicated that his corporation needed an audit, and he wished to discuss the matter with her. During the discussion, Potter was told that Tierra Corporation needed the audit to obtain a substantial amount of additional financing to acquire another company. Presently, Tierra Corporation is successful, profitable, and committed to growth. The audit fee for the engagement should be substantial.

Since Tierra Corporation appeared to be a good client prospect, Potter tentatively indicated that Tower & Tower wanted to do the work. Potter then mentioned that Tower & Tower's quality control policies require an investigation of new clients and approval by the managing partner, Lee Tower.

Potter obtained the authorizations of Edmond to make the necessary inquiries for the new client investigation. Edmond was found to be a highly respected member of the community. Also, Tierra corporation was highly regarded by its banker and its attorney, and the Dun & Bradstreet report on the corporation reflected nothing negative.

As a final part of the investigation process, Potter contacted Edmond's former tax accountant, Bill Turner. Potter was surprised to discover that Turner did not share the others' high opinion of Edmond. Turner related that on an IRS audit 10 years ago, Edmond was questioned about the details of a large capital loss reported on the sale of a tract of land to a trust. Edmond told the IRS agent that he had lost all of the supporting documentation for the transaction, and that he had no way of finding out the names of the principals of the trust. A search by an IRS auditor revealed that the land was recorded in the name of Edmond's married daughter and that Edmond himself was listed as the trustee. The IRS disallowed the loss and Edmond was assessed a civil fraud penalty. Potter was concerned about these findings, but eventually concluded that Edmond had probably matured to a point where he would not engage in such activities.

Required:
a. Present arguments supporting a decision to accept Tierra Corporation as an audit client.
b. Present arguments supporting a decision *not* to accept Tierra Corporation as an audit client.
c. Assuming that you are Lee Tower, set forth your decision regarding acceptance of the client, identifying those arguments from parts (*a*) or (*b*) that you found most persuasive.

Suggested references:
AICPA, *Professional Standards, Volume B,* Commerce Clearing House, *Statements on Quality Control Standards,* Section 10.07.
AICPA, *Professional Standards, Volume A,* Commerce Clearing House, *Statement on Auditing Standards 53,* "The Auditor's Responsibility to Detect and Report Errors and Irregularities," AU 316.

Internal control

Chapter 5 study objectives

After studying this chapter, you should be able to:

— Define internal control for a company.
— Describe the major components of a client's internal control structure: the overall control environment, the accounting system, and control procedures.
— Explain the characteristics of effective internal control.
— Describe the auditors' consideration of internal control.
— Explain the techniques used by auditors to obtain an understanding of internal control and describe the results in their working papers.
— Describe the auditors' responsibility for communication of internal control structure related matters.

Our consideration of internal control has three major objectives: first, to explain the meaning and significance of internal control; second, to outline the steps required to create and maintain strong internal control; and third, to show how auditors go about obtaining an understanding of internal control. No attempt is made in this chapter to present in detail the internal control procedures applicable to particular kinds of assets or to particular types of transactions, such as purchases or sales. Detailed information along these lines will be found in succeeding chapters as each phase of the auditors' examination is presented.

The meaning of internal control

Many people interpret the term *internal control* as the steps taken by a business to prevent employee fraud. Actually, such measures are a part of internal control. In the broadest sense, an organization's internal control structure (also referred to as internal control system) consists of the policies and procedures established to provide *reasonable assurance* that the organization's related objectives will be achieved. The concept of *reasonable assurance* recognizes that no structure is perfect and that the cost of an entity's internal control should not exceed the benefits expected to be derived. Those benefits include a structure's ability to (1) safeguard assets from waste, fraud, and inefficient use; (2) promote accurate and reliable accounting records; (3) encourage and measure compliance with company policies; and (4) evaluate the efficiency of operations. In short, internal control consists of all measures taken to assure management that everything is functioning as it should.

Internal control extends beyond the accounting and financial functions: its scope is companywide and touches all activities of the organization. It includes the methods by which top management delegates authority and assigns responsibility for such functions as selling, purchasing, accounting, and production. Internal control also includes the program for preparing, verifying, and distributing to various levels of supervision those current reports and analyses that enable executives to maintain control over the variety of activities and functions that constitute a large corporate enterprise. The use of budgetary techniques, production standards, inspection laboratories, time and motion studies, and employee training programs involves engineers and many other technicians far removed from accounting and financial activities; yet all of these devices are part of the mechanism now conceived as an internal control structure.

This broad, sweeping concept of internal control is most significant when viewed against the backdrop of a large nationwide industrial organization, for internal control has developed into a technique of vital importance in enabling management of large complex enterprises to function efficiently. Since internal control has attained greatest significance in large-scale business organizations, the greater part of the discussion in this chapter is presented in terms of the large corporation. A separate section is presented at the end of the chapter, however, dealing with the problem of achieving internal control in a small business.

The need for internal control

The long-run trend for corporations to evolve into organizations of gigantic size and scope, including a great variety of specialized technical operations and employees numbered in the tens of thousands, has made it impossible for corporate executives to exercise personal, firsthand supervision of operations. No longer able to rely upon personal observation as a means of appraising operating results and financial position, the corporate executive has, of necessity, come to depend upon a stream of accounting and statistical reports. These reports summarize current happenings and conditions throughout the enterprise; the units of measurement employed are not only dollars but labor-hours, material weights, customer calls, employee terminations, and a host of other denominators.

The information carried by this stream of reports enables management to control and direct the enterprise. It keeps management informed as to whether company policy is being carried out, whether governmental regulations are being observed, and whether financial position is sound, operations profitable, and interdepartmental relations harmonious.

Business decisions of almost every kind are based at least in part on accounting data. These decisions range from such minor matters as authorizing overtime work or purchasing office supplies to such major issues as a shift from one product to another or making a choice between leasing or buying a new plant. The internal control structure provides assurance to management of the dependability of the accounting data used in making these decisions.

Decisions made by management become company policy. To be effective, this policy must be communicated throughout the company and consistently followed. Internal control aids in securing compliance with company policy. Management also has the direct responsibility of maintaining accounting records and producing financial statements that are adequate and reliable. Internal control provides assurance that this responsibility is being met.

To the independent public accountants, internal control is of equal significance. The quality of the internal controls in force, more than any other factor, determines the pattern of their examination. The independent auditors obtain an understanding of the internal control structure in order to plan the audit and to determine the nature, timing, and extent of the other auditing work necessary to permit them to express an opinion as to the fairness of the financial statements.

Internal accounting controls versus internal administrative controls

Historically, professional standards have distinguished between internal accounting controls and internal administrative controls. *Internal accounting controls* are those bearing directly upon the dependability of the accounting records and the financial statements. For example, preparation of monthly bank reconciliations by an employee not authorized to issue checks or handle cash is an internal accounting control that increases the probability that cash transactions are presented fairly in the accounting records and financial statements.

Some internal controls have little or no bearing on the financial statements and consequently are not of direct interest to the auditors. Controls in this category are often referred to as *internal administrative controls.* Management is interested in maintaining strong internal control over factory operations and sales activities as well as over accounting and financial functions. Accordingly, management will establish administrative controls to provide for operational efficiency and for adherence to prescribed policies in all departments of the organization.

Professional standards for financial statement audits no longer distinguish accounting controls from administrative controls. They simply indicate that the auditors need only be concerned with internal controls that are designed to prevent or detect misstatements of the financial statements. However, the terms *internal accounting control* and *internal administrative control* are still used in many reference books on internal control, in the professional standards on opinions on internal control (discussed in Chapter 19 of the text), and in the Foreign Corrupt Practices Act.

Foreign Corrupt Practices Act

In the mid-1970s, a number of American corporations acknowledged having made payments (which could be interpreted as bribes) to officials in foreign countries. In most cases, the payments were legal under the laws of the countries in which they were made, but they were not in accordance with American business ethics. In some instances, these questionable payments were made without the authorization or knowledge of top executives of the corporations involved.

In the Foreign Corrupt Practices Act of 1977, Congress ordered an end to this practice. Payments to foreign officials for the purpose of securing business were specifically prohibited. However, the Act goes far beyond the issue of illegal payments and requires *every corporation under the jurisdiction of the SEC to maintain a system of internal accounting control that will provide reasonable assurance that transactions are executed only with the knowledge and authorization of management.* In addition, the Act requires the system of internal control to limit the use of corporate assets to those purposes approved by management. Finally, the Act calls for accounting records to be reconciled at reasonable intervals with assets actually on hand. These requirements are designed to prevent the creation of secret slush funds or other misuses of corporate resources. Violations of the Act can result in fines of up to $1 million and imprisonment of the responsible individuals. Thus, a strong system of internal accounting control, long viewed as essential to the operation of a large organization, is required by federal law.

Means of achieving internal control

Internal control structures vary significantly from one organization to the next. The specific control features used depend upon such factors as the size, nature of operations, and objectives of the organization for which the structure was designed. Yet certain features are essential to satisfactory internal control in almost any large-scale organization. For purposes of financial statement audits, the relevant features are generally those that pertain to the entity's ability to *record, process, summarize,* and *report* financial data. These features may be divided into three elements: (1) the *control environment;* (2) the *accounting system;* and (3) *control procedures.*

CONTROL ENVIRONMENT

The control environment consists of the overall set of factors designed to achieve the organization's policies and procedures. In this chapter we will emphasize internal factors, although you should recognize that external factors such as laws and regulatory requirements are also a part of a company's control environment. Internal environmental control factors include management philosophy and operating style; a logical plan of organization; effective personnel management methods; a forecasting and budgeting system; an internal audit function; and an effective audit committee.

Management philosophy and operating style

Managements differ in both their philosophies toward financial reporting and their attitudes toward taking business risks. Some managements are extremely aggressive in financial reporting and place great emphasis on meeting or exceeding earnings projections. They may be willing to undertake activities with high risk on the prospects of high returns. Other managements are extremely conservative and risk averse. These differing philosophies have an impact on the overall reliability of the financial statements.

Operating styles also vary from firm to firm. For example, companies differ as to the degree to which management decision making is centralized. When management decision making is centralized and dominated by one individual, that individual's moral character is extremely important to the auditors. When a decentralized style is used, procedures to monitor the decision making of the many managers involved become more important.

Organizational plan

Organizational independence of departments allows an entity to plan, direct, and control operations effectively. A *plan of organization* refers to the division of authority, responsibilities, and duties among members of an organization. A well-designed plan of organization is a first step to assure that transactions are executed in conformity with company policies, to enhance the efficiency of operations, to safeguard assets, and to promote the reliability of accounting data. These goals may be achieved in large part by an organization plan that separates responsibilities for (1) *authorization* of transactions, (2) *record keeping* for transactions, and (3) *custody* of assets. In addition, to the extent possible, execution of the *operation* involved should be segregated from these responsibilities. The effectiveness of such structure is usually obtained by having designated department heads who are evaluated on the basis of the performance of their respective departments. The top executives of the major departments should be of equal rank and should report directly to the president or to an executive vice president. The partial organization chart in Figure 5–1 illustrates such an arrangement. If, for example, the controller were a line subordinate to the vice president of production, the organizational independence of the accounting department would be greatly impaired.

Illustrative case

During an examination of the Foster Company, the auditors' study of organizational lines of authority and their use of an internal control questionnaire disclosed that the receiving department personnel were under the direction of the purchasing agent. Accounts payable department employees had also been instructed to accept informal memoranda from the purchasing agent as evidence of receipt of merchandise and propriety of invoices.

Because of this deficiency in internal control, the auditors made a very thorough examination of purchase invoices and came across a number of large December invoices from one supplier bearing the notation: "Subject to adjustment at time of delivery of merchandise." Investigation of these transactions disclosed that the merchandise had not yet been delivered, but the invoices had been paid. The purchasing agent explained that he had requested the advance billing in an effort to reduce taxable income for the year under audit, during which profits had been higher than usual. Further investigation revealed that the purchasing agent held a substantial personal interest in the supplier making the advance billings, and that top management of the client company was not aware of this conflict of interest.

Responsibilities of finance and accounting departments   Finance and accounting are the two departments most directly involved in the financial affairs of a business enterprise. The division of responsibilities between these departments illustrates the separation of the accounting function from operations and also from the custody of assets. Under the direction of the *treasurer,* the finance department is responsible for financial opera-

Figure 5–1   Partial organization chart

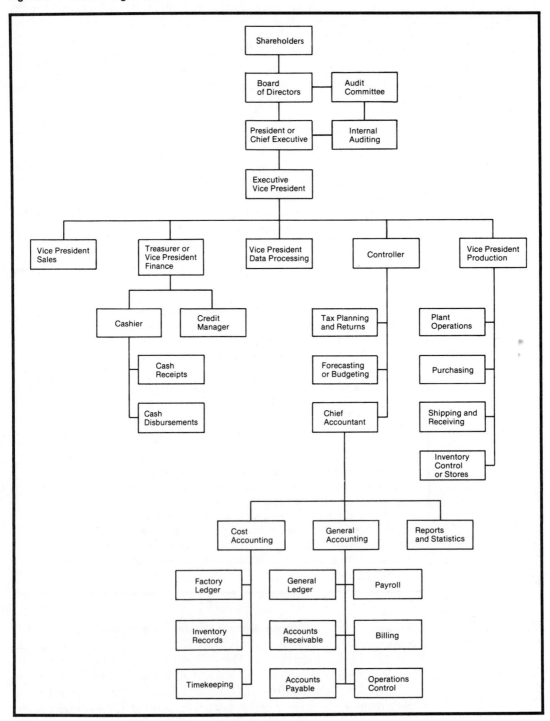

tions and custody of liquid assets. Activities of this department include planning future cash requirements, establishing customer credit policies, and arranging to meet the short- and long-term financing needs of the business. In addition, the finance department has custody of bank accounts and other liquid assets, invests idle cash, handles cash receipts, and makes cash disbursements. In short, it is the finance department that *conducts* financial activities.

The accounting department, under the authority of the **controller,** is responsible for all accounting functions and the design and implementation of internal control. With respect to financial activity, the accounting department *records* financial transactions but does not handle financial assets. Accounting records establish **accountability** over assets, as well as providing the information necessary for financial reports, tax returns, and daily operating decisions. With respect to internal control, the accounting department maintains the independent records with which quantities of assets and operating results are compared. Often, this reconciliation function is performed by the **operations control group** or some other subdepartment within accounting.

Many of the subdepartments often found within accounting are illustrated in Figure 5–1. It is important for many of these subdepartments to be relatively independent of one another. For example, if the operations control group reconciles assets on hand to the accounting records, it is essential that the operations control personnel not maintain those records.

Efficiency of operations   A well-designed organization plan should enhance the efficiency of operations as well as contribute to internal control. When two or more departments participate in every transaction, the work of one department is reviewed by another. Also, each department has an incentive to demand efficient performance from the others.

A typical purchase transaction may be used to illustrate how good organizational structure enhances both internal control and the efficiency of operations. If the purchasing department fails to place a purchase order promptly upon receipt of a purchase requisition from the material stores department, the latter department may find itself without materials required by production departments. The material stores department, therefore, has an incentive to follow up purchase requisitions and to demand prompt action by the purchasing agent. If the purchasing department orders an excessive or insufficient quantity, the responsibility for the error will be pinned down by reference to the purchase requisition, the purchase order, and the receiving report, each of which is prepared by an independent department.

Errors made by the receiving department in counting goods received will normally be brought to light by the accounting department when it compares the receiving report with the vendor's invoice and the purchase order. If defective materials are accepted by the receiving department, responsibility will be placed on the negligent department by personnel of the storeskeeping or production departments, which must utilize the materials in question.

On the other hand, if the various functional activities are not segregated by independent departments and all aspects of a purchase transaction are handled by employees reporting to the purchasing agent, then top management is less likely to learn of specific inefficiencies in purchasing activities.

Personnel management methods

Ultimately, the effectiveness of an internal control environment is affected by the characteristics of its personnel. Thus, personnel management methods and the business's policies for hiring, training, evaluating, promoting, and compensating employees have a significant effect on the effectiveness of the control environment. Effective personnel methods often can mitigate other weaknesses in the control environment.

Fidelity bonds Effective personnel management is not a guarantee against losses from dishonest employees. It is often the most trusted employees who engineer large embezzlements. The fact that they are so highly trusted explains why they have access to cash, securities, and company records and are in a position that makes embezzlement possible.

Fidelity bonds are a form of insurance in which a bonding company agrees to reimburse an employer, within limits, for losses attributable to theft or embezzlement by bonded employees. Most employers require employees handling cash or other negotiable assets to be bonded. Individual fidelity bonds may be obtained by concerns with only a few employees; larger concerns may prefer to obtain a blanket fidelity bond covering many employees. Before issuing fidelity bonds, underwriters investigate thoroughly the past records of the employees to be bonded. This service offers added protection by preventing the employment of persons with dubious records in positions of trust. Bonding companies are much more likely to prosecute fraud cases vigorously than are employers; general awareness of this fact is another deterrent against dishonesty on the part of bonded employees.

Financial forecasts and budgets

A financial forecast for an enterprise is an estimate of the expected financial position, results of operations, and cash flows for one or more future periods.[1] It establishes definite goals providing management with a yardstick for evaluating actual performance, and thereby serves as an instrument of control.

------

[1] AICPA, *Guide for Prospective Financial Statements* (New York, 1986), paragraph 200.04.

The simplest and most common application of forecasting is the cash forecast, in which the treasurer estimates, for perhaps a year in advance, the flow of cash receipts and disbursements classified by source of receipt and object of disbursement. The principal aim of the cash forecast is to ensure that sufficient funds are available at all times to meet maturing liabilities. In addition, the scheduling of anticipated receipts from all sources makes fraud involving the withholding of receipts more susceptible of detection. Similarly, the detailed planning of cash disbursements discourages the potential embezzler from any attempt to falsify the records of cash disbursements.

A more comprehensive forecasting program would include the preparation of:

1. A sales forecast, consisting of estimated sales by product and by territory.
2. A production forecast, detailing the quantity and cost of material, labor, and manufacturing overhead to meet the sales forecast.
3. A forecast of selling and administrative costs.
4. A plant and equipment forecast, consisting of estimates of acquisitions and retirements.
5. A cash forecast.
6. An estimated income statement, balance sheet, and statement of cash flows for the period encompassed by the forecast.

During the year, monthly reports should be prepared comparing actual operating results with forecast figures. These reports should be accompanied by explanations of all significant variations between forecast and actual results, with a definite fixing of responsibility for such variances. In brief, a forecast is a control device, involving the establishment of definite standards of performance throughout the business. Failure to attain these standards is promptly called to the attention of appropriate levels of management through variance reports.

Forecasts are also the basis for the company's budgets that are provided to managers throughout the organization. Budgets communicate the financial expectations of the company's top management and serve to motivate company personnel to achieve management's goals. A company's budgets may be identical to its forecasts, or they might reflect slightly higher expectations to challenge company personnel.

Internal auditing

Another basic component of the internal control environment is an internal auditing staff. The job of internal auditors is to investigate and appraise the system of internal control and the efficiency with which the various units of the business are performing their assigned functions, and to report their findings and make recommendations to top management. As representatives of top management, the internal auditors are interested in determining whether each branch or department has a clear understanding of its assignment, is adequately staffed, maintains good records, protects cash and inventories and other assets properly, cooperates harmoniously with other departments, and in general carries out effectively the function provided for in the overall plan and organization of the business.

Internal auditors are *not* responsible for performing routine control procedures, such as reconciling bank statements, balancing subsidiary ledgers, or verifying the mathematical accuracy of invoices. These functions are usually performed by a separate unit within the accounting department, such as the operations control group shown in Figure 5–1. Internal auditors provide a higher level of internal control; they design and carry out audit procedures that test the efficiency of virtually all aspects of company operations.

Internal auditors contrasted with independent auditors   The independent auditors' objective is the expression of an opinion on the client's financial statements; the internal auditors' objective is not to verify financial statements, but to aid management in achieving the most efficient administration of the business. To this end, they appraise the effectiveness of internal controls in various departments, branches, or other organizational units of the company. Internal auditors' work is not limited to accounting controls; they also monitor administrative controls.

The similarities between independent audits and internal auditing pertain to mechanics and techniques, not to objectives and end results. Both internal auditors and independent auditors examine accounting records and procedures and prepare working papers, but the reasons motivating the two lines of work and the end results obtained are quite different. Examinations by internal auditors are often called *operational audits* because the auditors are concerned with the *effect* of the existing policies and procedures upon the efficiency of operations. For example, in reviewing credit policies, independent CPAs are concerned primarily with determining the adequacy of the allowance for doubtful accounts. Internal auditors, on the other hand, are interested in whether employees are complying with existing policies and procedures and whether the existing policies and procedures might be changed to enhance the efficiency of operations. The end result of an operational audit is a report to management containing recommendations for improving operational performance. (Operational auditing is discussed further in Chapter 19.)

In companies that stress growth through acquisitions and mergers, the internal auditors may perform investigations of companies being considered for acquisition. In such an assignment, the role of the internal auditors is similar to that of an independent auditor. The investigation consists of gathering evidence to substantiate or disprove the other company's representations as to the collectibility of receivables, valuation of inventories, loss contingencies, volume of sales, trend of earnings, and related data in the financial statements.

Independence of internal auditors   Since internal auditors are employees of the company they serve, they obviously cannot achieve the CPAs' independence in fact and in appearance. However, if internal auditors report directly to the audit committee of the board of directors, the president, or other senior officer, they may achieve a greater degree of freedom, independence, and objectivity than if they report to an official of lesser rank in the organization.

Audit committee

As we discussed in Chapter 4, an audit committee should be composed of members of the board of directors who are neither officers nor employees of the client organization. Because of this independence from management of the firm, audit committees help maintain a direct line of communication between the board of directors and the entity's independent and internal auditors. They also monitor top management of the organization, serving as a deterrent to management override of other internal controls, including management fraud.

THE ACCOUNTING SYSTEM

To achieve the objectives of internal control, the accounting system must function effectively to properly record, process, summarize, and report transactions. In addition to the typical system of journals, ledgers, and other record-keeping devices, an accounting system should include:

1.   Adequate internal documentation to focus responsibility.
2.   A chart of accounts.
3.   A manual of accounting policies and procedures, and flowcharts depicting the established methods of processing transactions.

Adequate documentation

A system of well-designed forms and documents is necessary to create a record of the activities of all departments. For example, how is the accounting department notified when a credit sale takes place? Usually notification is through a sales ticket prepared by the salesclerk when the sale occurs. Without such documentation, there would be virtually no record or control over the activities of the operating departments. Internally created documents are also used to create accountability for assets transferred from one department to another. Copies of these documents provide a trail of evidence that focuses responsibility for any shortages that may develop as the assets move from department to department.

The reliability of internally created documents is increased if two parties with *opposing interests* participate in preparation of the document.

For example, when the stores department releases material to production, a ***production order*** is initialed by employees of each department. The stores department has an incentive to ascertain that quantities shown on the production order are not ***understated;*** otherwise, the stores department will be held responsible for goods no longer on hand. The production department, on the other hand, has an incentive to see that materials charged to its operations are not ***overstated.***

An internal control device of wide applicability is the use of serial numbers on documents. Serial numbers provide control over the number of documents issued. Checks, tickets, sales invoices, purchase orders, stock certificates, and many other business papers can be controlled in this manner. For some documents, such as checks, it may be desirable to account for every number of the series by a monthly or weekly inspection of the documents issued. For other documents, as in the case of serially numbered admission tickets, control may be achieved by noting the last serial number issued each day, and thereby computing the total value of tickets issued during the day. Adequate safekeeping and numerical control should be maintained at all times for unissued prenumbered documents.

Chart of accounts

A chart of accounts is a classified listing of all accounts in use, accompanied by a detailed description of the purpose and content of each. A chart of accounts helps companies to control the recording of transactions in a consistent, properly classified manner.

Manual of accounting policies and procedures

Every business organization, large or small, has a body of established methods of initiating, recording, and summarizing transactions. These procedures should be stated in writing, and documented in the form of flowcharts in a loose-leaf manual, and should be revised as the pattern of operating routines changes. If accounting procedures are clearly stated in writing, the policies set by management can be enforced efficiently and consistently. Uniform handling of like transactions is essential to the production of reliable accounting records and reports, and uniformity in the handling of transactions is possible only when definite patterns for processing routine transactions are made known to all employees.

CONTROL PROCEDURES

In addition to the control environment and the accounting system, management establishes other controls over particular types of transactions and assets. While there are many specific control procedures that may be implemented by a company, they all are designed to provide (1) proper authorization of transactions and activities, (2) appropriate segregation of duties, (3) adequate documentation and recording of transactions and events, (4) effective accountability for assets, and (5) proper valuation of recorded amounts. Although these specific controls are discussed in depth in succeeding chapters, an understanding of the concepts of segregation of duties and accountability for assets is essential to a general understanding of control procedures.

Segregation of duties   A fundamental concept of internal control is that *no one person or department should handle all aspects of a transaction from beginning to end.* If management is to direct the activities of a business according to plan, every transaction should involve five steps; it should be *authorized, initiated, approved, executed,* and *recorded.* Internal control will be enhanced if each of these steps is performed by relatively independent employees or departments. No single employee will then have *incompatible duties* that allow the employee to both perpetrate and conceal errors or irregularities in the normal course of a day's work.

A credit sales transaction may be used to illustrate an appropriate segregation of duties. Top management of a company may **authorize** the sale of merchandise at specified credit terms to customers who meet certain criteria. Orders from customers are *initiated* in the sales department and sent to the credit department for *approval.* The credit department reviews the transaction to ascertain that the extension of credit and terms of sale are in compliance with company policies. Once the sale is approved, the shipping department *executes* the transaction by obtaining the merchandise from the inventory stores department and shipping it to the customer. The accounting department uses copies of the documentation created by the sales, credit, and shipping departments as a basis for *recording* the transaction and billing the customer.

When responsibilities for authorizing, initiating, approving, executing, and recording transactions are separated in this manner, no one department can initiate and complete an unauthorized transaction. The possibility of unrecorded transactions is greatly reduced because of the documentation that must be prepared as information concerning the transaction moves from one department to another. (Sequential numbering of this documentation will assist the accounting department in determining that all transactions have been accounted for.) Also, segregation of duties permits specialization of labor, which should contribute to the overall efficiency of operations.

Accountability for assets   A traditional step in achieving internal control is separation of the record-keeping function from the custody of related assets. When the accounting and custodial departments are relatively independent, the work of each department serves to verify the accuracy of the work of the other. Periodic comparisons should be made of accounting records and the physical assets on hand. Investigation as to the cause of any discrepancies will uncover weaknesses either in procedures for safeguarding assets or in maintaining the related accounting records. If the accounting records were not independent of the custodial department, the records could be manipulated to conceal waste, loss, or theft of the related assets.

Illustrative case

A manufacturer of golf clubs operated a large storeroom containing thousands of sets of golf clubs ready for shipment. Detailed perpetual inventory records were maintained by the employee in charge of the storeroom. A shortage of several sets of clubs developed as a result of theft by another employee who had acquired an unauthorized key to the storeroom. The employee responsible for the storeroom discovered the discrepancy between the clubs in stock and the quantities of clubs as shown by the records. Fearing criticism of his record keeping, he changed the inventory records to agree with the quantities on hand. The thefts continued, and large losses were sustained before the shortages were discovered. If the inventory records had been maintained by someone not responsible for physical custody of the merchandise, there would have been no incentive or opportunity to conceal a shortage by falsifying the records.

Figure 5–2 illustrates the use of an independently maintained record to establish accountability for assets. It is not essential that **all three** parties in the diagram (A, B, and C) be employees of the company; one or more may be an outside party or a mechanical device. For example, if A is a bank with custody of cash on deposit, B would be the company employees maintaining records of cash receipts and disbursements, and C might be a computer program that performs periodic bank reconciliations. Or, if A is a salesclerk with custody of cash receipts from sales, B could be a

**Figure 5–2
Establishing
accountability for
assets**

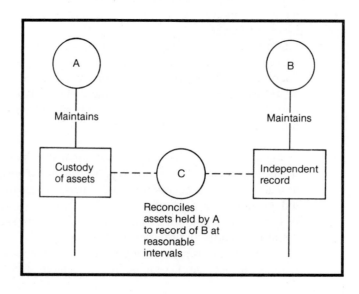

cash register with a locked-in tape, and C could be the departmental supervisor. Regardless of the nature of the parties involved, the principle remains the same: accounting records should be maintained independently of custody of the related assets and should be compared at reasonable intervals to asset quantities on hand.

Limitations of internal control

Internal control can do much to protect against fraud and assure the reliability of accounting data. Still, it is important to recognize the existence of inherent limitations in any internal control structure. Errors may be made in the performance of control procedures as a result of carelessness, misunderstanding of instructions, or other human factors. As dramatically illustrated in the Equity Funding case, internal control is not an effective deterrent to fraud by top management. Without active participation in management by the board of directors and an effective internal audit department, top management can easily override the internal control system. Also, those control procedures dependent upon separation of duties may be circumvented by collusion among employees.

The extent of the internal controls adopted by a business is limited by cost considerations. It is not feasible from a cost standpoint to establish a control system that provides absolute protection from fraud and waste; *reasonable assurance* in this regard is the best that generally can be achieved.

THE AUDITORS' CONSIDERATION OF INTERNAL CONTROL

The generally accepted auditing standards require the auditors to obtain an understanding of internal control. Specifically, the second standard of field work states:

> A sufficient understanding of the internal control structure is to be obtained to plan the audit and to determine the nature, timing, and extent of tests to be performed.

The auditors' understanding of their clients' internal control provides a basis both to (1) *plan* the audit and (2) *assess control risk.*

In planning an audit, it is essential that the auditors have a sufficient understanding of the client's control environment, accounting system, and control procedures. This understanding encompasses both the *design* of policies, procedures, and records and a knowledge of whether they have been *placed in operation* by the client. With this knowledge the auditors are able to (1) identify the types of potential misstatements of the financial statements, and (2) design effective substantive tests of the financial statement balances. It is difficult to imagine designing tests of financial statement balances without an understanding of the control structure. For example, auditors who do not understand the client's policies and procedures for executing and recording credit sales would have a difficult time substantiating the balances of accounts receivable and sales.

The auditors' understanding of the internal control structure also provides a basis for their assessment of control risk—the risk that material misstatements would not be prevented or detected by the client's internal control. If the auditors determine that the client's internal control is effective, they will assess control risk to be low. Thus, the auditors can accept a higher level of detection risk, and substantive testing can be decreased. Conversely, where internal controls are weak, control risk is high and the auditors must increase the extent of their substantive tests to limit detection risk. Therefore, the auditors' understanding of internal control is a major factor in determining the nature, timing, and extent of substantive testing necessary to verify the financial statement balances.

Since an adequate internal control structure is a major factor in an examination conducted by the auditors, the question arises as to what action they should take when internal control is found to be seriously deficient. Can the auditors complete a satisfactory audit and properly express an opinion on the fairness of financial statements of a company in which control risk is considered to be extremely high? The answer to this question depends on whether the auditors believe that inherent risk is at a satisfactory level so that substantive tests can be designed that will reduce audit risk to an acceptable level. The auditors of a small business often rely largely on an approach of restricting detection risk through substantive tests of financial statement balances, rather than relying on tests of internal control.

The steps in the auditors' consideration of the client's internal control consists of (1) obtaining an understanding of the internal control sufficient to plan the audit, (2) assessing control risk and designing additional tests of controls, (3) performing additional tests of controls, and (4) reassessing control risk and designing substantive tests.

Obtain an understanding of internal control sufficient to plan the audit

In every audit, the auditors must obtain an understanding of the internal control structure adequate to plan the audit—this includes an understanding of the control environment, the accounting system, and control procedures.

Control environment. The auditors must obtain sufficient knowledge to understand management's and the board of directors' attitudes, awareness, and actions concerning the control environment. It is important that the auditors concentrate on the substance of controls, rather than their form. For example, a budgetary reporting system may provide reports, but the reports may not be analyzed and acted upon by management.

Accounting system. To understand the accounting system the auditors must first understand the major types of transactions engaged in by the entity. Next, the auditors must become familiar with the treatment of transactions, including (1) how those transactions are initiated, (2) the related accounting records, and (3) the manner of processing the transactions. Finally, the auditors must understand the financial reporting process used to prepare the financial statements, including the approaches used to make accounting estimates and disclosures.

Control procedures. While obtaining an understanding of the control environment and the accounting system, the auditors will generally obtain some information on detailed control procedures. For example, while obtaining an understanding of documents relating to cash, it is likely that the auditors will discover whether bank accounts are reconciled. Auditors must use their judgment as to whether it is necessary to devote additional attention to obtaining an understanding of other control procedures.

In obtaining an understanding of the client's accounting system and the related control procedures, auditors generally find it useful to subdivide the overall system into its major transaction cycles. The term ***transaction cycle*** refers to the policies and the sequence of procedures for processing a particular type of transaction. For example, the system of internal control in a manufacturing business might be subdivided into the following major transaction cycles:

1. Sales and collection cycle—involving procedures and policies for obtaining orders from customers, approving credit, shipping merchandise, preparing sales invoices, recording revenue and accounts receivable, billing, and handling and recording cash receipts.
2. Purchase or acquisition cycle—including procedures for initiating purchases of inventory, other assets, or services; placing purchase orders; inspecting goods upon receipt and preparing receiving reports; recording liabilities to vendors; authorizing payment; and making and recording cash disbursements.
3. Production cycle—including procedures for storing materials, placing materials into production, assigning production costs to inventories, and accounting for the cost of goods sold.
4. Payroll cycle—including procedures for hiring, firing, and determining pay rates; timekeeping; computing gross payroll, payroll taxes, and amounts withheld from gross pay; maintaining payroll records and preparing and distributing paychecks.
5. Financing cycle—including procedures for authorizing, executing, and recording transactions involving bank loans, leases, bonds payable, and capital stock.

The transaction cycles within a particular company depend upon the nature of the company's business activities. A bank, for example, has no production cycle, but has both a lending cycle and a demand deposits cycle. Also, different auditors may elect to define a given company's transaction cycles in different ways. For example, the sales and collection cycle may alternatively be defined as two separate transaction cycles for (1) the processing and recording of credit sales and (2) the handling and recording of cash receipts. The important point to recognize is that subdividing internal control into transaction cycles enables the auditor to focus upon the internal control procedures that affect the reliability of specific elements of the financial statements.

Sources of information about internal control   How do auditors gain an understanding of the client's internal control structure? One approach is to review the audit working papers from examinations made in prior years. When auditors are involved in repeat engagements, they will of course use all information about the client obtained in previous engagements. Their investigation will then stress the areas shown as having questionable controls in prior years. It is imperative, however, that auditors recognize that the pattern of operations is an ever-changing one, that internal controls that were adequate last year may now be obsolete, and that the established use of a given control procedure is no assurance that it is currently being applied in an effective and intelligent manner.

Auditors may ascertain the duties and responsibilities of client employees from organization charts, job descriptions, and interviews with client personnel. Most clients have procedures manuals and flowcharts describing the approved practices to be followed in all phases of operations. Another excellent source of information is in the reports, working papers, and audit programs of the client's internal auditing staff.

As the auditors obtain an understanding of the internal control structure they consider the design of policies and procedures and whether they have been placed in operation. During this process they may sometimes also obtain information on the operating effectiveness of various controls. *Operating effectiveness* deals with how a control is applied, the consistency with which it is applied, and by whom. The distinction between knowing that a control has been *placed in operation* and obtaining evidence on its operating effectiveness is important. To properly plan the audit, auditors are required to determine that major controls have been placed in operation; they are not required to test operating effectiveness. However, when the auditors wish to assess control risk at a level lower than the maximum, they must have evidence of the operating effectiveness of the controls.

Information on operating effectiveness may be obtained in two ways at this first stage of the consideration of internal control. First, the very nature of obtaining information on whether a control has been placed in operation may provide information as to its operating effectiveness. The auditors, for example, may verify by observation that the segregations of duties designed by the client are not only placed in operation but are also operating effectively. The second way that the auditors may obtain information on operating effectiveness is to perform specific tests which address effectiveness. Both of these approaches in essence are "tests of controls." Tests of controls are discussed in greater detail later in this chapter.

As the independent auditors obtain a working knowledge of the internal control structure to plan the audit, they must document the information in their working papers. The form and extent of this documentation is affected by the size and complexity of the client, as well as the nature of the client's internal control structure. The documentation usually takes the form of internal control questionnaires, written narratives, or flowcharts.

Internal control questionnaire The traditional method of describing a system of internal control is to fill in a standardized internal control questionnaire. Many public accounting firms have developed their own questionnaires for this purpose. The questionnaire usually contains a separate section for each major transaction cycle, enabling the work of completing the questionnaire to be divided conveniently among several audit staff members.

Most internal control questionnaires are designed so that a "no" answer to a question indicates a weakness in internal control. In addition, questionnaires usually provide for a distinction between major and minor control weaknesses, indication of the sources of information used in answering questions, and explanatory comments regarding control deficiencies. A disadvantage of standardized internal control questionnaires is their lack of flexibility. They often contain many questions that are "not applicable" to specific systems, particularly systems for small companies. Also, the situation in which an internal control strength compensates for a weakness in the system is not obvious from examining a completed questionnaire. An internal control questionnaire relating to cash receipts is illustrated in Figure 5–3.

Written narrative of internal control An internal control questionnaire is intended as a means for the auditors to document their understanding of internal control. If completion of the questionnaire is regarded as an end in itself, there may be a tendency for the auditors to fill in the "yes" and "no" answers in a mechanical manner, without any real understanding or study of the problem. For this reason, some public accounting firms prefer to use written narratives or flowcharts in lieu of, or in conjunction with, questionnaires. Written narratives usually follow the flow of each major transaction cycle, identifying the employees performing various tasks, documents prepared, records maintained, and the division of duties. Figure 5–4 is a written narrative, describing internal control over cash receipts.

Flowcharts of internal control Many CPA firms now consider *systems flowcharts* to be more effective than questionnaires or narrative descriptions in developing an understanding of a client's data processing system and the related internal controls. A systems flowchart is a diagram—a symbolic representation of a system or a series of procedures with each procedure shown in sequence. To the experienced reader, a flowchart conveys a clear image of the system, showing the nature and sequence of

Figure 5–3

INTERNAL CONTROL QUESTIONNAIRE
CASH RECEIPTS – SALES CYCLE

Client _Bennington Co., Inc._   Audit Date _December 31, 198X_

Names and Positions of Client Personnel Interviewed:
Lorraine Martin – Cashier; Helen Ellis – head bookkeeper; Wm. Dale – Manager

QUESTION	NOT APPL.	YES	NO	WEAKNESS MAJOR	WEAKNESS MINOR	REMARKS
1. Are all persons receiving or disbursing cash bonded?		✔				
2. Is all incoming mail opened by a responsible employee who does not have access to accounting records and is not connected with the cashier's office?			✔	✔		H. Ellis is head bookkeeper
3. Does the employee assigned to the opening of incoming mail prepare a list of all checks and money received?			✔		✔	See mitigating control in #13
4. a) Is a copy of the listing of mail receipts forwarded to the accounts receivable department for comparison with the credits to customers' accounts?	✔					
b) Is a copy of this list turned over to an employee other than the cashier for comparison with the cash receipts book?	✔					
5. Are receipts from cash sales and other over-the-counter collections recorded by sales registers, cash registers, and serially numbered receipts?	✔					
6. Are the daily totals of cash registers or other mechanical devices verified by an employee not having access to cash?	✔					
7. Are physical facilities and mechanical equipment for receiving and recording cash adequate and conducive to good control?		✔				
8. Is revenue from investments, rent, concessions, and similar sources scheduled in advance so that nonreceipt on due date would be promptly investigated?	✔					
9. Do procedures for sale of scrap materials provide for direct reporting to accounting department concurrently with transfer of receipts to cashier?	✔					
10. Are securities and other negotiable assets in the custody of someone other than the cashier?	✔					
11. Are collections by branch offices deposited daily in a bank account subject to withdrawal only by home office executives?	✔					
12. Are each day's receipts deposited intact and without delay by an employee other than the accounts receivable bookkeeper?		✔				
13. Are the duplicate deposit tickets signed by the bank teller and compared with the cash receipts record and mailroom list of receipts by an employee other than the cashier or accounts receivable bookkeeper?		✔				W. Dale Manager
14. Are the duplicate deposit tickets properly filed and available for inspection by auditors?		✔				Chronological sequence
15. Are NSF checks or other items returned by the bank delivered directly to an employee other than the cashier and promptly investigated?		✔				W. Dale Manager
16. Is the physical arrangement of offices and accounting records designed to prevent employees who handle cash from having access to accounting records?			✔		✔	Small Company doesn't permit this.

Prepared by _V. M. Harris_   Date _Sept. 6, 8X_   Manager Review _____ Date _____

Senior Review _____ Date _____   Partner Review _____ Date _____

Figure 5–4

Bennington Co., Inc.
Cash Receipts Procedures
December 31, 198X

All cash receipts are received by mail in the form of checks. Lorraine Martin, cashier, picks up the mail every morning at the post office and delivers it unopened to Helen Ellis, the head bookkeeper.

Ellis opens and distributes the mail. Customers' checks are given to Martin, who records the remittances in the cash receipts journal, prepares duplicate deposit slips, and mails the day's receipts intact to First National Bank. The bank returns the validated duplicate deposit slips by mail, and Ellis files them in chronological order. Ellis posts the accounts receivable subsidiary ledger from the cash receipts journal on a daily basis.

Any customers' checks charged back by the bank are given by Ellis to the manager, William Dale, who follows up and redeposits the checks. Ellis also forwards monthly bank statements unopened to Dale. Dale reconciles the monthly bank statement, compares the dates and amounts of deposits with the entries in the cash receipts journal, and reviews the propriety of sales discounts recorded in the cash receipts journal.

Martin, Ellis, and Dale are all bonded.

Conclusion:
Internal control over cash receipts is weak; there is no separation of cash handling and record-keeping functions.

V.M.H.
September 6, 8X

---

procedures, division of responsibilities, sources and distribution of documents, and types and location of accounting records and files. The standard symbols used in systems flowcharting are illustrated in Figure 5–5; however, the symbols used and flowcharting technique vary somewhat among different public accounting firms.

Separate systems flowcharts are prepared for each major transaction cycle. In addition, each flowchart is subdivided into vertical columns

**Figure 5–5   Widely
used flowcharting
symbols**

Check

Document—any paper document, such as a check or sales invoice.

Prepare
sales
invoice

Manual process—any manual operation, such as preparation of a sales invoice or reconciling a bank statement.

Print
purchase
order

Process—any operation, whether performed manually, mechanically, or by EDP. Often used interchangeably with the manual process symbol.

4

Offline storage—a file or other storage facility for documents or EDP records.

Flowlines—lines indicating the directional flow of documents. Normally downward or to the right unless otherwise indicated by arrowheads.

Filed
by date

Annotation—used for explanatory comments, such as filing sequence (by date, alphabetical, etc.).

A

Connector—exit to or entry from another part of the flowchart. Used to avoid excessive crossing of flowlines. Exit and entry connectors are keyed by letters or numbers.

Customer

Off-page connector—indicates source or destination of items entering or exiting the flowchart.

Received
cash
from
customer

Input/Output—used in place of an off-page connector to indicate information entering or exiting the flowchart.

No
Yes

Decision—indicates alternative courses of action resulting from a yes or no decision.

Special symbols for EDP systems

Punched card   Punched tape   Drum or disk   Magnetic
tape

representing the various departments (or employees) involved in processing the transactions. Departmental responsibility for procedures, documents, and records is shown by reviewing the related flowcharting symbol
beneath the appropriate departmental heading. Flowcharts usually begin
in the upper left-hand corner; directional flowlines then indicate the sequence of activity. The normal flow of activity is from top to bottom and
from left to right. These basic concepts of systems flowcharting are illustrated in Figure 5–6.

The special advantage of a flowchart over a questionnaire or a narrative is that a flowchart provides a clearer, more specific portrayal of the
client's system. There is less opportunity for misunderstanding, blank
spots, or ambiguous statements when one uses lines and symbols rather
than words to describe internal control. Furthermore, in each successive
annual audit, updating a flowchart is a simple process requiring only that
the auditor add or change a few lines and symbols.

A possible disadvantage of flowcharts is that internal control weaknesses are not identified as prominently as in questionnaires. A "no"
answer in an internal control questionnaire is a conspicuous red flag calling attention to a dangerous situation. A flowchart may not provide so
clear a signal that a particular internal control is absent or is not being
properly enforced. For that reason, some CPA firms use both flowcharts
and questionnaires to describe internal control. The flowchart clearly
depicts the system, while the questionnaire serves to remind the auditors
of controls that should be present in the system.

Walk-through test   After describing internal control in their working
papers, the auditors will generally verify that the system has been placed
in operation by performing a walk-through of each transaction cycle. The
term **walk-through** refers to tracing several transactions (perhaps only
one or two) through each step in the cycle. To perform a walk-through of
the sales and collection cycle, for example, the auditors might begin by
selecting several sales orders and following the related transactions
through the client's sequence of procedures. The auditors would determine whether such procedures as credit approval, shipment of merchandise, preparation of sales invoices, recording of the accounts receivable,
and processing of the customers' remittances were performed by appropriate client personnel and in the sequence indicated in the audit working
papers. If the auditors find that the system functions differently from the
working paper description, they will amend the working papers to describe the actual system.

The primary purpose of the walk-through is to *test the completeness of
the auditor's working papers,* not the reliability of the client's control
procedures. To draw valid conclusions as to the reliability of specific
accounting controls for the entire year under audit usually requires a far
larger sample than one or two transactions.

Figure 5–6

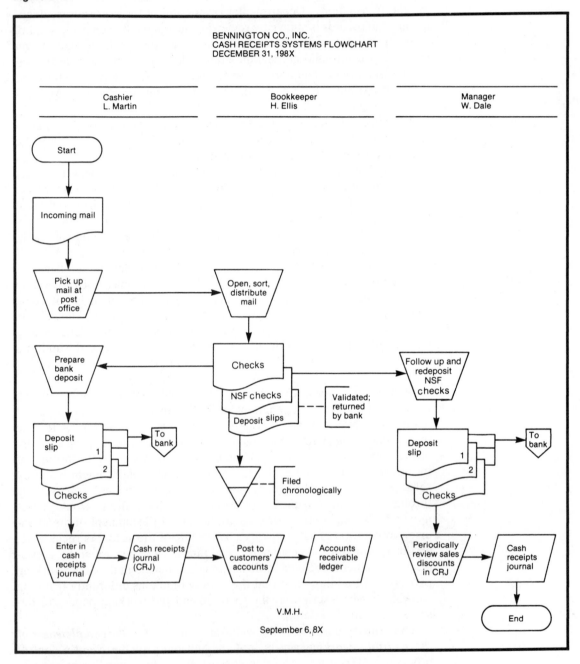

BENNINGTON CO., INC.
CASH RECEIPTS SYSTEMS FLOWCHART
DECEMBER 31, 198X

Cashier L. Martin	Bookkeeper H. Ellis	Manager W. Dale

Start

Incoming mail

Pick up mail at post office

Open, sort, distribute mail

Prepare bank deposit

Checks

NSF checks

Deposit slips

Validated; returned by bank

Follow up and redeposit NSF checks

Deposit slip 1 2

To bank

Checks

Filed chronologically

Deposit slip 1 2

To bank

Checks

Enter in cash receipts journal

Cash receipts journal (CRJ)

Post to customers' accounts

Accounts receivable ledger

Periodically review sales discounts in CRJ

Cash receipts journal

End

V.M.H.

September 6, 8X

Assess control risk and design additional tests of controls

After completing their working paper description of internal control, the auditors perform their initial assessment of control risk and design additional audit tests. The auditors' major objective at this point is to determine which internal controls, if any, merit additional testing. From a conceptual point of view this initial assessment and design of tests involves the following steps:

1. Identify the types of errors and irregularities that could occur in the client's financial statements.
2. Evaluate whether the client's controls are suitably designed to meet the control objectives of preventing such errors and irregularities.
3. Assess the control risk of the various types of errors and irregularities based on the design of the internal control structure and the results of any tests performed while obtaining an understanding of the design.
4. Identify additional controls, if any, that may be efficiently tested to reduce the assessed level of control risk of particular types of errors or irregularities.

This last consideration is highly subjective and requires both judgment and experience. The auditors would select a control for testing if reliance on the control would limit substantive testing sufficiently to justify the time required to test the control.

When auditing small businesses, the auditors may decide to stop their analysis of internal control at this point, feeling that further testing will not significantly reduce their assessment of control risk. The auditors would then use their understanding of the design of the internal control structure, and their current assessment of control risk to design the substantive tests for the audit.

To assess control risk at less than the maximum, the auditors must have evidence of the operating effectiveness of the controls; they must test the controls. While performing procedures to obtain an understanding of the design of internal controls, the auditors may have also gained some evidence that would allow them to assess control risk at less than the maximum for certain types of errors or irregularities. However, without performing additional tests of controls, the auditors would assess control risk at the maximum for the vast majority of the audit areas.

Perform additional tests of controls

Tests of controls are used by the auditors to obtain evidence about whether the tested policy or procedure operates in a manner that would prevent or detect material misstatements. That is, tests of controls are used to evaluate the effectiveness of both the design and operation of controls. Controls may be tested by (1) inquiries of appropriate client personnel, (2) inspection of documents and reports, (3) observation of the application of accounting policies or procedures, or (4) re-performance of the application of the policy or procedure by the auditors. Tests of controls focus on compliance with procedures rather than upon financial statement amounts or completed transactions. For example, assume that the client has implemented the control procedure of requiring a second person to review the quantities, prices, extensions, and footing of each sales invoice. The purpose of this control procedure is to prevent material errors in the billing of customers and the recording of sales transactions. To test the effectiveness of this control procedure, the auditors might select a sample of, say, 60 sales invoices prepared throughout the year. They would compare the quantities shown on each invoice to the quantities listed on the related shipping documents, compare unit prices to the client's price lists, and verify the extensions and footings. The results of this test provide the auditors with evidence as to whether they may rely on the dollar amounts produced by the client's billing process. If numerous errors are found in the invoices, the auditors will expand their substantive procedures of the validity of accounts receivable and sales transactions.

The control procedure described above leaves documentary evidence of compliance, allowing it to be tested by sampling. Other internal control procedures must be tested through observation by the auditors and inquiry of client personnel. Separation of duties, for example, is tested by observing the client's employees as they perform their duties, and inquiring as to who performed those duties throughout the period under audit. The auditors want to determine whether employees performed incompatible functions when other employees were absent from work on sick leave or vacation.

Reassess control risk and design substantive tests

After the auditors have carried out their tests of controls, they are in a position to perform a reassessment of control risk. Based on this final assessment, modifications are made in the auditors' substantive audit program; audit procedures are expanded in areas of maximum control risk and limited in areas in which control risk is restricted. Only after this reassessment of control risk are the auditors able to draft a complete audit program suitably tailored to the engagement.

The auditors' assessment of control risk will have identified those areas of maximum control risk and those areas where control risk is considered to be less than the maximum. The auditors will document these conclusions, as well as the basis for those assessments of control risk that are less than the maximum. These results are often summarized on a working paper that provides space for the auditors' assessment of control risk and references to the modifications in substantive procedures. A working paper used to summarize the auditors' final assessment of internal control is illustrated in Figure 5–7. Notice that the extensions and limitations of

Figure 5–7 The auditors' assessment of control risk

Denver Manufacturing Company
Assessment of Control Risk–Accounts Receivable
December 31, 198X

Potential error or irregularity	Control risk assessment	Modification of substantive tests
1. Accounts receivable may be recorded that are not valid due to inaccuracies in the recording of sales or collections.	Based on the design of internal control described on B-4-1 through B-4-7, and the results of the tests of control procedures summarized on B-7, control risk is assessed as *low*.	The extent of the sample size for confirmation of accounts receivable will be reduced to the minimum.
2. Accounts receivable may not be valued properly due to an inadequate allowance for uncollectible accounts.	Based on the design of internal control described on B-5, and the results of tests of control procedures summarized on B-5-1, control risk is assessed as *low*.	The adequacy of the allowance for uncollectible accounts will be tested solely with analytical procedures.
3. Accounts receivable may not be valid or complete due to failure to record sales in the proper accounting period.	Based on the design of internal control described on B-4-8, control risk is assessed at the *maximum*.	Tests of cut-off of sales transactions will be performed at year-end.

audit procedures are described in detail to facilitate drafting a final version of the audit program.

The auditors' consideration of internal control is very complex. Figure 5–8 is a flowchart that highlights the major steps in the auditors' consideration of internal control.

Decision aids for evaluation Modifying audit programs for strengths and weaknesses in internal control, while considering other factors such as levels of materiality and risk, involves complex judgments. How many additional items should the auditors sample to compensate for particular internal control weaknesses? Is control over a particular account strong enough to make it feasible to test the account at an interim date rather than at year-end? Without guidance from the CPA firm, different auditors within that firm might arrive at different answers to these questions. In fact, research on these types of audit judgments has revealed just that; there is a good deal of variance in auditors' program decisions.

CPA firms initially reacted to this problem by developing firm policies that put limits on individual auditor's decisions. The establishment of minimum audit sample sizes for particular types of tests is an example of such a policy. More recently, CPA firms have attempted to add even more

**Figure 5–8 The
auditors' consideration
of internal control**

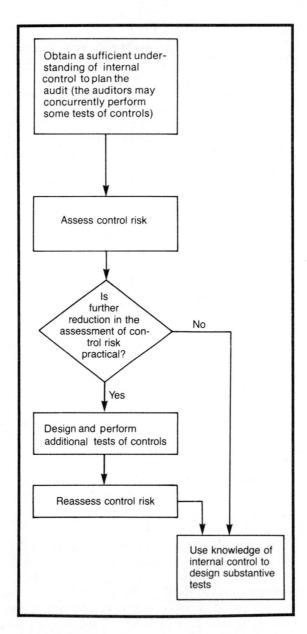

structure to auditors' program decisions through the use of decision aids
or guides. A ***decision aid*** is a checklist or standard form that helps the
auditors make a particular decision by ensuring that they consider all
relevant information or assisting them in combining the information to
make the decision. By reducing the variance in auditors' program judgments, decision aids promote the performance of audits that meet firm
and professional requirements.

Reliance on the work of internal auditors Many of the audit procedures performed by internal auditors are similar in nature to those employed by independent auditors. This raises the question of whether the independent auditors may rely on the work already performed by the internal auditors. The AICPA has addressed this issue in *SAS 9* (AU 322), "The Effect of an Internal Audit Function on the Scope of the Independent Auditor's Examination."

The position taken in *SAS 9* is that the work of internal auditors cannot be substituted for the work of independent auditors. However, the independent auditors should consider the existence and quality of an internal audit function in their assessment of the client's internal control structure. Through its contribution to internal control, the work of the internal auditors may reduce the amount of substantive testing performed by the independent auditors. In assessing the contribution of the internal audit function to internal control, the independent auditors should consider the *competence* and *objectivity* of the internal audit staff and *evaluate its work.*

In evaluating the objectivity of the internal auditors, the auditors consider the level in the organization to which the internal auditors report and compare the content of selected reports to related audit findings. Competence is evaluated by examining a sample of the work of the internal audit staff, considering such factors as the scope and quality of its audit procedures, the extent of the documentation in its working papers, and the appropriateness of its conclusions. In addition, the independent auditors should test specific transactions and compare their results with those obtained by the internal auditors. Upon completion of this investigation, the independent auditors have a sound basis for determining the extent to which they may limit their audit procedures in reliance upon the internal auditors' contribution to internal control.

To reduce the time and cost of an audit, the internal auditors may provide direct assistance to the CPAs in preparing working papers and performing certain audit procedures. The CPAs, however, should supervise and test any audit work done for them by the internal auditors. Also, the judgments regarding matters to be investigated, the effectiveness of internal control, and the fairness of the financial statements must be those of the independent auditors.

Communication of control structure related matters

Deficiencies in internal control brought to light by the auditors' assessment of the system should be communicated to the client, along with the auditors' recommendations for corrective action. *SAS 60* (AU XXX), "The Communication of Internal Control Structure Related Matters Noted in an Audit," uses the term *reportable conditions* to refer to those matters that must be communicated by the auditors to the audit committee of the board of directors (or an individual or group with equivalent responsibility if no audit committee exists). A *reportable condition* is a significant deficiency in the design or functioning of the internal control that could adversely affect the organization's ability to record, process, summarize, and report financial data. Reportable conditions may be communicated orally, but they are usually set forth in a letter, such as shown in Figure 5–9.

Figure 5–9 Report to audit committee

Wilson & Quinn
Certified Public Accountants
1134 California St.
San Diego, California 92110

March 12, 19X2

Audit Committee of the Board of Directors
Fleet Feet Shoe Stores, Inc.
2567 University Blvd.
San Diego, California 92105

Gentlemen:

In planning and performing our audit of the financial statements of the Fleet Feet Shoe Stores, Inc. for the year ended December 31, 19X1, we considered its internal control structure in order to determine our auditing procedures for the purpose of expressing our opinion on the financial statements and not to provide assurance on the internal control structure. However, we noted a matter involving the internal control structure and its operation that we consider to be a reportable condition under standards established by the American Institute of Certified Public Accountants. Reportable conditions involve matters coming to our attention relating to significant deficiencies in the design or operation of the internal control structure that, in our judgment, could adversely affect the organization's ability to record, process, summarize, and report financial data consistent with the assertions of management in the financial statements.

Our audit revealed that personnel at individual stores fail to prepare receiving reports for shipments of goods directly from wholesalers. This weakness increases the chance that the company will pay for merchandise that has not been received. We recommend that prenumbered receiving reports be prepared upon receipt of these shipments.

This report is intended solely for the information and use of the audit committee, management, and others in the organization.

Sincerely,

James Wilson

Wilson & Quinn, CPAs

A reportable condition may be so significant as to be considered a *material weakness in internal control;* that is, a condition that results in a higher than acceptable risk of material misstatement of the financial statements. Clients may also request the auditors to identify in their communication on internal control those *reportable conditions* that are considered to be *material weaknesses in internal control.*

Auditors often communicate both reportable conditions and lesser weaknesses in greater detail to management in a report called a *management letter.* This report serves as a valuable reference document for management and may also serve to minimize the auditors' legal liability in the event of a major defalcation or other loss resulting from a weakness in internal control. Many auditing firms place great emphasis upon providing clients with a thorough and well-planned management letter. These firms recognize that such a report can be a valuable and constructive contribution to the efficiency of the client's operations. The quality of the auditors' recommendations reflects their professional expertise and creative ability and the thoroughness of their investigation.

Internal control in the small company

The preceding discussion of internal control and its assessment by the independent auditors has been presented in terms of large corporations. In the large concern, excellent internal control may be achieved by extensive subdivision of duties, so that no one person handles a transaction completely from beginning to end. In the very small concern, however, with only one or two office employees, there is little or no opportunity for division of duties and responsibilities. Consequently, internal control tends to be weak, if not completely absent, unless the owner/manager recognizes the importance of internal control and participates in key activities.

Because of the absence of strong internal control in small concerns, the independent auditors must make a much more detailed examination of accounts, journal entries, and supporting documents than is required in larger organizations. Although it is well to recognize that internal control can seldom be strong in a small business, this limitation is no justification for ignoring available forms of control. Auditors can make a valuable contribution to small client companies by encouraging the installation of such control procedures as are practicable in the circumstances. The following specific practices are almost always capable of use in even the smallest business:

1. Record all cash receipts immediately.
   a. For over-the-counter collections, use cash registers easily visible to customers. Record register readings daily.
   b. Prepare a list of all mail remittances immediately upon opening the mail and retain this list for subsequent comparison with bank deposit tickets and entries in the cash receipts journal.

2. Deposit all cash receipts intact daily.
3. Make all payments by serially numbered checks, with the exception of small disbursements from petty cash.
4. Reconcile bank accounts monthly and retain copies of the reconciliations in the files.
5. Use serially numbered sales invoices, purchase orders, and receiving reports.
6. Issue checks to vendors only in payment of approved invoices that have been matched with purchase orders and receiving reports.
7. Balance subsidiary ledgers with control accounts at regular intervals, and prepare and mail customers' statements monthly.
8. Prepare comparative financial statements monthly in sufficient detail to disclose significant variations in any category of revenue or expense.

Adherence to these basic control practices significantly reduces the risk of material errors or major defalcation going undetected. If the size of the business permits a segregation of the duties of cash handling and record keeping, a fair degree of control can be achieved. If it is necessary that one employee serve as both accounting clerk and cashier, then active participation by the owner in certain key functions is necessary to guard against the concealment of fraud or errors. In a few minutes each day the owner, even though not trained in accounting, can create a significant amount of internal control by personally (1) reading daily cash register totals, (2) reconciling the bank account monthly, (3) signing all checks and canceling the supporting documents, (4) approving all general journal entries, and (5) critically reviewing comparative monthly statements of revenue and expense.

KEY TERMS INTRODUCED OR EMPHASIZED IN CHAPTER 5

Accounting controls   Internal controls of a nature that can directly affect the reliability of the accounting records and financial statements.

Administrative controls   Internal controls designed to promote operational efficiency in sales, production, and other nonfinancial areas, but having no direct bearing upon the reliability of accounting data.

Audit decision aids   Standard checklists or forms that assist auditors in making audit decisions by ensuring that they consider all relevant information, or aiding them in weighting and combining the information to make a decision.

Control risk   The possibility that a material error or irregularity will occur and not be prevented or detected by the client's internal control.

Fidelity bonds   A form of insurance in which a bonding company agrees to reimburse an employer for losses attributable to theft or embezzlement by bonded employees.

Foreign Corrupt Practices Act   Federal legislation prohibiting payments to foreign officials for the purpose of securing business. The act also requires all companies under SEC jurisdiction to maintain a system of internal accounting control providing reasonable assurance that transactions are executed only with the knowledge and authorization of management.

Incompatible duties   Assigned duties that put an individual in a position to both perpetrate and conceal errors or irregularities in the normal course of job performance.

Internal auditors   Corporation employees who design and execute audit programs to test the efficiency of all aspects of internal control. The primary objective of internal auditors is to evaluate and improve the efficiency of the various operating units of an organization rather than to express an opinion as to the fairness of financial statements.

Internal control questionnaire   One of several alternative methods of describing an internal control structure in audit working papers. Questionnaires are usually designed so that "no" answers prominently identify weaknesses in internal control.

Internal control structure (system)   An organization's policies and procedures that have been established to provide reasonable assurance that its related objectives will be achieved. An internal control structure is composed of the overall control environment, the accounting system, and control procedures.

Management letter   A report to management containing the auditors' recommendations for correcting any deficiencies disclosed by the auditors' consideration of internal control. In addition to providing management with useful information, a management letter may also help limit the auditors' liability in the event a control weakness subsequently results in a loss by the client.

Material weakness in internal control   A reportable condition (see definition) in which the control system design or the degree of compliance do not reduce to a relatively low level the risk that *material* errors or irregularities might occur and not be detected.

Operational audit   A review of a department or other unit of a business to evaluate the efficiency of operations.

Organization plan   The division of authority, responsibility, and duties among members of an organization.

Reportable condition   A matter coming to the auditors' attention that represents a significant deficiency in the design or functioning of the control structure, that could adversely affect the organization's ability to record, process, summarize, and properly report financial data.

Systems flowcharts   A symbolic representation of a system or series of procedures with each procedure shown in sequence. Systems flowcharts are a widely used method of describing a system of internal control in audit working papers.

Tests of controls   Tests directed toward the design or operation of an internal control structure policy or procedure to assess its effectiveness in preventing or detecting material misstatements of the financial statements.

Transaction cycle   The sequence of procedures applied by the client in processing a particular type of recurring transaction. The auditors' working paper description of internal control is organized around the client's major transaction cycles.

Walk-through of the system   A test of the accuracy and completeness of the auditors' working paper description of internal control. A walk-through is performed by tracing several transactions through each step of the related transaction cycle, noting whether the sequence of procedures actually performed corresponds to that described in the audit working papers.

Written narrative of internal control   A written summary of internal control for inclusion in audit working papers. Written narratives are more flexible than questionnaires, but are practical only for describing relatively small, simple systems.

GROUP I: REVIEW QUESTIONS

5–1.   What is the basic purpose of an internal control structure? What measures comprise the structure?

5–2.   Identify the three elements of an organization's internal control structure.

5–3.   List the factors that make up an organization's control environment.

5–4.   How does separation of the record-keeping function from custody of assets contribute to internal control?

5–5.   The owner of a medium-size corporation asks you to state two or three principles to be followed in dividing responsibilities among employees in a manner that will produce strong internal control.

5–6.   One basic concept of internal control is that no one employee should handle all aspects of a transaction. Assuming that a general category of transactions has been authorized by top management, how many employees (or departments) should participate in each transaction, as a minimum, to achieve strong internal control? Explain in general terms the function of each of these employees.

5–7.   Compare the objectives of the internal auditor with those of the independent auditor.

5–8.   How do the objectives of an operational audit differ from those of a financial audit?

5–9.   What reliance, if any, may independent auditors place upon the work of a client's internal audit staff?

5–10. What are the purposes of the consideration of internal control required by generally accepted auditing standards?

5–11. A prospective client informs you that all officers and employees of the company are bonded, and he requests that under these circumstances you forgo an assessment of internal control in order to reduce the cost of an audit. Construct a logical reply to this request.

5–12. Suggest a number of sources from which you might obtain the information needed to prepare a description of internal control in the audit working papers.

5–13. Distinguish between a walk-through test of a transaction cycle and a test of a control procedure.

5–14. Under what circumstances are tests of controls *efficient* audit procedures?

5–15. "All experienced auditors would design exactly the same audit program for a particular audit engagement." Do you agree? Explain.

5–16. What is a management letter? What is the letter's significance?

5–17. In view of the reliance the auditor places upon internal control, how do you account for the fact that the auditors' standard report makes no reference to internal control in describing the scope of the examination?

5–18. Name three factors you consider of greatest importance in protecting a business against losses through embezzlement.

5–19. You have discussed with the president of Vista Corporation several material weaknesses in internal control that have come to your attention during your audit. At the conclusion of this discussion, the president states that he will personally take steps to remedy these problems and that there is no reason for you to bring these matters to the attention of the board of directors. He explains that he believes the board should deal with major policy decisions and not be burdened with day-to-day management problems. How would you respond to this suggestion? Explain fully.

GROUP II: QUESTIONS REQUIRING ANALYSIS

5–20. The consideration of internal control is integral to financial statement audits.

Required:
a. For what two primary reasons do auditors consider internal control?
b. How is the auditors' understanding of the client's internal control structure documented in the audit working papers?
c. In what circumstances do auditors perform tests of control procedures?

5–21. The auditors' consideration of internal control begins with obtaining an understanding of the internal control structure.
a. Describe the remaining stages of the auditors' consideration.
b. Provide examples of audit procedures that are performed at each stage (including the stage of obtaining an understanding).

5–22. Henry Bailey, CPA, is planning the audit of The Neighborhood Store, a local grocery cooperative. Because The Neighborhood Store is a small business operated entirely by part-time volunteer personnel, internal controls are weak. Bailey has decided that he will not be able to rely on internal control to restrict audit procedures in any area. Under these circumstances, may Bailey omit the consideration of the internal control structure in this engagement?

5–23. Adherence to generally accepted auditing standards requires, among other things, a proper understanding of the existing internal control. The most common approaches to documenting the understanding of the system of internal control include the use of a questionnaire, preparation of a written narrative, preparation of a flowchart, and combinations of these methods.

Required:
a. Discuss the advantages to CPAs of documenting internal control by using:
(1) An internal control questionnaire.
(2) A written narrative.
(3) A flowchart.
b. If they are satisfied after completing their description of internal con-

trol that no material weaknesses exist in the system, is it necessary for the CPAs to conduct tests of controls? Explain.

(AICPA, adapted)

5–24. The process of gathering evidential matter to support an opinion on a client's financial statements involves several types of testing procedures. In the course of the examination, auditors perform detailed tests of samples of transactions from large-volume populations. Auditors may also audit various types of transactions by tracing a few transactions of each type through all stages of the accounting system.

Required:
What are the audit objectives associated with—
a. A sample of transactions from a large-volume population?
b. Tracing a few transactions of each type through all stages of the accounting system? (AICPA, adapted)

5–25. During your first examination of a manufacturing company with approximately 100 production employees, you find that all aspects of factory payroll are handled by one employee and that none of the usual internal controls over payroll is observed. What action will you take?

5–26. During your first examination of a medium-size manufacturing company, the owner, John Bell, explains that in order to establish clear-cut lines of responsibility for various aspects of the business, he has made one employee responsible for the purchasing, receiving, and storing of merchandise. A second employee has full responsibility for maintenance of accounts receivable records and collections from customers. A third employee is responsible for personnel records, timekeeping, preparation of payrolls, and distribution of payroll checks. Bell asks your opinion concerning this plan of organization. Explain fully the reasons supporting your opinion.

5–27. Internal auditing is a staff function found in virtually every large corporation. The internal audit function is also performed in many smaller companies as a part-time activity of individuals who may or may not be called internal auditors. The differences between the audits by independent auditors and the work of internal auditors are more basic than is generally recognized.

Required:
a. Briefly discuss the auditing work performed by the independent public accountant and the internal auditor with regard to—
   (1) Auditing objectives.
   (2) General nature of auditing work.
b. In conducting their audit, the independent auditors must evaluate the work of the internal auditors. Discuss briefly the reason for this evaluation.

5–28. Select the best answer for each of the following questions. Explain the reason for your selection.
a. Which of the following would be least likely to be considered an objective of internal control?
   (1) Checking the accuracy and reliability of accounting data.
   (2) Detecting management fraud.

    (3) Encouraging adherence to managerial policies.

    (4) Safeguarding assets.

b. Which of the following symbolic representations indicate that a file has been consulted?

    (1)

    (2)

    (3)

    (4)

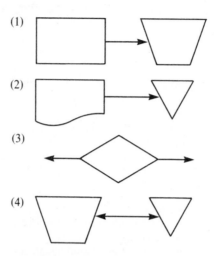

c. When an independent auditor decides that the work performed by internal auditors may have a bearing on the nature, timing, and extent of the independent auditor's procedures, the independent auditor should evaluate the competence and objectivity of the internal auditors. Relative to objectivity, the independent auditor should—

    (1) Consider the organizational level to which the internal auditors report the results of their work.

    (2) Test the internal auditors' work.

    (3) Consider the qualifications of the internal audit staff.

    (4) Review the training program in effect for the internal audit staff.

d. Effective internal control in a small company that has an insufficient number of employees to permit proper subdivision of responsibilities can best be enhanced by—

    (1) Employment of temporary personnel to aid in the separation of duties.

    (2) Direct participation by the owner in key record keeping and control activities of the business.

    (3) Engaging a CPA to perform monthly write-up work.

    (4) Delegation to each employee of full, clear-cut responsibility for a separate major transaction cycle.

e. Of the following statements about internal control, which one is *not* valid?

    (1) No one person should be responsible for the custodial responsibility and the recording responsibility for an asset.

    (2) Transactions must be properly authorized before such transactions are processed.

    (3) Because of the cost/benefit relationship, a client may apply control procedures on a test basis.

(4) Control procedures reasonably ensure that collusion among employees *cannot* occur.

 f. Proper segregation of functional responsibilities calls for separation of the

 (1) Authorization, recording, and custodial functions.
 (2) Authorization, execution, and payment functions.
 (3) Receiving, shipping, and custodial functions.
 (4) Authorization, approval, and execution functions.

GROUP III: PROBLEMS

5–29. At the Main Street Theatre the cashier, located in a box office at the entrance, receives cash from customers and operates a machine that ejects serially numbered tickets. To gain admission to the theater a customer hands the ticket to a door attendant stationed some 50 feet from the box office at the entrance to the theater lobby. The attendant tears the ticket in half, opens the door for the customer, and returns the stub to the customer. The other half of the ticket is dropped by the door attendant into a locked box.

Required:
 a. What internal controls are present in this phase of handling cash receipts?
 b. What steps should be taken regularly by the manager or other supervisor to give maximum effectiveness to these controls?
 c. Assume that the cashier and the door attendant decided to collaborate in an effort to abstract cash receipts. What action might they take?
 d. Continuing the assumption made in (c) of collusion between the cashier and the door attendant, what features of the control procedures would be likely to disclose the embezzlement?

5–30. Orange Corp., a high technology company, utilizes the following procedures for recording raw materials and transferring them to work in process.
 1. Upon receipt of raw materials by stores, the storeskeeper prepares a stock-in report with part number and quantities, files the original by date, and sends a copy to accounting.
 2. The inventory accounting clerk uses the stock-in report to post the perpetual inventory records using standard costs, and files the stock-in report by date.
 3. Raw materials requisitions, which show part number and quantity, are prepared by the manufacturing clerk and approved by the supervisor of manufacturing. A copy of the requisition is sent to accounting, and the original is filed by job order.
 4. The inventory accounting clerk reviews the requisitions for completeness, transfers the cost from raw materials to work in process, and files the requisitions by date.

Required:
Prepare a flowchart which describes the client's system of recording raw materials and transferring them to work in process.　　(CIA, adapted)

5–31. Island Trading Co., a client of your CPA firm, has requested your advice on the following problem. It has three clerical employees who must perform the following functions:

(1) Maintain general ledger.
(2) Maintain accounts payable ledger.
(3) Maintain accounts receivable ledger.
(4) Maintain cash disbursements journal and prepare checks for signature.
(5) Issue credit memos on sales returns and allowances.
(6) Reconcile the bank account.
(7) Handle and deposit cash receipts.

Required:

Assuming that there is no problem as to the ability of any of the employees, the company requests your advice on assigning the above functions to the three employees in such a manner as to achieve the highest degree of internal control. It may be assumed that these employees will perform no other accounting functions than the ones listed and that any accounting functions not listed will be performed by persons other than these three employees.

a. List four possible unsatisfactory combinations of the above-listed functions.

b. State how you would recommend distributing the above functions among the three employees. Assume that, with the exception of the nominal jobs of the bank reconciliation and the issuance of credits on returns and allowances, all functions require an equal amount of time.

(AICPA, adapted)

5–32. You have been asked by the board of trustees of a local church to review its accounting procedures. As part of this review you have prepared the following comments relating to the collections made at weekly services and record keeping for members' pledges and contributions:

(1) The church's board of trustees has delegated responsibility for financial management and internal audit of the financial records to the finance committee. This group prepares the annual forecast and approves major disbursements, but is not involved in collections or record keeping. No internal or independent audit has been considered necessary in recent years because the same trusted employee has kept church records and served as financial secretary for 15 years.

(2) The offering at the weekly service is taken by a team of ushers. The head usher counts the offering in the church office following each service. He then places the offering and a notation of the amount counted in the church safe. The next morning the financial secretary opens the safe and recounts the offering. He withholds about $100 to meet cash expenditures during the coming week and deposits the remainder of the offering intact. In order to facilitate the deposit, members who contribute by check are asked to draw their checks to cash.

(3) At their request a few members are furnished prenumbered, predated envelopes in which to insert their weekly contributions. The head usher removes the cash from the envelopes to be counted with the loose cash included in the offering and discards the envelopes. No record is maintained of issuance or return of the envelopes, and the envelope system is not encouraged.

(4) Each member is asked to prepare a contribution pledge card annually. The pledge is regarded as a moral commitment by the member to contribute a stated weekly amount. Based upon the amounts shown on the pledge cards, the financial secretary furnishes a letter to requesting members to support the tax deductibility of their contributions.

Required:
Describe the weaknesses and recommend improvements in procedures for—
a. Offerings given at weekly services.
b. Record keeping for members' pledges and contributions.
Organize your answer sheets as follows:

Weakness	Recommended improvement

(AICPA)

5–33. Prospect Corporation, your new audit client, processes its sales and cash receipts in the following manner:

1. Sales. Salesclerks prepare sales invoices in triplicate. The original and second copy are presented to the cashier, and the third copy is retained by the salesclerk in the sales book. When the sale is for cash, the customer pays the salesclerk, who presents the money to the cashier with the invoice copies.

A credit sale is approved by the cashier from an approved credit list. After receiving the cash or approving the invoice, the cashier validates the original copy of the sales invoice and gives it to the customer. At the end of each day the cashier recaps the sales and cash received, files the recap by date, and forwards the cash and the second copy of all sales invoices to the accounts receivable clerk.

The accounts receivable clerk balances the cash received with cash sales invoices and prepares a daily sales summary. Cash sales are posted by the accounts receivable clerk to the cash receipts journal, and the daily sales summary is filed by date. Cash from cash sales is included in the daily bank deposit (preparation of the bank deposit is described with cash receipts in the following section). The accounts receivable clerk posts credit sales invoices to the accounts receivable ledger and then sends all invoices to the inventory control clerk in the sales department.

The inventory clerk posts to the inventory control cards and files the sales invoices numerically.

2. Cash receipts. The mail is opened each morning by a mail clerk in the sales department. The mail clerk prepares a remittance advice (showing customer and amount paid) for each check and forwards the checks and remittance advices to the sales department supervisor. The supervisor reviews the remittance advices and forwards the checks and advices to the accounting department supervisor.

The accounting department supervisor, who also functions as credit manager in approving new credit and all credit limits, reviews all checks for payments on past-due accounts and then gives the checks and remittance advices to the accounts receivable clerk, who arranges the advices in alphabetical order. The remittance advices are posted directly to the accounts receivable ledger cards. The checks are endorsed by stamp and totaled. The total is posted to the cash receipts journal. The remittance advices are filed chronologically.

After receiving the cash from the previous day's cash sales from the cashier, the accounts receivable clerk prepares the daily deposit slip in triplicate. The original and second copy of the deposit slip accompany the bank deposit, and the third copy is filed by date. The bank deposit is sent directly to National Bank.

Required:
a. Prepare a systems flowchart of internal control over sales transactions as described in part 1 above.
b. Prepare a systems flowchart of internal control over cash receipts as described in part 2 above.

**GROUP IV:
RESEARCH AND
DISCUSSION CASE**

5–34. You are performing your first audit of Merit Drug Supply Company, a small company that is owned and managed by William Hicks. Merit employs only two other office workers, Tom Howe, the bookkeeper, and Glenda Monroe, the receptionist-secretary.

In your review of internal control over cash receipts, you ascertain that all cash receipts are received and deposited by Hicks. He prepares a list of the details of the receipts that is used by Howe to post the accounts receivable records. Neither Hicks nor Howe have any other incompatible duties in processing cash. You feel that this separation of responsibilities of custody of cash from record keeping is good, but you are uneasy about relying on controls applied by an owner/manager.

Required:
a. Present arguments for relying on the owner/manager control.
b. Present arguments against relying on the owner/manager control.
c. Express your own opinion, referring back to points from (a) or (b) that support your opinion.

Suggested references:
AICPA, *Statement on Auditing Standards No. 55,* "Consideration of the Internal Control Structure in a Financial Statement Audit," AU 321.

AICPA, *Professional Standards, Volume A,* Commerce Clearing House, *Statement on Auditing Standards No. 53,* "The Independent Auditor's Responsibility to Detect and Report Errors and Irregularities," AU 316.

Rayburn, D. D., *Auditing Research Monograph, No. 5,* "Audit Problems Encountered in Small Business Engagements" (New York: AICPA, 1982), pp. 77–81.

Internal control over EDP activities

Chapter 6 study objectives

After studying this chapter, you should be able to:

— Identify the characteristics of an EDP system that differ from a manual system.
— Distinguish between general controls and application controls in an EDP system.
— Describe the major types of general controls.
— Describe the major types of application controls.
— Discuss the nature of the controls over minicomputer systems.
— Discuss the characteristics and implications of advanced computer systems.
— Explain the manner in which the auditors obtain an understanding of internal control in an EDP environment.
— Describe the nature of generalized audit software programs and the ways that they are used by the auditors.

The rapid growth of electronic data processing (EDP) for business use is having a greater impact on public accounting than perhaps any other event in the history of the profession. No longer is the challenge of auditing EDP activities limited to a few large clients. With the advent of inexpensive minicomputer systems, even the smallest audit clients are likely to use a computer for many accounting functions. Thus, auditors must be prepared to work in an ever-changing environment in which the client's accounting records are maintained on anything from a personal computer to a multimillion dollar mainframe system.

Although the computer has created some challenging problems for professional accountants, it has also broadened their horizons and expanded the range and value of the services they offer. The computer is more than a tool for performing routine accounting tasks with unprecedented speed and accuracy. It makes possible the development of information that could not have been gathered in the past because of time and cost limitations. When a client maintains accounting records with a complex and sophisticated EDP system, auditors often find it helpful, and even necessary, to utilize the computer in performing many auditing procedures.

This chapter will consider some of the most significant ways in which auditing work is being affected by EDP, but it cannot impart extensive knowledge of technical computer skills. Independent auditors will find additional familiarity with the computer, including technical skills such as programming, to be of ever-increasing value in the accounting profession.

Nature of an electronic data processing system

Before considering the impact of electronic data processing systems on the work of the independent certified public accountant, some understanding of the nature of a computer and its capabilities is needed. A business EDP system usually consists of a digital computer and peripheral equipment known as *hardware* and equally essential *software,* consisting of various programs and routines for operating a computer.

Hardware   The principal hardware component of a digital computer is the *central processing unit* (CPU). The CPU consists of a *control unit,* which processes a program of instructions for manipulating data; a *storage unit* for storing the program of instructions and the data to be manipulated; and an *arithmetic unit* capable of addition, subtraction, multiplication, division, and comparison of data at speeds measured in *microseconds, nanoseconds,* or even *picoseconds.*

Peripheral to the central processing unit are devices for recording input and devices for auxiliary storage, output, and communications. Peripheral devices in direct communication with the CPU are said to be *online,* in contrast to *offline* equipment not in direct communication with the CPU.

A first step in electronic data processing is to convert the data to machine-sensible form. This is the role of recording and input devices, such as card readers, optical scanners, electronic cash registers, and intelligent terminals. Each of these devices either records data in some medium for later reading into the storage unit or communicates data direct to the CPU.

Secondary storage devices are utilized to augment the capacity of the storage unit of the CPU. Examples of secondary storage devices are magnetic tape, magnetic drums, and magnetic disk packs. Magnetic drums and disk packs have the advantage of *direct access,* which allows for faster location and retrieval of data. Data on magnetic tapes must be stored sequentially and is retrieved by a systematic search.

Digital computer circuitry has two states in that any given circuit may be "on" or "off." By using an internal code, or machine language, capable of representing with two symbols any kind of data, all data may be expressed internally by the computer by a combination of on and off circuits. An example of a machine language is the *binary* number system.

Machines must also be used to translate the output of the computer back into a recognizable code or language. Output equipment includes printers and display terminals.

Software   Computer systems use two major types of software: *system software* and *application software.* System software consists of programs that control and coordinate hardware components and provide other support to application software. Important components of system software are utility programs for recurring tasks of data processing, such as sorting, sequencing, and merging of data. The system software known as the *operating system* is important to the control of computer operations because it may be programmed to control access to programs and stored data and to maintain a log of all system activities.

Programs designed to perform a specific data processing task, such as payroll processing, are known as application software. Early application programs were laboriously written in machine language, but today, programming languages such as COBOL (common business-oriented language) are much like English. Programming in COBOL and other *source languages* is made possible by another element of software, the *compiler,* which is a computer program utilized in translating a *source-language program* into machine language. The machine-language version of a program is called an *object program.*

In some ways, computer systems enhance the reliability of financial information. Computers process transactions uniformly and eliminate the human errors that may occur in a manual system. On the other hand, defects in hardware or programs can result in a computer processing all transactions incorrectly. Also, errors or irregularities that do occur in computer processing may not be detected by the client's personnel because few people are involved with data processing. Thus, computer hardware precision does not assure that computer output will be reliable.

Auditors have the same responsibility in an EDP system as in a manual system, which is to satisfy themselves that the financial statements produced reflect the interpretation and processing of transactions in conformity with generally accepted accounting principles.

INTERNAL CONTROL IN THE ELECTRONIC DATA PROCESSING SYSTEM

The discussion of internal control in Chapter 5 stressed the need for a proper division of duties among employees operating a manual accounting system. In such a system, no one employee has complete responsibility for a transaction, and the work of one person is verified by the work of another handling other aspects of the same transaction. The division of duties gives assurance of accuracy in records and reports and protects the company against loss from fraud or carelessness.

When a company converts to an EDP system, however, the work formerly divided among many people is performed by the computer. Consolidation of activities and integration of functions are to be expected, since the computer can conveniently handle many related aspects of a transaction. For example, when payroll is handled by a computer, it is possible to carry out a variety of related tasks with only a single use of the master records. These tasks could include the maintenance of personnel files with information on seniority, rate of pay, insurance, and the like; a portion of the timekeeping function; distribution of labor costs; and preparation of payroll checks and payroll records.

Despite the integration of several functions in an EDP system, the importance of internal control is not in the least diminished. The essential factors described in Chapter 5 for satisfactory internal control in a large-scale organization are still relevant. Separation of duties and clearly defined responsibilities continue to be key ingredients despite the change in organization of activities. These traditional control concepts are augmented, however, by controls written into the computer programs and controls built into the computer hardware.

In auditing literature, internal controls over EDP activities often are classified as either *general controls* or *application controls.* General controls relate to all EDP applications and include such considerations as: (*a*) the organization of the EDP department; (*b*) procedures for documenting, testing, and approving the original system and any subsequent changes; (*c*) controls built into the hardware (equipment controls); and (*d*) security for files and equipment. Application controls, on the other hand, relate to specific accounting tasks performed by EDP, such as the preparation of payrolls. Controls of this nature include measures designed to assure the reliability of input, controls over processing, and controls over output.

Organizational controls in an electronic data processing system

Because of the ability of the computer to process data efficiently, there is a tendency to combine many data processing functions in an EDP department. In a manual or mechanical system, these combinations of functions may be considered incompatible from a standpoint of achieving strong internal control. For example, the function of recording cash disbursements is incompatible with the responsibility for reconciling bank statements. Since one of these procedures serves as a check upon the other, assigning both functions to one employee would enable the employee to conceal his own errors. A properly programmed computer, however, has no tendency or motivation to conceal its errors. Therefore, what appears to be an incompatible combination of functions may be combined in an EDP department without weakening internal control.

When apparently incompatible functions are combined in the EDP department, compensating controls are necessary to prevent improper human intervention with computer processing. A person with the opportunity to make unauthorized changes in computer programs or data files is in a position to exploit the concentration of data processing functions in the EDP department. For example, a computer program used to process accounts payable may be designed to approve a vendor's invoice for payment only when that invoice is supported by a purchase order and receiving report. An employee able to make unauthorized changes in that program could cause unsubstantiated payments to be made to specific vendors.

EDP programs and data files cannot be changed without the use of EDP equipment. With EDP equipment, however, they can be changed without leaving any visible evidence of the alteration. Thus, the organization plan of an EDP department should prevent EDP personnel from having unauthorized access to EDP equipment, programs, or data files. This is accomplished by providing definite lines of authority and responsibility, segregation of functions, and clear definition of duties for each employee in the department. The organizational structure of a well-staffed EDP department, as illustrated in Figure 6–1, should include the following separation of responsibilities:

Figure 6–1   Organization of EDP department

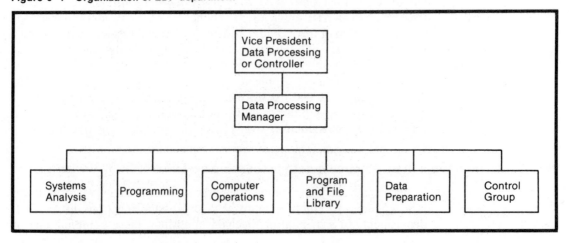

Data processing management A manager should be appointed to supervise the operation of the data processing department. The data processing manager should report to an officer who does authorize transactions for computer processing, perhaps to a vice president of data processing. When EDP is a section within the accounting department, the controller should not have direct contact with computer operations.

Systems analysis Systems analysts are responsible for designing the EDP system. After considering the objectives of the business and the data processing needs of the various departments using the computer output (*user groups*), they determine the goals of the system and the means of achieving these goals. Utilizing system flowcharts and detailed instructions, they outline the data processing system.

Programming Guided by the specifications provided by the systems analysts, the programmers design program flowcharts for computer programs required by the system. They then code the required programs in computer language, generally making use of specialized programming languages, such as COBOL, and software elements, such as assemblers, compilers, and utility programs. They test the programs with *test data* composed of genuine or dummy records and transactions and perform the necessary debugging. Finally, the programmers prepare necessary documentation, such as the computer operator instructions.

Computer operations The computer operators manipulate the computer in accordance with the instructions developed by the programmers. On occasion, the computer operators may have to intervene through the computer console during a run in order to correct an indicated error. The computer's operating system should be programmed to maintain a detailed log of all operator intervention. The separation of computer operations from programming is an important one from the standpoint of achieving internal control. An employee performing both functions would have an opportunity to make unauthorized changes in computer programs.

Program and file library The purpose of the file library is to protect computer programs, master files, transaction (detail) tapes, and other records from loss, damage, and unauthorized use or alteration. To assure adequate control, the librarian maintains a formal checkout system for making records available to authorized users.

In many systems, the library function is performed by the computer. The computer operators use special code numbers or passwords to gain access to programs and files stored within the system. The computer automatically maintains a log showing when these programs and files are used.

Data preparation   Personnel involved with this function prepare and verify input data for processing. A keypunch operation is a traditional example of a data preparation department. Keypunching is primarily associated with *batch processing* systems, in which a group (batch) of transactions is processed at one time. In an *online, real-time system,* data may be entered directly into the computer by user groups through remote *terminals* and computer files are immediately updated to reflect the new data. Even in the most sophisticated systems, however, many applications are still handled by batch processing of transactions entered directly by the user groups.

Control group   The control group of a data processing department reviews and tests all input procedures, monitors computer processing, handles the reprocessing of errors detected by the computer, and reviews and distributes all computer output. This group also reviews the computer log of operator interventions and the library log of program usage. In smaller organizations, control group functions may be performed by the user groups.

Besides segregation of functions, the data processing organization plan should provide for rotation of programmer assignments, rotation of operator assignments, mandatory vacations, and adequate fidelity bonds for EDP employees. At least two of the qualified data processing personnel should be present whenever the computer facility is in use. Careful screening procedures in the hiring of EDP personnel are also important in achieving strong internal control.

Organizational controls and computer-centered fraud

The history of computer-centered fraud shows that the persons responsible for frauds in many situations set up the system and control its use as programmer and operator.

Illustrative case

A programmer for a large bank wrote a program for identifying and listing all overdrawn accounts. Later, as operator of the bank's computer, he was able to insert a "patch" in the program to cause the computer to ignore overdrafts in his own account. The programmer-operator was then able to overdraw his bank account at will, without the overdraft coming to management's attention. The fraud was not discovered until the computer broke down and the listing of overdrawn accounts had to be prepared manually.

The number of personnel and the organizational structure will of course determine the extent to which segregation of duties is possible. As a minimum, the function of programming should be separated from the functions controlling input to the computer programs, and the function of the computer operator should be segregated from functions requiring detailed knowledge or custody of the computer programs. If one person is permitted to perform duties in several of these functions, internal control is weakened, and the opportunity exists for fraudulent data to be inserted in the system.

Access to assets by EDP personnel   Whenever the responsibilities for record keeping and custody of the related assets are combined, the opportunities for an employee to conceal the abstraction of assets are increased. Since EDP is basically a record-keeping function, it is highly desirable to limit the access of EDP personnel to company assets. However, EDP personnel have direct access to cash if EDP activity includes the preparation of signed checks. EDP personnel may also have indirect access to assets if, for example, EDP is used to generate shipping orders authorizing the release of inventory.

The combination of record keeping with access to assets seriously weakens internal control unless adequate *compensating controls* are present. One type of compensating control is the use of predetermined *batch totals,* such as document counts and totals of significant data fields, prepared in departments independent of EDP. For example, if EDP performs the function of printing checks, another department should be responsible for authorizing the preparation of the checks. The authorizing department should maintain a record of the total number and dollar amount of checks authorized. These independently prepared batch totals should then be compared with the computer output before the checks are released.

It is difficult for compensating controls to eliminate entirely the risk that results from EDP personnel having access to company assets. Auditors should therefore realize that the risk of computer-centered fraud is greatest in those areas in which EDP personnel have access to assets.

Management fraud   Organizational controls are reasonably effective in preventing an individual employee from perpetrating a fraud, but they do not prevent fraud involving collusion. If key employees or company officers conspire in an effort to commit fraud, internal controls that rely upon separation of duties can be rendered inoperative.

Illustrative case

Equity Funding Corporation of America went into bankruptcy after it was discovered that the company's financial statements had been grossly and

(Continued)

fraudulently misleading for a period of years. A subsidiary of the company had been manufacturing bogus insurance policies on fictitious persons and then selling these policies to other insurance companies. When the fraud was discovered, Equity Funding's balance sheet included more than $120 million in fictitious assets, far exceeding the $75 million net income reported over the 13-year life of the company.

Perhaps the most startling revelation of the Equity Funding scandal was that numerous officers and employees of the company had worked together for years to perpetrate and conceal the fraud. The fictitious transactions had been carefully integrated into the company's computer-based accounting system. A wide variety of fraudulent supporting documents had been prepared for the sole purpose of deceiving auditors and governmental regulatory agencies. Upon disclosure of the activities, several members of top management were convicted of criminal charges.

The Equity Funding scandal is often described as a computer-based fraud. It was not because of the use of computers, however, that the company was able to deceive auditors and government investigators. Rather, the fraudulent activities were successfully concealed for a number of years because of the unprecedented willingness of a large number of company officers and employees to participate in the scheme. Collusion of the magnitude existing at Equity Funding would render any system of internal control ineffective.

Documentation

Internal control in an EDP department requires not only subdivision of duties but also the maintenance of adequate documentation describing the system and procedures used in all data processing tasks. An effective system of documentation helps achieve control by providing users and operators with current operating instructions. It also aids programmers in revising existing programs.

The purpose of *system documentation* is to provide an overall description of a processing system including system flowcharts and descriptions of the nature of input, operations, and output. It also establishes responsibilities for entering data, performing control tasks, and correcting and reprocessing erroneous data. An example of system documentation is a *user's manual* that provides instructions for user tasks, such as preparing data for processing, applying control procedures, and operating computer terminals.

Another important type of documentation is *program documentation,* which contains a complete description of each application program. As a minimum, program documentation should include:

1. A description of the purpose of the program.

2. A list and explanation of processing controls associated with the program.
3. A record of layouts showing the placement of data on punched cards, magnetic tapes, disks, or drums.
4. Program flowcharts showing the major steps and logic of the computer program.
5. Program listings in source language.
6. Program approval and change sheets showing proper authorization for all initial programs and subsequent changes.
7. An operations manual, containing instructions for running the program.
8. Test data utilized in testing and debugging the program.

Complete program documentation may be utilized by systems analysts and programmers for making authorized changes in programs. Computer operators, on the other hand, should have access only to the *operations manual* that contains the instructions for processing the programs. If operators have access to detailed information about programs, the opportunities for an operator to change or patch a program are increased.

Documentation is helpful to the auditors in reviewing the controls over program changes, evaluating controls written into programs, and determining the program logic. The auditors must also refer to format and layout information in the documentation in order to prepare test decks or special audit programs for testing the client's processing programs and computerized files.

Hardware controls

Modern electronic data processing equipment is highly accurate and reliable. Most errors in computer output result from erroneous input or an error in the program. Auditors, however, should be familiar with the hardware controls within a given system in order to appraise the reliability of the hardware. Hardware (equipment) controls are built into the computer by the computer manufacturer. Among the more common hardware or equipment controls are the following:

1. **Echo check.** The purpose of the echo check is to ensure that peripheral equipment, such as a printer, complies with computer instructions. A signal is returned to the computer verifying transmitted data or acknowledging the performance of an assigned task.
2. **Self-diagnosis.** Many computers are supplied with hardware or software routines that allow the computer to test its own circuitry. Self-diagnosis routines can identify a defective circuit or memory module before the system fails.
3. **Duplicate process check.** A duplicate process check consists of performing an operation twice and comparing the two results. In the duplicate process check known as *read after write,* the computer

reads back data after they have been moved in the system and verifies their accuracy.

4. **Parity check.**   Data are processed by the computer in arrays of *bits* (binary digits of 1 or 0). In addition to bits necessary to represent the numeric or alphabetic character, a *parity* bit is added when necessary to make the sum of all the 1 bits always odd or even, depending upon the make of the computer. As data are transferred at rapid speeds between computer components, the parity check is applied by the computer to assure that bits are not lost during the transfer process.

A program of preventive maintenance also is essential to assure the proper functioning of computer hardware.

Security for files and equipment

Every EDP system should have adequate security controls to safeguard equipment, files, and programs against loss, damage, and access by unauthorized personnel. When programs or files can be accessed from minicomputers or intelligent terminals, users should be required to enter a *secret password* in order to gain access to the system. The computer's operating system should be programmed to maintain a log of all terminal usage and should produce a warning if repeated attempts are made to gain access to data by use of incorrect passwords. The importance of these controls has been illustrated by several highly publicized incidents of youthful "hackers" using home computers to gain entry to both military and commercial computer systems.

Another purpose of security controls is to enable a company to reconstruct its computer-based records in the event that files are lost or damaged. Magnetic tapes or disks can be damaged by exposure to magnetic fields or excessive heat. Also, it is possible that a program or a file will accidentally be erased while it is being processed by the computer. As a precaution against such accidents, duplicate copies should be made of all files and programs. These backup copies should be stored at a separate location from the originals. Records that are updated online should be transferred to disks or tapes at regular frequent intervals to prevent significant data loss in the event of power failure.

Files that are periodically updated, such as the accounts receivable files, are called master files. Generally, three generations of master files should be retained to enable reproduction of files lost or destroyed. Under this *grandfather-father-son* principle of file retention, the current updated master file is the *son,* the master file utilized in the updating run that produced the son is the *father,* and the previous father is the *grandfather.* Records of transactions for the current period and for the prior period also should be retained to facilitate updating the older master files in the event that the current master file is accidentally destroyed. The three generations should be stored in separate sections of the file library, or in separate locations, to minimize the risk of losing all three generations at once.

Safeguards are also necessary to protect the equipment against sabotage, fire, and water damage. The best way to prevent deliberate damage is to limit access to the facility to authorized personnel. Outsiders should be kept away from the facility, and EDP personnel should be carefully screened before employment. Management should always be alert to the possibility of damage by a disgruntled employee. Frequently, the location of the computer facility is kept relatively secret. The facility should have no windows and few doors; entrances should be controlled by guards or badge-activated locks. In addition, the computer room should be fire resistant, air conditioned, and above likely flood levels.

Controls over input

Input controls, the first type of application controls, are designed to provide assurance that data received for processing represent properly authorized transactions and are accurate and complete when read into the computer. Control over input begins with proper authorization for initiation of the transactions to be processed. EDP is primarily a record-keeping department and therefore should not be authorized to initiate transactions. When transaction data are originally recorded on hard-copy source documents, such as sales orders, authorization may be indicated by the appropriate person initialing the document. In online systems, transaction data may be entered directly into the computer from remote terminal devices located in the departments initiating the transactions. In these cases, access to the terminals must be limited to those persons authorized to initiate transactions. This may be accomplished by assigning to authorized terminal users an identification number that must be entered into the terminal before the computer will accept the input data.

In most systems, transaction documents are collected into batches for processing in sequence as one lot. Input controls are necessary in batch processing to determine that no data are lost or added to the batch. The sequence of serial numbers of source documents comprising each batch should be accounted for. In addition, such batch totals as item counts and totals for significant data fields should be developed for each batch; these totals may be verified during each stage of the processing of the batch.

Provision should be made for verifying the accuracy of the conversion of source documents to machine-readable media. For keypunch operations, a verifier punch should test the accuracy of the mechanical keystrokes, or, as an alternative, the punched cards may be interpreted and visually compared to the source documents. A *self-checking number* may also be utilized to promote the reliability of identification and account numbers included in the input data.

Control over processing

Processing controls are designed to assure the reliability and accuracy of data processing. A major method of achieving control over processing is the use of *program controls*, which are written into the computer programs. Common program controls include:

1. **Item (or record) count.** A count of the number of items or transactions to be processed in a given batch.
2. **Control total.** The total of one field of information for all items in a batch. An example would be total sales for a batch of sales orders. When compared to predetermined totals from user groups, this control protects against missing amounts, duplication, and transposition errors in input or processing.
3. **Hash total.** A total of one field of information for all items in a batch, used in the same manner as a control total. The difference between a hash total and a control total is that a hash total has no intrinsic meaning. An example of a hash total would be the sum of the employee social security numbers in a payroll application.
4. **Validity (code validity) test.** A comparison of employee, vendor, and other codes against a master file for authenticity.
5. **Limit test.** A test of the reasonableness of a field of data, given a predetermined upper and/or lower limit.
6. **Self-checking number.** A number containing redundant information, such as the sum of digits in another number, permitting a check for accuracy when the number is input, or after it has been transmitted from one device to another.
7. **File labels.** Labels used to ensure that the proper transaction file or master file is being used on a specific run. A *header label* is a machine-readable message on a tape or disk file, identifying the file and the date it was created. A *trailer label* is the last record in a file and contains such control devices as an item count and/or control totals. These internal labels are used in conjunction with gummed-paper external labels to prevent operators from accidentally processing the wrong file.

In cases of exceptions or errors disclosed by program controls, the computer processing will halt, or the errors will be printed out. Error printouts should be transmitted directly to the control group for follow-up. The control group's responsibility includes ascertaining that corrections of errors are properly entered and that duplicate corrections are avoided.

The control group also monitors the operator's activities. A log maintained by the operator should be available for review by the control group. The log records the description of each run, the elapsed time for the run, operator console interventions, machine halts, master files utilized, and so on.

Controls over output

Output controls are designed to assure the reliability of computer output and to determine that output is distributed only to authorized personnel. Departments external to EDP can appraise the reliability of output by maintaining independent control totals of input and by reviewing the output returned by the data processing department. The EDP control group should have the responsibility for distributing the computer output to the appropriate recipients and for following up on exceptions and errors reported by the recipients.

Control responsibilities of the internal auditors

An internal audit function should exist separate and distinct from the work of the control group in the data processing department. The control group is primarily concerned with day-to-day maintenance of the internal controls for data processing, whereas the internal auditors are interested in evaluating the overall efficiency of data processing operations and the related internal controls.

The internal auditors should participate in the design of the data processing system to ensure that the system provides a proper *audit trail* and includes adequate internal controls. Once the system becomes operative, internal auditors review all aspects of the system on a test basis to determine that prescribed internal controls are operating as planned. Among other things, the internal auditors will test to determine that no changes are made in the system without proper authorization, programming personnel are functionally separate from computer operating personnel, adequate documentation is maintained, input controls are functioning effectively, and the control group is performing its assigned functions.

Integrated test facility   One method used by internal auditors to test and monitor accounting controls in EDP applications is an *integrated test facility*. An integrated test facility is a subsystem of dummy records and files built into the regular data processing system. These dummy files permit test data to be processed simultaneously with regular (live) input without adversely affecting the live data files or output. The test data, which include all conceivable types of transactions and exceptions, affect only the dummy files and dummy output. For this reason, an integrated test facility is often called the "minicompany approach" to testing the system. Integrated test facilities may be used in either online, real-time, or batch processing systems.

The internal auditing staff monitors the processing of test data, studying the effects upon the dummy files, error reports and other output produced, and the follow-up of exceptions by the control group. An integrated test facility for payroll applications, for example, could be set up by including a fictitious department and records for fictitious employees in the payroll master file. Input data for the dummy department would be included with input data from actual departments. Internal auditors would monitor all output relating to the dummy department, including payroll records, error reports, and payroll checks. (In this situation, strict control would be necessary to prevent misuse of the dummy payroll checks.)

A problem with integrated test facilities is the risk that someone may manipulate the real data files by transferring data to or from the dummy files. Controls should exist to prevent unauthorized access to the dummy files, and the internal auditors should monitor all activity in these files. Also, the test facility must be carefully designed to ensure that real files are not *inadvertently* contaminated with the fictitious test data.

Control in minicomputer systems

The term *minicomputers* refers to a variety of small computers including computer workstations, microcomputers, and intelligent terminals. Although technology is reducing the extent of the differences between minicomputers and large computers, minicomputers generally are less flexible, smaller in memory capacity, and slower at processing data than large computers. However, minicomputers have the advantage of giving office personnel and salespeople direct access to the computer without the turnaround time associated with a centralized system. For that reason, even audit clients with sophisticated central systems are likely to use minicomputers for a variety of on-site record-keeping functions.

The advent of minicomputers has resulted in a decentralization of data processing activities. In a minicomputer environment, computers are located in user departments and operated by user personnel who have little or no computer training. Processing usually is performed with commercial software packages, thus eliminating the need for the client to employ programmers. For secondary storage when the computer is operating, minicomputers use hard (rigid) disk drives where programs and files are stored. Floppy (flexible) disks or magnetic tapes are used as *backup* for the hard disk.

Internal control over minicomputers is enhanced when data processing procedures are documented and operators are well trained. To assure that the client can reconstruct financial records, duplicate (backup) diskettes or tapes of files should be made frequently and stored away from the originals in a secure location. Since minicomputers are located in user departments, there is a greater risk of use by unauthorized personnel. Therefore, the minicomputer's operating system should require the operator to enter authorization codes to gain access to menus that control specific programs and files. As a means of detecting improper activities, there should be an independent review of activity logs generated by the minicomputer. In addition, management should consider locking away critical software or installing a locking on/off switch on the minicomputer to prevent unauthorized use of the machine after business hours.

Implications of advanced systems

Newer EDP systems are more efficient at processing transactions, and they store and retrieve data faster than their traditional counterparts. Many advanced systems offer users the ability to access large *data bases* from remote locations. They efficiently process individual transactions and instantaneously update accounting records. Some systems even automatically initiate transactions for the company with little or no human involvement. It should be recognized that these features are not restricted to large computer systems. Auditors are likely to encounter minicomputer systems that have advanced features, such as data communications capabilities and integrated data bases.

Advanced systems may offer improved information processing capabilities, but they present management and the auditors with challenging control problems. Such problems are best solved by designing systems with effective hardware controls and operating system controls. Adding controls to an existing system is very costly, and an advanced system with ineffective controls may not be auditable.

Data communication A common feature of computer systems is the ability to send and receive data among devices at different locations. Online, real-time systems (OLRT), for example, allow users to have direct (online) access to data stored in the system. Individual transactions may be entered from remote locations and relevant files updated instantaneously. Online, real-time systems are frequently encountered in banks and savings institutions. These systems allow a teller at any branch to update a customer's account immediately by recording deposits or withdrawals on a computer terminal. At many financial institutions, customers are able to transact business directly with the computer by inserting an identification card in an *automatic teller terminal.*

Financial institutions also are pioneers in the development of systems that have the ability to communicate data between firms. *Electronic funds transfer* systems transmit the details of a sale transaction, entered via a retailer's point-of-sale terminal, directly to the bank for processing. Funds in the amount of the sale are automatically transferred from the customer's bank account to the retailer's bank account.

Data communication also makes it feasible for users to do more of their own data processing through a system of **distributive data processing.** In these systems, smaller computers are located throughout the organization to allow users to perform certain information processing in their own departments. The smaller computers are linked to a main computer that allows information and programs to be shared by all the users. A distributive data processing system provides company executives with online access to the vast amount of data stored in the company's main computer. They may selectively retrieve data and process it to their personal specifications with minicomputers located on their desks.

In a computer system that has communication capabilities, data may be altered at any location that can access the system. Weak controls at a single location can jeopardize the reliability of the entire system. Accordingly, security should be provided at each location to assure that transactions are initiated or data is accessed only by authorized personnel. The computer's operating system should be programmed to check the validity of identification numbers before computer or terminal users can gain access to the system. A password or other authorization system should exist that allows only authorized personnel access to specific programs or files. Also, the operating system should maintain a log of activity at each location to be reviewed by the system's control group for evidence of unauthorized use. *Input validation (edit) checks,* such as limit tests, validity tests, and tests of self-checking numbers, should be performed on data as it is entered. These checks increase the accuracy of input data, because any data that fails to meet a test requirement is rejected by the system, and revised data is requested from the user.

Illustrative case

An outside computer consultant for a large bank was able to use the bank's electronic funds transfer system to transfer $10 million to his account at another bank. The consultant was able to perpetrate the fraud based on his extensive knowledge of the bank's security system. He was able to observe the process by which users were assigned identification codes, and he became aware that a notice on the wall of the wire transfer room listed "secret" code numbers used to validate transfers. Since the transaction was relatively small by normal bank standards, the fraud remained undetected for eight days. In the meantime, the consultant transferred the funds to a Swiss bank account and purchased $8 million worth of diamonds. The perpetrator might never have been apprehended, had he not returned to his home state and tried to sell some of the diamonds.

Data base management systems (DBMS)   In traditional computer systems, files are maintained for each application. An example of an application file is the master file of accounts receivable, which contains customer account activity for a period of time and information about each credit customer. Much of the information on this file would also be included on customer files maintained by the sales department. This *data redundancy* is expensive in terms of computer storage costs. Also, data inconsistencies may arise since the information may not be up-to-date on all files.

In data base management systems, separate files for each computer application are not necessary. Instead, all data are stored in a common data base with each information element being stored only once. This system of data integration eliminates data redundancy, and since the data base is normally stored on a direct access device, the system responds quickly to users' requests for information.

From a control standpoint, it is essential that the data base be secured against improper manipulation of data. A system of user identification numbers and passwords should be used to restrict specific data to personnel with a legitimate purpose for accessing the data. Terminal activity should be logged by the operating system to provide evidence that the data base has not been improperly altered. In addition, the quality of the data base may be enhanced if the responsibility for the accuracy of each data element is assigned to only one department.

Impact of EDP on the audit trail

In a manual or mechanical data processing system, an audit trail (also referred to as a transaction trail) of hard-copy documentation links individual transactions with the summary figures in the financial statements. Computers, on the other hand, are able to create, update, and erase data in computer-based records without any visible evidence of a change being made. During the early development of EDP systems, this capability led to some concern among accountants that electronic data processing would obscure or even eliminate the audit trail. Although it is technologically possible to design an EDP system that would leave no audit trail, such a system would be neither practical nor desirable. Valid business reasons exist for the inclusion of a hard-copy audit trail in even the most sophisticated EDP systems. An adequate audit trail is necessary to enable management to direct and control the operations of the business, to permit file reconstruction in the event of processing errors or computer failure, and to accommodate the needs of independent auditors and governmental agencies.

A problem with advanced systems is that audit trail information may not be printed; it may be generated only in machine readable form. Shortly after it is generated, the audit trail information may be transferred to a low-cost storage medium, such as microfiche. The auditors should consider such retention policies in planning the nature and timing of their audit procedures. Emphasis should be placed on coordinating the efforts of external and internal auditors to assure adequate audit coverage.

Fears that EDP would obscure the audit trail have not materialized. During the design of an EDP system, management will normally consult with both its internal auditors and independent auditors to assure that an adequate audit trail is built into the system. In an EDP system, of course, the audit trail may consist of computer printouts and data stored in machine readable form, rather than the more traditional handwritten source documents, journals, and ledgers.

**THE AUDITORS'
CONSIDERATION
OF INTERNAL
CONTROL IN AN
EDP SYSTEM**

Whether financial statements are produced by a manual, mechanical, or electronic data processing system, the auditors must conduct a proper study of internal control. This investigation provides the auditors with a basis for assessing control risk to determine the nature, timing, and extent of work necessary to complete the audit. In addition, their consideration of internal control serves as the basis for the auditors' recommendations to the client for improving the system.

Regardless of the type of data processing system used by the client, the auditors' consideration of internal control involves four distinct steps. The auditors must (1) obtain an understanding of internal control sufficient to plan the audit, (2) assess control risk and design additional tests of controls, (3) conduct additional tests of controls, and (4) reassess control risk and design substantive tests.

Obtain an understanding of internal control sufficient to plan the audit

Auditors usually begin their consideration of internal control over EDP systems with a review of the general controls. This is an efficient approach since the effectiveness of specific application controls is often dependent on the existence of effective general controls over all EDP activities. The auditors, for example, would get little audit evidence from testing program controls in an environment where programmers can easily make unauthorized changes in the programs. In the absence of controls over program modification, the auditors have no evidence that the program being tested is identical to the one used to process data during the year. Thus, when the auditors find significant weaknesses in general controls, they need go no further in their consideration of the system. Such weaknesses generally will prevent them from relying on any application controls, and control risk for the system would be assessed at, or near, the maximum.

Specialized skills may be needed to understand the flow of transactions or to design effective audit tests for clients with complex EDP systems. For this reason, many CPA firms have trained ***EDP specialists*** who act as consultants to the firm's other auditors. Other CPA firms may even rely on outside consultants to provide assistance on complex engagements. In either case, the auditor in charge of the engagement should have sufficient computer-related knowledge to review the adequacy of the procedures performed by the specialist. The results of the specialist's procedures must be considered when planning the nature, timing, and extent of other audit procedures.

Assess control risk and design additional tests of controls

After obtaining an understanding of the client's overall control environment, the flow of transactions through the EDP system, and basic control procedures, the auditors are in a position to make a preliminary assessment of the reliability of the client's internal controls. If it appears that the controls are not adequate to provide a basis for further reductions of control risk, the auditors will omit additional testing of controls. On the other hand, if it appears that the controls will prove sufficiently reliable to justify the audit effort of testing the procedures, the auditors will document those controls before designing and performing the additional tests of controls. EDP controls often are documented by the use of systems flowcharts or specially designed internal control questionnaires.

Systems flowcharts As explained in Chapter 5, systems flowcharts are the most commonly used technique for documenting internal control in audit working papers. An advantage of flowcharting, with respect to EDP systems, is that the EDP department should have systems flowcharts available for all computer applications as part of the standard documentation.

An illustration of a systems flowchart for sales, accounts receivable, illustrated procedures and processing steps should be helpful in studying the illustrated flowchart.

1. Orders are received from sales representatives, and sales invoices are generated on an intelligent terminal. A magnetic tape of sales transactions is generated by the terminal as a by-product of sales invoice preparation. Two copies of the invoice are mailed to the customer, one copy is sent to the shipping department, and one copy is filed offline. The items on the magnetic tape are then sorted into the proper sequence on another magnetic tape.
2. Individual cash remittances from customers are received from the mail room and verified to a batch total, which is also received from the mail room. These remittances are keypunched on cards, and the cards are verified. The deck of punched cards is then converted to magnetic tape. The items on the magnetic tape are in turn sorted into proper sequence on another magnetic tape.
3. The accounts receivable master file is updated by processing both the sales transactions tape and the cash receipts transactions tape. A byproduct of the updating of the accounts receivable master file is an *error report* for the run and a printout (on an online typewriter) of any job messages.

The client's documentation of EDP activities usually includes *program flowcharts* as well as systems flowcharts. Program flowcharts illustrate the detailed logic of specific computer programs. Auditors capable of interpreting program flowcharts may evaluate the program controls contained in specific computer applications and draw inferences regarding the computer output.

Internal control questionnaires for EDP systems The use of internal control questionnaires was discussed in Chapter 5. In the audit of EDP

Figure 6–2 System flowchart

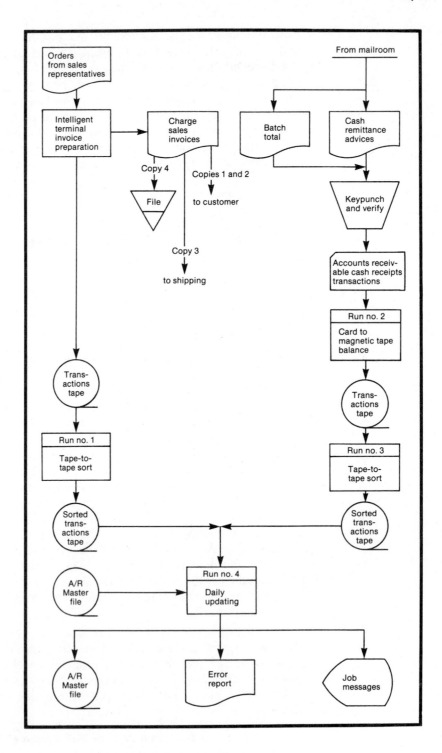

systems, questionnaires are best suited for a study of organizational controls and controls over input and output. The questionnaire approach is not well suited to studying the effectiveness of program controls because neither the auditor nor the respondent is usually aware of situations in which program controls are inadequate. A portion of the EDP control questionnaire used by one national CPA firm is illustrated in Figure 6–3.

Figure 6–3 Internal control questionnaire for EDP systems—input controls

Section C—Input controls	Application (if additional columns are required, use additional pages)					
	#1			#2		
	Yes	No	N/A	Yes	No	N/A
C-1 Are initiating departments required to establish control over data submitted for processing (through the use of batch totals, document counts or other)?	____	____	____	____	____	____
C-2 Are there adequate controls over the creation of data and its conversion to machine-readable form?	____	____	____	____	____	____
(a) Procedural controls	____	____	____	____	____	____
(b) Mechanical or visual verification	____	____	____	____	____	____
(c) Check digit	____	____	____	____	____	____
C-3 Is there adequate control over transmittal and input of data to detect loss or nonprocessing?	____	____	____	____	____	____
(a) Financial control totals	____	____	____	____	____	____
(b) Hash control totals	____	____	____	____	____	____
(c) Document counts	____	____	____	____	____	____
(d) Sequential numbering of input documents	____	____	____	____	____	____

Conduct additional tests of controls

The purpose of tests of controls is to provide reasonable assurance that the controls described in the audit working papers are actually operating as planned. Regardless of the nature of the client's data processing system, auditors must conduct tests of those controls they intend to rely on to reduce other audit procedures. The nature of the data processing system may, however, affect the specific procedures employed by the auditors in their testing of the controls.

Auditors usually test general controls by observing the performance of duties by client personnel; reviewing authorizations, documentation, and approvals of programs and program changes; inspecting the equipment in use; and observing the security measures in force. The nature of general controls is such that their presence usually must be observed rather than determined by the examination of accounting data.

Procedures used to test applications controls vary significantly from one system or application to another. In a batch system, for example, input controls may be tested by accounting for the serial sequence of source documents in selected batches, verifying the computation of batch control totals, and comparing control totals to computer output. In an online, real-time system, on the other hand, batch data are not available and the auditors must design entirely different tests of controls.

In testing processing controls, the auditors review the procedures performed by the EDP control group and review the working papers of any testing done by the client's internal auditors. To test the effectiveness of significant controls in the computer programs, auditors examine error reports and activity logs generated by the computer. These documents list the violations of program controls that occurred during computer processing, providing evidence of the application of those controls. Other techniques for testing program controls include auditing "around the computer" and auditing "through the computer" with the use of *computer-assisted audit techniques*. These techniques include the use of test decks, controlled programs, program analysis, tagging and tracing, and generalized audit software packages. Computer-assisted audit techniques are used by both external and internal auditors.

Auditing around the computer   One approach to testing processing controls in an EDP system is for the auditors to process input data manually on a test basis. The auditors' results are then compared to those obtained by the client's EDP department and any discrepancies are investigated. This technique is called auditing around the computer because the auditors bypass the computer rather than utilizing it in conducting their tests. Auditing around the computer can be an effective means of obtaining evidence of compliance with internal control in certain situations. However, auditing around the computer is unacceptable if the reason for this approach is merely that the auditors lack understanding of computer processing activities.

Test decks (data)   In the audit of a manual accounting system, the auditors trace sample transactions through the records from their inception to their final disposition. In the audit of an EDP system, a comparable approach is the use of a *test deck*. The test decks developed by the client's programmers may be utilized by the independent auditors once they have satisfied themselves by study of flowcharts and printouts that the tests are valid. As an alternative, the auditors may develop their own test decks, but this approach is often too time-consuming to be practicable.

Test decks should include all conceivable types of exceptions and errors in a process. Among these would be missing transactions, erroneous transactions, illogical transactions, out-of-balance batches, and out-of-sequence records. The auditors will carefully appraise the program controls and control group functions with respect to the test deck errors and exceptions. Dummy transactions and records used in test decks can be specially coded to avoid contamination of the client's genuine records and files. If the client's computer system includes an integrated test facility, the auditors may use this facility to prevent their test data from contaminating the client's files.

Controlled programs As an alternative or supplement to the test-deck approach, the auditors may monitor the processing of current data by using a duplicate program that is held under their control. They then compare their output to that developed by the client's copy of the program. They may also reprocess historical data with their controlled program for comparison with the original output. Reprocessing historical data may alert the auditors to undocumented changes in the client's programs.

Controlled programs are advantageous because the auditor may test the client's program with both genuine (live) and test data. Through controlled programs, auditors may test program controls without risk of contaminating the client's files. Also, the testing may be conducted at an independent computer facility without utilizing the client's computer or data processing personnel.

Program analysis techniques Many computers will accept programs that can generate computer-made flowcharts of other programs. A trained auditor can examine the flowcharts as a test of the logic of applications programs, and to ensure that the client's program documentation describes the program that is actually being used.

Tagging and tracing transactions This technique involves "tagging" transactions with an indicator when they are entered into the system. The computer provides the auditors with a printout of the details of the steps in processing tagged transactions. This printout is examined for evidence of unauthorized program steps.

Generalized audit software Many large CPA firms have developed *generalized audit software* (computer programs) that may be used to test the reliability of the client's programs as well as to perform many specific auditing functions. This audit software is suited for use on a wide variety of computer systems.

One application of computer audit software is to verify the reliability of the client's programs through a process termed *parallel simulation.* The generalized audit software may be directed to perform processing functions essentially equivalent to those of the client's programs. If the client's program is operating properly, the output of the client's processing of a group of transactions should be equivalent to the output from the generalized audit software package.

The value of generalized audit software lies in the fact that the auditors are able to conduct independent processing of live data. Often, the verification of the client's output would be too large a task to be undertaken manually, but can be done efficiently through a parallel computer program. Even when manual verification would be possible, the use of a parallel program allows the auditors to expand greatly the size of the sample of transactions to be tested. An extensive examination of the client's files may become a feasible and economic undertaking. It is not necessary, however, to duplicate all of the client's data processing. Testing should be performed only to the extent necessary to determine the reliability of the client's financial reporting systems.

Generalized audit software and substantive testing   Audit software is available for a wide variety of audit applications. It is most widely used for retrieving data from the client's system for use by the auditors in substantiating account balances. In performing retrieval functions, the audit software *interfaces* with the client's computer files and locates specific data requested by the auditors. The audit software may then be used to rearrange the data in a format more useful to the auditors, compare the data to other files, make computations, and select random samples. Applications of this nature include:

1. Examining the client's records for overall quality, completeness, and valid conditions.   In auditing a manual system, the auditors become aware of the general quality, accuracy, and validity of the client's records through visual observation. Since the auditors do not have the same physical contact with computer-based records, the audit software may be used to scan the client's files for various improprieties. For example, the accounts receivable file may be scanned for account balances in excess of credit limits, and the depreciation expense may be recomputed for each item in the plant assets file. The great speed of the computer often makes it possible to perform such calculations for each item in the population, rather than having to rely upon a sample-based test.

2. Rearranging data and performing analyses.   The audit software may be used to rearrange the data in the client's files into a format more useful to the auditors. For example, the accounts receivable file may be reorganized into the format of an aged trial balance. Data from the client's files may be printed out in the format of the auditors' working papers. In addition, the audit software can make analytical computations, such as computing turnover ratios to identify slow-moving inventory.

3. Selecting audit samples. Audit samples may be selected from the client's files on a random basis or using any other criteria specified by the auditors. Examples include selection of the inventory items to be test counted and the accounts receivable to be confirmed. An additional time savings may result if the audit software is used to print out the actual confirmation requests.

4. Comparing data on separate files. When similar data is contained in two or more files, the audit software can compare the files and identify any discrepancies. For example, the changes in accounts receivable over a period of time may be compared to the details of the cash receipts and credit sales transactions files. Also, actual operating results may be compared to forecasts.

5. Comparing the results of audit procedures with the client's records. Data obtained by the auditors may be converted to machine-readable form and compared to the data in computer-based files. For example, the results of the auditors' inventory test counts can be compared to the perpetual inventory file.

Using audit software: an illustration To illustrate some of the possible uses of generalized audit software, let us consider a specific example. Assume that an auditor is planning to observe a client's physical count of inventories at a specific date. All inventory is stored either in the client's distribution center or at a public warehouse. The client maintains computer-based perpetual inventory records, which are updated daily. This inventory file contains the following information:

Part number.   Cost per unit.
Description of item.   Date of last purchase.
Location.   Date of last sale.
Quantity on hand.   Quantity sold during the year.

The client has provided the auditor with a duplicate tape of the inventory file as of the date of the physical count.

The left-hand column in Figure 6–4 indicates typical inventory audit procedures the CPA might perform. The right-hand column indicates how the CPA's generalized audit software might be helpful in the performance of these procedures.

Auditors do not need extensive technical EDP knowledge in order to make use of generalized audit software. They will find it necessary to perform only a modest amount of programming. In fact, many CPA firms have found that they can train audit staff members to code specification sheets and operate a generalized audit program within a time span of a few days. Because of the simplified procedures that have been developed, auditors can, after limited training, program and operate the generalized audit software independently—that is, without assistance from the client's EDP personnel. On occasion, prepackaged software may not be available for a specific audit application. Most large CPA firms, however,

Figure 6–4 Illustration
of the uses of
generalized audit
software

Basic inventory audit procedure	How generalized audit software might be helpful
1. Observe the physical count, making appropriate test counts.	1. Determine which items are to be test counted by selecting from the inventory file a sample of items that provides the desired dollar coverage.
2. Test the mathematical accuracy of the inventory extensions and footings.	2. For each item in the inventory file, multiply the quantity on hand by the cost per unit and add the extended amounts.
3. Compare the auditors' test counts to the inventory records.	3. Arrange the test counts in a tape format identical to the inventory file and compare the two tapes.
4. Compare the client's physical count data to the inventory records.	4. Compare the quantity of each item counted to the quantity on hand in the inventory file.
5. Perform a lower-of-cost-or-market test by obtaining a list of current costs per item from vendors.	5. Compare the current costs per unit to the cost per unit in the inventory file; print out the extended value for each item, using the lower of two unit costs, and add extended amounts.
6. Test purchases and sales cut-off.	6. List a sample of items on the inventory file for which the date of last purchase or last sale is on, or immediately before, the date of the physical count.
7. Confirm the existence of items located in public warehouses.	7. List items located in public warehouses.
8. Analyze inventory for evidence of obsolescence or slow-moving items.	8. List items from the inventory file for which the turnover ratio (quantity sold divided by quantity on hand) is low or for which the date of last sale indicates a lack of recent transactions.

Source: AICPA, adapted from Uniform CPA Examination.

have technical support groups that can design software routines to meet the specifications of the audit staff.

As previously mentioned, a number of the larger CPA firms have developed their own generalized audit software. Similar programs are available to other members of the profession through the AICPA.

Reassess control risk and design substantive tests

Auditors assess internal control to determine the extent to which it may be relied upon to produce reliable accounting data and thereby reduce control risk. This assessment in turn determines the nature, timing, and extent of the substantive testing necessary for the auditors to express an opinion as to the fairness of the financial statements.

Conceptually, considering internal controls over EDP activities is no different from considering other aspects of the system. Substantive testing procedures must be expanded in those areas where internal controls are weak and may be restricted in areas where control is unusually strong. In assessing control over EDP activity, the auditors should consider the controls applied by user departments and internal auditing, as well as controls applied within the EDP department.

Computer service centers

Computer service centers provide data processing services to customers who do not do enough data processing to justify having their own computer facilities. Customers usually transmit data in batches to the service center, and the service center processes the data and returns the output to the customer.

Some computer centers operate on a time-sharing basis. The subscribers to a commercial time-sharing system can, through their terminals, run programs, store these programs in the computer for subsequent use, use the programs developed by the time-sharing company, and store files of data in the computer for subsequent use. In brief, the user of a time-sharing system has available most of the services that would be available through ownership of a computer.

When a service center performs data processing for a client, the center's internal controls interact with the client's control system. Accordingly, the auditors' understanding of the control system must be based, in part, on an understanding of processing activities at the computer service center. A visit to the center may be necessary to obtain this understanding. In addition, if the auditors plan to rely on certain controls, they must obtain evidence of their operational effectiveness regardless of whether those controls are applied by the client or by the service center.

The auditors may find that controls applied by the client are adequate to assure that errors or irregularities in transactions are detected. For example, the client's personnel may develop input control totals and compare them to the service center's output. They may also re-perform computer calculations on a test basis. When such controls are adequate, the auditors need test only client controls to reduce their assessment of control risk; there is no need to perform tests of controls at the service center.

In other situations, the controls performed at the computer service center are necessary to achieve the client's control objectives. This means that the auditors' assessment of control risk cannot be significantly reduced without evidence that controls at the center are operating effectively. To obtain this evidence, the auditors may have to perform tests at the service center.

Reviews by service auditors Most service centers perform similar processing services for numerous clients. If the auditors of each client (called *user auditors*) were to visit the service center for the purpose of reviewing internal controls, they would ask similar questions and perform similar tests of controls. It may be advantageous for the service center to engage its own auditors (called *service auditors*) to review their system of internal control and issue a report on the center's system. The user auditors may then elect to rely on this report as an alternative to visiting the service center themselves.

SAS 44 (AU 324), "Special-Purpose Reports on Internal Accounting Control at Service Organizations," states that service auditors may report on either the design of the service center's system or both the design of the system and the results of certain tests of controls. A report on system design provides information for the user auditors' understanding of the prescribed system, but it does not provide a basis for reliance on control procedures at the service center. To rely on service center controls, the user auditors must have evidence that controls *are being applied as prescribed.* This evidence can only be obtained from tests performed directly by the user auditors, or a report on the results of such tests performed by the service auditors. If the report covers tests of the controls on which the user auditors intend to rely to reduce their assessment of control risk, there usually is no need for the user auditors to perform their own tests at the center. They may decide to rely solely on the results of the service auditors' tests.

Before relying upon a service auditors' review, the user auditors should take steps to satisfy themselves as to the professional reputation of the service auditors. In addition, they should inquire of the service center management and the service auditors as to whether any significant changes have been made in internal control at the service center subsequent to the service auditors' review.

KEY TERMS INTRODUCED OR EMPHASIZED IN CHAPTER 6

Application controls Internal controls relating to a specific accounting task, such as preparation of a payroll.

Batch A group of transactions processed in sequence as one lot.

Control total A total of one information field for all the records of a batch, such as the total sales dollars for a batch of sales invoices.

Data base management system A system that eliminates data redundancy by storing data for two or more computer applications in an integrated data base.

Data communication In a system with this capability, data may be transmitted between computer devices at different locations.

Direct (random) access A storage technique in which each piece of data is assigned an address and may be retrieved without searching through other stored data. A magnetic disk drive is a direct access device.

File An organized collection of related records, such as a customer file.

File integrity The accuracy and reliability of data in a file.

General controls Internal controls that relate to all EDP applications. The category includes organizational controls, documentation, equipment controls, and security controls.

Generalized audit software A group of computer programs used by auditors to locate and process data contained in a client's EDP-based records. The audit programs perform such functions as rearranging the data in a format more useful to the auditors, comparing records, selecting samples, and making computations. This software is compatible with a wide variety of different computer systems.

Hard copy Computer output in printed form, such as printed listings, reports, and summaries.

Hash total A meaningless control total such as the total of all invoice numbers in a batch of sales invoices, used to determine whether data are lost, added, or processed incorrectly.

Header label A machine-readable record at the beginning of a file that identifies the file.

Integrated test facility A set of dummy records and files included in an EDP system enabling test data to be processed simultaneously with live input.

Intelligent terminals Visual display or keyboard/printer terminals that have a minimum amount of processing capabilities. They are often used to input transactions directly to magnetic tapes or disks for subsequent computer processing.

Interface To run two or more files or programs simultaneously in a manner permitting data to be transferred from one to another.

Master file A file of relatively permanent data or information that is generally updated periodically.

Offline Pertaining to peripheral devices or equipment not in direct communication with the central processing unit of the computer.

Online Pertaining to peripheral devices or equipment in direct communication with the central processing unit of the computer.

Operating system Software that coordinates and controls hardware components. Authorization procedures may be programmed into the operating system to restrict access to files and programs to authorized personnel.

Patch A new section of coding added in a rough or expedient way to modify a program.

Program analysis techniques Techniques for testing program controls that involve the examination of computer-generated flowcharts of application programs.

Program flowchart A graphic representation of the major steps and logic of a computer program.

Record A group of related items or fields of data handled as a unit.

Record layout   A diagram showing all the fields of data in a record and their arrangement in the record.

Self-checking number   A number that contains a redundant suffixed digit (check digit) permitting the number to be verified for accuracy after it has been transferred from one device or medium to another.

Sequential access   A storage technique in which data is read and written in numerical (i.e., account number) sequence. A magnetic tape drive is a sequential storage device.

Service auditors' review (of a computer service center)   A review and report by an independent auditor on the internal controls at a computer service center. Other auditors make use of this report in assessing the internal control over data processing performed for their clients by the service center.

Tagging and tracing   A technique for testing program controls in which selected transactions are tagged when they are entered for processing. A computer program provides a printout of the steps in processing the tagged transactions that may be reviewed by the auditors.

Test deck (data)   A set of dummy records and transactions developed to test the adequacy of a computer program or system.

GROUP I: REVIEW QUESTIONS

6–1.   Describe briefly the internal controls that should be established over the operation of a minicomputer to prevent use by unauthorized personnel.

6–2.   EDP systems use two types of software: system software and application software. Explain the difference between these two types of software.

6–3.   What are internal and external file labels? Why are they used?

6–4.   Distinguish general controls from application controls and give examples of the types of controls included in each of these broad categories.

6–5.   An EDP department usually performs numerous data processing functions that would be separated in a manual system. Does this imply that separation of duties is not a practical means of achieving internal control in a computerized system? Explain.

6–6.   Explain briefly "online, real-time system."

6–7.   Explain briefly the meaning of the term *documentation* as used in an EDP department. How might a client's documentation be used by the auditors?

6–8.   The number of personnel in an EDP department may limit the extent to which subdivision of duties is feasible. What is the minimum amount of segregation of duties that will permit satisfactory internal control?

6–9.   Compare the responsibilities and objectives of the EDP control group to those of the internal auditors with respect to EDP activities.

6–10. Define and give the purpose of each of the following program or equipment controls:
a. Record counts.
b. Limit test.
c. Duplicate processing.
d. Hash totals.   (AICPA, adapted)

6–11. Distinguish equipment controls from program controls and give examples of each.

6–12. Differentiate between a system flowchart and a program flowchart.

6–13. Auditors should be familiar with the terminology employed in electronic data processing. The following statements contain some of the terminology so employed. Indicate whether each statement is true or false.

   a. A recent improvement in computer hardware is the ability to automatically produce error listings. Previously, this was possible only when provisions for such a report were included in the program.

   b. The control of input and output to and from the EDP department should be performed by an independent control group.

   c. An internal-audit computer program that continuously monitors computer processing is a feasible approach for improving internal control in OLRT systems.

   d. An internal label is one of the controls built into the hardware by the manufacturer of a magnetic tape system.

   e. A limit test in a computer program is comparable to a decision that an individual makes in a manual system to judge a transaction's reasonableness.

   f. A principal advantage of using magnetic tape files is that data need not be recorded sequentially.

   g. A major advantage of disk files is the ability to gain random access to data on the disk.

   h. The term **grandfather-father-son** refers to a method of computer record security rather than to generations in the evolution of computer hardware.

   i. When they are not in use, tapes, disks, and card files should be stored apart from the computer room under the control of a librarian.

   j. Integrated data base systems are not available for minicomputers.

6–14. Explain briefly what is meant by a distributive data processing system.

6–15. Is it probable that the use of EDP will eventually eliminate the audit trail, making it impossible to trace individual transactions from their origin to the summary totals in the financial statements? Explain the reasons for your answer.

6–16. Do auditors usually begin their consideration of internal control over EDP activities with a review of general or application controls? Explain.

6–17. Describe the audit technique known as **tagging** and **tracing**. What is the purpose of the technique?

6–18. What is a service center? Are the auditors of a client that uses a service center concerned about the controls applied at the center? Explain.

**GROUP II:
QUESTIONS
REQUIRING
ANALYSIS**

6–19. Auditors encounter the use of minicomputers on almost every audit engagement.

   a. How do minicomputers differ from large computers?

   b. When are the auditors concerned with internal control over the use of minicomputers?

6–20. What are the purposes of each of the following categories of application controls?

   a. Input controls.

   b. Processing controls.

   c. Output controls.   (AICPA, adapted)

6-21. The first requirement of an effective system of internal control is a satisfactory plan of organization. Explain the characteristics of a satisfactory plan of organization for an EDP department, including the relationship between the department and the rest of the organization.

6-22. Distinguish between batch processing and online, real-time (OLRT) processing. In which of these systems is strong internal control over input most easily attained? Explain.

6-23. The use of test decks is one method of performing tests of processing controls in an EDP system. Identify and discuss several other methods by which auditors may test internal processing controls over EDP activity.

6-24. Discuss how generalized audit software can be used to aid the auditor in examining accounts receivable in a fully computerized system.

(AICPA, adapted)

6-25. An integrated test facility (ITF) is a method used by both internal and external auditors for testing EDP system controls. Discuss the advantages and disadvantages of implementing an ITF. (CIA, adapted)

6-26. Many companies have part or all of their data processing done by computer service centers.
  a. What controls should the company maintain to assure the accuracy of processing done by a service center?
  b. How do auditors assess internal control over applications processed for an audit client by a service center?
  c. What is a service auditors' review of a computer service center?
  d. What two types of reports are provided by service auditors as a result of their reviews?
  e. How do user auditors use each type of report?

6-27. Select the best answers for each of the following questions. Explain the reasons for your selection.
  a. Which of the following *best* describes a fundamental control weakness often associated with EDP systems?
    (1) EDP equipment is more subject to mechanical error than manual processing is subject to human error.
    (2) EDP equipment processes and records all similar transactions in a similar manner.
    (3) EDP procedures for detection of invalid transactions are less effective than manual control procedures.
    (4) Functions that normally would be separated in a manual system are combined in an EDP system.
  b. Which of the following is *not* a characteristic of a batch processed computer system?
    (1) The collection of like transactions that are sorted and processed sequentially against a master file.
    (2) Keypunching of transactions, followed by machine processing.
    (3) The production of numerous printouts.
    (4) The posting of a transaction, as it occurs, to several files, without intermediate printouts.
  c. When an online, real-time (OLRT) electronic data processing system is in use, internal control can be strengthened by:

    (1) Providing for the separation of duties between keypunching and error listing operations.

    (2) Attaching plastic file protection rings to reels of magnetic tape before new data can be entered on the file.

    (3) Making a validity check of an identification number before a user can obtain access to the computer files.

    (4) Preparing batch totals to provide assurance that file updates are made for the entire input.

d. Which of the following is an advantage of generalized audit software packages?

    (1) They are all written in one identical computer language.

    (2) They can be used for audits of clients that use differing EDP equipment and file formats.

    (3) They have reduced the need for the auditor to study input controls for EDP-related procedures.

    (4) Their use can be substituted for a relatively large part of the required tests of controls.

e. The auditors should be concerned about internal control in a data processing system because—

    (1) The auditors cannot follow the flow of information through the computer.

    (2) Fraud is more common in an EDP system than a manual system.

    (3) There is usually a high concentration of data processing activity and control by a small number of people in an EDP system.

    (4) Auditors most often "audit around the computer."

f. Which of the following employees normally would be assigned the operating responsibility for designing an electronic data processing installation, including flowcharts of data processing routines?

    (1) Computer programmer.

    (2) Data processing manager.

    (3) Systems analyst.

    (4) Internal auditor.   (AICPA, adapted)

GROUP III: PROBLEMS

6–28. The Ultimate Life Insurance Company recently established a data base management system. The company is now planning to provide its branch offices with terminals that have online access to the central computer facility.

Required:

a. Define a "data base."

b. Give one fundamental advantage of a data base.

c. Describe three security steps to safeguard the data base from improper access through the terminals.   (CIA, adapted)

6–29. CPAs may audit around or through computers in the examination of the financial statements of clients who utilize computers to process accounting data.

Required:

a. Describe the auditing approach referred to as "auditing around the computer."

    b. Under what conditions do CPAs decide to audit through the computer instead of around the computer?

    c. In auditing through the computer, CPAs may use test decks.

        (1) What is a test deck?

        (2) Why do CPAs use test decks?

    d. How can the CPAs be satisfied that the computer programs presented to them for testing are actually those used by the client for processing accounting data? (AICPA, adapted)

6–30. Johnson, CPA, was engaged to examine the financial statements of Horizon Incorporated, which has its own computer installation. While obtaining an understanding of the internal control structure, Johnson found that Horizon lacked proper segregation of the programming and operating functions. As a result, Johnson intensified the consideration of internal control surrounding the computer and concluded that the existing compensating general controls provided reasonable assurance that the objectives of internal control were being met.

Required:

    a. In a properly functioning EDP environment, how is the separation of the programming and operating functions achieved?

    b. What are the compensating general controls that Johnson most likely found? (AICPA, adapted)

6–31. As you are planning the annual audit of Norton Corporation, you are informed that the company has purchased a number of minicomputers for use in various locations. One of the machines has been installed in the stores department which has the responsibility for disbursing stock items and for maintaining stores records. In your audit, you find that an employee receives the requisitions for stores, disburses the stock, maintains the records, operates the computer, and authorizes adjustments to the total amounts of stock accumulated by the computer.

    When you discuss the applicable controls with the department manager, you are told that the minicomputer is assigned exclusively to that department. Therefore, the manager contends that it does not require the same types of controls applicable to large computer systems.

Required:

    a. Comment on the manager's contention.

    b. Discuss five types of control that would apply to this minicomputer application. (CIA, adapted)

6–32. A CPA's client, The Outsider, Inc., is a medium-size manufacturer of products for the leisure time activities market (camping equipment, scuba gear, bows and arrows, and so on). During the past year, a computer system was installed, and inventory records of finished goods and parts were converted to computer processing. The inventory master file is maintained on a disk. Each record of the file contains the following information:

Item or part number.
Description.
Size.
Unit of measure code.

Quantity on hand.
Cost per unit.
Total value of inventory on hand at cost.
Date of last sale or usage.
Quantity sold or used this year.
Economic order quantity.
Code number of major vendor.
Code number of secondary vendor.

In preparation for year-end inventory, the client has two identical sets of preprinted inventory count cards. One set is for the client's inventory counts and the other is for the CPA's use to make audit test counts. The following information has been keypunched into the cards and interpreted on their face:

Item or part number.
Description.
Size.
Unit of measure code.

In taking the year-end inventory, the client's personnel will write the actual counted quantity on the face of each card. When all counts are complete, the counted quantity will be keypunched into the cards. The cards will be processed against the disk file, and quantity-on-hand figures will be adjusted to reflect the actual count. A computer listing will be prepared to show any missing inventory count cards and all quantity adjustments of more than $100 in value. These items will be investigated by client personnel, and all required adjustments will be made. When adjustments have been completed, the final year-end balances will be computed and posted to the general ledger.

The CPA has available generalized audit software that can process both cards and disk files.

Required:

a. In general and without regard to the facts above, discuss the nature of generalized audit software and list the various types of uses of such software.

b. List and describe at least five ways general purpose audit software can be used to assist in the audit of inventory of The Outsider, Inc. (For example, the software can be used to read the disk inventory master file and list items of high unit cost or total value. Such items can be included in the CPA's test counts to increase the dollar coverage of the audit verification.) (AICPA, adapted)

6-33. You will be examining for the first time the financial statements of Central Savings and Loan Association for the year ending December 31. The CPA firm that examined the association's financial statements for the prior year issued an unqualified audit report.

At the beginning of the current year, the association installed an online, real-time computer system. Each teller in the association's main office and seven branch offices has an online, input-output terminal. Customers' mortgage payments and savings account deposits and withdrawals are recorded in the accounts by the computer from data input by the teller at the time of the transaction. The teller keys the proper account by account number and enters the information in the terminal keyboard to record the transaction. The accounting department at the main office has both punched card and typewriter input-output devices. The computer is housed at the main office.

Required:
You would expect the association to have certain internal controls in effect because an online, real-time computer system is employed. List the internal controls that should be in effect solely because this system is employed, classifying them as:
a.   Those controls pertaining to input of information.
b.   All other types of computer controls.   (AICPA, adapted)

6–34.   Lee Wong, CPA, is examining the financial statements of the Alexandria Corporation, which recently installed an offline electronic computer. The following comments have been extracted from Wong's notes on computer operations and the processing and control of shipping notices and customer invoices:

To minimize inconvenience Alexandria converted without change its existing data processing system, which utilized tabulating equipment. The computer company supervised the conversion and has provided training to all computer department employees (except keypunch operators) in systems design, operations, and programming.

Each computer run is assigned to a specific employee, who is responsible for making program changes, running the program, and answering questions. This procedure has the advantage of eliminating the need for records of computer operations because each employee is responsible for his or her own computer runs.

At least one computer department employee remains in the computer room during office hours, and only computer department employees have keys to the computer room.

System documentation consists of those materials furnished by the computer company—a set of record formats and program listings. These and the tape library are kept in a corner of the computer department.

The corporation considered the desirability of program controls, but decided to retain the manual controls from its existing system.

Company products are shipped directly from public warehouses, which forward shipping notices to general accounting. There a billing clerk enters the price of the item and accounts for the numerical sequence of shipping notices from each warehouse. The billing clerk also prepares daily adding machine tapes (control tapes) of the units shipped and the unit prices.

Shipping notices and control tapes are forwarded to the computer department for keypunching and processing. Extensions are made on the computer. Output consists of invoices (in six copies) and a daily sales register. The daily sales register shows the aggregate totals of units shipped and unit prices, which the computer operator compares to the control tapes.

All copies of the invoice are returned to the billing clerk. The clerk mails three copies to the customer, forwards one copy to the warehouse, maintains one copy in a numerical file, and retains one copy in an open invoice file that serves as a detailed accounts receivable record.

Required:

Describe weaknesses in internal control over information and data flows and the procedures for processing shipping notices and customer invoices, and recommend improvements in these controls and processing procedures. Organize your answer sheets as follows:

Weakness	Recommended improvement

(AICPA, adapted)

Evidence—what kind and how much?

Chapter 7 study objectives

After studying this chapter, you should be able to:

— Explain the concepts of competence and sufficiency as they apply to audit evidence.
— Describe the characteristics of accounts with high inherent risk.
— List and describe the types of evidence used to restrict detection risk.
— Describe appropriate accounting and auditing requirements related to subsequent events.
— Describe the auditors' responsibilities for subsequent discovery of omitted audit procedures and for related party transactions.

During financial statement audits the auditors gather and evaluate evidence to form an opinion on whether financial statements follow the appropriate criteria, usually generally accepted accounting principles. To form such an opinion, enough evidence must be gathered to adequately restrict audit risk, and provide an adequate basis for expressing an opinion on the financial statements. In short, gathering sufficient competent evidential matter is the very essence of auditing.

Sufficient competent evidential matter

The third standard of field work states:

> ***Sufficient competent evidential matter*** is to be obtained through inspection, observation, inquiries, and confirmations to afford a reasonable basis for an opinion regarding the financial statements under examination. [Emphasis added.]

What constitutes "sufficient competent evidential matter"? This question arises repeatedly when planning and performing every audit engagement. When an auditor is accused of negligence in the performance of an examination, the answer to this question may determine the CPA's innocence or guilt. To provide auditors with guidelines for answering this question, the Auditing Standards Board has issued *SAS 31* (AU 326), "Evidential Matter," specifically addressing the nature, competence, and sufficiency of audit evidence.

Nature of evidential matter   Evidential matter is *any information that corroborates or refutes a premise.* The auditors' premise is that the financial statements present fairly the client's financial position and operating results. One major source of evidential matter is the client's accounting system, including journals, ledgers, and supporting documentary materials (such as checks, invoices, and minutes of meetings). The client's accounting system by itself, however, cannot be considered sufficient evidential matter to support the auditors' opinion on the financial statements. The auditors must also gather evidence through firsthand observation of assets and from a variety of sources outside of the client company.

The evidence gathered by auditors during the course of an examination may assume many forms. For example, observation of assets, confirmation of transactions by third parties, the auditors' judgmental assessment of internal control, and information obtained in a telephone conversation may all be viewed as audit evidence.

Competence—a relative term   The competence of evidential matter refers to its *quality* or *reliability.* To be competent, evidence must be both *valid* and *relevant.* The relative competence of different types of evidential matter may vary greatly. Several factors contribute to the quality of evidential matter, including the following:

1. When auditors obtain evidence from independent sources *outside of the client company,* the reliability of the evidence is increased.
2. *Strong internal control* contributes substantially to the quality of accounting records and other evidence created within the client organization.
3. The quality of evidence is enhanced when the auditors obtain the information *directly*—that is, by firsthand observation, correspon-

dence, or computation, rather than by obtaining the information secondhand.

In addition, the competence of evidential matter is increased when the auditors are able to obtain additional information to support the original evidence. Thus, several pieces of related evidence may form a package of evidence that has greater competence than do any of the pieces viewed individually.

Sufficiency—a matter of judgment   The term *sufficient* relates to the *quantity* of evidence the auditors should obtain. The amount of evidential matter that is considered sufficient to support the auditors' opinion is a matter of professional judgment. However, the following considerations may be useful in evaluating the sufficiency of audit evidence:

1. The amount of evidence that is sufficient in a specific situation varies inversely with the competence of the evidence available. Thus, the more competent the evidential matter, the less the amount of evidence that is needed to support the auditors' opinion.
2. The need for evidential matter is closely related to the concept of materiality. The more material a financial statement amount, the greater the need for evidential matter as to its validity. Conversely, little or no evidence is needed to support items that are not material.
3. In every audit engagement, there is an element of risk that the auditors may overlook material error and issue an unqualified report when one is not warranted. This risk varies from one engagement to the next, depending upon such factors as the client's financial condition and line of business and the integrity of management. As the *relative risk* associated with a particular engagement increases, the auditors should require more evidence to support their opinion. In some special audit engagements the auditors are aware in advance that fraud is suspected and that the accounting records may include fictitious or altered entries. Perhaps the auditors have been engaged because of a dispute between partners or because of dissatisfaction on the part of stockholders with the existing management. The risk involved in such engagements will cause the auditors to assign different weight to various types of evidence than they otherwise would. Chapter 4 presented the factors that indicate a high overall risk of errors and irregularities in financial statements.

TYPES OF AUDIT EVIDENCE

When conducting audits, the auditors gather a combination of many types of evidence to adequately restrict audit risk. As described in Chapter 4, audit risk at the account balance level has three components—inherent risk, control risk, and detection risk. The evidence that the auditors gather pertaining to each of these risks differs. As a starting point, it is helpful to recognize that while the auditors gather evidence to assess inherent and control risk, they gather evidence to restrict detection risk to the appropriate level. Therefore, detection risk is the only risk that is completely a function of the effectiveness of the evidence gathered through the auditors' procedures.

Evidence about inherent risk

Just as risk differs for various audits, it also differs for various accounts within a given audit. *Inherent risk,* the risk of material error before considering internal control, is one source of this difference.

The very nature of some accounts makes the inherent risk of misstatement of those accounts greater than for others. Assume that in a given business the balance of the Cash account amounts to only one-tenth that of the Buildings account. Does this relationship indicate that the auditors should spend only one-tenth as much time in the verification of cash as in the verification of the buildings? Cash is much more susceptible to error or theft than are buildings, and the great number of cash transactions affords an opportunity for errors to be well hidden. The amount of time devoted to the verification of cash balances and of cash transactions during the year will generally be much greater in proportion to the dollar amounts involved than will be necessary for assets such as buildings.

Illustrative case

Bruce Henry, a resident of New York, owned a 90 percent stock interest in a California automobile agency. The other 10 percent of the stock was owned by James Barr, who also had a contract to act as general manager of the business. As compensation for his managerial services, Barr received a percentage of net income rather than a fixed salary. The reported net income in recent years had been large and increasing each year, with correspondingly larger payments to Barr as manager. However, during this period of reported rising income, the cash position of the business as shown by the balance sheet had been deteriorating rapidly. Working capital had been adequate when Barr took over as manager, but was now critically low.

Henry, the majority stockholder in New York, was quite concerned over these trends. He was further disturbed by reports that Barr was spending a great deal of time in Las Vegas and that he had placed several relatives on the payroll of the automobile agency. Henry decided to engage a CPA firm to audit the business. He explained fully to the CPAs his doubts as to the fairness of the reported net income and his misgivings as to Barr's personal integrity. Henry added that he wished to buy Barr's stockholdings, but first needed some basis for valuing the stock.

An audit initiated under these circumstances obviously called for a greater amount of evidence and a greater degree of caution by the auditors than would normally be required. Oral evidence from Barr could not be

(Continued)

given much weight. Documents created within the business might very possibly have been falsified. In brief, the degree of risk was great, and the auditors' approach was modified to fit the circumstances. More evidence and more conclusive evidence was called for than in a more routine audit of an automobile agency.

The outcome of the audit in question was a disclosure of a gross overstatement of inventories and the reporting of numerous fictitious sales. Commission payments were also found to have been made to persons not participating in the business.

Evidence about control risk

It is not practical for the auditors to examine every invoice, check, or other piece of documentary evidence. To do so would make an audit far too expensive. The solution lies in a study of the methods and procedures by which the company controls its accounting processes. If these procedures are well designed and consistently followed, the financial statements will be accurate and complete. An adequate internal control structure promotes accuracy and reliability in the accounting data. Errors are quickly and automatically brought to light by the built-in proofs and cross-checks that are inherent in the system. Therefore, the auditors' approach is to gather evidence about the effectiveness of internal control by performing a series of tests to determine that the company's control procedures are actually working as intended. Chapters 5 and 6 described the tests of internal controls that auditors perform to gather this evidence.

If the auditors find that the client company has carefully devised internal control for a particular account and that the prescribed practices are being consistently followed in day-to-day operations, they will assess control risk for that account to be low, and thereby accept a higher level of detection risk. Thus, the adequacy of the client's internal control is a major factor in determining how much evidence the auditors will gather to restrict detection risk.

Evidence that restricts detection risk

On all audits, a primary portion of the time is devoted to performing procedures that restrict detection risk—the risk that the auditors' procedures will fail to detect a material misstatement of the financial statements. The *major* types of evidence that are gathered to restrict detection risk may be summarized as follows:

1. Physical evidence.
2. Documentary evidence.
   a. Documentary evidence created outside the client organization and transmitted directly to the auditors.

      b. Documentary evidence created outside the client organization and held by the client.

      c. Documentary evidence created and held within the client organization.

3. Accounting records.
4. Analytical procedures.
5. Computations.
6. Evidence provided by specialists.
7. Oral evidence.
8. Client letters of representations.

1. Physical evidence.

Actual observation or count of certain types of assets is the best evidence of their physical existence. The amount of cash on hand is verified by counting; inventories are also observed and counted. The existence of property and equipment, such as automobiles, buildings, office equipment, and factory machinery, may also be established by physical observation.

At first thought, it might seem that physical observation of an asset would be conclusive verification, but this is often not true. For example, if the cash on hand to be counted by the auditors includes checks received from customers, counting provides no assurance that all of the checks will prove to be collectible when deposited. There is also the possibility that one or more worthless checks may have been created deliberately by a dishonest employee as a means of concealing from the auditors the existence of a cash shortage.

The physical observation of inventory may also leave some important questions unanswered. The quality and condition of merchandise or of goods in process are vital in determining salability. If the goods counted by the auditors contain hidden defects or are obsolete, a mere counting of units does not substantiate the dollar value shown on the balance sheet. Since auditors examine such widely differing businesses as breweries, mines, and jewelry stores, it is not possible for them to become expert in appraising the products of all their clients. However, CPAs should be alert to any clues that raise a doubt as to the quality or condition of inventories. CPAs sometimes request clients to hire independent specialists to provide the auditors with information on quality or condition of inventories.

Illustrative case

    During the observation of the physical inventory of a company manufacturing semiconductors—small chips of photographically etched silicon that channel electricity along microscopic pathways—one of the auditors

(Continued)

---

counted semiconductors purportedly worth several hundred thousand dollars. He then asked why apparently identical appearing semiconductors on another wall were not being counted. The client informed him that these semiconductors were defective and could not be sold. To the auditor, the defective semiconductors were identical in appearance with those included in the count. Shortly thereafter the auditor entered academics.

In the case of plant and equipment, the auditors' physical observation verifies the existence of the asset, but gives no proof of ownership. A fleet of automobiles used by salespeople and company executives, for example, might be leased rather than owned—or if owned might be subject to a mortgage. Also, physical observation does not substantiate the cost of the plant assets.

In summary, physical observation provides evidence as to the *existence* of certain assets, but generally needs to be supplemented by other types of evidence to determine the ownership, proper valuation, and condition of these assets. For some types of assets, such as accounts receivable or intangible assets, even the existence of the asset cannot be verified through physical evidence.

2. Documentary evidence.

The most important type of evidence relied upon by auditors consists of documents. The worth of a document as evidence depends in part upon whether it was created within the company (for example, a sales invoice) or came from outside the company (as in the case of a vendor's invoice). Some documents created within the company (checks, for example) are sent outside the organization for endorsement and processing; because of this critical review by outsiders, these documents are regarded as very reliable evidence.

In appraising the reliability of documentary evidence, the auditors should consider whether the document is of a type that could easily be forged or created in its entirety by a dishonest employee. A stock certificate evidencing an investment in marketable securities is usually elaborately engraved and would be most difficult to falsify. On the other hand, a note receivable may be created by anyone in a moment merely by filling in the blank spaces in one of the standard note forms available at any bank.

Documentary evidence created outside the client organization and transmitted directly to the auditors The best quality of documentary evidence consists of documents created by independent parties outside the client's organization and transmitted directly to the auditors without passing through the client's hands. For example, in the verification of accounts receivable, the customer is requested by the client to write directly to the auditors to confirm the amount owed to the auditors' client. To assu e that the customer's reply comes directly to the auditors and not to the client, the auditors will enclose with the confirmation request a return envelope addressed to the auditors' office. If the replies were addressed to the auditors at the client's place of business, an opportunity would exist for someone in the client's organization to intercept the customer's letter and alter the amount of indebtedness reported, or even destroy the letter.

Similar precautions are taken in the verification of cash in a bank. The client will request the bank to advise the auditors directly in writing of the amounts the client has on deposit.

Another type of document created outside the client's organization and transmitted directly to the auditors is a letter from the client's attorneys describing any pending litigation. Again, the client requests the outsider to furnish the information directly to the auditors in an envelope addressed to the auditors' office, and the auditors mail the request.

Documentary evidence created outside the client organization and held by the client Many of the externally created documents referred to by the auditors will be in the client's possession. Examples include bank statements, vendors' invoices and statements, property tax bills, notes receivable, contracts, customers' purchase orders, and stock and bond certificates. In deciding how much reliance to place upon this type of evidence, the auditors should consider whether the document is of a type that could be easily created or altered by someone in the client's employ. The auditors should be particularly cautious in accepting as evidence any documents that have been altered in any way. Of course, an alteration may have been made by the company originating the document to correct an accidental error. In general, however, business concerns do not send out documents marred by errors and corrections. The auditors cannot afford to overlook the possibility that an alteration on a document may have been made deliberately to misstate the facts and to mislead auditors or others who relied upon the document.

In pointing out the possibility that externally created documents in the client's possession *might* have been forged or altered, it is not intended to discredit this type of evidence. Externally created documents in the possession of the client are used extensively by auditors and are considered, in general, as a stronger type of evidence than documents created by the client.

Documentary evidence created and held within the client organization No doubt the most dependable single piece of documentary evidence created within the client's organization is a paid check. The check bears the endorsement of the payee and a perforation or stamp indicating payment by the bank. Because of this review and processing of a check by outsiders, the auditors will usually look upon a paid check as a strong type of evidence. The paid check may be viewed as evidence that an asset was acquired at a given cost, or as a proof that a liability was paid or an expense incurred.

Most companies place great emphasis on proper internal control of cash disbursements by such devices as the use of serial numbers on checks, signature (or two signatures) by responsible officials, and separation of the check-signing function from the accounting function. This emphasis on internal control over cash payments lends additional assurance that a paid check is a valid document.

Most documents created within the client organization represent a lower quality of evidence than a paid check because they circulate only within the company and do not receive critical review by an outsider. Examples of internally created documents that do not leave the client's possession are sales invoices, shipping notices, purchase orders, receiving reports, and credit memoranda. Of course, the original copy of a sales invoice or purchase order is sent to the customer or supplier, but the carbon copy available for the auditors' inspection has not left the client's possession.

The degree of reliance to be placed on documents created and used only within the organization depends on the adequacy of the internal control. If the accounting procedures are so designed that a document prepared by one person must be critically reviewed by another, and if all documents are serially numbered and all numbers in the series accounted for, these documents may represent reasonably good evidence. Adequate internal control will also provide for extensive subdivision of duties so that no one employee handles a transaction from beginning to end. An employee who maintains records or creates documents, such as credit memoranda, should not have access to cash. Under these conditions there is no incentive for an employee to falsify a document, since the employee creating documents does not have custody of assets.

On the other hand, if internal control is weak, the auditors cannot place much reliance on documentary evidence created within the organization and not reviewed by outsiders. If an employee is authorized to create documents such as sales invoices and credit memoranda and also has access to cash, an incentive exists to falsify documents to conceal a theft. If documents are not controlled by serial numbers, the possibility arises that the auditors are not being given access to all documents or that duplicates are being used to support fictitious transactions. There is the danger not only of fictitious documents created to cover theft by an employee but also the possibility, however remote, that management is purposely presenting misleading financial statements and has prepared false supporting documents for the purpose of deceiving the auditors.

3. Accounting records as evidence.

When auditors attempt to verify an amount in the financial statements by tracing it back through the accounting records, they will ordinarily carry this tracing process through the ledgers to the journals and on back to such basic documentary evidence as a paid check, invoice, or other original papers. To some extent, however, the ledger accounts and the journals constitute worthwhile evidence in themselves.

The dependability of ledgers and journals as evidence is indicated by the extent of internal control covering their preparation. Whenever possible, subsidiary ledgers for receivables, payables, and plant equipment should be maintained by persons not responsible for the general ledger. All general journal entries should be approved in writing by the controller or other official. If ledgers and journals are produced by an electronic data processing system, the safeguards described in Chapter 6 should be in effect. When controls of this type exist and the records appear to be well maintained, the auditors may regard the ledgers and journals as affording some support for the financial statements.

As a specific example, assume that the auditors wish to determine that the sale of certain old factory machinery during the year under audit was properly recorded. By reference to the subsidiary ledger for plant and equipment, they might ascertain that the depreciation accumulated during the years the machine was owned agreed with the amount cleared out of the Accumulated Depreciation account at the time of sale. They might also note that the original cost of the machine as shown in the plant ledger agreed with the credit to the Plant and Equipment control account when the machine was sold, and that the proceeds from sale were entered in the cash receipts journal. Assuming that the plant ledger, general ledger, and the cash receipts journal are independently maintained by three different employees, or are produced by an electronic data processing department with effective internal control, the agreement of these records offers considerable evidence that the sale of the machine was a legitimate transaction and properly recorded. Whether the auditors should go beyond this evidence and examine original documents, such as the bill of sale or a work order authorizing the sale, would depend upon the relative importance of the amount involved and upon other circumstances of the audit.

In addition to journals and ledgers, other accounting records providing evidential matter for independent auditors include sales summaries, trial balances, interim financial statements, and operating and financial reports prepared for management.

4. Analytical procedures.

Analytical procedures involve evaluations of financial statement information by a study of relationships among financial and nonfinancial data. *SAS 56* (AU 329) provides guidance and examples of applications of these procedures.[1]

Essentially, the process of performing analytical procedures consists of four steps:

1. Develop an expectation of an account balance.

---

[1] AICPA, *Statement on Auditing Standards 56,* "Analytical Procedures" (New York, 1988), AU 329.

2. Determine the amount of difference from the expectation that can be accepted without investigation.
3. Compare the company's account balance with the expected account balance.
4. Investigate significant deviations from the expected account balance.

Techniques used in performing analytical procedures range in sophistication from straightforward comparisons and ratios to complex models involving many relationships and data from many previous years. Examples of analytical procedures include comparisons of revenue and expense amounts for the current year to those of prior periods, to industry averages, to budgeted levels, and to relevant nonfinancial data, such as units produced or hours of direct labor. A more sophisticated analytical procedure might involve the development of a multiple regression model to estimate the amount of sales for the year using economic and industry data. In addition, analytical procedures may involve computations of percentage relationships of various items in the financial statements, such as gross profit percentages. When the relationships turn out as expected, auditors are provided with evidence that the data being reviewed are free from material error. On the other hand, unusual fluctuations in these relationships may indicate serious problems in the financial statements and should be investigated fully by the auditors.

Illustrative case

In performing analytical procedures for a marine supply store, the auditors noticed that uncollectible accounts expense, which normally had been running about 1 percent of net sales for several years, had increased in the current year to 4 percent of net sales. This significant variation caused the auditors to make a careful investigation of all accounts written off during the year and those presently past due. Most of the uncollectible accounts examined were found to be fictitious, and the cashier-bookkeeper then admitted that he had created those accounts to cover up his abstraction of cash receipts.

Comparisons with industry averages Average statistics for various industries are available through such reporting services as Dun & Bradstreet's *Key Business Ratios* and Robert Morris Associates' *Annual Statement Studies*. Such averages provide a potentially rich source of information for analytical procedures. Comparisons with industry statistics may alert auditors to classification errors, improper applications of accounting principles, or other errors in specific items in the client's financial statements. In addition, these comparisons may highlight the client's strengths and weaknesses relative to similar companies, thus providing the auditors with a basis for making constructive recommendations to the client.

One problem with the use of industry averages for analytical procedures is the degree of comparability. Other companies in the same industry may be larger or smaller, engage in other lines of business that affect their financial ratios, or use different accounting methods than does the auditors' client. Thus, auditors should carefully consider the extent of comparability before drawing conclusions based upon comparisons with industry averages.

Comparisons with internal client data Every audit client generates internal information that may be used in performing analytical procedures. Forecasts, production reports, and monthly performance reports are but a few data sources that may be expected to bear predictable relationships to financial statement amounts. In establishing these relationships, auditors may use dollar amounts, physical quantities, ratios, or percentages. Separate relationships may be computed for each division or product line.

Trend analysis is a technique for identifying consistent patterns in the relationships of data from successive time periods. For example, a review of the client's sales for the past three years might reveal a consistent growth rate of about 7 percent. This information would assist the auditors in evaluating the reasonableness of the sales reported in the client's income statement for the current year.

Timing of analytical procedures Analytical procedures are used at various times throughout the audit. They are useful in the early *planning* stage for assisting in planning the nature, timing, and extent of other audit procedures and directing the auditors' attention to areas requiring special investigation. Some of the problems that may be brought to light by the application of specific analytical procedures are illustrated in Figure 7–1. Analytical procedures also may be applied during the audit as *substantive tests* to provide evidence as to the reasonableness of specific account balances. Finally, analytical procedures are performed at the end of the engagement as a final overall review of the audited figures. This last application provides assurance that the auditors have not "failed to see the forest because of the trees." *SAS 56* (AU 329) requires the performance of analytical procedures at two of these stages: (1) during the planning stage, and (2) as a final overall review near the completion of the engagement.

The quality or competence of evidence obtained from analytical procedures depends upon the strength of the relationships among the data being compared. However, analytical procedures usually are highly efficient in that they may be performed quickly and inexpensively (often on a microcomputer using generalized audit software) in relation to the value of the evidence obtained.

Figure 7–1 Potential
problems disclosed by
analytical procedures

Analytical procedure	Potential problems
1. Comparison of inventory levels for the current year to that of prior years.	Misstatement of inventory; inventory obsolescence problem.
2. Comparison of research and development expense to the budgeted amount.	Misclassification of research and development expenses.
3. Comparison of accounts receivable turnover for the current year to that of prior years.	Misstatement of sales or accounts receivable; misstatement of the allowance for uncollectible accounts.
4. Comparison of the client's gross profit percentage to published industry averages.	Misstatement of sales and accounts receivable; misstatement of cost of goods sold and inventory.
5. Comparison of production records in units to sales.	Misstatement of sales; misstatement of inventory.
6. Comparison of interest expense to the average outstanding balance of interest bearing debt.	Understatement of liabilities; misstatement of interest expense.

5. Computations.

Another form of audit evidence consists of computations made independently by the auditors to prove the arithmetical accuracy of the client's records. Computations differ from analytical procedures. Analytical procedures involve the analysis of relationships among financial data, whereas computations simply verify mathematical processes. In its simplest form, an auditor's computation might consist of footing a column of figures in a sales journal or in a ledger account to prove the column total.

Independent computations may be used to prove the accuracy of such client calculations as earnings per share, depreciation expense, allowance for uncollectible accounts, revenue recognized on a percentage-of-completion basis, and provisions for federal and state income taxes. The computation of a client's pension liability normally involves actuarial assumptions and computations beyond an auditor's area of expertise. Therefore, auditors usually enlist the services of an actuary to verify this liability.

6. Evidence provided by specialists.

We have pointed out that CPAs may not be experts in such technical tasks as judging the quality of a client's inventory or making the actuarial computations to verify pension liabilities. Other phases of an audit in which CPAs lack the special qualifications necessary to determine the fairness of the client's representations include assessing the probable outcome of pending litigation and estimating the number of barrels of oil in an underground oil field.

In *SAS 11* (AU 336), "Using the Work of a Specialist," the AICPA recognized the necessity for CPAs to consult with experts, when appropriate, as a means of gathering competent audit evidence. *SAS 11* defined a **specialist** as a person or firm possessing special skill or knowledge in a field other than accounting or auditing, giving as examples actuaries, appraisers, attorneys, engineers, and geologists. It is desirable that the specialist consulted by the auditors be unrelated to the client; however, in some instances it is acceptable for the specialist to have an existing relationship with the client. For example, the most logical specialist to consult regarding pending litigation would be the client's legal counsel. In any event, the auditors are responsible for ascertaining the professional qualifications and reputation of the specialist consulted.

Auditors cannot accept a specialist's findings blindly; they must obtain an understanding of the methods or assumptions used by the specialist and test accounting data furnished to the specialist by the client. The CPAs may accept the specialist's findings as competent audit evidence unless their tests cause them to believe the findings are unreasonable.

7. Oral evidence.

Throughout their examination the auditors will ask a great many questions of the officers and employees of the client's organization. Novice auditors are sometimes afraid to ask questions for fear of seeming to be uninformed and inexperienced. Such an attitude is quite illogical; even the most experienced and competent auditors will ask a great many questions. These questions cover an endless range of topics—the location of records and documents, the reasons underlying an unusual accounting procedure, the probabilities of collecting a long past-due account receivable.

The answers auditors receive to these questions constitute another type of evidence. Generally, oral evidence is not sufficient in itself, but it may be useful in disclosing situations that require investigation or in corroborating other forms of evidence. For example, after making a careful analysis of all past-due accounts receivable, an auditor will normally sit down with the credit manager and get that official's views on the prospects for collection of accounts considered doubtful. If the opinions of the credit manager are in accordance with the estimates of uncollectible accounts losses that have been made independently by the auditor, this oral evidence will constitute significant support of the conclusions reached. In repeat examinations of a business, the auditor will be in a better position to evaluate the opinions of the credit manager based on how well the manager's estimates in prior years have worked out.

8. Client letters of representations.

At the conclusion of the examination, auditors obtain from the client a written letter of representations summarizing the most important oral representations made during the engagement. Many specific items are included in this representations letter. For example, management usually represents that all liabilities known to exist are reflected in the financial statements. Most of the representations fall into the following broad categories:

1. All accounting records, financial data, and minutes of directors' meetings have been made available to the auditors.
2. The financial statements are complete and prepared in conformity with generally accepted accounting principles.
3. All items requiring disclosure (such as loss contingencies, illegal acts, and related party transactions) have been properly disclosed.

SAS 19 (AU 333), "Client Representations," requires auditors to obtain a representations letter on every engagement and provides suggestions as to its form and content. These letters are dated as of the last day of field work (which also is the date of the audit report) and usually are signed by both the client's chief executive officer and chief financial officer.

A client representations letter is a low grade of audit evidence and *should never be used as a substitute for performing other audit procedures.* The financial statements already constitute written representations by the client; hence, a representations letter does little more than assert that the original representations were correct.

Illustrative case

The income statement of National Student Marketing Corporation (NSMC) included total gains of $370,000 from the sale of two subsidiary companies to employees of the subsidiaries. Consideration for the sales was notes receivable collateralized by 7,700 shares of NSMC stock. Because both subsidiaries had been operating at substantial losses, NSMC's independent auditors obtained written representations from three officers of NSMC that there were no indemnification or repurchase commitments given to the purchasers.

The SEC criticized the auditors for too great reliance on management representations regarding the sales. The SEC considered the sales to be sham transactions that would have been brought to light had the auditors sufficiently extended their auditing procedures. NSMC had executed various side agreements to assume all risks of ownership after the "sale" of one subsidiary, and had agreed to make cash contributions and guarantee a bank line of credit after the "sale" of the other subsidiary. Further, the NSMC stock collateralizing the notes receivable had been given to the subsidiaries' "purchasers" by officers of NSMC.

Although representation letters are not a substitute for other necessary auditing procedures, they do serve several important audit purposes. One purpose is to *remind the client officers of their primary and personal responsibility for the financial statements.* Another purpose is to document in the audit working papers the client's responses to many questions asked by the auditors during the engagement. Also, a representation by management may be the only evidence available with respect to management's *future intentions.* For example, whether maturing debt is classified as a current or a long-term liability may depend upon whether management has both the ability to and the *intention* of refinancing the debt.

The cost of obtaining evidence

CPAs can no more disregard the cost of alternative auditing procedures than a store manager can disregard a difference in the costs of competing brands of merchandise. Cost is not the primary factor influencing the auditors in deciding what evidence should be obtained, but cost is always an important consideration.

The cost factor may preclude gathering the ideal form of evidence and necessitate the substitution of other forms of evidence that are of lesser quality, yet still satisfactory. For example, assume that the auditors find that the client has a large note receivable from a customer. What evidence should the auditors obtain to be satisfied that the note is authentic and will be paid at maturity? One alternative is for the auditors to correspond directly with the customer and obtain written confirmation of the amount, maturity date, and other terms of the note. This confirmation is evidence that the customer issued the note and regards it as a valid obligation. Second, the auditors might test the collectibility of the note by obtaining a credit report on the customer from Dun & Bradstreet, Inc., or from a local credit association. They might also obtain copies of the customer's most recent financial statements accompanied, if possible, by the opinion of an independent CPA. To carry our illustration to an extreme, the auditors might obtain permission to make an audit of the financial statements of the customer. The cost of conducting this separate audit could amount to more than the note receivable the auditors wished to verify.

The point of this illustration is that auditors *do not* always insist upon obtaining the strongest possible evidence. They do insist upon obtaining evidence that is adequate under the circumstances. The more material the item to be verified, the stronger the evidence required by the auditors, and the greater the cost they may be willing to incur in obtaining it.

EVIDENCE PROVIDED BY SUBSEQUENT EVENTS

Evidence not available at the close of the period under audit often becomes available before the auditors finish their field work and write their audit report. The CPA's opinion on the fairness of the financial statements may be changed considerably by these *subsequent events.* The term *subsequent event* refers to an event or transaction that occurs after the date of the balance sheet but prior to the completion of the audit and issuance of the audit report. Subsequent events may be classified into two broad categories: (1) those providing additional evidence as to facts existing on or before the balance sheet date and (2) those involving facts coming into existence after the balance sheet date.

Type 1 subsequent events   The first type of subsequent event provides additional evidence as to *conditions that existed at the balance sheet date* and affects the estimates inherent in the process of preparing financial statements. This type of subsequent event requires that the financial statement amounts be *adjusted* to reflect the changes in estimates resulting from the additional evidence.

As an example, let us assume that a client's accounts receivable at December 31 included one large account and numerous small ones. The large amount due from the major customer was regarded as good and collectible at the year-end, but during the course of the audit engagement the customer entered bankruptcy. As a result of this information, the auditors might have found it necessary to insist on an increase in the December 31 allowance for uncollectible accounts. The bankruptcy of the customer shortly after the balance sheet date indicates that the financial strength of the customer had probably deteriorated before December 31, and the client was simply in error in believing the receivable to be good and collectible at that date. Evidence becoming available after the balance sheet date should be used in making judgments about the valuation of receivables on the balance sheet date.

Other examples of this first type of subsequent event include the following:

1.   Customers' checks included in the cash receipts of the last day of the year prove to be uncollectible and are charged back to the client's account by the bank. If the checks were material in amount, an adjustment of the December 31 cash balance may be necessary to exclude the checks now known to be uncollectible.

2.   A new three-year union contract signed two weeks after the balance sheet date provides evidence that the client has materially underestimated the total cost to complete a long-term construction project on which revenue is recognized by the percentage-of-completion method. The amount of income (or loss) to be recognized on the project in the current year should be recomputed using revised cost estimates.

3.   Litigation pending against the client is settled shortly after the balance sheet date, and the amount owed by the client is material. This litigation was to be disclosed in notes to the financial statements, but no liability had been accrued because at year-end no reasonable estimate could be made of the amount of the client's loss. Now that competent evidence exists as to the dollar amount of the loss, this loss contingency meets the criteria for accrual in the financial statements, rather than mere footnote disclosure.[2]

---

[2] *FASB Statement No. 5* requires accrual of loss contingencies in the accounting records when both of the following criteria are met: (1) It is probable that a loss has been incurred and (2) the amount of loss can be reasonably estimated.

Type 2 subsequent events The second type of subsequent event involves conditions *coming into existence after the balance sheet date.* These events do not require adjustment to the dollar amounts shown in the financial statements, *but they should be disclosed if the financial statements otherwise would be misleading.* To illustrate, assume that shortly after the balance sheet date a client sustains an uninsured fire loss destroying most of its plant assets. The carrying value of plant assets should not be reduced in the balance sheet because these assets were intact at year-end. However, anyone analyzing the financial statements would be misled if they were not advised that most of the plant assets are no longer in a usable condition.

Not all events occurring after the balance sheet date warrant disclosure in the financial statements. For example, assume that the following events occurred after the balance sheet date but prior to completion of the audit field work:

1. Business combination with a competing company.
2. Early retirement of bonds payable.
3. Adoption of a new pension plan requiring large, near-term cash outlays.
4. Death of the company treasurer in an airplane crash.
5. Introduction of a new line of products.
6. Plant closed by a labor strike.

Although these events may be significant in the future operations of the company and of interest to many who read the audited financial statements, none of these occurrences has any bearing on the results of the year under audit, and their bearing on future results is not easily determinable. The question facing the independent auditors is: Which, if any, of these events should be reflected in footnotes to the financial statements in order to achieve adequate informative disclosure?

It is generally agreed that subsequent events involving business combinations, substantial casualty losses, and other significant changes in a company's financial position or financial structure should be disclosed in footnotes. Otherwise the financial statements might be misleading rather than informative. Consequently, the first three of the preceding examples (combination with a competing company, early retirement of bonds payable, and adoption of a new pension plan) should be disclosed in notes to the financial statements. The last three subsequent events (personnel changes, product line changes, and strikes) are *nonaccounting matters* and are *not disclosed in footnotes* unless particular circumstances make such information essential to the proper interpretation of the financial statements.

Pro forma statements as a means of disclosure Occasionally subsequent events may be so material that supplementary *pro forma financial statements* should be prepared giving effect to the events as if they had occurred as of the balance sheet date. The pro forma statements (usually a balance sheet only) may be presented in columnar form next to the primary audited financial statements. This form of disclosure is used only when the subsequent event has a significant effect upon the asset structure or capital structure of the business. An example would be a business combination.

Distinguishing between the two types of subsequent events In deciding whether a particular subsequent event should result in adjustment to the financial statements or footnote disclosure, the auditor should carefully consider *when the underlying conditions came into existence.* For example, assume that shortly after the balance sheet date, a major customer of the audit client declares bankruptcy, with the result that a large receivable previously considered fully collectible now appears to be uncollectible. If the customer's bankruptcy resulted from a steady deterioration in financial position, the subsequent event provides evidence that the receivable actually was uncollectible at year-end, and the allowance for doubtful accounts should be increased. On the other hand, if the customer's bankruptcy stemmed from a casualty (such as a fire) occurring after year-end, the conditions making the receivable uncollectible came into existence after the balance sheet date. In this case, the subsequent event should be disclosed in a note to the financial statements.

Audit procedures relating to subsequent events

The period of time between the balance sheet date and the last day of field work is called the subsequent period. During this period, the auditors should determine that proper cutoffs of cash receipts and disbursements and sales and purchases have been made, and should examine data to aid in the evaluation of assets and liabilities as of the balance sheet date. In addition, the auditors should—

1. Review the latest available interim financial statements and minutes of directors', stockholders', and appropriate committees' meetings.
2. Inquire about matters dealt with at meetings for which minutes are not available.
3. Inquire of appropriate client officials as to loss contingencies; changes in capital stock, debt, or working capital; changes in the current status of items estimated in the financial statements under audit, or any unusual adjustments made subsequent to the balance sheet date.
4. Obtain a letter from the client's attorney describing as of the last day of field work any pending litigation, unasserted claims, or other loss contingencies.
5. Obtain a letter of representations from the client concerning subse-

quent events. This letter also should be dated as of the last day of field work.

Generally, the auditors' responsibility for performing audit procedures to gather evidence as to subsequent events extends only through the last day of field work. However, even after completing normal audit procedures, the auditors have the responsibility to evaluate subsequent events *that come to their attention.* Suppose, for example, that the auditors completed their field work for a December 31 audit on February 3 and thereafter began writing their report. On February 12, before completing their report, the auditors were informed by the client that a lawsuit, which had been footnoted as a loss contingency in the December 31 financial statements, had been settled on February 11 by a substantial payment by the client. The auditors would have to insist that the loss contingency be changed to a real liability in the December 31 balance sheet and that the footnote be revised to show the settlement of the lawsuit subsequent to the balance sheet date. If the client agreed, the auditors would *dual-date* their report "February 3, except for Note __, as to which the date is February 12." Alternatively, the auditors might decide to return to the client's facilities for further review of subsequent events through February 12; in this case, the audit report would bear that date only.

Dual dating extends the auditors' liability for disclosure through the later date *only with respect to the specified item.* Using the later date for the date of the report will extend the auditors' liability with respect to all areas of the financial statements.

Figure 7–2 summarizes the auditors' responsibilities for subsequent events with respect to the balance sheet date, the last day of field work, and the date upon which the audit report is actually issued.

The auditors' S-1 review in an SEC registration   The Securities Act of 1933 (Section 11[a]) extends the auditors' liability in connection with the registration of new securities with the SEC to the *effective date* of the registration statement—the date on which the securities may be sold to the public. In many cases, the effective date of the registration statement may be several days or even weeks later than the date the auditors completed their field work. Accordingly, on or as close as practicable to the effective date, the auditors return to the client's facilities to conduct an S-1 review, so-called because of the "Form S-1" title of the traditional SEC registration statement for new securities issues. In addition to completing the subsequent events review described in the preceding section, the auditors should read the entire prospectus and other pertinent portions of the registration statement. They should also inquire of officers and other key executives of the client whether any events not reported in the registration statement have occurred that require amendment of the registration statement to prevent the audited financial statements therein from being misleading.

Figure 7–2 Subsequent events

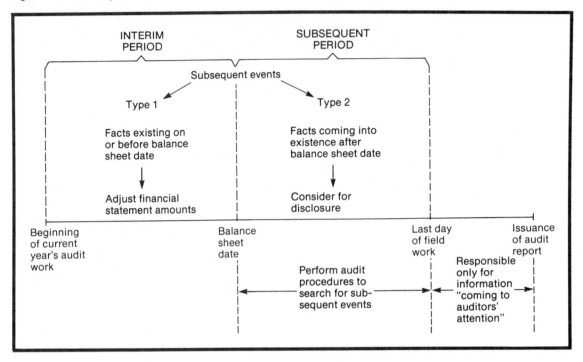

The auditors' subsequent discovery of facts existing at the date of their report

After the issuance of its audit report, a CPA firm may encounter evidence indicating that the client's financial statements contained material error or lacked required disclosures. The auditors must investigate immediately such subsequently discovered facts. If the auditors ascertain that the facts are significant and existed at the date of the audit report, they should advise the client to make appropriate disclosure of the facts to anyone actually or likely to be relying upon the audit report and the related financial statements. If the client refuses to make appropriate disclosure, the CPAs should inform each member of the client's board of directors of such refusal and then should notify regulatory agencies having jurisdiction over the client, and, if practicable, each person known to be relying upon the audited financial statements, that the CPAs' report can no longer be relied upon.

Subsequent discovery of omitted audit procedures

What actions should the auditors take if after issuing an audit report they find that they failed to perform certain significant audit procedures? The omission of appropriate audit procedures in a particular engagement might be discovered during a peer review or other subsequent review of the auditors' working papers. Unlike the situation described in the previous section, the auditors do not have information indicating that the financial statements are in error. Instead, the subsequent review has revealed that they may have issued their audit report without having gathered sufficient evidential matter. In addressing this sensitive problem, *SAS 46* (AU 390) states that if the auditors believe their report is still being relied upon by third parties, they should attempt to perform the omitted procedures.[3] Because of the legal implications of these situations, the auditors should consider consulting their legal counsel.

EVIDENCE FOR RELATED PARTY TRANSACTIONS

How should auditors react if a corporation buys a parcel of real estate from one of its executive officers at an obviously excessive price? This situation illustrates the problems that may arise for auditors when the client company enters into *related party transactions.* The term *related parties* refers to the client entity and any other party with which the client may deal where one party has the ability to influence the other to the extent that one party to the transaction may not pursue its own separate interests. Examples of related parties include officers, directors, principal owners, and members of their immediate families; and affiliated companies, such as subsidiaries. A related party transaction is any transaction between related parties (except for normal compensation arrangements, expense allowances, and similar transactions arising in the ordinary course of business).

The primary concern of the auditors is that material related party transactions are *adequately disclosed* in the client's financial statements or footnotes.[4] Disclosure of related party transactions should include: the nature of the relationship; a description of the transactions, including dollar amounts; and amounts due to and from related parties, together with terms and manner of settlement.

Since transactions with related parties are not conducted at arm's length, the auditors should be aware that the *economic substance* of these transactions may differ from their form. For example, a long-term, interest-free loan to an officer includes in substance an element of executive compensation equal to a realistic interest charge. If the auditors believe that related party transactions were executed at unrealistic prices or terms, and the dollar amounts are material, they must insist that the financial statements properly describe the substance of the transactions.

SAS 45 (AU 334) suggests guidelines for identifying related parties and related party transactions.[5] Common methods of identifying related par-

---

[3] AICPA, *Statement on Auditing Standards 46*, "Consideration of Omitted Procedures after the Report Date" (New York, 1983), AU 390.

[4] *FASB Statement 57*, "Related Party Disclosures," contains requirements for disclosure of related party transactions.

[5] AICPA, *Statement on Auditing Standards 45*, "Omnibus Statement on Auditing Standards—1983" (New York, 1983), AU 334.

ties include making inquiries of management and reviewing SEC filings, stockholders' listings, and conflict-of-interest statements obtained by the client from its executives. A list of all known related parties should be prepared at the beginning of the audit so that the audit staff may be alert for related party transactions throughout the engagement. This list is retained in the auditors' permanent file for reference and updating in successive engagements.

KEY TERMS INTRODUCED OR EMPHASIZED IN CHAPTER 7

Analytical procedures   Evaluations of financial information made by a study of plausible relationships among both financial and nonfinancial data. Typical analytical procedures involve comparisons of current financial data to that of prior periods, to industry averages, to budgeted performance, and to nonfinancial data.

Competence   The competence of evidential matter relates to its quality. To be competent, evidence must be both valid and relevant.

Confirmation   A type of documentary evidence created outside the client organization and transmitted directly to the auditors.

Evidential matter   Any information that corroborates or refutes the auditors' premise that the financial statements present fairly the client's financial position and operating results.

Letter of representations   A single letter or separate letters prepared by officers of the client company at the auditors' request setting forth certain representations about the company's financial position or operations.

Material   Of substantial importance. Significant enough to affect evaluations or decisions by users of financial statements. Information that should be disclosed in order that financial statements constitute a fair presentation. Involves both qualitative and quantitative considerations.

Observation   The auditors' evidence-gathering technique that provides physical evidence.

Pro forma financial statements   Financial statements that give effect to subsequent events as though they had occurred as of the balance sheet date.

Related party transaction   A transaction in which one party has the ability to influence significantly the management or operating policies of the other party, to the extent that one of the transacting parties might be prevented from pursuing fully its own separate interests.

Relative risk   The danger in a specific audit engagement of substantial error and misstatement in the accounts and the financial statements.

S-1 review   Procedures carried out by auditors at the client company's facilities on or as close as practicable to the effective date of a registration statement filed under the Securities Act of 1933.

Specialist   A person or firm possessing special skill or knowledge in a field other than accounting or auditing, such as an actuary.

Subsequent event   An event occurring after the date of the balance sheet but prior to completion of the audit and issuance of the audit report.

Sufficient   Sufficient evidential matter is a measure of the quantity of the evidence.

GROUP I: REVIEW QUESTIONS

7-1. In a conversation with you, Mark Rogers, CPA, claims that both the *sufficiency* and the *competence* of audit evidence are a matter of judgment in every audit. Do you agree? Explain.

7-2. Distinguish between the components of audit risk that the auditors gather evidence to assess versus the component of audit risk that they collect evidence to restrict.

7-3. Identify and explain the considerations that guide the auditors in deciding how much evidence they must examine as a basis for expressing an opinion on a client's financial statements.

7-4. "The best means of verification of cash, inventory, office equipment, and nearly all other assets is a physical count of the units; only a physical count gives the auditors complete assurance as to the accuracy of the amounts listed on the balance sheet." Evaluate this statement.

7-5. As part of the verification of accounts receivable as of the balance sheet date, the auditors might inspect copies of sales invoices. Similarly, as part of the verification of accounts payable, the auditors might inspect purchase invoices. Which of these two types of invoices do you think represents the stronger type of evidence? Why?

7-6. In verifying the asset accounts Notes Receivable and Marketable Securities, the auditors examined all notes receivable and all stock certificates. Which of these documents represents the stronger type of evidence? Why?

7-7. When in the course of an audit might the auditor find it useful to apply analytical procedures?

7-8. Give at least four examples of *specialists* whose findings might provide competent evidence for the independent auditors.

7-9. What are the major purposes of obtaining letters of representations from audit clients?

7-10. "In deciding upon the type of evidence to be gathered in support of a given item on the financial statements, the auditors should not be influenced by the differences in cost of obtaining alternative forms of evidence." Do you agree? Explain.

7-11. The cost of an audit might be significantly reduced if the auditors relied upon a representations letter from the client instead of observing the physical counting of inventory. Would this use of a representations letter be an acceptable means of reducing the cost of an audit?

7-12. What are subsequent events?

7-13. What are *related party transactions?*

7-14. What disclosures should be made in the financial statements regarding material related party transactions?

7-15. Evaluate the following statement: "Identifying related parties and obtaining a client letter of representations are two required audit procedures normally performed on the last day of field work."

7-16. "The gathering of evidence by auditors is guided by the standards of field work developed by the AICPA. To comply with these standards, the auditors must obtain the strongest possible evidence for each item in the financial statements, regardless of the cost or difficulties that may be encountered.''

Do you agree with the two sentences quoted above? Explain.

7–17. One of the assets of Vista Corporation is 6,000 acres of land in a remote area of the Arizona desert. The land is held as a long-term investment and is carried in the accounting records at a cost of $200 per acre. A recent topographical map prepared by the U.S. Soil Conservation Service shows the land to be nearly flat with no standing bodies of water. The land is accessible only by aircraft or four-wheel-drive vehicles. Evaluate the merits of the auditors personally observing this land as a means of obtaining audit evidence.

7–18. Analytical procedures are extremely useful in the initial audit planning stage.

Required:
a. Explain why analytical procedures are considered substantive tests.
b. Explain how analytical procedures are useful in the initial audit planning stage.
c. Should analytical procedures be applied at any other stages of the audit process? Explain.
d. List several types of comparisons a CPA might make in performing analytical procedures.   (AICPA, adapted)

7–19. When analytical procedures disclose unexpected changes in financial relationships relative to prior years, the auditors consider the possible reasons for the changes. Give several possible reasons for the following significant changes in relationships:
a. The rate of inventory turnover (ratio of cost of goods sold to average inventory) has declined from the prior year's rate.
b. The number of days' sales in accounts receivable has increased over the prior year.   (AICPA, adapted)

7–20. Comment on the competence of each of the following examples of audit evidence. Arrange your answer in the form of a separate paragraph for each item. Explain fully the reasoning employed in judging the competence of each item.
a. Copies of client's sales invoices.
b. Auditors' independent computation of earnings per share.
c. Paid checks returned with a bank statement.
d. Response from customer of client addressed to auditors' office confirming amount owed to client at balance sheet date.
e. Letter of representations by controller of client company stating that all liabilities of which she has knowledge are reflected in the company's accounts.

7–21. Marshall Land Company owns substantial amounts of farm and timber lands, and consequently property taxes represent one of the more important types of expense. What specific documents or other evidence should the auditors examine in verifying the Property Taxes Expense account?

7–22. Auditors are required on every engagement to obtain a letter of representations from the client.

Required:

a. What are the objectives of the client's representations letter?

b. Who should prepare and sign the client's representations letter?

c. When should the client's representations letter be obtained?

7–23. The auditor's opinion on the fairness of financial statements may be affected by subsequent events.

Required:

a. Define what is commonly referred to in auditing as a subsequent event, and describe the two general types of subsequent events.

b. Identify those auditing procedures that the auditor should apply at or near the completion of field work to disclose significant subsequent events. (AICPA, adapted)

7–24. On July 27, 1989, Arthur Ward, CPA, issued an unqualified audit report on the financial statements of Dexter Company for the year ended June 30, 1989. Two weeks later, Dexter Company mailed annual reports, including the June 30 financial statements and Ward's audit report, to 150 stockholders and to several creditors of Dexter Company. Dexter Company's stock is not actively traded on national exchanges or over the counter.

On September 5, the controller of Dexter Company informed Ward that an account payable for consulting services in the amount of $170,000 had inadvertently been omitted from Dexter's June 30 balance sheet. As a consequence, net income for the year ended June 30 was overstated $90,500, net of applicable federal and state income taxes. Both Ward and Dexter's controller agreed that the misstatements were material to Dexter's financial position at June 30, 1989, and operating results for the year then ended.

Required:

What should Arthur Ward's course of action be in this matter? Discuss.

7–25. In your examination of the financial statements of Wolfe Company for the year ended April 30, you find that a material account receivable is due from a company in reorganization under Chapter 10 of the Bankruptcy Act. You also learn that on May 28 several former members of the bankrupt company's management formed a new company and that the new company had issued a note to Wolfe Company that would pay off the bankrupt customer's account receivable over a four-year period. What presentation, if any, should be made of this situation in the financial statements of Wolfe Company for the year ended April 30? Explain.

7–26. What would you accept as satisfactory documentary evidence in support of entries in the following?

a. Sales journal.

b. Sales returns register.

c. Voucher or invoice register.

d. Payroll register.

e. Check register. (AICPA, adapted)

7–27. Select the best answer for each of the following questions. Explain the reasons for your selection.

a. As part of their examination, auditors must obtain a letter of representations from their client. Which of the following is *not* a valid purpose of such a letter?

(1) To increase the efficiency of the audit by eliminating the need for such audit procedures as personal observation, inspection, and confirmation.

(2) To remind the client's management of its primary and personal responsibility for the financial statements.

(3) To document in the audit working papers the client's responses to certain verbal inquiries made by the auditors during the engagement.

(4) To provide evidence in those areas dependent upon management's future intention.

b. Which of the following statements best describes why auditors should investigate related party transactions?

(1) Related party transactions are illegal acts.

(2) The substance of related party transactions may differ from their form.

(3) All related party transactions must be eliminated as a step in preparing consolidated financial statements.

(4) Related party transactions are a form of management fraud.

c. On August 15, the CPA completed field work on the audit of Cheyenne Corporation's financial statements for the year ended June 30. On September 1, before issuance of the auditor's report, an event occurred that the CPA and Cheyenne agree should be disclosed in a footnote to the June 30 financial statements. The CPA has not otherwise reviewed events subsequent to the completion of field work. The auditor's report should be dated:

(1) September 1.

(2) June 30, except for the footnote, which should be dated September 1.

(3) August 15, except for the footnote, which should be dated September 1.

(4) August 15.

d. Which event that occurred after the balance sheet date but prior to issuance of the auditor's report would not require disclosure in the financial statements?

(1) Sale of a bond or capital stock issue.

(2) A major drop in the quoted market price of the company's capital stock.

(3) Destruction of a factory as a result of a fire.

(4) Settlement of litigation when the event giving rise to the claim took place after the balance sheet date.

e. Of the following, which is the *least* persuasive type of audit evidence?

(1) Documents mailed by outsiders to the auditors.

(2) Correspondence between the auditors and vendors.

(3) Copies of sales invoices inspected by the auditors.

(4) Cancelled checks returned in the year-end bank statement directly to the client.

f. One reason why the independent auditors apply analytical procedures to the client's operations is to identify probable—

(1) Weaknesses of a material nature in internal control.
(2) Unusual transactions.
(3) Noncompliance with prescribed control procedures.
(4) Improper separation of accounting and other financial duties.

(AICPA, adapted)

7–28. John Reed is engaged in the audit of Brooke Corporation. While reviewing the company's notes payable, Reed encounters a three-year, 16 percent note in the amount of $1.5 million payable to Alan Davis, president of Brooke Corporation. The note was issued in conjunction with the purchase of a parcel of commercial real estate from Davis during the current year at a total price of $2.5 million. Discuss the audit significance of these findings and the actions, if any, that Reed should take.

**GROUP III:
PROBLEMS**

7–29. Assume that the auditors find serious weaknesses in the internal control of Oak Canyon, Inc., a producer and distributor of fine wines. Would these internal control weaknesses cause the auditors to rely more or less upon each of the following types of evidence during their audit of Oak Canyon?
a. Documents created and used only within the organization.
b. Physical evidence.
c. Evidence provided by specialists.
d. Analytical procedures.
e. Accounting records.

Required:
For each of the above five items, state your conclusion and explain fully the underlying reasoning.

7–30. In the examination of financial statements, auditors must judge the validity of the audit evidence they obtain.

Required:
Assume that the auditors have considered internal control and found it satisfactory.
a. In the course of examination, the auditors ask many questions of client officers and employees.
(1) Describe the factors that the auditors should consider in evaluating oral evidence provided by client officers and employees.
(2) Discuss the validity and limitations of oral evidence.
b. Analytical procedures include the computation of various balance sheet and operating ratios for comparison to prior years and industry averages. Discuss the validity and limitations of ratio analysis as evidential matter.
c. In connection with an examination of the financial statements of a manufacturing company, the auditors are observing the physical inventory of finished goods, which consists of expensive, highly complex electronic equipment. Discuss the validity and limitations of the audit evidence provided by this procedure.   (AICPA, adapted)

7–31. In connection with her examination of the financial statements of Flowmeter, Inc. for the year ended December 31, 1990, Joan Hirsch, CPA, is aware that certain events and transactions that took place after December 31, 1990, but before she issues her report dated February 28, 1991, may affect the company's financial statements.

The following material events or transactions have come to her attention:

a. On January 3, 1991, Flowmeter, Inc. received a shipment of raw materials from Canada. The materials had been ordered in October 1990 and shipped FOB shipping point in November 1990.

b. On January 15, 1991, the company settled and paid a personal injury claim of a former employee as the result of an accident that had occurred in March 1990. The company had not previously recorded a liability for the claim.

c. On January 25, 1991, the company agreed to purchase for cash the outstanding stock of Porter Electrical Co. The business combination is likely to double the sales volume of Flowmeter, Inc.

d. On February 1, 1991, a plant owned by Flowmeter, Inc. was damaged by a flood, resulting in an uninsured loss of inventory.

e. On February 5, 1991, Flowmeter, Inc. issued to an underwriting syndicate $2 million in convertible bonds.

Required:

For each of the above items, indicate how the event or transaction should be reflected in Flowmeter's financial statements and explain the reasons for selecting this method of disclosure.   (AICPA, adapted)

7–32. The financial statements of Wayne Company indicate that large amounts of notes payable to banks were retired during the period under audit. Evaluate the reliability of each of the following types of evidence supporting these transactions:

a. Debit entries in the Notes Payable account.

b. Entries in the check register.

c. Paid checks.

d. Notes payable bearing bank perforation stamp PAID and the date of payment.

e. Statement by client's treasurer that notes had been paid at maturity.

f. Letter received by auditors directly from bank stating that no indebtedness on part of client existed as of the balance sheet date.

7–33. During your examination of the accounts receivable of Hope Ranch, a new client, you notice that one account is much larger than the rest, and you therefore decide to examine the evidence supporting this customer's account. Comment on the relative reliability and adequacy of the following types of evidence:

a. Computer printout from accounts receivable subsidiary ledger.

b. Copies of sales invoices in amount of the receivable.

c. Purchase order received from customer.

d. Shipping document describing the articles sold.

e. Letter received by client from customer acknowledging the correctness of the receivable in the amount shown on client's accounting records.

f. Letter received by auditors directly from customer acknowledging the correctness of the amount shown as receivable on client's accounting records.

7–34. Robertson Company had accounts receivable of $200,000 at December 31,

1990, and had provided an allowance for uncollectible accounts of $6,000. After performing all normal auditing procedures relating to the receivables and to the valuation allowance, the independent auditors were satisfied that this asset was fairly stated and that the allowance for uncollectible accounts was adequate. Just before completion of the audit field work late in February, however, the auditors learned that the entire plant of Thompson Corporation, a major customer, had been destroyed by a flood early in February and that as a result Thompson Corporation was hopelessly insolvent.

The account receivable from Thompson Corporation in the amount of $44,000 originated on December 28; terms of payment were net 60 days. The receivable had been regarded as entirely collectible at December 31, and the auditors had so considered it in reaching their conclusion as to the adequacy of the allowance for uncollectible accounts. In discussing the news concerning the flood, the controller of Robertson Company emphasized to the auditors that the probable loss of $44,000 should be regarded as a loss of the year 1991 and not of 1990, the year under audit.

What action, if any, should the auditors recommend with respect to the receivable from Thompson Corporation?

7–35. In connection with your examination of the financial statements of Hollis Mfg. Corporation for the year ended December 31, 1990, your review of subsequent events disclosed the following items:

(1) January 7, 1991: The mineral content of a shipment of ore en route to Hollis Mfg. Corporation on December 31, 1990, was determined to be 72 percent. The shipment was recorded at year-end at an estimated content of 50 percent by a debit to Raw Materials Inventory and a credit to Accounts Payable in the amount of $82,400. The final liability to the vendor is based on the actual mineral content of the shipment.

(2) January 15, 1991: Culminating a series of personal disagreements between Ray Hollis, the president, and his brother-in-law, the treasurer, the latter resigned, effective immediately, under an agreement whereby the corporation would purchase his 10 percent stock ownership at book value as of December 31, 1990. Payment is to be made in two equal amounts in cash on April 1 and October 1, 1991. In December, the treasurer had obtained a divorce from his wife, who is Ray Hollis's sister.

(3) January 31, 1991: As a result of reduced sales, production was curtailed in mid-January and some workers were laid off. On February 5, 1991 all the remaining workers went on strike. To date the strike is unsettled.

Required:
Assume that the above items came to your attention before completion of your audit field work on February 15, 1991. For each of the above items, discuss the disclosure that you would recommend for the item, listing all details that you would suggest should be disclosed. Indicate those items or details, if any, that should not be disclosed. Give your reasons for recommending or not recommending disclosure of the items or details.

(AICPA, adapted)

7–36.   You are the partner on the audit of Datasave, Inc., a small publicly held corporation that manufactures high-speed tape drives for the computer industry. The audit of Datasave had been progressing satisfactorily until you were about a month away from issuing your opinion. Suddenly, and quite mysteriously, Carl Wagner, the financial vice president, resigned. John Ross, who had been a manager with a large CPA firm, was quickly hired to replace Wagner. Although the change in Datasave's chief financial officer caused some disruption, the audit was completed on a timely basis.

As the last step in the audit process, you have the representations letter prepared for signing. You wanted the letter to be signed by William Cox, the president; Robert Star, the controller; and Wagner, who occasionally came to the company's offices to resolve matters regarding his past compensation. The signatures of Cox and Star were obtained, and you approached Wagner for his signature. In response to your request, Wagner replied, "I no longer am employed with this crazy company. Why should I take any responsibility for the financial statements?" Despite your attempts to persuade him, Wagner refused to sign the letter. Wagner also refused to discuss the reasons for his resignation, other than to say the reasons were personal.

When you discussed the problem of Wagner's refusal to sign with Cox, he indicated that there was no problem because Ross would sign the letter. You see this as a possible solution, but you are aware that Ross knows very little about the financial statements for the year under audit. Also, you are still somewhat concerned about the reasons for Wagner's resignation.

Required:
a.   Describe fully the alternatives that are available to you in this situation.
b.   Express your personal opinion as to the appropriate course of action and provide reasoning to support your opinion.

Suggested references:
AICPA, *Professional Standards, Volume A,* Commerce Clearing House, *Statements on Auditing Standards,* Sections 333 and 508.

Audit sampling

Chapter 8 study objectives

After studying this chapter, you should be able to:

— Explain the important similarities and differences between statistical and nonstatistical sampling.

— Describe the basic sampling concepts as applied to audit sampling.

— Explain the effects of changes in various population characteristics and changes in sampling risk on required sample size.

— Plan, execute, and evaluate sampling plans for tests of controls.

— Plan, execute, and evaluate sampling plans for substantive tests.

— Distinguish among attributes, discovery, sequential, variables, and probability-proportional-to-size sampling plans.

The preceding chapter discussed the need for sufficient, competent evidential matter as the basis for audit reports. As business entities have evolved in size, auditors increasingly have had to rely upon sampling procedures as the only practical means of obtaining this evidence. This reliance upon sampling procedures is one of the basic reasons that audit reports are regarded as expressions of opinion, rather than absolute certifications of the fairness of financial statements.

Sampling, whether statistical or nonstatistical (judgmental), is the process of selecting a group of items (called the *sample*) from a large group of items (called the *population* or *field*) and using the characteristics of the sample to draw inferences about the characteristics of the entire population of items. The underlying assumption is that the sample is *representative* of the population, meaning that the sample will possess essentially the same characteristics as the population. Basic to audit sampling is sampling risk—the risk that the auditors' conclusion based on a sample might be different from the conclusion they would reach if they examined every item in the entire population.

Sampling risk is reduced by increasing the size of the sample. When sample size is 100 percent of the population, the sample is by definition perfectly representative, and sampling risk is eliminated entirely. Large samples, however, are costly and time-consuming. A key element in efficient sampling is to balance the sampling risk against the cost of using larger samples.

Auditors may also draw erroneous conclusions because of ***nonsampling errors***—errors due to factors not directly caused by sampling. For example, the auditors may fail to apply appropriate audit procedures, or they may fail to recognize errors in the documents or transactions that are examined. The risk pertaining to nonsampling errors is referred to as ***nonsampling risk.*** Nonsampling risk can generally be reduced to low levels through effective planning and supervision of audit engagements and through implementation of appropriately designed quality control procedures within the CPA firm. The procedures discussed throughout this text help control nonsampling risk. In the remainder of this chapter, we will emphasize sampling risk.

Comparison of statistical and nonstatistical sampling

A sample is said to be nonstatistical (or judgmental) when the auditors estimate sampling risk by using professional judgment rather than by using statistical techniques. This is not to say that nonstatistical samples are haphazard samples. Indeed, both nonstatistical and statistical audit samples should be selected in a way that is expected to result in them being representative of the population. In addition, the errors found in either a nonstatistical or a statistical sample should be used to estimate the total amount of error in the population (called the ***projected error***). However, nonstatistical sampling provides no means of ***quantifying*** sampling risk—that is, mathematically measuring the possibility that the actual amount of error in the population is ***significantly greater*** (or smaller) than that indicated by the results of the sample. Thus, the auditors may find themselves taking larger and more costly samples than are necessary, or unknowingly accepting a higher than acceptable degree of sampling risk.

The use of statistical sampling does not eliminate professional judgment from the sampling process. It does, however, allow sampling risk to be measured and controlled. Through statistical sampling techniques, the auditors may specify *in advance* the sampling risk they want in their sample results and may then compute a sample size that controls sampling risk at the desired level. Since statistical sampling techniques are based upon the laws of probability, the auditors are able to control the extent of their risk in relying upon sample results. Thus, statistical sampling may assist auditors in (1) designing efficient samples, (2) measuring the sufficiency of the evidence obtained, and (3) objectively evaluating sample results. However, these advantages are not often obtained without additional costs of training audit staff, designing sampling plans, and selecting items for examination. For these reasons, nonstatistical samples are widely used by auditors, especially for tests of relatively small populations. Both statistical and nonstatistical sampling can provide auditors with sufficient competent evidential matter.[1]

Random selection

A common misinterpretation of statistical sampling is to equate this process with random sampling. Random sampling is simply a method of *selecting* items for inclusion in a sample; it can be used in conjunction with either statistical or nonstatistical sampling. To emphasize this distinction, we will use the term *random selection* rather than random ''sampling'' to refer to the procedure of selecting the items for inclusion in a sample.

The principle involved in unrestricted random selection is that every item in the population has an equal chance of being selected for inclusion in the sample. Although random selection results in an *unbiased sample,* the sample is not necessarily representative. The risk still exists that purely by chance a sample will be selected that does not possess essentially the same characteristics as the population. However, since the risk of a nonrepresentative random sample stems from the laws of probability, this risk may be measured by statistical formulas.

The sample may also not be representative of the actual population because the population being sampled from differs from the correct population. That is, the *physical representation* of the actual population may not be complete. For example, if the auditors are using a computer printout of recorded accounts payable from which to sample, any conclusions based on the sample relate only to the population on that computer printout. The auditors' statistical conclusions do not consider situations such as those in which certain creditors (with balances due) are completely omitted from the printout. It is essential that the auditors consider whether the physical representation includes the entire population.

The concept of a random sample requires that the person selecting the sample will not influence or bias the selection either consciously or un-

---

[1] *SAS 39* (AU 350), ''Audit Sampling,'' and the AICPA Audit and Accounting Guide, *Audit Sampling,* provide auditors with guidelines for planning, performing, and evaluating both statistical and nonstatistical samples.

consciously. Thus, some type of impartial selection process is necessary to obtain a truly random sample. Techniques often used for selecting random samples include *random number tables, random number generators,* and *systematic selection.*

Random number tables

Perhaps the easiest method of selecting items at random is the use of a random number table. A portion of a random number table is illustrated in Figure 8–1.

Figure 8–1 Table of random numbers

Row	Columns				
	(1)	(2)	(3)	(4)	(5)
1	04734	39426	91035	54839	76873
2	10417	19688	83404	42038	48226
3	07514	48374	35658	38971	53779
4	52305	86925	16223	25946	90222
5	96357	11486	30102	82679	57983
6	92870	05921	65698	27993	86406
7	00500	75924	38803	05386	10072
8	34862	93784	52709	15370	96727
9	25809	21860	36790	76883	20435
10	77487	38419	20631	48694	12638

The random numbers appearing in Figure 8–1 are arranged into columns of five digits. Except that the columnar arrangement permits the reader of the table to select numbers easily, the columns are purely arbitrary and otherwise meaningless. Each digit on the table is a random digit; the table does *not* represent a listing of random five-digit numbers. The columnar arrangement is for convenience only.

In using a random number table, the first step is to establish correspondence between the digits in the table and the items in the population. This is most easily done when the items in the population are consecutively numbered. On occasion, however, auditors may find it necessary to re-number the population to obtain correspondence. For example, if transactions are numbered A–001, B–001, and so on, the auditors may assign numbers to replace the alphabetic characters. Next, the auditors must select a starting point and a systematic route to be used in reading the random number table. Any route is permissible, as long as it is followed consistently.

To illustrate the use of a random number table, assume that a client's accounts receivable are numbered from 0001 to 5,000 and that the auditors want to select a random sample of 200 accounts for confirmation. Using the table in Figure 8–1, the auditors decide to start at the top of Column 2 and to proceed from top to bottom. Reading only the first four digits of the numbers in Column 2, the auditors would select 3942, 1968, and 4837 as three of the account numbers to be included in their sample. The next number, 8692, would be ignored, since there is no account with that number. The next numbers to be included in the sample would be 1148, 592, 2186, and so on.

Duplicate numbers   In using a random number table, it is possible that the auditors will draw the same number more than once. If the auditors ignore a number that is drawn a second time and go on to the next number, they are *sampling without replacement.* This term means that an item once selected is not replaced into the population of eligible items, and consequently it cannot be drawn for inclusion in the sample a second time.

The alternative to sampling without replacement is *sampling with replacement.* This method requires that if a particular number is drawn two or more times, the number must be included two or more times in the sample. Sampling with replacement means that once an item has been selected, it is immediately replaced into the population of eligible items and may be selected a second time.

Statistical formulas can be used to compute sample size either with or without replacement. Sampling without replacement is the more efficient technique because it requires slightly smaller sample sizes.

Random number generators

Even when items are assigned consecutive numbers, the selection of a large sample from a random number table may be a very time-consuming process. Computer programs called *random number generators* may be used to provide any length list of random numbers applicable to a given population. Random number generators may be programmed to select random numbers with specific characteristics, so that the list of random numbers provided to the auditors includes only numbers present in the population. A random number generator is a standard program in all generalized audit software packages.

Systematic selection

An approach that is less time-consuming than selecting a random number for each item to be included in the sample is *systematic selection.* This technique involves selecting every *n*th item in the population following one or more *random starting points.*

To illustrate systematic selection, assume that auditors wish to examine 200 paid checks from a population of 10,000 checks. If only one random starting point is used, the auditors would select every 50th check (10,000 ÷ 200) in the population. As a starting point, the auditors would select at random one of the first 50 checks. If the random starting point is check No. 37, check Nos. 37, 87 (37 + 50), and 137 (87 + 50) would be included in the sample, as well as every 50th check number after 137. If the auditors had elected to use five random starting points, 40 checks (200 ÷ 5) would have to be selected from each random start. Thus, the auditors would select every 250th check number (10,000 ÷ 40) after each of the five random starting points between one and 250.

Selecting every nth item in the population results in a random sample only when positions in the population were assigned in random order. For example, if expensive inventory parts are always assigned an identification number ending in 9, systematic selection could result in a highly biased sample that would include too many expensive items or too many inexpensive items.

To prevent drawing a nonrandom or biased sample when systematic selection is used, the auditors should first determine that the population is arranged in random order. If the population is not in random order, each item to be included in the sample should be selected independently, or the auditors should use several random starting points for their systematic selection process.

The systematic selection technique has the advantage of enabling the auditors to obtain a sample from a population of unnumbered documents or transactions. If the documents to be examined are unnumbered, there is no necessity under this method to number them either physically or mentally, as required under the random number table selection technique. Rather, the auditors merely count off the sampling interval to select the documents or use a ruler to measure the interval. Generalized audit software packages include routines for systematic selection of audit samples from computer-based files.

Stratification

Auditors often *stratify* a population before computing the required sample size and selecting the sample. Stratification is the technique of dividing a population into relatively homogeneous subgroups called strata. These strata then may be sampled separately; the sample results may be evaluated separately, or combined, to provide an estimate of the characteristics of the total population. Whenever items of extremely high or low values, or other unusual characteristics, are segregated into separate populations, each population becomes more homogeneous. It is easier to draw a representative sample from a relatively homogeneous population. Thus, it is generally true that a smaller number of items must be examined to evaluate several strata separately than to evaluate the total population.

Besides increasing the efficiency of sampling procedures, stratification enables auditors to relate sample selection to the materiality, turnover, or other characteristics of items and to apply different audit procedures to each stratum. Frequently, auditors examine 100 percent of the stratum containing the most material items.[2] For example, in selecting accounts receivable for confirmation, auditors might stratify and test the population as follows:

Stratum	Composition of stratum	Method of selection used	Type of confirmation request*
1	All accounts of $10,000 and over	100% confirmation	Positive
2	Wholesale accounts receivable (under $10,000), all numbered with numbers ending in zero.	Random number table selection	Positive
3	All other accounts (under $10,000) in random order	Systematic selection	Negative

* A positive confirmation request asks the respondent to reply, indicating the amount owed; a negative request asks for a response only if the respondent does not agree with the amount indicated on the request. Confirmation of accounts receivable is discussed in more detail in Chapter 12.

Block samples

A block sample consists of all items in a selected time period, numerical sequence, or alphabetical sequence. For example, in testing internal control over cash disbursements, the auditors might decide to vouch all disbursements made during the months of April and December. In this case, the sampling unit is months rather than individual transactions. Thus, the sample consists of two blocks selected from a population of 12. Block sampling cannot be relied upon to produce a representative sample unless a relatively large number of blocks are selected from the population.

Sampling plans

The statistical sampling procedures used to accomplish specific audit objectives are called sampling plans. Sampling plans may be used to estimate many different characteristics of a population, but every estimate is either of (1) an occurrence rate or (2) a numerical quantity. The sampling terms corresponding to *occurrence rates* and *numerical quantities* are, respectively, *attributes* and *variables*.

Attributes sampling plans are used in testing of internal control procedures. In tests of controls, the auditors are interested in estimating the

---

[2] Any item sufficiently material that it may, by itself, constitute a material error in the balance should be substantiated separately, rather than by reliance upon sample results. Also, some populations (such as minutes of directors meetings) should be examined on a 100 percent basis, rather than on a sampling basis.

rate of compliance with (or deviation from) prescribed control procedures. ***Variables sampling plans,*** on the other hand, are widely used in substantive tests because they provide auditors with an estimate of a numerical quantity, such as an account balance. Sometimes one sampling plan may be used for the ***dual purposes*** of (1) testing an internal control procedure and (2) substantiating the dollar amount of an account balance. For example, a single sampling plan might be used to evaluate the effectiveness of the client's internal controls over recording the cost of sales and to estimate the total overstatement or understatement of the cost of goods sold account.[3]

In order to understand statistical sampling plans, you must first have a general familiarity with the meanings and interrelationships among certain statistical concepts. One of these concepts, sampling risk, has already been described. The other two include ***allowance for sampling risk*** (or ***precision***) and ***sample size***.

Allowance for sampling risk (precision)

Whether the auditors' objective is estimating attributes or variables, the sample results may not be ***exactly*** representative of the population. Some degree of ***sampling error***—the difference between the actual rate or amount in the population and that of the sample—is usually present. In utilizing statistical sampling techniques, auditors are able to measure and control the risk of material sampling error by deciding on the appropriate levels for sampling risk and the allowance for sampling risk.

The allowance for sampling risk is the range, set by + and − limits from the sample results, within which the true value of the population characteristic being measured is likely to lie. For example, assume a sample is taken to determine the occurrence rate of a certain type of error in the preparation of invoices. The sample indicates an error rate of 2.1 percent. We have little assurance that the error rate in the population is exactly 2.1 percent, but we know that the sample result probably approximates the population error rate. Therefore, using statistical sampling techniques, we may set an interval around the sample result within which we expect the population error rate to be. An allowance for sampling risk of ±1 percent would indicate that we expect the true population error rate to lie between 1.1 and 3.1 percent.

The wider the interval we allow, the more confident we may be that the true population characteristic is within it. In the preceding example, an allowance for sampling risk ±2 percent would mean that we assume the population error rate to be between .1 percent and 4.1 percent.

The allowance for sampling risk may also be used to construct a dollar value interval. For example, we may attempt to establish the total dollar

---

[3] The size of a sample selected for a dual purpose test should be the larger of the samples that would have been designed for the two separate purposes.

value of receivables with an interval of ±$10,000. As is discussed later in this chapter, the allowance for sampling risk required by auditors usually is determined in light of the amount of a tolerable error. ***Tolerable error*** is an estimate of the maximum monetary error that may exist in an account, that, when combined with the error in other accounts, will not cause the financial statements to be materially misstated.

Sample size

The size of the sample has a direct effect upon both the allowance for sampling risk and sampling risk. With a very small sample, we cannot have low sampling risk unless we allow a large allowance for sampling risk (precision). On the other hand, a sample of 100 percent of the population allows us no sampling risk with an allowance for sampling risk of zero.

The allowance for sampling risk and sampling risk can be decreased by increasing sample size. In other words, the smaller the allowance for sampling risk or the sampling risk desired by the auditors, the larger the required sample.

Sample size is also affected by certain characteristics of the population being tested. As the population increases in size, the sample size necessary to estimate the population with specified sampling risk and allowance for sampling risk will increase, but not in proportion to the increase in population size. In attributes sampling, sample size also increases as the expected population deviation rate increases. Finally, in variables sampling, greater variability among the item values in the population (a larger standard deviation) increases the required sample size. These relationships are summarized in Figure 8–2.

Figure 8–2 Factors affecting sample size

Factor	Change in factor*	Effect upon required sample size
Auditors' requirements:		
Sampling risk.	Increase (higher)	Decrease
Allowance for sampling risk . .	Increase (wider)	Decrease
Population characteristics:		
Size	Increase	Small increase†
Population deviation rate or Variability of item values	Increase	Increase

* As one factor changes, other factors are assumed to remain constant.
† This assumes sampling without replacement is used. If sampling with replacement is used, the population size has no effect on sample size.

AUDIT SAMPLING FOR TESTS OF CONTROLS

Sampling is used for tests of controls to estimate the frequency of *deviations or exceptions* from a prescribed internal control procedure. As discussed in Chapter 5, sampling cannot be used to test all internal control procedures. In general, sampling can be used only when performance of the internal control procedures leaves *evidence* such as a completed document or the initials of the person performing the procedure. This evidence allows the auditors to determine whether or not the control procedure was applied to each item included in their sample. The deviation rate in the sample can then be used to estimate the deviation rate in the entire population of items processed during the period.

Audit sampling for tests of controls generally involves the following procedures:

1. Determine the objective of the test.
2. Define a deviation.
3. Define the population to be sampled.
4. Determine the method of sample selection.
5. Determine the sample size.
6. Select the sample and examine the sample items.
7. Evaluate the sample results.
8. Document the sampling procedures.

Defining a "deviation"

When sampling is used for tests of controls, the population usually consists of all transactions subject to a specific control procedure during the period under audit. Deviations are defined as those *control failures* the auditors consider relevant to their evaluation of the effectiveness of the control procedure. The auditors' interpretation of the estimated deviation rate will depend largely on how they have defined deviations. If deviations are defined to include every departure from prescribed procedures, no matter how trivial, a population could contain a relatively high deviation rate without significantly increasing control risk. On the other hand, if deviations are defined only as fictitious transactions recorded in the accounting records, even a very low occurrence rate has serious implications.

Auditors may combine several types of exceptions in their definition of a deviation. However, it is important that these deviations be of similar audit significance. If both serious and minor types of exceptions are combined in the definition, the significance of the deviation rate to the auditors' assessment of control risk is obscured.

If a document selected for testing cannot be located, the auditors will not in general be able to apply alternate procedures to determine whether the control procedure was applied. Simply selecting another item is *not* appropriate. In such circumstances, at a minimum, the misplaced document should be treated as a deviation for evaluation purposes. Also, because the disappearance of documents is consistent with many possible explanations, ranging from unintentional misfiling to material irregularities, the auditors must carefully consider the overall implications of the situation.

Sampling risk for tests of controls

In performing tests of control procedures, the auditors are concerned with two aspects of sampling risk:

1. **The risk of underreliance on internal control.**   This is the possibility that the sample results will cause the auditors to rely too little on a control procedure. Thus, control risk is assessed at too high of a level.
2. **The risk of overreliance on internal control.**   This more important risk is the possibility that the sample results will cause the auditors to erroneously place *more reliance* upon an internal control procedure than is justified by the true effectiveness of that control. Thus, control risk is assessed at too low of a level.

The risk of underreliance on internal control relates to the *efficiency* of the audit process. When the sampling results cause the auditors to assess control risk at a higher level than it actually is, the auditors will perform more substantive testing than is necessary in the circumstance. This unnecessary testing reduces the *efficiency* of the audit process, but it does not lessen the *effectiveness* of the audit in disclosing material errors in the financial statements. The auditors usually do not attempt to directly control the risk of underreliance.

The risk of *overreliance,* on the other hand, is of utmost concern to the auditors. If the auditors assess control risk to be lower than it actually is, they will inappropriately *reduce* the intensity of their substantive tests. An unwarranted reduction in substantive testing lessens the overall *effectiveness* of the audit as a means of detecting material errors in the client's financial statements. In designing tests of controls, therefore, auditors should *carefully control the risk of overreliance* upon internal control procedures.

The allowance for sampling risk

Tests of controls are designed to provide the auditors with assurance that deviation rates do not exceed acceptable levels. Assume, for example, that the auditors anticipate a deviation rate of 3 percent and stipulate an allowance for sampling risk of ±1 percent. The relevant question is whether the auditors can accept a deviation rate of up to 4 percent, not whether they can accept a deviation rate of less than 2 percent. The lower limit is not pertinent to the objective of the test. For this reason, auditors generally use one-sided tests in attributes sampling; they generally only consider the *tolerable deviation rate* that will still permit them to assess control risk at the planned level.

Attributes sampling

Statistical sampling applied to attributes enables auditors to estimate the frequency with which specified characteristics occur within a population. Attributes sampling does not provide dollar value information—that is, the sample results do not indicate the dollar amount of the deviations or their effect upon the fairness of the financial statements. For example, the definition of a deviation from a control procedure might include failure to secure management approval for a specific transaction. If an unapproved transaction is properly recorded in the accounting records, it is a deviation in internal control but it does not result in an error in the financial statements. The major factors that determine the sample size for an attributes sampling plan include the risk of overreliance, the tolerable deviation rate, and the expected population deviation rate.

Determining risk of overreliance and the tolerable deviation rate   How do auditors determine the appropriate risk of overreliance and the tolerable deviation rate for a test of a control? The answer, in short, is ***professional judgment.*** In making these decisions, the auditors must consider such factors as: the types of errors that might occur if the control is not operating effectively, the nature of the transactions involved, the extent of reliance that the auditors plan to place upon the procedure in assessing control risk, and the existing compensating controls.

The risk of overreliance[4] upon a control procedure—that is, the risk that the actual deviation rate *exceeds* the tolerable deviation rate—is the critical risk in tests of controls. Since the results of tests of controls play a major role in determining the nature, timing, and extent of other audit procedures, auditors usually specify a low level of risk or overreliance for these tests. In practice, the risk of overreliance for tests of controls often is set at 5 to 10 percent. Auditors specify the tolerable deviation rate based on the degree to which they plan to rely on the control procedure to reduce substantive testing. Typically the rates are set between 2 and 20 percent.

---

[4] Some sources use the term *confidence level* to represent the complement of the risk of overreliance. Thus, a 95 percent confidence level is identical to a 5 percent risk of overreliance (100 percent − 5 percent).

> The AICPA's *Audit Sampling Guide* includes the following overlapping ranges to illustrate the relative reliance auditors might place on an internal control procedure:
>
> | Planned degree of reliance | Tolerable rate |
> |---|---|
> | Substantial | 2%– 7% |
> | Moderate | 6%–12% |
> | Little | 11%–20% |
> | None | omit test |

Estimating the expected population deviation rate   In addition to the tolerable deviation rate and the risk of overreliance, the expected population deviation (occurrence) rate affects sample size in attribute sampling. This expected deviation rate is significant because it represents the rate that the auditors expect to discover in their sample from the population.

In estimating the expected population deviation rate, the auditors often use the sample results from prior years, as documented in their working papers. The auditors may also base the estimate on their experience with similar tests for other clients or on examination of a small pilot sample.

Tables for use in attributes sampling   To enable auditors to use attributes sampling without resorting to complex mathematical formulas, tables such as the ones in Figures 8–3 and 8–4 have been developed. All of the information in these figures is based on a risk of overreliance of 5 percent. Similar tables are available for other levels of risk, such as 1 percent and 10 percent.

The horizontal axis of Figure 8–3 is the tolerable deviation rate specified by the auditors. The vertical axis is the deviation rate estimated by the auditors to exist within the population. The numbers in the body of the table indicate the *required sample sizes*. The number in parenthesis shown after the required sample size is the maximum number of deviations that may be observed in the sample for the results to support the auditors' planned reliance upon the control procedure.[5]

To use Figure 8–3, one must stipulate (1) the permissible risk of overreliance, (2) the expected deviation rate in the population, and (3) the tolerable deviation rate.[6] An appropriate table is selected based on the specified

---

[5] Some readers may notice that the number of deviations allowable in a sample sometimes exceeds the estimated deviation rate multiplied by the sample size. This is because the allowable number of deviations is always rounded up to the nearest whole number, as it is not possible to observe a partial deviation in a sample item. The sample sizes have been adjusted to reflect this rounding.

[6] Some tables require the auditors to specify population size. Figures 8–3 and 8–4 assume an infinite population. The effect on sample size when populations are finite but of significant size is not material.

Figure 8–3 Statistical sample sizes for tests of controls 5 percent risk of overreliance (with number of allowable deviations in parentheses)

Expected population deviation rate (in percentage)	Tolerable deviation rate										
	2%	3%	4%	5%	6%	7%	8%	9%	10%	15%	20%
0.00%	149(0)	99(0)	74(0)	59(0)	49(0)	42(0)	36(0)	32(0)	29(0)	19(0)	14(0)
0.25	236(1)	157(1)	117(1)	93(1)	78(1)	66(1)	58(1)	51(1)	46(1)	30(1)	22(1)
0.50	*	157(1)	117(1)	93(1)	78(1)	66(1)	58(1)	51(1)	46(1)	30(1)	22(1)
0.75	*	208(2)	117(1)	93(1)	78(1)	66(1)	58(1)	51(1)	46(1)	30(1)	22(1)
1.00	*	*	156(2)	93(1)	78(1)	66(1)	58(1)	51(1)	46(1)	30(1)	22(1)
1.25	*	*	156(2)	124(2)	78(1)	66(1)	58(1)	51(1)	46(1)	30(1)	22(1)
1.50	*	*	192(3)	124(2)	103(2)	66(1)	58(1)	51(1)	46(1)	30(1)	22(1)
1.75	*	*	227(4)	153(3)	103(2)	88(2)	58(1)	51(1)	46(1)	30(1)	22(1)
2.00	*	*	*	181(4)	127(3)	88(2)	77(2)	68(2)	46(1)	30(1)	22(1)
2.25	*	*	*	208(5)	127(3)	88(2)	77(2)	68(2)	61(2)	30(1)	22(1)
2.50	*	*	*	*	150(4)	109(3)	77(2)	68(2)	61(2)	30(1)	22(1)
2.75	*	*	*	*	173(5)	109(3)	95(3)	68(2)	61(2)	30(1)	22(1)
3.00	*	*	*	*	195(6)	129(4)	95(3)	84(3)	61(2)	30(1)	22(1)
3.25	*	*	*	*	*	148(5)	112(4)	84(3)	61(2)	30(1)	22(1)
3.50	*	*	*	*	*	167(6)	112(4)	84(3)	76(3)	40(2)	22(1)
3.75	*	*	*	*	*	185(7)	129(5)	100(4)	76(3)	40(2)	22(1)
4.00	*	*	*	*	*	*	146(6)	100(4)	89(4)	40(2)	22(1)
5.00	*	*	*	*	*	*	*	158(8)	116(6)	40(2)	30(2)
6.00	*	*	*	*	*	*	*	*	179(11)	50(3)	30(2)
7.00	*	*	*	*	*	*	*	*	*	68(5)	37(3)

Note: This table assumes a large population.
* Sample size is too large to be cost-effective for most audit applications. Source: AICPA, Audit and Accounting Guide, *Audit Sampling* (New York, 1983).

Figure 8–4   Statistical sampling results evaluation table for tests of controls: achieved upper deviation rate at 5 percent risk of overreliance

Sample size	Actual number of deviations found										
	0	1	2	3	4	5	6	7	8	9	10
25	11.3	17.6	*	*	*	*	*	*	*	*	*
30	9.5	14.9	19.6	*	*	*	*	*	*	*	*
35	8.3	12.9	17.0	*	*	*	*	*	*	*	*
40	7.3	11.4	15.0	18.3	*	*	*	*	*	*	*
45	6.5	10.2	13.4	16.4	19.2	*	*	*	*	*	*
50	5.9	9.2	12.1	14.8	17.4	19.9	*	*	*	*	*
55	5.4	8.4	11.1	13.5	15.9	18.2	*	*	*	*	*
60	4.9	7.7	10.2	12.5	14.7	16.8	18.8	*	*	*	*
65	4.6	7.1	9.4	11.5	13.6	15.5	17.4	19.3	*	*	*
70	4.2	6.6	8.8	10.8	12.6	14.5	16.3	18.0	19.7	*	*
75	4.0	6.2	8.2	10.1	11.8	13.6	15.2	16.9	18.5	20.0	*
80	3.7	5.8	7.7	9.5	11.1	12.7	14.3	15.9	17.4	18.9	*
90	3.3	5.2	6.9	8.4	9.9	11.4	12.8	14.2	15.5	16.8	18.2
100	3.0	4.7	6.2	7.6	9.0	10.3	11.5	12.8	14.0	15.2	16.4
125	2.4	3.8	5.0	6.1	7.2	8.3	9.3	10.3	11.3	12.3	13.2
150	2.0	3.2	4.2	5.1	6.0	6.9	7.8	8.6	9.5	10.3	11.1
200	1.5	2.4	3.2	3.9	4.6	5.2	5.9	6.5	7.2	7.8	8.4

Note: This table presents upper limits as percentages. This table assumes a large population.
* Over 20 percent.
Source: AICPA, Audit and Accounting Guide, *Audit Sampling* (New York, 1983).

risk of overreliance. Then, one may read the sample size from the table at the intersection of the stipulated tolerable deviation rate and the expected population deviation rate. For example, assume that the auditors specify a risk of overreliance of 5 percent, allowing them to use Figure 8–3 to determine sample size. They estimate the deviation rate for the population at 3 percent and specify a 7 percent tolerable deviation rate to justify their planned reliance upon this control procedure. Figure 8–3 shows that these specifications indicate a sample size of 129 items, which must contain no more than four control procedure deviations if the auditors' planned reliance upon the control procedure is to be justified by the test.

After the sample has been taken, if four or less deviations are found in the sample, the results would support the auditors' degree of planned reliance on the control procedure. If more than four deviations are found, Figure 8–4 may be used to evaluate the results.

Figure 8–4 allows auditors to obtain the *achieved upper deviation rate* from a sample result. The achieved upper deviation rate is the actual maximum deviation rate which the results obtained in the sample statistically support. When the achieved upper deviation rate is in excess of the tolerable deviation rate, the planned degree of reliance on the control procedure is not justified. To illustrate evaluation of a sample, assume that 5 deviations are found in the sample of 129. Referring to Figure 8–4, we find that the exact sample size of 129 does not appear. When this happens the auditors may interpolate; use more detailed tables, sometimes generated by generalized audit software; or use the largest sample size listed on the table that does not exceed the sample size actually selected. Using the latter approach, we evaluate the results using a slightly smaller size of 125. Figure 8–4 reveals that when 5 deviations are found for a sample size of 125, the achieved upper deviation rate is 8.3 percent. This tells the auditors that, statistically, there is a 5 percent chance that the actual deviation rate is higher than 8.3 percent. Therefore, there is more than a 5 percent chance that the actual deviation rate exceeds 7 percent, the tolerable rate. The most likely effect on the audit will be an increased assessment of control risk and an increase in the scope of substantive testing for accounts affected by the control being tested. Only when the upper deviation rate found in Table 8–4 is less than or equal to the tolerable deviation rate would the sample results support the planned reliance (assessment of control risk).

Detailed illustration of attributes sampling

The following procedures for applying attribute sampling are based upon the use of the tables in Figures 8–3 and 8–4; however, only slight modifications of the approach are necessary if other tables are used.

1. Determine the objective of the test Assume that the auditors wish to test the effectiveness of the client's internal control procedure of matching receiving reports with purchase invoices as a step in authorizing payments for purchases of materials. They are, therefore, interested in the clerical accuracy of the matching process and in determining whether the control procedure that requires the matching of purchase invoices and receiving reports is working.

2. Define a deviation The auditors define a deviation as any one or more of the following with respect to each invoice and the related receiving report:

a. Any invoice not supported by a receiving document.

b. Any invoice supported by a receiving document that is applicable to another invoice.

c. Any difference between the invoice and the receiving document as to quantities shipped.

For this type of test, the only testing procedure needed is inspection of the documents and matching receiving reports with invoices.

3. Define the population to be sampled The client prepares a serially numbered voucher for every purchase of materials. The receiving report and purchase invoice are attached to each voucher. Therefore, the sampling unit for the test is an individual voucher. Since the test of controls is being performed during the interim period, the population to be tested consists of 3,600 vouchers for purchases of material during the first 10 months of the year under audit. If at any point the auditor determines that the physical representation of the population (the 3,600 vouchers) has omitted vouchers that should be included in the first 10 months, the auditor should also analyze those vouchers as is appropriate.

4. Determine the method of sample selection Since the vouchers are serially numbered, the auditors decide to use a generalized audit software program to generate a list of random numbers to select a sample for testing.

5. Determining the sample size In the audits of the previous three years, the auditors observed that exceptions of the type described above produced deviation rates of 0.5 percent, 0.9 percent, and 0.7 percent. Therefore, the auditors conservatively select an *expected deviation rate* of 1 percent.

The auditors realize that errors in matching receiving reports with purchase orders can affect the financial statements through overpayments to vendors and misstatements of purchases and accounts payable. They also would like to rely upon this internal control procedure to limit their substantive testing of accounts payable, inventories, and the cost of goods sold. Based on these considerations, the auditors decide upon a tolerable deviation rate of 4 percent, with a risk of overreliance of 5 percent.

Since the stipulated risk of overreliance is 5 percent, Figure 8–3 is applicable. At the intersection of the column for a tolerable deviation rate of 4 percent and the row for a 1 percent expected deviation rate, the sample size is found to be 156 items. The expected number of deviations in the sample is two.

6. Select the sample and examine the sample items The auditors proceed to select 156 vouchers, and examine the vouchers and supporting documents for each of the types of deviations previously defined.

7. Evaluate the sample results In evaluating the sample results, the auditors must consider not only the actual number of deviations observed, but also the nature of the deviations. We will discuss three possible sets of circumstances: (1) the actual deviation rate is equal to, or less than, the expected rate; (2) the actual deviation rate is more than the expected rate; and (3) one or more deviations observed contain evidence of a deliberate manipulation or circumvention of internal control.

First, assume that one deviation has been identified and there is no evidence of a deliberate manipulation or circumvention of the internal control structure. Recall that the expected number of deviations from Figure 8–3 was two. Because the number of deviations (here, one) did not exceed the expected number, the auditors may conclude that there is less than a 5 percent risk that the population deviation rate is greater than 4 percent. In this case, the sample results support the auditors' planned reliance on the control and, therefore, their planned assessment of control risk.

Next, assume that the number of deviations observed in the sample is three, and none of the observed deviations indicate deliberate manipulation or circumvention of internal control. Because this exceeds the expected number of two deviations, the upper deviation rate is greater than 4 percent. Referring to Figure 8–4 for a sample size of 150 (the highest number still less than the sample size), the auditors find that when three deviations are observed the achieved upper deviation rate is 5.1 percent. In light of these results, the auditors should reduce their reliance upon the clients' internal control in this area and increase their reliance upon their substantive testing procedures. As a preliminary step to any modification of their audit program, the auditors should investigate the cause of the unexpectedly high deviation rate.

Finally, assume that one or more of the deviations discovered by the auditors indicates an irregularity such as circumvention of the internal control structure. In such a circumstance other auditing procedures become necessary. The auditors must evaluate the effect of the deviation on the financial statements and adopt auditing procedures that are specifically designed to protect against the type of deviation observed. Indeed, the nature of the deviation may be more important than its rate of occurrence.

8. Documenting the sampling procedures Finally, each of the seven prior steps, as well as the basis for overall conclusions, should be documented in the auditors' working papers.

Other statistical attributes sampling approaches

Discovery sampling Discovery sampling is actually a modified case of attributes sampling. The purpose of a discovery sample is to detect at least *one deviation,* with a predetermined risk of overreliance, if the deviation rate in the population is greater than the specified tolerable deviation rate. One important use of discovery sampling is to locate examples of a suspected fraud.

Although discovery sampling is designed to locate relatively rare items, it cannot locate a needle in a haystack. If an extremely small number of deviations exist within a population (e.g., .1 percent or less), no sample of reasonable size can provide adequate assurance that an example of the deviation will be encountered. Still, discovery sampling can (with a very high degree of confidence) ensure detection of deviations occurring at a rate as low as .3 to 1 percent.

Discovery sampling is used primarily to search for *critical errors*. When a deviation is critical, such as evidence of fraud, any deviation rate may be intolerable. Consequently, if such deviation is discovered, the auditors may abandon their sampling procedures and undertake a thorough examination of the population. If no deviations are found in discovery sampling, the auditors may conclude (with the specified risk of overreliance) that the critical error does not occur to the extent of the tolerable deviation rate.

To use discovery sampling, the auditors must specify their desired risk of overreliance and the tolerable deviation rate for the test. The required sample size then may be determined by referring to an appropriate attribute sampling table, *with the assumption that the expected deviation rate in the population is 0 percent.*

To illustrate discovery sampling, assume that auditors have reason to suspect that someone has been preparing fraudulent purchase orders, receiving reports, and purchase invoices in order to generate cash disbursements for fictitious purchase transactions. In order to determine whether this has occurred, it is necessary to locate only one set of the fraudulent documents in the client's file of paid vouchers.

Assume the auditors desire a 5 percent risk of overreliance that their sample will not bring to light a fraudulent voucher if the population contains 2 percent or more fraudulent items. Referring to Figure 8–3, the auditors find that a sample size of 149 is required for an expected population deviation rate of zero percent and a tolerable deviation rate of 2 percent. Assuming that the auditors select and examine the 149 vouchers and no fraudulent vouchers are found, the auditors will have only a 5 percent risk that there are more than 2 percent fraudulent vouchers in the population.

Sequential (stop-or-go) sampling   Another approach used in practice is *sequential (stop-or-go) sampling.* Under a sequential sampling plan, the audit sample is taken in several stages. The auditors start by examining a small sample. Then, based on the results of this initial sample, they decide whether (1) to place their planned reliance on the internal control procedures, (2) to reduce their planned reliance on internal control, or (3) to examine additional sample items to get more information. If the sample results do not provide enough information to make a clear-cut decision about reliance on internal control, the auditors examine additional items and repeat the decision process until the tables being used indicate that a decision as to internal control reliance can be made.

The primary advantage of a sequential approach is that for very low population deviation rates lower sample sizes may be required as compared to the fixed sample size plans. Disadvantages of sequential approaches include the fact that sample sizes may be larger for populations with moderate error rates and that the process of drawing samples at several stages may not be cost efficient.

Nonstatistical attributes sampling

The major differences between statistical and nonstatistical sampling in attributes sampling are the steps for determining sample size and for evaluating sample results. As is the case with statistical sampling, auditors who use nonstatistical sampling need to consider the risk of overreliance and the tolerable deviation rate when determining the required sample size. But these factors need not be quantified. When evaluating results, the auditors should compare the deviation rate of the sample to the tolerable deviation rate. If the sample size was appropriate and the sample deviation rate is somewhat lower than the tolerable deviation rate, the auditors can generally conclude that the risk of overreliance is at an acceptable level. As the sample deviation rate gets closer to the tolerable deviation rate, it becomes less and less likely that the population's deviation rate is lower than the tolerable level. The auditors must use their professional judgment to determine the point at which reliance on internal control should be reduced.

AUDIT SAMPLING FOR SUBSTANTIVE TESTS

Substantive tests are designed to detect errors and irregularities that may exist in the financial statements. Accordingly, the sampling plans that are used for substantive tests are designed to estimate the dollar amount of error in a particular account balance. Based on the sample results, the auditors then conclude whether there is an unacceptably high risk of material error in the balance. The actual steps involved may be summarized as:

1. Determine the objective of the test.
2. Define the population.
3. Choose an audit sampling technique.
4. Determine the sample size.
5. Choose the method of sample selection.
6. Select the sample and examine the sample items.
7. Evaluate the sample results.
8. Document the sampling procedures.

Statistical procedures that typically are used for substantive tests include classical variables and probability-proportional-to-size sampling plans. This chapter emphasizes the classical variables plans, especially the *mean-per-unit estimation* method. Appendix 1 presents an overview of the probability-proportional-to-size method.

Sampling risk for substantive tests

In performing substantive tests of account balances, there are two types of sampling risk:

1.   The risk of *incorrect rejection* (alpha risk) of a population. This is the possibility that sample results will indicate that a population is materially misstated when, in fact, it is not materially misstated.
2.   The risk of *incorrect acceptance* (beta risk) of a population. This is the possibility that sample results will indicate that a population is *not* materially misstated when, in fact, it is materially misstated.

The nature of these risks parallel the sampling risks of tests of controls. If the auditors make the first type of error and incorrectly reject an account balance, their audit will lack *efficiency* since they will perform additional audit procedures that will eventually reveal that the account is not materially misstated. Thus, the risk of incorrect rejection relates to the efficiency, but not the effectiveness, of the audit.

The risk of incorrect acceptance of a population relates to the *effectiveness* of the audit in detecting material errors. This risk is of primary concern to auditors; failure to detect a material misstatement may lead to accusations of negligence and to extensive legal liability.

Variables sampling

Although attributes sampling approaches are useful for testing internal control, they do not provide results stated in dollars. Techniques that enable auditors to estimate dollar amounts are called variables sampling plans. These techniques are very useful in such audit applications as estimating the dollar value of a client's inventories or accounts receivable. Widely used classical variables sampling plans include *mean-per-unit estimation, ratio estimation,* and *difference estimation.*

Mean-per-unit estimation

Mean-per-unit estimation enables auditors to estimate the *average* dollar value of items in a population, with specified sampling risk and allowance for sampling risk (precision) by determining the *average* dollar value of items in a sample. An estimate of the total dollar value of the population may be obtained by multiplying the average audited value in the sample (the *sample mean*) times the number of items in the population. The *projected error* may then be calculated as the difference between this estimated total value of the population and the client's book value.

The assumption underlying mean-per-unit estimation is that the mean of a sample will, within a certain sampling risk and allowance for sampling risk, represent the true mean of the population. For variables sampling, even if tables are used to determine the required sample size, the auditor needs some familiarity with statistical theory and terminology. Of particular importance are the concepts of *normal distribution* and *standard deviation.*

Normal distribution   Many populations, such as the heights of all men, may be described as normal distributions. A normal distribution is illustrated by the familiar bell-shaped curve, illustrated in Figure 8–5, in which the values of the individual items tend to congregate around the population *mean.* Notice that the distribution of individual item values is symmetrical on both sides of the mean. There is no tendency for deviations to be to one side rather than the other.

Figure 8–5   Normal distribution

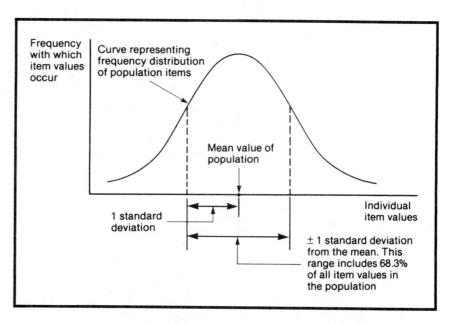

Even when the items within the population are not normally distributed, the concept of a normal distribution is relevant to sampling theory. If auditors were to draw from any population hundreds of samples of a given size, *the means of these samples would form a normal distribution* around the true population mean. This characteristic allows auditors to apply mean-per-unit estimation to populations that are not normally distributed, even though only one sample is usually taken.

Standard deviation   The standard deviation of a population is a measure of the *variability* or *dispersion* of individual item values about the population means.[7] The less variation among item values, the smaller the standard deviation; the greater the variation among item values, the larger the standard deviation. It is inherent in the definitions of normal distribution and standard deviation that 68.3 percent of the item values in a normal distribution fall within ±1 standard deviation of the population mean, that 95.4 percent fall within ±2 standard deviations, and that 99.7 percent fall within ±3 standard deviations. These percentage relationships hold true by definition; however, the dollar amount of the standard deviation will vary from one population to another.

Auditors may obtain a reliable estimate of the dollar amount of the standard deviation by taking a *pilot sample* of approximately 50 items.[8] (The items examined in this pilot sample become part of the larger sample used for estimating the population mean.) Generalized audit software packages also include routines designed to estimate the standard deviation of the book values of a population either from a sample or from the population itself.

Controlling sampling risk

The risks of incorrect acceptance and of incorrect rejection may be controlled independently of one another. For example, auditors may design a sample that limits both risks to 10 percent, or they may hold the risk of incorrect acceptance to 5 percent while allowing the risk of incorrect rejection to rise to 40 percent or more. In establishing the planned level of the risk of incorrect acceptance, auditors must consider the extent of the evidence that must be obtained from this test about the fairness of the

---

[7] The standard deviation is the square root of the following quotient: the sum of the squares of the deviation of each item value from the population mean, divided by the number of items in the population. Symbolically, the formula for calculating the standard deviation is:

$$\sqrt{\frac{\Sigma(x - \overline{X})^2}{N}}$$

[8] An *estimate* of the standard deviation may be made from a sample by taking the square root of the following quotient: the sum of the squares of the deviation of each sample item value from the sample mean, divided by one less than the number of items in the sample. Symbolically, the formula for estimating the standard deviation is:

$$\sqrt{\frac{\Sigma(x - \overline{x})^2}{n - 1}}$$

account. This is determined by the extent to which the auditors need to restrict detection risk for the account. In stipulating the planned risk of incorrect rejection, on the other hand, they should consider the *time* and *cost* involved in performing additional audit procedures when the sample results *erroneously* indicate that a correct book balance is materially misstated. In mean-per-unit estimation, as was the case with attributes sampling, the allowance for sampling risk is used to control sampling risk. The appropriate planned allowance for sampling risk may be determined from the following formula:

$$\text{Planned allowance for sampling risk} = \frac{\text{Tolerable error}}{1 + \dfrac{\text{Incorrect acceptance coefficient}}{\text{Incorrect rejection coefficient}}}$$

The tolerable error is the maximum monetary error that may exist in the account without causing the financial statements to be materially misstated. The *risk coefficients* are taken from a table, such as the one in Figure 8–6. Notice that the coefficients are different for the two types of risks.

Figure 8–6 Risk coefficients

Acceptable level of risk	Incorrect acceptance coefficient	Incorrect rejection coefficient
1.0%	2.33	2.58
4.6	1.68	2.00
5.0	1.64	1.96
10	1.28	1.64
15	1.04	1.44
20	0.84	1.28
25	0.67	1.15
30	0.52	1.04
40	0.25	0.84
50	0.00	0.67

Determination of sample size

The factors directly included in the sample size formula in mean-per-unit estimation are the (1) population size, (2) planned risk of incorrect rejection, (3) estimated variability (standard deviation) among item values in the population, and (4) planned allowance for sampling risk. The relationship of these factors to the required sample size is expressed by the following:[9]

$$\text{Sample size} = \left(\frac{\begin{array}{c} \text{Population size} \times \text{Incorrect rejection} \\ \text{coefficient} \times \text{Estimated standard deviation} \end{array}}{\text{Planned allowance for sampling risk}} \right)^2$$

Evaluating the sample results

Recall that the auditors determined sample size based on the planned sampling risks and on an estimate of the standard deviation of the population. When the auditors' estimate of the population's standard deviation is exactly the same as that of the subsequent sample, the planned allowance for sampling risk may be used for evaluation purposes. However, this is seldom the case. The auditors' estimate of the population standard deviation usually differs from that of the subsequent sample. When this occurs, the sample taken does not control both risks at their planned levels, because the auditors have under- or overestimated the variability of the population in computing the required sample size. Although there are various ways of adjusting the allowance for sampling risk, one that maintains the risk of incorrect acceptance at its planned level is described below:

$$\begin{array}{l} \text{Adjusted allowance} \\ \text{for sampling risk} \end{array} = \begin{array}{l} \text{Tolerable} \\ \text{error} \end{array} - \frac{\begin{array}{c} \text{(Population size} \times \text{Incorrect} \\ \text{acceptance coefficient} \times \\ \text{Sample standard deviation)} \end{array}}{\sqrt{\text{Sample size}}}$$

Once the auditors calculate the adjusted allowance for sampling risk, the client's book value is accepted or rejected based on whether it falls within

---

[9] This formula is based upon an infinite population. The effect on sample size when the population is finite but of significant size is small. Symbolically, this formula may be stated:

$$n = \left(\frac{N \times U_r \times SD}{A} \right)^2$$

where n = sample size, N = Population size, U_r = Incorrect rejection coefficient, SD = Estimated standard deviation, and A = Allowance for sampling risk.

the interval constructed by the audited sample mean ± the adjusted allowance for sampling risk. If the book value falls within the interval, the sample results support the conclusion that the account balance is materially correct. On the other hand, the sample results indicate that there is too great a risk that the account balance is materially misstated, if the client's book value does *not* fall within the interval.

Detailed illustration of mean-per-unit estimation

1. Determine the objective of the test Assume that the auditors wish to test the validity of recorded accounts receivable of a small public-utility client. They wish to test the book value of accounts receivable by confirming a sample of the accounts through direct correspondence with the customers.

2. Define the population The client's records have 100,000 accounts recorded at a total book value of $6,250,000.

3. Choose the audit sampling technique The auditors have decided to use the mean-per-unit technique.

4. Determine the sample size To calculate the required sample size the auditors must determine (1) the tolerable error for accounts receivable, (2) planned levels of sampling risk (the risks of incorrect acceptance and rejection), (3) an estimate of the population standard deviation, and (4) the population size.

Based on their evaluation of internal control, the auditors believe that all accounts are included in the 100,000 accounts in the clients' subsidiary ledger. In view of the materiality of the dollar amounts involved, the auditors assess tolerable error to be $364,000. Since internal control is weak the auditors recognize that detection risk must be restricted to a low level. Therefore, the auditors decide on a 5 percent risk of incorrect acceptance. Also, based on a consideration of costs of performing the procedures, a 4.6 percent risk of incorrect rejection is planned by the auditors. From this information and by using risk coefficients obtained from Figure 8–6, the planned allowance for sampling risk may be calculated as follows:

$$\text{Planned allowance for sampling risk} = \frac{\text{Tolerable error}}{1 + \dfrac{\text{Incorrect acceptance coefficient}}{\text{Incorrect rejection coefficient}}}$$

$$= \frac{\$364,000}{1 + \dfrac{1.64}{2.00}} = \$200,000$$

To estimate the standard deviation of the population, the auditors used a generalized audit software program to calculate the standard deviation of the recorded book values of the individual customers' accounts. The result was $15.

Using the sample size formula, the required sample size may now be computed:

$$\text{Sample size} = \left(\frac{\text{Population size} \times \text{Incorrect rejection coefficient} \times \text{Estimated standard deviation}}{\text{Planned allowance for sampling risk}} \right)^2$$

$$= \left(\frac{100,000 \times 2.00 \times \$15}{\$200,000} \right)^2 = \left(\frac{\$3,000,000}{\$\ 200,000} \right)^2$$

$$= 225 \text{ accounts}$$

5. Choose the method of sample selection   The client's receivables are from residential customers and do not vary greatly in size. For this reason, the auditors decide to use a random number table to select an unstratified random sample.

6. Select the sample and examine the sample items   The auditors send the confirmations and perform additional procedures as appropriate.

7. Evaluate the sample results   Confirmation of the 225 accounts results in a sample with a mean value of $61 per account and a standard deviation of $15. Since the sample's standard deviation equals that used in planning, the adjusted allowance for sampling risk equals the planned allowance of $200,000. Therefore, the auditors' estimate of the total value of the population is $6,100,000 ($61 × 100,000 accounts) plus or minus the allowance for sampling risk of $200,000 ($5,900,000 to $6,300,000). Because the client's book value of $6,250,000 falls within this interval, the sample results indicate that the client's valuation of accounts receivable is not materially in error. However, the sample results indicate a ***projected error*** of $150,000 ($6,250,000 − $6,100,000). This projected error will be considered when the auditors are analyzing the total amount of potential error in the financial statements. Also, the auditors will suggest that the client correct any accounts that their test revealed to be in error, even though the errors are less than the tolerable error amount.

How do the auditors evaluate the results if the sample's standard deviation differs from the estimate? The auditors may use the formula discussed above to calculate the adjusted allowance for sampling risk. For example, if the sample's standard deviation had instead been equal to $16, the adjusted allowance for sampling risk may be calculated as follows:

$$
\begin{aligned}
\text{Adjusted allowance} &= \text{Tolerable} - \frac{(\text{Population size} \times \text{Incorrect acceptance coefficient} \times \text{Sample standard deviation})}{\sqrt{\text{Sample size}}} \\[2mm]
\text{for sampling risk} \quad & \quad \text{error} \\[2mm]
&= \$364{,}000 - \frac{(100{,}000 \times 1.64 \times \$16)}{\sqrt{225}} \\[2mm]
&= \$189{,}067
\end{aligned}
$$

Thus, the interval would be constructed as $6,100,000 ± $189,067 ($5,910,933 to $6,289,067). Because the book value ($6,250,000) falls within this interval, the sample results still indicate that the account does not contain a material error.

In cases in which the client's book value falls *outside* the interval, the auditor must decide whether: (1) the client's book value is actually materially misstated or (2) the sample is not representative of the population. To decide which is the case, the auditors should carefully examine the errors found in the sample. If few errors were found, this indicates that the sample may not be representative. Based on the results of this error analysis, the auditors may decide to (1) increase the sample size of the test, (2) perform other audit tests of the account, or (3) work with the client's personnel to locate the errors in the account.

As in other types of sampling, the auditors should consider the qualitative aspects of any errors found in their sample. "What caused the errors?" "Do any of the errors indicate fraud?" and "What are the implications of the errors for other audit areas?" are questions the auditors would attempt to answer in their qualitative evaluation of the results.

8. Document the sampling procedures   Each of the prior seven steps, as well as the basis for overall conclusions, should be documented.

Ratio and difference estimation

Mean-per-unit estimation estimates the average item value as the basis for estimating the total value of the population. Two alternatives to this approach are ratio and difference estimation. Although closely related, ratio estimation and difference estimation are two distinct sampling plans; each is appropriate under slightly different circumstances.

In ratio estimation, the auditors use a sample to estimate the *ratio* of the audited (correct) value of a population to its book value. This ratio is estimated by dividing the total audited value of a sample by the total book value of the sample items.[10] An estimate of the correct population value is obtained by multiplying this estimated ratio by the total book value of the population.

In applying difference estimation, the auditors use a sample to estimate the ***average difference*** between the audited value and book value of items in a population. The average difference is estimated by dividing the net difference between the audited value and book value of a sample by the number of items in the sample.[11] The total difference between the book value of the population and its estimated correct value is determined by multiplying the estimated average difference by the number of items in the population.

Use of ratio and difference estimation   The use of ratio or difference estimation techniques requires that (1) each population item has a book value, (2) an audited value may be ascertained for each sample item, and (3) differences between audited and book values are relatively frequent. If the occurrence rate of differences is very low, a prohibitively large sample is required to disclose a representative number of errors. However, when these requirements are met, ratio estimation or difference estimation is often more efficient than mean-per-unit estimation.

Ratio estimation is most appropriate when the size of errors is nearly proportional to the book values of the items. In many cases, the size of transactions affecting an account may be nearly proportional to the account balance. Thus, mistakes in processing transactions affecting large accounts generally are larger than those affecting small accounts. In these situations ratio estimation is more appropriate than difference estimation.

---

[10] Symbolically, this process is expressed:

$$\hat{R} = \frac{\Sigma a_j}{\Sigma b_j}$$

where $\hat{R}$ (pronounced R caret) represents the estimated ratio of audited value to book value, a_j represents the audited value of each sample item, and b_j represents the book value of each sample item.

[11] Symbolically, the estimated difference is computed:

$$\hat{d} = \frac{1}{n} \sum_{j=1}^{n} (a_j - b_j)$$

where $\hat{d}$ represents the estimated average difference between audited value and book value; n represents the number of items in the sample; and a_j and b_j represent the audited and book values, respectively.

When the size of errors is not approximately proportional to book value, difference estimation is the more appropriate technique.

Illustration of ratio and difference estimation

To illustrate the use of ratio and difference estimation techniques, assume that auditors wish to estimate the total value of a client's accounts payable. The population consists of 4,000 accounts with an aggregate book value of $5 million. The auditors calculate the required sample size, randomly select the accounts to be sampled, and apply auditing procedures to determine the correct account balances. Assume that the sample consists of 200 accounts with a book value of $240,000 and that the audited amount is determined to be $247,500.

Using ratio estimation, the auditors would estimate the ratio of audited value to book value to be 1.03125 ($247,500/$240,000). Their estimate of the total population value, therefore, would be $5,156,250 ($5,000,000 × 1.03125). The ratio approach thus indicates a projected error of a $156,250 understatement ($5,156,250 − $5,000,000) of payables.

If difference estimation is used, the auditors would estimate the average difference per item to be a $37.50 understatement, the $7,500 (net difference of $247,500 − $240,000) divided by 200 items. Multiplying $37.50 by the 4,000 accounts in the population indicates that the projected error for accounts payable is a $150,000 understatement. The estimated total audited value would be $5,150,000 ($5,000,000 + $150,000).

Each of these estimates would have a sampling risk and an allowance for sampling risk that would be related to the auditors' sample size. The procedures for determining the required sample size in these sampling plans are similar to those in mean-per-unit estimation. To provide auditors with assistance in this area, the AICPA audit guide, *Audit Sampling*, is helpful.

Nonstatistical variables sampling

The major difference between statistical and nonstatistical sampling in substantive testing are in the steps for determining sample size and for evaluating sample results. When using nonstatistical sampling the auditors may choose not to explicitly quantify the factors used to arrive at a sample size, although they should consider the relationships summarized in Figure 8–2. In evaluating the sample results, the auditors should project the errors found in the sample to the population and consider sampling risk, but they do not quantify the risk.

Conceptually, projecting the errors to the population may be performed using various approaches. The AICPA's audit guide uses two approaches which are in essence applications of the difference and ratio methods. To illustrate the two approaches, assume that the auditors have used a nonstatistical approach and have obtained a total audited value of

$10,000 for a sample of 50 items, with a book value of $10,500. Further, assume the sample was selected from a population of 1,000 items with a total book value of $195,000.

Using the ratio approach, the auditors would estimate the ratio of audited value to book value to be .95238 ($10,000/$10,500) and their estimate of the total population value, therefore, would be $185,714 ($195,000 × .95238). The test thus indicates a projected error for the account of a $9,286 overstatement ($195,000 − $185,714).

If the difference approach is used, the auditors would estimate the average difference per item to be $10, the $500 (net difference) divided by 50 items. Multiplying the $10 difference per item by the 1,000 items in the population indicates that the projected error for the account is a $10,000 overstatement.

Certainly, if the projected error exceeds the tolerable error, the auditor should conclude that the population is probably materially misstated. When the projected error is less than tolerable error, the auditors must judgmentally determine whether to accept the population as being materially correct. The closer the projected error is to the tolerable error, the higher the risk of a material error in the account.

KEY TERMS INTRODUCED OR EMPHASIZED IN CHAPTER 8

Allowance for sampling risk (ASR, precision)   An interval around the sample results in which the true population characteristic is expected to lie.

Attributes sampling   A sampling plan enabling the auditors to estimate the rate of deviation (occurrence) in a population.

Confidence level   The complement of the risk of overreliance on internal control (or of incorrect acceptance in an attributes sampling plan).

Deviation rate (occurrence rate, exception rate)   A defined rate of departure from prescribed control procedures. This is the characteristic measured in tests of controls.

Difference estimation   A sampling plan for estimating the average difference between the audited (correct) values of items in a population and their book values. Difference estimation is used in lieu of ratio estimation when the differences are not nearly proportional to book values.

Discovery sampling   A sampling plan for locating at least one exception, providing that the exception occurs in the population with a specified frequency.

Dual-purpose test   A test designed to test an internal control procedure and to substantiate the dollar amount of an account using the same sample.

Effective audit   An audit that achieves the planned degree of effectiveness in detecting any material errors in the client's financial statements.

Efficient audit   An effective audit that is performed at the lowest possible cost.

Exception rate   See deviation rate.

Expected deviation rate   An advance estimate of a deviation rate. This estimate is necessary for determining the required sample size in an attributes sampling plan.

Mean   The average item value, computed by dividing total value by the number of items comprising total value.

Mean-per-unit estimation A sampling plan enabling the auditors to estimate the average dollar value (or other variable) of items in a population by determining the average value of items in a sample.

Nonsampling risk The aspects of audit risk not due to sampling. This risk normally relates to "human" rather than "statistical" errors.

Normal distribution A frequency distribution in which item values tend to congregate around the mean with no tendency for deviation toward one side rather than the other. A normal distribution is represented graphically by a bell-shaped curve.

Physical representation of population The population from which the auditors sample. The physical representation of the population differs from the true population when it does not include items that exist in the true population. For example, the auditors sample from a trial balance of receivables which may or may not include all actual receivables.

Population The entire field of items from which a sample might be drawn.

Precision See allowance for sampling risk.

Random selection Selecting items from a population in a manner in which every item has an equal chance of being included in the sample.

Ratio estimation A sampling plan for estimating the ratio of the audited (correct) values of items to their book values. Extending the book value of the population by this ratio provides an estimate of audited total population value. Ratio estimation is a highly efficient technique when errors are nearly proportional to item book values.

Reliability See confidence level.

Representative sample A sample possessing essentially the same characteristics as the population from which it was drawn.

Risk of incorrect acceptance (beta risk) The risk that sample results will indicate that a population is *not* materially misstated when, in fact, it is materially misstated.

Risk of incorrect rejection (alpha risk) The risk that sample results will indicate that a population is materially misstated when, in fact, it is not.

Sampling error The difference between the actual rate or amount in the population and that of the sample. For example, if an actual (but unknown) deviation rate of 3 percent exists in the population, and the sample's deviation rate is 2 percent, the sampling error is 1 percent.

Sampling risk The risk that the auditors' conclusion based on a sample might be different from the conclusion they would reach if the test were applied to the entire population. For tests of controls, sampling risks include the risks of overreliance and underreliance; for substantive testing, sampling risks include the risks of incorrect acceptance and rejection.

Sequential sampling A sampling plan in which the sample is selected in stages, with the need for each subsequent stage being conditional on the results of the previous stage.

Standard deviation A measure of the variability or dispersion of item values within a population; in a normal distribution, 68.3 percent of all item values fall within ± 1 standard deviation of the mean, 95.4 percent fall within ± 2 standard deviations, and 99.7 percent fall within ± 3 standard deviations.

Stratification   Dividing a population into two or more relatively homogeneous subgroups (strata). Stratification increases the efficiency of most sampling plans by reducing the variability of items in each stratum. The sample size necessary to evaluate the strata separately is often smaller than would be needed to evaluate the total population.

Systematic selection   The technique of selecting a sample by drawing every nth item in the population, following one or more random starting points.

Tolerable error   An estimate of the maximum monetary error that may exist in an account balance, when combined with error in other accounts, without causing the financial statements to be materially misstated.

Tolerable rate   The maximum population rate of deviations from a prescribed control procedure that the auditor will tolerate without modifying the planned reliance on internal control (assessment of control risk).

Variables sampling   Sampling plans designed to estimate a numerical measurement of a population such as a dollar value.

GROUP I: REVIEW QUESTIONS

8–1.   Describe the difference between sampling risk and nonsampling risk.

8–2.   Define, and differentiate between, nonstatistical (judgmental) sampling and statistical sampling.

8–3.   What statistical sampling plan appears to be most useful in accomplishing the basic objectives of tests of controls? Explain.

8–4.   Distinguish between attributes sampling and variables sampling.

8–5.   Explain the meaning of *sampling without replacement* and *sampling with replacement*.

8–6.   In selecting items for examination, an auditor considered three alternatives: (a) random number table selection, (b) systematic selection, and (c) random number generator selection. Which, if any, of these methods would lead to a random sample if properly applied?

8–7.   Explain briefly the term *systematic selection* as used in auditing and indicate the precautions to be taken if a random sample is to be obtained. Is systematic selection applicable to unnumbered documents? Explain.

8–8.   Explain briefly how the auditors using statistical sampling techniques may measure the possibility that the sample drawn has characteristics not representative of the population.

8–9.   What would be the difference in an attributes sampling plan and a variables sampling plan in a test of inventory extensions?

8–10.   Describe what is meant by a *sequential sampling plan.*

8–11.   If a sample of 100 items indicates an error rate of 3 percent, should the auditors conclude that the entire population also has approximately a 3 percent error rate?

8–12.   What relationship exists between the expected population deviation rate and sample size?

8–13.   Explain what is meant by an allowance for sampling risk of ±1 percent with a risk of overreliance of 10 percent.   (AICPA, adapted)

8–14.   The 10 following statements apply to unrestricted random sampling with replacement. Indicate whether each statement is true or false. Briefly discuss each false statement.

a. When sampling from the population of accounts receivable, for certain objectives the auditor might sample only active accounts with balances.

b. To be random, every item in the population must have an equal chance of being selected for inclusion in the sample.

c. In general, all items in excess of a material error need to be examined and sampling of them is inappropriate.

d. It is likely that five different random samples from the same population could produce five different estimates of the true population mean.

e. A 100 percent sample would have to be taken to attain an allowance for sampling risk range of $\pm\$0$ with no sampling risk.

f. The effect of the inclusion by chance of a very large or very small item in a random sample can be lessened by increasing the size of the sample.

g. The standard deviation is a measure of the variability of items in a population.

h. The larger the standard deviation of a population, the smaller the required sample size.

i. Unrestricted random sampling with replacement results in a larger sample size than unrestricted random sampling without replacement.

j. Unrestricted random sampling normally results in a smaller sample size than does stratified sampling.

8–15. In performing a substantive test of the book value of a population, auditors must be concerned with two aspects of sampling risk. What are these two aspects of sampling risk, and which aspect is of greater importance to auditors? Explain.

GROUP II: QUESTIONS REQUIRING ANALYSIS

8–16. An auditor used a nonstatistical sampling plan to audit the inventory of an auto supply company. The auditor tested the recorded cost of a sample of inventory items by reference to vendors' invoices. In performing the test, the auditor verified all the items on two pages selected at random from the client's 257-page inventory listing. The sampling plan resulted in a test of $50,000 of the total book value of $5,000,000, and the auditor found a total of $5,000 in overstatement errors in the sample. Since the senior indicated that a material error in the Inventory account was $100,000, the auditor concluded that the recorded inventory value was materially correct.

Required:
Evaluate the auditor's sampling plan and the manner in which the results were evaluated.

8–17. Increasing attention is being given by CPAs to the application of statistical techniques to audit testing.

Required:
a. List and explain the advantages of applying statistical sampling techniques to audit testing.

b. List and discuss the decisions involving professional judgment that must be made by the CPAs in applying statistical sampling techniques to tests of controls.

    c. You have applied attributes sampling to the client's pricing of the inventory and discovered from your sampling that the sample deviation rate exceeds your maximum tolerable deviation rate. Discuss the courses of action you can take.   (AICPA, adapted)

8–18. The professional development department of a large CPA firm has prepared the following illustration to familiarize the audit staff with the relationships of sample size to population size and variability and the auditors' specifications as to the allowance for sampling risk (ASR) and the risk of incorrect acceptance.

	Characteristics of population 1 relative to population 2		Audit specifications as to a sample from population 1 relative to a sample from population 2	
	Size	Variability	Planned ASR	Planned risk of incorrect acceptance
Case 1	Larger	Equal	Equal	Equal
Case 2	Equal	Larger	Wider	Equal
Case 3	Larger	Equal	Tighter	Equal
Case 4	Smaller	Smaller	Equal	Lower
Case 5	Smaller	Equal	Wider	Higher

Required:

For each of the five cases in the above illustration, indicate the relationship of the sample size to be selected from population 1 relative to the sample from population 2. Select your answer from the following numbered responses and state the reasoning behind your choice. The required sample size from population 1 is:

1. Larger than the required sample size from population 2.
2. Equal to the required sample size from population 2.
3. Smaller than the required sample size from population 2.
4. Indeterminate relative to the required sample size from population 2.
    (AICPA, adapted)

8–19. In performing a test of controls for sales order approvals, the CPAs stipulate a maximum tolerable deviation rate of 8 percent with a risk of overreliance of 5 percent. They anticipate a deviation rate of 2 percent.

Required:

    a. What type of sampling plan should the auditors use for this test?

    b. Using the appropriate table or formula from this chapter, compute the required sample size for the test.

    c. Assume that the sample indicates four deviations. May the CPAs conclude with a 5 percent risk of overreliance that the population deviation rate does not exceed their maximum tolerable rate of 8 percent?

8–20. An auditor has reason to suspect that fraud has occurred through forgery of the treasurer's signature on company checks. The population under consideration consists of 3,000 checks. Can discovery sampling rule out the possibility that any forged checks exist among the 3,000 checks? Explain.

8–21. During an audit of Potter Company, an auditor needs to estimate the total value of the 5,000 invoices processed during June. The auditor estimates the standard deviation of the population to be $30. Determine the size sample the auditor would select to achieve an allowance for sampling risk (precision) of ±$25,000 with 4.6 percent risk of incorrect rejection.

(AICPA, adapted)

8–22. Robert Rotter, CPA, is considering the use of a mean-per-unit estimation sampling plan. Explain the factors that Rotter would consider in determining—

a. The acceptable risk of incorrect rejection.
b. The maximum tolerable error in the population.
c. The acceptable risk of incorrect acceptance.

8–23. Cathy Williams is auditing the financial statements of Westerman Industries. In the performance of a mean-per-unit estimation of credit samples, Williams has decided to limit the risk of incorrect rejection to 25 percent and the risk of incorrect acceptance to 10 percent. Williams considers the maximum tolerable error in this revenue account to be ±$500,000. Calculate the planned allowance for sampling risk.

8–24. Select the best answer for each of the following questions. Explain the reasons for your selection.

a. Which of the following is an element of sampling risk?
1. Choosing an audit procedure that is inconsistent with the audit objective.
2. Concluding that no material error exists based on taking a sample that includes no errors from a materially misstated population.
3. Failing to detect an error on a document that has been inspected by an auditor.
4. Failing to perform audit procedures that are required by the sampling plan.

b. What is the primary purpose of using stratification as a sampling method in auditing?
1. To decrease the nonsampling risk of a given sample.
2. To determine the exact occurrence rate of a given characteristic in the population being studied.
3. To decrease the effect of variance in the total population.
4. To determine the allowance for sampling risk of the sample selected.

c. Approximately 4 percent of the homogeneous items included in Gooba's finished goods inventory are believed to be defective. The CPAs examining Gooba's financial statements decide to test this estimated 4 percent defective rate. They learn that a sample of 146 items from the inventory will permit a specified risk of overreliance of 5 percent with a tolerable rate of 8 percent. If the specified tolerable rate is changed to 9 percent and the risk of incorrect acceptance

remains at 5 percent, the planned sample size becomes (solve without use of tables)—
1. 100
2. 335
3. 436
4. 1,543

d. In assessing sampling risk, the risk of incorrect rejection and the risk of underreliance on internal control relate to the—
1. Efficiency of the audit.
2. Effectiveness of the audit.
3. Selection of the sample.
4. Audit quality controls.

e. If certain forms are not consecutively numbered—
1. Selection of a random sample probably is not possible.
2. Systematic sampling may be appropriate.
3. Stratified sampling should be used.
4. Random number tables cannot be used.

f. If the auditors are concerned that a population may contain exceptions, the determination of a sample size sufficient to include at *least* one such exception is a characteristic of—
1. Discovery sampling
2. Variables sampling
3. Random sampling
4. Attributes sampling   (AICPA, adapted)

8–25. Ratio estimation and difference estimation are two widely used variables sampling plans.

Required:
a. Under what conditions are ratio estimation or difference estimation appropriate sampling plans for estimating the total dollar value of a population?
b. What relationship determines which of these two plans will be most efficient in a particular situation?

8–26. One of the generally accepted auditing standards states that sufficient competent evidential matter is to be obtained through inspection, observation, inquiries, and confirmation to afford a reasonable basis for an opinion regarding the financial statements under examination. Some degree of uncertainty is implicit in the concept of "a reasonable basis for an opinion," because the concept of sampling is well established in auditing practice.

Required:
a. Explain the auditor's justification for accepting the uncertainties that are inherent in the sampling process.
b. Discuss the nature of the sampling risk and nonsampling risk. Include the effect of sampling risk on substantive tests of details and on tests of internal control.   (AICPA, adapted)

GROUP III: PROBLEMS

8–27. The use of statistical sampling techniques in an examination of financial statements does not eliminate judgmental decisions.

Required:

a. Identify and explain four areas in which judgment may be exercised by CPAs in planning a statistical test of a control.

b. Assume that the auditors' sample shows an unacceptable deviation rate. Discuss the various actions that they may take based upon this finding.

c. A nonstratified sample of 80 accounts payable vouchers is to be selected from a population of 3,200. The vouchers are numbered consecutively from 1 to 3,200 and are listed, 40 to a page, in the voucher register. Describe four different techniques for selecting a random sample of vouchers for review. (AICPA, adapted)

8–28. To test the pricing and mathematical accuracy of sales invoices, the auditors selected a sample of 208 sales invoices from a total of 41,600 invoices that were issued during the years under examination. The 208 invoices represented total recorded sales of $20,800. Total sales for the year amounted to $5 million. The examination disclosed that of the 208 invoices audited, 5 were not properly priced or contained errors in extensions and footings. The 5 incorrect invoices represented $720 of the total recorded sales, and the errors found resulted in a net understatement of these invoices by $300.

Required:

Explain what conclusions the auditors may draw from the above information, assuming the sample was selected—

a. Using nonstatistical sampling.

b. As part of an attributes sampling plan using a stipulated maximum deviation rate of 5 percent, and a risk of overreliance of 5 percent.

c. As part of a difference estimation plan for estimating the total population value.

8–29. In the audit of Potomac Mills, the auditors wish to test the costs assigned to manufactured goods. During the year, the company has produced 2,000 production lots with a total recorded cost of $5.9 million. The auditors select a sample of 200 production lots with an aggregate book value of $600,000 and vouch the assigned costs to the supporting documentation. Their examination discloses errors in the cost of 52 of the 200 production lots; after adjustment for these errors, the audited value of the sample is $582,000.

Required:

a. Show how the auditors would compute an estimate of the total cost of production lots manufactured during the year using each of the following sampling plans. (Do not compute the allowance for sampling risk or risk of incorrect acceptance of the estimates.)

(1) Mean-per-unit estimation.

(2) Ratio estimation.

(3) Difference estimation.

b. Explain why mean-per-unit estimation results in a higher estimate of the population value than does ratio estimation in this particular instance.

8–30. The auditors wish to use mean-per-unit sampling to evaluate the reasonableness of the book value of the accounts receivable of Smith, Inc. Smith has 10,000 receivable accounts with a total book value of $1,500,000. The auditors estimate the population's standard deviation to be equal to $25. After examining the overall audit plan, the auditors believe that the account's tolerable error is $60,000, and that a risk of incorrect rejection of 5% and a risk of incorrect acceptance of 10% are appropriate.

Required:

a. Calculate the required sample size.

b. Assuming the following results:

Average audited value   = $146
Standard deviation of sample = $ 28

Use the mean-per-unit method to:

(1) Calculate the point estimate of the account's audited value.
(2) Calculate the projected error for the population.
(3) Calculate the adjusted allowance for sampling risk.
(4) State the auditors' conclusion in this situation.

APPENDIX 1: PROBABILITY-PROPORTIONAL-TO-SIZE (PPS) SAMPLING

Probability-proportional-to-size (PPS) sampling[12] is a technique that applies the theory of attributes sampling to estimate the total dollar amount of error in a population. It has gained popularity in practice because: (1) its use may result in smaller-size samples than classical approaches, especially for populations with low error rates; (2) the method automatically results in a stratified sample in which individually significant items are identified; (3) the sample can be designed and sample selection can begin prior to the availability of the entire population; and (4) many auditors consider it easier to apply than classical variables sampling.

Whereas classical variables sampling plans define the population as a group of accounts or transactions, PPS sampling defines the population as the *individual dollars* comprising the population's book value. Thus, a population of 5,000 accounts receivable with a total value of $2,875,000 is viewed as a population of 2,875,000 items (dollars), rather than 5,000 items (accounts).

Determination of sample size

The factors affecting sample size in PPS sampling are (1) the recorded dollar amount of the population, (2) the reliability factor, (3) the tolerable error, (4) the expected error in the account, and (5) the expansion factor. Specifically, the sample size for PPS may be computed as follows:

$$\text{Sample size} = \frac{\text{Book value of population} \times \text{Reliability factor}}{\text{Tolerable error} - (\text{Expected error} \times \text{Expansion factor})}$$

---

[12] Variations of this sampling technique are called dollar-unit sampling and monetary-unit sampling.

Several of the factors in the PPS formula need very little additional explanation. The book value of the population is the recorded amount of the population being audited. The tolerable error is the maximum monetary error that may exist in the population without causing the financial statements to be materially misstated. The expected error is the auditors' estimate of the dollar amount of error in the population. The auditors estimate the expected error using professional judgment based on prior experience and knowledge of the client. The other factors used to calculate sample size are based on the auditors' desired risk of incorrect acceptance and are obtained from tables, such as the ones in Figures 8–7 and 8–8. The "zero errors" row of Figure 8–7 is always used for obtaining the reliability factor for determining sample size. Thus, if a 10 percent risk of incorrect acceptance is desired, the factor is 2.31. The expansion factor comes directly from Figure 8–8. For a 10 percent risk, the factor is 1.5.

Figure 8–7 Reliability factors for errors of overstatement

Number of over-statement errors	Risk of incorrect acceptance								
	1%	5%	10%	15%	20%	25%	30%	37%	50%
0*	4.61	3.00	2.31	1.90	1.61	1.39	1.21	1.00	.70
1	6.64	4.75	3.89	3.38	3.00	2.70	2.44	2.14	1.68
2	8.41	6.30	5.33	4.72	4.28	3.93	3.62	3.25	2.68
3	10.05	7.76	6.69	6.02	5.52	5.11	4.77	4.34	3.68
4	11.61	9.16	8.00	7.27	6.73	6.28	5.90	5.43	4.68
5	13.11	10.52	9.28	8.50	7.91	7.43	7.01	6.49	5.68
6	14.57	11.85	10.54	9.71	9.08	8.56	8.12	7.56	6.67
7	16.00	13.15	11.78	10.90	10.24	9.69	9.21	8.63	7.67
8	17.41	14.44	13.00	12.08	11.38	10.81	10.31	9.68	8.67
9	18.79	15.71	14.21	13.25	12.52	11.92	11.39	10.74	9.67
10	20.15	16.97	15.41	14.42	13.66	13.02	12.47	11.79	10.67

* Always used for reliability factor in sample size formula and for basic precision.
Source: AICPA, Audit and Accounting Guide, *Audit Sampling* (New York, 1983).

Figure 8–8 Expansion factors for expected errors

	Risk of incorrect acceptance								
	1%	5%	10%	15%	20%	25%	30%	37%	50%
Factor	1.9	1.6	1.5	1.4	1.3	1.25	1.2	1.15	1.0

Source: AICPA, Audit and Accounting Guide, *Audit Sampling* (New York, 1983).

Controlling sampling risk

As is the case with classical variables approaches, the auditors decide on an appropriate level of risk of incorrect acceptance. This level of risk is then used to obtain the appropriate factors to calculate sample size. The risk of incorrect rejection is indirectly controlled by the auditors' estimate of expected error that is used to calculate the PPS sample size. If the auditors underestimate the expected error, the sample size will not be large enough and additional testing may be necessary in order to accept the account balance as being materially correct.

Method of sample section

Auditors generally use a systematic selection approach when using PPS. However, since the sampling unit is based on dollars, not individual accounts, the sampling interval is also based on dollars. The sampling interval is calculated as follows:

$$\text{Sampling interval} = \frac{\text{Book value of population}}{\text{Sample size}}$$

To illustrate this method of selection, assume that the auditors are sampling from a population of accounts receivable totaling $300,000, and the sampling interval is calculated to be $1,500. A random starting point is selected between $1 and $1,500, say, $412. Then, the sample will include the accounts receivable that contain every $1,500 from the starting point, as illustrated in Figure 8–9. The accounts included in Figure 8–9 are considered "logical units" because when applying PPS the auditors generally *cannot* audit only the dollar selected but must audit the entire account, invoice, or voucher. Consider the confirmation of accounts receivable. Sending a confirmation of a specific dollar in a selected balance is not generally feasible. The auditors usually must confirm the entire account.

Figure 8–9 PPS selection process

Account number	Book value	Cumulative total	Dollar selected	Sample item book value
0001	$1,000	$1,000	$ 412	$1,000
0002	42	1,042		
0003	1,700	2,742	1,912	1,700
0004	666	3,408		
0005	50	3,458	3,412	50
		$300,000		

Evaluation of sample results

After the sample has been selected and procedures applied to arrive at audited values for the individual accounts, the PPS sample may be evaluated. The PPS evaluation procedure involves calculating an *upper limit on errors,* which is an estimate of the maximum amount of error in the account. The upper limit on errors has two already familiar components—the *projected error* and the *allowance for sampling risk.* However, in PPS sampling, the allowance for sampling risk is made up of two other components, the *basic precision* and the *incremental allowance.* Mathematically, these relationships may be described as follows:

$$
\underset{\text{on errors}}{\text{Upper limit}} = \underset{\text{error}}{\text{Projected}} + \overbrace{\underset{\text{precision}}{\text{Basic}} + \underset{\text{allowance}}{\text{Incremental}}}^{\substack{\text{Allowance for}\\\text{sampling risk}}}
$$

As is the case with the classical approaches, the projected error may be viewed as the auditors' "best guess" of the error in the population. The *projected error* in the population is determined by summing the projected error for each account, or other logical unit, in the sample. Thus, when the sample includes no errors, the projected error is zero. When errors do exist in the sample, the method used to project the error in a particular account depends on whether or not the book value of the account found to be in error is less than the sampling interval. For accounts with book values that are less than the amount of the sampling interval, the projected error is calculated by multiplying the percent of error in the account, known as the *tainting,* times the sampling interval. Thus, if an account with a book value of $100 is found to have an audited value of $60, the error in the account is $40 ($100 − $60) and the tainting is 40 percent ($40/$100). The tainting of 40 percent would then be multiplied by the sampling interval to get the projected error for that account.

For accounts with book values equal to or greater than the sampling interval, the actual error in the account is equal to the projected error. The reason for the difference in the methods of calculation of the projected error is that every account with a book value equal to or greater than the sampling interval will be included in the sample. These items do not represent other unselected items in the population; therefore, the actual error in the account is equal to the projected error. Accounts with balances less than the sampling interval represent other unselected items of similar size in the population. For these accounts the error must be weighted by the sampling interval to arrive at the projected error for the account.

The next step in determining the upper limit on errors involves calculating the two components of the allowance for sampling risk—the basic precision and the incremental allowance. The basic precision is always found by multiplying the reliability factor for zero errors from Figure 8–7 by the sampling interval.

The way in which the incremental allowance is calculated varies depending on the number of accounts with book values less than the sampling interval that are found to be in error. When no such errors are found in the sample, the incremental allowance is zero. When errors are discovered in the sample, the incremental allowance is found by (1) ranking the projected errors for the accounts with book values less than the sampling interval from largest projected error to smallest projected error, (2) multiplying each projected error by an incremental factor calculated from the reliability factors in Figure 8–7, and (3) summing the resulting amounts.

To complete the quantitative evaluation of the sample results, the auditors compute the upper limit on errors. When errors are found, the upper limit is computed by adding together the projected error, the basic precision, and the incremental allowance. Of course, if no errors are found in the sample, the upper limit on errors consists only of the basic precision.

After the upper limit on errors is calculated, the auditors compare it to the tolerable error for the account. If the upper limit on errors is less than or equal to tolerable error, the sample results support the conclusion that the population is not misstated by more than tolerable error at the specified level of sampling risk. On the other hand, if the upper limit on errors exceeds the amount of tolerable error, the sample results do not provide the auditor with enough assurance that the misstatement in the population is less than tolerable error.

Illustration of PPS sampling

The case used to illustrate mean-per-unit sampling on pages 285 to 287 will be used to illustrate PPS sampling. The population, in that case, had a book value of $6,250,000 and the auditors decided on a tolerable error for the account of $364,000 and a 5 percent risk of incorrect acceptance. Additionally, assume that based on prior audits, the auditors expected $50,000 of error in the population.

Since the auditors are using a risk of incorrect acceptance of 5 percent, the reliability factor from Figure 8–7 is 3.00, and the expansion factor from Figure 8–8 is 1.6. Remember for calculating sample size that the zero error row of Figure 8–7 is always used. Using this information, the sample size and sampling interval may be calculated as follows:

$$\text{Sample size} = \frac{\text{Recorded amount of population} \times \text{Reliability factor}}{\text{Tolerable error} - (\text{Expected error} \times \text{Expansion factor})}$$

$$= \frac{\$6,250,000 \times 3}{\$364,000 - (50,000 \times 1.6)} = 66$$

(Continued)

$$\frac{\text{Sampling}}{\text{interval}} = \frac{\text{Recorded amount of population}}{\text{Sample size}}$$

$$= \frac{\$6,250,000}{66} = \$95,000 \text{ (approximately)}$$

Using the PPS selection method, the auditors select the accounts for confirmation, perform confirmation procedures, and find the following three errors:

Book value	Audited value
$ 100	$ 90
2,000	1,900
102,000	102

Based on the above results, the projected error, basic precision, and the incremental allowance are calculated in Figure 8–10.

The calculation of projected error is straightforward, and no table values are required. Note that the tainting percentages for the first two errors are computed by dividing the error amount by the book value of the account. Then, the tainting percentages are multiplied by the sampling

Figure 8–10   PPS illustration of calculation of upper limit on errors

PROJECTED ERROR

Book value	Audited value	Error	Tainting percentage	Sampling interval	Projected error	
$ 100	$ 90	$ 10	10%	$95,000	$ 9,500	
2,000	1,900	100	5	95,000	4,750	
102,000	102	101,898	NA	NA	101,898	
$104,100	$2,092	$102,008				$116,148

BASIC PRECISION = Reliability factor × Sampling interval

3.0	×	$95,000	=	$285,000

INCREMENTAL ALLOWANCE

Reliability factor	Increment	(Increment − 1)	Projected error	Incremental allowance	
3.00		—	—	—	
4.75	1.75	.75	$9,500	$7,125	
6.30	1.55	.55	4,750	2,613	9,738

UPPER LIMIT ON ERRORS $410,886

interval to calculate the projected error. Because the book value of the account containing the third error is greater than the sampling interval, the projected error for that account is equal to the amount of the error.

The second element of the upper limit on errors, basic precision, is simply the reliability factor for zero errors and a risk of incorrect acceptance of 5 percent from Figure 8–7 multiplied by the sampling interval.

The calculation of the incremental allowance uses the projected errors of the accounts with book values less than the sampling interval. These projected errors are ranked by size from largest projected error to smallest and multiplied by the incremental reliability factors, minus one. These incremental reliability factors are derived from the factors in Figure 8–7. Because a 5 percent risk of incorrect acceptance was selected and two errors were found in accounts with balances less than the sampling interval, the factors of 3.00, 4.75, and 6.30 are taken from Figure 8–7. An incremental factor is calculated as the difference between successive factors. For example, the incremental factor for the first error is 4.75 − 3.00, or 1.75. Then one is subtracted from each incremental factor to arrive at the factor that is multiplied by the first projected error, in this case .75. This process is repeated for each additional projected error.

Because the upper limit ($410,886) is in excess of the tolerable error ($364,000), the auditors would not accept the population as being materially correct. Thus, adjustment of the account, expansion of the sample, or audit report modification would be appropriate.[13] In this situation, the most logical approach would be to persuade the client to adjust for the $102,008 in actual errors found in the sample. This would reduce the upper limit on errors to $308,878 ($410,886 − $102,008) and enable the auditors to accept the account as being materially correct.

Final comments   Although the formulas for PPS sampling at first seem difficult, once a user becomes familiar with them, they are easier to apply in practice than the classical sampling methods. The method also provides smaller sample sizes when few errors are expected in the account. However, the existence of a moderate or high error rate in the account usually means that classical techniques would be more efficient. Finally, the mathematics behind PPS sampling is only developed to estimate overstatement type errors. CPA firms use various methods to test for understatements in the accounts.

**APPENDIX 2:
AUDIT RISK**

What level of risk of incorrect acceptance is acceptable for a substantive test? Recall that in Chapter 4 the concept of audit risk presented in *SAS 47* (AU 312) was introduced. That chapter suggested that audit risk resulted from three sources—inherent risk, control risk, and detection

---

[13] In many circumstances such as this, the client requests that the auditors expand the sample to either identify the specific errors or to determine that the account is not materially misstated.

risk. Although not meant to be a formula rigidly applied in practice, those relationships may be described as follows:

$$AR = IR \times CR \times DR$$

where:

AR = Audit risk, the risk that the auditor may unknowingly fail to appropriately modify his opinion on financial statements that are materially misstated.

IR = Inherent risk, the risk of material error[14] in an account, assuming there were no related internal controls.

IC = Control risk, the risk of a material error occurring in an account and not being prevented or detected on a timely basis by the internal control structure.

DR = Detection risk, the risk that the auditors' procedures will lead them to conclude an account is not materially in error, when in fact such error does exist.

Conceptually, if the auditors can quantify the planned level of audit risk and the estimated levels of inherent risk and control risk, the appropriate planned level of detection risk may be determined. This planned level of detection risk is a function of the risk of incorrect acceptance of the test being performed and of any other substantive procedures bearing on the account (e.g., analytical procedures).

Implementing this formula in practice is difficult. For example, immaterial errors in two or more accounts may accumulate to a material amount, and the disaggregation of a material amount to "tolerable errors" for individual accounts is difficult, both conceptually and practically. In addition, quantifying the various risks is difficult. Despite these difficulties, we know from the formula that in circumstances in which the auditors assess inherent risk and control risk as high, a low detection risk (the combination of the risk related to analytical procedures and tests of details) becomes appropriate. Decreases in inherent risk or control risk allow the auditors to accept a higher detection risk.

To illustrate, assume the auditors are willing to accept a 5 percent audit risk of a larger than tolerable error in the client's accounts receivable. They believe that the inherent risk of the account is 75 percent. After considering internal control over sales and cash receipts transactions, they decide that control risk is at a level of 70 percent. The acceptable level of detection risk is:

---

[14] Formally, all of the component risks (inherent risk, control risk, and detection risk) relate to account balances *or* class of transactions and to error either material by itself or when aggregated with other balances or classes. *SAS 47* (AU 312) discusses this in more detail.

$$DR = \frac{AR}{IR \times CR} = \frac{.05}{(.75)(.70)} = .095$$

Thus, the auditors must plan a combination of substantive tests to control detection risk at approximately a 10 percent level.

Reconciling *SAS 39* and *SAS 47*

SAS 39 (AU 350) uses a modification of the above formula.[15] First, as a conservative measure, inherent risk is set at 1.00, or 100 percent, and the above formula becomes:

$$AR = CR \times DR$$

The second modification is to separate detection risk into two components, *AP*, analytical procedures and other relevant substantive tests, and *TD*, test of details, the allowable risk of incorrect acceptance. Algebraically:

$$AR = CR \times DR$$
$$AR = CR \times AP \times TD$$

Mathematically we may rearrange the terms in the formula as follows to calculate the appropriate test of details risk (risk of incorrect acceptance) for a substantive test:

$$TD = \frac{AR}{CR \times AP}$$

KEY TERMS INTRODUCED OR EMPHASIZED IN CHAPTER 8 APPENDICES

Audit risk   The risk that the auditors may unknowingly fail to appropriately modify their opinion on financial statements that are materially misstated.

Basic precision   In probability-proportional-to-size sampling, the reliability factor (for zero errors at the planned risk of incorrect acceptance) times the sampling interval.

Control risk   The risk of a material error occurring in an account and not being detected on a timely basis by internal control.

---

[15] *SAS 39* uses somewhat different terminology (and symbols) to represent these risks. We maintain the *SAS 47* terminology for the sake of consistency.

Detection risk The risk that the auditors' procedures will lead them to conclude that an account is not materially in error, when in fact such error does exist.

Dollar-unit sampling See probability-proportional-to-size sampling.

Incremental allowance In probability-proportional-to-size sampling, an amount determined by ranking the errors for logical units that are less than the sampling interval and considering incremental changes in reliability factors.

Inherent risk The risk of material error in an account, assuming there were no related internal controls.

Probability-proportional-to-size sampling A variables sampling procedure that uses attributes theory to express a conclusion in monetary (dollar) amounts.

Projected error In probability-proportional-to-size sampling, an amount calculated for logical units less than the size of the sampling interval by multiplying the percentage of error (the "tainting") times the sampling interval.

Tainting In probability-proportional-to-size sampling, the percentage of error of an item (error amount divided by book value).

Upper limit on errors In probability-proportional-to-size sampling, the sum of projected error, basic precision, and the incremental allowance. This total is used to evaluate sample results.

QUESTIONS AND PROBLEMS FROM APPENDICES

8–A–1. Barker Company has an inventory with a book value of $4,583,231, which includes 116 product lines and a total of 326,432 units. How many items comprise this population for purposes of applying a probability-proportional-to-size sampling plan? Explain.

8–A–2. Chris York, CPA, is considering the use of probability-proportional-to-size sampling in examining the sales transactions and accounts receivable of Carter Wholesale Company.

Required:
a. How does the definition of the items in an accounts receivable population vary between probability-proportional-to-size sampling and mean-per-unit sampling?
b. Should a population of accounts receivable be stratified by dollar value before applying probability-proportional-to-size sampling procedures? Discuss.

8–A–3. The auditors of Dunbar Electronics want to limit the risk of material error in the valuation of inventories to 2 percent. They believe that there exists only a 20 percent risk that a material error could have bypassed the client's internal control and that the inherent risk in the account is 50 percent. What is the maximum detection risk the auditor may allow in their substantive tests for inventories?

8–A–4. The auditors wish to test the valuation of accounts receivable in the audit of Desert Enterprises of Bullhead City. The client has $500,000 of total recorded receivables, composed of 850 accounts. The auditors have determined the following:

Tolerable error	$25,000
Risk of incorrect acceptance	.05
Expected error	$ 2,000

The auditors have decided to use probability-proportional-to-size sampling.

Required:

a. For the planning of the sample, calculate:
   (1) Required sample size
   (2) Sampling interval

b. Assume that the auditors have tested the sample and discovered three errors:

Book value	Audited value
$ 50	47
800	760
8,500	8,100

Calculate:
   (1) Projected error.
   (2) Basic precision.
   (3) Incremental allowance.
   (4) Upper limit on errors.

c. Explain how the auditors would consider the results calculated in b.

8–A–5. Edwards has decided to use probability-proportional-to-size (PPS) sampling, sometimes called dollar-unit sampling, in the audit of a client's accounts receivable balance. Few, if any, errors of account balance overstatement are expected.

Edwards plans to use the following PPS sampling table:

Table
Reliability factors for errors of overstatement

Number of over- statement errors	Risk of incorrect acceptance				
	1%	5%	10%	15%	20%
0	4.61	3.00	2.31	1.90	1.61
1	6.64	4.75	3.89	3.38	3.00
2	8.41	6.30	5.33	4.72	4.28
3	10.05	7.76	6.69	6.02	5.52
4	11.61	9.16	8.00	7.27	6.73

Required:

a. Identify the advantages of using PPS sampling over classical variables sampling.

b. Calculate the sampling interval and the sample size Edwards should use given the following information:

Tolerable error $15,000
Risk of incorrect acceptance 5%
Number of errors allowed 0
Recorded amount of accounts receivable $300,000

Note: Requirements b and c are *not* related.

c. Calculate the total projected error if the following three errors were discovered in a PPS sample:

	Recorded amount	Audit amount	Sampling interval
1st error	$ 400	$ 320	$1,000
2nd error	500	0	1,000
3rd error	3,000	2,500	1,000

(AICPA, adapted)

Audit working papers: Quality control for audits

Chapter 9 study objectives

After studying this chapter, you should be able to:

— Describe the function of audit working papers.
— Explain the relationship between the working papers and legal liability of the auditors.
— Describe the factors that affect the independent auditors' judgment as to the quality, type, and content of the working papers.
— Describe the types of working papers, and the way they are organized.
— Explain the purpose of quality control procedures for a CPA firm.
— Describe the objectives of each of the elements of quality control for a CPA firm.

Working papers are vitally important tools of the auditing profession. To an auditor, the ability to design and use working papers efficiently is just as essential as is the surgeon's ability to use surgical instruments. In this chapter, we shall discuss the basic characteristics of working papers and the roles that these papers play in the audit process. We also shall discuss the related topic of quality control within a CPA firm.

What are audit working papers?

Working papers are the connecting link between the client's accounting records and the auditors' report. They document all of the work done by the auditors and provide the justification for the auditors' report. The third standard of field work states that:

> Sufficient, competent evidential matter is to be obtained through inspection, observation, inquiries, and confirmations to afford a reasonable basis for an opinion regarding the financial statements under examination.

All of this evidence must be clearly documented in the auditors' working papers.

Some working papers take the form of bank reconciliations or analyses of ledger accounts; others may consist of photocopies of minutes of directors' meetings; still others might be organization charts or flowcharts of the client's internal control structure. Working trial balances, audit programs, internal control questionnaires, letters of representation obtained from the client and from the client's legal counsel, returned confirmation forms—all of these schedules, lists, notes, and documents are part of the auditors' working papers.

Thus, the term *audit working papers* is quite comprehensive. Remember that the partner who writes and signs the auditors' report did not personally perform most of the audit procedures. The partner's opinion was developed primarily by reviewing the working papers prepared by the audit staff. Therefore, the working papers must include absolutely all of the information that is *relevant to expressing an opinion on the fairness of the client's financial statements.*

Most large CPA firms send new staff assistants to special training schools to learn the firm's working paper "techniques." Of course, no one standard set of working papers is suitable for all engagements. As auditors move from one client to another they encounter different business operations and different kinds of accounting records and internal controls. It follows that the auditors must tailor the form and content of their working papers to fit the circumstances of each engagement.[1]

---

[1] AICPA, *Statements on Auditing Standards 41,* "Working Papers" (New York, 1982), AU 339.01.

Functions of working papers

Audit working papers assist auditors in several major ways: they (*a*) provide a means of assigning and coordinating audit work; (*b*) aid seniors, managers, and partners in supervising and reviewing the work of assistants; (*c*) provide the support for the auditors' report; (*d*) document the auditors' compliance with the generally accepted auditing standards relating to field work; and (*e*) aid in planning and conducting future audits of the client. In addition, working papers provide information useful in rendering additional professional services, such as preparing income tax returns, making recommendations for improving internal control, and providing management advisory services.

Assigning and coordinating audit work Most audits are a joint effort. Several auditors, perhaps even several different offices of a CPA firm, usually are involved in each engagement. The work of these different auditors is coordinated through the audit working papers. Work may be conveniently delegated by assigning different assistants responsibility for completing different working papers. The senior auditor might fill in the column headings on a working paper and enter one or two sample transactions, requesting that a staff assistant complete the paper. In this manner, a senior can initiate and supervise the work of several assistants simultaneously.

If an audit is to progress efficiently, information often must pass from one auditor to another. For example, assume that Smith prepared the flowcharts of a client's internal control and was then transferred to another job. Jones and Reed are now assigned responsibility for performing tests of the significant control procedures. Obviously Jones and Reed must understand how the client's control procedures operate—information previously obtained by Smith. This information is readily available in the flowchart—the audit working paper in which Smith documented his work.

Often it is not possible to complete all of the work on an account at one time. For example, cash on hand may be counted at the balance sheet date, but confirmations of bank balances may not be received until a week or so later. As each step in the verification of the client's cash balance is completed, a working paper is filed, to be expanded and updated as additional information is obtained. Thus, the audit work on a given account might be started early in the engagement by one assistant and completed later by another.

Supervising and reviewing the work of assistants As working papers are completed by staff assistants, they are *reviewed* by the senior running the job. If the senior finds any shortcomings in the assistants' work, the senior will explain the problem to the assistant and ask that the working paper be revised. Once the senior is satisfied with the working paper, it will be passed on to the manager, who will perform a similar review. If the

manager has any questions or finds any problems, the working paper is
again returned to the audit staff. After the manager is satisfied that the
working paper documents complete and thorough audit work, the working paper is reviewed by one or more partners. This process of successive
levels of review provides assurance that work of the audit staff is carefully
reviewed and supervised. As each review is completed, the reviewer
"signs off" by initialing the working paper.

Support for the report The working papers must contain adequate
evidence and documentation to convince the partner on the engagement
that it is appropriate for the CPA firm to issue a particular type of opinion
on the client's financial statements. The partner knows that some risk
always exists that investors may sustain losses and bring a lawsuit against
the CPAs alleging an improper audit. Therefore, the partner will want to
be certain that the auditors' report is supported and justified by the evidence contained in the working papers.

Compliance with the three standards of field work As discussed in
Chapter 3, auditors may find themselves liable for losses sustained by
financial statement users if the auditors' examination was not performed
in accordance with generally accepted auditing standards. The working
papers are the principal means by which auditors can demonstrate their
compliance with the standards of field work. Thus, the working papers
should document adequate planning and proper supervision of assistants
(the first standard of field work), a proper understanding of internal control (second standard), and the gathering of sufficient competent evidential matter to afford a reasonable basis for opinion (third standard).

Planning and conducting the next audit The working papers from the
previous audit of a particular client provide a wealth of information that is
useful in planning and conducting the next audit. For example, the prior
year's working papers show how much time was required to perform the
audit, provide insight into the client's internal control structure, and refresh the auditors' memory of any special problems encountered during
the engagement. In addition, some working papers, such as the substantiation of land, bonds payable, or capital stock may be updated from one
year to the next with very little effort.

Finally, how do inexperienced staff assistants know how to document
the results of the audit procedures they perform? Often they look at the
prior year's audit working papers. The procedures performed in the prior
year probably were similar to those scheduled for the current year. Furthermore, the prior year's working papers were reviewed and "signed
off" by a senior, a manager, and at least one partner, thus providing
assurance that they represent satisfactory documentation of the audit
work performed.

Some care should be taken in using the working papers of the prior year as a model. The auditor must always be alert to changes in the client's operations or internal control structure that may make last year's approach inappropriate for the current year. In addition, the auditor should always be looking for ways to make the current year's audit more efficient than that of the prior year. Nonetheless, the audit staff usually finds the prior year's working papers to be an invaluable guide in conducting the current year's audit.

Confidential nature of working papers

To conduct a satisfactory audit, the auditors must be given unrestricted access to all information about the client's business. Much of this information is confidential, such as the profit margins on individual products, tentative plans for business combinations with other companies, and the salaries of officers and key employees. Officers of the client company would not be willing to make available to the auditors information that is carefully guarded from competitors, employees, and others unless they could rely on the auditors maintaining a professional silence on these matters.

Much of the information gained in confidence by the auditors is recorded in their working papers; consequently, the working papers are confidential in nature. The *Code of Professional Conduct* developed by the AICPA includes the rule that "a member in public practice shall not disclose any confidential information obtained in the course of a professional engagement except with the consent of the client." In interpreting this rule, the AICPA Professional Ethics Executive Committee has expressed the opinion that one CPA firm selling its practice to another should not give the purchaser access to working papers without first obtaining permission from the clients involved.

Although the auditor is as careful as an attorney or physician to hold in confidence all information concerning a client, the communication between a client and a CPA is not privileged under the common law. In most states and under federal laws, a CPA firm may legally be required to produce its working papers in a court case and to disclose information regarding a client. In some states, however, statutes have granted a privileged status to communications between a client and the CPA.

Under normal circumstances, auditors think of confidential information as being information that must not be divulged *outside* of the client organization. But the confidential nature of information in the auditors' working papers has another dimension—it often must not be divulged *within* the client organization. If, for example, the client does not want certain employees to know the levels of executive salaries, the auditors obviously should not defeat this policy by exposing their working papers to unauthorized client personnel. Also, the working papers may identify particular accounts, branches, or time periods to be tested by the auditors; to permit the client's employees to learn of these in advance would weaken the significance of the tests.

Since audit working papers are highly confidential, they must be safeguarded at all times. Safeguarding working papers usually means keeping them locked in a file cabinet or an audit case during lunch and after working hours.

Ownership of audit working papers

Audit working papers are the ***property of the auditors,*** not of the client. At no time does the client have the right to demand access to the auditors' working papers. After the audit, the working papers are retained by the auditors.

Clients may sometimes find it helpful to refer to information from the auditors' working papers from prior years. Auditors usually are willing to provide this information, but the auditors' working papers should not be regarded as a substitute for the client's own accounting records. As part of any audit engagement, the auditors should provide the client with any information that could be regarded as the client's accounting records.

Working papers and auditors' liability

The auditors' working papers are the principal record of the extent of the procedures applied and evidence gathered during the audit. If the auditors, after completing an engagement, are charged with negligence, their audit working papers will be a major factor in refuting or substantiating the charge. Working papers, if not properly prepared, are as likely to injure the auditors as to protect them.

If a lawsuit is brought against the auditors, the plaintiffs will go over the auditors' working papers with a fine-tooth comb, looking for contradictions, omissions, or any evidence of carelessness or fraud. This possibility suggests the need for public accounting firms to make their own critical review of the working papers at the end of each engagement. During this review, the auditors should bear in mind that any contradictory statements, or evidence that is not consistent with the conclusions finally reached, may be used at a later date to support a charge of improper auditing.

Part of the difficulty in avoiding inconsistent and conflicting evidence in working papers is that the papers are prepared in large part by less experienced staff members. When the papers are reviewed by a supervisor or partner, the reviewer will give careful consideration to any questionable points. In studying these points, the reviewer often gives consideration to many other aspects of the audit and of the client's records with which he or she is familiar. These other factors may lead the reviewer to the conclusion that an issue raised in the working papers does not warrant any corrective action. In some instances, the reviewer may conclude that the assistant who prepared the paper has misinterpreted the situation. Years later, if a dispute arises and the working papers are being subjected to critical study by attorneys representing an injured party, these questionable points in the papers may appear in a different light. The reviewer who cleared the issue based on personal knowledge of the client's business may not be available to explain the reasoning involved. This long-range responsibility suggests that the reviewer should insert in the working papers a carefully written *memorandum* explaining the decision.

Differences of opinion   On occasion, inconsistencies will arise in the working papers because different members of the audit staff—say, a senior and the engagement partner—will reach different conclusions on some complex auditing or accounting issue. In such cases, the disagreeing auditors should discuss the matter to see if they can reach agreement. If they are able to do so, the working papers should be revised to reflect their common opinion. If they are not able to reach agreement, the opinion of the partner in charge of the engagement will prevail with respect to the content of the auditors' report. However, all other members of the audit team have the right to document in the working papers *their disagreement* with the ultimate decision.[2] In the event that a staff person elects to document his or her disagreement, the partner in charge obviously should be extremely thorough in documenting the rationale underlying the firm's ultimate decision.

From time to time, a public accounting firm should make a critical evaluation of its policies for preparation, review, and preservation of working papers. Recent experience in cases involving legal liability may lead some firms to modifications in the traditional handling of working papers.

Types of working papers

Since the audit working papers document a variety of information gathered by the auditors, there are innumerable types of papers. However, there are certain general categories into which most working papers may be grouped; these are: (1) audit administrative working papers; (2) working trial balance and lead schedules; (3) adjusting journal entries and reclassification entries; (4) supporting schedules, analyses, reconciliations, and computational working papers; and (5) corroborating documents.

Audit administrative working papers   Auditing is a sophisticated activity requiring planning, supervision, control, and coordination. Certain

---

[2] AICPA, *Statement on Auditing Standards 22*, "Planning and Supervision" (New York, 1978), AU 311.14.

working papers are specifically designed to aid the auditors in the planning and administration of engagements. These working papers include audit plans and programs, internal control questionnaires and flowcharts, engagement letters, and time budgets. Memoranda of the planning process and significant discussions with client management are also considered administrative working papers.

Working trial balance The working trial balance is a schedule listing the balances of accounts in the general ledger for the current and previous year, and also providing columns for the auditors' adjustments and reclassifications and for the final amounts that will appear in the financial statements. A working trial balance is the "backbone" of the entire set of audit working papers; it is the key schedule that controls and summarizes all supporting papers. This type of working paper will usually appear as shown below.

Process Company Inc.
Working Trial Balance   TB-1
December 31, 1990

Working Paper Reference	Caption	Final Dec. 31, 89	Balance per Ledger Dec. 31, 90	Adjustments Dr. (Cr.)	Adjusted Dec. 31, 90	Reclassifications Dr. (Cr.)	Final Balance Dec. 31, 90
	Assets						
	Current Assets:						
A	Cash	481 413	742 186		742 186		742 186
B	Short-Term Investments		149 413		149 413		149 413
C	Accounts Receivable—Net	2 298 722	2 053 918	(91 096)	1 962 822		1 962 822
D	Inventories	2 701 814	2 942 117	(129 799)	2 812 318		2 812 318

Although most of these column headings are self-explanatory, a brief discussion of the third and fourth columns is appropriate. In the third column, the final adjusted balances from the previous year's audit are listed. Inclusion of the previous year's figures facilitates comparison with the corresponding amounts for the current year and focuses attention upon any unusual changes. Inclusion of the final figures from the prior year's audit also gives assurance that the correct starting figure is used if the auditors verify the year's transactions in a balance sheet account in order to determine the validity of the ending balance.

The fourth column provides for the account balances at the close of the year under audit; these balances usually are taken directly from the general ledger. The balances of the Revenue and Expense accounts should be included, even though these accounts have been closed into the Retained Earnings account prior to the auditors' arrival. Since the auditors ordinarily express an opinion on the income statement as well as the balance sheet, it is imperative that the audit working papers include full information on the revenue and expense accounts. The amount to be listed for the Retained Earnings account is the balance at the *beginning* of the year under audit. Dividends declared during the year are listed as a separate item, as is the computed net income for the year.

In many audits, the client furnishes the auditors with a working trial balance after all normal end-of-period journal entries have been posted. Before accepting the trial balance for their working papers, the auditors should trace the amounts to the general ledger for evidence that the trial balance is prepared accurately.

Lead schedules   Separate lead schedules (also called *grouping sheets* or *summary schedules*) are set up to combine similar general ledger accounts, the total of which appears on the working trial balance as a single amount. For example, a lead schedule for Cash might combine the following general ledger accounts: Petty Cash, $500; General bank account, $196,240; Factory Payroll bank account, $500; and Dividend bank account, $1,000. Similar lead schedules would be set up for Accounts Receivable, Inventories, Stockholders' Equity, Net Sales, and for other balance sheet or income statement captions.

Adjusting journal entries and reclassification entries   During the course of an audit engagement, the auditors may discover various types of errors in the client's financial statements and accounting records. These errors may be large or small in amount; they may arise from the omission of transactions or from the use of incorrect amounts; or they may result from improper classification or cutoff, or from misinterpretation of transactions. Generally, these errors are accidental; however, the auditors may discover irregularities in the financial statements or accounting records.

To correct *material* errors or irregularities discovered in the financial statements and accounting records, the auditors draft *adjusting journal entries* (AJEs), which they recommend for entry in the client's accounting records. In addition, the auditors develop *reclassification journal entries* (RJEs) for items that, although correctly recorded in the accounting records, must be reclassified for fair presentation in the client's financial statements. For example, accounts receivable with large credit balances should be *reclassified* as a liability in the balance sheet. Reclassification entries affect only the financial statement presentation; therefore, they are *not recorded* in the client's accounting records. Reclassification entries appear only in the auditors' working papers.

Supporting schedules Although all types of working papers may loosely be called schedules, auditors prefer to use this term to describe a listing of the elements or details comprising the balance in an asset or liability account at a specific date. Thus, a list of amounts owed to vendors making up the balance of the Trade Accounts Payable account is properly described as a *schedule*.

Analysis of a ledger account An analysis of a ledger account is another common type of audit working paper. The purpose of an analysis is to show on one paper *all changes* in an asset, liability, equity, revenue, or expense account during the period covered by the audit. If a number of the changes are individually immaterial, they may be recorded as a single item in the analysis working paper. Account analyses are most useful in substantiating those accounts affected by relatively few transactions during the year. Examples include plant asset accounts, long-term debt accounts, capital stock accounts, and retained earnings.

To analyze a ledger account, the auditors first list the beginning balance and indicate the nature of the items comprising this balance. Next, the auditors list and investigate the nature of all debits and credits to the account during the period. These entries, when combined with the beginning balance, produce a figure representing the balance in the account as of the audit date. If any errors or omissions of importance are detected during this analysis of the account, the necessary adjusting journal entry approved by the client is entered on the working paper to produce the adjusted balance required for the financial statements.

Reconciliations Frequently, auditors wish to prove the relationship between amounts obtained from different sources. When they do so, they prepare working papers known as reconciliations. These reconciliations provide evidence as to the accuracy of one or both of the amounts and are important to the audit of many accounts, including cash, accounts receivable, and inventories.

Computational working papers Another type of supporting working paper is the computational working paper. The auditors' approach to verifying certain types of accounts and other figures is to make an independent computation and compare their results with the amounts shown by the client's records. Examples of amounts that might be verified by computation are interest expense, depreciation, payroll taxes, income taxes, pension liabilities, and earnings per share.

Corroborating documents Auditing is not limited to the examination of financial records, and working papers are not confined to schedules and analyses. During the course of an audit, the auditors may gather much purely expository material to substantiate their report. One common example is copies of minutes of directors' and stockholders' meetings. Other examples include copies of articles of incorporation and bylaws; copies of important contracts, bond indentures, and mortgages; memoranda pertaining to examination of records; audit confirmations; and letters of representations from the client and from the client's legal counsel.

Organization of the working papers

The auditors usually maintain two files of working papers for each client: (1) current files for every completed examination and (2) a permanent file of relatively unchanging data. The current file (as for the 1990 audit) pertains solely to that year's examination; the permanent file contains such things as copies of the articles of incorporation, which are of continuing audit interest.

The current files The auditors' report for a particular year is supported by the working paper contained in the current files. Many CPA firms have found it useful to organize the current files around the arrangement of the accounts in the client's financial statements. The administrative working papers usually begin the current files, including a draft of the financial statements and the auditors' report. These working papers are followed by the working trial balance and the adjusting and reclassification entries. The remaining portion of the current files consists of working papers supporting the balances and other representations in the client's financial statements. It begins with working papers for each asset account and continues with papers for liabilities, owners' equity accounts, and revenue and expense accounts.

Each working paper in a file is assigned a reference number, and information is tied together through a system of cross-referencing. In this way, a reviewer may trace amounts on the working trial balance back to the supporting working papers. Figure 9–1 illustrates a system of cross-referencing and a typical arrangement of the current files after the administrative working papers.

The permanent file The permanent file serves three purposes: (1) to refresh the auditors' memory on items applicable over a period of many years; (2) to provide for new staff members a quick summary of the policies and organization of the client; and (3) to preserve working papers on items that show relatively few or no changes, thus eliminating the necessity for their preparation year after year.

Much of the information contained in the permanent file is gathered during the course of the first audit of a client's records. A considerable portion of the time spent on a first audit is devoted to gathering and appraising background information, such as copies of articles of incorporation and bylaws, leases, patent agreements, pension plans, labor con-

Figure 9–1 Organization of the current files

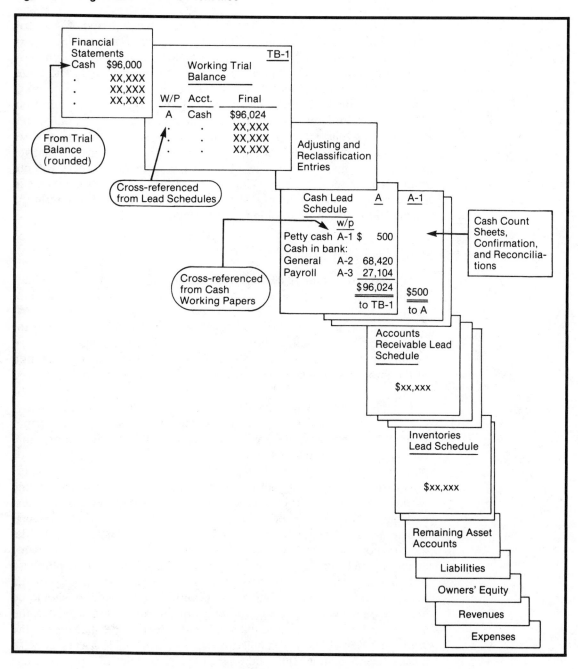

tracts, long-term construction contracts, charts of accounts, and prior years' tax returns.

Analyses of accounts that show few changes over a period of years are also included in the permanent file. These accounts may include land, buildings, accumulated depreciation, long-term investments, long-term liabilities, capital stock, and other owners' equity accounts. The initial investigation of these accounts must often include the transactions of many years. But once these historical analyses have been brought up to date, the work required in subsequent examinations will be limited to a review of the current year's transactions in these accounts. In this respect, the permanent file is a timesaving device because current changes in such accounts need only be added to the permanent papers without reappearing in the current working papers. Adequate cross-referencing in the working papers, of course, should be provided to show where in the permanent file such information is to be found.

Guidelines for preparation of working papers

We can now summarize in a few short paragraphs our basic guidelines for preparing working papers that will meet current professional standards.

A separate, properly identified working paper should be prepared for each topic. Proper identification of a working paper is accomplished by a heading that includes the name of the client company, a clear description of the information presented, and the applicable date or the period covered.

Complete and specific identification of documents examined, employees interviewed, and sites visited is essential for good working paper practice. The preparer of a working paper should date and sign or initial the working paper; the signatures or initials of the senior, manager, or partner who reviewed the working paper should also appear on the paper.

All working papers should be referenced and cross-referenced to the working trial balance or relevant lead schedule. Where reference is necessary between working papers, there must be adequate cross-referencing.

The nature of verification work performed by the auditors should be indicated on each working paper. A review of paid purchase invoices, for example, might be supplemented by inspection of the related purchase orders and receiving documents to substantiate the authenticity of the invoices examined; a description of this verification procedure should be included on the working paper. As audit working papers are prepared, the auditors will use several different symbols to identify specific steps in the work performed. These symbols, or *tick marks,* provide a very concise means of indicating the auditing procedures applied to particular amounts. Whenever tick marks are employed, they must be accompanied by a legend explaining their meaning.

The working papers should include comments by the auditors indicat-

Figure 9–2   Preparation of a working paper

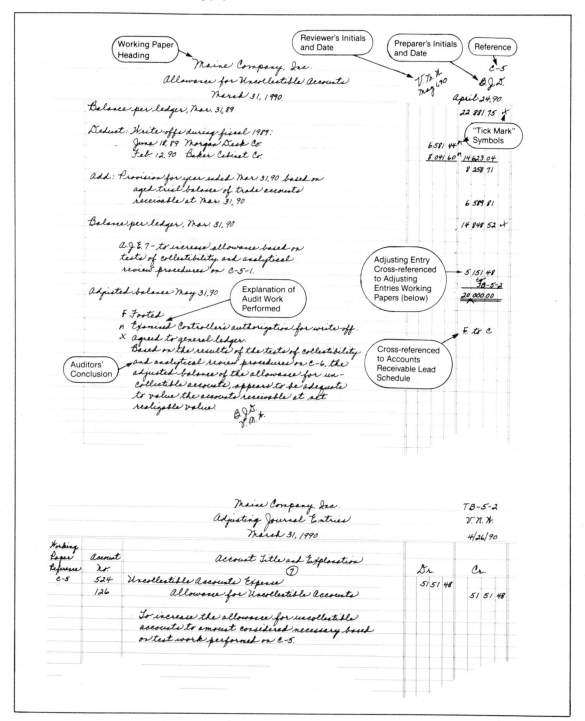

ing their conclusions on each aspect of the work. In other words, the auditors should clearly express the opinion they have formed as a result of having performed the auditing procedures summarized in the working paper. Figure 9–2 illustrates such a conclusion related to the audit of the allowance for uncollectible account, along with other aspects of a properly prepared working paper.

Computer-generated working papers

Traditionally working papers have been prepared in pencil on columnar paper. Today, many working papers are prepared on portable personal computers carried by the auditors to the work site. When an adjustment is entered on computer-based working papers, it appears instantly on the appropriate lead schedules, the adjustments schedule, and the working trial balance. The necessary cross-references are automatically entered on each schedule. If the adjustment affects taxable income, the income tax expense account and the tax liability are automatically adjusted using the client's marginal tax rate. In addition, all of the subtotals, column totals, and cross-footings in the working papers are instantly adjusted.

When working papers are maintained manually, all of these entries and changes must be made by hand with a pencil, an eraser, and a "ten-key." With a personal computer, an adjustment that might take a half hour or more to "push through" manual working papers can be entered in a few seconds. Thus, personal computers have taken much of the "pencil pushing" and the "number crunching" out of working paper preparation.

Illustrative case

An advertisement for computer software appearing in the *Journal of Accountancy* illustrates the time savings that can be achieved by preparing audit working papers on a personal computer. The advertisement showed time comparisons for preparing various working papers manually and by computer. The following were among the comparisons made:

		Hours	
		Manual	**Computer**
1.	Prepare 30 lead schedules and a working trial balance	9	1
2.	Perform initial analytical procedures	8	½
3.	Prepare accounts receivable confirmation letter reports and analysis of results	20	5

(Continued)

	Hours	
	Manual	Computer
4. Prepare 50 adjusting and reclassifying journal entries and post to lead schedules and working trial balance	4	½
5. Prepare comparative balance sheet, income statements, and statement of changes in financial position worksheet	10	1
6. OOPS! Post two *late* adjusting journal entries to lead schedules and working trial balance. Update *all* working papers as required.	10	½

The review of audit working papers

Working papers are reviewed at every supervisory level of a CPA firm. Senior auditors review the working papers of staff assistants; managers review all working papers prepared by staff assistants and by senior auditors; the partner in charge of the engagement reviews the entire set of working papers. Many CPA firms also require a review by a second partner.

What do the reviewers look for?   All of the reviewers look to see that the working papers properly document the audit. However, there are differences in the nature of the reviews. The senior's review is the most technical, and it generally is performed promptly after the completion of the individual working paper. Seniors look primarily to see that the staff assistant has performed the audit procedures properly and that the assistant's findings and conclusions are clearly expressed.

The reviews by managers and partners are often performed near the *end* of the engagement, when the reviewer may examine at one time the entire set of working papers. These reviewers are primarily interested in determining that the audit was performed in accordance with generally accepted auditing standards and that the working papers properly support the auditors' report that will be issued on the financial statements. There are several advantages to reviewing all of the working papers at once. The reviewer can determine that the working papers "tie together"—that is, that amounts are properly carried forward from one working paper to another. As we mentioned earlier in the chapter, these reviewers should look critically for any inconsistencies, omissions, or "loose ends" that might later support a plaintiff's allegations of improper auditing. In addition, the reviewer should consider whether the various immaterial discrepancies that were passed without adjustment might *cumulatively* have a material effect upon the financial statements.

The purposes of a *second partner review* are to provide assurance that all of the CPA firm's in-house *quality control policies* have been complied with, as well as to provide a "second opinion" that the audit was performed in accordance with generally accepted auditing standards. The second partner review, sometimes called a "cold review," usually is performed by a partner with no personal or professional ties to the audit client. Multioffice CPA firms sometimes bring in a partner from another office to perform the second partner review.

Not until all of these reviewers have "signed off" on the audit working papers is the CPA firm's name signed to the auditors' report.

QUALITY CONTROL IN CPA FIRMS

A CPA firm should establish adequate quality control policies and procedures to provide reasonable assurance that the firm conforms with generally accepted auditing standards on every audit engagement.[3] To provide CPA firms with guidance in establishing quality control policies, the AICPA has issued *Statement on Quality Control Standards 1,* which identifies nine "elements" of quality control.[4] The "elements" of quality control may be regarded as the *areas* in which the AICPA considers it desirable for a CPA firm to maintain quality control procedures.

The AICPA did not require specific quality control procedures. In fact, it stated that the specific procedures should depend upon the size of the firm, the number of offices, and the nature of the firm's practice. Thus, the quality control procedures employed by a 200-office international firm will differ considerably from those employed by a single-office firm that only audits small businesses. Technically, the AICPA's quality control *Statement* applies only to auditing and accounting services for which professional standards have been established by the AICPA. As a practical matter, however, every CPA firm should have quality control procedures applicable to *every aspect of its practice.* In the broad sense, the concept of "quality control" means that CPA firms should establish controls to provide assurance that they meet their responsibilities to their clients and to the public.

Figure 9–3 indicates the nine areas in which the AICPA has indicated that quality control procedures are appropriate. In addition, the table explains the basic objective to be achieved in each area and provides an example of a procedure that a CPA firm might implement as a step toward achieving the objective.

Division for CPA firms

In 1977, the AICPA took another step toward establishing quality control standards within the profession with the formation of the AICPA

---

[3] AICPA, *Statement on Auditing Standards 25,* "The Relationship of Generally Accepted Auditing Standards to Quality Control Standards" (New York, 1979), AU 161.

[4] AICPA, *Statement on Quality Control Standards 1,* "System of Quality Control for a CPA Firm" (New York, 1979), Professional Standards QC 10.

Figure 9–3　Elements of quality control

Element of quality control	Basic objective	Example of procedure
Independence	Firm personnel should meet the independence requirements of the AICPA *Code of Professional Conduct*	An investigation is made to determine the firm's independence before accepting a new audit client
Assigning personnel to engagements	Work should be performed by personnel with appropriate technical training and proficiency	Periodic meetings of audit managers are held to assign staff to upcoming jobs
Consultation	Advice should be sought from qualified persons to help resolve complex problems	A "technical center" is maintained by a large CPA firm to provide research and consulting services to any practice office in the firm
Supervision	Personnel should be properly supervised	Working papers are reviewed by the field supervisor and any deficiencies are discussed with the preparer
Hiring	New employees should possess the characteristics to handle their job	Prospective employees are interviewed by both the personnel partner and by a technical partner in the area in which they will work
Professional development	Personnel should continue to expand their knowledge as required to meet their responsibilities	Each professional must annually receive at least 40 hours of continuing education
Advancement	Persons promoted should be qualified to assume their new responsibilities	Professionals are evaluated by their supervisors at the end of each engagement; the evaluations are placed in their personnel files
Acceptance and continuation of clients	Care should be taken to avoid association with clients lacking in integrity	Background information is gathered on all prospective audit clients and is discussed at a partners' meeting before accepting the client
Inspection	Controls should exist to provide reasonable assurance that established quality control procedures are being effectively applied	A quality control partner should periodically test the application of quality control procedures

Division for CPA Firms. This action represented a positive response to certain congressional committees and other critics of the profession's system of self-regulation. Prior to forming the Division, CPAs joined the AICPA only as individuals; no mechanism existed for enforcing professional standards for CPA firms. In the Division for CPA Firms, membership is granted to CPA firms, not to individual CPAs.

The Division for CPA Firms actually includes two separate sections, the **SEC Practice Section** and the **Private Companies Practice Section.** CPA firms voluntarily join either, or both, sections based on the type of clients that they serve. Both sections require member firms to establish and maintain an adequate system of quality control and adhere to certain membership requirements. For example, the SEC Practice Section requires audit partners on SEC audit clients to be rotated at least every seven years. Audit engagements for such clients must be subjected to review by a second partner. Members of the SEC Practice Section are also prohibited from performing certain management advisory services for SEC clients, including executive recruiting activities. Regular *peer reviews* and mandatory continuing education for firm personnel (120 hours every 3 years) are part of the membership requirements of both firm sections.

The executive committees of the two sections have the power to sanction member firms for substandard performance. These sanctions may include additional education requirements for firm personnel, special peer reviews, fines, and suspension or expulsion from the division.

The Public Oversight Board

A vital aspect of the profession's system of self-regulation is the Public Oversight Board, which is made up of prominent individuals who are not members of the accounting profession. The Board oversees the activities of the SEC Practice Section and can intervene when the members of the Board think that the public's interest is not being served. Periodic reports inform the SEC and Congress about the activities of the Public Oversight Board.

Peer reviews

An important feature of the AICPA Division for Firms is the mandatory peer reviews that are required periodically of members of both sections. Member firms must subject their practice to an intensive review of their quality control policies and procedures by another CPA firm, or a review team authorized or appointed by one of the peer review committees of the two sections. Many firms that are not members of the AICPA Division for CPA Firms voluntarily submit their practice to periodic peer review. As discussed in Chapter 1, a new AICPA requirement of membership for individuals in public practice is peer review of the member's practice every three years. As a result, peer review should become almost universal within the profession.

A peer review involves a study of the adequacy of the firm's established quality control policies and tests to determine the extent of the firm's compliance with these policies. In large part, these tests of compliance consist of a review of working paper files and audit reports for selected engagements. These engagements are evaluated for compliance with established quality control policies and generally accepted auditing standards.

The reviewers also examine many internal records of the CPA firm.

They are especially interested in records concerning the promotion of employees, continuing education of firm personnel, staffing of audit engagements, client acceptance, and the employment of professional personnel. Based on the reviewers' study and tests of the quality controls, they issue a report that includes an opinion as to the adequacy of the reviewed firm's quality control system. Suggestions for improvement to the system are outlined in a "letter of comments" issued by the reviewers to the reviewed firm.

Underreporting of time

A special quality control problem for CPA firms is understating the hours they have actually worked—a practice informally called *"eating time."* Everyone in public accounting is under time pressure, working to stay within the *time budget* and finish each step of the audit on schedule. Staff members, with some justification, believe they will "look bad" if they cannot perform procedures in the budgeted time. They also may feel that they can impress their supervisor by coming in "under budget." The senior auditor, in turn, is anxious to bring the whole engagement in under budget, or, at least avoiding going way over the original time estimate.

One means of coming in under budget is to understate the number of hours actually worked. This can be accomplished by arriving early, staying late, or working through lunch or on weekends without recording the extra hours on the time sheet. When staff members "eat time," however, problems are created for the public accounting firm. For one thing, the firm is underbilling its clients, considering the amount of services actually rendered. For another, the time reported this year for each step of the audit will be a major factor in determining next year's time budget. If next year's time budget is based on understated hours, the staff members will have to "eat" more time next year if they are to stay on schedule. In the long run, underreporting may lead staff members to feel that they are being abused, leading to lower staff morale and to cases of individual employee "burnout."

Unfortunately, underreporting is not uncommon in public accounting. It is a difficult problem to eliminate because the field supervisors tend to benefit from the practice.

KEY TERMS INTRODUCED OR EMPHASIZED IN CHAPTER 9

Adjusting journal entry A journal entry drafted by the auditors to correct a material error discovered in the financial statements and accounting records.

Administrative working papers Working papers specifically designed to help the auditors in planning and administration of the engagement, such as audit programs, internal control questionnaires and flowcharts, time budgets, and engagement memoranda.

Analysis A working paper showing all changes in an asset, liability, equity, revenue, or expense account during the period covered by the audit.

Corroborating documents Documents and memoranda included in the working papers that substantiate representations contained in the client's financial statements. These working papers include audit confirmations, lawyers' letters, copies of contracts, copies of minutes of directors' and stockholders' meetings, and letters of representations from the client's management.

Division for CPA Firms   A division of the AICPA providing a mechanism to regulate CPA firms. Firms may voluntarily join either or both sections; the SEC Practice Section and the Private Companies Practice Section.

Lead schedule   A working paper with columnar headings similar to those in a working trial balance, set up to combine similar ledger accounts, the total of which appears in the working trial balance as a single amount.

Peer review   The study and evaluation of a CPA firm's quality control policies and procedures by another CPA firm or a team of qualified CPAs.

Permanent file   A file of working papers containing relatively unchanging data, such as copies of articles of incorporation and bylaws, copies of minutes of directors', stockholders', and committee meetings, and analyses of such ledger accounts as land and retained earnings.

Public Oversight Board   An independent group of prominent nonaccountants who monitor the activities of the SEC Practice Section to provide assurance that the section is serving the public's interest.

Quality control standards   Standards for establishing quality control policies and procedures that provide reasonable assurance that all of a CPA firm's audits are conducted in accordance with generally accepted auditing standards.

Reclassification entry   A working paper entry drafted by the auditors to assure fair presentation in the client's financial statements, such as an entry to transfer accounts receivable credit balances to the current liabilities section of the client's balance sheet. Since reclassification entries do not correct errors in the client company's accounting records, they are not posted to the client's ledger accounts.

Tick mark   A symbol used in working papers by the auditor to indicate a specific step in the work performed. Whenever tick marks are used, they must be accompanied by a legend explaining their meaning.

Working papers   Papers that document the evidence gathered by auditors to show the work they have done, the methods and procedures they have followed, and the conclusions they have developed in an examination of financial statements or other type of engagement.

Working trial balance   A working paper that lists the balances of accounts in the general ledger for the current and the previous year and also provides columns for the auditor's adjustments and reclassifications and for the final amounts that will appear in the financial statements.

GROUP I: REVIEW QUESTIONS

9–1.   What are the major functions of audit working papers?

9–2.   Why are the prior year's audit working papers a useful reference to staff assistants during the current examination?

9–3.   Why are the final figures from the prior year's audit included in a working trial balance or lead schedules? Explain.

9–4. Should the working trial balance prepared by the auditors include revenue and expense accounts if the balances of these accounts for the audit year have been closed into retained earnings prior to the auditors' arrival? Explain.

9–5. Explain the meaning of the term *permanent file* as used in connection with audit working papers. What kinds of information are usually included in the permanent file?

9–6. List the major types of audit working papers and give a brief explanation of each. For example, one type of audit working paper is an account analysis. This working paper shows the changes that occurred in a given account during the period under audit. By analyzing an account, the auditors determine its nature and content.

9–7. List several rules to be observed in the preparation of working papers that will reflect current professional practice.

9–8. In their review of audit working papers, what do managers and partners look for?

9–9. Should the auditors prepare adjusting journal entries to correct all errors they discover in the accounting records for the year under audit? Explain.

9–10. "Audit working papers are the property of the auditors, who may destroy the papers, sell them, or give them away." Criticize this quotation.

9–11. Describe a situation in which a set of audit working papers might be used by third parties to support a charge of gross negligence against the auditors.

9–12. "I have finished my testing of footings of the cash journals," said the assistant auditor to the senior auditor. "Shall I state in the working papers the periods for which I verified footings, or should I just list the totals of the receipts and disbursements I have proved to be correct?" Prepare an answer to the assistant's question, stressing the reasoning involved.

9–13. What is the purpose of a "second partner review?" What should be the extent of the second partner's association with the engagement being reviewed?

9–14. What has the AICPA done to help assure adequate quality control by CPA firms?

9–15. Explain the basic objective of establishing quality control procedures in the following areas:
  a. Consultation.
  b. Acceptance and continuation of clients.
  c. Inspection.

9–16. Does the AICPA's *Statement of Quality Control Standards 1* require every CPA firm to implement similar quality control procedures? Explain.

9–17. What is the Public Oversight Board? What is its purpose?

9–18. Your CPA firm has been requested to perform a peer review of the firm of William & Stafford. What is involved in the performance of such an engagement? Discuss.

9–19. What problems are created for a CPA firm when audit staff members underreport the amount of time spent in performing specific auditing procedures?

GROUP II:
QUESTIONS
REQUIRING
ANALYSIS

9–20. An important part of every examination of financial statements is the preparation of audit working papers.

Required:

a. Discuss the relationship of audit working papers to each of the standards of field work.

b. You are instructing an inexperienced staff assistant on her first auditing assignment. She is to examine an account. An analysis of the account has been prepared by the client for inclusion in the audit working papers. Prepare a list of the comments, commentaries, and notations that the staff assistant should make or have made on the account analysis to provide an adequate working paper as evidence of her examination. (Do not include a description of auditing procedures applicable to the account.) (AICPA, adapted)

9–21. The preparation of working papers is an integral part of the auditors' examination of financial statements. On a recurring engagement the auditors review the working papers from their prior examination while planning the current examination to determine the papers' usefulness for the current engagement.

Required:

a. (1) What are the purposes or functions of audit working papers?

(2) What records of the auditors may be included in audit working papers?

b. What factors affect the auditors' judgment of the type and content of the working papers for a particular engagement?

c. To comply with generally accepted auditing standards, the auditors include certain evidence in their working papers, for example, "evidence that the engagement was planned and work of assistants was supervised and reviewed." What other evidence should the auditors include in audit working papers to comply with generally accepted auditing standards? (AICPA, adapted)

9–22. The partnership of Smith, Frank & Clark, a CPA firm, has been the auditor of Greenleaf, Inc. for many years. During the annual examination of the financial statements for the year ended December 31, 198X, a dispute developed over whether certain disclosures should be made in the financial statements. The dispute resulted in Smith, Frank & Clark's being dismissed and Greenleaf's engaging another CPA firm. Greenleaf demanded that Smith, Frank & Clark turn over all working papers applicable to the Greenleaf audits or face a lawsuit. Smith, Frank & Clark refused. Greenleaf has instituted a suit against Smith, Frank & Clark to obtain the working papers.

Required:

a. Will Greenleaf succeed in its suit? Explain.

b. Discuss the rationale underlying the rule of law applicable to the ownership of audit working papers. (AICPA, adapted)

9–23. "Working papers should contain facts and nothing but facts," said student A. "Not at all," replied student B. "The audit working papers may also include expressions of opinion. Facts are not always available to settle all issues." "In my opinion," said student C, "a mixture of facts and opinions in the audit working papers would be most confusing if the papers were produced as a means of supporting the auditors' position when their report has been challenged." Evaluate the issues underlying these arguments.

9–24. At 12 o'clock, when the plant whistle sounded, George Green, an assistant auditor, had his desk completely covered with various types of working papers. Green stopped work immediately, but not wanting to leave the desk with such a disorderly appearance he took a few minutes to sort the papers into proper order, place them in a neat pile, and weight them down with a heavy ash tray. He then departed for lunch. The auditor-in-charge, who had been observing what was going on, was critical of the assistant's actions. What do you think was the basis for criticism by the auditor-in-charge?

9–25. You have been assigned by your CPA firm to complete the examination of the financial statements of Hamilton Manufacturing Corporation because the senior auditor and his inexperienced assistant, who began the engagement, were hospitalized as the result of an accident. The engagement is about one-half completed. Your audit report must be delivered in three weeks, as agreed when your firm accepted the engagement. You estimate that by utilizing the client's staff to the greatest possible extent consonant with independence you can complete the engagement in five weeks. Your firm cannot assign an assistant to you.

The working papers show the status of work on the examination as follows:
(1) *Completed*—Cash, property and equipment, depreciation, mortgage note payable, and stockholders' equity.
(2) *Completed except as noted later*—Inventories, accounts payable, tests of controls over purchase transactions and payrolls.
(3) *Nothing done*—Trade accounts receivable, inventory price testing, accrued expenses payable, unrecorded liability test, tests of controls over sales transactions, tests of controls over payroll deductions and observation of payroll check distribution, analysis of other expenses, analytical procedures, vouching of December purchase transactions, audit report, assessment of control risk, letter on internal control structure weaknesses, minutes, preparation of tax returns, subsequent events, and supervision and review.

Your review discloses that the assistant's working papers are incomplete and were not reviewed by the senior accountant. For example, the inventory working papers present incomplete notations, incomplete explanations, and no cross-referencing.

Required:
a. What field work standards have been violated by the senior accountant who preceded you on this assignment? Explain why you think the standards you list have been violated.
b. In planning your work to complete this engagement, you should scan working papers and schedule certain work as soon as possible and also identify work that may be postponed until after the audit report is rendered to the client.

(1) List the areas on which you should plan to work first, say in your first week of work, and for each item explain why it deserves early attention.

(2) State which work you believe could be postponed until after the audit report is rendered to the client, and give reasons why the work may be postponed.   (AICPA, adapted)

9–26. Select the best answer for each of the following and give reasons for your choice:

a. Which of the following is *not* a factor that affects the independent auditors' judgment as to the quality, type, and content of working papers?

(1) The timing and the number of personnel to be assigned to the engagement.

(2) The nature of the financial statements, schedules, or other information upon which the auditor is reporting.

(3) The need for supervision of the engagement.

(4) The nature of the auditors' report.

b. Audit working papers are used to record the results of the auditors' evidence-gathering procedures. When preparing working papers the auditors should remember that working papers should be—

(1) Kept on the client's premises so that the client can have access to them for reference purposes.

(2) The primary support for the financial statements being examined.

(3) Considered as a part of the client's accounting records that is retained by the auditors.

(4) Designed to meet the circumstances and the auditors' needs on each engagement.

c. During the course of an audit engagement, auditors prepare and accumulate audit working papers. The primary purpose of the audit working papers is to—

(1) Aid the auditors in adequately planning their work.

(2) Provide a point of reference for future audit engagements.

(3) Support the underlying concepts included in the preparation of the basic financial statements.

(4) Support the auditors' opinion.

d. In pursuing a CPA firm's quality control objectives, a CPA firm may maintain records indicating which partners or employees of the CPA firm were previously employed by the CPA firm's clients. Which quality control objective would this be *most* likely to satisfy?

(1) Professional relationship.

(2) Supervision.

(3) Independence.

(4) Advancement.

e. A difference of opinion concerning accounting and auditing matters relative to a particular phase of the audit arises between an assistant auditor and the auditor responsible for the engagement. After appropriate consultation, the assistant auditor asks to be disassociated from the resolution of the matter. The working papers would probably be—

    (1) Silent on the matter since it is an internal matter of the auditing firm.

    (2) Expanded to note that the assistant auditor is completely dissociated from responsibility for the auditor's opinion.

    (3) Expanded to document the additional work required, since all disagreements of this type will require expanded substantive testing.

    (4) Expanded to document the assistant auditor's position, and how the difference of opinion was resolved.

f. Williams & Co., a large international CPA firm, is to have an "external peer review." The peer review will most likely be performed by

    (1) Employees and partners of Williams & Co. who are *not* associated with the particular audits being reviewed.

    (2) Audit review staff of the Securities and Exchange Commission.

    (3) Audit review staff of the American Institute of Certified Public Accountants.

    (4) Employees and partners of another CPA firm.

(AICPA, adapted)

GROUP III: PROBLEMS

9–27. Criticize the working paper on the following page that you are reviewing as senior auditor on the December 31, 1990, audit of Pratt Company.

9–28. One of the practical problems confronting the auditors is that of determining whether adjusting journal entries or other corrective actions are warranted by errors, omissions, and inconsistencies. The following items were noted by the auditors during their year-end examination of a small manufacturing partnership having net sales of approximately $1.6 million; net income of approximately $40,000; total assets of nearly $2 million; and total partners' capital of $300,000.

(1) Proceeds of $250 from the sale of fully depreciated office equipment were credited to Miscellaneous Revenue rather than to Gain and Loss on Sale of Equipment, a ledger account that had not been used for several years.

(2) The Trade Accounts Receivable control account showed a balance of $79,600. The individual accounts comprising this balance included three with credit balances of $320, $19, and $250, respectively.

(3) Several debits and credits to general ledger accounts had been made directly without use of journal entries. The amounts involved did not exceed $500.

(4) Credit memoranda were not serially numbered or signed, but a file of duplicates was maintained.

(5) General journal entries did not include explanations for any but unusual transactions.

(6) Posting references were occasionally omitted from entries in general ledger accounts.

(7) An expenditure of $200 for automobile repairs was recorded as a December expense, although shown by the invoice to be a November charge.

(8) The auditors' count of petty cash disclosed a shortage of $20.

Pratt Company
Cash   E-2

Per bank   44,874.50 √

Deposit in transit   837.50 √

Bank charges   2.80
                                      _____
                                      45,714.80
Outstanding checks
                    46.40
                    10.00
                    30.00
                 1,013.60 √
                 1,200.00 √
                    10.00
                    25.00 √
                    15.00 √
                    50.00 √
                 1,002.00 √   3,402.00
                                  _____
Per ledger   42,312.80 √

        √- Verified

            R. G H.
            1-15-91

(9) Expenditures for advertising amounting to $8,000 were charged to the Advertising Expense account; other advertising expenses amounting to $3,000 had been charged to Miscellaneous Expense.

(10) On September 12, the client borrowed $288,000 from First Bank by signing a 120-day note payable in the face amount of $300,000. The note matures on January 10. The client's accountant had charged the entire $12,000 interest included in the face amount of the note to the interest expense of the current year. He stated that he did not consider deferring part of the interest to the following year to be warranted by the dollar amounts involved.

Required:

You are to state clearly the position the auditors should take with respect to each of the above items during the course of an annual audit. If adjusting journal entries are necessary, include them in your solution.

9–29. You are a new staff assistant with the Houston office of a national public accounting firm. Yesterday you read an article in *The Wall Street Journal* in which the managing partner of your firm's New York office discussed the problems caused for the public accounting profession by auditors underreporting the number of hours worked on audits.

You found this article interesting because of the experience you are having on the audit of Regal Industries, one of your office's largest clients. The field work at Regal is being run by Mark Thomas, a very hard-working senior who is highly regarded within your office. Thomas made senior in record time, and has established a reputation for bringing jobs in on schedule. Four staff assistants, including yourself, are working under Thomas. At the end of the engagement, Thomas will write a performance report on each assistant, which will be placed in the assistant's personnel file. The manager on the engagement also writes a performance evaluation on each assistant and on Thomas. You have heard, however, that managers usually agree with whatever the senior has said about an assistant's performance.

The budgeted time estimates for almost every audit procedure being performed at Regal seem too short. No one is able to finish anything on schedule. Last week, Thomas approached all of the staff assistants about working Saturday to "catch up." He said that he was going to work a short day on Saturday and would not report the hours on his time sheet. He said that if you would do the same, he would buy lunch after you finished up on Saturday. You and two other assistants agreed. The fourth assistant, Dave Scott, declined, saying that he was going to a baseball game on Saturday.

The work on Saturday ran smoothly, and it was nice to wear jeans instead of dress clothes. You did quit a little early, although it was about 3:30, not noon. Afterwards, Thomas bought everyone lunch at a popular restaurant.

During the following workweek, you noticed that Thomas seemed quite friendly toward you and the other two assistants who had worked on Saturday. He also was complimentary of your work. He was not complimentary of Scott's work; in fact, you heard him comment to the engagement manager that he thought Scott would be a "short-timer," a phrase used to describe staff assistants who do not last long in public accounting. You were not too sympathetic to Scott's plight, however, as you and the other staff assistants also feel that Scott's work on the engagement has been substandard.

It is now Thursday afternoon, and Thomas has just asked the three of you who worked last Saturday if you will do the same thing again this week. He did not ask Scott. Again, Thomas offered to buy lunch if you would leave the hours off of your time sheets. You suspect that Thomas has read the article in *The Wall Street Journal*, because he seemed a little defensive about asking you to underreport your time. He pointed out that you are not paid by the hour anyway, so leaving the extra hours off of your time sheet "doesn't really cost you anything."

Required:

a.   Briefly explain why the managing partner of an office would probably oppose the practice of underreporting hours worked by the audit staff.

b.   Briefly explain why a senior might *not* oppose the practice.

c.   Explain how you think the other two staff assistants asked to work Saturday will probably respond. If you would respond differently, explain.

d.   Suggest quality control procedures that you think could be implemented by a CPA firm to discourage the underreporting of time by audit staff members.

**GROUP IV:
RESEARCH AND
DISCUSSION CASE**

9–30.   Marshall and Wyatt, CPAs, have been the independent auditors of Interstate Land Development Corporation for several years. During these years, Interstate prepared and filed its own annual income tax returns.

During 1990, Interstate requested Marshall and Wyatt to examine all the necessary financial statements of the corporation to be submitted to the Securities and Exchange Commission (SEC) in connection with a multistate public offering of 1 million shares of Interstate common stock. This public offering came under the provisions of the Securities Act of 1933. The examination was performed carefully and the financial statements were fairly presented for the respective periods. These financial statements were included in the registration statement filed with the SEC.

While the registration statement was being processed by the SEC, but before the effective date, the Internal Revenue Service (IRS) obtained a federal court subpoena directing Marshall and Wyatt to turn over all of its working papers relating to Interstate for the years 1986–90. Marshall and Wyatt initially refused to comply for two reasons. First, Marshall and Wyatt did not prepare Interstate's tax returns. Second, Marshall and Wyatt claimed that the working papers were confidential matters subject to the privileged communications rule. Subsequently, however, Marshall and Wyatt did relinquish the subpoenaed working papers.

Upon receiving the subpoena, Wyatt called Dunkirk, the chairman of Interstate's board of directors, and asked him about the IRS investigation. Dunkirk responded, "I'm sure the IRS people are on a fishing expedition and that they will not find any material deficiencies."

A few days later Dunkirk received a written memorandum from the

IRS that it was contending Interstate had underpaid its taxes during the period under review. The memorandum revealed that Interstate was being assessed $800,000, including penalties and interest for the three years. Dunkirk forwarded a copy of this memorandum to Marshall and Wyatt.

This $800,000 assessment was material relative to the financial statements as of December 31, 1990. The amount for each year individually exclusive of penalty and interest was not material relative to each respective year.

Required:

a. In general terms, discuss the extent to which a CPA firm's potential liability to third parties is increased in an SEC registration audit.

b. Discuss the implications of the IRS investigation, if any, relative to Marshall and Wyatt's examination of Interstate's 1990 financial statements. Discuss any additional investigative procedures that the auditors should undertake or any audit judgments that should be made as a result of this investigation.

c. Can Marshall and Wyatt validly refuse to surrender the subpoenaed working papers to the IRS? Explain.   (AICPA, adapted)

Suggested references:

Part a:

This textbook, pages 87–88.

Part b:

This textbook, pages 243–48.

AICPA, Professional Standards, Volume A, Commerce Clearing House, *Statement on Auditing Standards 1,* Section 560.

FASB Statement 5, "Accounting for Contingencies."

Part c:

This textbook, pages 62–63 and 314–15.

Designing audit programs; examination of the general records

Chapter 10 study objectives

After studying this chapter, you should be able to:

— Distinguish between the systems portion of the audit program and the substantive test portion.

— Describe the general objectives of audit programs for financial statement accounts.

— Explain the way in which the general objectives of audit programs are used to develop the specific objectives that are then used to determine the audit procedures to be applied to an asset account.

— Describe the type of general records that are examined by the auditors.

— Explain the auditors' responsibilities regarding illegal acts by clients.

— Describe the auditors' review and testing of the client's accounting records.

An audit program is a detailed list of the audit procedures to be performed in the course of the examination. As discussed in Chapter 4, a tentative audit program is developed as part of the advance planning of an audit. This tentative program, however, requires frequent modification as the audit progresses. For example, the nature, timing, and extent of substantive test procedures are influenced by the auditor's assessment of control risk. Thus, not until the consideration of internal control has been completed can a final version of the audit program be drafted. Even this final version may require modification if the auditors revise their preliminary estimates of materiality or risk for the engagement or if their substantive tests disclose unexpected problems.

The audit program usually is divided into two major sections. The first section deals with the procedures to obtain an understanding of the client's internal control structure, and the second section deals with the substantiation of specific financial statement amounts, as well as the adequacy of financial statement disclosures.

The systems portion of the program

The first part of the audit program is organized around the major *transaction cycles* in the client's internal control. For example, the systems portion of the audit program for a manufacturing company might be subdivided into separate programs for such areas as: (1) sales and collections cycle, (2) purchase cycle, (3) production cycle, (4) payroll cycle, and (5) financing cycle. (The activities comprising these specific transaction cycles are described in Chapter 5.) Audit procedures in the systems portion of the program typically include preparation of flowcharts for each transaction cycle, tests of the significant internal controls, identification of strengths and weaknesses, and assessment of control risk.

In conjunction with their consideration of internal control, the auditors will make appropriate modifications in the substantive test portion of the audit program. For example, as a result of weaknesses in internal control in the sales cycle, the auditors may assess control risk for accounts receivable to be high and decide to perform more extensive substantive tests of receivables.

The substantive test portion of the program

The portion of the audit program aimed at substantiating financial statement amounts usually is organized in terms of major balance sheet topics, such as cash, accounts receivable, inventories, and plant and equipment. Considering the importance of the income statement, why do audit programs emphasize the substantiation of balance sheet items? In part, this method of organizing the work may be a carryover from the days when the auditor's objective was verification of the balance sheet alone. Even though present-day auditors are very much concerned with the reliability of the income statement, they still find the balance sheet approach to be an effective method of organizing their substantive audit procedures.

One advantage of the balance sheet approach is that highly competent evidence generally is available to substantiate assets and liabilities. Assets usually are subject to direct verification by such procedures as physical observation, inspection of externally created documentary evidence, and confirmation by outside parties. Liabilities usually can be verified by externally created documents, confirmation, and inspecting paid checks after the liability has been paid.

In contrast, consider the nature of revenues and expenses in double-entry accounting. The entry to record revenues or expenses has two parts: first, the recognition of the revenue or expense; and second, the corresponding change in an asset or liability account. Revenues and expenses have no tangible form; they exist only as entries in the client's accounting records, representing changes in owners' equity. Consequently, the best evidence supporting the existence of revenues or expenses usually is the verifiable change in the related asset or liability account.

Indirect verification of income statement accounts   Figure 10–1 shows the relationship between income statement accounts and the related changes in cash or other balance sheet items. By substantiating the changes in the asset and liability accounts, the auditors indirectly verify revenue, cost of goods sold, and expenses. For example, most revenue transactions involve a debit to either Cash or Accounts Receivable. If the auditors are able to satisfy themselves that all cash receipts and all changes in accounts receivable during the year have been properly recorded, they have indirect evidence that revenue transactions have been accounted for properly.

Direct verification of income statement accounts   Not all of the audit evidence pertaining to income statement accounts is indirect. The verification of a major balance sheet item often involves several closely related income statement accounts that can be verified through computation or other direct evidence. For example, in substantiating the marketable securities owned by the client, it is a simple matter to compute the related interest revenue, dividends revenue, and gains or losses on sales of securities. In substantiating the balance sheet items of plant assets and accumulated depreciation, the auditors make computations that also substantiate depreciation expense. Uncollectible accounts expense is substantiated in conjunction with the balance sheet item Allowance for Doubtful Accounts. In addition to these computations, the auditors' *analytical procedures* provide direct evidence as to the reasonableness of various revenues and expenses.

Figure 10–1

	Income statement items		Cash transactions		Balance sheet items		
Financial statement relationships	Revenue	=	Cash receipts from customers	−	Beginning balance of Accounts Receivable	+	Ending balance of Accounts Receivable
	Cost of goods sold	=	Cash payments for merchandise	−	Beginning balance of Accounts Payable	+	Ending balance of Accounts Payable
				+	Beginning balance of Inventory	−	Ending balance of Inventory
	Expenses	=	Cash payments for expenses	−	Beginning balances of Accrued Expenses	+	Ending balances of Accrued Expenses
				+	Beginning balances of Prepaid Expenses	−	Ending balances of Prepaid Expenses
Auditors' approach to substantiation	Verify indirectly by substantiating right-hand side of equation; also analytical procedures and (if possible) direct computations.		Substantiate by testing transactions; also reconciliations of cash accounts.		Substantiate by reference to last year's audit working papers.		Substantiate by substantive tests in current year.

Comparison of the systems approach and the substantive approach
Auditing literature frequently refers to a CPA firm following a systems approach or a substantive approach to an audit. The *systems approach* involves heavy reliance upon the client's internal control, whereas the substantive approach relies more heavily upon substantive testing as the basis for the auditors' opinion. Actually, every audit involves a blend of reliance on internal control and substantive testing. Thus, *systems approach* and *substantive approach* are relative terms, indicating the emphasis that a particular CPA firm places in the systems or substantive portions of its audit program on a given engagement. Some CPA firms may lean toward one approach or the other as a matter of firm policy. However, in the audit of a client with weak internal control, the auditor has no choice but to emphasize the substantive approach.

Objectives of audit programs

An audit program is designed to accomplish certain objectives with respect to each major account in the financial statements. These objectives follow directly from the assertions that are contained in the client's financial statements.

Management assertions Assertions are representations of management that are set forth in the financial statements. Broadly speaking, a set of financial statements contains the following five management assertions:

1. *Existence or occurrence*—assets, liabilities, and owners' equity reflected in the financial statements exist; the recorded transactions have occurred.
2. *Completeness*—all transactions, assets, liabilities, and owners' equity that should be presented in the financial statements are included.
3. *Rights and obligations*—the client has rights to assets and obligations to pay liabilities that are included in the financial statements.
4. *Valuation or allocation*—assets, liabilities, owners' equity, revenues, and expenses are presented at amounts that are determined in accordance with generally accepted accounting principles.
5. *Presentation and disclosure*—accounts are described and classified in the financial statements in accordance with generally accepted accounting principles, and all material disclosures are provided.

From these assertions, general objectives may be developed for each major type of balance sheet account, including assets, liabilities, and owners' equity.

General objectives of audit programs for asset accounts

The audit program for each financial statement account must be tailored to accomplish the specific audit objectives for that account. The specific objectives for auditing cash are not identical to the specific objectives for auditing inventory. Although the specific audit objectives and, therefore, the audit procedures differ for each account, it is useful to realize that each audit program follows basically the same approach to verifying the balance sheet items and related income statement amounts. The audit program for every asset category includes procedures designed to accomplish the following *general objectives:*

**Audit program for accounts
stated in terms of general objectives**

I. Consideration of internal control.
   A. Obtain an understanding of internal control sufficient to plan the audit.
   B. Assess control risk and design additional tests of controls.
   C. Conduct additional tests of controls.
   D. Reassess control risk and design substantive tests.

II. Substantiate account balances (substantive tests).
   A. Establish the *existence* of assets.
   B. Establish that the company has *rights* to the assets.
   C. Establish *completeness* of recorded assets.
   D. Determine the appropriate *valuation* of the assets.
   E. Establish the *clerical accuracy* of the underlying records.
   F. Determine the appropriate financial statement *presentation and disclosure* of the assets.

These general objectives are *common to all audit programs for asset accounts.* Changes in these audit objectives, with respect to audit programs for liability and owners' equity accounts, will be discussed in later chapters.

Substantiation of account balances

The central purpose of the auditors' consideration of internal control is to assess control risk for each major *assertion* concerning a financial statement account to determine the nature and extent of the audit work necessary to substantiate the account balance. In previous chapters, considerable attention has been given to the consideration of internal control; let us now discuss the objectives of the auditors' substantiation procedures.

Existence of assets

The first step in substantiating the balance of an asset account is to verify the existence of the asset. For assets such as cash on hand, marketable securities, and inventories, existence of the asset usually may be verified by physical inspection. When assets are in the custody of others, such as cash in banks and inventory on consignment, the appropriate audit procedure may be direct confirmation with the outside party. The existence of accounts receivable normally is verified by confirming with customers the amounts receivable. Verifying the existence of intangibles is more difficult; the auditors must gather evidence that costs have been incurred and that these costs represent probable future economic benefits.

Rights to the assets

Usually, the same procedures that verify existence also establish the company's rights to the asset. For example, confirming cash balances in bank accounts establishes existence of the cash and the company's ownership rights to that cash. Similarly, inspecting marketable securities verifies both existence and ownership because the registered owner's name usually appears on the face of the security certificate.

With other assets, such as plant and equipment, physical inspection establishes existence *but not ownership*. Plant and equipment may be rented or leased rather than owned. To verify the client's rights to plant assets, the auditors must inspect documentary evidence such as property tax bills, purchase documents, and deeds.

The client may not hold legal title to all assets that are appropriately included in the financial statements. Instead, the client may own *rights* to use the assets conveyed by contracts, such as leases. The ownership of these rights may be established by reviewing the underlying contracts.

Establishing completeness

Designing substantive tests that are effective at detecting assets that are not recorded in the client's accounting records is difficult. Thus, the auditors often find it preferable to rely heavily on tests of the client's internal controls to establish the completeness of recorded assets.

Many tests for unrecorded assets involve *tracing* from the documents created when the assets were acquired to entries recording the assets in the accounting records. To test for unrecorded accounts receivable, for example, the auditors may select a sample of shipping documents issued during the year and trace the details to recorded sales transactions. Observation is important to testing the completeness of recorded physical assets. During their observation of the client's physical inventory, the auditors are alert for inventory items that are not counted and included in the inventory summary.

Analytical procedures also may be used to bring conditions to light that indicate that all assets may not be recorded. For example, a low gross profit percentage for the current year in comparison to prior years may indicate that the client has a substantial amount of unrecorded inventory.

Verifying the cutoff of transactions As a part of the auditors' procedures for establishing completeness as well as existence of recorded assets, the auditors will verify the client's cutoff of transactions included in the period. The financial statements should reflect all transactions occurring through the end of the period and none that occur subsequently. The term *cutoff* refers to the process of determining that transactions occurring near the balance sheet date are assigned to the proper accounting period.

The impact of cutoff errors upon the financial statements varies with the nature of the error. For example, a cutoff error in recording acquisitions of plant assets affects the balance sheet, but probably does not affect the income statement since depreciation usually is not recorded on assets acquired within a few days of year-end. On the other hand, a cutoff error in recording shipments of merchandise to customers affects both inventory and the cost of sales. In order to improve their financial picture, some clients may "hold their records open" to include in the current year cash receipts and revenue from the first part of the next period.

To verify the client's cutoff of transactions, the auditors should review transactions recorded shortly before and after the balance sheet date to ascertain that these transactions are assigned to the proper period. When such documents as checks, receiving reports, and shipping documents are serially numbered, noting the last serial number issued during the period will assist the auditors in determining that a proper cutoff has been made in recording transactions.

Valuation of assets

Determining the proper valuation of assets requires a thorough knowledge of generally accepted accounting principles. The auditors must not only establish that the accounting method used to value a particular asset is generally accepted, they must also determine that the method of valuation is appropriate in the circumstances. Once the auditors are satisfied as to the appropriateness of the method, the auditors will perform procedures to test the accuracy of the client's application of the method of valuation to the asset.

Most assets are valued at cost. Therefore, a common audit procedure is to vouch the acquisition cost of assets to paid checks and other documentary evidence. If the acquisition cost is subject to depreciation or amortization, the auditors must evaluate the reasonableness of the cost allocation program and verify the computation of the remaining unallocated cost. Assets valued at lower of cost or market necessitate an investigation of current market prices as well as acquisition costs.

Clerical accuracy of records

The amount appearing as an asset on a financial statement is almost always the accumulation of many smaller items. For example, the amount of inventory on a financial statement might consist of the cost of thousands or, perhaps, hundreds of thousands of individual products. Before auditing these individual items, the auditors must test the clerical accuracy of the underlying records to determine that they accumulate to the total appearing in the general ledger and, therefore, the amount in the financial statements. The auditors often use their generalized audit programs to perform these tests of clerical accuracy of the records.

Financial statement presentation and disclosure

Even after all dollar amounts have been substantiated, the auditors must perform procedures to assure that the financial statement presentation conforms to the requirements of authoritative accounting pronouncements and the general principle of adequate disclosure. Procedures falling into this category include the review of subsequent events; search for related party transactions; investigation of loss contingencies; review of disclosure of such items as leases, compensating balances, pledged assets, and inventory profits; and review of the categories and descriptions used on all of the financial statements.

An illustration of program design

The above general objectives apply to all types of assets. Audit procedures for a particular asset account must be designed to accomplish the *specific audit objectives* regarding that asset. These specific objectives vary with the nature of the asset and the generally accepted accounting principles that govern its valuation and presentation.

In designing an audit program for a specific account, the auditors start by developing general objectives from the financial statement assertions. Then, specific objectives are developed for the account under audit and, finally, audit procedures are designed to accomplish each specific audit objective. Figure 10–2 provides a description of this process for accounts receivables and illustrates the relationship between management assertions, audit objectives, and audit procedures.

Figure 10–2 includes only one example of audit procedure for each specific objective. Usually, additional procedures must be performed to accomplish the audit objectives. For example, the audit objective of determining that receivables are properly presented in the balance sheet is not achieved solely by a procedure focusing on the disclosure of pledged accounts. The audit program must include procedures that focus on other aspects of presentation and disclosure, such as procedures designed to identify receivables from related parties.

The audit objectives relating to the auditors' consideration of internal control are not included in Figure 10–2. The auditors' consideration of internal control can provide evidence regarding any of the assertions for an account. Any evidence provided by internal control regarding an asser-

Figure 10–2   Relationship of assertions, objectives, and procedures

Management assertions	General audit objectives for assets	Specific audit objectives for accounts receivable	Example audit procedures
Existence and occurrence	Existence of assets	Validity of recorded receivables	Confirm a sample of receivables by direct communication with the debtors
Rights and obligations	Rights to assets		
Completeness	Completeness	All receivables are recorded	Compare a sample of shipping documents to related sales invoices
Valuation or allocation	Valuation of assets	Receivables are presented at net realizable value	Investigate the credit ratings for delinquent and large receivables accounts
	Clerical accuracy of records	Receivables records are accurate and agree with general ledger	Obtain an aged trial balance of receivables, test its clerical accuracy, and reconcile to the ledgers
Presentation and disclosure	Financial statement presentation	Receivables are properly presented in the balance sheet, including the appropriate disclosures	Review standard bank confirmations for indications of receivables pledged for loans

tion results in a reduction in the extent of the substantive tests required to accomplish the related objective.

In the next four chapters, we will consider the audit work to be done on the major asset categories, beginning with cash and concluding with plant assets and intangible assets. Specific audit objectives and a sample audit program will be presented for each asset category to provide a framework for our discussion. It is important to remember that the audit programs presented in the textbook are merely illustrations of *typical* audit procedures. In actual practice, audit programs must be tailored to each client's business environment and internal control structure. The audit procedures comprising audit programs may vary substantially from one engagement to the next.

Verification of related income statement accounts

Income statement amounts often can be verified conveniently in conjunction with the substantiation of the related asset account. For example, after notes receivable have been verified, the related interest revenue can be substantiated by mathematically computing the interest applicable to the notes. In other cases, income statement amounts are determined by the same audit procedures used in determining the valuation of the related asset. Determining the undepreciated cost of plant assets, for example, necessitates computing (or testing) the depreciation expense for the period. Similarly, determining the net valuation of accounts receivable involves estimating the uncollectible accounts expense.

Some income statement items, such as sales revenue, do not lend themselves to verification by such direct audit procedures. However, when the auditors establish that accounts receivable are legitimate assets, and have been properly recorded, they have substantial *indirect* evidence that sales on account also have been properly measured.

EXAMINATION OF THE GENERAL RECORDS

In the early stages of an audit, the independent auditors must become familiar with many aspects of the client's business. For example, the auditors must obtain a knowledge of the client's organization plan, financial structure, physical facilities, products, accounting policies, and control procedures. However, information about the internal activities of the client is not in itself sufficient. If this information is to be interpreted and evaluated in a proper perspective, the auditors must also understand the business environment in which the client operates. State and federal laws and regulations, pending or threatened litigation, affiliations with other companies, and contracts with suppliers and customers are only a few of the factors in the business environment that may affect the client's internal activities. The auditors can gain considerable information about both the client's business environment and internal operations by examining the client's general records. The term *general records* is used to include the following categories.

1. Nonfinancial records.
   a. Articles of incorporation and bylaws.
   b. Partnership contract.
   c. Minutes of directors' and stockholders' meetings.
   d. Contracts with customers and suppliers.
   e. Contracts with officers and employees, including union agreements and stock option, profit-sharing, bonus, and pension plans.
   f. Governmental regulations directly affecting the enterprise.
   g. Correspondence files.
2. Financial records.
   a. Income tax returns of prior years.
   b. Financial statements and annual reports of prior years.
   c. Registration statements and periodic reports filed with the SEC.
3. Accounting records.
   a. General ledger.
   b. General journal.

Examining these records should assist the auditors in identifying problems requiring more extensive audit attention. Also, the auditors obtain an understanding of the client's business characteristics, policies, and plans that enable them to determine whether the transactions reflected in the accounts were properly authorized and executed in accordance with the directives of management. If audit staff members are thoroughly familiar with the history and problems of the business, the duties and responsibilities of key officials, and the nature and quality of the accounting records and procedures, then they are prepared to carry out each phase of the audit with confidence and understanding. If they do not acquire this background information before beginning the work of analyzing transactions and substantiating account balances, they are almost certain to proceed in a mechanical and routine manner, unaware of the real significance of much of the evidence examined.

Articles of incorporation and bylaws

In the first audit of a client's financial statements, a senior auditor will obtain copies of the articles of incorporation (or corporate charter) and bylaws. The *articles of incorporation* is the basic document filed with the state to evidence the legal existence of a corporation. It includes such information as the name of the company, date and state of incorporation, and number of authorized directors. In addition, the articles of incorporation describe the authorized capital structure, including classes of capital stock, number of shares authorized, par or stated values, liquidating preferences, voting rights, and dividend rates for preferred stock.

The *bylaws* help define the internal administrative structure of a corporation; they include the organizational structure, rules, and procedures adopted by the corporate stockholders. For example, the bylaws may stipulate the frequency of stockholders' meetings, the date and method for election of directors and selection of officers, and the powers and duties of directors and officers. Copies of both the articles of incorporation and the bylaws are retained in the auditors' permanent file for convenient reference during repeat engagements.

Partnership contract

In the audit of a business organized as a partnership, the partnership contract should be examined in much the same manner as the articles of incorporation and bylaws of corporate clients. The partnership contract represents an agreement among partners on the rules to be followed in the operation of the enterprise. The information available in a copy of the partnership contract usually includes the following:

1. The name and address of the firm.
2. The names and addresses of the individual partners.
3. The amount, date, and nature of the investment made by each partner.
4. The profit-sharing ratio, partners' salaries, interest on partners' capital, and restrictions on withdrawals.
5. The duties, responsibilities, and authority of each partner.
6. The provision for insurance on lives of partners.

7.   The provisions concerning liquidation of the firm and distribution of assets.

In repeat examinations, the auditors must ascertain whether any modification of the partnership contract has been made and obtain copies of the modifications for the permanent file. If no change has occurred since the preceding audit, a notation to that effect should be made.

Corporate minutes book

The corporate minutes book is an official record of the actions taken at meetings of directors and stockholders. Typical of the actions taken at meetings of stockholders is the extension of authority to management to acquire or dispose of subsidiaries and to adopt or modify pension or profit sharing plans for officers and employees. The stockholders also customarily approve the selection of a firm of independent auditors. Representatives of the auditing firm attend the stockholders' meeting for the purpose of answering questions that may arise concerning internal control and the financial operations of the business.

Minutes of the directors' meetings usually contain authorizations for important transactions and contractual arrangements, such as the establishment of bank accounts, setting of officers' salaries, declaration of dividends, and formation of long-term agreements with vendors, customers, and lessors. In addition, the minutes may document discussions by the board of pending litigation, investigations by regulatory agencies, or other loss contingencies.

Committees of the board   In large corporations, the board of directors often works through committees appointed to deal with special phases of operations. Common examples include an audit committee and an investment committee. As discussed in Chapters 4 and 5, the audit committee maintains close contact with both the independent CPAs and the company's internal auditors and may be involved in discussions of weaknesses in internal control, accounting policies, and possible illegal or fraudulent acts by management. The investment committee periodically reviews and approves the investment activities of management. Minutes of the meetings of such committees are just as essential to the auditors' investigation as are the minutes covering the meetings of the entire board.

Procedure for review of minutes   In the first audit of a client, it may be necessary to review minutes recorded in prior years. Copies of these minutes will be preserved in the permanent file; as succeeding annual audits are made, the file will be appropriately expanded.

The auditor-in-charge will obtain from the secretary or other corporate officer copies of all minutes, including those of board committees, directors, and stockholders, for both regular and special meetings. These copies should be certified by a corporate officer and should be compared with the official minutes book to an extent sufficient to establish their completeness and authenticity.

In reviewing the minutes, the auditors will (1) note the date of the meeting and whether a quorum was present and (2) underscore or highlight such actions and decisions that in their judgment should influence the conduct of the audit. Nonessential material can be scanned rapidly, and highlighting can be limited to issues that warrant investigation during the course of the audit. For this phase of the audit work, there is no substitute for breadth of experience and maturity of judgment; the minutes include a wide range of information from matters of real importance to the audit and to those that may safely be passed by.

Major decisions in the minutes, such as declaration of dividends or authorization for borrowing, usually result in actions that need to be recorded in the accounting records. As the audit progresses, the auditors should trace authorized events from the minutes into the accounting records and cross-reference their copies of the minutes to the underlying account analyses. Similarly, events recorded in the accounting records that normally require authorization by directors should be traced and cross-referenced to the auditors' copies of the minutes.

Determining that all minutes are made available   How do the auditors know that copies of all minutes have been made available to them? First, they can review their permanent file to determine the identities of the boards' committees and the scheduled dates for regular meetings. Next, a typical practice at board and committee meetings is to approve the minutes of the preceding meeting. This practice enables the auditors to work backward from the most recent minutes to the oldest, noting the date of the previous minutes approved in the later meeting. Also, the auditors should obtain from management a letter representing that all minutes have been made available. The client's refusal to provide the auditors with copies of all minutes is a serious limitation of the scope of the auditors' examination. *SAS 58* (AU 508) advises auditors to issue a disclaimer of opinion on the financial statements when significant scope limitations are imposed by the client.[1]

Relationship of corporate minutes to audit objectives   The nature of the information to be highlighted in the minutes and the usefulness of this information to the auditors can be made clear by a few examples. Figure 10–3 shows several audit objectives and indicates for each objective certain relevant events that are likely to be documented in the minutes of the board and its committees.

---

[1] AICPA, *Statement on Auditing Standards 58,* "Reports on Audited Financial Statements" (New York, 1988), par. 42, AU 508.42.

Figure 10–3   Relationship of minutes to audit objectives

Audit objectives	Relevant information likely to be included in minutes of the board and its committees
1. Establishing the completeness of cash balances.	1. The opening and closing of bank accounts require authorization by the board of directors.
2. Financial statement presentation and disclosure of marketable securities.	2. Pledging of securities as collateral for a loan requires approval of the investments committee of the board.
3. Establishing the completeness of liabilities.	3a. The obtaining of bank loans requires advance approval by the board.
	b. Authority for the declaration of dividends payable rests with the board.
	c. The issuance of bonds payable or other long-term debt requires approval by the board.
4. Financial statement presentation and disclosure of loss contingencies.	4a. Such issues as pending litigation, income tax disputes, accommodation endorsements, and other loss contingencies discussed by the board are documented in the minutes.
	b. Unusual purchase commitments and sales commitments may be submitted to the board for approval.
	c. The selection of legal counsel, who in turn may have information regarding pending litigation or other loss contingencies, is approved by the board.

Contracts held or issued by client

Early in the audit engagement the auditors should obtain copies of the major contracts to which the client is a party. Information obtained from an analysis of contracts may be helpful in interpreting such accounts as Advances from Suppliers, Progress Payments under Government Contracts, and Stock Options. In addition to production contracts with governmental agencies and other companies, the auditors may review contracts with suppliers for future delivery of materials, royalty agreements for use of patents, union labor contracts, leases, pension plans, stock options, and bonus contracts with officers.

The terms of existing contracts are often material factors in measuring debt-paying ability and estimating future earnings. When examinations are being made on behalf of prospective investors, creditors, or purchasers of a business, the nature of contracts with customers may outweigh all other considerations in determining a market value for the business.

The auditors may at times require the assistance of engineers, attorneys, and other specialists in the interpretation of important contracts. Most contracts include such accounting concepts as net income or working capital, but unfortunately those who draft the contracts may not in all cases understand the true meaning of the accounting terminology they employ. Skill in analyzing and interpreting the financial aspects of contracts appears to be a qualification of increasing importance to independent auditors.

Among the items auditors should usually note in reviewing contracts are the names and addresses of parties, effective date and duration of the contract, schedule for performance, provisions for price redetermination (such as cost-of-living adjustments), procedures for settlement of disputes, cancellation clauses, and provisions requiring audit of records to determine amounts owed.

Government laws and regulations

Although independent auditors are not licensed to give legal advice or to interpret federal or state laws, they must be familiar with laws and regulations that affect the client's financial statements. Auditors should consult with the client's legal counsel—and their own attorneys if necessary—when they believe a legal problem affects performance of the audit or requires disclosure in the financial statements.

Among the laws and regulations with which auditors should be familiar are the following:

Foreign Corrupt Practices Act   This legislation has two major parts: (1) it prohibits bribes of foreign government officials for the purpose of securing business and (2) it requires companies to maintain reasonably complete accounting records and an adequate system of internal accounting control. The specific requirements regarding the internal accounting control provisions were discussed in Chapter 5.

State corporations codes   These laws govern the formation and operation of corporations and include provisions that affect such matters as legal or stated capital, par or no-par-value stock, dividend declarations, and treasury stock.

Uniform Partnership Act This Act, in effect in most states, governs the operations of partnerships in areas not covered by the partnership agreement.

State and federal corporate securities laws Most states have blue-sky laws regulating the issuance of corporate debt and equity securities within their jurisdictions. In addition, the federal Securities Act of 1933 governs the interstate issuance of corporate securities, while the Securities Exchange Act of 1934 deals with the trading of securities on national exchanges or over the counter.

Uniform Commercial Code This Code regulates sales of goods, commercial paper (such as checks, warehouse receipts, and bills of lading), investment securities, and secured transactions in personal property.

Antitrust laws Federal antitrust laws are designed to promote competition; these laws provide civil and, in some cases, criminal liability for offenders.

Labor laws Federal laws regulating labor include provisions that relate to such matters as minimum wage, overtime premiums, and equal pay for equal work.

Social security The Social Security Act of 1935 provides for payroll taxes on employers and employees to finance retirement and medical benefits for retired persons and certain surviving dependents.

Employee Retirement Income Security Act of 1974 (ERISA) This legislation, also known as the Pension Reform Act, regulates the administration and funding of private retirement plans.

Cost Accounting Standards These standards establish accounting methods to be used by contractors to determine *cost* for cost-plus government contracts.

Regulations for specific industries Clients in regulated industries, such as insurance companies, banks, savings and loan associations, public utilities, airlines, and railroads, are subject to additional specific controls often administered by federal and state regulatory commissions.

Temporary controls Various temporary regulations have been occasionally imposed affecting wages, prices, and dividends.

The Single Audit Act The Single Audit Act of 1984 requires any state or local government receiving $100,000 or more in federal financial assistance to have an annual audit. In performing a "single audit" the auditors must adhere to the standards of the Governmental Accounting Office (GAO) for financial and compliance audits. In addition to determining whether the financial statements are presented fairly in accordance with generally accepted accounting principles, the auditors must also determine and report whether: (1) the client has internal control systems to provide reasonable assurance that it is managing its federal assistance programs in accordance with applicable laws and regulations, and (2) the client has complied with laws and regulations that may have a material effect on major federal assistance programs.

Illegal acts by clients Laws and regulations vary in their relation to the client's financial statements. Certain laws have a direct effect on the financial statements and are considered on every audit. An example is the income tax law which affects the amount of income tax expense in the financial statements of most clients. The auditors' responsibility for detecting violations of these laws is greater than their responsibility to detect illegal acts arising from laws that only indirectly affect the client's financial statements, such as violations of antitrust laws. An illegal act may need to be reflected in the client's financial statements, and may even affect the future viability of the client's business.

As explained in *SAS 54* (AU 317), ''Illegal Acts by Clients,'' an auditors' examination carried out in accordance with generally accepted auditing standards should be designed to provide reasonable assurance of detecting illegal acts having a material *direct* affect on the financial statements—this is the same responsibility the auditors have for material errors and irregularities. An audit does *not* generally provide a basis for detecting violations of laws or regulations which have an *indirect* affect on the financial statements. Unfortunately, the media and the public sometimes tend to blame auditors because illegal acts by a client company are not brought to light during an audit. Only those persons who understand the scope and limitations of an audit realize that audits by their very nature cannot be relied on to detect all types of illegal acts by the client. Of course, audit procedures such as reading minutes of the board of directors and inquiring of management and the client's legal counsel, sometimes will result in the discovery of certain illegal acts. Also, the auditors are alert throughout their audit for information that raises a question regarding the possibility of illegal acts, such as transactions that are unauthorized or improperly recorded, investigations of governmental agencies, and excessive or unusual payments.

Under no circumstances should the CPAs condone or ignore actions they *know* to be dishonest or illegal. This does not mean that the CPAs should report such acts to governmental authorities; it does mean that they should not permit their firm's name to be associated with financial statements that are misleading or that conceal morally indefensible actions by a client.

If the CPAs have knowledge of dishonest or clearly illegal actions by a client, they should attempt to assess the impact of the actions on the financial statements. This usually requires consulting legal council or other specialists. The auditors should also discuss the situation with top management and notify the audit committee of the board of directors so that action can be taken to remedy the situation and make disclosures or adjustments to the financial statements. If the client fails to take appropriate corrective action, the CPAs should withdraw from the engagement. This action on the part of the CPAs makes clear that they will not be associated in any way with dishonorable or illegal activities.

Detection of fraud   In recent years, investors have been deceived by a few gigantic frauds including falsified financial statements. In considering the responsibility of auditors for detection of fraud, it is helpful to distinguish employee fraud from management fraud. *Employee fraud* consists of dishonest actions that occur within a company despite management's efforts to prevent such actions. Protection against employee fraud is provided by a strong internal control structure, as discussed in Chapter 5. The independent auditors' contribution in preventing employee fraud is to study internal control and to make recommendations for improvements.

Management fraud   Fraud involving management occurs when the top executives of a company deliberately deceive stockholders, creditors, and independent auditors. The purpose of management fraud is generally to issue misleading financial statements that exaggerate corporate earnings and financial strength. Management fraud is of significant concern to the profession, so much so that a National Commission on Fraudulent Financial Reporting was created by the major professional accounting organizations to identify factors that may contribute to fraudulent reporting and ways of preventing it from occurring including the role of independent and internal auditors. The Commission basically endorsed the statement of auditors' responsibility for the detection of fraud as set forth in *SAS 53* (AU 316). As discussed in Chapter 4, the auditors have a responsibility to design their audit to provide reasonable assurance of detecting errors or irregularities that have a material effect on the financial statements and to conduct their examination with due care and skill. The auditors should be alert for circumstances that might motivate management to exaggerate financial results, such as a marginal financial position, a "shakeout" in the company's industry, or the need to maintain earnings growth to support the company's stock price.

Correspondence files

The general correspondence files of the client may contain much information of importance to the independent auditors, but it would be quite out of the question for them to plow through the great mass of general correspondence on file in search of pertinent letters. When the reading of corporate minutes, contract files, or other data indicates the existence of significant correspondence on matters of concern to the auditors, they should request the client to provide them with copies of such letters. In addition, the audit staff will usually review the client's correspondence with banks and other lending institutions, attorneys, and governmental agencies. Correspondence may generally be accepted as authentic, but if reason for doubt exists, the auditors may wish to confirm the contents of letters directly with the responsible persons.

Income tax returns of prior years

A review of federal, state, and foreign income tax returns of prior years will aid the auditors in planning any tax services required by the terms of the engagement. The possibility of assessment of additional income taxes exists with respect to the returns of recent years not yet cleared by tax authorities. By reviewing tax returns and revenue agents' reports, the auditors may become aware of any matters that pose a threat of additional assessments; they may also find a basis for filing a claim for a tax refund.

Financial statements and annual reports of prior years

Study of the financial statements and annual reports of prior years and of any available monthly or quarterly statements for the current year is a convenient way for the auditors to gain a general background knowledge of the financial history and problems of the business. If independent auditors have submitted audit reports in prior years, these documents may also be useful in drawing attention to matters requiring special consideration.

Reports to the SEC

Registration statements and periodic reports filed by the client with the SEC contain valuable information for the auditors—especially in a first audit. Included in this information will be the client's capital structure, a summary of earnings for the past five years, identity of affiliated companies, descriptions of the business and property of the client, pending legal proceedings, names of directors and executive officers of the client and their remuneration, stock option plans, and principal shareholders of the client.

Review and testing of the accounting records

Early in the examination the auditors should review the client's accounting system and assess the quality of the accounting records. A review of these records will inform the auditors as to the client's accounting procedures, the accounting records in use, and the control procedures in effect. Testing of the accounting records verifies the mechanical accuracy of the records and provides assurance that the journals and ledger are actually achieving their respective purposes of recording and classifying transaction data.

The quality of accounting records may vary widely from one engagement to the next. Many clients maintain records that are carefully designed, well maintained, and easy to comprehend. The journals and ledgers of such clients are generally up to date, in balance, and virtually free from mechanical error. When the auditors ascertain that a client's accounting records are highly reliable, the audit work necessary to substantiate account balances may justifiably be minimized. At the other extreme, the accounting records of some clients may be typified by unrecorded transactions, unsupported entries, and numerous mechanical errors. In these cases, the auditors may have to perform extensive audit work to substantiate account balances. On occasion, the accounting records may be so inadequate that the auditors must disclaim an opinion on the financial statements.

Extent of testing   If the client's accounting records and procedures are well designed and efficiently maintained, it is reasonable to devote less audit time to verifying the mechanical accuracy of the records than would be required in audits in which less satisfactory conditions prevail. The extent to which the auditors test the accounting records depends upon two factors: (1) the general appearance of the records, and (2) the frequency and relative importance of any errors discovered during the actual testing. The first of these factors, the general appearance of the records, deserves some explanation. High-quality accounting records have basic characteristics that are readily apparent: journal entries include adequate written explanations, general journal entries are reviewed and approved by an officer before processing, and the records are up to date and properly cross-referenced. When records do not possess these characteristics, the existence of errors is a virtual certainty.

Testing of the accounting records may be done on a judgmental basis, or the auditors may use statistical sampling techniques. Attributes sampling, as discussed in Chapter 8, is a statistical sampling plan that may be used to estimate deviation rates with specified levels of risk of overreliance on internal control.

The general ledger

The function of the general ledger is to accumulate and classify the transaction data posted from the journals. To ascertain that the ledger is being properly maintained, the auditors should conduct tests to determine that (1) account balances are mathematically correct, (2) entries in the ledger were posted from journal entries, and (3) journal entries were properly posted.

To test the mathematical accuracy of account balances, the auditors should verify the footings of some or all of the ledger accounts. The term **footings** is used among practicing accountants to designate column totals. "To foot," on the other hand, means to verify the total by adding the column.

For the second group of tests, the auditors must satisfy themselves that entries in the general ledger were posted from authentic sources; that is, from entries in the journals. This procedure is important because the financial statements are drawn from the general ledger balances, and these balances conceivably could be falsified through the recording of unsupported debits or credits in the general ledger. The auditors can determine that entries in the ledger are properly supported by *tracing a sample of ledger entries back into the journals.* Ledger entries included in this sample are normally selected at random from entries made throughout the year. Of course, the auditors may test most or all of the entries in excess of some specified dollar amount.

Finally, to test the accuracy of the client's posting procedures, the auditors should *trace a sample of entries from the journals into the general and subsidiary ledgers.*

Direction of testing   In the two preceding paragraphs, two similar tests are described. In one test, ledger entries are traced to journals; in the other, journals are traced forward into the ledgers. The direction of testing is crucial to the effectiveness of the tests. The reasoning behind the direction of testing becomes apparent when we consider the nature of the errors for which the auditors are testing.

In the first test, the auditors are testing for unsupported entries into the ledger. Tracing ledger entries back to journal entries may reveal transactions that are not supported and, possibly, not valid. By extending the test and vouching the journalized transactions to the supporting documents, such as receiving reports and canceled checks, the auditors may also obtain evidence of the validity of the journalized transactions. On the other hand, transactions that are not supported *can never* be found by tracing forward from journal entries or source documents to the ledgers.

In the second test, the auditors are testing the *completeness* of posted transactions. If a transaction was never posted, this omission can be detected only by tracing from the source documents or the journals to the ledgers. Transactions improperly omitted from ledger accounts *cannot* be brought to light by tracing existing ledger entries back to their source. Of course, some errors, such as transposition errors in entering transactions and postings to the wrong account, may be discovered by tracing in either direction.

Computer-based systems   It is likely that a client's accounting system will involve some form of electronic data processing. In these computer-based systems, transactions are entered into the computer either individually or in batches. The computer system then creates a journal of the transactions, and posts the transactions to the general ledger and appropriate subsidiary ledgers. Entries in the journals are linked to the ledger postings by the *audit trail* that allows journal entries to be traced to or from the ledgers. The audit trail also allows journal entries to be traced to and from the documents supporting the transactions.

Tests of the mechanical accuracy of computer-based accounting records may be performed manually by the auditors. It is generally more efficient, however, to perform the tests using *computer-assisted audit techniques,* as described in Chapter 6. Generalized audit software programs may be used to foot accounting ledgers, and tools to test controls, such as controlled programs and integrated test facilities, may be used to test the accuracy with which the system enters transactions to journals and ledgers.

The general journal

The general journal is an accounting record used to record all transactions for which special journals have not been provided. In its simplest form, the general journal has only a single pair of columns for the recording of debit and credit entries, but many variations from this basic design are encountered. A third column may be added to provide for entries to subsidiary ledgers, or various multicolumn forms may be used.

Some companies maintain a system of journal vouchers. These are serially numbered documents, each containing a single, general journal entry, with full supporting details and bearing the signature of the controller or other officer authorized to approve the entry. A general journal in traditional form may be prepared from the journal vouchers, or that series of documents may be utilized in lieu of a general journal. Companies having electronic data processing equipment generally enter journal vouchers to serve as one of the transaction sources for printouts of the ledgers and the trial balance.

The auditors should conduct tests to determine that entries in the general journal are based upon actual transactions and that these transactions have been properly recorded. Suggested procedures for testing the general journal follow:

1.   Foot column totals of the journal.

The testing of footings in the general journal follows the pattern previously described for verification of ledger balances. The footings may be performed manually or by using computer assisted audit techniques.

2.   Vouch selected entries to original documents.

To vouch a journal entry means to examine the original papers and documents supporting the entry. The term *voucher* is used to describe any type of supporting documentary evidence. For example, a journal entry recording the trade-in of a machine would be vouched by comparing it with a purchase order, supplier's invoice, sales contract, receiving report, and paid check—the vouchers for this entry. The auditors might not consider it necessary to examine all these documents if the evidence first examined appeared to provide adequate support for the entry. All general journal entries selected for testing should be vouched.

Entries in the general journal should include clear, informative explanations; but, unfortunately, deviations from this principle are frequently encountered. The auditors should determine whether (1) the explanation is in agreement with the supporting documentation, and (2) the entry reflects the transaction properly in the light of generally accepted accounting principles.

The supporting evidence to be examined during the review of general journal entries may include purchase orders, invoices, receiving reports, sales contracts, correspondence, the minutes book, and the partnership contract. Journal vouchers represent an internal control device; however, they should not be considered as original source documents supporting entries in the general journal. Verification of journal entries requires that the auditors refer to original invoices and other evidence previously described.

3. Scan the general journal for unusual entries.

The importance of certain types of transactions that are recorded in the general journal makes it desirable for auditors to scan this record for the entire period under audit, in addition to vouching all entries selected for testing. The following list is illustrative of the type of significant transactions for which the auditors should look in this scanning of the general journal:

1. The write-off of assets, particularly notes and accounts receivable: Collections from customers abstracted by employees and not recorded in the accounts may be permanently concealed if the accounts in question are written off as uncollectible. Any general journal entries involving loans receivable from officers require full investigation to provide assurance that such transactions are proper and have been authorized.

2. Assumption of liabilities: Transactions that create liabilities are normally recorded in special journals. Common examples of such transactions are the purchase of merchandise, materials, or equipment and the receipt of cash. General journal entries that bring liabilities into the record warrant close investigation to determine that they have received proper authorization and are adequately supported.

3. Any debits or credits to Cash accounts, other than for bank charges and other bank reconciliation items: Most transactions affecting cash are recorded in special journals.

4. Creation of revenue: Transactions affecting operating revenue accounts are usually recorded in special journals. Operating revenue would be recorded in the general journal only if the underlying transaction was of an unusual nature or, for some reason, was being pro-

cessed in a special manner. In either case, the auditors should verify the authenticity of the transaction and the propriety of the entry.

5. Unexplained or fragmentary transactions, the purpose and nature of which are not apparent from the journal entry: General journal entries with inadequate or unintelligible explanations suggest that the person making the entry did not understand the issues involved or was unwilling to state the facts clearly. Entries of this type, and entries that affect seemingly unrelated accounts, should be fully investigated.

6. Related party transactions: Transactions between the client and affiliated companies, directors, officers, and principal owners and their immediate families are not at arm's length and should be investigated to determine that the substance of the transactions has been fairly recorded. These transactions, as discussed in Chapter 7, should be reviewed by the auditors as to reasonableness of amounts, business purpose, and adequacy of disclosure.

Illustrative case

In a widely publicized management fraud, the financial statements of Equity Funding Corporation of America were inflated over a period of years by more than $120 million in fictitious assets and revenue. Although falsified journal entries were prepared to record fictitious transactions, there was frequently no documentation to support the journal entries. Large amounts of revenue were also recognized in journal entries that involved debits and credits to an illogical combination of accounts. Thorough investigation of unusual revenue-creating journal entries could have alerted the company's independent auditors to the fraud long before it reached mammoth proportions.

---

4. Determine that general journal entries have received the approval of an officer.

An adequate internal control structure includes procedures for regular review and written approval of all general journal entries by the controller or other appropriate executive. The auditors should determine that such procedures have been consistently followed. In those cases in which a client official does not regularly review and approve journal entries, the auditors may deem it desirable to review the general journal with the controller and request an approval signature on each page. In such cases, the report to the client on internal control structure and related matters should include a suggestion that the client undertake regular review and approval of journal entries.

Audit working papers for the examination of accounting records

Upon completing the review and testing of the accounting records, the auditors should prepare a working paper describing the records in use, the tests of controls and other audit procedures followed, the nature and significance of errors discovered, any suggestions for improving the accounting system, and the auditors' conclusion as to the overall quality of the accounting records. This working paper summarizes an important part of the auditors' consideration of internal control and may serve as a reference for determining appropriate modifications in the audit program. At the beginning of the next annual audit, a review of this working paper will enable the auditors to concentrate upon the most significant aspects of the accounting records.

KEY TERMS INTRODUCED OR EMPHASIZED IN CHAPTER 10

Articles of incorporation   That part of the application to the state for a corporate charter that includes detailed information concerning the financial structure and other details of the business.

Bylaws   Rules adopted by the stockholders at the inception of a corporation to serve as general guidelines in the conduct of the business.

Cutoff   The process of determining that transactions occurring near the balance sheet date are assigned to the proper accounting period.

Employee fraud   Dishonest actions (usually involving the theft of assets) that occur within a company despite management's efforts to prevent such actions.

Journal voucher   A serially numbered document describing the details of a single journal entry and bearing the signature of the officer who approved the entry.

Management assertions   Representations of management that are communicated, explicitly or implicitly, by the financial statements.

Management fraud   Exists when the client management makes a deliberate effort to present misleading financial statements, supported by falsified accounting records.

Minutes book   A formal record of the issues discussed and actions taken in meetings of stockholders and of the board of directors.

Substantive approach (to an audit)   An approach to auditing in which the auditors' opinion is based primarily upon the evidence obtained by substantiating the individual financial statement items. This approach places less emphasis upon the consideration of internal control than does the systems approach and is particularly appropriate when internal control is weak.

Substantive tests   Tests of account balances and transactions designed to detect any material errors in the financial statements.

Systems approach (to an audit)   An approach to auditing in which the auditors place a relatively high degree of reliance upon their consideration of the client's internal control and, therefore, perform a minimum of substantive testing. Whether an auditor follows a systems approach or a substantive approach is merely a matter of degree; every engagement involves both an assessment of control risk and substantive testing.

Trace   To follow data from one accounting record to another.

Transaction cycle   The sequence of procedures applied by the client in processing a particular type of recurring transaction. The term *cycle* reflects the idea that the same sequence of procedures is applied to each similar transaction.

The auditors' consideration of internal control often is organized around the client's major transactions cycles.

Vouch To verify the accuracy and authenticity of entries in the accounting records by examining the original source documents supporting the entries.

10–1. Why is audit work usually organized around balance sheet accounts rather than income statement items?

10–2. Identify the general objectives of the auditors' substantiation procedures with respect to any major asset category.

10–3. What is meant by making a proper year-end *cutoff?* Explain the effects of errors in the cutoff of sales transactions in both the income statement and the balance sheet.

10–4. Since an audit is an examination of financial statements, why need auditors be concerned with records of a nonfinancial nature?

10–5. During the first audit of a corporate client, the auditors will probably obtain a copy of the bylaws and review them carefully.

Required:
a. What are bylaws of a corporation?
b. What provisions of the bylaws are of interest to the independent auditors?

10–6. State five significant provisions for which an auditor should particularly look in examining the articles of incorporation of a company and any amendments thereto. (AICPA)

10–7. In connection with an annual audit of a corporation engaged in manufacturing operations, the auditors have regularly reviewed the minutes of the meetings of stockholders and of the board of directors. Name 10 important items that might be found in the minutes of the meetings held during the period under review that would be of interest and significance to the auditors. (AICPA)

10–8. What should be the scope of an auditors' review of the corporate minutes book during the first audit of a client? During a repeat engagement?

10–9. What type of entities are subject to the Single Audit Act? How does a "single audit" differ from a typical audit in accordance with generally accepted auditing standards?

10–10. Explain briefly the auditors' responsibility for detecting illegal acts by clients.

10–11. Distinguish between management fraud and employee fraud.

10–12. Should the auditors make a complete review of all correspondence in the client's files? Explain.

10–13. What are the purposes of the audit procedures of (a) tracing a sample of journal entries forward into the ledgers and (b) tracing a sample of ledger entries back into the journals?

10–14. List three types of general journal entries that the auditors would investigate in scanning the general journal for unusual entries, and explain why the journal entries you list are unusual.

10–15. Charles Halstead, CPA, has a number of clients who desire audits at the end of the calendar year. In an effort to spread his work load more uniformly throughout the year, he is preparing a list of audit procedures that could be performed satisfactorily before the year-end balance sheet date. What work, if any, might be done on the general records in advance of the balance sheet date?

10–16. What is the nature of the working papers used by the auditors to summarize the audit work performed on the accounting records?

GROUP II: QUESTIONS REQUIRING ANALYSIS

10–17. Financial statements contain five broad assertions regarding the accounts and classes of transactions included in the statements.

Required:
a. Who makes the assertions?
b. List and describe each of the assertions.

10–18. Auditing literature frequently makes reference to the substantive approach and the systems approach to auditing.
a. Distinguish between the substantive approach and the systems approach to an audit.
b. Explain the circumstances under which each approach would be most appropriate.

10–19. Listed below are several of the auditors' general objectives in performing substantive tests of an asset account:
1. Establish the existence of assets.
2. Establish that the company has rights to the assets.
3. Establish the completeness of recorded assets.
4. Determine the appropriate valuation of the assets.
5. Establish the clerical accuracy of the underlying records.
6. Determine the appropriate financial statement presentation and disclosure of the assets.

Required:
Indicate the general objective (or objectives) of each of the following audit procedures:
a. Count petty cash on hand.
b. Locate on the client's premises a sample of the equipment items listed in the subsidiary plant and equipment ledger.
c. Obtain a listing of shipping documents to recorded sales transactions.
d. Trace a sample of shipping documents to recorded sales transactions.
e. Obtain a letter of representations from management stating that no inventory or accounts receivable have been pledged to secure specific liabilities.
f. Vouch selected purchases of securities to brokers' advices.

10–20. Richard Foster, an assistant auditor, was assigned to the year-end audit work of Sipher Corporation. Sipher is a small manufacturer of language translation equipment. As his first assignment, Foster was instructed to test the cutoff of year-end sales transactions. Since Sipher uses a calendar year-end for its financial statements, Foster began by obtaining the computer-generated sales ledgers and journals for December and January. He then traced ledger postings for a few days before and after

December 31 to the sales journals, noting the dates of the journal entries. Foster noted no journal entries that were posted to the ledger in the wrong accounting period. Thus, he concluded that the client's cutoff of sales transactions was effective.

Required:
Comment on the validity of Foster's conclusion. Explain fully.

10–21. In a recent court case, the presiding judge criticized the work of a senior in charge of an audit in approximately the following language: "As to minutes, the senior read only what the secretary (of the company) gave him, which consisted only of the board of directors' minutes. He did not read such minutes as there were of the executive committee of the board. He did not know that there was an executive committee, hence he did not discover that the treasurer had notes of executive committee minutes which had not been written up."

Required:
How can the independent auditors be certain the client has provided them with minutes of all meetings of the board and committees thereof? Explain.

10–22. Bonnie Cogan, CPA, is a senior auditor assigned to the first examination of the financial statements of Pioneer Mfg. Company, Inc. for the current year ended December 31. In scanning the client's general journal, Cogan noted the following entry dated June 30 of the current year:

Cost of Sales	186,453	
Raw materials		84,916
Work in process		24,518
Finished goods		77,019
To adjust perpetual inventories to amounts of physical inventory taken this date.		

The client-prepared income statement shows net sales and net income of approximately $5,500,000 and $600,000, respectively.

Required:
Do you think Cogan should investigate the above entry? Explain fully.

10–23. Fred Murray, an assistant auditor, was instructed to use a discovery sampling plan to search for entries in the client's ledger that were not supported by entries in the journals. Murray defined the population as all journal entries made during the year. A statistical table for that size population indicated that a sample size of 149 was necessary to provide 95 percent confidence of finding at least one exception if the occurrence rate is 2 percent or greater. In conducting his test, Murray traced 149 randomly selected journal entries into the ledger and found no exceptions. Based upon this test, may Murray conclude with 95 percent confidence that at least 98 percent of the entries in the ledger are supported by journal entries? Explain fully.

10–24. Select the best answer for each of the following and give the reasons for your choice.

a. Which of the following is not a basic objective of the audit procedures applied to any major asset category?

(1) Verifying the appropriate valuation of the asset.

(2) Determining that all assets are recorded.

(3) Determining that the asset is fully insured against possible loss.

(4) Establishing that the company has rights to the asset.

b. Generally, the decision to notify parties outside the client's organization regarding an illegal act is the responsibility of the

(1) Independent auditors.

(2) Management.

(3) Outside legal counsel.

(4) Internal auditors.

c. If an illegal act is discovered during the audit of a publicly held company, the auditors should—

(1) Notify the regulatory authorities.

(2) Determine who was responsible for the illegal act.

(3) Intensify the examination.

(4) Report the act to high-level personnel within the client's organization and the audit committee of the board of directors.

d. An auditor should examine the minutes of board of directors' meetings:

(1) Through the date of the financial statements.

(2) Through the date of the audit report.

(3) On a test basis.

(4) Only at the beginning of the audit.

e. Which of the following statements most appropriately summarizes the auditor's responsibility for reviewing the client's correspondence files?

(1) The auditor should review all correspondence for items relevant to the audit.

(2) The auditor should not review any correspondence; to do so would waste time more productively spent on gathering other evidence.

(3) The auditor should apply statistical selection techniques to draw a random sample of correspondence for review.

(4) The auditor should review correspondence with banks, other lending institutions, attorneys, and governmental agencies.

f. As one step in testing sales transactions, a CPA traces a random sample of sales journal entries to debits in the accounts receivable subsidiary ledger. This test provides evidence as to whether:

(1) Each recorded sale represents a bona fide transaction.

(2) All sales have been recorded in the sales journal.

(3) All debit entries in the accounts receivable subsidiary ledger are properly supported by sales journal entries.

(4) Recorded sales have been properly posted to customer accounts. (AICPA, adapted)

GROUP III: PROBLEMS

10–25. Precision Industries, Inc. is a manufacturer of electronic components. When a purchase order is received from a customer, a salesclerk prepares a serially numbered sales order and sends copies to the shipping and accounting departments. When the merchandise is shipped to the customer, the shipping department prepares a serially numbered shipping advice and sends a copy to the accounting department. Upon receipt of the appropriate documents, the accounting department records the sale in the accounting records. All shipments are *FOB shipping point*.

Required:

a. How can the auditors determine whether Precision Industries, Inc. has made a proper year-end cutoff of sales transactions?

b. Assume all shipments for the first five days of the following year were recorded as occurring in the current year. If not corrected, what effect will this cutoff error have upon the financial statements for the current year?

10–26. Kenneth J. Bryan, secretary of Jensen Corporation, has given you the minutes of the meetings of the board of directors. Summarize, in good form for the audit working papers, those contents of the following minutes that you consider to be of significance in the conduct of an annual audit.

Meeting of February 15, 19X2

The meeting was called to order at 2:15 P.M. by H. R. Jensen, chairman of the board. The following directors were present:

John J. Savage	Ruth Andrews
Helen R. King	Dale H. Lindberg
Lee McCormick	Ralph Barker
H. R. Coleman	H. R. Jensen
George Anderson	Kenneth J. Bryan
Harold Bruce Smith	

Absent was Director J. B. Adams, who was in New York City on company business in connection with the opening of a sales office.

The minutes of the preceding meeting, December 15, 19X1, were read by the secretary and duly approved as read.

Upon a motion by Ms. King, seconded by Mr. Savage, and unanimously carried, the secretary was instructed to notify the firm of Black, Bryson & MacDougal, Certified Public Accountants, of its selection to conduct an annual audit of the company's financial statements as of March 31, 19X2.

President John J. Savage outlined the current status of negotiations leading toward the acquisition of a new factory site in San Diego, California, and recommended to the board the purchase of said property at a price not to exceed $600,000.

Ms. King offered the following resolution, which was seconded by Mr. Smith, and unanimously carried:

Resolved: That Mr. Savage hereby is authorized to acquire on behalf of

(Continued)

---

the company the factory site located at Exmont and Donaldson Avenues, San Diego, California, at a price not in excess of $600,000, to be paid for in cash from the general funds of the corporation.

Upon a motion by Mr. Savage, seconded by Ms. King and carried unanimously, the secretary was instructed to arrange for the purchase from the estate of J. B. Williams, former director, 100 shares of the company's own stock at a price not in excess of $110 per share.

Mr. Savage, after discussing the progress of the company in recent months and its current financial condition, submitted the following resolution, which was seconded by Mr. Coleman and unanimously passed:

Resolved: That the following cash dividends are hereby declared, payable April 10, 19X2, to stockholders of record on March 31, 19X2.

a.   The regular quarterly dividend of $1 per share of capital stock.
b.   A special dividend of 50 cents per share of capital stock.

There being no further business brought before the meeting, the meeting was adjourned at 4 P.M.

Kenneth J. Bryan
Secretary

Meeting of March 15, 19X2

The meeting was called to order at 2:15 P.M. by H. R. Jensen, chairman of the board. The following directors were present:

John J. Savage	Ruth Andrews
Helen R. King	Dale H. Lindberg
Lee McCormick	J. B. Adams
H. R. Coleman	H. R. Jensen
George Anderson	Kenneth J. Bryan
Harold Bruce Smith	

Absent was Director Ralph Barker.

The minutes of the preceding meeting, February 15, 19X2, were read by the secretary and duly approved as read.

Chairman H. R. Jensen stated that nominations for the coming year were in order for the positions of president, vice president in charge of sales, vice president in charge of manufacturing, treasurer, controller, and secretary.

The following nominations were made by Ms. King, and there being no further nominations the nominations were declared closed:

President	John J. Savage
Vice president—sales	Otis Widener
Vice president—manufacturing	Henry Pendleton
Treasurer	Ruth Andrews
Controller	Roger Dunn
Secretary	Kenneth J. Bryan

The above nominees were duly elected.

(Continued)

Mr. McCormick then offered the following resolution, which was seconded by Mr. Coleman and unanimously carried:

Resolved: That the salaries of all officers be continued for the next year at the same rates currently in effect. These rates are as follows:

John J. Savage—president	$150,000
Otis Widener—vice president—sales	70,000
Henry Pendleton—vice president—manufacturing	70,000
Ruth Andrews—treasurer	70,000
Roger Dunn—controller	70,000
Kenneth J. Bryan—secretary	50,000

Mr. Bryan offered the following resolution, which was seconded by Mrs. Andrews and unanimously carried:

Resolved: That the company establish a bank account at the United National Bank, San Diego, California, to be subject to check by either John J. Savage or Ruth Andrews.

There being no further business to come before the meeting, the meeting was adjourned at 4 P.M.

Kenneth J. Bryan
Secretary

10–27. A normal procedure in the audit of a corporate client consists of a careful reading of the minutes of meetings of the board of directors. One of the CPAs' objectives in reading the minutes is to determine whether the transactions recorded in the accounting records are in agreement with actions approved by the board of directors.

Required:

a. What is the reasoning underlying this objective of reconciling transactions in the corporate accounting records with actions approved by the board of directors? Describe fully how the CPAs achieve the stated objective after they have read the minutes of directors' meetings.

b. Discuss the effect each of the following situations would have on specific audit steps in the CPAs' examination and on the auditors' opinion:

(1) The minutes book does not show approval for the sale of an important manufacturing division that was consummated during the year.

(2) Some details of a contract negotiated during the year with the labor union are different from the outline of the contract included in the minutes of the board of directors.

(3) The minutes of a meeting of directors held after the balance sheet date have not yet been written, but the corporation's secretary shows the CPAs' notes from which the minutes are to be prepared when the secretary has time.

c. What corporate actions should be approved by stockholders and recorded in the minutes of the stockholders' meetings?

(AICPA, adapted)

10–28. Enormo Corporation is a large multinational audit client of your CPA firm. One of Enormo's subsidiaries, Ultro, Ltd., is a successful electronics assembly company that operates in a small Caribbean country. The country in which Ultro operates has very strict laws governing the transfer of funds to other countries. Violations of these laws may result in fines or the expropriation of the assets of the company.

During the current year, you discover that $50,000 worth of foreign currency was smuggled out of the Caribbean country by one of Ultro's employees and deposited in one of Enormo's bank accounts. Ultro's management generated the funds by selling company automobiles, which were fully depreciated on Ultro's books, to company employees.

You are concerned about this illegal act by Ultro's management and decide to discuss the matter with Enormo's management and the company's legal counsel. Enormo's management and board of directors seemed to be unconcerned with the matter and expressed the opinion that you were making far too much of a situation involving an immaterial dollar amount. They also believe that it is unnecessary to take any steps to prevent Ultro's management from engaging in illegal activities in the future. Enormo's legal counsel indicated that the probability was remote that such illegal acts would ever be discovered, and that if discovery occurred, it would probably result in a fine that would not be material to the client's consolidated financial statements.

Your CPA firm is ready to issue its opinion on Enormo's consolidated financial statements for the current year, and you are trying to decide on the appropriate course of action regarding the illegal act.

Required:
a. Discuss the implications of these illegal acts by Ultro's management.
b. Describe the courses of action that are available to your CPA firm regarding this matter.
c. State your opinion as to the course of action that is appropriate. Explain.

Suggested references:
AICPA, *Statement on Auditing Standards No. 53,* "The Auditor's Responsibility to Detect and Report Errors and Irregularities" (New York, 1988), AU 316.

AICPA, *Statement on Auditing Standards No. 54,* Illegal Acts by Clients" (New York, 1988), AU 317.

FASB Statement No. 5, "Accounting for Contingencies," pars. 8–12.

AICPA, *Professional Standards, Volume B,* Commerce Clearing House, *Statements on Quality Control Standards,* Section 10.

Cash and marketable securities

Chapter 11 study objectives

After studying this chapter, you should be able to:

— Describe the nature of cash and marketable securities.
— Explain the nature of the receipts and disbursements cycles.
— Explain the fundamental internal controls over cash receipts, cash disbursements, and marketable securities and be able to identify weaknesses.
— Describe the auditors' objectives for the audit of cash and marketable securities.
— Describe the nature of appropriate procedures to accomplish the auditor's objectives for the audit of cash and marketable securities.

The manner in which auditors approach cash and marketable securities is discussed in this chapter. Because both types of accounts are usually extremely liquid and because companies often transfer funds between them, their consideration is combined in the chapter.

CASH

Sources and nature of cash

Cash normally includes general, payroll, petty cash and, less frequently, savings accounts. General accounts are checking accounts similar in nature to those maintained by individuals. Cash sales, collections of receivables, and investment of additional capital typically increase the account; business expenditures decrease it. Under the terms of a bank loan agreement, the cash in a company's general account sometimes must be maintained at a specified minimum balance referred to as a ***compensating balance.*** In other circumstances, separate compensating balance cash accounts are established.

Payroll and petty cash accounts are "imprest" at a low balance. When payroll is paid, a check from the general account is drawn to deposit funds into the payroll account. Petty cash, used for very small expenditures, is replenished as necessary.

Normal client supervision and review procedures (e.g., reconciliation of bank accounts) detect most errors that occur in these accounts. On the other hand, the liquid nature of cash increases the risk of undetected irregularities.

The auditors' approach in examination of cash

The auditors' ***objectives*** in the examination of cash are to determine that:

1. ***Internal control*** over cash transactions is adequate.
2. The recorded cash is valid (***existence and rights***).
3. All cash accounts are recorded (***completeness***).
4. Cash schedules are mathematically correct and agree with general ledger accounts (***clerical accuracy***).
5. The ***presentation*** and ***disclosure*** of cash, including restricted funds (such as compensating balances and bond sinking funds) is adequate.

In connection with the audit of cash the auditors will also verify the amounts of any interest revenue from cash deposits. As is the case with other assets, auditors are especially concerned with the likelihood of overstatements of the account; therefore, objective 2, the validity of the recorded amount of cash, is of utmost importance.

Illustrative note

A recent research study reports the results of a study of lawsuits against accountants. A total of 129 cases were examined and none of the suits concerned misstatements involving undervalued ***assets.***

In addition to concerns about the overstatement of cash, auditors are aware that cash may have been improperly abstracted during the period, even though the year-end cash may be properly stated. To distinguish between the situations assume that the client's balance sheet shows "Cash . . . . . $250,000." For most clients, the primary risks are that errors or irregularities either (1) create a situation in which $250,000 overstates actual cash, or (2) have improperly reduced the balance to $250,000.

Concerning the first risk (overstated cash), a shortage may have been concealed merely by the insertion of a fictitious check in the cash on hand at year-end or by the omission of an outstanding check from the year-end bank reconciliation. Note that the omission of an outstanding check may be indicative of either an error or an irregularity. For example, poor internal control may result in a situation in which human error resulted in the check not being recorded in disbursements. On the other hand, although recorded in cash disbursements, the check may be omitted from the outstanding checklist to allow the individual who has embezzled that amount of cash to hide an irregularity.

Concerning the second risk—when the year-end cash is correct, but should be higher—the auditors' problem is not misstated cash, but the irregularity itself and its effect on other accounts. Consequently, the auditors have in mind such basic questions as: (1) do the client's records reflect all cash transactions that took place during the year, and (2) were all cash payments properly authorized and for a legitimate business purpose? Examples of irregularities that may be disclosed in searching for answers to these questions are:

1. Interception of cash receipts before any record is made.
2. Payment for materials not received.
3. Duplicate payments.
4. Overpayments to employees or payments to fictitious employees.
5. Payments for personal expenditures of officers or related parties.

Exceptions exist to the general rule that auditors are primarily concerned with overstatements of cash (and other assets). For example, the management of a privately held company may be motivated to understate assets (including cash) to minimize income taxes. Also, a client may maintain bank accounts not recorded on the books for purposes such as making illegal bribes. Thus, the auditors must consider whether all amounts of cash accounts are recorded (the completeness objective).

We have not included a "valuation" objective for cash. Valuation of cash is less a concern than for other assets because no allowance need be considered to arrive at a realizable value. However, when foreign subsidiaries are involved, the auditors must determine that translated currency is properly valued.

How much audit time for cash?

The factor of materiality applies to audit work on cash as well as to other sections of the examination. The counting of a small petty cash fund, which is inconsequential in relation to the company's overall financial position, accomplishes little in achieving the auditors' objective of expressing an independent opinion on the financial statements. Nevertheless, auditors do devote a larger proportion of the total audit hours to cash than might be suggested by the relatively small amount of cash shown on the balance sheet. Although the year-end balance of cash may appear relatively small, the amount flowing into and out of the Cash account during the year is often greater than for any other account. Consequently, work on cash is important in virtually every audit.

Several reasons exist to explain the auditors' traditional emphasis on cash transactions. Liabilities, revenue, expenses, and most other assets flow through the Cash account; that is, these items either arise from or result in cash transactions. Thus, the examination of cash transactions assists the auditors in the substantiation of many other items in the financial statements.

Another reason contributing to extensive auditing of cash is that cash is the most liquid of assets and offers the greatest temptation for theft, embezzlement, and misappropriation. Inherent risk is high for liquid assets, and auditors tend to respond to high-risk situations with more intensive investigation. However, the detection of fraud is relevant to overall fairness of the client's financial statements only if such fraud is material in amount.

On occasion, auditors may encounter evidence of small-scale employee fraud. After determining that such fraud could **not** have a material effect upon the financial statements, the auditors should review the situation with the management and the audit committee of the board of directors before investigating the matter further. This discussion will alert the client to the situation, protect the auditors from charges of incompetence, and avoid wasting audit time on matters that are not material with respect to the financial statements and that may better be pursued by client personnel.

Internal control over cash transactions

Most of the functions relating to cash handling are the responsibility of the finance department, under the direction of the treasurer. These functions include handling and depositing cash receipts; signing checks; investing idle cash; and maintaining custody of cash, marketable securities, and other negotiable assets. In addition, the finance department must forecast cash requirements and make both short-term and long-term financing arrangements.

Ideally, the functions of the finance department and the accounting department should be integrated in a manner that provides assurance that—

1. All cash that should have been received *was* in fact received, recorded accurately, and deposited promptly.
2. Cash disbursements have been made only for authorized purposes and have been properly recorded.
3. Cash balances are maintained at adequate, but not excessive, levels by forecasting expected cash receipts and payments related to normal operations. The need for obtaining loans or for investing excess cash is thus made known on a timely basis.

A detailed study of the operating routines of the individual business is necessary in developing the most efficient control procedures, but there are some general guidelines to good cash-handling practices in all types of business. These universal rules for achieving internal control over cash may be summarized as follows:

1. Do not permit any one employee to handle a transaction from beginning to end.
2. Separate cash handling from record keeping.
3. Centralize receiving of cash as much as possible.
4. Record cash receipts immediately.
5. Encourage customers to obtain receipts and observe cash register totals.
6. Deposit each day's cash receipts intact.
7. Make all disbursements by check, with the exception of small expenditures from petty cash.
8. Have monthly bank reconciliations prepared by employees not responsible for the issuance of checks or custody of cash. The completed reconciliation should be reviewed promptly by an appropriate official.

Several good reasons exist for the rule that each day's cash receipts should be deposited intact. Daily deposits mean that less cash will be on hand to invite "borrowing"; moreover, the deposit of each day's cash receipts as a unit tends to prevent the substituting of later cash receipts to cover a shortage. Any delay in depositing customers' checks increases the risk that the checks will be uncollectible. Furthermore, undeposited receipts represent idle cash, which is not a revenue-producing asset.

Internal control over cash receipts

Cash sales Control over cash sales is strongest when two or more employees (usually a salesclerk and a cashier) participate in each transaction with a customer. Restaurants and cafeterias often use a centrally located cashier who receives cash from the customer along with a sales ticket prepared by another employee. Theaters generally have a cashier selling prenumbered tickets, which are collected by a door attendant when the customer is admitted. If tickets or sales checks are serially numbered and all numbers accounted for, this separation of responsibility for the transaction is an effective means of preventing fraud. In many retail establishments, the nature of the business is such that one employee must make over-the-counter sales, deliver the merchandise, receive cash, and record the transaction. In this situation, dishonesty may be discouraged by proper use of cash registers, electronic point-of-sale systems, or form-writing machines. The protective features of cash registers include (1) visual display of the amount of the sale in full view of the customer; (2) a printed receipt, which the customer is urged to take with the merchandise; and (3) accumulation of a locked-in total of the day's sales.

Electronic point-of-sale (POS) systems   Many retail stores use various types of electronic cash registers, including online computer terminals. With some of these registers, an electronic scanner is used to read the sales price and other data from specially prepared product tags. The salesperson need only pass the tag over the scanner for the register to record the sale at the product's sale price. Thus, the risk of a salesperson recording sales at erroneous prices is substantially reduced. Besides providing strong control over cash sales, electronic registers often may be programmed to perform numerous other control functions. For example, online registers may verify the credit status of charge account customers, update accounts receivable and perpetual inventory records, and provide special printouts accumulating sales data by product line, salesperson, department, and type of sale.

Control features of form-writing machines   Some businesses making sales over the counter find that internal control is strengthened by use of a machine containing triplicate sales tickets. As each sales check is written, two copies are ejected by the machine and a third copy is retained in a locked compartment. The retention of the third copy, which is not available to the salesclerk, tends to prevent a dishonest employee from reducing the store's copy of the sales check to an amount less than that shown on the customer's copy.

Collections from credit customers   In many manufacturing and wholesale companies, cash receipts consist principally of checks received through the mail. This situation poses little threat of defalcation unless one employee is permitted to receive and deposit these checks and also to record the credits to the customers' accounts. A typical system of internal control over cash received through the mail is described below.

Incoming mail usually is opened in the mail room, where an employee prepares a *control listing* of the incoming cash receipts. This listing shows the amount received from each customer and identifies the customer by name or account number. A copy of the control listing is forwarded to the controller. Another copy of the control listing and the cash receipts are forwarded to the cashier. The remittance advices and a copy of the control listing are forwarded to the employee responsible for the customers' accounts.

Which controls tend to prevent the mail room employee from abstracting the receipts from several customers, destroying the remittance advices, and omitting these receipts from the control listing? First, incoming cash receipts consist primarily of checks made payable to the company. Second, if customers' accounts are not credited for payments made, the customers will complain to the company. If these customers can produce paid checks supporting their claims of payment, and these checks do not appear on the mail room control listings, responsibility for the abstraction is quickly focused upon the mail room employee.

The cashier uses the control listing and customers' remittance advices to record the cash received in the cash receipts journal. Then the cashier deposits the day's receipts intact in the bank. Control is exercised over the cashier by periodic reconciliation of the controller's copies of the mail room control listings with the cash receipts journal and the details of daily bank deposits.

The employee responsible for the customers' accounts ledger reconciles the remittance advices to his copy of the control listing and, when satisfied that all remittance advices are accounted for, posts credits to the customers' accounts. Strong internal control requires that the accounts receivable clerk have no access to the cash receipts, and that the customers' accounts be periodically reconciled with the general ledger. When the nature of operations permits, different employees should be assigned responsibility for (1) preparation of sales invoices, (2) maintenance of customers' accounts, (3) reconciling customers' ledgers with controlling accounts, (4) initial listing of cash receipts, (5) custody and depositing of cash receipts, and (6) collection activity and past-due accounts.

The division of responsibilities, sequence of procedures, and internal controls over cash sales and collections from customers are illustrated in the systems flowchart in Figure 11–1.

Lockbox control over cash receipts Businesses receiving a large volume of cash through the mail often use a lockbox system to strengthen internal control and hasten the depositing of cash receipts. The lockbox is actually a post office box controlled by the company's bank. The bank picks up mail at the post office box several times a day, credits the company's checking account for cash received, and sends the remittance advices to the company. Internal control is strengthened by the fact that the bank has no access to the company's accounting records.

Internal control over cash disbursements

All disbursements should be made by check, except for payment of minor items from petty cash funds. A principal advantage is the obtaining of a receipt from the payee in the form of an endorsement on the check. Other advantages include (1) the centralization of disbursement authority in the hands of a few designated officials—the only persons authorized to sign checks; (2) a permanent record of disbursements; and (3) a reduction in the amount of cash kept on hand.

To secure in full the internal control benefits implicit in the use of checks, it is essential that all checks be prenumbered and all numbers in the series be accounted for. Unissued prenumbered checks should be adequately safeguarded against theft or misuse. Voided checks should be defaced to eliminate any possibility of further use and filed in the regular sequence of paid checks. Dollar amounts should be printed on all checks by the computer or a check-protecting machine. This practice prevents anyone from altering a check by raising its amount.

Officials authorized to sign checks should review the documents supporting the payment and perforate (deface) these documents at the time of signing the check to prevent them from being submitted a second time. The official signing checks should maintain control of the checks until they are placed in the mail. Typically the check comes to the official complete except for signature. It is imperative that the signed checks not be returned to the custody of the employee who prepared them for signature.

Most companies issuing a large volume of checks use check-signing machines. These machines print the authorized signature, usually that of the treasurer, on each check by means of a facsimile signature plate. An item count of checks signed is provided by the machine, and a key is required to retrieve the signed checks. The facsimile signature plate should be removed from the machine and safeguarded when the machine is not in use.

Reconciliation of monthly bank statements is essential to adequate internal control over cash receipts and disbursements. Bank statements should be reconciled by an employee having no part in authorizing or accounting for cash transactions, or in handling cash. Statements from the bank should come unopened to this employee. Each month the completed bank reconciliation should be reviewed by a responsible company official and approved in writing.

Figure 11–1

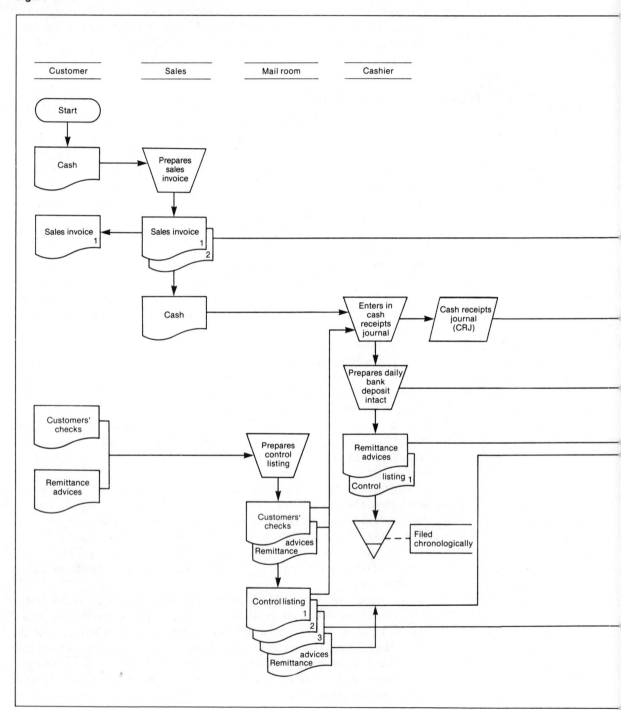

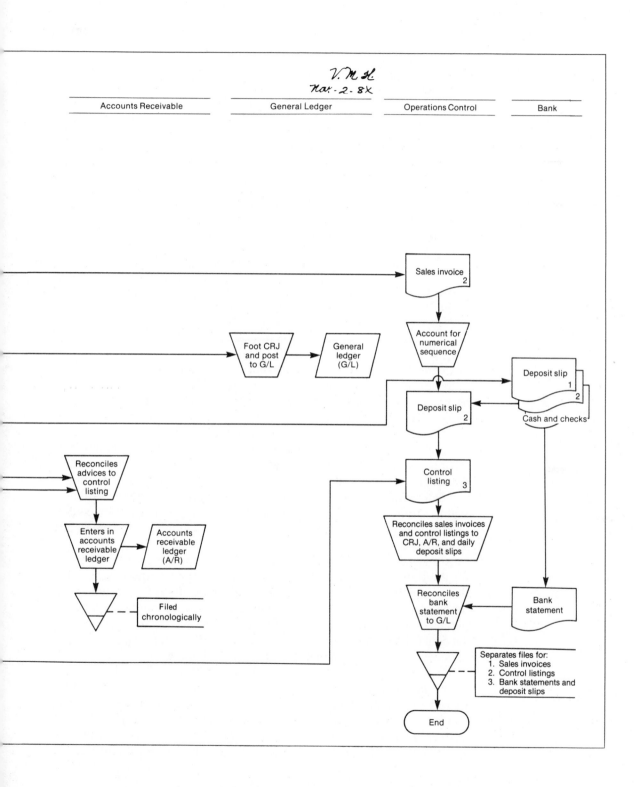

V. M. H.
Mar. 2. 8X

Accounts Receivable	General Ledger	Operations Control	Bank

Sales invoice 2

Account for numerical sequence

Foot CRJ and post to G/L

General ledger (G/L)

Deposit slip 1 2

Deposit slip 2

Cash and checks

Reconciles advices to control listing

Control listing 3

Enters in accounts receivable ledger

Accounts receivable ledger (A/R)

Reconciles sales invoices and control listings to CRJ, A/R, and daily deposit slips

Filed chronologically

Reconciles bank statement to G/L

Bank statement

Separates files for:
1. Sales invoices
2. Control listings
3. Bank statements and deposit slips

End

Illustrative case

One large construction company ignored basic controls over cash disbursements. Unissued checks were stored in an unlocked supply closet, along with Styrofoam coffee cups. The company check-signing machine deposited signed checks into a box that was equipped with a lock. Despite warnings from their independent auditors, company officials found it "too inconvenient" to keep the box locked or to pay attention to the check-counter built into the machine. The company maintained very large bank balances and did not bother to reconcile bank statements promptly.

A three-week-old bank statement and a group of paid checks were given to an employee with instructions to prepare a bank reconciliation. The employee noticed that the group of paid checks accompanying the bank statement was not complete. No paid checks could be found to support over $700,000 in charges on the bank statement. Further investigation revealed that more than $1 million in unauthorized and unrecorded checks had been paid from various company bank accounts. The checks had been issued out of sequence and had been signed by the company check-signing machine. The company was unable to determine who was responsible for the theft, and the money was never recovered.

Control features of a voucher system   A voucher system is one method of achieving strong internal control over cash disbursements by providing assurance that all disbursements are properly authorized and reviewed before a check is issued. In a typical voucher system, the accounting department is responsible for assembling the appropriate documentation to support every cash disbursement. For example, before authorizing payment for merchandise purchased, the accounting department assembles copies of the purchase order, receiving report, and vendor's invoice, and determines that these documents are in agreement. After determining that the transaction is properly supported, an accounting employee prepares a voucher, which is filed in a tickler file according to the date upon which payment will be made.

A voucher, in this usage, is an authorization sheet that provides space for the initials of the employees performing various authorization functions. Authorization functions include such procedures as extending and footing the vendor's invoice; determining the agreement of the invoice, purchase order, and receiving report; and recording the transaction in the accounts. Transactions are recorded in a *voucher register* (which normally replaces a purchases journal) by an entry debiting the appropriate asset, liability, or expense accounts, and crediting Vouchers Payable.

On the payment date, the voucher and supporting documents are removed from the tickler file. A check is prepared **but not signed.** The voucher, supporting papers, and the check (complete except for signature) are forwarded to the finance department. The treasurer reviews the voucher before signing the check; the check is then mailed directly to the payee, and the voucher and all supporting documents are perforated to prevent reuse. The canceled vouchers are returned to the accounting department, where an entry is made to record the cash disbursement (a debit to Vouchers Payable and a credit to Cash). Paid vouchers usually are filed by voucher number in a paid voucher file.

Strong internal control is inherent in this system because every disbursement is authorized and reviewed before a check is issued. Also, neither the accounting department nor the finance department is in a position to disburse cash without a review of the transaction by the other department. The operation of a voucher system is illustrated in the flowchart in Figure 11–2.

Internal control aspects of petty cash funds

Internal control over payments from an imprest petty cash fund is achieved at the time the fund is replenished to its fixed balance, rather than at the time of handing out small amounts of cash. When the custodian of a petty cash fund requests replenishment of the fund, the documents supporting each disbursement should be reviewed for completeness and authenticity and perforated to prevent reuse.

Audit tests of petty cash emphasize transactions rather than the year-end balance. The auditors may test one or more replenishment transactions by examining petty cash vouchers and verifying their numerical sequence.

Petty cash funds are sometimes kept in the form of separate bank accounts. The bank should be instructed in writing not to accept for deposit in such an account any checks payable to the company. The deposits will be limited to checks to replenish the fund and drawn payable to the bank or to the custodian of the fund. The prohibition against deposit of checks payable to the company is designed to prevent the routing of cash receipts into petty cash, since this would violate the basic assumption of limited disbursements and review at time of replenishing the fund.

Internal control and the computer

Computer processing of cash transactions can contribute to strong internal control over cash. As previously discussed, control over cash sales may be strengthened by the use of online register terminals. Remittance advices or mail room listings of customers' payments can be processed by computer. Many companies use computers to issue checks and, subsequently, to prepare bank reconciliations. The daily computer processing of cash receipts and checks can provide management with a continually up-to-date cash receipts journal, check register, customers' accounts ledger, and cash balance. In addition to this, the computer can prepare reliable bank reconciliations even when thousands of checks are outstanding and can provide current information for cash planning and forecasting.

Figure 11–2   Flowchart of a voucher system

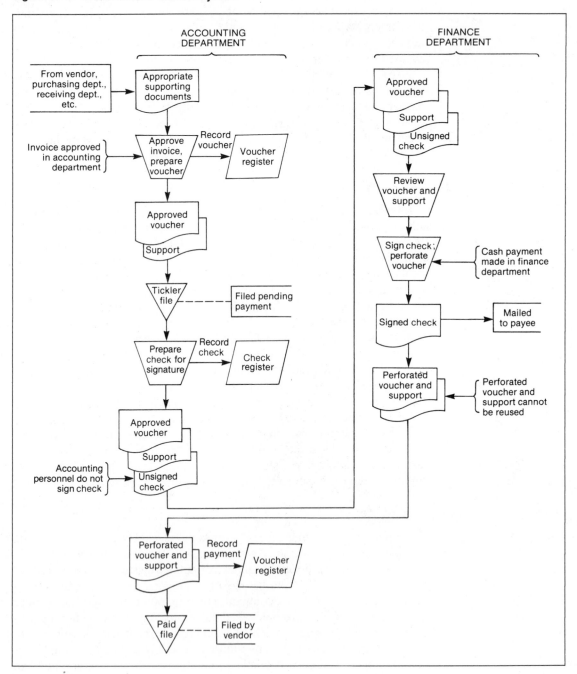

Audit working papers for cash

Auditors' working papers for cash usually include a flowchart or a written description of internal controls. An internal control questionnaire is also often used, especially in larger companies. A related working paper will summarize tests of controls for cash transactions and the assessment of internal control over cash.

Additional cash working papers include a lead schedule, cash counts, bank confirmations, bank reconciliations, outstanding checklists, lists of checks being investigated, recommendations to the client for improving internal control, and notes concerning proper presentation of cash in the client's balance sheet.

AUDIT PROGRAM FOR CASH

The following audit program indicates the general pattern of work performed by the auditors in the verification of cash. Selection of the most appropriate procedures for a particular audit will be guided, of course, by the nature of the internal controls in force and by other circumstances of the engagement.

A. Consider internal control for cash

1. *Obtain an understanding of internal control* for cash.
2. *Assess control risk* and *design additional tests of controls* for cash.
3. *Perform tests of controls* for those controls which the auditors plan to rely upon to restrict their assessment of control risk, and reduce the extent of substantive testing, such as:
   a. Prove footings of cash journals and trace postings to ledger accounts.
   b. Compare the detail of a sample of cash receipts listings to the cash receipts journal, accounts receivable postings, and authenticated deposit slips.
   c. Compare the detail of a sample of recorded disbursements in cash payments journal to accounts payable postings, purchase orders, receiving reports, invoices, and paid checks.
4. *Reassess control risk* and *design substantive tests* for cash.

B. Perform substantive tests of cash transactions and balances

5. Obtain analyses of cash balances and reconcile to the general ledger.
6. Send confirmation letters to banks to verify amounts on deposit.
7. Obtain or prepare reconciliations of bank accounts as of the balance sheet date and consider need to reconcile bank activity for additional months.
8. Obtain a cutoff bank statement containing transactions of at least seven business days subsequent to balance sheet date.
9. Count and list cash on hand.

10. Verify the client's cutoff of cash receipts and cash disbursements.

11. Trace all bank transfers for last week of audit year and first week of following year.

12. Investigate any checks representing large or unusual payments to related parties.

13. Evaluate proper financial statement presentation and disclosure of cash.

Figure 11–3 relates these substantive tests to the primary audit objectives.

Figure 11–3 Objectives of major substantive tests of cash transactions and balances

Substantive tests	Primary audit objectives
Obtain analyses of cash balances and reconcile to general ledger	*Clerical accuracy*
Send confirmation letters to banks Obtain reconciliations of bank balances and consider reconciling bank activity Obtain bank cutoff statement Count cash on hand	*Validity (existence and rights)*
Verify the client's cutoff of cash transactions Trace bank transfers occurring around year-end	*Validity (existence and rights)* *Completeness*
Investigate payments to related parties Evaluate financial statement presentation and disclosure	*Presentation and disclosure*

A. Consider internal control for cash

1. Obtain an understanding of internal control.

In the audit of a small business, auditors may prepare a written description of controls in force, based upon the questioning of owners and employees and upon firsthand observation. For larger companies, a flowchart or internal control questionnaire is usually employed to describe the internal control structure. An internal control questionnaire for cash receipts was illustrated in Chapter 5. Among the questions included in a questionnaire for cash disbursements are whether all disbursements (except those from petty cash) are made by prenumbered checks and whether voided checks are mutilated, preserved, and filed. The existence of these controls permits the auditors to determine that all disbursements have been recorded by accounting for the sequence of checks issued or voided during the period.

Other points to be made clear by the questionnaire include: (*a*) whether check-signing authority is restricted to selected executives not having access to accounting records or to vouchers and other documents supporting checks submitted for signature, and (*b*) whether checks are mailed directly to the payees after being signed.

The internal control questionnaire will also cover cash disbursements for payroll and for dividends, as well as bank reconciliation procedures. All questions on the internal control questionnaire are designed to require affirmative answers when satisfactory controls exist.

After the auditors have prepared a flowchart (or other description) of internal control, they should conduct a walk-through of the system. The term *walk-through* means to trace a few transactions through each step of the system to determine that transactions actually are being processed in the manner indicated by the flowchart.

2.   Assess control risk and design additional tests of controls.

Control risk for a financial statement assertion may be assessed below the maximum only when tests indicate that related controls are designed and operating effectively. The auditors must decide which additional tests of controls will likely result in cost justified restrictions of substantive tests.

3.   Perform additional tests of controls.

Tests directed toward the effectiveness of controls help to evaluate the client's internal control structure and determine the extent to which the auditors are justified in relying upon the client's controls to restrict control risk for the cash account. The following are examples of typical tests.

a.   Prove footings of cash journals and trace postings to ledger accounts.

The purpose of proving footings and postings of the cash records is to verify the mechanical accuracy of the journals and ledgers. In a computer-based system, journal and ledger entries are created simultaneously from the same source documents. The auditors might choose to use a test data approach to test controls over the postings of ledgers. The accuracy of footings may be proved with the auditors' generalized audit software.

In a manual system, information on source documents is entered first in a journal; at a later date the information is summarized and posted from journals to ledgers. Therefore, in a manual system, the auditors must manually determine that journals are accurately footed and the data properly posted to the ledgers.

The auditors also should trace the monthly postings of column totals from the cash receipts journal to the Cash account and to the controlling account for Accounts Receivable. Similar verification may be made for the totals posted from the cash payments journal to the Cash account and to the Accounts Payable account in the general ledger. If the testing of postings and footings discloses sloppy accounting work, with numerous errors and corrections, indistinct figures, and ambiguous totals, the scope of the auditors' work should be increased, for these are often the hallmarks of fraudulent manipulation of the records.

b.   Compare detail of cash receipts listings to cash receipts journal, accounts receivable postings, and authenticated deposit slips.

Satisfactory internal control over cash receipts demands that each day's collections be deposited intact no later than the next banking day.

This practice will minimize the opportunity for employees handling cash to "borrow" from the funds in their custody and will facilitate comparison by the auditors of the cash receipts journal with the deposits per the bank.

To provide assurance that cash receipts have been deposited intact, the auditors should compare the detail of the original cash receipts listings (mail room listings and register tapes) to the detail of the daily deposit tickets. The *detail* of cash receipts refers to a listing of the amount of each individual check and the total amount of currency comprising the day's receipts. In making a comparison of receipts and deposits, the auditors must emphasize the detail of cash receipts rather than relying upon daily or periodic totals. Agreement of total receipts and deposits for a period gives no assurance that worthless checks have not been substituted for currency or that shortages occurring early in the period have not been made up by subsequent deposits.

Comparison of the daily entries in the cash receipts journal with bank deposits may disclose a type of fraud known as *lapping*. Lapping means the concealment of a cash shortage by delaying the recording of cash receipts. If cash collected from customer A is withheld by the cashier, a subsequent collection from customer B may be entered as a credit to A's account. B's account will not be shown as paid until a collection from customer C is recorded as a credit to B. Unless the money abstracted by the cashier is replaced, the accounts receivable as a group remain overstated; but judicious shifting of the overstatement from one account receivable to another may avert protests from customers receiving monthly statements. The following schedule makes clear how a lapping activity may be carried on. In companies in which the cashier has access to the general accounting records, shortages created in this manner have sometimes been transferred to inventory accounts or elsewhere in the records for temporary concealment.

Date	Actually received from	Actual cash receipts	Recorded as received from	Receipts recorded and deposited	Receipts withheld
Dec. 1	Abbott	$ 750			$ 750
	Crane	1,035	Crane	$1,035	
2	Barstow	750	Abbott	750	
	White	130	White	130	
3	Crawford	1,575	Barstow	750	825
	Miller	400	Miller	400	
		$4,640		$3,065	$1,575

Lapping is most easily carried on when an employee who receives collections from customers is responsible for the posting of customers' accounts. Familiarity with customers' accounts makes it relatively easy to lodge a shortage in an account that will not be currently questioned.

Duplicate deposit tickets in the possession of the client may be subject to alteration. If the auditors suspect that the duplicate slips have been altered, they should compare them with the originals on file at the bank. Most banks are willing to furnish auditors with copies of deposit tickets for comparison with the client's record of cash receipts.

c.   Compare the detail of a sample of recorded disbursements in cash payments journal, accounts payable postings, purchase orders, receiving reports, invoices, and paid checks.

Satisfactory internal control over cash disbursements requires that controls exist to provide assurance that disbursements are properly authorized. Testing cash disbursements involves tracing selected items back through the cash payments journal to original source documents, including vouchers, purchase orders, receiving reports, invoices, and paid checks. While examining these documents, the auditors have an opportunity to test many of the controls over cash disbursements. For example, they will notice whether all paid vouchers and supporting documents have been perforated or cancelled. Also, they will determine whether agreement exists among the supporting documents and note the presence of all required authorization signatures. The auditors also may review the file of paid checks to test the client's procedures for accounting for the numerical sequence of checks.

Cash discounts on purchases may be tested if the auditors are concerned that the company may be losing money by failing to take advantage of the discounts or that purchase discounts may have been fraudulently manipulated by employees. Numerous case histories of fraud relating to cash disbursements have involved the drawing of checks for the gross amount of an invoice paid within the discount period. The dishonest employee was then in a position to request a refund from the creditor, to substitute the refund check for currency, and to abstract cash in this amount without any further manipulation of the records. When testing disbursements, the auditors will investigate and obtain explanations for any payments made within the discount period on which discounts have not been taken.

4.   Reassess control risk and design substantive tests.

When the auditors have completed the procedures described in the preceding sections, they should assess the extent of control risk for each financial statement assertion regarding cash. As illustrated in Chapter 5, the control risk assessment involves identification of weaknesses and unusual strengths in internal control, related extensions or limitations of auditing procedures, and recommendations for inclusion in the internal control report to the client. The auditors then draft the portion of the audit program devoted to the substantive tests of cash transactions and balances.

B. Substantive tests

5. Obtain analyses of cash balances and reconcile to general ledger.

The auditors will prepare or obtain a schedule that lists all of the client's cash accounts. For cash in bank accounts, this schedule will typically list the bank, the account number, account type, and the year-end balance per books. The auditors will trace and reconcile all accounts to the general ledger as necessary.

6. Send confirmation letters to banks to verify amounts on deposit.

One of the objectives of the auditors' work on cash is to substantiate the validity of the amount of cash shown on the balance sheet. A direct approach to this objective is to confirm amounts on deposit, count the cash on hand, and obtain or prepare reconciliations between bank statements and the accounting records.

Confirmation of amounts on deposit by direct communication with bank officials is normally obtained in all cases, even when unopened bank statements are made available to the auditors. The confirmation letters are prepared by the client, but they must be mailed personally by the auditors, with return envelopes enclosed that are addressed to the auditors' office. A standard form of bank confirmation request agreed upon by the AICPA and the Bank Administration Institute is widely used by the public accounting profession. This form is prepared in duplicate, the original to be mailed to the auditors and the duplicate to be retained by the bank. An illustration of this form appears in Figure 11–4.

Generally, information identifying the accounts, loans, and other transactions are typed on the standard bank confirmation to assist bank officials in confirming the information. Thus, the confirmation primarily *corroborates* the validity of recorded information. However, the confirmation may also lead to the *discovery* of additional accounts, loans, or other transactions.

An important element of the confirmation letter is the request for disclosure of all indebtedness of the client to the bank. This request thus serves to bring to light any unrecorded liabilities to banks, as well as to confirm the existence of assets. Auditors should normally send confirmation letters to all banks in which the client has had deposits during the year, even though a deposit account may have been closed out during the period. It is entirely possible that a bank loan may continue after the closing of the deposit account. The same line of reasoning leads to the conclusion that confirmation letters are necessary even when the auditors obtain the bank statements and paid checks directly from the bank. Since every client maintains one or more bank accounts, the independent auditors will use bank confirmation requests on every audit engagement.

Figure 11–4

STANDARD BANK CONFIRMATION INQUIRY
Approved 1966 by
AMERICAN INSTITUTE OF CERTIFIED PUBLIC ACCOUNTANTS
and
BANK ADMINISTRATION INSTITUTE (FORMERLY NABAC)

| ORIGINAL |
| To be mailed to accountant |

January 3 , 19 8X

Your completion of the following report will be sincerely appreciated. **IF THE ANSWER TO ANY ITEM IS "NONE,"
PLEASE SO STATE.** Kindly mail it in the enclosed stamped, addressed envelope *direct* to the accountant named below.

Report from   Yours truly,   The Fairview Corporation
                                                              (ACCOUNT NAME PER BANK RECORDS)

(Bank) Security National Bank   By _Earl J. Foster_
                                                                   Authorized Signature

          1000 Wilshire Boulevard

          Los Angeles, California 90017   Bank customer should check here if confirma-
                                                 tion of bank balances only (item 1) is desired. ☐

                                                 NOTE—If the space provided is inadequate,
                                                 please enter totals hereon and attach a state-
Accountant   ment giving full details as called for by the
   Douglas and Troon, CPAs   columnar headings below.
   800 Hill Street
   Los Angeles, California 90014

1. At the close of business on _December 31_ 19_XX_ our records showed the following balance(s) to the
credit of the above named customer. In the event that we could readily ascertain whether there were any balances
to the credit of the customer not designated in this request, the appropriate information is given below.

AMOUNT	ACCOUNT NAME	ACCOUNT NUMBER	Subject to With-drawal by Check?	Interest Bearing? Give Rate
$ 44,874.50	General account	123-5828	Yes	No
3,215.89	Payroll account	123-6451	Yes	No

2. The customer was directly liable to us in respect of loans, acceptances, etc., at the close of business on that
date in the total amount of $_20,000.00_, as follows:

AMOUNT	DATE OF LOAN OR DISCOUNT	DUE DATE	INTEREST Rate	INTEREST Paid to	DESCRIPTION OF LIABILITY, COLLATERAL, SECURITY INTERESTS, LIENS, ENDORSERS, ETC.
$ 20,000.00	10-1-8X	4-1-8X	12%		Unsecured

3. The customer was contingently liable as endorser of notes discounted and/or as guarantor at the close of
business on that date in the total amount of $_None_, as below:

AMOUNT	NAME OF MAKER	DATE OF NOTE	DUE DATE	REMARKS
$				

4. Other direct or contingent liabilities, open letters of credit, and relative collateral, were   None

5. Security agreements under the Uniform Commercial Code or any other agreements providing for restrictions,
not noted above, were as follows (if officially recorded, indicate date and office in which filed):   None

Yours truly, (Bank) _Security National Bank_

Date _January 7,_ 19 _8X_   By _Elizabeth Richards_
                                               Authorized Signature

Additional copies of this form are available from the American Institute of CPAs, 1211 Avenue of the Americas, New York, N. Y. 10036

7. Obtain or prepare reconciliations of bank accounts as of the balance sheet date and consider need to reconcile bank activity for additional months.

Determination of a company's cash position at the close of the period requires a reconciliation of the balance per the bank statement at that date with the balance per the company's accounting records. Even though the auditors may not be able to begin their field work for some time after the close of the year, they will prepare a bank reconciliation as of the balance sheet date or review the one prepared by the client.

If the year-end reconciliation has been made by the client before the arrival of the auditors, there is no need for duplicating the work. However, the auditors should examine the reconciliation in detail to satisfy themselves that it has been properly prepared. Inspection of a reconciliation prepared by the client will include verifying the arithmetical accuracy, tracing balances to the bank statement and ledger account, and investigating the reconciling items. The importance of a careful review of the client's reconciliation is indicated by the fact that a cash shortage may be concealed merely by omitting a check from the outstanding check list or by purposely making an error in addition on the reconciliation.

There are many satisfactory forms of bank reconciliations. The form most frequently used by auditors begins with balance per bank and ends with unadjusted balance per the accounting records. The format permits the auditors to post adjusting entries affecting cash directly to the bank reconciliation working paper, so that the final adjusted balance can be cross-referenced to the cash grouping sheet or to the working trial balance.

The mechanics of balancing the ledger account with the bank statement by no means completes the auditors' verification of cash on deposit. The authenticity of the individual items making up the reconciliation must be established by reference to their respective sources. The balance per the bank statement, for example, is not accepted at face value but is verified by direct confirmation with the bank, as described in the preceding pages. Other verification procedures associated with the reconciliation of the bank statement will now be discussed.

The auditors should investigate any checks outstanding for a year or more. If checks are permitted to remain outstanding for long periods, internal control over cash disbursements is weakened. Employees who become aware that certain checks have long been outstanding and may never be presented have an opportunity to conceal a cash shortage merely by omitting the old outstanding check from the bank reconciliation. Such omissions will serve to increase the apparent balance of cash on deposit and may thus induce an employee to abstract a corresponding amount of cash on hand. Payroll and dividend checks are the types most commonly misplaced or lost. It is good practice for the client to eliminate long-outstanding checks of this nature by an entry debiting the Cash account and crediting Unclaimed Wages or another special liability account. This will reduce the work required in bank reconciliations, as well as lessen the opportunity for irregularities.

When internal control over the recording of cash receipts and disbursements is considered weak, the auditors may use additional reconciliation procedures such as preparing a *proof of cash*, which allows a more detailed study of the cash transactions occurring within a specified period. This is essentially a fraud detection procedure which may be used for the last month of the year or for selected months during the year.

A proof of cash for the test period of September is illustrated in Figure 11–5. Notice that this working paper is so organized that the first and last columns reconcile the cash balance per bank and the balance per accounting records at the beginning of the test period (Column 1) and at the end of this period (Column 4). These outside columns are equivalent to typical monthly bank reconciliations. The two middle columns reconcile the bank's record of deposits with the client's record of cash receipts (Column 2) and the bank's record of paid checks with the client's record of cash disbursements (Column 3).

Next consider the source of the figures used in this reconciliation. The amounts in Column 1 (Balance, August 31) are taken from the client's bank reconciliation as of August 31. Similarly, the figures for Column 4 (Balance, September 30) are taken from the client's bank reconciliation as of September 30. For Column 2 (Deposits), the auditors arrive at the $46,001 of deposits per the bank by adding the deposits appearing on the September bank statement. The $45,338.50 of receipts per the books is obtained from the debits of Cash in Bank account in the general ledger. In Column 3, the auditors compute the $40,362.90 of checks paid by the bank by cross-footing the top line of the reconciliation and prove the figure by adding the paid checks. The bottom figure in Column 3 represents the disbursements per the accounting records during September and is taken from the general ledger account. The reconciling items listed in Columns 2 and 3 are computed by the auditors from analysis of the reconciling items at the beginning and end of September.

After completing the four-column bank reconciliation form, the auditors should prove the footings of all four columns and make a detailed verification of the figures used in the reconciliation. The balances taken from the client's bank reconciliations as of August 31 and September 30 should be traced to the bank statements and to the Cash in Bank account in the general ledger.

Verification of cash receipts and deposits during the test period To verify receipts and deposits for the month being tested, deposits listed on the bank statement should be compared with the client's cash receipts record. This step will include a comparison of the total receipts with the total deposits and also a comparison of the date of each deposit with the date such funds were received by the company. Any failure to deposit each day's receipts intact should be investigated.

Figure 11–5

The Fairview Corporation

Acct. No. 101   Proof of Cash for September 198X   A-4
December 31, 198X

	Balance Aug. 31/8X	Deposits	Checks	Balance Sept. 30/8X
Per bank statement	39,236.40 #	46,001.00 ②	40,362.90	44,874.50 z
Deposits in transit:				
at Aug. 31/8X	600.00 z	(600.00)		
at Sept. 30/8X		837.50		837.50
Outstanding checks				
at Aug. 31/8X	(1,241.00) X		(1,241.00)	
at Sept. 30/8X			3,402.00	(3,402.00) √
Bank service charge:				
August	4.60		4.60	
September			(2.80)	2.80
Check of customer G. B. Speeler charged back by bank Sept. 12/8X, redeposited Sept. 15/8X		(900.00)	(900.00)	
Per books	38,600.00 u	45,338.50 u	41,625.70 u ①	42,312.80 u A-1

z = Traced to clients' Aug. 31/8X bank reconciliation and/or to September bank statement.
# = Per adding machine tape at A-4-1.
X = Per adding machine tape at A-4-2.
√ = Per adding machine tape at A-4-3.
u = Traced to general ledger.
① = Vouched selected September disbursements to paid vouchers and other supporting documents.
② = Obtained authenticated deposit slips for September from bank and compared with cash receipts journal. Compared detail of 10 deposit slips with original control listings and postings to customers' accounts.

Footed cash receipts journal and check register for September, 198X. Accounted for numerical sequence of all checks issued September 198X-nos. 610-792. No exceptions to tests.

V. M. H. Oct./16/8X

The misappropriation of cash receipts may sometimes be concealed by crediting the customers' accounts but debiting Sales Discounts rather than Cash. For this reason, auditors may verify all sales discounts recorded during the test period by computing the allowable discounts and noting the dates of invoices and customers' payments.

Verification of cash disbursements during the test period Reconciling the client's record of cash disbursements to the bank's record of paid checks provides the auditors with assurance that all disbursements clearing the bank during the test period have been recorded in the accounting records. To determine that the nature of these disbursements is properly reflected in the accounts, the auditors will vouch disbursements for the test period to supporting evidence such as vouchers, approved vendors' invoices, and payroll records.

An important step in the verification of cash disbursements is to account for the sequence of check numbers issued during the period. All checks used should be paid, voided, or listed as outstanding on September 30. The auditors will examine any checks either recorded as voided or not included in the sequence of recorded checks during the period. They may also obtain the October bank statement to examine checks listed as outstanding on September 30.

Omitting an outstanding check from a bank statement may conceal a cash shortage. Auditors should therefore determine that all check numbers not paid or voided during the test period are listed as outstanding on September 30. Another test of the client's bank reconciliation function is to determine that all checks listed as outstanding on August 31 were either paid in September or listed as outstanding in the September 30 bank reconciliation.

8. Obtain a cutoff bank statement containing transactions of at least seven business days subsequent to balance sheet date.

A *cutoff bank statement* is a statement covering a specified number of *business days* (usually 7 to 10) following the end of the client's fiscal year. The client will request the bank to prepare such a statement and deliver it directly to the auditors. This statement is used to test the accuracy of the year-end reconciliation of the company's bank accounts. It allows the auditors to examine firsthand the checks listed as outstanding and the details of deposits in transit on the company's reconciliation.

With respect to checks that were shown as outstanding at year-end, the auditors should determine the dates on which these checks were paid by the bank. By noting the dates of payment of these checks, the auditors can determine whether the time intervals between the dates of the check and the time of payment by the bank were unreasonably long. Unreasonable delay in the presentation of these checks for payment constitutes a strong implication that the checks were not mailed by the client until some time after the close of the year. The appropriate adjusting entry in such cases consists of a debit to Cash and a credit to a liability account.

In studying the cutoff bank statement, the auditors will also watch for any paid checks issued, or clearing a bank, on or before the balance sheet date but not listed as outstanding on the client's year-end bank reconciliation. Thus, the cutoff bank statement provides assurance that the amount of cash shown on the balance sheet was not overstated by omission of one or more checks from the list of checks outstanding.

9. Count and list cash on hand.

Cash on hand ordinarily consists of undeposited cash receipts, petty cash funds, and change funds. The petty cash funds and change funds may be counted at any time before or after the balance sheet date; many auditors prefer to make a surprise count of these funds. If the client's internal audit staff regularly performs surprise counts of petty cash and change funds, the CPAs may review the internal auditors' working papers for these counts and conclude that it is unnecessary to include a count of petty cash and change funds among the procedures of the annual independent audit. If undeposited cash receipts and any other cash on hand constitute a material factor, a count at the balance sheet date is desirable; otherwise the auditors may verify the deposit in transit at year-end by referring to the date of deposit shown on the cutoff bank statement.

The count of cash on hand is of special importance in the audit of banks and other financial institutions. Whenever auditors make a cash count, they should insist that the *custodian of the funds be present throughout the count*. At the completion of the count, the auditors should obtain from the custodian a signed and dated acknowledgment that the funds were counted in the custodian's presence and were returned intact by the auditors. Such procedures avoid the possibility of an employee trying to explain a cash shortage by claiming that the funds were intact when turned over to the auditors.

A first step in the verification of cash on hand is to establish control over all negotiable assets, such as cash funds, securities and other investments, notes receivable, and warehouse receipts. Unless all negotiable assets are verified at one time, an opportunity exists for a dishonest officer or employee to conceal a shortage by transferring it from one asset category to another.

Illustrative case

John Sidell, a key office employee in a small business, misappropriated $30,000 by withholding cash collections and postponing the required credits to accounts receivable from customers. The accounting records were in balance; but Sidell was aware that when the independent auditors confirmed the balances due from customers the shortage would be disclosed. He therefore "borrowed" negotiable securities from the office safe

(Continued)

shortly before the annual audit and used them as collateral to obtain a short-term loan of $34,000. He intermingled the proceeds of this loan with the cash receipts on hand and credited the customers' accounts with all payments received to date. Mr. Sidell knew that unless the auditors insisted on verifying the securities owned by the business concurrently with their verification of cash, he would be able to abstract funds again after the cash had been counted, use these funds to pay off his loan, and return the "borrowed" securities to the safe before the auditors began their verification of investments. The defalcation was discovered when the auditors insisted on a simultaneous verification of all negotiable assets.

It is not uncommon to find included in cash on hand some personal checks cashed for the convenience of officers, employees, and customers. Such checks, of course, should not be entered in the cash receipts journal because they are merely substitutes for currency previously on hand. The auditors should determine that these checks are valid and collectible, thus qualifying for inclusion in the balance sheet figure for cash. This may be accomplished by the auditors taking control of the last bank deposit for the period and determining that it includes all checks received through year-end. The auditors will retain a validated deposit slip from this deposit for comparison to any checks subsequently charged back by the bank.

10.   Verify the client's cutoff of cash transactions.

The balance sheet figure for cash should include all cash received on the final day of the year and none received subsequently. In other words, an accurate cutoff of cash receipts (and of cash disbursements) at year-end is essential to a proper statement of cash on the balance sheet. If the auditors can arrange to be present at the client's office at the close of business on the last day of the fiscal year, they will be able to verify the cutoff by counting the undeposited cash receipts. It will then be impossible for the client to include in the records any cash received after this cutoff point without the auditor being aware of such actions.

All customers' checks included in cash receipts should have been entered in the cash receipts journal before the auditors' cash count. The auditors should compare these checks, both as to name and amount, with the cash journal entries. If checks have been credited to accounts other than those of the drawers of the checks, a likelihood of lapping or other fraudulent activity is indicated.

Of course, auditors cannot visit every client's place of business on the last day of the fiscal year, nor is their presence at this time essential to a satisfactory verification of cash. As an alternative to a count on the balance sheet date, auditors can verify the cutoff of cash receipts by determining that deposits in transit as shown on the year-end bank reconciliation appear as credits on the bank statement on the first business day of the new year. Failure to make *immediate* deposit of the closing day's cash receipts would suggest that cash received at a later time might have been included in the deposit, thus overstating the cash balance at the balance sheet date.

To ensure an accurate cutoff of cash disbursements, the auditors should determine the serial number of the last check written on each bank account on the balance sheet date and should inquire whether all checks up to this number have been placed in the mail. Some companies, in an effort to improve the current ratio, will prepare checks payable to creditors and enter these checks as cash disbursements on the last day of the fiscal year, although there is no intention of mailing the checks until several days or weeks later. When the auditors make a note of the number of the last check issued for the period, they are in a position to detect at once any additional checks that the client might later issue and seek to show as disbursements of the year under audit.

11. Trace all bank transfers for the last week of audit year and first week of following year.

The purpose of tracing bank transfers is to disclose overstatements of cash balances resulting from *kiting*. Many businesses maintain checking accounts with a number of banks and often find it necessary to transfer funds from one bank to another. When a check drawn on one bank is deposited in another, several days (called the float period) usually pass before the check clears the bank on which it is drawn. During this period, the amount of the check is included in the balance on deposit at both banks. Kiting refers to manipulations that utilize such temporarily overstated bank balances to conceal a cash shortage or meet short-term cash needs.

Auditors can detect manipulations of this type by preparing a schedule of bank transfers for a few days before and after the balance sheet date. This working paper lists all bank transfers and shows the dates that the receipt and disbursement of cash were recorded in the cash journals and on the bank statements. A partial illustration of a schedule of bank transfers is shown below.

	Bank accounts			Date of disbursement		Date of receipt	
Check No.	From	To	Amount	Books	Bank	Books	Bank
5897	General	Payroll	$30,620	12/28	1/3	12/28	12/28
6006	General	Branch 4	24,018	1/2	1/4	12/30	12/30
6029	Branch 2	General	10,000	1/3	1/5	1/3	12/31

Disclosure of kiting   By comparing the dates in this working paper, auditors can determine whether any manipulation of the cash balance has taken place. The increase in one bank account and decrease in the other bank account should be recorded in the cash journals in the same accounting period. Notice that Check No. 6006 in the transfer schedule was recorded in the cash journals as a receipt on December 30 and a disbursement of January 2. As a result of recording the debit and credit parts of the transaction in different accounting periods, cash is overstated on December 31. For the cash receipts journal to remain in balance, some account must have been credited on December 30 to offset the debit to Cash. If a revenue account was credited, the results of operations were overstated along with cash.

Kiting may also be used to conceal a cash shortage. Assume, for example, that a financial executive misappropriates $10,000 from a company's general checking account. To conceal the shortage on December 31, the executive draws a check transferring $10,000 from the company's branch bank account to the general account. The executive deposits the transfer check in the general account on December 31, but records the transfer in the accounting records as occurring early in January. As of December 31, the shortage in the general account has been replaced, no reduction has yet been recorded in the branch account, and no shortage is apparent. Of course, the shortage will reappear in a few days when the transfer check is paid from the branch account.

A bank transfer schedule should disclose this type of kiting because the transfer deposit appears on the general account bank statement in December, while the transaction was not recorded in the cash journals until January. Check No. 6029 in the transfer schedule illustrates this discrepancy.

A third type of kiting uses the float period to meet short-term cash needs. For example, assume that a business does not have sufficient cash to meet the month-end payroll. The company might draw a check on its general account in one bank, deposit it in a payroll account in another bank, and rely upon subsequent deposits being made to the general account before the transfer check is presented for payment. If the transfer is properly recorded in the accounting records, this form of kiting will not cause a misstatement of the cash balance for financial reporting purposes (e.g., Check No. 5897). However, banks discourage this practice and may not allow the customer to draw against the deposit until the check has cleared the other account. In some deliberate schemes to defraud banks, this type of kiting has been used to create and conceal overdrafts of millions of dollars.

12. Investigate any checks representing large or unusual payments to related parties.

Any large or unusual checks payable to directors, officers, employees, affiliated companies, or cash should be carefully reviewed by the auditors to determine whether the transactions (*a*) were properly authorized and recorded and (*b*) are adequately disclosed in the financial statements. If checks have been issued payable to cash, the auditors should determine who received these payments and why this form of check was used.

To provide assurance that cash disbursements to related parties were authorized transactions and were properly recorded, the auditors should determine that each such transaction has been charged to the proper account, is supported by adequate vouchers or other records, and was specifically approved in advance by an officer other than the one receiving the funds.

The need for financial statement disclosure of transactions with related parties was discussed in Chapter 7. To determine that such transactions are adequately disclosed, the auditors must obtain evidence concerning the relationship between the parties, the substance of each transaction (which may differ from its form), and the effect of each transaction upon the financial statements. Disclosure of related party transactions should include the nature of the relationships, a description of the transactions, and the dollar amounts involved.

13. Determine proper financial statement presentation and disclosure of cash.

The balance sheet figure for cash should include only those amounts that are available for use in current operations. Most users of the balance sheet are not interested in the breakdown of cash by various bank accounts or in the distinction between cash on hand and on deposit. Consequently, all cash on hand and in banks that is available for general use is presented as a single amount on the balance sheet. Change funds and petty cash funds, although somewhat lacking in the general availability test, are usually not material in amount and are included in the balance sheet figure for cash.

A bank deposit that is restricted in use (for example, cash deposited with a trustee for payments on long-term debt) should not be included in cash. Agreements to maintain *compensating balances* should be disclosed. The auditors must also make sure that the caption, cash or cash and equivalents, on the client's balance sheet corresponds to that used in the statement of cash flows.

Window dressing The term *window dressing* refers to actions taken shortly before the balance sheet date to improve the cash position or in other ways to create an improved financial picture of the company. For example, if the cash receipts journal is held open for a few days after the close of the year, the balance sheet figure for cash is improperly increased to include cash collections actually received after the balance sheet date. Another approach to window dressing is found when a corporate officer who has borrowed money from the corporation repays the loan just before the end of the year and then promptly obtains the loan again after the balance sheet has been prepared. This second example is not an outright misrepresentation of the cash position (as in the case of holding the cash receipts journal open), but nevertheless creates misleading financial statements that fail to portray the underlying economic position and operations of the company.

Not all forms of window dressing require action by the auditors. Many companies make strenuous efforts at year-end to achieve an improved financial picture by rushing shipments to customers, by pressing for collection of receivables, and sometimes by paying liabilities down to an unusually low level. Such efforts to improve the financial picture to be reported are not improper. Before giving approval to the balance sheet presentation of cash, the auditors must exercise their professional judgment to determine whether the client has engaged in window dressing of a nature that causes the financial statements to be misleading.

Interim audit work on cash

To avoid a concentration of audit work shortly after the year-end, CPA firms try to complete as many auditing procedures as possible on an interim basis during the year. The consideration of internal control over cash, for example, can be performed in advance of the client's year-end. The audit work on cash at year-end can then be limited to such substantive tests as a review of the client's bank reconciliation, confirmation of year-end bank balances, investigation of the year-end cutoff, and a general review of cash transactions during the interval between the interim work on cash and the end of the period.

MARKETABLE SECURITIES

The most important group of investments, from the viewpoint of the auditors, consists of stocks and bonds because they are found more frequently and usually are of greater dollar value than other kinds of investment holdings. Bank certificates of deposit, commercial paper issued by corporations, mortgages and trust deeds, and the cash surrender value of life insurance policies are other types of investments often encountered.

Investment of temporarily idle cash in selected types of marketable securities is an element of good financial management. Such holdings are regarded as a secondary cash reserve, capable of quick conversion to cash at any time, although producing a steady rate of return. Management may also choose to maintain some investments in marketable securities on a semipermanent basis. The length of time such investments are held may be determined by current security yields and by the company's income tax position, as well as by its cash requirements. Investments in securities made for the purpose of maintaining control or influence over affiliated companies should *not* be classified under marketable securities.

The auditors' objectives in examination of marketable securities

The auditors' *objectives* in the examination of marketable securities are to determine that:

1. *Internal control* over marketable securities is adequate.
2. Marketable securities are valid in that they exist and are the property of the client (*existence and rights*).

3. All marketable securities are recorded (*completeness*).
4. Valuation of marketable securities is in accordance with the lower of cost or market method of accounting (*valuation*).
5. Marketable security records and schedules are mathematically correct and agree with general ledger accounts (*clerical accuracy*).
6. The *presentation* and *disclosure* of marketable securities, including current/noncurrent classifications and necessary disclosures, is adequate.

In conjunction with their audit of marketable securities, the auditors will also verify the related accounts of interest income and dividends, accrued interest revenue, and gains and losses on the sale of securities.

The liquid nature of marketable securities makes the potential for irregularities high. Auditors must coordinate their cash and marketable securities audit procedures to detect any possible irregularities involving unauthorized substitution (e.g., sale of securities to hide a cash shortage) between the accounts. The overall audit approach is one of assessing control over securities, inspecting certificates, and confirming securities held by third parties such as banks.

Internal control for marketable securities

The major elements of adequate internal control over marketable securities include the following:

1. Separation of duties between the executive *authorizing* purchases and sales of securities, the *custodian* of the securities, and the person maintaining the *record* of investments.
2. Complete detailed records of all securities owned and the related revenue from interest and dividends.
3. Registration of securities in the name of the company.
4. Periodic physical inspection of securities by an internal auditor or an official having no responsibility for the authorization, custody, or record keeping of investments.

In many concerns, segregation of the functions of custody and record keeping is achieved by the use of an independent safekeeping agent, such as a stockbroker, bank, or trust company. Since the independent agent has no direct contact with the employee responsible for maintaining accounting records of the investments in securities, the possibilities of concealing fraud through falsification of the accounts are greatly reduced. The risks of physical loss or destruction are also minimized because the independent agent generally has fireproof vaults and other facilities especially designed to safeguard valuable documents. If securities are not placed in the custody of an independent agent, they should be kept in a bank safe-deposit box under the joint control of two or more of the company's officials. *Joint control* means that neither of the two custodians may have access to the securities except in the presence of the other. A list of securities in the box should be maintained there, and the deposit or withdrawal of securities should be recorded on this list along with the date and signatures of all persons present. The safe-deposit box rental should be in the name of the company, not in the name of an officer having custody of securities.

Complete detailed records of all securities owned, and of any securities held for others, are essential to a satisfactory internal control structure. These records frequently consist of a subsidiary record for each security, with such identifying data as the exact name, face amount or par value, certificate number, number of shares, date of acquisition, name of broker, cost, and any interest or dividends payments received. The purchase and sale of securities often is entrusted to a responsible financial executive, subject to frequent review by an investment committee of the board of directors.

The auditors occasionally may find that securities owned by the client are registered in the name of an officer or other individual rather than in the name of the company. Immediate registration in the company's name at date of purchase is the preferred practice, since this reduces the likelihood of fraudulent transfer or unauthorized use of the securities as collateral. Some bonds are payable to *bearer* and cannot be registered in the name of the owner.

An internal auditor or other responsible employee should at frequent intervals inspect the securities on hand, compare the serial numbers and other identifying data of the securities examined with the accounting records, and reconcile the subsidiary record for securities with the control account. This procedure supplements the internal control inherent in the segregation of the functions of authorization, record keeping, and custodianship.

Internal control questionnaire

A questionnaire used by the auditors in assessing internal controls relating to securities will include such questions as the following. Are securities and similar instruments under the joint control of responsible officials? Are all persons having access to securities properly bonded? Is an independent safekeeping agent retained? Are all purchases and sales of securities authorized by a financial executive and reviewed by an investment committee of the board of directors?

Audit program for securities

Listed below are procedures typically performed by auditors to achieve the objectives described earlier.

A. Consider internal control for securities

1. *Obtain an understanding of internal control* for securities.
2. *Assess control risk* and *design additional tests of controls* for securities.
3. *Perform additional tests of controls* for those controls the auditors plan to rely upon to restrict their assessment of control risk, and reduce the extent of substantive testing such as:
   a. Trace transactions for purchases and sales of securities through the system.
   b. Review reports by internal auditors on their periodic inspection of securities.
   c. Review monthly reports by officers of the client's company on securities owned, purchased, and sold, and revenue earned.
4. *Reassess control risk* and *design substantive tests* for securities.

B. Perform substantive tests of securities transactions and year-end balances

5. Obtain or prepare analyses of the securities investment account and related revenue accounts and reconcile to the general ledger.
6. Inspect securities on hand and compare serial numbers with those shown on previous examinations.
7. Obtain confirmation of securities held by others.
8. Vouch purchases and sales of securities during the year.
9. Determine market value of securities at date of balance sheet.
10. Perform analytical procedures.
11. Make independent computations of revenue from securities.
12. Verify the client's cutoff of securities transactions.
13. Evaluate the method of accounting for securities.
14. Evaluate financial statement presentation and disclosure of securities.

Figure 11–6 relates these substantive tests to the primary audit objectives.

Audit procedures and working papers

The audit working papers describing internal control may include a flowchart, questionnaire, or a written narrative. Next, selected transactions for purchase or sale of securities will be traced through the system to verify that the controls are being followed in actual practice. For example, a purchase of securities should be approved in minutes of the meetings of the investment committee, and documents from the stockbrokerage firm should show receipt of the order and its execution. Other evidence will be the broker's month-end statement, the stock certificate acquired, the entry in the subsidiary ledger for securities, and the monthly report of the treasurer showing all purchases, sales, current holdings, and revenue received from investments.

Figure 11–6 Objectives of major substantive tests of securities

Substantive tests	Primary audit objectives
Obtain analyses of securities and related accounts and reconcile to ledgers	*Clerical accuracy*
Inspect securities on hand Obtain confirmation of securities held by others	*Validity (existence and rights)*
Vouch purchases and sales of securities during the year Determine market value of securities	*Validity (existence and rights)* *Valuation*
Perform analytical procedures Make independent computations of revenue from securities Verify the client's cutoff of securities transactions	*Validity (existence and rights)* *Completeness*
Evaluate method of accounting for securities	*Valuation* *Presentation and disclosure*
Evaluate financial statement presentation and disclosure	*Presentation and disclosure*

In large companies, the internal auditors may make surprise counts of all company-owned securities held in a bank safe-deposit box or other location. The independent auditors may reconcile the listing of securities at a given date as prepared by the internal auditors with the subsidiary ledger for securities and with the CPA firm's own working papers from the preceding year's audit.

A written monthly report of securities transactions can be a valuable internal control device. In many companies, the treasurer will submit a monthly report to the investment committee of the board of directors showing securities owned at the beginning of the month, all purchases, sales, gains and losses during the month, the dividends and interest received, and the month-end holdings. Such reports are important evidence to the auditors in assessing internal control.

The auditors will count the securities owned by the client at year-end, verify that the securities are registered in the company's name, and compare the serial numbers on the certificates with those shown on previous examinations. This step *proves the existence and ownership of the securities*. The count ideally is made at the balance sheet date concurrently with the count of cash and other negotiable securities. If the securities are kept in a bank safe-deposit box, the client may instruct the bank in writing on the balance sheet date that no one is to have access to the box unless accompanied by the auditors. This arrangement makes it possible to count the securities at a more convenient time after the balance sheet date. The auditors should insist that a representative of the client be present throughout the count of the securities. To expedite the counting process, the auditors should have available a complete list of securities so that securities can quickly be checked off as counted.

Often, most client-owned securities will be in the hands of brokers or banks for transfer or safekeeping. In such cases, the client-prepared confirmation request should be sent *by the auditors* directly to the holders and the reply mailed directly to the auditors' office in a self-addressed return envelope. When a confirmation letter is received from a reliable financial institution independent of the client, the auditors will often choose not to inspect the securities.

In addition to vouching selected purchases and sales of investments during the year to *brokers' advices and statements* and cash records, the auditors should review securities transactions for two or three weeks *after* the balance sheet date. The purpose is to assure that a correct cutoff of transactions was made. Sometimes sales occur shortly before the balance sheet date but go unrecorded until delivered to the broker early in the next period.

The auditors can make an independent computation of dividends that should have been received and recorded by referring to dividend record books published by investment advisory services. These books show dividend declarations, amounts, and payment dates for all listed stocks. Interest earned on bonds and notes also can be computed independently by the auditors and compared with recorded amounts in the client's records. This provides evidence both that the employees are not embezzling investment income and that the client actually owns the securities recorded in the accounting records.

Current market quotations for all marketable securities owned by the client should be obtained by the auditors and included in the audit working papers. The presentation of marketable equity securities in financial statements is presently guided by *FASB Statement No. 12,* which requires use of the lower of the aggregate cost or market value determined at the balance sheet date.[1]

Investments accounted for by the equity method   Investments in common stock that give the investor company the ability to exercise significant influence over operating and financial policies of the investee require use of the equity method of accounting. Ownership of 20 percent of the voting stock of an investee is used as a general indication of ability to exert influence in the absence of evidence to the contrary. Such factors as investor representation on the investee's board of directors and material intercompany transactions also suggest an ability to exercise influence.

When auditing an investment accounted for by the equity method, the auditors must verify that the investment was recorded properly initially. They must also obtain evidence regarding subsequent amounts of income

---

[1] FASB, *Statement of Financial Accounting Standards No. 12,* "Accounting for Certain Marketable Securities" (Stamford, Conn., 1975).

from the investment and of other adjustments to the investment account. This evidence is usually obtained from *audited* financial statements of the investee.

If audited financial statements of an investee are not available for the period covered by the independent auditors' report on the investor, the auditors should perform a sufficient investigation of the investee's financial statements to determine the fairness of amounts recorded by the investor.

KEY TERMS INTRODUCED OR EMPHASIZED IN CHAPTER 12

Brokers' advice   A notification sent by a stockbrokerage firm to a customer reporting the terms of a purchase or sale of securities.

Certificate of deposit   A receipt issued by a bank for a deposit of funds for a specified time. Usually in denominations of $100,000 or more and bearing interest at a higher rate than for most bank savings accounts.

Check register   A journal used in a voucher system to record payment of vouchers. Since the cost distribution relating to voucher transactions is made in the voucher register, entries in the check register represent debits to Vouchers Payable and credits to Cash.

Confirmation letter (from bank)   Documentary evidence sent by the bank directly to the auditors confirming the client's bank account balances, outstanding loans, and other transactions involving the bank.

Confirmation request—securities   A letter prepared by the client and addressed to the broker, bank, or other holder of client-owned securities, requesting the holder to respond directly to the independent auditors giving full identification of the securities and the purpose for which held.

Cutoff bank statement   A bank statement covering a specified number of business days (usually 7 to 10) after the client's balance sheet date. Auditors use this statement to determine that checks issued on or before the balance sheet date and paid during the cutoff period were listed as outstanding on the year-end bank reconciliation. Another use is to determine that reconciling items shown on the year-end bank reconciliation have cleared the bank within a reasonable time.

Dividend record book   A reference book published monthly by investment advisory services reporting much detailed information concerning all listed and many unlisted securities. Includes dividend dates and amounts, current prices of securities, and other condensed financial data.

Kiting   Manipulations causing an amount of cash to be included simultaneously in the balance of two or more bank accounts. Kiting schemes are based on the float period—the time necessary for a check deposited in one bank to clear the bank on which it was drawn.

Lockbox   A post office box controlled by a company's bank at which cash remittances from customers are received. The bank picks up the remittances, immediately credits the cash to the company's bank account, and forwards the remittance advices to the company.

Proof of cash   An audit procedure that reconciles the bank's record of cash activity with the client's accounting records for a test period. The working paper used for the proof of cash is a four-column bank reconciliation.

Remittance advice   A document that accompanies cash remittances from customers identifying the customer and the amount of the remittance.

Voucher   A document authorizing a cash disbursement. A voucher usually provides space for employees performing various approval functions to initial. (The term *voucher* may also be applied to the group of documents that support a cash disbursement.)

Voucher register   A special journal used to record the liabilities for payment originating in a voucher system. The debit entries are the cost distribution of the transaction, and the credits are to Vouchers Payable. Every transaction recorded in a voucher register corresponds to a voucher authorizing future payment of cash.

Window dressing   Action taken by the client shortly before the balance sheet date to improve the financial picture presented in the financial statements.

GROUP I: REVIEW QUESTIONS

11–1.   It is sometimes said that audit work on cash is facilitated by the existence of two independent records of the client's cash transactions, which are available for comparison by the auditors. Identify these two independent records.

11–2.   "If the auditors discover any evidence of employee fraud during their work on cash, they should extend their investigation as far as necessary to develop a complete set of facts, regardless of whether the amounts involved are or are not material." Do you agree with the quoted statement? Explain.

11–3.   Give two reasons why audit work on cash is likely to be more extensive than might appear to be justified by the relative amount of the balance sheet figure for cash.

11–4.   The auditors' work on cash may include preparing a description of internal controls and making tests of controls. Which of these two steps should be performed first? What is the purpose of tests of controls?

11–5.   Among the departments of J-R Company are a purchasing department, receiving department, accounting department, and finance department. If you were preparing a flowchart of a voucher system to be installed by the company, in which department would you show—
 a.   The assembling of the purchase order, receiving report, and vendor's invoice to determine that these documents are in agreement.
 b.   The preparation of a check.
 c.   The signing of a check.
 d.   The mailing of a check to the payee.
 e.   The perforation of the voucher and supporting documents.

11–6.   Describe circumstances that might cause a client to understate assets such as cash and marketable securities.

11–7.   What prevents the person who opens incoming mail from being able to abstract cash collections from customers?

11–8.   Should an internal control questionnaire concerning cash receipts and disbursements be filled out for all audits? At what stage of an audit would you recommend use of the questionnaire?

11–9.   An internal control questionnaire includes the following items. For each item, explain what is accomplished by the existence of the controls involved:

    a. Are each day's cash receipts deposited intact and without delay?

    b. If an imprest fund is represented by a bank account, has the bank been notified that no checks payable to the company should be accepted for deposit?

    c. Are payroll disbursements made from an imprest bank account restricted to that purpose?

    d. Are vouchers or other supporting documents stamped or perforated when checks are signed?   (AICPA, adapted)

11–10. How can an auditor obtain assurance that cash receipts are being deposited intact?

11–11. Prepare a simple illustration of lapping of cash receipts, showing actual transactions and the cash receipts journal entries.   (AICPA)

11–12. During your audit of a small manufacturing firm, you find numerous checks of large amount drawn payable to the treasurer and charged to the Miscellaneous Expense account. Does this require any action by the auditor? Explain.

11–13. What information do CPAs request from a bank in the Standard Bank Confirmation Inquiry?

11–14. What action should be taken by the auditors when the count of cash on hand discloses a shortage?

11–15. "The auditors should send confirmation requests to all banks with which the client has had deposits during the year, even though some of these accounts have been closed prior to the balance sheet date." Do you agree? Explain.

11–16. State one broad general objective of internal control for each of the following: cash receipts, cash disbursements, and cash balances.

11–17. In preparing a proof of cash, how does the auditor account for all checks issued during the test period?

11–18. During your reconciliation of bank accounts in an audit, you find that a number of checks of small amount have been outstanding for more than a year. Does this situation call for any action by the auditor? Explain.

11–19. Explain the objectives of each of the following audit procedures for cash:

    a. Obtain a cutoff bank statement subsequent to the balance sheet date.

    b. Compare paid checks returned with bank statement to list of outstanding checks in previous reconciliation.

    c. Trace all bank transfers during the last week of the audit year and the first week of the following year.

    d. Investigate any checks representing large or unusual payments to related parties.

11–20. Explain two procedures by which auditors may verify the client's cutoff of cash receipts.

11–21. What is the meaning of the term *window dressing* when used in connection with year-end financial statements? How might the term be related to the making of loans by a corporation to one or more of its executives?

11–22. An audit client that has never before invested in securities recently acquired more than a million dollars in cash from the sale of real estate no longer used in operations. The president intends to invest this money in marketable securities until such time as the opportunity arises for advantageous acquisition of a new plant site. He asks you to enumerate the principal factors you would recommend to create strong internal control over marketable securities.

11–23. Under what conditions would CPAs accept a confirmation of the securities in the possession of a custodian in lieu of inspecting the securities themselves? (AICPA)

11–24. What documents should be examined in verifying the purchases and sales of securities made during the year under audit?

11–25. How can the auditors determine that all dividends applicable to marketable securities owned by the client have been received and recorded?

11–26. What information should be noted by the auditors during their inspection of securities on hand?

11–27. Under what circumstances may securities owned by the client not be on hand at the balance sheet date?

11–28. Are the auditors concerned with securities transactions subsequent to the balance sheet date? Explain.

11–29. Assume that it is not possible for you to be present on the balance sheet date to inspect the securities owned by the client. What variation in audit procedures is appropriate if the inspection is not made until two weeks after the balance sheet date?

11–30. A well-financed audit client of your CPA firm invests large amounts in marketable securities. As part of its internal control, the company uses a monthly report of securities transactions. The report is prepared by the treasurer and presented to the Investment Committee of the board of directors. What information should this report contain?

GROUP II: QUESTIONS REQUIRING ANALYSIS

11–31. "When auditors are verifying a client's bank reconciliation, they are particularly concerned with the possibility that the list of outstanding checks may include a nonexistent or fictitious check, and also are concerned with the possibility of omission from the reconciliation of a deposit in transit." Criticize the above quotation and revise it into an accurate statement.

11–32. During the first few months of the year, John Smith, the cashier in a small company, was engaged in lapping operations. However, he was able to restore the amount of cash "borrowed" by March 31, and he refrained from any fraudulent acts after that date. Will the year-end audit probably lead to the discovery of his lapping activities? Explain.

11–33. An assistant auditor received the following instructions from her supervisor: "Here is a cutoff bank statement covering the first seven business days of January. Compare the paid checks returned with the statement and dated December 31 or earlier with the list of checks outstanding at December 31." What type of irregularity might this audit procedure bring to light? Explain.

11–34. Henry Mills is responsible for preparing checks, recording cash disbursements, and preparing bank reconciliations for Signet Corporation. While reconciling the October bank statement, Mills noticed that several checks totaling $937 had been outstanding for more than one year. Concluding that these checks would never be presented for payment, Mills prepared a check for $937 payable to himself, forged the treasurer's signature, and cashed the check. Mills made no entry in the accounts for this disbursement and attempted to conceal the theft by destroying the forged check and omitting the long-outstanding checks from subsequent bank reconciliations.

Required:

a.   Identify the weaknesses in Signet Corporation's internal control.

b.   Explain several audit procedures that might disclose the fraudulent disbursement.

11–35.   Fluid Controls, Inc., a manufacturing company, has retained you to perform an audit for the year ended December 31. Prior to the year-end, you begin to obtain an understanding of the new client's internal controls over cash.

You find that nearly all of the company's cash receipts are in the form of checks received through the mail, but there is no prelisting of cash receipts before they are recorded in the accounts. You find that the incoming mail is opened either by the cashier or by the employee maintaining the accounts receivable subsidiary ledger, depending on which employee has time available. The controller stresses the necessity of flexibility in assignment of duties to the 20 employees comprising the office staff, in order to keep all employees busy and achieve maximum economy of operation.

Required:

a.   Explain how prelisting of cash receipts strengthens internal control.

b.   List specific duties that should not be performed by an employee assigned to prelist the cash receipts in order to avoid any opportunity for that employee to conceal embezzlement of cash receipts.

(AICPA, adapted)

11–36.   Although the primary objective of an independent audit is not the discovery of fraud, the auditors in their work on cash take into consideration the high inherent risk associated with this asset. One evidence of this attitude is evidenced by the CPA's alertness for signs of lapping.

Required:

a.   Define *lapping*.

b.   Explain the audit procedures that CPAs might utilize to uncover lapping.

11–37.   During the examination of cash, the CPAs are alert for any indications of kiting.

Required:

a.   Define *kiting*.

b.   Explain the audit procedures that should enable the CPAs to uncover kiting.

11–38.   Explain how each of the following items would appear in a four-column proof of cash for the month of November. Assume the format of the proof of cash begins with bank balances and ends with the unadjusted balances per the accounting records.

a. Outstanding checks at November 30.

b. Deposits-in-transit at October 31.

c. Check issued and paid in November, drawn payable to Cash.

d. The bank returned $1,800 in NSF checks deposited by the client in November; the client redeposited $1,450 of these checks in November and $350 in December, making no additional entries in the accounting records.

11–39. In the audit of a client with a fiscal year ending June 30, the CPAs obtain a July 10 bank statement directly from the bank. Explain how this cutoff bank statement will be used:

a. In the review of the June 30 bank reconciliation.

b. To obtain other audit information. (AICPA, adapted)

11–40. In the audit of Wheat, Inc. for the year ended December 31, you discover that the client had been drawing checks as creditors' invoices became due but had not been mailing the checks immediately. Because of a working capital shortage, some checks have been held for two or three weeks.

The client's controller informs you that unmailed checks totaling $48,500 were on hand at December 31 of the current year. He states that these December-dated checks had been entered in the cash disbursements journal and charged to the respective creditors' accounts in December because the checks were prenumbered. However, these checks were not actually mailed until early January. The controller wants to adjust the cash balance and accounts payable at December 31 by $48,500 because the Cash account had a credit balance. He objects to submitting to his bank your audit report showing an overdraft of cash.

Discuss the propriety of adjusting the cash balance and accounts payable by the indicated amount of outstanding checks.

11–41. You are retained to audit the financial statements of John Brown, an individual with extensive investments in real estate and ranching. In reviewing the general ledger, you notice an account entitled Davis Company, which has a debit balance of $150,000. Your investigation shows this to be the name of a local stockbrokerage firm with which your client had made a deposit for purchase of securities on margin. The only security transaction to date had been the purchase on December 10 of 3,000 shares of National Environmental Products at a price per share of $80. The brokerage fee on the transaction had been $1,566. No entry had been made for this purchase.

Give the adjusting entry or entries that you consider necessary for a proper presentation of these facts in the balance sheet at December 31.

11–42. Select the best answer for each of the following situations and give reasons for your choice.

a. You have been assigned to the year-end audit of a financial institution and are planning the timing of audit procedures relating to cash. You decide that it would be preferable for the auditors to:

(1) Count the cash in advance of the balance sheet date in order to disclose any kiting operations at year-end.

      (2) Coordinate the count of cash with the cutoff of accounts payable.

      (3) Coordinate the count of cash with the count of marketable securities and other negotiable assets.

      (4) Count the cash immediately upon the return of the bank confirmation letters.

b. To gather evidence on the balance per bank in a bank reconciliation, the auditors would examine all of the following *except—*

      (1) Cutoff bank statement.

      (2) Year-end bank statement.

      (3) Bank confirmation.

      (4) General ledger.

c. It is most likely that the auditors would detect an unrecorded check issued during the last week of the year when the—

      (1) Check register for the last month is reviewed.

      (2) Cutoff bank statement is reconciled.

      (3) Search for unrecorded liabilities is performed.

      (4) Bank confirmation is received.

d. Which of the following is an internal control procedure that would prevent a paid voucher from being presented for payment a second time?

      (1) Vouchers should be prepared by individuals who are responsible for signing checks.

      (2) Vouchers should be approved by at least two responsible officials.

      (3) The date on a voucher should be within a few days of the date the voucher is presented for payment.

      (4) The official signing the check should compare the check with the voucher and should perforate or otherwise deface the voucher and supporting documents.

e. In order to guard against the misappropriation of company-owned marketable securities, which of the following is the **best** course of action that can be taken by a company with a large portfolio of marketable securities?

      (1) Require that one trustworthy and bonded employee be responsible for access to the safekeeping area where securities are kept.

      (2) Require that employees who enter and leave the safekeeping area sign and record in a log the exact reason for their access.

      (3) Require that employees involved in the safekeeping function maintain a subsidiary control ledger for securities on a current basis.

      (4) Require that the safekeeping function for securities be assigned to a bank or stockbroker that will act as a custodial agent.

f. Hall Company had large amounts of funds to invest on a temporary basis. The board of directors decided to purchase marketable securities and assigned the future purchase and sale decisions to a responsible financial executive. The best person(s) to make periodic reviews of the investment activity would be:

      (1) An investment committee of the board of directors.

(2) The chief operating officer.

(3) The corporate controller.

(4) The treasurer.

**GROUP III:
PROBLEMS**

11–43. The Art Appreciation Society operates a museum for the benefit and enjoyment of the community. During hours when the museum is open to the public, two clerks who are positioned at the entrance collect a five-dollar admission fee from each nonmember patron. Members of the Art Appreciation Society are permitted to enter free of charge upon presentation of their membership cards.

At the end of each day one of the clerks delivers the proceeds to the treasurer. The treasurer counts the cash in the presence of the clerk and places it in a safe. Each Friday afternoon the treasurer and one of the clerks deliver all cash held in the safe to the bank, and receive an authenticated deposit slip that provides the basis for the weekly entry in the cash receipts journal.

The board of directors of the Art Appreciation Society has identified a need to improve their internal control over cash admission fees. The board has determined that the cost of installing turnstiles, sales booths, or otherwise altering the physical layout of the museum will greatly exceed any benefits which may be derived. However, the board has agreed that the sale of admission tickets must be an integral part of its improvement efforts.

Smith has been asked by the board of directors of the Art Appreciation Society to review the internal control over cash admission fees and provide suggestions for improvement.

Required:

Indicate weaknesses in the existing internal control over cash admission fees, which Smith should identify, and recommend one improvement for each of the weaknesses identified.

Organize the answer as indicated in the following illustrative example:

Weakness	Recommendation
1. There is no documentation to establish the number of paying patrons.	1. Prenumbered admission tickets should be issued upon payment of the admission fee.

(AICPA, adapted)

11–44. The following are typical questions that might appear on an internal control questionnaire for marketable securities.

1. Is custody of investment securities maintained by an employee who does not maintain the detailed records of the securities?

2. Are securities registered in the company name?

Required:

a. Describe the purpose of each of the above internal control procedures.

b. Describe the manner in which each of the above procedures might be tested.

c. Assuming that the operating effectiveness of each of the above procedures is found to be inadequate, describe how the auditors might alter their substantive tests to compensate for the internal control weakness.

11–45. The following client-prepared bank reconciliation is being examined by Kautz, CPA, during an examination of the financial statements of Cynthia Company:

CYNTHIA COMPANY
Bank Reconciliation
Village Bank Account 2
December 31, 1987

Balance per bank (a)		$18,375.91
Deposits in transit (b)		
12/30	$1,471.10	
12/31	2,840.69	4,311.79
Subtotal		22,687.70
Outstanding checks (c)		
837	6,000.00	
1941	671.80	
1966	320.00	
1984	1,855.42	
1985	3,621.22	
1987	2,576.89	
1991	4,420.88	(19,466.21)
Subtotal		3,221.49
NSF check returned		
12/29 (d)		200.00
Bank charges		5.50
Error Check No. 1932		148.10
Customer note collected		
by the bank ($2,750 plus		
$275 interest) (e)		(3,025.00)
Balance per books (f).		$ 550.09

Required:
Indicate one or more audit procedures that should be performed by Kautz in gathering evidence in support of each of the items (a) through (f) above. (AICPA, adapted)

11–46. The cashier of Mission Corporation intercepted customer A's check, payable to the company in the amount of $500, and deposited it in a bank account that was part of the company petty cash fund, of which he was custodian. He then drew a $500 check on the petty cash fund bank account payable to himself, signed it, and cashed it. At the end of the month, while processing the monthly statements to customers, he was able to change the statement to customer A to show that A had received credit for the $500 check that had been intercepted. Ten days later he made an entry in the cash receipts journal that purported to record receipt of a remittance of $500 from customer A, thus restoring A's account to its proper balance but overstating cash in the bank. He covered the overstatement by omitting from the list of outstanding checks in the bank reconciliation two checks, the aggregate amount of which was $500.

Required:
Discuss briefly what you regard as the more important deficiencies in internal control in the above situation and in addition include what you consider a proper remedy for each deficiency.

(AICPA, adapted)

11–47. You are the senior in charge of the July 31, 198X, audit of Reliable Auto Parts, Inc. Your newly hired staff assistant reports to you that she is unable to complete the four-column proof of cash for the month of April 198X, which you instructed her to do as part of the consideration of internal control for cash.

Your assistant shows you the following working paper that she has prepared:

RELIABLE AUTO PARTS, INC.
Proof of Cash for April 198X
July 31, 198X

	Balance 3/31/8X	Deposits	Checks	Balance 4/30/8X
Per bank statement	71,682.84	61,488.19	68,119.40	65,051.63
Deposits in transit:				
At 3/31/8X	2,118.18			(2,118.18)
At 4/30/8X		4,918.16		4,918.16
Outstanding checks:				
At 3/31/8X	(14,888.16)		14,888.16	
At 4/30/8X			(22,914.70)	22,914.70
Bank service charges:				
March 198X	(22.18)		22.18	
April 198X			(19.14)	19.14
Note receivable collected by bank 4/30/8X		18,180.00		18,180.00
NSF check of customer L. G. Waite, charged back by bank 3/31/8X, redeposited and cleared 4/3/8X	(418.19)	418.19		
Balances as computed	58,472.49	85,004.54	60,095.90	108,965.45
Balances per books	59,353.23	45,689.98	76,148.98	28,894.23
Unlocated difference	(880.74)	39,314.56	(16,053.08)	80,071.22

Your review of your assistant's work reveals that the dollar amounts of all of the items in her working paper are correct. You learn that the accountant for Reliable Auto Parts, Inc., makes no journal entries for bank services charges or note collections until the month following the bank's recording of the item and that Reliable's accountant makes no journal entries whatsoever for NSF checks that are redeposited and cleared.

Required:

Prepare a corrected four-column proof of cash in good form for Reliable Auto Parts, Inc., for the month of April 198X.

11–48. During the audit of Sunset Building Supply, you are given the following year-end bank reconciliation prepared by the client:

SUNSET BUILDING SUPPLY
Bank Reconciliation
December 31

Balance per 12/31 bank statement.	$48,734
Add: Deposits in transit.	4,467
	53,201
Less: Checks outstanding.	20,758
Balance per ledger, 12/31	$32,443

According to the client's accounting records, checks totaling $31,482 were issued between January 1 and January 14 of the following year. You have obtained a cutoff bank statement dated January 14 containing paid checks amounting to $50,440. Of the checks outstanding at December 31, $3,600 were not returned in the cutoff statement, and of those issued per the accounting records in January, $8,200 were not returned.

Required:

a. Prepare a working paper comparing (1) the total of all checks returned by the bank or still outstanding with (2) the total per the client's records of checks outstanding at December 31 plus checks issued from January 1–14.

b. Suggest four possible explanations for the situation disclosed in your working paper. State what action you would take in each case, including any adjusting entry you would propose.

11–49. In connection with an examination of the financial statements of Morton, Inc., Jane Hill, CPA, is considering the necessity of inspecting marketable securities on the balance sheet date, May 31, or at some other date. The marketable securities held by Morton include negotiable bearer bonds, which are kept in a safe in the treasurer's office, and miscellaneous stocks and bonds kept in a safe-deposit box at The City Bank. Both the negotiable bearer bonds and the miscellaneous stocks and bonds are material to proper presentation of Morton's financial position.

Required:

a. What are the factors that Hill should consider in determining the necessity for inspecting these securities on May 31, as opposed to other dates?

b. Assume that Hill plans to send a member of her staff to Morton's offices and The City Bank on May 31 to make the security inspection. What instructions should she give to this staff member as to the conduct of the inspection and the evidence to be included in the audit working papers? (*Note:* Do not discuss the valuation of securities, the revenue from securities, or the examination of information contained in the accounting records of the company.)

c. Assume that Hill finds it impracticable to send a member of her staff to Morton's offices and The City Bank on May 31. What alternative procedures may she employ to assure herself that the company had physical possession of its marketable securities on May 31, if the securities are inspected (1) May 28? (2) June 5?

(AICPA, adapted)

11–50. MLG Company's auditor received confirmations and cutoff statements with related checks and deposit tickets for MLG's three general-purpose bank accounts directly from the banks. The auditor determined that internal control over cash was satisfactory and will be relied upon. The proper cutoff of external cash receipts and disbursements was established. No bank accounts were opened or closed during the year.

Required:

Prepare the audit program of substantive procedures to verify MLG's bank balances. Ignore any other cash accounts.   (AICPA, adapted)

11–51. You are in charge of the audit of the financial statements of Hawk Corporation for the year ended December 31. The corporation has had the policy of investing its surplus cash in marketable securities. Its stock and bond certificates are kept in a safe-deposit box in a local bank. Only the president or the treasurer of the corporation has access to the box.

You were unable to obtain access to the safe-deposit box on December 31 because neither the president nor the treasurer was available. Arrangements were made for your staff assistant to accompany the treasurer to the bank on January 11 to examine the securities. Your assistant has never examined securities that were being kept in a safe-deposit box and requires instructions. To inspect all the securities on hand should not require more than one hour.

Required:

a. List the instructions that you would give to your assistant regarding the examination of the stock and bond certificates kept in the safe-deposit box. Include in your instructions the details of the securities to be examined and the reasons for examining these details.

b. Upon returning from the bank, your assistant reported that the treasurer had entered the box on January 4. The treasurer stated that the purpose of the January 4 visit to the safe-deposit box had been to remove an old photograph of the corporation's original building. The photograph was reportedly loaned to the local chamber of commerce for display purposes. List the additional audit procedures that are required because of the treasurer's action. (AICPA)

GROUP IV: RESEARCH AND DISCUSSION CASE

11–52. On October 21, Rand & Brink, a CPA firm, was retained by Suncraft Appliance Corporation to perform an audit for the year ended December 31. A month later James Minor, president of the corporation, invited the CPA firm's partners, George Rand and Alice Brink, to attend a meeting of all officers of the corporation. Mr. Minor opened the meeting with the following statement:

"All of you know that we are not in a very liquid position, and our October 31 balance sheet shows it. We need to raise some outside capital in January, and our December 31 financial statements (both balance sheet and income statement) must look reasonably good if we're going to make a favorable impression upon lenders or investors. I want every officer of this company to do everything possible during the next month to ensure that, at December 31, our financial statements look as strong as possible, especially our current position and our earnings."

"I have invited our auditors to attend this meeting so they will understand the reason for some year-end transactions that might be a little unusual. It is essential that our financial statements carry the auditors' approval, or we'll never be able to get the financing we need. Now what suggestions can you offer?"

The vice president for sales was first to offer suggestions: "I can talk some of our large customers into placing some orders in December that they wouldn't ordinarily place until the first part of next year. If we get those extra orders shipped, it will increase this year's earnings and also increase our current assets."

The vice president in charge of production commented: "We can ship every order we have now and every order we get during December before the close of business on December 31. We'll have to pay some overtime in our shipping department, but we'll try not to have a single unshipped order on hand at year-end. Also, we could overship some orders, and the customers wouldn't make returns until January."

The controller spoke next: "If there are late December orders from customers that we can't actually ship, we can just label the merchandise as sold and bill the customers with December 31 sales invoices. Also, there are always some checks from customers dated December 31 that don't reach us until January—some as late as January 10. We can record all those customers' checks bearing dates of late December as part of our December 31 cash balance."

The treasurer offered the following suggestions: "I owe the company $50,000 on a call note I issued to buy some of our stock. I can borrow $50,000 from my mother-in-law about Christmas time and repay my note to the company. However, I'll have to borrow the money from the company again early in January, because my mother-in-law is buying an apartment building and will need the $50,000 back by January 15.

"Another thing we can do to improve our current ratio is to write checks on December 31 to pay most of our current liabilities. We might even wait to mail the checks for a few days or mail them to the wrong addresses. That will give time for the January cash receipts to cover the December 31 checks.''

The vice president of production made two final suggestions: "Some of our inventory, which we had tentatively identified as obsolete, does not represent an open and shut case of being unsalable. We could defer any write-down until next year. Another item is some machinery we have ordered for delivery in December. We could instruct the manufacturer not to ship the machines and not to bill us before January.''

After listening to these suggestions, the president, James Minor, spoke directly to Rand and Brink, the auditors. "You can see I'm doing my best to give you full information and cooperation. If any of these suggested actions would prevent you from giving a clean bill of health to our year-end statements, I want to know about it now so we can avoid doing anything that would keep you from issuing an unqualified audit report. I know you'll be doing a lot of preliminary work here before December 31, but I'd like for you not to bill us before January. Will you please give us your reactions to what has been said in this meeting?''

Required:

a. Put yourself in the role of Rand & Brink, CPAs, and evaluate *separately* each suggestion made in the meeting. What general term is applicable to most of the suggested actions?

b. Could you assure the client that an unqualified audit report would be issued if your recommendations were followed on all the matters discussed? Explain.

c. Would the discussion in this meeting cause you to withdraw from the engagement?

Suggested references:

Appropriate chapters from any intermediate accounting textbook.

This textbook, pages 402–3.

Accounts receivable, notes receivable, and sales transactions

Chapter 12 study objectives

After studying this chapter, you should be able to:

— Describe the nature of receivables.
— Explain the nature of the sales and collection transaction cycle.
— Identify and explain the fundamental internal controls over sales transactions and receivables.
— Describe the auditors' objectives for the audit of receivables.
— Describe the nature of the audit procedures to accomplish the auditors' objectives for the audit of receivables.

Because sales transactions and receivables from customers are so closely related, the two can best be considered jointly in a discussion of auditing objectives and procedures. In broad terms, the sales and collection cycle includes the receiving of orders from customers, the delivery and billing of merchandise to customers, and the recording and collection of accounts receivable. Receivables from customers include both accounts receivable and various types of notes receivable.

RECEIVABLES

Sources and nature of accounts receivable

Accounts receivable include not only claims against customers arising from the sale of goods or services, but also a variety of miscellaneous claims such as loans to officers or employees, loans to subsidiaries, uncollected stock subscriptions, claims against various other firms, claims for tax refunds, and advances to suppliers.

Trade notes and accounts receivable usually are relatively large in amount and should appear as separate items in the current assets section of the balance sheet at their net realizable value. Auditors are especially concerned with the presentation and disclosure of loans to officers, directors, and affiliated companies. These related party transactions are commonly made for the convenience of the borrower rather than to benefit the lending company. Consequently, such loans are often collected only at the convenience of the borrower. It is a basic tenet of financial statement presentation that transactions not characterized by arm's-length bargaining should be fully disclosed.

Sources and nature of notes receivable

Typically, notes receivable are used for handling transactions of substantial amount; these negotiable documents are widely used by both industrial and commercial concerns. In banks and finance companies, notes receivable usually constitute the single most important asset.

An installment note or contract is a negotiable instrument that grants possession of the goods to the purchaser but permits the seller to retain a lien on the goods until the final installment under the note has been received. Installment notes are widely used in the sale of industrial machinery, farm equipment, tractors, and automobiles. Other transactions that may lead to the acquisition of notes receivable include the disposal of items of plant and equipment, the sale of divisions of a company, the issuance of capital stock, and the making of loans to officers, employees, and affiliated companies.

The auditors' objectives in examination of receivables

The auditors' objectives are to determine that:

1. *Internal control* over receivables is adequate.
2. The recorded receivables are valid (*existence and rights*).
3. All receivables are recorded (*completeness*).
4. Receivable records and supporting schedules are mathematically correct and agree with general ledger accounts (*clerical accuracy*).

5. The *valuation* of receivables approximates their realizable values.
6. The *presentation* and *disclosure* of receivables is adequate, including the separation of receivables into appropriate categories, and adequate reporting of any receivables pledged as collateral and related party receivables.

In conjunction with the audit of receivables, the auditors will also obtain evidence concerning the recorded amounts of sales revenue and interest income from receivables.

The objective of determining the validity of the recorded receivables deals with (1) determining the genuineness of customers' accounts and notes and (2) determining whether generally accepted accounting principles have been followed in the establishment of the receivables. The genuineness of receivables may be addressed by examining client controls over issuance of sales invoices, shipping documents, and other evidence of claims against customers. Establishing whether generally accepted accounting principles have been followed often includes an analysis of estimates made by management in areas such as the capitalization of leases and the sale of franchises.

Completeness addresses the question of whether other receivables have been omitted. Improper cutoffs of either sales or collections may result in errors affecting both validity and completeness. For example, cash received after year-end may be treated as having been received prior to year-end (resulting in a validity problem), or credit sales made toward the end of the year may have been included in the subsequent year's first month (resulting in a completeness problem).

Proper valuation, the fifth objective, requires that receivables be recorded at their expected net realizable value. Analysis of the allowance for doubtful accounts and bad debt expense helps the auditors to meet this objective. The balances of these accounts are based almost entirely on management's estimates (aided by past results) and are therefore considered to have a high degree of inherent risk. The final objective, determining the adequacy of presentation and disclosure, includes consideration of the separate classification of receivables into appropriate categories, reporting of receivables pledged as collateral, and related party transactions.

Internal control of sales transactions and accounts receivable

Our discussion of internal control will be developed primarily in terms of the sales activities of manufacturing companies. When internal controls over sales on account are inadequate, large credit losses are almost inevitable. For example, merchandise may be shipped to customers whose credit standing has not been approved. Shipments may be made to customers without notice being given to the billing department; consequently, no sales invoice is prepared. Sales invoices may contain errors in prices and quantities; and if sales invoices are not controlled by serial numbers, some may be lost and never recorded as accounts receivable. To avoid such difficulties, strong internal controls over credit sales are necessary. Usually internal control over credit sales is strengthened by a division of duties so that different departments or individuals are responsible for (1) preparation of the sales order, (2) credit approval, (3) issuance of merchandise from stock, (4) shipment, (5) billing, (6) invoice verification, (7) maintenance of control accounts, (8) maintenance of customers' ledgers, (9) approval of sales returns and allowances, and (10) authorization of write-offs of uncollectible accounts. When this degree of subdivision of duties is feasible, accidental errors are likely to be detected quickly through the comparison of documents and amounts emerging from independent units of the company, and the opportunity for fraud is reduced to a minimum.

Controlling customers' orders   The controlling and processing of orders received from customers require carefully designed operating procedures and numerous control devices if costly errors are to be avoided. Important initial steps include the registering of the customer's purchase order, a review of items and quantities to determine whether the order can be filled within a reasonable time, and the preparation of a sales order. The sales order is a translation of the terms of the customer's order into a set of specific instructions for the guidance of various divisions, including the credit, finished goods stores, shipping, billing, and accounts receivable units. The action to be taken by the factory upon receipt of a sales order will depend upon whether the goods are standard products carried in stock or are to be produced to specifications set by the customer.

Credit approval   Before sales orders are processed, the credit department must determine whether goods may be shipped to the customer on open account. This department is supervised by a credit manager who reports to the treasurer or the vice president of finance. The credit department monitors the financial condition of prospective and continuing customers by study of the customers' financial statements and by reference to reports of credit agencies.

Issuance of merchandise   Companies that carry standard products in stock maintain a finished goods storeroom supervised by a storeskeeper. The storeskeeper issues the goods covered by a sales order to the shipping department only after the sales order has been approved by the credit department. Perpetual inventory records of finished goods are maintained in the accounting department, not by the storeskeeper.

The shipping function   When the goods are transmitted by the finished goods storeroom to the shipping department, this group must arrange for space in railroad cars, aircraft, or motor freight carriers. Shipping documents, such as bills of lading, are created at the time of loading the goods into cars or trucks. The shipping documents are numerically controlled and are entered in a shipping register before being forwarded to the billing department. When shipments are made by truck, some type of gate control is also needed to ensure that all goods leaving the plant have been recorded as shipments. This may require the surrender to the gatekeeper of special copies of shipping documents.

The billing function   The term *billing* means notifying the customer of the amount due for goods or services delivered. This notification is accomplished by preparing and mailing a sales invoice. Billing should be performed by a department not under the control of sales executives. The function is generally assigned to a separate section within the accounting, data processing, or finance departments. The billing section has the responsibility of (1) accounting for the serially numbered shipping documents, (2) comparing shipping documents with sales orders and customers' purchase orders and change notices, (3) entering pertinent data from these documents on the sales invoice, (4) applying prices and discounts from price lists to the invoice, (5) making the necessary extensions and footings, and (6) accumulating the total amounts billed. In the case of government contracts, the formal contract usually specifies prices, delivery procedures, inspection and acceptance routines, method of liquidating advances, and numerous other details, so that the contract is a more important source of information for preparation of the sales invoice.

Before invoices are mailed to customers, they should be reviewed to determine the propriety and accuracy of prices, credit terms, transportation charges, extensions, and footings. Daily totals of amounts invoiced should be transmitted directly to the general ledger accounting section for entry in controlling accounts. Copies of individual invoices should be transmitted to the accounts receivable section under the control of transmittal letters, with a listing by serial number of all invoices being submitted.

Collection of receivables   Most receivables held by manufacturing companies are collected by receipt of customers checks and remittance advices through the mails. The cashier will control and deposit checks. The remittance advices or a listing of the receipts will then be forwarded to the accounts receivable section or the data processing department, which will record them in the appropriate accounts in the customers' ledger. The total reduction in accounts receivable will be posted periodically to the general ledger control account from the total of the accounts receivable column in the cash receipts journal. Internal control over collections from customers is shown in the cash receipt flowchart in Figure 11–1 of Chapter 11.

An *aged trial balance* of customers' accounts should be prepared at regular intervals for use by the credit department in carrying out its collection program. Under this system the general ledger and the subsidiary ledger for accounts receivable are developed from separate data by employees working independently of each other, thus assuring detection of nearly all accidental errors. Fraud becomes unlikely except in the event of collusion of two or more employees. The subsidiary ledger should be balanced periodically with the control account by an employee from the operations control group.

Write-off of receivables Receivables judged by management to be uncollectible should be written off (after review by the credit department) and transferred to a separate ledger and control account. This record may be of a memorandum nature rather than part of the regular accounting structure, but it is essential that the accounts that are written off be properly controlled. Also, statements should continue to be mailed to the debtors requesting payment. Otherwise, any subsequent collections may be abstracted by employees without the necessity of any falsification of the records to conceal the theft.

Internal audit of receivables In some large companies, the internal auditors periodically take over the mailing of monthly statements to customers and investigate any discrepancies reported; or they may make extensive reviews of shipping reports, invoices, credit memoranda, and aged trial balances of receivables to determine whether authorized procedures are being carried out consistently.

The division of responsibility, sequence of procedures, and basic documentation of the handling of credit sales transactions are illustrated in the systems flowcharts in Figure 12–1.

Internal control of notes receivable

As previously stated, a basic element of internal control consists of the subdivision of duties. As applied to notes receivable, this principle requires that—

1. The custodian of notes receivable not have access to cash or to the general accounting records.
2. The acceptance and renewal of notes be authorized in writing by a responsible official who does not have custody of the notes.
3. The write-off of defaulted notes be approved in writing by responsible officials and effective procedures adopted for subsequent follow-up of such defaulted notes.

These rules are obviously corollaries of the general proposition that the authorization and recording functions should be entirely separate from the custodial function, especially for cash and receivables.

If the acceptance of a note from a customer requires written approval of a responsible official, the likelihood of fictitious notes being created to offset a theft of cash is materially reduced. The same review and approval

Figure 12–1

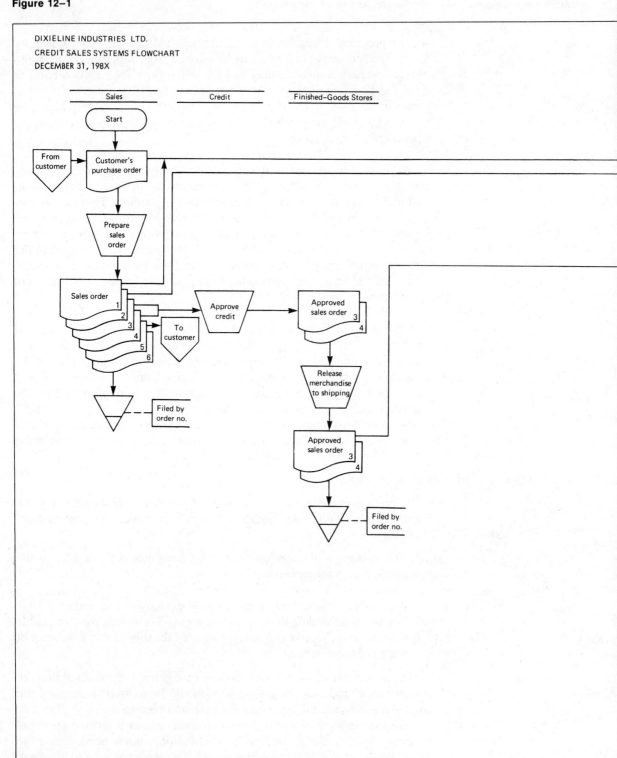

DIXIELINE INDUSTRIES LTD.
CREDIT SALES SYSTEMS FLOWCHART
DECEMBER 31, 198X

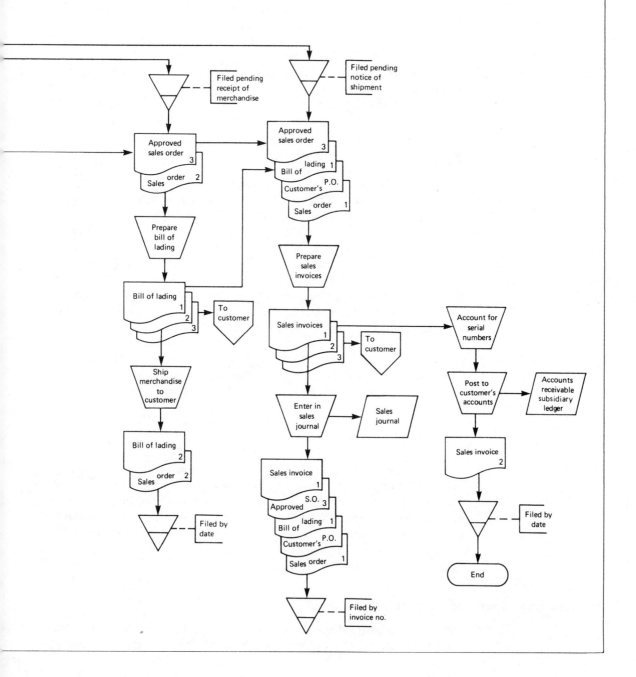

should be required for renewal of a note; otherwise, an opportunity is created for the diversion of cash when a note is collected and the concealment of a shortage by unauthorized renewal of the paid note. The protection given by this procedure for executive approval of notes will be stronger if the internal auditing department periodically confirms notes directly with the makers.

The abstraction of cash receipts is sometimes concealed by failing to make any entry to record receipt of a partial payment on a note. Satisfactory control procedures for recording partial payments require that the date and amount of the payment and the new unpaid balance should be entered on the back of the instrument, with proper credit being given the debtor in the note register. Any notes written off as uncollectible should be kept under accounting control because occasionally debtors may attempt to reestablish their credit in later years by paying old dishonored notes. Any credit memoranda or journal vouchers for partial payments, write-offs, or adjustment of disputed notes should be authorized by proper officials and kept under numerical control.

Adequate internal controls over notes receivable secured by mortgages and trust deeds must include follow-up procedures that assure prompt action on delinquent property taxes and insurance premiums, as well as for nonpayment of interest and principal installments.

In many companies, internal control is strengthened by the preparation of monthly reports summarizing notes receivable transactions during the month and the details of notes owned at the end of the reporting period. These reports are often designed to focus executive attention immediately upon any delinquent notes and to require advance approval for renewals of maturing notes. In addition, a monthly report on notes receivable ordinarily will show the amounts collected during the month, the new notes accepted, notes discounted, and interest earned. The person responsible for reporting on note transactions should be someone other than the custodian of the notes.

Internal control and the computer

EDP systems permit instantaneous verification of customers' credit limits, recording of sales transactions, preparation of sales invoices, updating of customer account balances, and maintenance of inventory records. In such systems, the chance of mechanical error is virtually eliminated. However, the auditors must consider internal control over EDP operations to determine that no individual is in a position to make unauthorized changes in programs or files.

Audit working papers for receivables and sales

Besides preparing lead schedules for receivables and net sales, the auditors obtain or prepare the following working papers, among others:

1. Aged trial balance of trade accounts receivable (often a computer printout).
2. Analyses of other accounts receivable.
3. Analysis of notes receivable and related interest.
4. Analysis of allowance for uncollectible accounts and notes.
5. Comparative analyses of sales transactions by month, by product or territory, or relating forecasted sales to actual sales.

AUDIT PROGRAM FOR RECEIVABLES AND SALES TRANSACTIONS

The following audit procedures are typical of the work done in the verification of notes, accounts receivable, and sales transactions.

A. **Consider internal control for receivables and sales**
   1. *Obtain an understanding of internal control* for receivables and sales.
   2. *Assess control risk* and *design additional tests of controls* for receivables and sales.
   3. *Perform additional tests of controls* for those controls which the auditors plan to rely upon to restrict their assessment of control risk and, thus, reduce the extent of substantive testing, such as:
      a. Examine significant aspects of a sample of sales transactions.
      b. Compare a sample of shipping documents to related sales invoices.
      c. Review the use and authorization of credit memoranda.
      d. Reconcile selected cash register tapes and sales tickets with sales journals.
   4. *Reassess control risk* and *design substantive tests* for receivables and sales.

B. **Perform substantive tests of receivables and sales transactions**
   5. Obtain an aged trial balance of trade accounts receivables and analyses of other accounts receivable and reconcile to ledgers.
   6. Obtain analyses of notes receivable and related interest.
   7. Inspect notes on hand and confirm those not on hand with holders.
   8. Confirm receivables with debtors.
   9. Review the year-end cutoff of sales transactions.
   10. Perform analytical procedures for accounts receivable, sales, notes receivable, and interest revenue.
   11. Verify interest earned on notes and accrued interest receivable.
   12. Determine adequacy of allowance for uncollectible accounts.
   13. Ascertain whether any receivables have been pledged.
   14. Investigate fully any notes or accounts receivable from related parties.
   15. Evaluate financial statement presentation and disclosure of receivables and sales.

16. Review propriety of client's accounting for transactions resulting in receivables and sales.

Figure 12–2 relates these major substantive tests of receivables and sales
to their primary audit objectives.

**Figure 12–2 Objectives
of major substantive
tests of receivables and
sales transactions**

Substantive tests	Primary audit objectives
Obtain aged listing of receivables and recon- cile to ledgers Obtain analyses of notes receivable and related interest	*Clerical accuracy*
Inspect notes on hand and confirm those not on hand Confirm receivables with debtors	*Validity (existence and rights)*
Review the year-end cutoff of sales transactions Perform analytical procedures Verify interest earned on notes receivable	*Validity (existence and rights) Completeness*
Determine adequacy of allowance for uncollect- ible accounts	*Valuation*
Ascertain the existence of pledged receivables Investigate receivables from related parties Evaluate financial statement presentation and disclosure	*Presentation and disclosure*
Review propriety of client's accounting for transactions	*All objectives*

A. Consider internal control for receivables and sales
1. Obtain an understanding of internal control.

The auditors' consideration of internal controls over receivables and
sales may begin with the preparation of a written description or flowchart
or the filling in of an internal control questionnaire. Typical of the questions comprising an internal control questionnaire for receivables and
sales are the following: Are orders from customers recorded and reviewed
by a sales department? Are sales invoices prenumbered and all numbers
accounted for? Are all sales approved by the credit department before
shipment? The questionnaire should be viewed as an enumeration of matters to be investigated, rather than as questions to be disposed of with
yes or no answers.

2. Assess control risk and design additional tests of controls.

Control risk for a financial statement assertion may be assessed below
the maximum only when tests indicate that related controls are designed
and operating effectively. The auditors must decide which additional tests

of controls will likely result in cost justified restrictions of substantive tests.

3. Perform additional tests of controls.

a. Examine all significant aspects of a sample of sales transactions.

To determine that the internal controls portrayed in the flowchart are actually functioning in everyday operations, the auditors will examine significant aspects of a sample of sales transactions. The size of the sample and the transactions included therein may be determined by either statistical or nonstatistical sampling techniques. The auditors often use generalized computer audit programs to select the transactions to be tested.

In manufacturing companies, the audit procedure for verification of a sales transaction that has been selected for testing may begin with a comparison of the customer's purchase order, the client's sales order, and the duplicate copy of the sales invoice. The descriptions of items and the quantities are compared on these three documents and traced to the duplicate copy of the related shipping document. The credit manager's signature denoting approval of the customer's credit should appear on the sales order.

The extensions and footings on each invoice in the sample should be proved to be arithmetically correct. In addition, the date of each invoice should be compared with two other dates:

a. The date on the related shipping document.
b. The date of entry in the accounts receivable subsidiary ledger.

Prices on the invoices can be verified by comparison with price lists, catalogs, or other sources used in preparing invoices. Bills of lading and freight bills may also be compared with invoices as a further test of validity of the invoices.

After proving the accuracy of selected individual invoices, the auditors next trace the invoices to the sales journal. The footing of the sales journal is proven, and the total is traced to the general ledger account for sales.

In summary, this process of testing consists of tracing each selected transaction through the system from the receipt of the customer's order to the shipment of the goods and the subsequent collection of the account receivable. Testing in the opposite direction may also be used; for example, entries in the sales journal may be selected for vouching to supporting invoices, customer purchase orders, and shipping documents. By these tests, the auditors should obtain evidence that all sales are being accurately and promptly billed, that billings do not include any anticipated sales or extraneous transactions, and that the amounts billed are accurately and promptly recorded in customer's ledgers and in controlling accounts. If these conditions prevail, the auditors are entitled to rely upon the changes appearing in customers' accounts.

When performing tests of sales transactions, the auditors should be alert for indications of consignment shipments treated as sales. Some concerns that dispose of only a small portion of their total output by consignment shipments fail to make any distinction between consignment shipments and regular sales.

If the subsidiary records for receivables include some accounts with large debit entries and more numerous small credit entries, this should suggest to the auditors that goods have been shipped on consignment and that payments are being received only as the consignee makes sales. Notations such as "Consignment shipment" or "On approval" are sometimes found in subsidiary ledgers or on the duplicate copies of sales invoices. Numerous large returns of merchandise are also suggestive of consignment shipments.

A clearly defined company policy with respect to *cash discounts on sales* is a necessary element of good internal control over sales transactions. After discussing the policy with management, the auditors will scan the cash receipts journal to observe any deviations from established rates.

Another approach in reviewing the propriety of recorded cash discounts is to analyze by months the dollar amount of collections on receivables, the dollar amount of cash discounts allowed, and the percentage relationship of discounts to collections. Any significant variations should be fully investigated. Comparison, period by period, of the ratio of cash discounts to net credit sales is also a useful step in bringing to light variations of substantial amount.

The auditors should also investigate the controls for sales to related parties. Effective control over intercompany or interbranch transfers of merchandise often requires the same kind of formal procedures for billing, shipping, and collection functions as for sales to outsiders; hence, these movements of merchandise are often invoiced and recorded as sales. When the operations of the several organizational units are combined or consolidated into one income statement, however, it is apparent that any transactions not representing sales to outsiders should be eliminated from consolidated sales. In the examination of a client that operates subsidiaries or branches, the auditors should investigate the procedures for recording movements of merchandise among the various units of the company.

b.   Compare a sample of shipping documents to related sales invoices.

The preceding step in the audit program called for an examination of selected sales transactions and a comparison of the invoices with sales records and shipping documents. That procedure would not, however, disclose orders that had been shipped but not billed. To assure that all shipments are billed, it is necessary for the auditors to obtain a sample of shipping documents issued during the year and to compare these to sales invoices. In making this test, particular emphasis should be placed upon accounting for all shipping documents by serial number. Any voided shipping documents should have been mutilated and retained in the files. The purposeful or accidental destruction of shipping documents before the creation of a sales invoice might go undetected if this type of test were not made. Correlation of serial numbers of sales orders, shipping advices, and sales invoices is highly desirable.

c. Review the use and authorization of credit memoranda.

All allowances to customers for returned or defective merchandise should be supported by serially numbered credit memoranda signed by an officer or responsible employee having no duties relating to handling cash or to the maintenance of customers' ledgers. Good internal control over credits for returned merchandise usually includes a requirement that the returned goods be received and examined before credit is given. The memoranda should then bear the date and serial number of the receiving report on the return shipment.

In addition to establishing that credit memoranda were properly authorized, the auditors should make tests of these documents similar to those suggested for sales invoices. Prices, extensions, and footings should be verified, and postings traced from the sales return journal or other accounting record to the customers' accounts in the subsidiary receivable ledgers.

d. Reconcile selected cash register tapes and sales tickets with sales journals.

In the audit of clients that make a substantial amount of sales for cash, the auditors may compare selected daily totals in the sales journal with cash register readings or tapes. The serial numbers of all sales tickets used during the selected periods should be accounted for and the individual tickets examined for accuracy of calculations and traced to the sales summary or journal.

4. Reassess control risk and design substantive tests.

When the auditors have completed the procedures described in the preceding sections, they should assess the extent of control risk for each financial statement assertion regarding receivables and sales transactions. In their assessment, the auditors will identify those weaknesses that require extension of substantive procedures and those strengths that permit curtailment of procedures.

B. Substantive tests

5. Obtain an aged trial balance of trade accounts receivable and analyses of other accounts receivable and reconcile to ledgers.

An aged trial balance of trade accounts receivable at the audit date is commonly prepared by employees of the client for the auditors, often in the form of a computer printout. The client-prepared schedule illustrated in Figure 12–3 is a multipurpose format designed to display the aging of customers' accounts, the estimate of probable credit losses, and the confirmation control information. The summary of so many phases of the examination of receivables in a single working paper is practicable only for small concerns with a limited number of customers. If the client has any accounts receivable other than trade accounts, the auditors also should obtain similar analyses of those accounts.

When trial balances or analyses of accounts receivable are furnished to

Figure 12–3

The Coast Company
Accounts Receivable—Trade
December 31, 198X

Acct. No. 121   G-1

Confirmation No.	Customer	Balance Dec. 31, 8X	Billed In December	Billed In November	Billed In October	Prior Months	Credit Balances	Collections Subsequent to Dec. 31, 8X	Estimated Uncollectible Amount Acct. No. 125
1	Adams & Sons	cx 8255.60 u	7921.60 λ		334.00 λ			7921.60	
2	Baker Company, Inc.	c 205.00 u		205.00 λ				205.00	
3	Cross Mfg. Co., Inc.	c 7310.20 u	1500.20 λ	1210.00 λ	500.00	4100.00 λ		4100.00	
	Douglas Supply Co.	22.00 u							22.00
4	Elastic Mfg. Co., Inc.	c 1250.00 u	1250.00 λ					1250.00	
	J. R. Farmer	3000.00 u	3000.00 λ						
64	Young Industries	cx 1825.00 u	1575.00 λ			250.00		47.19	91250
	Zenith Co.	47.19 u	47.19 λ						
		78624.62	48801.67	21245.60	2875.30	6302.15	(600.00)		4100.00
A.J.E. 12—Quest J.R. Farmer G-2		(3000.00)	(3000.00)						
		75624.62 u✓	45801.67 u✓	21245.60 u	2875.20 u	6302.15 u	(600.00)		4100.00 u
		G							G

A.J.E. 12
Accounts Receivable—Officers   3000.00
    Accounts Receivable—Trade   3000.00
Correct classification of account
receivable from J. R. Farmer,
President.

Prepared by client

u = Footed and cross-footed   ✓ = Agreed to general ledger } no differences noted
λ = Traced to accounts receivable subsidiary ledger.
ι = Verified aging.
c = Confirmed; no exceptions.
cx = Confirmed with exceptions. See G-1-1.

    See audit program (B-2) for extent of confirmation and
other auditing procedures.

Conclusion:
    The results of the confirmation and other tests described in the audit program (B-2)
provide sufficient appropriate evidence of existence of, and rights to, trade
accounts receivable in the aggregate amount of $75,624.62.

                                                                V.M.H.
                                                                Jan. 20, 8X

the auditors by the client's employees, some independent verification of the listing is essential. Determination of the proper extent of testing should be made in relation to the adequacy of the internal controls over receivables. The auditors should test footings, crossfootings, and agings. In testing the aging, it is important to test some accounts classified as current, as well as those shown as past due. These selected accounts should be traced to the subsidiary ledgers. The totals of schedules prepared by client personnel should also be compared with related controlling accounts. In addition, the balances of the subsidiary ledger records should be verified by footing the debit and credit columns on a test basis. Generalized computer audit programs may be used to perform these tests when the client's accounts receivable are processed by an electronic data processing system.

6. Obtain analyses of notes receivable and related interest.

An analysis of notes receivable supporting the general ledger controlling account may be prepared for the auditors by the client's staff. The information to be included in the analysis normally will include the name of the maker, date, maturity, amount, and interest rate. In addition to verifying the accuracy of the analysis prepared by the client, the auditors should trace selected items to the accounting records and to the notes themselves.

7. Inspect notes on hand and confirm those not on hand with holders.

The inspection of notes receivable on hand should be performed concurrently with the count of cash and securities to prevent the concealment of a shortage by substitution of cash for misappropriated negotiable instruments, or vice versa. Any securities held by the client as collateral for notes receivable should be inspected and listed at the same time. Complete control over all negotiable instruments should be maintained by the auditors until the count and inspection are completed.

Notes receivable owned by the client may be held by others at the time of the examination. Confirmation in writing from the *holder* of the note is considered as an acceptable alternative to inspection; it does not, however, eliminate the need for securing confirmation from the *maker* of the note. The confirmation letter sent to a bank, collection agency, secured creditor, or other holder should contain a request for verification of the name of the maker, the balance of the note, the interest rate, and the due date.

Confirmation of notes receivable discounted or pledged as collateral with banks is obtained in connection with the verification of cash on deposit, since the standard form of bank confirmation request includes specific inquiry on these matters.

Printed note forms are readily available at any bank; an unscrupulous officer or employee of the client company desiring to create a fictitious note could do so by obtaining a bank note form and filling in the amount, date, maturity, and signature. The relative ease of creating a forged or fictitious note suggests that physical inspection by the auditors represents a less significant and conclusive audit procedure in verification of notes receivable than for cash or securities.

8. Confirm receivables with debtors.

The term *confirmation* was defined in Chapter 7 as a type of documentary evidence secured from outside the client organization and transmitted directly to the auditors. Direct communication with debtors is the most essential and conclusive step in the verification of accounts and notes receivable. By confirming an account receivable, the auditors prove that the customer *exists.* Written acknowledgment of the debt by the debtor serves the dual purposes of (*a*) establishing the existence of the asset and (*b*) providing some assurance that no lapping or other manipulations affecting receivables is being carried on at the balance sheet date. However, the confirmation of a receivable does not mean that it is collectible.

A better understanding of the emphasis placed on confirmation of receivables can be gained by a brief review of auditing history. Audit objectives and procedures were drastically revised in the late 1940s. Before that time the usual audit did not include procedures to assure that the receivables were genuine claims against existing companies or that inventories actually existed and had been accurately counted. For the auditors to confirm receivables (or to observe the taking of physical inventory) was considered too expensive and not particularly important. Auditors generally relied in that early era upon a written statement by management concerning the validity of receivables and the existence of inventories. This approach was drastically revised after some spectacular fraud cases involving millions of dollars in fictitious receivables and inventories showed the need for stronger audit evidence.

The following quotation from *SAS 1* summarizes the current status of the confirmation procedure.

> Confirmation of receivables . . . (is a) generally accepted auditing procedure. The independent auditor who issues an opinion when he has not employed . . . (confirmation) must bear in mind that he has the burden of justifying the opinion expressed.[1]

The circumstances of a particular audit engagement may make it impracticable or impossible for the auditors to confirm accounts receivable. If the auditors can satisfy themselves by using alternative procedures, the audit report need not mention the omission of the confirmation process.

An example of a situation in which it is sometimes impracticable or impossible to confirm receivables arises when sales are made to governmental agencies. The operating records and procedures of some agencies will not ordinarily enable them to confirm the amounts payable under government contracts and purchase orders. The auditors will, therefore, resort to alternative methods of verification—such as the examination of contracts, purchase orders, shipping documents, sales invoices, subsequent payments, and other similar evidence—to satisfy themselves that the receivable resulted from an actual order and shipment.

An important part of confirming notes and accounts receivable is determining the validity of the debtors' addresses. The auditors should investi-

---

[1] AICPA, *Statement on Auditing Standards 1,* "Codification of Auditing Standards and Procedures" (New York, 1973), sec. 331, par. .01.

gate thoroughly if an excessive number of *individual* debtors have addresses that are post office boxes; the boxes may have been rented under fictitious debtors' names by employees of the client company engaged in accounts receivable fraud.

Illustrative case

In the Equity Funding Corporation of America fraud, fictitious receivables selected for confirmation by the auditors bore addresses of employees who were conspirators in the fraud. The fictitious confirmation requests were thus signed and returned to the auditors by the recipients.

All requests for confirmation of notes and accounts receivable should be mailed in envelopes bearing the CPA firm's return address. A stamped or business reply envelope addressed to the office of the auditors should be enclosed with the request. The confirmation requests should be deposited personally by the auditors at the post office or in a government mailbox. These procedures are designed to prevent the client's employees from having any opportunity to alter or intercept a confirmation request or the customer's reply thereto. The entire process of confirming receivables will obviously contribute nothing toward the detection of overstated or fictitious accounts if the confirmation requests or replies from customers pass through the hands of the client. Requests returned as undeliverable by the post office may be of prime significance to the auditors and hence should be returned directly to their office.

Positive and negative confirmation requests There are two methods of confirming receivables by direct communication with the debtor. In each type of communication, the *client* makes the formal request for confirmation, although the auditors *control* the entire confirmation process.

The *positive method* consists of a request addressed to the debtor company asking it to confirm directly to the auditors the accuracy of the dollar amount shown on the confirmation request. The positive method calls for a reply in every case; the customer is asked to state whether the balance shown is correct or incorrect. See Figure 12–4.

The *negative method* consists of a communication addressed to the debtor company asking it to advise the auditors *only* if the balance shown is incorrect. A negative confirmation request may be in the form of a letter or it may be made merely by applying a rubber stamp to the customer's regular monthly statement, or by attaching a gummed label bearing the words shown in Figure 12–5.

The greater reliability of the positive form of confirmation arises from the fact that the auditors are alerted to the need for further investigation if

Figure 12–4   Positive form of accounts receivable confirmation request

Smith & Co. ♦♦♦♦ Ltd.

1416 EIGHTEENTH STREET, LOS ANGELES, CALIFORNIA 90035

December 31, 198X

Martin, Inc.
6700 Holmes Street
Kansas City, Missouri 64735

Dear Sirs:

Please confirm directly to our auditors

ADAMS AND BARNES
Certified Public Accountants
1800 Avenue of the Stars
Los Angeles, California 90067

the correctness of the balance of your account payable to us as shown below
and on the enclosed statement at December 31, 198X. If the amount is not in
agreement with your records at that date, please provide any information which
will aid our auditors in reconciling the difference.

Your prompt return of this form in the enclosed stamped envelope is
essential to the completion of the auditors' examination of our financial statements and will be appreciated.

Smith & Co.

By _M. J. Crowley_
(Controller)

THIS IS NOT A REQUEST FOR PAYMENT, BUT MERELY FOR
CONFIRMATION OF YOUR ACCOUNT.

- -

The statement of our account showing a balance of $24,689.00 due Smith & Co.
at December 31, 198X is correct except as noted below.

Martin, Inc.

Date _January 16, 198X_   By _Howard Martin_

Exceptions: _None_

Figure 12–5 Negative form of accounts receivable confirmation request

Please examine this statement carefully. If it does not agree with your records, please report any differences to our auditors

Adams and Barnes
Certified Public Accountants
1800 Avenue of the Stars
Los Angeles, California 90064

A business reply envelope requiring no postage is enclosed for your convenience.

THIS IS NOT A REQUEST FOR PAYMENT

a reply is not received. When the negative form of confirmation is used, the lack of a reply from a given customer is interpreted as satisfactory evidence when in fact the customer may simply have ignored the confirmation request. The expense of sending negative confirmation requests is considerably less than for the positive form; thus, more customers can be contacted for the same cost.

The Auditing Standards Board of the AICPA has commented as follows on the positive and negative methods of confirming receivables:

> Because the use of the positive form results in either (a) the receipt of a response from the debtor constituting evidence regarding the debt or (b) the use of other procedures to provide evidence as to the validity and accuracy of significant nonresponding accounts, the use of the positive form is preferable when individual account balances are relatively large or when there is reason to believe that there may be a substantial number of accounts in dispute or with inaccuracies or irregularities. The negative form is useful particularly when internal control surrounding accounts receivable is considered to be effective, when a large number of small balances are involved, and when the auditor has no reason to believe the persons receiving the requests are unlikely to give them consideration. If the negative rather than the positive form of confirmation is used, the number of requests sent or the extent of the other auditing procedures applied to the receivable balance should normally be greater in order for the independent auditor to obtain the same degree of satisfaction with respect to the accounts receivable balance.
>
> In many situations a combination of the two forms may be appropriate, with the positive form used for large balances and the negative form for small balances.[2]

---

[2] Ibid., sec. 331, pars. .05–.06.

Size of sample In the audit of most companies, the confirmation process is limited to a sample of the accounts receivable. The sample should generally be sufficiently large to account for most of the dollar amount of the receivables, and it should always be sufficiently representative to warrant the drawing of valid inferences about the entire population of receivables.

The size of the sample will vary with the materiality of accounts receivable in comparison with total assets. If accounts receivable are a relatively large asset, the size of the sample should be relatively large. The auditors' assessment of control risk is also a factor; weaknesses in internal control call for larger samples than when internal control is strong. The results of confirmation tests in prior years serve as another guide to the auditors in setting sample size; significant exceptions in prior years' confirmations signal the need for extensive confirmation of this year's receivables. Finally, the choice between the positive and negative forms of confirmation request influence the size of the sample. The number of confirmations is usually increased when the negative form is used.

In selecting the individual accounts to be confirmed, it is customary to include all customers with balances above a selected dollar amount and to select accounts on a random basis from the remaining receivables. Generalized computer audit programs are useful in stratifying computer-processed accounts receivable to facilitate the selection process described above.

Discrepancies in customers' replies The auditors should resolve unusual or significant differences reported by customers; other exceptions may be turned over to employees of the client with the request that investigation be made and explanations furnished to the auditors. The majority of such reported discrepancies arise because of normal lags in the recording of cash receipts or sales transactions, or because of misunderstanding on the part of the customer company as to the date of the balance it is asked to confirm. Some replies may state that the balance listed is incorrect because it does not reflect recent cash payments; in such instances, the auditors normally trace the reported payments to the cash records.

Alternative audit procedures for nonrespondents The percentage of replies to be expected for positive confirmation requests will vary greatly according to the type of debtor. Second and third requests, the latter usually by registered mail, telegram, or telephone are often found necessary to produce replies. When replies are not received on notes or accounts with significant balances, the auditors should apply alternative procedures to the accounts. The auditors may verify the existence, location, and credit standing of the debtor by reference to credit agencies or other independent sources. The authenticity of the underlying transactions can be established by examination of subsequent cash receipts, contracts, customer purchase orders, sales order, sales invoices, and bills of lading.

Putting the confirmation process in perspective When all expected replies to confirmation requests have been received, a summary should be prepared outlining the extent and nature of the confirmation program and the overall results obtained. Such a summary is a highly important part of the audit working papers.

After resolving all differences disclosed by confirming accounts receivable, the auditors may decide to reassess control risk for receivables. For example, if the number of significant errors exceeded what was anticipated from the auditors' original assessment of control risk, the original evaluation was not valid. A new assessment is necessary, and that may alter the remaining course of the audit.

The auditors face more than one type of risk in relying upon the confirmation process to form an opinion about the fairness of the accounts receivable as a whole. We have already recognized the risk that some accounts with erroneous balances may not be included in the sample confirmed, and also the risk that replies may not be received from some customers having erroneous balances. Finally, there is the risk that customers may routinely return confirmation requests without actually comparing the balance with their records. Such responses would give the auditors a false sense of security. Despite these risks, however, the confirming of accounts receivable provides valuable evidence and represents an important part of the auditors' work.

It has sometimes been said that the best proof available to the auditors as to the validity of an account receivable is its collection during the course of their examination. But this statement requires qualification, as indicated by the following situation:

Illustrative case

During the first audit of a small manufacturing company, the auditors sent confirmation requests to all customers whose accounts showed balances in excess of $1,000. Satisfactory replies were received from all but one account, which had a balance of approximately $30,000. A second confirmation request sent to this customer produced no response; but before the auditors could investigate further, they were informed by the cashier-accountant that the account had been paid in full. The auditors asked to examine the customer's check and the accompanying remittance advice, but were told that the check had been deposited and the remittance advice destroyed. Further questioning concerning transactions with this customer evoked such vague responses that the auditors decided to discuss the account with the officers of the company. At this point the

(Continued)

cashier-accountant confessed that the account in question was a fictitious
one created to conceal a shortage and that to satisfy the auditors he had
"collected" the account receivable by diverting current collections from
other customers whose accounts had already been confirmed.

Reviewing and confirming accounts and notes written off as uncollectible   If any accounts or notes receivable of significant amount were written off as uncollectible during the year, the auditors should determine that these write-offs were properly authorized. In the absence of proper authorization procedures, a dishonest employee could conceal permanently a theft of cash merely by a charge to accounts or notes receivable followed by a write-off of that asset.

A systematic review of the notes and accounts written off can conveniently be made by obtaining or preparing an analysis of the Allowance for Doubtful Accounts and Notes. Debits to the allowance may be traced to the authorizing documents and to the control record of accounts and notes written off; confirmation requests may be mailed to some of the debtors to determine that the account or note was genuine when it was first recorded in the accounts. Credit entries should be compared with the charges to Uncollectible Accounts and Notes Expense. Any write-off that appears unreasonable should be fully investigated. Charge-off of a note or account receivable from an officer, stockholder, or director is unreasonable on its face and warrants the most searching investigation by the auditors. The computation of percentages relating the year's write-offs to net credit sales, to uncollectible accounts expense, and to the allowance for doubtful accounts and notes may be useful in bringing to light any abnormal write-offs.

9.   Review the year-end cutoff of sales transactions.
One of the more common methods of falsifying accounting records is to inflate the sales for the year by holding open the sales journal beyond the balance sheet date. Shipments made in the first part of January may be covered by sales invoices bearing a December date and included in December sales. The purpose of such misleading entries is to present a more favorable financial picture than actually exists. Since sales are frequently used as the base for computation of bonuses and commissions, an additional incentive for padding the Sales account is often present. A related abuse affecting accounts receivable is the practice of holding the cash journals open beyond the balance sheet date; auditing procedures designed to detect this practice were described in connection with the audit of cash transactions in Chapter 11.

To guard against errors in the cutoff of sales records (whether accidental or intentional), the auditors should compare the sales recorded for several days before and after the balance sheet date with the duplicate sales invoices and shipping documents. The effectiveness of this step is largely dependent upon the degree of segregation of duties between the shipping, receiving, and billing functions. If warehousing, shipping, billing, and receiving are independently controlled, it is most unlikely that records in all these departments will be manipulated to disguise shipments of one period as sales of the preceding period. On the other hand, one individual who had control over both shipping records and billing documents could manipulate both sets of records if overstatement of the year's sales were attempted.

Fictitious sales, as well as predated shipments, are occasionally recorded at year-end as a means of "window dressing" the financial statements. The merchandise in question may even be shipped to customers without their prior knowledge, and subsequently returned. To guard against such manipulation, the auditors should review carefully all substantial sales returns following the balance sheet date that may apply to receivables originating in the year under audit. Consideration should be given to reflecting these returns in the current year's business by means of adjusting entries. Confirmation of accounts receivable, if made at the balance sheet date, should also serve to bring any large unauthorized shipments to the attention of the auditors.

10. Perform analytical procedures for accounts receivable, sales, notes receivable, and interest revenue.

Several ratios and relationships can be computed to indicate the overall reasonableness of the amounts shown for accounts receivable, sales, notes receivable, and interest revenue. Examples include: (*a*) the gross profit rate, (*b*) accounts receivable turnover, (*c*) the ratio of accounts receivable to the year's net credit sales, (*d*) the ratio of accounts written off during the year to the ending balance of accounts receivable, (*e*) the ratio of the valuation allowance to accounts receivable, and (*f*) the ratio of interest revenue to notes receivable.

These ratios and relationships should be compared with corresponding data for the preceding years and with comparable industry averages.

11. Verify interest earned on notes and accrued interest receivable.

The most effective verification of the Interest Earned account consists of an *independent computation* by the auditors of the interest earned during the year on notes receivable. The working paper used to analyze notes receivable should show the interest rate and date of issuance of each note. The interest section of this working paper consists of four columns, which show for each note receivable owned during the year the following information:

a. Accrued interest receivable at the beginning of the year (taken from the preceding year's audit working papers).

b. Interest earned during the year (computed from the terms of the notes).

c. Interest collected during the year (traced to cash receipts records).

d. Accrued interest receivable at the end of the year (computed by the auditors).

These four columns comprise a self-balancing set. The beginning balance of accrued interest receivable (first column) plus the interest earned during the year (second column) and minus the interest collected (third column) should equal the accrued interest receivable at the end of the year (fourth column). The totals of the four columns should be cross-footed to ensure that they are in balance; in addition, the individual column totals should be traced to the balances in the general ledger.

If the interest earned for the year as computed by the auditors does not agree with interest earned as shown in the accounting records, the next step is an analysis of the ledger account. Any unaccounted-for credits in the Interest Earned account deserve particular attention because these credits may represent interest received on notes that have never been recorded.

Illustrative case

In an examination of a company that held numerous notes receivable, the auditors made an independent computation of the interest earned during the year. The amount of interest earned shown by the accounting records was somewhat larger than the amount computed by the auditors. Careful analysis of entries in the Interest Earned account revealed one credit entry not related to any of the notes shown in the Notes Receivable account. Further investigation of this entry disclosed that a note had been obtained from a customer who was delinquent in paying his account receivable. The note receivable had not been recorded as an asset, but the account receivable that was replaced by the note had been written off as uncollectible.

Because of this situation the auditors made a thorough investigation of all accounts written off in recent years. Several of the former customers when contacted stated that they had been asked to sign demand notes for the balances owed and had been assured there would be no pressure for collection as long as interest was paid regularly. The existence of notes receivable totaling nearly a million dollars was brought to light; these notes were not recorded as assets and were not known to the officers of the client company. The note transactions had been arranged by a trusted employee who admitted having abstracted the interest payments received with the exception of one payment which, through oversight, he had permitted to be deposited and recorded as interest earned.

For financial institutions or other clients having numerous notes receivable, the auditors may verify interest computations on only a sample of the notes. In addition, they should test the reasonableness of total interest earned for the year by applying a weighted average rate of interest to the average balance of the Notes Receivable ledger account during the year.

12.   Determine adequacy of allowance for uncollectible accounts.

If the balance sheet is to reflect fairly the financial position of the business, the receivables must be stated at net realizable value, that is, at face value less an adequate allowance for doubtful notes and accounts receivable. The measurement of income requires an impartial matching of revenue and related expenses. Since one of the expenses involved is the expense caused by uncollectible notes and accounts, the auditors' review of doubtful receivables should be looked upon as the verification of both income statement and balance sheet accounts.

As the audit approaches completion, considerable time will have elapsed since the balance sheet date. Consequently, many of the accounts receivable that were past due at the balance sheet date will have been collected; the others will be further past due. Thus, the auditors have the advantage of hindsight in judging the collectibility of the receivables owned at the balance sheet date.

The auditors' best evidence of *collectibility* of accounts and notes receivable is payment in full by the debtors subsequent to the balance sheet date. The auditors should note in the working papers any such amounts received; in the illustrated trial balance of trade accounts receivable (Figure 12–3), a special column has been provided for this purpose. Since one of the auditors' objectives in the examination of notes and accounts receivable is the determination of their collectibility, it is important for the auditors to be aware of any collections on past-due accounts or matured notes during the period subsequent to the balance sheet date.

A note receivable, especially one obtained in settlement of a past-due account receivable, may involve as much credit risk as an account receivable. Provision for loss may reasonably be made for notes that have been repeatedly renewed, for installment notes on which payments have been late and irregular, for notes received in consequence of past-due accounts receivable, for defaulted notes, and for notes of companies known to be in financial difficulties. To appraise the collectibility of notes receivable, the auditors may investigate the credit standing of the makers of any large or doubtful notes. Reports from credit-rating agencies and financial statements from the makers of notes should be available in the client's credit department.

Evaluation of any collateral supplied by the makers of notes is another step in determining the collectibility of notes receivable. The auditors should determine current market value of securities held as collateral by the client by reference to market quotations or by inquiry from brokers. Attention of the client should be called to any cases in which the market value of the collateral is less than the note; the deficiency might have to be considered uncollectible.

To conclude, as to the adequacy of management's accounting estimate for the allowance for doubtful accounts the auditors may take the following steps:

a. Compare the details to the aging of accounts receivable to prior years' aging. Examine the past-due accounts receivable listed in the aging schedule that have not been paid subsequent to the balance sheet date, noting such factors as the size and recency of payments, settlement of old balances, and whether recent sales are on a cash or a credit basis. The client's correspondence file may furnish much of this information.

b. Investigate the credit ratings for delinquent and unusually large accounts. An account with a single customer may represent a major portion of the total receivables.

c. Review confirmation exceptions for indication of amounts in dispute or other clues as to possible uncollectible accounts.

d. Summarize in a working paper those accounts considered to be doubtful of collection based on the preceding procedures. List customer names, doubtful amounts, and reasons considered doubtful.

e. Review with the credit manager the current status of significant doubtful accounts, ascertaining the collection action taken and the opinion of the credit manager as to ultimate collectibility. Indicate on the doubtful accounts working paper the credit manager's opinion as to the collectible portion of each account listed, and provide for the estimated losses on accounts considered by the auditors to be uncollectible.

f. Compute ratios, such as the number-of-days-sales in accounts receivable and the relationship of the valuation allowance, to (1) accounts receivable, (2) net credit sales, and compare to comparable ratios for prior years and industry averages. Investigate any significant variations.

13. Ascertain whether any receivables have been pledged.

The auditors should inquire directly whether any notes or accounts receivable have been pledged or assigned. Evidence of the pledging of receivables may also be disclosed through the medium of bank confirmation requests, which specifically call for a description of the collateral securing bank loans. Analysis of the interest expense accounts may reflect charges from the pledging of receivables to finance companies.

Accounts receivable that have been pledged should be plainly labeled by stamping on the copy of the sales invoice a notice such as "Pledged to First National Bank under loan agreement of December 198X," and by inserting an identifying code in the accounts receivable records. Accounts labeled in this manner would be identified by the auditors in their initial review of receivables and confirmed by direct correspondence with the bank to which pledged. The auditors cannot, however, proceed on the assumption that all pledged receivables have been labeled to that effect, and they must be alert to detect any suggestions of an unrecorded pledging of accounts receivable.

14. Investigate fully any notes or accounts receivable from related parties.

Loans by a corporation to its officers, directors, stockholders, or affiliates require particular attention from the auditors because these related party transactions are not the result of arm's-length bargaining by parties of opposing interests. Furthermore, such loans are often prohibited by state law or by the corporation's bylaws. It is somewhat difficult to reconcile substantial loans to insiders by a nonfinancial corporation with the avowed operating objectives of such an organization. The independent auditors have an obligation to stockholders, creditors, and others who rely upon audited statements to require disclosure of any self-dealing on the part of the management. It seems apparent that most loans to officers, directors, and stockholders are made for the convenience of the borrower rather than for the profit of the corporation. Because of the somewhat questionable character of such loans, they are sometimes paid off just before the balance sheet date and renewed shortly thereafter in an effort to avoid disclosure in financial statements. Under these circumstances, the renewed borrowing may be detected by the auditors through a scanning of notes and accounts receivable transactions subsequent to the balance sheet date.

15. Evaluate financial statement presentation and disclosure.

The auditors must ascertain that the financial presentation of accounts and notes receivable and the related disclosures are in accordance with generally accepted accounting principles. Related party receivables should be shown separately with disclosure of the nature of the relationships and the amounts of the transactions. Any unusual terms of notes receivable should be disclosed in the footnotes. Also, the amounts of allowances for uncollectible receivables should be shown as deductions from the related receivables.

16. Review propriety of client's accounting for transactions resulting in receivables and sales.

An analysis of the overall propriety of treatment of transactions is necessary. For example, consider the following:

1. Goods shipped on a consignment basis might incorrectly be recorded as sales.
2. An allowance for sales returns may not be set up for goods shipped to customers who are given the right to return the goods under certain circumstances.
3. Cash receipts from franchise fees may be included in receivables and revenues when services have not been rendered to the franchisees.
4. Leases properly accounted for using the operating method of accounting may be improperly accounted for as a sales-type capital lease that overstates receivables and revenues.

5. Management might use the percentage-of-completion method in inappropriate circumstances or might recognize more income from the contract than is appropriate.

The above examples make clear that auditors must also be accountants who understand generally accepted accounting principles. Recent research has revealed that a number of "audit failures" have involved situations in which the accounting methods used by the client were not proper and the auditors did not detect the problem. In all of the above circumstances the auditors must carefully examine the various documents pertaining to the transactions involved and determine whether proper accounting procedures have been followed.

Interim audit work on receivables and sales

Much of the audit work on receivables and sales can be performed one or two months before the balance sheet date. The interim work may consist of the consideration of internal controls and, in some cases, the confirmation of accounts receivable as well. A decision to carry out the confirmation of receivables at an interim date rather than at year-end is justified only if internal controls for receivables are reasonably strong.

If interim audit work has been done on receivables and sales, the year-end audit work may be modified considerably. For example, if the confirmation of accounts receivable was performed at October 31, the year-end audit program would include preparation of a summary analysis of postings to the Accounts Receivable controlling account for the period from November 1 through December 31. This analysis would list the postings by month, showing the journal source of each. These postings would be traced to the respective journals, such as the sales journal and cash receipts journal. The amounts of the postings would be compared with the amounts in preceding months and with the corresponding months in prior years. The purpose of this work is to bring to light any significant variations in receivables during the months between the interim audit work and the balance sheet date.

In addition to this analysis of the entries to the receivable accounts for the intervening period, the audit work at year-end would include obtaining the aging of the accounts receivable at December 31, confirmation of any large accounts in the year-end trial balance that are new or delinquent, and the usual investigation of the year-end cutoff of sales and cash receipts.

**KEY TERMS
INTRODUCED OR
EMPHASIZED IN
CHAPTER 12**

Aged trial balance   A listing of individual customers' accounts classified by age. Serves as a preliminary step in estimating the collectibility of accounts receivable.

Confirmation   A type of documentary evidence that is created outside the client organization and transmitted directly to the auditors.

Consignment   A transfer of goods from the owner to another person who acts as the sales agent of the owner.

Interim audit work   Those audit procedures that can be performed before the balance sheet date. The purpose is to facilitate earlier issuance of the audit report and to spread the auditors' work more uniformly over the year.

Negative confirmation   A confirmation request addressed to the debtor requesting a reply only if the balance shown on the monthly statement is incorrect.

Pledging of receivables   To assign to a bank, factor, finance company, or other lender an exclusive claim against accounts receivable as security for a debt.

Positive confirmation   A confirmation request sent to the debtor asking it to confirm directly to the auditors the accuracy of the dollar amount shown on the request. Calls for a reply regardless of whether the amount is correct or incorrect.

GROUP I: REVIEW QUESTIONS

12–1.   Give an example of a type of receivable originating without arm's-length bargaining. Comment on the presentation of such receivables in the balance sheet.

12–2.   State briefly the objective of the billing function. What important document is created by the billing department?

12–3.   Criticize the following quotation: "A credit memorandum should be issued only when an account receivable is determined to be uncollectible."

12–4.   Explain the difference between a ***customer's order*** and a ***sales order,*** as these terms might be used by a manufacturing company making sales on credit.

12–5.   Describe the role of the credit department in a manufacturing company.

12–6.   In selecting accounts receivable for confirmation, the auditors discover that the client company's records show the addresses of several individual customers to be post office boxes. What should be the auditors' reaction to this situation?

12–7.   Cite various procedures auditors employ that might lead to the detection of an inadequate allowance for doubtful accounts receivable.

(AICPA, adapted)

12–8.   A CPA firm wishes to test the client's sales cutoff at June 30, 198X. Describe the steps that the auditors should include in this test.

(AICPA, adapted)

12–9.   Several accounts receivable confirmations have been returned with the notation "verifications of vendors' statements are no longer possible because of our data processing system." What alternative auditing procedures could be used to verify these accounts receivable?

(AICPA, adapted)

12–10.   The confirmation of accounts receivable is an important auditing procedure. Should the formal request for confirmation be made by the client or by the auditors? Should the return envelope be addressed to the client, to the auditors in care of the client, or to the auditors' office? Explain.

12–11. The controller of a new client operating a medium-size manufacturing business complains to you that he believes the company has sustained significant losses on several occasions because certain sales invoices were misplaced and never recorded as accounts receivable. What internal control procedure can you suggest to guard against such problems?

12–12. In the examination of an automobile agency, you find that installment notes received from the purchasers of automobiles are promptly discounted with a bank. Would you consider it necessary to confirm these notes by a communication with the bank? With the makers? Explain.

12–13. Your review of notes receivable from officers, directors, stockholders, and affiliated companies discloses that several notes of small amounts were written off to the allowance for uncollectible notes during the year. Have these transactions any special significance? Explain.

12–14. In the examination of credit memoranda covering allowances to customers for goods returned, how can the auditors ascertain whether the customer actually did return merchandise in each case in which accounts receivable were reduced?

12–15. What auditing procedures, if any, are necessary for notes receivable but are not required for accounts receivable?

12–16. Among specific procedures that contribute to good internal control over accounts receivable are (*a*) the approval of uncollectible account write-offs and credit memoranda by an executive and (*b*) the sending of monthly statements to all customers. State three other procedures conducive to strong internal control. (AICPA)

12–17. What additional auditing procedures should be undertaken in connection with the confirmation of accounts receivable where customers having substantial balances fail to reply after second request forms have been mailed directly to them? (AICPA, adapted)

12–18. In your first examination of Hydro Manufacturing Company, a manufacturer of outboard motors, you discover that an unusually large number of sales transactions were recorded just before the end of the fiscal year. What significance would you attach to this unusual volume?

12–19. In connection with a regular annual audit, what are the purposes of a review of sales returns and allowances subsequent to the balance sheet date? (AICPA, adapted)

12–20. An inexperienced clerk assigned to the preparation of sales invoices in a manufacturing company became confused as to the nature of certain articles being shipped, with the result that the prices used on the invoices were far less than called for in the company's price lists. What internal control procedures could be established to guard against such errors?

12–21. The accounts receivable section of the accounting department in Wind Power, Inc. maintains subsidiary ledgers that are posted from copies of the sales invoices transmitted daily from the billing department. How may the accounts receivable section be sure that it receives promptly a copy of each sales invoice prepared?

12–22. A company that ships goods to its customers must establish procedures to ensure that a sales invoice is prepared for every shipment. Describe procedures to meet this requirement.

12–23. State briefly the *audit objective* that is achieved by the audit procedure of "Confirm accounts receivable and notes receivable by direct communication with debtors."

GROUP II: QUESTIONS REQUIRING ANALYSIS

12–24. During the audit of Solar Technologies, Inc., the auditors sent confirmation requests to customers whose accounts had been written off as uncollectible during the year under audit. An executive of Solar protested, saying: "You people should be verifying that the receivables on the books are collectible. We know the ones we wrote off are no good."

Required:
a. What purpose, if any, is served by this audit procedure?
b. Does the Solar executive's statement suggest some misunderstanding of audit objectives? Explain.

12–25. If you were preparing a credit sales system flowchart, what document would you show as—
a. The source for posting debits to a customer's account in the accounts receivable ledger.
b. Authorization to the finished goods stores to release merchandise to the shipping department.
c. The source for preparing a sales order.
d. The source for preparing a bill of lading.
e. The source for an entry in the sales journal.

12–26. During preliminary conversations with a new staff assistant you instruct her to send out confirmation requests for both accounts receivable and notes receivable. She asks whether the confirmation requests should go to the makers of the notes or to the holders of the notes in the case of notes that have been discounted. Provide an answer to her question and give reasons for your answer.

12–27. Lakeside Company has retained you to conduct an audit so that it will be able to support its application for a bank loan with audited financial statements. The president of Lakeside states that you will have unlimited access to all records of the company and may carry out any audit procedures you consider necessary, except that you are not to communicate with customers. The president feels that contacts with customers might lead them to believe that Lakeside was in financial difficulty. Under these circumstances, will it be possible for you to issue the auditors' standard unqualified audit report? Explain.

12–28. Tom Jones, CPA, is examining the financial statements of a manufacturing company with a significant amount of trade accounts receivable. Jones is satisfied that the accounts are properly summarized and classified, and are valued in accordance with generally accepted accounting principles. Jones plans to use accounts receivable confirmation requests to satisfy the third standard of field work as to trade accounts receivable.

Required:

    a. Identify and describe the two forms of accounts receivable confirmation requests and indicate what factors Jones should consider in determining when to use each.

    b. Assume Jones has received a satisfactory response to the confirmation requests. Describe how Jones could evaluate collectibility of the trade accounts receivable.   (AICPA, adapted)

12–29. In their work on accounts receivable and elsewhere in an audit, the independent auditors often make use of confirmations.

    a. What is an audit confirmation?

    b. What characteristics should an audit confirmation possess if a CPA firm is to consider it as valid evidence?

    c. Distinguish between a positive confirmation and a negative confirmation in the auditors' examination of accounts receivable.

    d. In confirming a client's accounts receivable, what characteristics should be present in the accounts if the CPA firm is to use negative confirmations?   (AICPA, adapted)

12–30. Elizabeth Cole, the senior auditor-in-charge of auditing statements of Thorne Company, a small manufacturer, was busy writing the audit report for another engagement. Accordingly, she sent Martin Joseph, a recently hired staff assistant of the CPA firm, to begin the audit of Thorne Company, with the suggestion that Joseph start with the accounts receivable. Using the preceding year's audit working papers for Thorne Company as a guide, Joseph prepared a trial balance of Thorne's trade accounts receivable, aged them, prepared and mailed positive confirmation requests, examined underlying documents plus other support for charges and credits to the Accounts Receivable ledger account, and performed such other work as he deemed necessary to assure the validity and collectibility of the accounts receivable. At the conclusion of Joseph's work, Cole traveled to Thorne Company to review Joseph's working papers. Cole found that Joseph had carefully followed the prior year's audit working papers.

Required:

State how the three generally accepted auditing standards of field work were fulfilled, or were not fulfilled, in the audit of the accounts receivable of Thorne Company.   (AICPA, adapted)

12–31. What are the implications to the auditors if, during their examination of accounts receivable, some of a client's customers do not respond to the auditors' request for positive confirmation of their accounts receivable?

    What procedures should the auditors perform if there is no response to a second request for a positive confirmation?   (AICPA, adapted)

12–32. You are considering using the services of a reputable outside mailing service for the confirmation of accounts receivable balances. The service would prepare and mail the confirmation requests and remove the returned confirmations from the envelopes and give them directly to you.

    What reliance, if any, could you place on the services of the outside mailing service? Discuss and state the reasons in support of your answer.   (AICPA)

12-33. An assistant auditor was instructed to "test the aging of accounts receivable as shown on the trial balance prepared by the client." In making this test, the assistant traced all past-due accounts shown on the trial balance to the ledger cards in the accounts receivable subsidiary ledger and computed the aging of these accounts. The assistant found no discrepancies and reported to the senior auditor that the aging work performed by the client was satisfactory.

Comment on the logic and adequacy of this test of the aging of accounts receivable.

12-34. Your regular annual audit of Palisades, Inc. included the confirmation of accounts receivable. You decided to use the positive form of confirmation request. Satisfactory replies were received from all but one of the large accounts. You sent a second and third request to this customer, but received no reply. At this point an employee of the client company informed you that a check had been received for the full amount of the receivable. Would you regard this as a satisfactory disposition of the matter? Explain.

12-35. Early in your examination of Sierra Products, Inc., you make a careful study of the division of responsibility, the sequence of procedures, and the basic documentation used in handling credit sales transactions. Your study included preparation of a systems flowchart similar to the one shown early in this chapter. Information disclosed included the following.

Customers' orders are received by the sales order department. After each customer's order is registered and reviewed to determine if it can be filled promptly, employees of the sales order department prepare a sales order that translates the terms of the customer's order into specific instructions for the guidance of the credit, finished goods stores, shipping, billing, and accounts receivable units. The sales order department sends a copy of the sales order to the credit department for approval. After written credit approval, a copy of the sales order is routed through the finished goods storeroom and the shipping department as authorization for the respective departments to release and ship the goods. Shipping department personnel pack the order and prepare a multicopy bill of lading. One copy goes to the billing department.

In the billing department, the bill of lading is matched with the sales order and the sales invoice is prepared in several copies. After review of the prices, extensions, and footings, the customer's copy is mailed directly to the customer, and another copy is transmitted to the accounts receivable department.

In the accounts receivable department, an employee enters the invoice data in a sales–accounts receivable journal, posts the customer's account in the accounts receivable subsidiary ledger, and files the sales invoice in the sales invoice file. The sales invoices are prenumbered and filed in sequence.

Required:
From the above description, select the best answer for each of the four multiple-choice questions shown below and explain fully the reasons for your answer.

a. In order to determine whether internal control operated effectively to minimize errors of failure to post invoices to the accounts receivable subsidiary ledger, the auditors would select a sample of transactions from the population represented by the—
   (1) Sales order file.
   (2) Bill of lading file.
   (3) Accounts receivable subsidiary ledger.
   (4) Sales invoice file.
b. In order to gather audit evidence concerning the proper credit approval of sales, the auditors would select a sample of transaction documents from the population represented by the—
   (1) Sales order file.
   (2) Bill of lading file.
   (3) Accounts receivable subsidiary ledger.
   (4) Sales invoice file.
c. In order to gather audit evidence that uncollected items in customers' accounts represented valid trade receivables, the auditors would select a sample of items from the population represented by the—
   (1) Sales order file.
   (2) Bill of lading file.
   (3) Accounts receivable subsidiary ledger.
   (4) Sales invoice file.
d. In order to determine whether internal control operated effectively to minimize errors of failure to invoice a shipment, the auditors would select a sample of transactions from the population represented by the—
   (1) Sales order file.
   (2) Bill of lading file.
   (3) Accounts receivable subsidiary ledger.
   (4) Sales invoice file.

12–36. Select the best answer for each of the questions shown below and explain fully the reason for your answers.
a. Customers having substantial year-end past due balances failed to reply after second confirmation request forms had been mailed directly to them. Which of the following is the most appropriate audit procedure?
   (1) Examine the bill of lading that is matched with the sales order and sales invoice.
   (2) Review cash collections during the year being examined.
   (3) Intensify the consideration of the client's internal control with respect to receivables.
   (4) Increase the balance in the accounts receivable allowance (contra) account.
b. Which of the following internal control procedures will most likely prevent the concealment of a cash shortage resulting from the improper write-off of a trade account receivable?
   (1) Write-offs must be approved by a responsible officer after review of credit department recommendations and supporting evidence.

(2) Write-offs must be supported by an aging schedule showing that only receivables overdue several months have been written off.

(3) Write-offs must be approved by the accounts receivable department which is in a position to know if the receivables have, in fact, been collected.

(4) Write-offs must be authorized by the shipping department which is in a position to determine that the goods have actually been shipped.

GROUP III: PROBLEMS

12–37. The following are typical questions that might appear on an internal control questionnaire for accounts receivable:

1. Are sales invoices checked for proper pricing, terms, and clerical accuracy?

2. Are shipping documents prenumbered and all numbers accounted for?

3. Is customer credit approval obtained from the credit department prior to shipment of goods?

Required:

a. Describe the purpose of each of the above internal control procedures.

b. Describe the manner in which the operating effectiveness of each of the above procedures might be tested.

c. Assuming that the operating effectiveness of each of the above procedures is found to be inadequate, describe how the auditors might alter their substantive tests to compensate for the internal control weakness.

12–38. You are conducting an annual audit of Granite Corporation, which has total assets of approximately $1 million and operates a wholesale merchandising business. The corporation is in good financial condition and maintains an adequate accounting system. Granite Corporation owns about 25 percent of the capital stock of Desert Sun, Inc., which operates a dude ranch. This investment is regarded as a permanent one and is accounted for by the equity method.

During your examination of accounts and notes receivable, you develop the information shown below concerning three short-term notes receivable due in the near future. All three of these notes receivable were discounted by Granite Corporation with its bank shortly before the balance sheet date.

1. A 13 percent, 60-day note for $50,000 received from a customer of unquestioned financial standing.

2. A 15 percent, six-month note for $60,000 received from the affiliated company, Desert Sun, Inc. The affiliated company is operating profitably, but is presently in a weak cash position because of recent additions to buildings and equipment. The president of Granite Corporation intends to make an $80,000 advance with a five-year maturity to Desert Sun, Inc. The proposed advance will enable Desert Sun, Inc. to pay the existing 15 percent, $60,000 note at maturity and to meet certain other obligations.

3. A 14 percent, $20,000 note from a former key executive of Granite

Corporation whose employment had been terminated because of chronic alcoholism and excessive gambling. The maker of the note is presently unemployed and without personal resources.

Required:

Describe the proper balance sheet presentation with respect to these discounted notes receivable. Use a separate paragraph for each of the three notes, and state any assumptions you consider necessary.

12–39. Milton Chambers, CPA, was retained by Hall Corporation to perform an audit of its financial statements for the year ending December 31. In a preliminary meeting with company officials, Chambers learned that the corporation customarily accepted numerous notes receivable from its customers. At December 31, the client company's controller provided Chambers with a list of the individual notes receivable owned at that date. The list showed for each note the date of the note, amount, interest rate, maturity date, and name and address of the maker. After a careful consideration of the internal control relating to notes receivable, Chambers turned his attention to the list of notes receivable provided to him by the controller.

Chambers proved the footing of the list and determined that the total agreed with the general ledger control account for notes receivable and also with the amount shown in the balance sheet. Next he selected 20 of the larger amounts on the list of notes receivable for detailed investigation. This investigation consisted of confirming the amount, date, maturity, interest rate, and collateral, if any, by direct communication with the makers of the notes. By selection of the larger amounts, Chambers was able to verify 75 percent of the dollar amount of notes receivable by confirming only 20 percent of the notes. However, he also selected a random sample of another 20 percent of the smaller notes on the list for confirmation with the makers. Satisfactory replies were received to all confirmation requests.

The president of Hall Corporation informed Chambers that the company never required any collateral in support of the notes receivable; the replies to confirmation requests indicated no collateral had been pledged.

No notes were past due at the balance sheet date, and the credit manager stated that no losses were anticipated. Chambers verified the credit status of the makers of all the notes he had confirmed by reference to audited financial statements of the makers and Dun & Bradstreet, Inc. credit ratings.

By independent computation of the interest accrued on the notes receivable at the balance sheet date, Chambers determined that the accrued interest receivable as shown on the balance sheet was correct.

Since Chambers found no deficiencies in any part of his examination, he issued an unqualified audit report. Some months later, Hall Corporation became insolvent and the president fled the country. Chambers was sued by creditors of the company, who charged that his audit was inadequate and failed to meet minimum professional standards. You are to comment on the audit program followed by Chambers with respect to notes receivable *only*.

12-40. As part of his examination of the financial statements of Marlborough Corporation for the year ended March 31, 198X, Mark Wayne, CPA, is reviewing the balance sheet presentation of a $1,200,000 advance to Franklin Olds, Marlborough's president. The advance, which represents 50 percent of current assets and 10 percent of total assets, was made during the year ended March 31, 198X. It has been described in the balance sheet as "miscellaneous accounts receivable" and classified as a current asset.

Olds informs the CPA that he has used the proceeds of the advance to purchase 35,000 shares of Marlborough's common stock, in order to forestall a take-over raid on the company. He is reluctant to have his association with the advance described in the financial statements because he does not have voting control and fears that this will "just give the raiders ammunition."

Olds offers the following four-point program as an alternative to further disclosure:

(1) Have the advance approved by the board of directors. (This can be done expeditiously because a majority of the board members are officers of the company.)

(2) Prepare a demand note payable to the company with interest of 12 percent (the average bank rate paid by the company).

(3) Furnish an endorsement of the stock to the company as collateral for the loan. (During the year under audit, despite the fact that earnings did not increase, the market price of Marlborough common rose from $20 to $40 per share. The stock has maintained its $40 per share market price subsequent to year-end).

(4) Obtain a written opinion from the company attorney supporting the legality of the company's advance and the use of the proceeds.

Required:

a. Discuss the proper balance sheet classification of the advance to Olds and other appropriate disclosures in the financial statements and footnotes. (Ignore SEC regulations and requirements, tax effects, creditors' restrictions on stock repurchase, and the presentation of common stock dividends and interest revenue.)

b. Discuss each point of Olds's four-point program as to whether or not it is desirable and as to whether or not it is an alternative to further disclosure.

c. If Olds refuses to permit further disclosure, what action should the CPA take? Discuss.

d. In his discussion with the CPA, Olds warns that the raiders, if successful, probably will appoint new auditors. What consideration should the CPA give to this factor? Explain.   (AICPA, adapted)

12-41. Lawrence Company maintains its accounts on the basis of a fiscal year ending October 31. Assume that you were retained by the company in August to perform an audit for the fiscal year ending October 31, 198X. You decide to perform certain auditing procedures in advance of the balance sheet date. Among these interim procedures is the confirmation of accounts receivable, which you perform at September 30.

The accounts receivable at September 30 consisted of approximately 200 accounts with balances totaling $956,750. Seventy-five of these accounts with balances totaling $650,725 were selected for confirmation. All but 20 of the confirmation requests have been returned; 30 were signed without comments, 14 had minor differences that have been cleared satisfactorily, and 11 confirmations had the following comments:

1. We are sorry, but we cannot answer your request for confirmation of our account because Moss Company uses a computerized accounts payable voucher system.
2. The balance of $1,050 was paid on September 23, 198X.
3. The above balance of $7,750 was paid on October 5, 198X.
4. The above balance has been paid.
5. We do not owe you anything at September 30, 198X, since the goods represented by your invoice dated September 30, 198X, Number 25,050, in the amount of $11,550, were received on October 5, 198X, on FOB destination terms.
6. An advance payment of $2,500 made by us in August 198X should cover the two invoices totaling $1,350 shown on the statement attached.
7. We never received these goods.
8. We are contesting the propriety of the $12,525 charge. We think the charge is excessive.
9. Amount okay. As the goods have been shipped to us on consignment, we will remit payment upon selling the goods.
10. The $10,000, representing a deposit under a lease, will be applied against the rent due to us during 1990, the last year of the lease.
11. Your credit dated September 5, 198X, in the amount of $440 cancels the above balance.

Required:

What steps would you take to clear satisfactorily each of the above 11 comments?   (AICPA, adapted)

12–42. During your examination of the financial statements of Martin Mfg. Co., a new client, for the year ended March 31, 198X, you note the following entry in the general journal dated March 31, 198X:

Notes Receivable	550,000	
Land		500,000
Gain on Sale of Land		50,000
To record sale of excess plant-site land to Ardmore Corp. for 8 percent note due five years from date. No interest payment required until maturity of note.		

Your review of the contract for sale between Martin and Ardmore, your inquiries of Martin executives, and your study of minutes of Martin's directors' meetings develop the following facts:

(1)   The land has been carried in your client's accounting records at its cost of $500,000.

(2)   Ardmore Corp. is a land developer and plans to subdivide and resell the land acquired from Martin Mfg. Co.

(3)   Martin had originally negotiated with Ardmore on the basis of a 12 percent interest rate on the note. This interest rate was established by Martin after a careful analysis of Ardmore's credit standing and current money market conditions.

(4)   Ardmore had rejected the 12 percent interest rate because the total outlay on a 12 percent note for $550,000 would amount to $880,000 at the end of five years, and Ardmore thought a total outlay of this amount would leave it with an inadequate return on the subdivision. Ardmore held out for a total cash outlay of $770,000, and Martin Mfg. Co. finally agreed to this position. During the discussions, it was pointed out that the present value of $1 due five years hence at an annual interest rate of 12 percent is approximately $0.567.

Required:

Ignoring income tax considerations, is the journal entry recording Martin's sale of the land to Ardmore acceptable? Explain fully and draft an adjusting entry if you consider one to be necessary.

12–43.   The July 31, 198X, general ledger trial balance of Aerospace Contractors, Inc., reflects the following accounts associated with receivables. Balances of the accounts are after all adjusting journal entries proposed by the auditors and accepted by the client.

Accounts receivable—commercial	$ 595,000
Accounts receivable—U.S. government.	3,182,000
Allowance for uncollectible accounts and notes	75,000 cr.
Claims receivable—public carriers.	7,000
Claims receivable—U.S. government terminated contracts	320,000
Due from Harwood Co., investee	480,000
Notes receivable—trade	15,000

Remember that two or more ledger accounts are often combined into one amount in the financial statements in order to achieve a concise presentation. The need for brevity also often warrants the disclosure of some information parenthetically, as for example, the amount of the allowance for doubtful accounts.

Required:

a.   Draft a partial balance sheet for Aerospace Contractors at July 31, 198X. In deciding upon which items deserve separate listing, consider materiality as well as the nature of the accounts.

b.   Write an explanation of the reasoning employed in your balance sheet presentation of these accounts.

Inventories and cost of goods sold

Chapter 13 study objectives

After studying this chapter, you should be able to:
— Describe the nature of inventories and cost of goods sold.
— Explain the nature of the purchase and production cycles.
— Identify the fundamental internal controls over inventories.
— Describe the auditors' objectives for the audit of inventories.
— Describe the nature of the audit procedures to accomplish the auditors' objectives for the audit of inventories.

The interrelationship of inventories and cost of goods sold makes it logical for the two topics to be considered together. The internal controls that assure the fair valuation of inventories are found in the purchase (or acquisition) cycle. These controls include procedures for selection of vendors, ordering merchandise or materials, inspecting goods received, recording the liability to the vendor, and authorizing and making cash disbursements. In a manufacturing business, the valuation of inventories also is affected by the production cycle, in which various manufacturing costs are assigned to inventories, and the cost of inventories is then transferred to the cost of goods sold.

The selection of a valuation method and the need for consistency in its application also affect both inventories and cost of goods sold. During periods of inflation, the inadequacies of historical cost affect the validity of cost of goods sold as much as they affect inventories. Thus, it is not surprising that FASB recently experimented with requiring supplemental disclosure of current replacement cost of inventories.[1]

---

[1] The requirement for mandatory disclosure of current cost information was rescinded by *FASB Statement No. 89,* "Financial Reporting and Changing Prices."

Sources and nature of inventories and cost of goods sold

The term inventories is used in this chapter to include (1) goods on hand ready for sale, either the merchandise of a trading concern or the finished goods of a manufacturer; (2) goods in the process of production; and (3) goods to be consumed directly or indirectly in production, consisting of raw materials, purchased parts, and supplies.

Inventories have received much attention in both the accounting and auditing literature, as well as in discussions among professional accountants. The reasons for the special significance attached to inventories are readily apparent:

1. Inventories usually constitute the largest current asset of an enterprise and are very susceptible to major errors and irregularities.
2. Numerous alternative methods for valuation of inventories are sanctioned by the accounting profession, and different methods may be used for various classes of inventories.
3. The determination of inventory value directly affects the cost of goods sold and has a major impact upon net income for the year.
4. The determination of inventory quality, condition, and value is inherently a more complex and difficult task than is the case with most elements of financial position. Many items, such as precious gems, sophisticated electronic parts, and construction in progress, present significant problems of identification and valuation.

The auditors' approach in examination of inventories and cost of goods sold

The auditors' *objectives* in the examination of inventories (and cost of goods sold) are to determine that

1. *Internal control* over inventories is adequate.
2. The recorded inventories are valid (*existence and rights*).
3. All inventory is recorded (*completeness*).
4. Inventory records and supporting schedules are mathematically correct and agree with general ledger accounts (*clerical accuracy*).
5. The *valuation* of inventories approximate the lower-of-cost-or-market method.
6. The *presentation* and *disclosure* of inventories is adequate.

In conjunction with the audit of inventories and cost of goods sold, the auditors will also obtain evidence about the related purchases, sales, purchase returns, and sales returns accounts.

The responsibilities of independent auditors with respect to the validity of inventories can best be understood by turning back to the time of the spectacular *McKesson & Robbins* fraud case. The hearings conducted by the SEC in 1939 disclosed that the audited financial statements of McKesson & Robbins, Inc., a drug company listed on the New York Stock Exchange, contained $19 million of fictitious assets, about one fourth of the total assets shown on the balance sheet. The fictitious assets included $10 million of nonexistent inventories. How was it possible for the independent auditors to have conducted an audit and to have issued an unqualified report without discovering this gigantic fraud? The audit program followed for inventories in this case was in accordance with customary auditing practice of the 1930s. The significant point is that in that period it was customary to limit the audit work on inventories to an examination of records only; the standards of that era did not require any observation, physical count, or other actual contact with the inventories.

Up to the time of the *McKesson & Robbins* case, auditors had avoided taking responsibility for verifying the accuracy of inventory quantities and the physical existence of the goods. With questionable logic, many auditors had argued that they were experts in handling figures and analyzing accounting records but were not qualified to identify and measure the great variety of raw materials and manufactured goods found in the factories, warehouses, and store buildings of their clients.

The *McKesson & Robbins* case brought a quick end to such limited views of the auditors' responsibility. The public accounting profession was faced with the necessity of accepting responsibility for verifying the physical existence of inventories or of confessing that its audit function offered no real protection to investors or other users of financial statements. The profession met the challenge by adopting new standards requiring the auditors to establish the validity and completeness of inventories by observing the taking of the physical inventory.

Subsequently, the AICPA issued *Statement on Auditing Standards 1* and *2*, which reaffirmed the importance of the auditors' observation of physical inventories but authorized the substitution of other auditing procedures under certain circumstances. *SAS 1* (AU 331.09–.11) made a distinction between companies that determine inventory quantities solely by an annual physical count and companies with well-kept perpetual inventory records. The latter companies often have strong internal control over inventories and may employ statistical sampling techniques to verify the records by occasional test counts rather than by a complete annual count of the entire inventory. For these clients the auditors' observation of physical inventory may be limited to such counts as they consider appropriate, and may occur during or after the end of the period being audited.

A difficult part of the professional standards to interpret is the provision that permits the auditors to substitute other audit procedures for the observation of inventories because it is *impracticable* or *impossible* for them to observe the physical inventory. The difficulty lies in defining the circumstances that make it *impracticable* or *impossible* to observe physical inventory. When observation of the physical inventory is determined to be impracticable or impossible but the auditors are able to obtain competent evidence through the use of other auditing procedures, they may issue an unqualified opinion without making any disclosure of the omission of an observation of the physical inventory. However, the importance of physical contact with items of inventory, as well as inspection of records and documents, is stressed by *SAS 1* in stipulating that the use of alternative auditing procedures must always include observing or making some physical counts of inventories even though this occurs after the balance sheet date.

The auditors' approach to the verification of inventories and cost of goods sold should be one of awareness to the possibility of intentional misstatements, as well as to the prevalence of accidental error in the determination of inventory quantities and amounts. Purposeful misstatement of inventories has often been employed to evade income taxes, to conceal shortages arising from various irregularities, and to mislead stockholders or other inactive owners as to a company's profits and financial position.

Internal control over inventories and cost of goods sold

The importance of adequate internal control over inventories and cost of goods sold from the viewpoint of both management and the auditors can scarcely be overemphasized. In some companies, management stresses internal controls over cash and securities but pays little attention to control over inventories. Since many types of inventories are composed of items not particularly susceptible to theft, management may consider internal controls to be unnecessary in this area. Such thinking ignores the fact that internal control performs other functions just as important as fraud prevention.

Good internal control is a means of providing accurate cost data for inventories and cost of goods sold as well as accuracy in reporting physical quantities. Inadequate internal control may cause losses by permitting erroneous cost data to be used by management in setting prices and in making other decisions based on reported profit margins. If the accounts do not furnish a realistic picture of the cost of inventories on hand, the cost of goods manufactured, and the cost of goods sold, the financial statements may be grossly misleading both as to earnings and as to financial position.

Internal control procedures for inventories and cost of goods sold affect nearly all the functions involved in producing and disposing of the company's products. Purchasing, receiving, storing, issuing, processing, and shipping are the physical functions directly connected with inventories; the cost accounting system and the perpetual inventory records comprise the recording functions. Since the auditors are interested in the final products of the recording functions, it is necessary for them to understand and appraise the cost accounting system and the perpetual inventory records, as well as the various procedures and original documents underlying the preparation of financial data.

The purchasing function   Adequate internal control over purchases requires, first of all, an organizational structure that delegates to a separate department of the company exclusive authority to make all purchases of materials and services. The purchasing, receiving, and recording functions should be clearly separated and lodged in separate departments. In small companies, this type of departmentalized operation may not be possible; but even in very small enterprises, it is usually feasible to make one person responsible for all purchase transactions.

Serially numbered purchase orders should be prepared for all purchases, and copies forwarded to the accounting and receiving departments. The copy sent to receiving should have the quantities blacked out to increase the probability that receiving personnel will make independent counts of the merchandise received. Even though the buyer may actually place an order by telephone, the formal purchase order should be prepared and forwarded. In many large organizations, purchase orders are issued only after compliance with extensive procedures for (1) determining the need for the item, (2) obtaining competitive bids, and (3) obtaining approval of the financial aspect of the commitment.

The receiving function   All goods received by the company—without exception—should be cleared through a receiving department that is independent of purchasing, storing, and shipping departments. The receiving department is responsible for (1) the determination of quantities of goods received, (2) the detection of damaged or defective merchandise, (3) the preparation of a receiving report, and (4) the prompt transmittal of goods received to the stores department.

The storing function   As goods are delivered to stores, they are counted, inspected, and receipted for. The stores department will then notify the accounting department of the amount received and placed in stock. In performing these functions, the stores department makes an important contribution to overall control of inventories. By signing for the goods, it fixes its own responsibility, and by notifying the accounting department of actual goods stored, it provides verification of the receiving department's work.

The issuing function   The stores department, being responsible for all goods under its control, has reason to insist that for all items passing out of its hands it be given a prenumbered requisition, which serves as a signed receipt from the department accepting the goods. Requisitions are usually prepared in triplicate. One copy is retained by the department making the request; another acts as the stores department's receipt; and the third is a notice to the accounting department for cost distribution. To prevent the indiscriminate writing of requisitions for questionable purposes, some organizations establish policies requiring that requisitions be drawn only upon the authority of a bill of materials, an engineering order, or a sales order. In mercantile concerns, shipping orders rather than factory requisitions serve to authorize withdrawals from stores.

The production function   Responsibility for the goods must be fixed, usually on factory supervisors or superintendents. Thus, from the time materials are delivered to the factory until they are completed and routed to a finished goods storeroom, a designated supervisor should be in control and be prepared to answer for their location and disposition.

The system of internal control over goods in process may include regular inspection procedures to reveal defective work. This aids in disclosing inefficiencies in the productive system and also tends to prevent inflation of the goods in process inventory by the accumulation of cost for goods that will eventually be scrapped.

Control procedures should also assure that goods scrapped during the process of production are promptly reported to the accounting department so that the decrease in value of goods in process inventories may be recorded. Scrapped materials may have substantial salvage value, and this calls for segregation and control of scrap inventories.

The shipping function   Shipments of goods should be made only after proper authorization has been received. This authorization will normally be a sales order approved by the credit department, although the shipping function also includes the returning of defective goods to suppliers. In this latter case, the authorization may take the form of a shipping advice from a purchasing department executive.

One copy of the shipping authorization will go to the stores department; a second copy will be retained by the shipping department as evidence of shipment; and a third copy will be enclosed as a packing slip with the goods when they are shipped. These forms should be prenumbered and kept under accounting control. The control aspect of this procedure is strengthened by the fact that an outsider, the customer, will inspect the packing slip and notify the company of any discrepancy between this list, the goods ordered, and the goods actually received.

When the goods have been shipped, the shipping department will attach to a fourth copy of each shipping order the related evidence of shipment: bills of lading, trucking bills, carriers' receipts, freight bills, and so on. This facilitates subsequent audit by grouping together the documents showing that shipments were properly authorized and carried out. The shipping advice, with supporting documents attached, is then sent to the billing department, where it is used as the basis for invoicing the customer.

Established shipping routines should be followed for all types of shipments, including the sale of scrap, return of defective goods, and forwarding of materials and parts to subcontractors.

The cost accounting system   To account for the usage of raw materials and supplies, to determine the content and value of goods in process inventories, and to compute the finished goods inventory, an adequate cost accounting system is necessary. This system comprises all the records, orders, requisitions, time tickets, and the like needed in a proper accounting for the disposition of materials as they enter the flow of production and as they continue through the factory in the process of becoming finished goods. The cost accounting system also serves to accumulate labor costs and indirect costs that contribute to the goods in process and the finished goods inventories. The cost accounting system thus forms an integral part of the internal control for inventories.

The figures produced by the cost system should be controlled by general ledger accounts. Two general types of systems are widely used. Under one, all transactions in a factory are passed through a factory ledger. The net balance of this ledger is represented by a factory ledger controlling account in the general ledger. The other system records the cost of materials, labor, and factory overhead in individual goods in process accounts for each production order or process. These goods in process accounts are controlled by a single general ledger goods in process inventory account. In effect, a subsidiary goods in process ledger is produced by the cost system, which must at all times be represented in the general records.

Underlying this upper level of control between the factory records and the general ledger is found a system of production orders, material requisitions, job tickets or other labor distributions, and factory overhead distributions. Control is effected by having each production order properly authorized, recorded, and followed up. Payroll records are compiled only after all time tickets have been verified for accuracy. Indirect costs are distributed to the various job orders or processes through predetermined rates, which are adjusted to actual cost at the period's end. In addition, many cost systems have introduced methods of determining spoilage, idle labor, and idle machine time. These systems, known as standard costing, provide for the prompt pricing of inventories and for a control over operations through a study of variances between actual and standard figures. All these various types of cost accounting systems are alike in that all are designed to contribute to effective internal control by tracing the execution of managerial directives in the factory, by providing reliable inventory figures, and by safeguarding company assets.

The perpetual inventory system Perpetual inventory records constitute a most important part of internal control. These records, by showing at all times the quantity of goods on hand, provide information essential to intelligent purchasing, sales, and production-planning policies. With such a record it is possible to guide procurement by establishing points of minimum and maximum quantities for each standard item stocked.

The use of a perpetual inventory system allows companies to control the high costs of holding excessive inventory, while minimizing the risk of running out of stock. The company can control inventories through reorder points and economic order quantities, including *just-in-time* systems in which inventory levels are kept to a minimum.

If perpetual inventory records are to produce the control implicit in their nature, it is desirable that the subsidiary records be maintained both in quantities and dollars for all stock, that the subsidiary records be controlled by the general ledger, that trial balances be prepared at reasonable intervals, and that both the detailed records and the general ledger control accounts be adjusted to agree with physical counts whenever taken.

Perpetual inventory records discourage inventory theft and waste, since storeskeepers and other employees are aware of the accountability over goods established by this continuous record of goods received, issued, and on hand. The records, however, must be periodically verified through the physical counting of goods.

Audit working papers for inventories and cost of goods sold

A great variety of working papers may be prepared by the auditors in their verification of inventories and cost of goods sold. These papers will range in form from written comments on the manner in which the physical inventory was taken to elaborate analyses of production costs of finished goods and goods in process. Selected working papers will be illustrated in connection with the audit procedures to be described in later sections of this chapter.

AUDIT PROGRAM FOR INVENTORIES AND COST OF GOODS SOLD

The following audit procedures for the verification of inventories and cost of goods sold will be discussed in detail in the succeeding pages. The program is appropriate for a manufacturing company that takes a complete physical inventory to verify the perpetual inventories at the close of each fiscal year.

A. Consider internal control for inventories and cost of goods sold
1. *Obtain an understanding of internal control* for inventories and cost of goods sold.
2. *Assess control risk* and *design additional tests of controls* for inventories and cost of goods sold.

3. ***Perform additional tests of controls.*** For controls which the auditors plan to rely upon to restrict their assessment of control risk, and, thus, reduce the extent of substantive testing, perform tests of controls such as:

 a. Examining significant aspects of a sample of purchase transactions.

 b. Testing the cost accounting system.

4. ***Reassess control risk*** and ***design substantive tests*** for inventories and cost of goods sold to plan the audit and to assess control risk.

B. Perform substantive tests of inventories and cost of goods sold transactions

5. Obtain listings of inventory and reconcile to ledgers.

6. Evaluate the client's planning of physical inventory.

7. Observe the taking of physical inventory and make test counts.

8. Review the year-end cutoff of purchases and sales transactions.

9. Obtain a copy of the completed physical inventory, test its clerical accuracy, and trace test counts.

10. Review inventory quality and condition.

11. Evaluate the bases and methods of inventory pricing.

12. Test the pricing of inventories.

13. Perform analytical procedures.

14. Determine whether any inventories have been pledged and review purchase and sales commitments.

15. Evaluate financial statement presentation of inventories and cost of goods sold, including the adequacy of disclosure.

Figure 13–1 relates the objectives of the major substantive tests of inventories and cost of goods sold to the primary audit objectives.

A. Consider internal control for inventories and cost of goods sold

1. Obtain an understanding of internal control.

As previously indicated, the consideration of internal controls may involve the filling out of a questionnaire, the writing of descriptive memoranda, or the preparation of flowcharts depicting organizational structure and the flow of materials and documents. All these approaches utilize the same basic investigative techniques of interview and the conduct of a walk-through of the system to determine that the system is accurately described.

During the review of internal controls over inventory, the auditors should become thoroughly conversant with the procedures for purchasing, receiving, storing, and issuing goods and for controlling production, as well as acquiring an understanding of the cost accounting system and the perpetual inventory records.

The auditors should also give consideration to the physical protection for inventories. Any deficiencies in storage facilities, in guard service, or

Substantive tests	Primary audit objectives
Obtain listings of inventory and reconcile to ledgers	*Clerical accuracy*
Evaluate the client's planning of physical inventory Observe the taking of the physical inventory Review the year-end cutoff of purchases and sales transactions Obtain a copy of the completed physical inventory and test its accuracy	*Validity (existence and rights)* *Completeness*
Review inventory quality and condition Evaluate the bases and methods of inventory pricing Test the pricing of inventories	*Valuation*
Perform analytical procedures	*Validity (existence and rights)* *Completeness* *Valuation*
Determine whether any inventories have been pledged and review commitments	*Valuation* *Presentation and disclosure*
Evaluate financial statement presentation and disclosure	*Presentation and disclosure*

in physical handling that may lead to losses from weather, fire, flood, or theft may appropriately be called to the attention of management.

Should the auditors' consideration of internal control over inventories (or plant and equipment) include study of the client's insurance coverage? Management's policy as to the extent of insuring assets against fire, flood, earthquake, and other hazards will vary greatly from one company to another. The auditors' responsibility does not include a determination of what constitutes adequate insurance coverage. Consequently the auditors' report on financial statements need not contain any disclosure on the client's policies with respect to insurance coverage.

The matters to be investigated in the auditors' consideration of internal controls over inventory and cost of sales are fairly well indicated by the following questions: Are perpetual inventory records maintained for each class of inventory? Are the perpetual inventory records verified by physical inventories at least once each year? Do the procedures for physical inventories include the use of prenumbered tags, with all tag numbers accounted for? Are differences between physical inventory counts and perpetual inventory records investigated before the perpetual records are adjusted? Is a separate purchasing department responsible for purchasing all materials, supplies, and equipment? Are all incoming shipments, including returns by customers, processed by a separate receiving department? Are materials and supplies held in the custody of a stores department and issued only on properly approved requisitions?

2. Assess control risk and design additional tests of controls.

Control risk for a financial statement assertion may be assessed below the maximum only when tests indicate that related controls are designed and operating effectively. The auditors must decide which additional tests of controls will likely result in cost justified restrictions of substantive tests.

3. Perform additional tests of controls.

a. Examine significant aspects of a sample of purchase transactions.

The proper recording of purchase transactions and of cash disbursements is essential to reliable accounting records. Therefore, the auditors test the key control procedures in the client's purchasing transaction cycle. Tests of this cycle may include the following steps:

1. Select a sample of purchase transactions.
2. Examine the purchase requisition or other authorization for each purchase transaction in the sample.
3. Examine the related vendor's invoice, receiving report, and paid check for each purchase order in the sample. Trace transactions to the voucher register and check register.
4. Review invoices for approval of prices, extensions, footings, freight and credit terms, and account distribution.
5. Compare quantities and prices in the invoice, purchase order, and receiving report.
6. Trace postings from voucher register to general ledger and any applicable subsidiary ledgers.

b. Test the cost accounting system.

For a client in the manufacturing field, the auditors must become familiar with the cost accounting system in use as a part of their consideration of internal control. A wide variety of practices will be encountered for the costing of finished units. The cost accounting records may be controlled by general ledger accounts or operated independently of the general accounting system. In the latter case, the cost of completed units may be difficult or impossible to verify and may represent nothing more than a well-reasoned guess. Because cost accounting methods vary so widely, even among manufacturing concerns in the same industry, audit procedures for a cost accounting system must be designed to fit the specific circumstances encountered in each case.

In any cost accounting system, the three elements of manufacturing cost are direct materials costs, direct labor costs, and manufacturing overhead. Cost accounting systems may accumulate either actual costs or standard costs according to *processes* or *jobs.* The auditors' tests of the client's cost accounting system are designed to determine that costs allocated to specific jobs or processes are appropriately compiled.

To achieve this objective, the auditors test the propriety of direct materials quantities and unit costs, direct labor-hours and hourly rates, and overhead rates and allocation bases. Quantities of direct materials charged to jobs or processes are vouched to materials requisitions, and unit materials costs are traced to the raw materials perpetual inventory records or purchase invoices. The auditors examine job tickets or time summaries supporting direct labor-hours accumulations and trace direct labor hourly rates to union contracts or individual employee personnel files.

The auditors must recognize that a variety of methods are generally accepted for the application of manufacturing overhead to inventories. A predetermined rate of factory overhead applied on the basis of machine-hours, direct labor dollars, direct labor-hours, or some similar basis is used by many manufacturing companies. The predetermined overhead rate is usually revised periodically, but nevertheless leads each year to some underabsorbed or overabsorbed overhead. The auditors will ordinarily insist that any significant amount of under- or overabsorbed overhead be applied to a proportionate reduction in inventory and cost of sales.

A distinction between factory overhead, on the one hand, and overhead costs pertaining to selling or general administration of the business, on the other, must be made under generally accepted accounting principles because selling expenses and general and administrative expenses are written off in the period incurred. The difference in the accounting treatment accorded to factory overhead and to nonmanufacturing overhead implies a fundamental difference between these two types of cost. Nevertheless, as a practical matter it is often impossible to say with finality that a particular expenditure, such as the salary of a vice president in charge of production, should be classified as factory overhead, as general and administrative expense, or perhaps be divided between the two. Despite this difficulty, a vital procedure in the audit of cost of goods sold for a manufacturing concern is determining that factory overhead costs are reasonably allocated in the accounts. Failure to distribute factory costs to the correct accounts can cause significant distortions in the client's predetermined overhead rate and in over- or underapplied factory overhead. The auditors may find it necessary to obtain or prepare analyses of a number of the factory overhead subsidiary ledger accounts and to verify the propriety of the charges thereto. Then, the auditors must determine the propriety of the total machine-hours, direct labor-hours, or other aggregate allocation base used by the client company to predetermine the factory overhead rate.

If standard costs are in use, it is desirable to compare standard costs with actual costs for representative items and to ascertain whether the standards reflect current materials and labor usage and unit costs. The composition of factory overhead, the basis for its distribution by department and product, and the effect of any change in basis during the year should be reviewed. The standard costs of selected products should be verified by testing computations, extensions, and footings and by tracing charges for labor, material, and overhead to original sources.

The auditors' study of a manufacturing company's cost accounting system should give special attention to any changes in cost methods made during the year and the effect of such changes on the cost of sales. Close attention should also be given to the methods of summarizing costs of completed products and to the procedures for recording the cost of partial shipments.

If the client company has supply contracts with U.S. government agencies, the auditors should determine whether standards issued by the Cost Accounting Standards Board were complied with. Cost accounting standards issued to date have dealt with such matters as consistency in estimating, accumulating, allocating and reporting costs, and depreciation of plant assets.

4. Reassess control risk and design substantive tests.

The description and tests of controls of the client's internal control for inventories and cost of goods sold provide the auditors with evidence as to weaknesses and strengths of the system. Based on this information, the auditors reassess control risk and design their substantive testing of inventories and cost of sales accordingly.

B. Substantive tests

5. Obtain listings of inventory and reconcile to ledgers.

The auditor will obtain a schedule of listings of inventory which will be reconciled to both the general ledger and appropriate subsidiary ledgers. The nature of the listings will vary depending upon whether the client engages in manufacturing or simply sells products at retail. The auditors' goal in performing this step is to make sure the inventory records agree with what is recorded in the accounting system.

6. Evaluate the client's planning of physical inventory.

Efficient and effective inventory taking requires careful planning in advance. Cooperation between the auditors and client personnel in formulating the procedures to be followed will prevent unnecessary confusion and will aid in securing a complete and well-controlled count. A first step is the designation by the client management of an individual employee, often a representative of the controller, to assume responsibility for the physical inventory. This responsibility will begin with the drafting of procedures and will carry through to the final determination of the dollar value of all inventories.

In planning the physical inventory, the client should consider many factors, such as (1) selection of the best date or dates, (2) suspending production in certain departments of the plant, (3) segregating obsolete and defective goods, (4) establishing control over the counting process through the use of inventory tags or sheets, (5) achieving proper cutoff of sales and purchase transactions, and (6) arranging for services of engineers or other specialists to determine the quantity or quality of certain goods or materials.

Once the plan has been developed, it must be documented and communicated in the form of written instructions to the personnel taking the physical inventory. These instructions normally will be drafted by the client and reviewed by the auditors, who will judge their adequacy. In evaluating the adequacy of the instructions, the auditors should consider the nature and materiality of the inventories, as well as the existing internal control. Normally, the auditors will insist that the inventory be taken at or near the balance sheet date. However, if the client has an effective system of internal control, including perpetual records, the auditors may be satisfied to observe inventory counts performed during the year. If the client plans to use a statistical sampling technique to estimate the quantities of inventories, the auditors will evaluate the statistical validity of the sampling method and the adequacy of the confidence level and precision. If the instructions for taking inventory are adequate, then the auditors' responsibility during the count is largely a matter of seeing that the instructions are followed conscientiously.

Some companies prepare two sets of instructions for the physical inventory: one set for the supervisors who will direct the count and a second set for the employees who will perform the detailed work of counting and listing merchandise. A set of instructions prepared by the controller of a large clothing store for use by supervisors is shown in Figure 13–2.

Advance planning by the senior auditor-in-charge is also necessary to assure efficient use of audit staff members during the inventory taking. The auditor-in-charge should determine the dates of the counts, the extent of the test counts, the number of auditors needed at each location, and the estimated time required. The senior should then assign auditors to specific locations and provide them with a written statement of their duties. The senior may also wish to arrange for the cooperation of the client's internal auditing staff during the count, and possibly for the assistance of the company's engineers or independent specialists.

When written instructions are prepared by the auditing firm for use of its staff in a particular engagement, these instructions are not made available to the client. Their purpose is to make sure that all auditors understand their assignments and can therefore work efficiently during the physical inventory. An example of inventory instructions prepared by a public accounting firm for the use of its own staff members is presented in Figure 13–3. These instructions relate to the same audit engagement described in the client's instructions to supervisors illustrated in Figure 13–2. The audit staff members should have copies of the client's inventory instructions in their possession during the inventory observation.

7. Observe the taking of physical inventory and make test counts.

It is not the auditors' function to *take* the inventory or to control or supervise the taking; this is the responsibility of management. The audi-

Figure 13–2

GLEN HAVEN DEPARTMENT STORES, INC.

Instructions for Physical Inventory,
August 5, 198X

TO ALL SUPERVISORS:

A complete physical inventory of all departments in each store will
be taken Sunday, August 5, 198X, beginning at 8:30 a.m. and continuing
until completed. Employees are to report at 8:15 a.m. to receive their
final briefing on their instructions, which are appended hereto.

Within one week prior to August 5, supervisors should make sure
that merchandise in departments is well organized. All merchandise with
the same stock number should be located together. Merchandise that is
damaged should be segregated for separate listing on inventory sheets.

Each count team should be formed and started by a supervisor, and
should be periodically observed by that supervisor to assure that instructions are being complied with in the counting and listing processes.

A block of sequential prenumbered inventory sheets will be issued
to each supervisor at 8:00 a.m. August 5, for later issuance to count
teams. Each supervisor is to account for all sheets--used, unused, or
voided. In addition, each supervisor will be furnished at that time with
a listing of count teams under his supervision.

When a count team reports completion of a department, that team's
supervisor should accompany a representative of the independent auditors,
McDonald & Company, in performing test counts. A space is provided on
each inventory sheet for the supervisor's signature as reviewer. When
the independent auditors have "cleared" a department, the supervisor
responsible should take possession of the count sheets. All completed
count sheets are to be placed in numerical sequence and turned over to
me when the entire inventory had been completed.

Before supervisors and employees leave the stores Saturday evening,
August 4, they are to make certain that "housekeeping" is in order in
each department, and that all merchandise bears a price ticket.

If you have any questions about these instructions or any other aspect of the physical inventory, please see me.

J. R. Adams

J. R. Adams
Controller
July 24, 198X

Figure 13–3

McDONALD and COMPANY

CERTIFIED PUBLIC ACCOUNTANTS

Glen Haven Department Stores, Inc.
Inventory Observation--Instructions for Audit Staff
August 5, 198X

We will observe physical inventory taking at the following stores of
Glen Haven Department Stores, Inc., on August 5, 198X:

Store	Store Manager	Our Staff
Wilshire	J. M. Baker	John Rodgers, Faye Arnold
Crenshaw	Roberta Bryan	Weldon Simpkins
Valley	Hugh Remington	Roger Dawson

Report to assigned stores promptly at 8:00 a.m. Attached are copies of
the company's detailed instructions to employees who are to take the physical
inventories and to supervisors who are to be in charge. These instructions
appear to be complete and adequate; we should satisfy ourselves by observation
that the instructions are being followed.

All merchandise counted will be listed on prenumbered inventory sheets.
We should make test counts of approximately 5 percent of the stock items
to ascertain the accuracy of the physical counts. Test counts are to be
recorded in working papers, with the following information included:
    Department number
    Inventory sheet number
    Stock number
    Description of item, including season letter and year
    Quantity
    Selling price per price tag

We should ascertain that adequate control is maintained over the prenumbered inventory sheets issued. Also, we should prepare a listing of the
last numbers used for transfers, markdowns, and markups in the various departments and stores. Inventory sheets are not to be removed from the departments
until we have "cleared" them; we should not delay this operation.

Each staff member's working papers should include an opinion on the
adequacy of the inventory taking. The papers should also include a summary of
time incurred in the observation.

No cash or other cutoff procedures are to be performed as an adjunct to
the inventory observation.

tors *observe* the inventory taking in order to obtain sufficient competent evidence as to the existence and completeness of audit objectives. In brief, observation of inventory taking gives the auditors a basis for an opinion as to the credibility of representations by management of inventory quantities.

To observe the inventory taking, however, implies a much more active role than that of a mere spectator. Observation by the auditors also includes determining that all usable inventory owned by the client is included in the count and that the client's employees comply with the written inventory instructions. As part of the process of observing the physical inventory, the auditors will be alert to detect any obsolete or damaged merchandise included in inventory. Such merchandise should be segregated by the client and written down to net realizable value. In short, during the inventory observation, the auditors are alert for, and follow up on, any unusual problems not anticipated in the client's written inventory instructions or improperly dealt with by the client's inventory teams.

The auditors will also **make a record of the serial number of the final receiving and shipping documents issued before the taking of inventory** so that the accuracy of the cutoff can be determined at a later date. Shipments or receipts of goods taking place during the counting process should be closely observed and any necessary reconciliations made. Observation of the physical inventory by the auditors also stresses determining that the client is controlling properly the inventory tags or sheets. These should be prenumbered so that all tags can be accounted for.

During their inventory observation, the auditors will make test counts of selected inventory items. The extent of the test counts will vary widely, depending upon the inherent risk and materiality of the client's inventory and the extent of the client's internal controls. A representative number of test counts should be recorded in the audit working papers for subsequent comparison with the completed inventory listing.

Serially numbered inventory count tags are usually attached to each lot of goods during the taking of a physical inventory. The design of the tag and the procedures for using it are intended to guard against two common pitfalls: (*a*) accidental omission of goods from the count and (*b*) double counting of goods.

Many companies use two-employee teams to count the inventories. Each team is charged with a sequence of the serially numbered tags and is required to turn in to the physical inventory supervisor any tags voided or not used.

The actual counting, the filling in of inventory tags, and the pulling of these tags are done by the client's employees. While the inventory tags are still attached to the goods, the auditors may make such test counts as they deem appropriate in the circumstances. The auditors will list in their working papers the tag numbers for which test counts were made. The client employees will ordinarily not collect (pull) the inventory tags until the auditors indicate that they are satisfied with the accuracy of the count.

In comparing their test counts to the inventory tags, the auditors are alert for errors not only in quantities but also in part numbers, descriptions, units of measure, and all other aspects of the inventory item. For test counts of goods in process inventory, the auditors must ascertain that the percentage or stage of completion indicated on the inventory tag is appropriate.

If the test counts made by the auditors indicate discrepancies, the goods are recounted at once by the client's employees and the error corrected. If an excessive number of errors is found, the inventory for the entire department or even for the entire company should be recounted.

The information listed on the inventory tags often is transferred by the client to serially numbered inventory sheets. These sheets are used in pricing the inventory and in summarizing the dollar amounts involved. After the inventory tags have been collected, the client employee supervising the inventory will determine that all tags are accounted for by serial number. The auditors should ascertain that numerical control is maintained over both inventory tags and inventory sheets.

Clients using electronic data processing equipment may facilitate inventory counting and summarizing through machine readable inventory tags. Prior to the physical inventory, the tags may be encoded with tag numbers, part numbers, descriptions, and unit prices. After the physical inventory, the information from the tags is entered into the computer, which extends quantity times unit price for each inventory item and prints out a complete inventory summary.

The test counts and tag numbers listed by the auditors in their working papers will be traced later to the client's inventory summary sheets. A discrepancy will be regarded not as an error in counting but as a mistake in copying data from the tags, a purposeful alteration of a tag, or creation of a fictitious tag.

Illustrative case

The auditors of Cenco Incorporated did not adequately review the control of physical inventory tags, even though their CPA firm's procedures required such a review. According to the SEC (Accounting and Auditing Enforcement Release No. 1, par. 4552), Cenco personnel altered quantities on the final inventory computer listings and created bogus inventory tags; the result was a $39 million overstatement of inventory with a reported value of $119 million. The auditors ignored several indications of the inventory overstatement, including numerous differences between the client's inventory computer listings and the auditors' test counts, lack of vendor invoices to support the purchase of quantities of certain inventory items reported to be on hand, and unusual adjustments of perpetual records to physical counts.

During the observation of physical inventories, the auditors should make inquiries to ascertain whether any of the materials or goods on hand are the property of others, such as goods held on consignment or customer-owned materials sent in for machine work or other processing.

Audit procedures applicable to goods held by the client on consignment may include a comparison of the physical inventory with the client's records of consigned goods on hand, review of contracts and correspondence with consignors, and direct written communication with the consignors to confirm the quantity and value of goods held at the balance sheet date and to disclose any client liability for unremitted sales proceeds or from inability to collect consignment accounts receivable.

Working papers will be prepared by each auditor participating in the observation of the inventory. These papers should indicate the extent of test counts, describe any deficiencies noted, and express a conclusion as to whether the physical inventory appeared to have been properly taken in accordance with the client's instructions. The auditor-in-charge should prepare a concise summary memorandum indicating the overall extent of observation and the percentage of inventory value covered by quantity tests. The memorandum may also include comments on the consideration given to the factors of quality and condition of stock, the treatment of consigned goods on hand, and the control of shipments and receipts during the counting process. Figure 13–4 illustrates this type of memorandum.

Inventories in public warehouses and on consignment   The examination of warehouse receipts is not sufficient verification of goods stored in public warehouses. The AICPA has recommended direct confirmation in writing from outside custodians of inventories, and supplementary procedures when the amounts involved represent a significant proportion of the current assets or of the total assets of a concern. These supplementary procedures include review of the client's procedures for investigating prospective warehouses and evaluating the performance of warehouses having custody of the client's goods. The auditors should also consider obtaining accountants' reports on the warehouses' internal controls relevant to custody of stored goods. If the amounts are quite material, or if any reason for doubt exists, the auditors may decide to visit the warehouses and observe a physical inventory of the client's merchandise stored at the warehouses.

The verification of goods in the hands of consignees may conveniently be begun by obtaining from the client a list of all consignees and copies of the consignment contracts. Contract provisions concerning the payment of freight and other handling charges, the extension of credit, computation of commissions, and frequency of reports and remittances require close attention. After review of the contracts and the client's records of consignment shipments and collections, the auditors should communicate directly with the consignees and obtain full written information on con-

Figure 13–4

THE WILSHIRE CORPORATION
Comments on Observation of Physical Inventory   D9

December 31, 198X

1. Advance Planning of Physical Inventory.

A physical inventory was taken by the client on December 31, 198X. Two
weeks in advance of this date we reviewed the written inventory instructions
prepared by L. D. Frome, Controller. These instructions appeared entirely
adequate and reflected the experience gained during the counts of previous
years. The plan called for a complete closing down of the factory on
December 31, since the preceding year's count had been handicapped by movements of productive material during the counting process. Training meetings
were conducted by Frome for all employees assigned to participate in the
inventory; at these meetings the written instructions were explained and
discussed.

2. Observation of Physical Inventory.

We were present throughout the taking of the physical inventory on
December 31, 198X. Prior to the count, all materials had been neatly arranged, labeled, and separated by type. Two-employee inventory teams were
used: one employee counting and calling quantities and descriptions; the
other employee filling in data on the serially numbered inventory tags. As
the goods were counted, the counting team tore off the "first count" portion
of the inventory tag. A second count was made later by another team working
independently of the first; this second team recorded the quantity of its
count on the "second count" portion of the tag.
We made test counts of the numerous items, covering approximately 30
percent of the total inventory value. These counts were recorded on our
working papers and used as noted below. Our observation throughout the plant
indicated that both the first and second counts required by the inventory instructions were being performed in a systematic and conscientious manner. The
careful and alert attitude of employees indicated that the training meetings
preceding the count had been quite effective in creating an understanding of
the importance of an accurate count. Before the "second count" portions of
the tags were removed, we visited all departments in company with Frome and
satisfied ourselves that all goods had been tagged and counted.
No goods were shipped on December 31. We ascertained that receiving reports
were prepared on all goods taken into the receiving department on this day.
We recorded the serial numbers of the last receiving report and the last
shipping advice for the year 198X. (See D-9-1.) We compared the quantities
per the count with perpetual inventory records and found no significant discrepancies.

3. Quality and Condition of Materials.

Certain obsolete parts had been removed from stock prior to the count and
reduced to a scrap carrying value. On the basis of our personal observation
and questions addressed to supervisors, we have no reason to believe that any
obsolete or defective materials remained in inventory. During the course of
inventory observation, we tested the reasonableness of quantities of 10 items,
representing 40 percent of the value of the inventory, by comparing the
quantity on hand with the quantity used in recent months; in no case did we
find that the quantity in inventory exceeded three months' normal usage.

                                        V. M. L.
                                        Jan. 3, 8X

signed inventory, receivables, unremitted proceeds, and accrued expenses and commissions as of the balance sheet date.

Often, the client may own raw materials that are processed by a subcontractor before being used in the client's production process. The auditors should request the subcontractor to confirm quantities and descriptions of client-owned materials in the subcontractor's possession.

Inventory verification when auditors are engaged after the end of the year   A company desiring an independent audit should engage the auditors well before the end of the year, so they can participate in advance planning of the physical inventory and be prepared to observe the actual counting process. Occasionally, however, auditors are not engaged until after the end of the year and therefore find it impossible to observe the taking of inventory at the close of the year. For example, the illness or death of a company's individual practitioner CPA near the year-end might lead to the engagement of new auditors shortly after the balance sheet date.

Under these circumstances, the auditors may conclude that sufficient competent evidence cannot be obtained concerning inventories to permit them to express an opinion on the overall fairness of the financial statements. On the other hand, if circumstances are favorable, the auditors may be able to obtain satisfaction concerning the inventories by alternative auditing procedures. These favorable circumstances might include the existence of strong internal control, perpetual inventory records, availability of instructions and other records showing that the client had carried out a well-planned physical inventory at or near the year-end, and the making of test counts by the newly appointed auditors. If the auditors are to express an unqualified opinion, their investigation of inventories must include some physical contact with items of inventory and must be thorough enough to compensate for the fact that they were not present when the physical inventory was taken. Whether such alternative auditing procedures will be feasible and will enable the auditors to satisfy themselves depends upon the circumstances of the particular engagement.

8.   Review the year-end cutoff of purchases and sales transactions.

An accurate cutoff of purchases is one of the most important factors in verifying the accuracy and completeness of the year-end inventory. Assume that a shipment of goods costing $10,000 is received from a supplier on December 31, but the purchase invoice does not arrive until January 2 and is entered as a January transaction. If the goods are included in the December 31 physical inventory but there is no December entry to record the purchase and the liability, the result will be an overstatement of both net income for the year and retained earnings and an understatement of accounts payable, each error being in the full amount of $10,000 (ignoring income taxes).

An opposite situation may arise if a purchase invoice is received and recorded on December 31, but the merchandise covered by the invoice is not received until several days later and is not included in the physical inventory taken at the year-end. The effect on the financial statements of recording a purchase without including the goods in the inventory will be to understate net income, retained earnings, and inventory.

How can the auditors determine that the liability to suppliers has been recorded for all goods included in inventory? Their approach is to *examine on a test basis the purchase invoices and receiving reports for several days before and after the inventory date.* Each purchase invoice in the files should have a receiving report attached; if an invoice recorded in late December is accompanied by a receiving report dated December 31 or earlier, the goods must have been on hand and included in the year-end physical inventory. However, if the receiving report carried a January date, the goods were not included in the physical count made on December 31.

A supplementary approach to the matching of purchase invoices and receiving reports is to examine the records of the receiving department. For each shipment received near the year-end, the auditors should determine that the related purchase invoice was recorded in the same period.

The effect on the financial statements of failing to include a year-end in-transit purchase as part of physical inventory is often not a serious one, *provided* the related liability is not recorded until the following period. In other words, a primary point in effecting an accurate *cutoff of purchases is that both sides of a purchase transaction must be reflected in the same accounting period.* If a given shipment is included in the year-end physical inventory of the purchaser, the entry debiting Inventories and crediting Accounts Payable must be made. If the shipment is not included in the purchaser's year-end physical inventory, the purchase invoice must not be recorded until the following period.

Adjustments to achieve an accurate cutoff of purchases should, of course, be made by the client's staff; the function of the auditors should be to review the cutoff and determine that the necessary adjustments have been made.

Chapter 12 includes a discussion of the audit procedures for determining the accuracy of the sales cutoff. The sales cutoff is mentioned again at this point to emphasize its importance in determining the fairness of the client's inventory and cost of goods sold as well as accounts receivable and sales.

9. Obtain a copy of the completed physical inventory, determine its clerical accuracy, and trace test counts.

The testing of extensions and footings on the final inventory listing may disclose misstatements of physical inventories. Often this test consists of "sight-footing" to the nearest hundred dollars or thousand dollars of the inventory listings. Generalized audit software may also be used to test extensions and footings.

In testing extensions, the auditors should be alert for two sources of substantial errors—misplaced decimal points and incorrect extension of *count* units by *price* units. For example, an inventory listing that extends 1,000 units times $1C (per hundred) as $1,000 will be overstated by $990. An inventory extension of 1,000 sheets of steel times $1 per pound will be substantially understated if each sheet of steel weighs more than one pound.

The auditors also should trace to the completed physical inventory their test counts made during the observation of physical inventory. During this tracing, the auditors should be alert for any indications that inventory tags have been altered or that fictitious inventory tags have been created. The auditors also compare inventory tag number sequences in the physical inventory listing to tag numbers noted in their audit working papers for the inventory observation. This procedure is designed to determine that the client has not omitted inventory items from the listing, or included additional items that were not present during the physical inventory.

Another test of the clerical accuracy of the completed physical inventory is the reconciliation of the physical counts to inventory records. Both the quantities and the values of the items should be compared to the company's perpetual records. The totals of various sections of inventory should also be compared with the corresponding control accounts. All substantial discrepancies should be investigated fully. The number, type, and cause of the discrepancies revealed by such comparisons are highly significant in appraising the adequacy of the internal control over inventories.

10. Review inventory quality and condition.

The auditors should also be alert during the course of their inventory observation for any inventory of questionable quality or condition. Excessive dust or rust on raw materials inventory items may be indicative of obsolescence or infrequent use.

The auditors should also review perpetual inventory records for indications of slow-moving inventory items. Then, during the course of observing inventory taking, the auditors should examine these slow-moving items and determine that the client has identified the items as obsolete if appropriate.

To discharge their responsibility for inventory quality and condition, the auditors may also have to rely upon the advice of a specialist. For example, the auditors of a retail jeweler might request the client to hire an independent expert in jewelry to assist the auditors in identifying the precious stones and metals included in the client's inventory. Similarly, the auditors of a chemical producer might rely upon the expert opinion of an independent chemist as to the identity of components of the client's inventories. Guidelines for using the work of a specialist are in Chapter 7.

11. Evaluate the bases and methods of inventory pricing.

The auditors are responsible for determining that the bases and methods of pricing inventory are in accordance with generally accepted accounting principles. The investigation of inventory pricing often will emphasize the following three questions:

1. What method of pricing does the client use?
2. Is the method of pricing the same as that used in prior years?
3. Has the method officially selected by the client been applied consistently and accurately in practice?

For the first question—a method of pricing—a long list of alternatives is possible, including such methods as cost; cost or market, whichever is lower; the retail method; and quoted market price (as for metals and staple commodities traded on organized exchanges). The cost method, of course, includes many diverse systems, such as last-in, first-out (LIFO); first-in, first-out (FIFO); specific identification; weighted average; and standard cost.

The second question raised in this section concerns a change in method of pricing inventory from one year to the next. For example, let us say that the client has changed from the FIFO method to the LIFO method. The nature and justification of the change in method of valuing inventory and its effect on income should be disclosed in accordance with the provisions of *APB Opinion No. 20,* "Accounting Changes." In addition, the auditors must insert in the audit report an explanatory paragraph concerning the lack of consistency between the two years.

The third question posed deals with consistent accurate application in practice of the method of valuation officially adopted by the client. To answer this question the auditors must test the pricing of a representative number of inventory items.

12. Test the pricing of inventories.

The testing of prices applied to inventories of raw materials, purchased parts, and supplies by a manufacturing company is similar to the testing of prices of merchandise in a trading business. In both cases, cost of inventory items, whether LIFO, FIFO, weighted average, or specific identification, is readily verified by reference to purchase invoices. An illustration of a working paper prepared by an auditor in making price tests of an inventory of raw materials and purchased parts is presented in Figure 13–5.

Audit procedures for verification of the inventory values assigned to goods in process and finished goods are not so simple and conclusive as in the case of raw materials or merchandise for which purchase invoices are readily available. To determine whether the inventory valuation method used by the client has been properly applied, the auditors must make tests of the pricing of selected items of finished goods and goods in process. The items to be tested should be selected from the client's inventory summary sheets after the quantities established by the physical inventory have been priced and extended. Items of large total value may be selected

Figure 13–5

The Wilshire Corporation
Test of Pricing–Raw Materials and Purchased Parts (RM) D-5
December 31, 198X

Part No.	Description	Per Inventory Quantity	Price	Vendor	Per Vendor's Invoice Date	No.	Quantity	Price
8Z 182	Aluminum 48×144×.025	910 sheets	10.10	Hardy & Co.	Dec. 18, 8X	5418	1,000	10.10 ✓
8Z 195	Aluminum 45×72×.032	804 sheets	9.01	Watson Mfg. Co.	Nov. 28, 8X	225	500	9.01 ✓
					Dec. 22, 8X	3207	500	9.01 ✓
K1125	Stainless steel .025×23	80,625 lbs.	.80	Ajax Steel Co.	Dec. 3, 8X	K182	100,000	.80 ✓
K1382	Stainless steel .031×17	65,212 lbs.	.82	Ajax Steel Co.	Dec. 3, 8X	K182	75,000	.82 ✓
XL 3925	10 H.P. Electronic Motor	50 ea.	400.00	Cronyn Mfg. Co.	Nov. 18, 8X	253	100	400.00 ✓
XJ 3821	¾ H.P. Electronic Motor	645 ea.	30.50	Long & Co.	Dec. 29, 8X	E9821	650	30.50 ✓

Inventory value of raw materials and purchased parts selected for price testing — $301,825.56.

% of total raw materials and purchased parts selected for price testing — $\frac{\$301,825.56}{503,615.10} = 60\%$

See audit program B-4 for method of selecting raw materials and purchased parts for price testing

✓ – agreed to prices on the vendor's invoice.

<u>Conclusion</u>:
     Based on our tests, it appears that the pricing of raw materials and purchased parts is materially correct.
      Prepared by: C.M.B
               Jan. 4, 8Y

      Reviewed by: W.B
               Jan. 7, 8Y

for testing so that the tests will encompass a significant portion of the dollar amount of inventories.

Lower-of-cost-or-market test   As a general rule, inventories should not be carried at an amount in excess of net realizable value. The lower-of-cost-or-market rule is a common means of measuring any loss of utility in the inventories. If the inventory includes any discontinued lines or obsolete or damaged goods, the client should reduce these items to net realizable value, which is often scrap value.

Illustrative case

During the first audit of an automobile agency, the auditors were observing the taking of the physical inventory of repair parts. They noticed a large number of new fenders of a design and shape not used on the current model cars. Closer inspection revealed that the fenders (with a total inventory valuation of several thousand dollars) were for a model of automobile made seven years ago. The records showed that only one of this type of fender had been sold during the past two years. The automobile dealer explained that these fenders had been included in the parts inventory when he purchased the agency two years ago and that he had no idea as to why such a large stock had originally been acquired. He agreed that few, if any, of this model of fender would ever be sold. It had not occurred to him to write down the carrying value of these obsolete parts, but he readily agreed with the auditors' suggestion that the fenders, being virtually unsalable, should be reduced to scrap value.

---

13.   Perform analytical procedures.

Material errors in counting, pricing, and calculating the physical inventory, as well as fictitious or obsolete inventory, may be disclosed by analytical procedures designed to establish the general reasonableness of the inventory figures.

A comparative summary of inventories classified by major types, such as raw materials, goods in process, finished goods, and supplies, should be obtained or prepared. Explanations should be obtained for all major increases or decreases from the prior year's amounts.

In certain lines of business, particularly retail and wholesale companies, gross profit margins may be quite uniform from year to year. Any major difference between the ending inventory estimated by the gross profit percentage method and the count of inventory at year-end should be investigated fully. The discrepancy may reflect theft of merchandise, or unrecorded or fictitious purchases or sales. On the other hand, it may be the result of changes in the basis of inventory valuation or of sharp changes in sales prices.

Another useful test is the computation of rates of inventory turnover, based on the relationship between the cost of goods sold for the year and the average inventory as shown on the monthly financial statements. These turnover rates should be compared with the rates prevailing in prior years. A decreasing rate of turnover suggests the possibility of obsolescence or of unnecessarily large inventories. Deliberate stockpiling in anticipation of higher prices or shortages of certain strategic materials will, of course, be reflected by a declining inventory turnover rate. Rates of turnover are most significant when computed for individual products or by departments; if compared on a company-wide basis, substantial declines in turnover in certain sections of the client company's operations may be obscured by compensating increases in the turnover rates for other units of the organization.

The auditors should also make certain that aggregate or unit inventories do not exceed the capacity of the client's production or storage facilities. For example, in the audit of a manufacturer of chemicals, the auditors should ascertain the total storage capacity of the client's containers, and determine that the aggregate quantity of chemicals reported in inventories does not exceed that capacity.

The auditors' analytical procedures for purchase transactions will often include a comparison of the volume of transactions from period to period. In this study, the purchase transactions may be classified by vendor and also by type of product; comparisons made in this manner sometimes disclose unusual variations of quantities purchased or unusual concentration of purchases with particular vendors, indicating a possible conflict of interest.

In addition to performing analytical procedures, the auditors should review all general ledger accounts relating to cost of sales to make certain that they contain no apparent irregularities. Adjustments of substantial amount should be investigated to determine the propriety of their inclusion in the cost of goods sold. If this review of general ledger accounts were not made, the door would be left open for all types of gross errors to remain undetected—such obvious errors, for example, as closing miscellaneous revenue and expense into cost of goods sold.

The auditors of a manufacturer client should obtain from the client or prepare an analysis of cost of sales by month, broken down into raw materials, direct labor, and factory overhead elements. The analysis should also include a description of all unusual and nonrecurring charges or credits to cost of goods sold.

14.   Determine whether any inventories have been pledged and review purchase and sales commitments.

The verification of inventories includes a determination by the auditors as to whether any goods have been pledged or subjected to a lien of any kind. Pledging of inventories to secure bank loans should be brought to light when bank balances and indebtedness are confirmed.

A record of outstanding purchase commitments is usually readily available, since this information is essential to management in maintaining day-to-day control of the company's inventory position and cash flow.

In some lines of business, it is customary to enter into firm contracts for the purchase of merchandise or materials well in advance of the scheduled delivery dates. Comparison by the auditors of the prices quoted in such commitments with the vendors' prices prevailing at the balance sheet date may indicate substantial losses if firm purchase commitments are not protected by firm sales contracts. Such losses should be reflected in the financial statements.

The quantities of purchase commitments should be reviewed in the light of current and prospective demand, as indicated by past operations, the backlog of sales orders, and current conditions within the industry. If quantities on order appear excessive by these standards, the auditors should seek full information on this phase of operations. Purchase commitments may need to be disclosed in the financial statements.

Sales commitments are indicated by the client's **backlog** of unfilled sales orders. Losses inherent in firm sales commitments are generally recognized in the lower-of-cost-or-market valuation of inventories, with **market** being defined as the net realizable value of the goods in process or finished goods inventories applicable to the sales commitments. In addition, the backlog may include sales orders for which no production has been started as of the balance sheet date. The auditors must review the client's cost estimates for these sales orders. If estimated total costs to produce the goods ordered exceed fixed sales prices, the indicated loss and a related liability should be recorded in the client's financial statements for the current period.

15. Evaluate financial statement presentation of inventories and cost of goods sold, including the adequacy of disclosure.

One of the most important factors in proper presentation of inventories in the financial statements is disclosure of the inventory pricing method or methods in use. To say that inventories are stated at *cost* is not sufficient, because cost may be determined under several alternative assumptions, each of which leads to a substantially different valuation.

From the standpoint of analyzing the current earnings of the company, it is extremely important to know whether the reported profits have been inflated by price changes, as has often been the case under FIFO, or that the effect of price rises has been limited through the LIFO method of valuation. The users of the financial statements also need to know whether the carrying value of inventory approximates current cost (as with FIFO) or whether inventories are stated at cost of an earlier period (as with the LIFO method).

Other important points in presenting inventories in the financial statements include the following:

1. Changes in methods of valuing inventory should be disclosed and the dollar effect and justification for the change reported, in accordance

with *APB Opinion No. 20*. The auditors' report will contain an explanatory paragraph because of the lack of consistency between years.

2. A separate listing is desirable for the various classifications of inventory, such as finished goods, goods in process, and raw materials.
3. If any portion of the inventory has been pledged to secure liabilities, full disclosure of the arrangement should be made.
4. Deduction of valuation allowance for inventory losses from the related inventory.
5. Disclosure of the existence and the terms of inventory purchase commitments.

Examples of disclosures of inventory pricing methods In many large companies, the cost of certain portions of the inventory is determined on one basis and the cost of other portions of inventory on some other basis. Typical of the disclosure of inventory pricing methods are the following examples taken from published financial statements:

ALPHA PORTLAND CEMENT COMPANY

Inventories—at cost or market, whichever is lower:

Finished cement at cost under LIFO method	$ 2,547,980
Raw materials, in process, packages, and operating supplies, principally at average cost	1,907,376
Maintenance supplies and repair parts at or below cost	2,155,742

LEAR SIEGLER, INC.

Inventories—at the lower of cost (determined by the FIFO method) or market:

Raw materials	$16,969,758
Work in process	8,110,027
Finished goods	17,068,834
	$42,148,619

Cost of goods sold is reported as a deduction from net sales to arrive at gross profit on sales for a multiple-step income statement. In a single-step income statement, cost of goods sold is included among the costs and expenses section of the income statement.

Problems associated with inventory of first year audit clients

The need for the auditors to be present to observe the taking of the ending inventory has been strongly emphasized in auditing literature. However, the figure for beginning inventory is equally significant in determining the cost of goods sold and the net income for the year. In the initial examination of a client, the auditors may not have been present to observe the taking of inventory at the beginning of the year. What procedures can they follow to obtain evidence that the beginning inventories are fairly stated?

The first factor to consider is whether the client was audited by another firm of independent public accountants for the preceding year. If a review of the predecessor firm's working papers indicates compliance with generally accepted auditing standards, the new auditors can accept the beginning inventories with a minimum of investigation. That minimum might include the following steps: (a) study of the inventory valuation methods used; (b) review of the inventory records; (c) review of the inventory sheets used in taking the preceding year's physical inventory; and (d) comparison of the beginning and ending inventories, broken down by product classification.

If there had been no satisfactory audit for the preceding year, the investigation of the beginning inventories would include not only the procedures mentioned above but also the following steps: (a) discussion with the person in the client's organization who supervised the physical inventory at the preceding balance sheet date; (b) study of the written instructions used in planning the inventory; (c) tracing of numerous items from the inventory tags or count sheets to the final summary sheets; (d) tests of the perpetual inventory records for the preceding period by reference to supporting documents for receipts and withdrawals; and (e) tests of the overall reasonableness of the beginning inventories in relation to sales, gross profit, and rate of inventory turnover. An investigation along these lines will sometimes give the auditors definite assurance that the beginning inventory was carefully compiled and reasonable in amount; in other cases, these procedures may raise serious doubts as to the validity of the beginning inventory figure. In these latter cases, the auditors will not be able to issue an unqualified opinion *as to statements of income and cash flows.* They may be able, however, to give an unqualified opinion on the *balance sheet,* since this financial statement does not reflect the beginning inventories.

Unaudited replacement cost information

In years of double-digit inflation, many investors question the usefulness of historical cost-based financial statements. They contend that such statements must be supplemented with measures of the effects of changing prices on the earnings and major assets of the company. In recognition of this problem, the FASB issued *FASB Statement No. 33,* "Financial Reporting and Changing Prices," requiring the supplementary disclosure of replacement costs and changing price information by certain companies. An integral part of the requirements was the disclosure of the current replacement cost of the company's inventories. Subsequently, the FASB rescinded these requirements for mandatory presentation of the current cost information, but a number of companies still present the information voluntarily.

Supplementary information is not required for fair presentation of the basic financial statements. Consequently, *the auditors are not required to audit the information* in order to express an opinion on the financial statements, even if disclosure of the supplementary information is required by the FASB or the GASB. Instead, the Auditing Standards Board established limited procedures to be applied to all FASB-required supplementary information.[2] These procedures require the following of auditors:

---

a. Inquire whether the information is presented in accordance with FASB requirements, whether the methods have changed from the prior period, and as to significant underlying assumptions.
b. Compare the information with management's responses, audited financial statements, and other information known to the auditors.
c. Consider obtaining written representations from management concerning the supplementary information.
d. Apply additional procedures as specified in Statements on Auditing Standards specifically related to the particular required supplementary information.
e. Make additional inquiries if the preceding procedures indicate that the information may not be appropriately presented.

The auditors are no longer required to apply these procedures to current cost information. However, companies who voluntarily present the information may request the auditors to do so. When the auditors are required or requested to review supplementary information, they should add an additional paragraph to their reports to indicate any (1) omission of required information, (2) presentation that does not conform to FASB or GASB requirements, (3) inability to complete the review procedures, or (4) substantial doubts about whether the information conforms to prescribed guidelines. Since the information is not required for fair presentation of the financial statements, the inclusion of the additional paragraph does not constitute a qualification of the auditors' opinion.

KEY TERMS INTRODUCED OR EMPHASIZED IN CHAPTER 13

Bill of lading   A document issued by a common carrier acknowledging the receipt of goods and setting forth the provisions of the transportation agreement.

Confirmation   A type of documentary evidence that is created outside the client organization and transmitted directly to the auditors.

---

[2] AICPA, *Statement on Auditing Standards 27,* "Supplementary Information Required by the Financial Accounting Standards Board" (New York, 1979), AU 553.

Consignment   A transfer of goods from the owner to another person who acts as the sales agent of the owner.

Cost Accounting Standards Board   A five-member board established by Congress to narrow the options in cost accounting that are available under generally accepted accounting principles. Companies having significant supply contracts with certain U.S. government agencies are subject to the cost accounting standards established by the board.

Observation   The auditors' evidence-gathering technique that provides physical evidence.

Periodic inventory system   A method of accounting in which inventories are determined solely by means of a physical inventory at the end of the accounting period.

Perpetual inventory system   A method of accounting for inventories in which controlling accounts and subsidiary ledgers are maintained to record receipts and issuances of goods, both in quantities and in dollar amounts. The accuracy of perpetual inventory records is tested periodically by physical inventories.

Purchase commitment   A contractual obligation to purchase goods at fixed prices, entered into well in advance of scheduled delivery dates.

Replacement cost information   Supplementary information which was required by *FASB Statement No. 33*. The information could be presented in "unaudited" notes to the financial statements or in supplementary schedules. The disclosures are no longer required.

Sales commitment   A contractual obligation to sell goods at fixed prices, entered into well in advance of scheduled delivery dates.

Specialist   A person or firm possessing special skill or knowledge in a field other than accounting or auditing, such as an actuary.

GROUP I: REVIEW QUESTIONS

13–1.   Many auditors consider the substantiation of the figure for inventory to be a more difficult and challenging task than the verification of most other items on the balance sheet. List several specific factors that support this view.

13–2.   Explain the significance of the purchase order to adequate internal control over purchase transactions.

13–3.   What segregation of duties would you recommend to attain maximum internal control over purchasing activities in a manufacturing concern?

13–4.   Do you believe that the normal review of purchase transactions by the auditors should include examination of receiving reports? Explain.

13–5.   The client's cost accounting system is often the focal point in the auditors' examination of the financial statements of a manufacturing company. For what purposes do the auditors review the cost accounting system?   (AICPA)

13–6.   What part, if any, do the independent auditors play in the planning for a client's physical inventory?

13–7.   What are general objectives or purposes of the auditors' observation of the taking of the physical inventory? (Do not discuss the procedures or techniques involved in making the observation.)   (AICPA)

13–8. For what purposes do the auditors make and record test counts of inventory quantities during their observation of the taking of the physical inventory? Discuss. (AICPA)

13–9. Once the auditors have completed their test counts of the physical inventory, will they have any reason to make later reference to the inventory tags used by the client's employees in the counting process? Explain.

13–10. When perpetual inventory records are maintained, is it necessary for a physical inventory to be taken at the balance sheet date? Explain.

13–11. What charges and credits may be disclosed in the auditors' analysis of the Cost of Goods Sold account of a manufacturing concern?

13–12. A client company wishes to conduct its physical inventory on a sampling basis. Many items will not be counted. Under what general conditions will this method of taking inventory be acceptable to the auditors?

13–13. "A well-prepared balance sheet usually includes a statement that the inventories are valued at cost." Evaluate this quotation.

13–14. Darnell Equipment Company uses the LIFO method of valuation for part of its inventories and weighted-average cost for another portion. Would you be willing to issue an unqualified opinion under these circumstances? Explain.

13–15. "If the auditors can determine that all goods in the physical inventory have been accurately counted and properly priced, they will have discharged fully their responsibility with respect to inventory." Evaluate this statement.

13–16. How do the independent auditors use the client's backlog of unfilled sales orders in the examination of inventories?

13–17. The controller of a new client company informs you that most of the inventories are stored in bonded public warehouses. He presents warehouse receipts to account for the inventories. Will careful examination of these warehouse receipts constitute adequate verification of these inventories? Explain.

13–18. Hana Ranch Company, which has never been audited, is asked on October 1 by its bank to arrange for a year-end audit. The company retains you to make this audit and asks what measures, if any, it should take to ensure a satisfactory year-end physical inventory. Perpetual inventories are not maintained. How would you answer this inquiry?

13–19. Enumerate specific steps to be taken by the auditors to ascertain that a client's inventories have not been pledged or subjected to a lien of any kind.

GROUP II: QUESTIONS REQUIRING ANALYSIS

13–20. You are engaged in the audit of Reed Company, a new client, at the end of its first fiscal year, June 30, 19X1. During your work on inventories, you discover that all of the merchandise remaining in stock on June 30, 19X1, had been acquired July 1, 19X0, from Andrew Reed, the sole shareholder and president of Reed Company, for an original selling price of $10,000 cash and a note payable due July 1, 19X3, with interest at 15 percent, in the amount of $90,000. The merchandise had been used by the president when he operated a similar business as a single proprietor.

How can you verify the pricing of the June 30, 19X1, inventory of Reed Company? Explain.

13–21. The observation of a client's physical inventory is a mandatory auditing procedure when practicable and possible for the auditors to carry out and when inventories are material.

Required:
a. Why is the observation of physical inventory a mandatory auditing procedure? Explain.
b. Under what circumstances is observation of physical inventory impracticable or impossible?
c. Why is the auditors' review of the client's control of inventory tags important during the observation of physical inventory? Explain.

13–22. You have been asked to examine the financial statements of Wilson Corporation, a roadbuilding contractor that has never before been audited by CPAs. During your interim work, you learn that Wilson excludes a significant inventory item from its annual balance sheet. This inventory item, which Wilson management claims is approximately the same amount each year, is gravel that has been processed for use in road building and is placed at different road construction sites wherever it might be used. Wilson's controller states that any unused gravel at the completion of a construction contract is never moved to another job site; in fact, the gravel often disappears because of thefts during winter months when road construction is suspended.

Would you be able to issue an unqualified opinion on the financial statements of Wilson Corporation? Explain.

13–23. Grandview Manufacturing Company employs standard costs in its cost accounting system. List the audit procedures that you would apply to ascertain that Grandview's standard costs and related variance amounts are acceptable and have not distorted the financial statements. (Confine your audit procedures to those applicable to raw materials.)

(AICPA, adapted)

13–24. At the beginning of your annual audit of Crestview Manufacturing Company's financial statements for the year ended December 31, 198X, the company president confides in you that Henry Ward, an employee, is living on a scale in excess of that which his salary would support.

The employee has been a buyer in the purchasing department for six years and has charge of purchasing all general materials and supplies. He is authorized to sign purchase orders for amounts up to $500. Purchase orders in excess of $500 require the countersignature of the general purchasing agent.

The president understands that the usual examination of financial statements is not designed, and cannot be relied upon, to disclose fraud or conflicts of interest, although their discovery may result. The president authorizes you, however, to expand your regular audit procedures and to apply additional audit procedures to determine whether there is any evidence that the buyer has been misappropriating company funds or has been engaged in activities that were conflicts of interest.

Required:
List the audit procedures you would apply to the company records and documents in an attempt to discover evidence within the purchasing department of defalcations being committed by the buyer. Give the purpose of each audit procedure.   (AICPA, adapted)

13–25.   A number of companies employ outside service companies that specialize in counting, pricing, extending, and footing inventories. These service companies usually furnish a certificate attesting to the value of the physical inventory.

Assuming that the service company took the client company's inventory on the balance sheet date:

a.   How much reliance, if any, can the auditors place on the inventory certificate of outside specialists? Discuss.

b.   What effect, if any, would the inventory certificate of outside specialists have upon the type of report the auditors would render? Discuss.

c.   What reference, if any, would the auditors make to the certificate of outside specialists in their audit report?   (AICPA)

13–26.   Santa Rosa Corporation is a closely held furniture manufacturing company employing approximately one thousand employees. On December 15, the corporation retained the firm of Warren and Wood, Certified Public Accountants, to perform a December 31 year-end audit. The president of the corporation explained that perpetual inventory records were maintained and that every attention was given to maintaining strong internal control. A complete count of inventories had been made at November 30 by the company's own employees; in addition, extensive test counts had been made in most departments at various intervals during the year. Although the company was not large, it employed an internal auditor and an assistant who had devoted their full time to analysis of internal control and appraisal of operations in the various organizational units of the company.

The certified public accountant who had audited Santa Rosa Corporation for several years had died during the current year, and the company had decided to forgo an annual audit. The physical inventory had therefore been taken at November 30 without being observed by an independent public accountant. Shortly thereafter, a major stockholder in the company had demanded that new auditors be retained. The president explained to Warren and Wood that the company was too far behind on its delivery schedules to take time out for another physical inventory, but that all the papers used in the recent count were available for their review. The auditors reviewed these papers, made a thorough analysis of the internal controls over inventory, and made test counts at December 31 of large items representing 10 percent of the total value of inventory. The items tested were traced to the perpetual inventory records, and no significant discrepancies were found. Inventories at December 31 amounted to $4 million out of total assets of $9 million.

Required:
Assume that the auditors find no shortcomings in any aspect of the examination apart from the area of inventories. You are to prepare:

  a. An argument setting forth the factors that indicate the issuance of an unqualified audit opinion.

  b. An opposing argument setting forth the factors that indicate the auditors should not issue an unqualified opinion.

13–27. One of the problems faced by the auditors in their verification of inventory is the possibility that slow-moving and obsolete items may be included in the goods on hand at the balance sheet date. In the event that such items are identified in the physical inventory, their carrying value should be written down to an estimated scrap value or other recoverable amount.

  Prepare a list of the auditing procedures that the auditors should employ to determine whether slow-moving or obsolete items are included in the physical inventory.

13–28. During your observation of the November 30, 198X, physical inventory of Jay Company, you note the following unusual items:

  a. Electric motors in finished goods storeroom not tagged. Upon inquiry, you are informed that the motors are on consignment to Jay Company.

  b. A cutting machine (one of Jay's principal products) in the receiving department, with a large REWORK tag attached.

  c. A crated cutting machine in the shipping department, addressed to a nearby U.S. naval base, with a Department of Defense "Material Inspection and Receiving Report" attached, dated November 30, 198X, and signed by the Navy Source Inspector.

  d. A small, isolated storeroom with five types of dusty raw materials stored therein. Inventory tags are attached to all of the materials, and your test counts agree with the tags.

Required:

What additional procedures, if any, would you carry out for each of the above? Explain.

13–29. Ace Corporation does not conduct a complete annual physical count of purchased parts and supplies in its principal warehouse, but uses statistical sampling instead to estimate the year-end inventory. Ace maintains a perpetual inventory record of parts and supplies and believes that statistical sampling is highly effective in determining inventory values and is sufficiently reliable to make a physical count of each item of inventory unnecessary.

Required:

  a. Identify the audit procedures that should be used by the independent auditor that change or are in addition to normal required audit procedures when a client utilizes statistical sampling to determine inventory value and does not conduct a 100 percent annual physical count of inventory items.

  b. List at least 10 normal audit procedures that should be performed *to verify physical quantities* whenever a client conducts a periodic physical count of all or part of its inventory. (AICPA, adapted)

13–30. Nolan Manufacturing Company retains you on April 1 to perform an audit for the fiscal year ending June 30. During the month of May, you made extensive studies of internal control over inventories.

All goods purchased pass through a receiving department under the direction of the chief purchasing agent. The duties of the receiving department are to unpack, count, and inspect the goods. The quantity received is compared with the quantity shown on the receiving department's copy of the purchase order. If there is no discrepancy, the purchase order is stamped "OK—Receiving Dept." and forwarded to the accounts payable section of the accounting department. Any discrepancies in quantity or variations from specifications are called to the attention of the buyer by returning the purchase order to him with an explanation of the circumstances. No records are maintained in the receiving department, and no reports originate there.

As soon as goods have been inspected and counted in the receiving department, they are sent to the factory production area and stored alongside the machines in which they are to be processed. Finished goods are moved from the assembly line to a storeroom in the custody of a stock clerk, who maintains a perpetual inventory record in terms of physical units, but not in dollars.

What weaknesses, if any, do you see in the internal control over inventories?

13–31. Select the best answer for each of the following and explain fully the reason for your selection.

    a. When perpetual inventory records are maintained in quantities and in dollars, and internal control over inventory is weak, the auditor would probably—

        (1) Want the client to schedule the physical inventory count at the end of the year.

        (2) Insist that the client perform physical counts of inventory items several times during the year.

        (3) Increase the extent of tests for unrecorded liabilities at the end of the year.

        (4) Have to disclaim an opinion on the income statement for that year.

    b. Which of the following is the best audit procedure for the discovery of damaged merchandise in a client's ending inventory?

        (1) Compare the physical quantities of slow-moving items with corresponding quantities of the prior year.

        (2) Observe merchandise and raw materials during the client's physical inventory taking.

        (3) Review the management's inventory representations letter for accuracy.

        (4) Test overall fairness of inventory values by comparing the company's turnover ratio with the industry average.

    c. McPherson Corp. does not make an annual physical count of year-end inventories, but instead makes weekly test counts on the basis of a statistical plan. During the year, Sara Mullins, CPA, observes such counts as she deems necessary and is able to satisfy herself as to the reliability of the client's procedures. In reporting on the results of her examination, Mullins—

      (1) Can issue an unqualified opinion without disclosing that she did not observe year-end inventories.

      (2) Must comment in the scope paragraph as to her inability to observe year-end inventories, but can nevertheless issue an unqualified opinion.

      (3) Is required, if the inventories were material, to disclaim an opinion on the financial statements taken as a whole.

      (4) Must, if the inventories were material, qualify her opinion.

    d. The primary objective of a CPA's observation of a client's physical inventory count is to—

      (1) Discover whether a client has counted a particular inventory item or group of items.

      (2) Obtain direct knowledge that the inventory exists and has been properly counted.

      (3) Provide an appraisal of the quality of the merchandise on hand on the day of the physical count.

      (4) Allow the auditor to supervise the conduct of the count so as to obtain assurance that inventory quantities are reasonably accurate.

    e. Which of the following situations would most likely require special audit planning by the auditors?

      (1) Some sales transactions are to related parties.

      (2) Perpetual inventory records are maintained on items with a value in excess of $50.

      (3) Purchase orders are required for all inventory purchases.

      (4) Inventory is comprised of precious stones.

    f. When verifying debits to the perpetual inventory records of a non-manufacturing company, the auditors would be most interested in examining a sample of purchase—

      (1) Approvals.

      (2) Requisitions.

      (3) Invoices.

      (4) Orders.   (AICPA, adapted)

GROUP III: PROBLEMS

13–32. You have been engaged by the management of Alden, Inc., to review its internal controls over the purchase, receipt, storage, and issue of raw materials. You have prepared the following comments, which describe Alden's procedures.

    (1) Raw materials, which consist mainly of high-cost electronic components, are kept in a locked storeroom. Storeroom personnel include a supervisor and four clerks. All are well-trained, competent, and adequately bonded. Raw materials are removed from the storeroom only upon written or oral authorization of one of the production first-line supervisors.

    (2) There are no perpetual-inventory records; hence, the storeroom clerks do not keep records of goods received or issued. To compensate for the lack of perpetual records, a physical-inventory count is taken monthly by the storeroom clerks, who are well supervised. Appropriate procedures are followed in making the inventory count.

(3) After the physical count, the storeroom supervisor matches quantities counted against a predetermined reorder level. If the count for a given part is below the reorder level, the supervisor enters the part number on a materials requisition list and sends this list to the accounts payable clerk. The accounts payable clerk prepares a purchase order for a predetermined reorder quantity for each part and mails the purchase order to the vendor from whom the part was last purchased.

(4) When ordered materials arrive at Alden, they are received by the storeroom clerks. The clerks count the merchandise and agree the counts to the carrier's bill of lading. All bills of lading are initialed, dated, and filed in the storeroom to serve as receiving reports.

Required:

Describe the weaknesses in internal control and recommend improvements of Alden's procedures for the purchase, receipt, storage, and issuance of raw materials. Organize your answer sheet as follows:

Weaknesses	Recommended improvements

(AICPA, adapted)

13–33. The following are typical questions that might appear on an internal control questionnaire for inventory:

1. Are written procedures prepared by the client for the taking of the physical inventory?
2. Do the client's inventory taking procedures include a requirement to identify damaged inventory items?
3. Does the client maintain perpetual inventory records?

Required:

a. Describe the purpose of each of the above internal control procedures.
b. Describe the manner in which each of the above procedures might be tested.
c. Assuming that the operating effectiveness of each of the above procedures is found to be inadequate, describe how the auditors might alter their substantive tests to compensate for the internal control weakness.

13–34. David Anderson, CPA, is engaged in the examination of the financial statements of Redondo Manufacturing Corporation for the year ended June 30, 198X. Redondo's inventories at year-end include finished merchandise on consignment with consignees and finished merchandise stored in public warehouses. The merchandise in public warehouses is pledged as collateral for outstanding debt.

Required:

Normal inventory and notes payable auditing procedures have been satisfactorily completed. Describe the specific additional auditing procedures that Anderson should undertake with respect to—

a. Consignments out.

b. Finished merchandise in public warehouses pledged as collateral for outstanding debt. (AICPA, adapted)

13–35. You are an audit manager of the rapidly growing CPA firm of Raye and Coye. You have been placed in charge of three new audit clients, which have the following inventory features:

1. Canyon Cattle Co., which maintains 15,000 head of cattle on a 1,000 square mile ranch, mostly unfenced, near the south rim of the Grand Canyon in Arizona.

2. Rhoads Mfg. Co., which has raw materials inventories consisting principally of pig iron loaded on gondola freight cars on a siding at the company's plant.

3. Strawser Company, which is in production around the clock on three shifts, and which cannot shut down production during the physical inventory.

Required:

What problems do you anticipate in the observation of physical inventories of the three new clients, and how would you deal with the problems?

13–36. Royal Meat Processing Company buys and processes livestock for sale to supermarkets. In connection with the examination of the company's financial statements, you have prepared the following notes based on your review of inventory procedures:

1. Each livestock buyer submits a daily report of his or her purchases to the plant superintendent. This report shows the dates of purchase and expected delivery, the vendor and the number, and weights and type of livestock purchased. As shipments are received, any available plant employee counts the number of each type received and places a check mark beside this quantity on the buyer's report. When all shipments listed on the report have been received, the report is returned to the buyer.

2. Vendors' invoices, after a clerical review, are sent to the appropriate buyer for approval and returned to the accounting department. A disbursement voucher and a check for the approved amount are prepared in the accounting department. Checks are forwarded to the treasurer for signature. The treasurer's office sends signed checks directly to the buyer for delivery to the vendor.

3. Livestock carcasses are processed by lots. Each lot is assigned a number. At the end of each day a tally sheet reporting the lots processed, the number and type of animals in each lot, and the carcass weight is sent to the accounting department, where a perpetual inventory record of processed carcasses and their weights is maintained.

4. Processed carcasses are stored in a refrigerated cooler located in a small building adjacent to the employee parking lot. The cooler is locked when the plant is not open, and a company guard is on duty when the employees report for work and leave at the end of their shifts. Supermarket truck drivers wishing to pick up their orders have been instructed to contact someone in the plant if no one is in the cooler.

5. Substantial quantities of by-products are produced and stored, either in the cooler or elsewhere in the plant. By-products are initially accounted for as they are sold. At this time the sales manager prepares a two-part form: one copy serves as authorization to transfer the goods to the customer, and the other becomes the basis for billing the customer.

Required:
For each of the numbered notes 1 to 5 above, state the weaknesses, if any, in the present inventory procedures and your suggestions, if any, for improvement.   (AICPA, adapted)

13–37. Payne Press Company is engaged in the manufacture of large-size presses under specific contracts and in accordance with customers' specifications. Customers are required to advance 25 percent of the contract price. The company records sales on a shipment basis and accumulates costs by job orders. The normal profit margin over the past few years has been approximately 5 percent of sales, after provision for selling and administrative expenses of about 10 percent of sales. Inventories are valued at the lower of cost or market.

Among the jobs you are reviewing in the course of your annual examination of the company's December 31 financial statements is Job No. 2357, calling for delivery of a three-color press at a firm contract price of $50,000. Costs accumulated for the job at the year-end aggregated $30,250. The company's engineers estimated that the job was approximately 55 percent complete at December 31. Your audit procedures have been as follows:
1. Examined all contracts, noting pertinent provisions.
2. Observed physical inventory of jobs in process and reconciled details to job order accounts.
3. Tested controls over input of labor, material, and overhead charges into the various jobs to determine that such charges were authentic and had been posted correctly.
4. Confirmed customers' advances at year-end.
5. Reconciled goods in process job ledger with control account.

Required:
With respect to Job No. 2357:
a. State what additional audit procedures, if any, you would follow and explain the purpose of the procedures.
b. Indicate the manner and the amount at which you would include Job No. 2357 in the balance sheet.   (AICPA, adapted)

13–38. Late in December, your CPA firm accepted an audit engagement at Nash Jewelers, Inc., a corporation that deals largely in diamonds. The corporation has retail jewelry stores in several eastern cities and a diamond wholesale store in New York City. The wholesale store also sets the diamonds in rings and other quality jewelry.

The retail stores place orders for diamond jewelry with the wholesale store in New York City. A buyer employed by the wholesale store purchases diamonds in the New York diamond market; the wholesale store then fills orders from the retail stores and from independent customers and maintains a substantial inventory of diamonds. The corporation values its inventory by the specific identification cost method.

Required:

Assume that at the inventory date you are satisfied that Nash Jewelers, Inc. has no items left by customers for repair or sale on consignment and that no inventory owned by the corporation is in the possession of outsiders.

a. Discuss the problems the auditors should anticipate in planning for the observation of the physical inventory on this engagement because of the—

   (1) Different locations of inventories.

   (2) Nature of the inventory.

b. Assume that a shipment of diamond rings was in transit by corporation messenger from the wholesale store to a retail store on the inventory date. What additional audit steps would you take to satisfy yourself as to the gems that were in transit from the wholesale store on the inventory date? (AICPA, adapted)

13–39. Smith is the partner in charge of the audit of Blue Distributing Corporation, a wholesaler that owns one warehouse containing 80 percent of its inventory. Smith is reviewing the working papers that were prepared to support the firm's opinion on Blue's financial statements, and Smith wants to be certain essential audit records are well-documented.

Required:

What substantive tests should Smith expect to find in the working papers to document management's assertion about completeness as it relates to the inventory quantities at the end of the year? (AICPA, adapted)

**GROUP IV:
RESEARCH AND
DISCUSSION CASE**

13–40. Western Trading Company is a sole proprietorship engaged in the grain brokerage business. At December 31, 198X, the entire grain inventory of the company was stored in outside bonded warehouses. The company's procedure of pricing inventories in these warehouses includes comparing the actual cost of each commodity in inventory with the market price as reported for transactions on the commodity exchanges at December 31. A write-down is made on commodities in which cost is in excess of market. During the course of the 198X examination, the auditors verified the company's computations. In addition to this, they compared the book value of the inventory with market prices at February 15, 198Y, the last day of field work. The auditors noted that the market price of several of the commodities had declined sharply subsequent to year-end, until their market price was significantly below the commodities' book values.

The inventory was repriced by the auditors on the basis of the new market price, and the book value of the inventory was found to be in excess of market value on February 15 by approximately $21,000. The auditors proposed that the inventories be written down by $17,000 to this new market value, net of gains on the subsequent sales. The management protested this suggestion, stating that in their opinion the market decline was only temporary and that prices would recover in the near future. They refused to allow the write-down to be made. Accordingly, the auditors qualified their audit opinion for a departure from generally accepted accounting principles.

Required:

a. Were the auditors justified in issuing a qualified opinion in this situation? Discuss fully, including alternative courses of action.

b. State your opinion as to the course of action that was appropriate in this situation.

Suggested references:

AICPA, *Professional Standards, Volume A,* Commerce Clearing House, *Statements on Auditing Standards 1,* Sections 560.01–.09.

AICPA, *Professional Standards, Volume C,* Commerce Clearing House, *Statements on Financial Accounting Standards,* Sections 4311.09–.19 and 5121.08–.10.

Property, plant, and equipment: Depreciation and depletion

Chapter 14 study objectives

After studying this chapter, you should be able to:

— Describe the nature of property, plant, and equipment, and depreciation.
— Explain the fundamental internal controls over property, plant, and equipment.
— Describe the auditors' objectives for the audit of property, plant, and equipment.
— Describe the nature of the procedures to accomplish the auditors' objectives for the audit of property, plant, and equipment, and depreciation.

The term *property, plant, and equipment* includes all tangible assets with a service life of more than one year that are used in the operation of the business and are not acquired for the purpose of resale. Three major subgroups of such assets are generally recognized:

1. *Land,* such as acres of property used in the operation of the business, has the significant characteristic of not being subject to depreciation.
2. *Buildings, machinery, equipment, and land improvements,* such as fences and parking lots, have limited service lives and are subject to depreciation.

3. *Natural resources* (wasting assets), such as oil wells, coal mines, and tracts of timber, are subject to depletion as the natural resources are extracted or removed.

Acquisitions and disposals of property, plant, and equipment are usually large in dollar amount, but concentrated in only a few transactions. Individual items of plant and equipment may remain unchanged in the accounts for many years.

The auditors' approach in examination of property, plant, and equipment

The auditors' *objectives* are to determine that:

1. *Internal control* over property, plant, and equipment *is adequate.*
2. The recorded property, plant, and equipment is valid (*existence* and *rights*).
3. All property, plant, and equipment is recorded (*completeness*).
4. Property, plant, and equipment records and supporting schedules are mathematically correct and agree with general ledger accounts (*clerical accuracy*).
5. The *valuation* of property, plant, and equipment is proper.
6. The *presentation* and *disclosure* of property, plant, and equipment, including disclosure of depreciation methods, is adequate.

In conjunction with the audit of property, plant, and equipment, the auditors also obtain evidence about the related accounts of depreciation expense, accumulated depreciation, and repairs and maintenance expense.

Contrast with audit of current assets

In many companies, the investment in plant and equipment amounts to 50 percent or more of the total assets. However, the audit work required to verify these properties is usually a much smaller proportion of the total audit time spent on the engagement. The verification of plant and equipment is facilitated by several factors not applicable to audit work on current assets.

First, a typical unit of property or equipment has a high dollar value, and relatively few transactions may lie behind a large balance sheet amount. Second, there is usually little change in the property accounts from year to year. The Land account often remains unchanged for a long span of years. The durable nature of buildings and equipment also tends to hold accounting activity to a minimum for these accounts. By way of contrast, such current assets as accounts receivable and inventory may have a complete turnover several times a year.

A third point of contrast between the audit of plant assets and the audit of current assets is the significance of the year-end cutoff of transactions. For current assets, the year-end cutoff is a critical issue; for plant assets, it is generally not. For example, in our discussion of inventories in Chapter 13, we emphasized the importance of an accurate year-end cutoff of the transactions for purchases and sales of merchandise. An error in the cutoff of a $50,000 purchase or sales transaction may cause a $50,000 error in the year's pretax net income. The possibility of such errors is substantial because a large volume of merchandise transactions is normal at year-end. For plant assets, on the other hand, a year-end cutoff error in recording an acquisition or retirement ordinarily will not affect net income for the year. Moreover, for many companies, there may be no transactions in plant assets occurring at the year-end. Of course, a cutoff error relating to acquisition or retirement of plant assets could cause slight inaccuracies in depreciation or in the timing of gains or losses on disposals. The problem of year-end cutoff for plant assets, however, must be considered a minor one in contrast to the audit of current assets.

Internal controls over plant and equipment

The principal purpose of internal controls relating to plant and equipment *is to obtain maximum efficiency from the dollars invested in plant assets.*

The amounts invested in plant and equipment represent a large portion of the total assets of many industrial concerns. The expenses of maintenance, rearrangement, and depreciation of these assets are a major factor in the income statement. The sheer size of the amounts involved makes strong internal controls essential to the production of reliable financial statements. Errors in measurement of income will be material if assets are scrapped without their cost being removed from the accounts or if the distinction between capital and revenue expenditures is not maintained consistently. The losses that inevitably arise from uncontrolled methods of acquiring, maintaining, and retiring plant and equipment are often greater than the losses from fraud in cash handling.

The plant and equipment budget

In large enterprises, the auditors may expect to find an annual plant budget used to forecast and to control acquisitions and retirements of plant and equipment. Many small companies also forecast expenditures for plant assets. Successful utilization of a plant budget presupposes the existence of reliable and detailed accounting records for plant and equipment. A detailed knowledge of the kinds, quantities, and condition of existing equipment is an essential basis for intelligent forecasting of the need for replacements and additions to the plant.

If the auditors find that acquisitions of plant and equipment, whether by purchase or construction, are made in accordance with prior budgetary authorizations and that any necessary expenditures not provided for in the budget are made only upon approval of a top level executive, they will be able to minimize the routine testing of the year's acquisitions. Reference to the reports of the internal auditors is often a convenient method for the independent auditors to become familiar with the scope and dependability of the budgetary controls over plant and equipment.

Other major control devices

Other important controls applicable to plant and equipment are as follows:

1. A subsidiary ledger consisting of a separate record for each unit of property. An adequate plant and equipment ledger facilitates the auditors' work in analyzing additions and retirements, in verifying the depreciation provision and maintenance expenses, and in comparing authorizations with actual expenditures.
2. A system of authorizations requiring advance executive approval of all plant and equipment acquisitions, whether by purchase, lease, or construction. Serially numbered capital work orders are a convenient means of recording authorizations.
3. A reporting procedure assuring prompt disclosure and analysis of variances between authorized expenditures and actual costs.
4. An authoritative written statement of company policy distinguishing between capital and revenue expenditures. A dollar minimum ordinarily will be established for capitalization; any expenditures of lesser amount automatically are classified as charges against current revenue.
5. A policy requiring all purchases of plant and equipment to be handled through the purchasing department and subjected to standard routines for receiving, inspection, and payment.
6. Periodic physical inventories, designed to verify the existence, location, and condition of all property listed in the accounts and to disclose the existence of any unrecorded units.
7. A system of retirement procedures, including serially numbered retirement work orders, stating reasons for retirement and bearing appropriate approvals.

Audit working papers

The key audit working paper for property, plant, and equipment is a summary analysis such as that illustrated in Figure 14–1. This working paper follows the approach we have previously described of *emphasizing changes during the year under audit.* The working paper shows the beginning balances for the various types of plant assets; these amounts are the ending balances shown in the prior year's working papers. Next, the working paper shows the additions and retirements during the year. These are the transactions upon which the auditors' attention will be focused. A final column shows the ending balances that must equal the beginning balances plus the additions and minus the retirements. A similar set of four columns is used to summarize the changes in the accounts for accumulated depreciation.

Among the other audit working papers for property, plant, and equipment are analyses of the year's additions and retirements, analyses of repairs and maintenance expense accounts, and tests of depreciation. The analyses of plant additions and retirements and the tests of depreciation are cross-indexed to the summary analysis, as illustrated in Figure 14–1. In the audit of larger companies, it is common practice for the client to prepare for the auditors both a listing of the year's additions and a schedule of the year's disposals.

Initial audits and repeat engagements

The auditing procedures listed in subsequent pages are applicable to repeat engagements and therefore concern only transactions of the current year. In the auditors' first examination of a new client that has changed auditors, the beginning balances of plant and equipment may be substantiated by reference to the predecessor firm's working papers. If, in previous years, audits were made by other reputable firms of public accountants, it is not customary in a first audit to go beyond a general review of the past history of the plant and equipment as recorded in the accounts.

In a first audit of a company for which audits by independent public accountants have not been made previously, the ideal approach is a complete historical analysis of the property accounts. By thorough review of all major charges and credits to the property accounts since their inception, the auditors can determine whether the company has consistently followed good accounting practices in recording capital additions and retirements and in providing for periodic depreciation.

If the client has been in business for many years, the review of transactions in earlier years necessarily must be performed on a test basis in order to stay within reasonable time limits. However, the importance of an analysis of transactions of prior years deserves emphasis. Only by this approach can the auditors be in a sound position to express an opinion as

Figure 14–1

The Nashville Corporation
Summary of Property, Plant and Equipment and Accumulated Depreciation
December 31, 1991   K-1

Account No.	Description	Assets						Accumulated Depreciation			
		Balance Dec. 31, 90	Additions	Retirements	Balance Dec. 31, 91	Method	Rate	Balance Dec. 31, 90	Provision	Retirements	Balance Dec. 31, 91
151	Land	500000	15100.00		65 100.00						
152/3	Land Improvements	135000	1000.00		145000 4	SL	5%	135000	7000		21000 4
154/5	Buildings	4500000	495000.00		4995000 4	SL	3%	292000.00	142400		434400 4
156/7	Equipment	7000000	1100000	600000	85000.00 4	SL	10%	2350000	706000	504000	2552000 4
		53150000	7160000	600000	6641000.00			5140500	2203400	504000	7102900
			X-1-1		X			X-1-2	X-1-2	X-1-1	X

4 — Footed plant and equipment and equipment subsidiary ledger cards. No exceptions.

Conclusions:
As a result of our audit procedures for plant
and equipment and related depreciation, it is our
opinion that the Dec 31, 89 balances above are fairly
stated.

2/14/74
Jan 9, 1992

to the propriety of the current period's depreciation. If repair and maintenance expenses have been capitalized, or asset additions have been recorded as operating expenses, or retirements of property have gone unrecorded, the depreciation expense will be misstated regardless of the care
taken in the selection of depreciation rates. The auditors should make
clear to the client that the initial examination of plant and equipment
requires procedures that need not be duplicated in subsequent engagements.

AUDIT PROGRAM FOR PROPERTY, PLANT, AND EQUIPMENT

The following procedures are typical of the work required in many
engagements for the verification of property, plant, and equipment. The
procedures for accumulated depreciation are covered in a separate program on pages 524–25.

A. Consider internal control for property, plant, and equipment
  1. *Obtain an understanding* of the internal control for property,
     plant, and equipment.
  2. *Assess control risk* for each of the major financial statement
     assertions about property, plant, and equipment, *and design
     additional tests of controls.*
  3. *Perform additional tests of controls* for those controls on which
     the auditors plan to rely to reduce their assessment of control
     risk and, thus, the extent of substantive testing.
  4. *Reassess control risk* for each of the major financial statement
     assertions about property, plant, and equipment based on the
     results of tests of controls, *and design substantive tests.*

**B. Perform substantive tests of property, plant, and equipment, and
related revenue and expenses**
  5. Obtain a summary analysis of changes in property owned and
     reconcile to ledgers.
  6. Vouch additions to property during the year.
  7. Make physical inspection of major acquisitions of plant and
     equipment.
  8. Analyze repair and maintenance expense accounts.
  9. Investigate the status of property not in current use.
  10. Test the client's provision for depreciation.
  11. Verify retirements of property during the year.
  12. Verify legal ownership of property, plant, and equipment.
  13. Review rental revenue from land, buildings, and equipment
      owned by the client but leased to others.
  14. Examine lease agreements on property, plant, and equipment
      leased to and from others.
  15. Perform analytical procedures for property, plant, and equip-
      ment.
  16. Evaluate financial statement presentation and disclosure for
      plant assets and for related revenue and expenses.

These substantive audit procedures are summarized in Figure 14–2 along with the primary audit objectives.

Figure 14–2 Objectives of major substantive tests of property, plant, and equipment, and depreciation

Substantive tests	Primary audit objectives
Obtain a summary analysis of changes in property owned and reconcile to ledgers	*Clerical accuracy*
Vouch additions during year Make physical inspection of major acquisitions	*Validity (existence and rights)* *Valuation or allocation*
Analyze repair and maintenance expense accounts Investigate the status of property not in current use Test the client's provision for depreciation	*Valuation or allocation*
Verify retirements of property during the year Verify legal ownership Review rental revenue	*Validity (existence and rights)*
Examine lease agreements Perform analytical procedures	*Validity (existence and rights)* *Completeness* *Valuation or allocation*
Evaluate financial statement presentation and disclosure	*Presentation and disclosure*

A. Consider internal control for property, plant, and equipment

1. Obtain an understanding of the internal control.

In the study of internal control for plant and equipment, the auditors may utilize a written description, flowcharts, or an internal control questionnaire. The following are typical of the questions included in a questionnaire: Are plant ledgers regularly reconciled with general ledger controlling accounts? Are periodic physical inventories of plant assets compared with the plant ledgers? Are variances between plant budgets and actual expenditures for plant assets subject to review and approval of executives? Does the sale, transfer, or dismantling of equipment require written executive approval on a serially numbered retirement work order? Is there a written policy for distinguishing between capital expenditures and revenue expenditures?

2. Assess control risk and design additional tests of controls.

Control risk for a financial statement assertion may be assessed below the maximum only when tests indicate that related controls are designed and operating effectively. The auditors must decide which additional tests of controls will likely result in cost justified restrictions of substantive tests.

3. Perform additional tests of controls.

The purpose of tests of controls for plant assets is to determine whether the internal controls established by the client are being followed consistently in practice. For example, if the client uses serially numbered retirement work orders to authorize the disposal of plant assets, the auditors may test this control by matching known retirements with retirement work orders and by comparing individual work orders with entries in the subsidiary ledgers for plant and equipment. Another test is to examine copies of reconciliations of the subsidiary ledgers with general ledger controlling accounts to determine whether these reconciliations have, in fact, been regularly prepared and have been approved by an appropriate official.

4. Reassess control risk and design substantive tests.

The final step in the auditors' consideration of internal control involves a reassessment of control risk based on the results of the tests of controls. The auditors then select the substantive tests necessary to provide sufficient competent evidence as to the audit objectives for the client's property, plant, and equipment. The extent of the substantive tests is determined in relation to the auditors' final assessment of control risk.

B. Substantive tests

5. Obtain a summary analysis of changes in property owned and reconcile to ledgers.

The auditors may verify the beginning balances of plant and equipment assets by reference to the prior year's audit working papers. In addition to beginning balances, the summary analysis will show the additions and retirements of plant and equipment during the year under audit. As the audit progresses, the auditors will verify in detail these additions and retirements. The detailed working papers showing this verification will support and be cross-indexed to the summary analysis worksheet.

Before making a detailed analysis of changes in property accounts during the year, the auditors will want to be sure that the amounts in the subsidiary ledgers agree in total with the balances in the controlling accounts. This is also a desirable prerequisite to any tests of the ledger by firsthand observation of plant and equipment. Reconciliation of the subsidiary ledgers with the controlling accounts can be performed very quickly with the use of generalized audit software.

6. Vouch additions to property during the year.

The vouching of additions to the property accounts during the period under audit is one of the most important substantive tests of plant and equipment. The extent of the vouching is dependent upon the auditors' assessment of control risk for plant and equipment expenditures. The vouching process utilizes a working paper analysis of the general ledger controlling accounts and includes the tracing of entries through the journals to original documents, such as contracts, deeds, construction work orders, invoices, canceled checks, and authorization by directors.

The specific steps to be taken in investigating the year's property additions usually will include the following:

1. Examine authorizations for all major additions, including assets purchased and assets constructed.
2. Review changes during the year in construction in progress and examine supporting work orders, both incomplete and closed.
3. Trace transfers from the Construction in Progress account to the property accounts, observing propriety of classification. Determine that all completed items have been transferred.
4. On a test basis, vouch purchases of plant and equipment to invoices, deeds, contracts, or other supporting documents. Test extensions, footings, and treatment of discounts. Make certain revenue expenditures were not improperly capitalized.
5. Investigate all instances in which the actual cost of acquisitions substantially exceeded authorized amounts. Determine whether such excess expenditures were analyzed and approved by appropriate officials.
6. Investigate fully any debits to property accounts not arising from acquisition of physical assets.
7. Determine that the total cost of any plant and equipment assets purchased on the installment plan is reflected in the asset accounts and that the unpaid installments are set up as liabilities. Ascertain that all plant and equipment leases that in effect are installment purchases are accounted for as assets acquired. Interest charges should not be capitalized as a cost of the asset acquired.

The accounting for plant assets acquired in a trade-in or other exchange is specified by *APB Opinion No. 29*, "Accounting for Nonmonetary Transactions." No gain is recognized when a plant asset is exchanged for a similar plant asset. The asset acquired in the exchange is valued at the carrying amount of the asset given up plus any additional cash paid or amount financed.

Assets constructed by a company for its own use should be recorded at the cost of direct material, direct labor, and applicable overhead cost. However, auditors usually apply the additional test of comparing the total cost of self-constructed equipment with bids or estimated purchase prices for similar equipment from outside suppliers, and they take exception to the capitalization of costs substantially in excess of the amount for which the asset could have been purchased and installed.

Related party transactions Assets acquired from affiliated corporations, from promoters or stockholders, or by any other type of related party transaction not involving arm's-length bargaining between buyer and seller, have sometimes been recorded at inflated amounts. The auditors should inquire into the methods by which the sales price was determined, the cost of the property to the vendor, length of ownership by vendor, and any other available evidence that might indicate an arbitrarily determined valuation. Related party transactions must be disclosed in the notes to the financial statements.

7. Make a physical inspection of major acquisitions of plant and equipment.

The auditors usually make a physical inspection of major units of plant and equipment acquired during the year under audit. This step is helpful in maintaining a good working knowledge of the client's operations and also in interpreting the accounting entries for both additions and retirements. Physical inspection is particularly appropriate if there appear to be weaknesses in the client's internal controls over plant assets.

The audit procedure of physical inspection may flow in either direction between the plant assets and the records of plant assets. By tracing items in the plant ledger to the physical assets, the auditors prove that the assets shown in the accounting records *actually exist* and are in current use. The alternative testing procedure is to inspect selected assets in the plant and trace these assets to the detailed records. This test provides evidence that existing assets are recorded.

The physical inspection of plant assets may be limited to major units acquired during the year or may be extended to include tests of older equipment as well. In a few situations (especially when internal controls are weak), the auditors may conclude that the taking of a complete physical inventory is needed. Bear in mind, however, that a complete physical inventory of plant and equipment is a rare event. If such an inventory is required, the auditors' role is to *observe* the physical inventory.

Let us consider an example of a situation in which the auditors might conclude that a complete physical inventory of plant and equipment was needed. Assume that a client is engaged in commercial construction work and that the client owns and operates a great many units of costly mobile equipment. Such equipment may often be scrapped or sold upon the authorization of a field supervisor. Under these circumstances, the auditors might regard a complete physical inventory of plant and equipment as essential. Similarly, in the audit of clients owning a large number of automobiles and trucks, the auditors may insist upon observing a physical count, as well as making verification of legal title.

Some large companies, as part of their internal control, perform occasional physical inventories of plant and equipment at certain locations or in selected departments. The *observation* of these limited counts is often carried out by the client's internal auditing staff rather than by the independent auditors.

8. Analyze repair and maintenance expense accounts.

The auditors' principal objective in analyzing repair and maintenance expense accounts is to discover items that should have been capitalized. Many companies have a written policy setting the minimum expenditure to be capitalized. For example, company policy may prescribe that no expenditure for less than $300 shall be capitalized regardless of the service life of the item purchased. In such cases, the auditors will analyze the repair and maintenance accounts with a view toward determining the consistency of application of this policy as well as compliance with generally accepted accounting principles. To determine that the accounts contain only bona fide repair and maintenance charges, the auditors will trace the larger expenditures to written authorizations for the transaction. Correctness of the amounts involved may be verified by reference to vendors' invoices, to material requisitions, and to labor time records.

One useful means of identifying any capital expenditures that are buried in the repair and maintenance accounts is to obtain or prepare an analysis of the monthly amounts of expense with corresponding amounts listed for the preceding year. Any significant variations from month to month or between corresponding months of the two years should be fully investigated. If maintenance expense is classified by the departments serviced, the variations are especially noticeable.

9. Investigate the status of property not in current use.

Land, buildings, and equipment not in current use should be investigated thoroughly to determine the prospects for their future use in operations. Plant assets that are temporarily idle need not be reclassified, and depreciation may be continued at normal rates. On the other hand, idle equipment that has been dismantled, or that for any reason appears unsuitable for future operating use, should be written down to an estimated realizable value and excluded from the plant and equipment classification. In the case of standby equipment and other property not needed at present or prospective levels of operation, the auditors should consider whether the carrying value is recoverable through future use in operations.

Illustrative case

During the 1970s, many large public utility companies began the construction of nuclear power plants which were believed to be the best source of electricity for the future. By the mid-1980s, however, these projects had turned into financial nightmares. In many cases, the cost to date of a half-completed nuclear plant was several times the original estimate of total cost. Construction had ground virtually to a halt, and the prospects for getting these nuclear plants into operation were dim. Efforts of the antinuclear lobby and legal battles combined with engineering problems to raise doubts whether nuclear plants representing investments in the billions would ever become operational.

These developments created a most difficult situation for the CPA firms having "nuclear utilities" as clients. Should the costly nuclear facilities be written off even though such action would wipe out the stockholders' equity? Should the uncompleted facilities be carried at cost in the companies' financial statements despite the distinct possibility they would never be completed? Most auditing firms felt that they must modify their audit reports to indicate that the future solvency of the client company rested on a favorable solution to the problem of the uncompleted nuclear plant.

10. Test the client's provision for depreciation.

See the separate *depreciation* program following this audit program.

11. Verify retirements of property during the year.

The principal purpose of this procedure is to determine whether any property has been replaced, sold, dismantled, or abandoned without such action being reflected in the accounting records. Nearly every thorough physical inventory of plant and equipment reveals missing units of property: units disposed of without a corresponding reduction of the accounts.

It is not unusual for a factory supervisor to order that a machine be scrapped without realizing that the accounting department has an interest in such action. How is the accounting department expected to know when a factory asset is retired? If a machine is sold for cash or traded in on a new machine, the transaction will presumably involve the use of documents, such as a cash receipts form or a purchase order; the processing of these documents may bring the retirement to the attention of accounting personnel. However, many plant assets are scrapped rather than being sold or traded in on new equipment; consequently, there may be no paper work to evidence the disappearance of a machine.

One method of guarding against unrecorded retirements is enforcement of a company-wide policy that no plant asset shall be retired from use without prior approval on a special type of serially numbered work order. A copy of the retirement work order is routed to the accounting department, thus providing some assurance that retirements will be reflected in the accounting records.

What specific steps should the auditors take to discover any unrecorded retirements? The following measures often are effective:

1. If major additions of plant and equipment have been made during the year, ascertain whether old equipment was traded in or replaced by the new units.
2. Analyze the Miscellaneous Revenue account to locate any cash proceeds from sale of plant assets.
3. If any of the company's products have been discontinued during the year, investigate the disposition of plant facilities formerly used in manufacturing such products.
4. Inquire of executives and supervisors whether any plant assets have been retired during the year.
5. Examine retirement work orders or other source documents for authorization by the appropriate official or committee.
6. Investigate any reduction of insurance coverage to determine whether this was caused by retirement of plant assets.

12. Verify legal ownership of property, plant, and equipment.

To determine that plant assets are the property of the client, the auditors look for such evidence as a deed, title insurance policy, property tax bills, receipts for payments to mortgagee, and fire insurance policies. Additionally, the fact that rental payments are not being made is supporting evidence of ownership.

It is sometimes suggested that the auditors may verify ownership of real property and the absence of liens by examination of public records. This step is seldom taken. Inspection of the documentary evidence listed above usually provides adequate proof of ownership. If some doubt exists as to whether the client has clear title to property, the auditors should obtain the opinion of the client's legal counsel or request that a title search be performed by a title insurance company.

Possession of a deed is not proof of present ownership because when real property is sold, a new deed is prepared and the old one is retained by the seller. This is true of title insurance policies as well. Better evidence of continuing ownership is found in property tax bills made out in the name of the client and in fire insurance policies, rent receipts from lessees, and regular payments of principal and interest to a mortgagee or trustee.

The disclosure of liens on property is considered during the examination of liabilities, but in the audit work on plant and equipment the auditors should be alert for evidence indicating the existence of liens. Purchase contracts examined in verifying the cost of property may reveal unpaid balances. Insurance policies may contain loss payable endorsements in favor of a secured party.

The ownership of automobiles and trucks can readily be ascertained by the auditors by reference to certificates of title and registration documents. The ease of transfer of title to automotive equipment, plus the fact that it is often used as collateral for loans, makes it important that the auditors verify title to such property.

13. Review rental revenue from land, buildings, and equipment owned by the client but leased to others.

In verifying rental revenue from land and buildings, it is often desirable for the auditors to obtain or to sketch a map of the property and to make a physical inspection of each unit. This may disclose that premises reported as vacant are in fact occupied by lessees and are producing revenue not reflected in the accounting records. If the client's property includes an office or apartment building, the auditors should obtain a floor plan of the building as well as copies of all lease contracts. In this way, they can account for all available rental space as revenue producing or vacant and can verify reported vacancies by physical inspection at the balance sheet date. If interim audit work is being performed, vacancies should also be verified by inspection and discussion with management during the year.

Examination of leases will indicate whether tenants are responsible for the cost of electricity, water, gas, and telephone service. These provisions should be reconciled with utility expense accounts. Rental revenue accounts should be analyzed in all cases and the amount compared with lease agreements and cash records.

14. Examine lease agreements on property, plant, and equipment leased to and from others.

The preceding step addressed rental revenue from leases. Also related to leases, the auditors must be aware that generally accepted accounting principles require differing accounting treatments, depending upon whether they qualify as an operating or a capital lease. The auditors should carefully examine lease agreements to determine whether the accounting for the assets involved is proper. For example, the auditors must determine whether assets leased by the client should be capitalized.

15. Perform analytical procedures for property, plant, and equipment.

The specific trends and ratios used in judging the overall reasonableness of recorded amounts for plant and equipment will vary with the nature of the client's operations. Among the ratios and trends often used by auditors for this purpose are the following:

a. Total cost of plant assets divided by annual output in dollars, pounds, or other units.
b. Total cost of plant assets divided by cost of goods sold.
c. Comparison of repairs and maintenance expense on a monthly basis and from year to year.
d. Comparison of acquisitions for the current year with prior years.
e. Comparison of retirements for the current year with prior years.

Acquisitions and retirements may vary widely from year to year; however, it is essential that the auditors be aware of these variations and judge their reasonableness in the light of trends in the client's past and present operations. Analytical procedures relating to depreciation are discussed later in this chapter as part of the audit program for depreciation.

16. Evaluate financial statement presentation and disclosure for plant assets and for related revenue and expenses.

The balance sheet or accompanying notes should disclose balances of major classes of depreciable assets. Accumulated depreciation may be shown by major class or in total, and the method or methods of computing depreciation should be stated. The total amount of depreciation should be disclosed in the income statement or supporting notes.

In addition, adequate financial statement presentation and disclosure will ordinarily reflect the following principles:

a. The basis of valuation should be explicitly stated. At present, cost is the generally accepted basis of valuation for plant and equipment; property not in use should be valued at estimated realizable value.
b. Property pledged to secure loans should be clearly identified.
c. Property not in current use should be segregated in the balance sheet.

DEPRECIATION

The auditors' perspective toward depreciation

The auditors' approach to verification of depreciation expense is influenced by two factors not applicable to most other expenses. First, we must recognize that depreciation expense is an *estimate*. Determining the annual depreciation expense involves two rather arbitrary decisions by the client company: first, an estimate of the useful economic lives of various groups of assets; and second, a choice among several depreciation methods, each of which would lead to a different answer. The wide range of possible amounts for annual depreciation expense because of these decisions by the client suggests that the auditors should maintain a perspective of looking for assurance of overall reasonableness. Specifically, overall tests of the year's depreciation expense are of special importance.

A second unusual characteristic of depreciation expense is that, unlike other expenses, it typically has not been verified during the auditors' consideration of internal control. The *tests of controls* performed during the auditors' work on internal control include exchange transactions with outsiders, such as payments for advertising or rent, but often do not include the internal allocations of cost that establish depreciation expense. Consequently, the auditors must place more emphasis upon the verification of year-end balances than would be needed if the reliability of the depreciation data had been established through tests of controls.

Among the methods of computing depreciation expense most frequently encountered are the straight-line method and the declining-balance methods. Far less common, although quite acceptable, are methods based on units of output or hours of service. The most widely adopted types of accelerated depreciation methods are fixed percentage of declining balance, and sum-of-the-years' digits. The essential characteristic of these and other similar methods is that depreciation is greatest in the first year and becomes smaller in succeeding years.

Accelerated Cost Recovery System (ACRS)

For assets acquired after January 1, 1981, federal income tax rules require the use of either straight-line depreciation or a special accelerated method called the Accelerated Cost Recovery System (ACRS), or the Modified Cost Recovery System after 1986. ACRS speeds up the write-off of cost in two ways. First, it designates "recovery periods" over which the cost of various types of assets are to be written off. For example, buildings acquired prior to 1987 are considered "18-year property," which means that they are depreciated over 18 years even though the estimated useful life may be much longer.

A second element of ACRS is that it requires the use of an accelerated depreciation rate, similar to the declining-balance method. Under ACRS, assets are depreciated to a book value of zero; residual values are ignored.

ACRS is a systematic method of depreciating the cost of an asset; therefore, it may be acceptable for financial statement purposes. However, if the client elects to use ACRS for financial statement purposes, the auditors must evaluate whether the recovery periods are reasonable in relation to the useful lives of the assets. Even when the ACRS method is used solely for income tax purposes, the auditors must satisfy themselves as to the reasonableness of the year's write-off of assets for tax purposes, as well as verify the depreciation shown on the financial statements.

The auditors' objectives in auditing depreciation

As we discussed earlier, depreciation relates most directly to the **valuation or allocation** audit objective. To meet this objective, the auditors in examining depreciation methods and amounts determine (*a*) that the methods in use are acceptable, (*b*) that the methods are being followed consistently, and (*c*) that the calculations required by the chosen methods are accurate. A more detailed picture of the auditors' objectives is conveyed by the audit program in the following section.

Audit program—depreciation expense and accumulated depreciation

The following outline of substantive tests to be performed by the auditors in reviewing depreciation is stated in sufficient detail to be largely self-explanatory. Consequently, no point-by-point discussion will be presented. Techniques for testing the client's provision of depreciation for the year and for analyzing the accumulated depreciation accounts are, however, discussed immediately following the audit program.

1. Review the depreciation policies set forth in company manuals or other management directives. Determine whether the methods in use are designed to allocate costs of plant and equipment assets equitably over their service lives.
    a. Inquire whether any extra working shifts or other conditions of accelerated production are present that might warrant adjustment of normal depreciation rates.
    b. Discuss with executives the possible need for recognition of obsolescence resulting from inventions or economic developments. For example, assume that a new, improved model of computer has recently become available and that it would fit the company's needs most effectively. Should the remaining estimated useful life of an older computer presently owned by the company be reevaluated in the light of this technological advance?
2. Obtain or prepare a summary analysis (see Figure 14–1) of accumulated depreciation for the major property classifications as shown by the general ledger control accounts, listing beginning balances, provisions for depreciation during the year, retirements, and ending balances.
    a. Compare beginning balances with the audited amounts in last year's working papers.
    b. Determine that the totals of accumulated depreciation recorded in the plant and equipment subsidiary records agree with the applicable general ledger controlling accounts.

3. Verify the provisions for depreciation.
   a. Compare rates used in the current year with those employed in prior years, and investigate any variances.
   b. Test computations of depreciation provisions for a representative number of units and trace to individual records in the property ledger. Be alert for excessive depreciation on fully depreciated assets. Generalized audit software can be used to prove the depreciation calculations in the client's subsidiary ledger for plant and equipment. The computation of depreciation expense for groups of assets can be verified quickly if the client maintains a computer-based subsidiary ledger.
   c. Compare credits to accumulated depreciation accounts for the year's depreciation provisions with debit entries in related depreciation expense accounts.
4. Verify deductions from accumulated depreciation for assets retired.
   a. Trace deductions to the working paper analyzing retirements of assets during the year.
   b. Test the accuracy of accumulated depreciation to date of retirement.
5. Review the most recent audit report on depreciation made by the revenue agents from the Internal Revenue Service. Determine whether provisions and rates have been adjusted, when necessary, to agree with the findings of the Internal Revenue Service.
6. Perform analytical procedures for depreciation.
   a. Compute the ratio of depreciation expense to total cost of plant and compare with prior years.
   b. Compare the percentage relationships between accumulated depreciation and related property accounts with that prevailing in prior years. Discuss significant variations from the normal depreciation program with appropriate members of management.

Testing the client's provision for depreciation

We have emphasized the importance of determining the overall reasonableness of the amount of depreciation expense, which is usually a very material amount on the income statement. An *overall* test of the annual provision for depreciation requires the auditors to perform the following steps:

1. List the balances in the various asset accounts at the beginning of the year.
2. Deduct any fully depreciated assets, since these items should no longer be subject to depreciation.
3. Add one half of the asset additions for the year.
4. Deduct one half of the asset retirements for the year (exclusive of any fully depreciated assets).

These four steps produce average amounts subject to depreciation at the regular rates in each of the major asset categories. By applying the appropriate rates to these amounts, the auditors determine on an overall average basis the amount of the provision for depreciation. The computed amount is then compared with the client's figures. Precise agreement is not to be expected, but any material difference between the depreciation expense computed in this manner and the amount set up by the client should be investigated fully.

Verification of natural resources

In the examination of companies operating properties subject to depletion (mines, oil and gas deposits, timberlands, and other natural resources), the auditors follow a pattern similar to that used in evaluating the provision for depreciation expense and accumulated depreciation. They determine whether depletion has been recorded consistently and in accordance with generally accepted accounting principles, and they test the mathematical accuracy of the client's computations.

The depletion of timberlands is usually based on physical quantities established by cruising. (The term *cruising* means the inspection of a tract of forestland for the purpose of estimating the total lumber yield.) The determination of physical quantities to use as a basis for depletion is more difficult in many mining ventures and for oil and gas deposits. The auditors often rely upon the opinions of such specialists as mining engineers and geologists about the reasonableness of the depletion rates being used for such resources. Under these circumstances, the auditors must comply with the provisions of *SAS 11* (AU 336), "Using the Work of a Specialist" (discussed in Chapter 7).

If the number of tons of ore in a mining property could be accurately determined in advance, an exact depletion cost per ton could be computed by dividing the cost of the mine by the number of tons available for extraction. In reality, the contents of the mine can only be estimated, and the estimates may require significant revision as mining operations progress.

The auditors verify the ownership and the cost of mining properties by examining deeds, leases, tax bills, vouchers, paid checks, and other records in the same manner that they verify the plant and equipment of a manufacturing or trading concern. The costs of exploration and development work in a mine customarily are capitalized until such time as commercial production begins. After that date additional development work generally is treated as expense. The costs of drilling oil wells are capitalized if the wells are productive. Under this "successful efforts" policy, the costs of drilling wells which prove not to be productive are immediately written off. However, some smaller companies follow an alternative of "full-cost" policy, under which all drilling costs are capitalized and amortized over future years.

Verification of intangible assets

The balance sheet caption *Intangible Assets* includes a variety of assets. All intangible assets are characterized by a lack of physical substance. Furthermore, they do not qualify as current assets, and they are nonmonetary—that is, they do not represent fixed claims to cash.

Among the more prominent intangible assets are goodwill, patents, trademarks, franchises, and leaseholds. Notice that investment in securities is *not* included in our list of intangibles. Since intangible assets are lacking in physical substance, their value lies in the rights or economic advantages afforded in their ownership. Because of their intangible nature, these assets may be more difficult to identify than units of plant and equipment. When a client treats an expenditure as creating an intangible asset, the auditors must look for objective evidence that a genuine asset has come into existence.

The auditors' substantiation of intangible assets may begin with an analysis of the ledger accounts for these assets. Debits to the accounts should be traced to evidence of payment having been made, and to documentary evidence of the rights or benefits acquired. Credits to the accounts should be reconciled with the client's program of amortization or traced to appropriate authorization for the write-off of the asset.

One intangible asset that may be large in amount yet of questionable future economic benefit is *goodwill.* Goodwill arises in accounting for business combinations in which the price paid to acquire another company exceeds the fair value of the identifiable net assets acquired. When business combinations result in the recording of goodwill, the auditors should review the allocation of the lump-sum acquisition cost among tangible assets, identifiable intangible assets, and goodwill. Any allocation of total acquisition cost to goodwill should be considered for reasonableness and also traced to the authorization and subsequent approval in the minutes of the directors' meetings.

As part of an analysis of intangible asset accounts, the auditors should review the reasonableness of the client's amortization program. Amortization is ordinarily computed by the straight-line method over the years estimated to be benefited, but not in excess of 40 years.

Examination of plant and equipment in advance of the balance sheet date

Most of the audit work on plant and equipment can be done in advance of the balance sheet date. For the initial audit of a new client, the time-consuming task of reviewing the records of prior years and establishing the beginning balances in the plant accounts for the current period should be completed before the year-end.

In repeat engagements, as well as in first examinations, the consideration of internal control can be carried out at any convenient time during the year. Many auditing firms lighten their year-end work loads by performing interim work during October and November, including the analysis of the plant and equipment ledger accounts for the first 9 or 10 months of the year. After the balance sheet date, the work necessary on property accounts is then limited to the final two or three months' transactions. One of the major problems in managing an accounting practice is arranging a uniform work load for the staff throughout the year. A step toward the solution of this problem lies in performing most of the work on plant and equipment in advance of the balance sheet date.

Unaudited replacement cost information

In an environment of inflation, such as that experienced by the United States in the latter part of the 1970s and the early part of the 1980s, the SEC and the FASB saw the need for disclosure of the effects of changing price levels on financial statements. Both the SEC and the FASB acted to require large corporations meeting certain size tests to disclose supplementary information of this nature. An important element of this information was the estimated current replacement, and price level adjusted, cost of plant and equipment. The SEC's action several years ago (Rule 3.17 of Regulation S-X) called upon large corporations to include replacement cost information in a separate supplement to financial statements. The SEC did not require that the replacement cost information be audited, but urged that standards be developed for the guidance of auditors. Later the Financial Accounting Standards Board in *FASB Statement No. 33* took broader action in requiring large corporations to disclose information on the effects of changing price levels.

These disclosure requirements called for replacement cost information (including depreciation) to be shown in a footnote or in a supplementary section accompanying the financial statements. Notice that replacement cost information was not substituted for historical cost in the financial statements.

As discussed in Chapter 14, the requirements for mandatory disclosure of this current cost information has been rescinded by *FASB Statement No. 89,* "Financial Reporting and Changing Prices." However, many large corporations still voluntarily disclose the information in their annual reports. Also, they still request auditors to perform limited procedures for the review of the replacement cost information as outlined in *SAS 27* (AU 553). Remember, this and other supplementary information is not required for fairness of the basic financial statements.

Most large corporations in making the supplementary disclosure of replacement cost information present a three-column income statement. The three columns show (1) historical cost, (2) constant dollar amounts, and (3) current costs. The largest variation from historical cost is likely to be depreciation expense. The following excerpt from the annual report of

Standard Oil Company of California is a good example of this type of disclosure.

DATA ADJUSTED FOR CHANGING PRICES (dollars in millions, except per share amounts)			
1983 Statement of Income	As reported	Constant dollar	Current cost
Revenues.	$29,182	$29,182	$29,182
Costs and Expenses			
Cost of products sold and operating expenses	21,967	22,119	22,226
Depreciation, depletion and amortization	1,294	2,428	2,829
Taxes other than on income	2,914	2,914	2,914
Interest and debt expense	75	75	75
Provision for taxes on income.	1,342	1,342	1,342
Net income	$ 1,590	$ 304	$ (204)

KEY TERMS INTRODUCED OR EMPHASIZED IN CHAPTER 14

Capital expenditure   An expenditure for property, plant, and equipment that is properly charged to an asset account.

Cruising   The inspection of a tract of forestland for the purpose of estimating the total lumber yield.

Disclosure of replacement cost information   Supplementary information which may be shown in annual reports to shareholders. Designed to reflect the effects of inflation by reporting the cost of replacing the plant and equipment at current prices and by computing the amount of depreciation based on replacement cost of depreciable assets in use.

Loss payable endorsement   A clause in a fire or other casualty insurance policy providing for payments to lienholders of the insured property to the extent of their unpaid loans or the face amount of the insurance, whichever is less.

Operating method   A method of accounting for lease revenue in which aggregate rentals are reported as revenue over the life of the lease, usually as rent becomes receivable under terms of the lease.

Revenue expenditure   An expenditure for property, plant, and equipment that is properly charged to an expense account.

Work order   A serially numbered accounting document authorizing the acquisition of plant assets. A separate series of retirement work orders may be used to authorize the retirement or disposal of plant assets, and a third variety consists of documents authorizing repair or maintenance of plant assets.

GROUP I: REVIEW QUESTIONS

14–1.   With respect to previously required disclosure by large corporations of their plant assets, answer the following questions:
   a.   How did this disclosure relate to changing price levels?
   b.   Summarize the position of the FASB on this disclosure.
   c.   Was this disclosure requirement primarily a response to possibly overstated corporate earnings or to possibly understated balance sheet totals?

    d. How did the required disclosure of replacement cost appear in the financial statements?

14–2. Identify at least three elements of strong internal control for property, plant, and equipment.

14–3. What documentary evidence is usually available to the auditors in the client's office to substantiate the legal ownership of property, plant, and equipment?

14–4. Moultrie Company discovered recently that a number of its property and equipment assets had been retired from use several years ago without any entries being made in the accounting records. The company asks you to suggest procedures that will prevent unrecorded retirement of assets.

14–5. Does a failure to record the retirement of machinery affect net income? Explain.

14–6. The auditors' verification of plant and equipment is facilitated by several factors not applicable to audit work on current assets. What are these factors?

14–7. Do the auditors question the service lives adopted by the client for plant assets, or do they accept the service lives without investigation? Explain.

14–8. Should the independent auditors observe a physical inventory of property and equipment in every audit engagement? Discuss.

14–9. Hamlin Metals Company has sales representatives covering several states and provides automobiles for them and for its executives. Describe any substantive tests you would consider appropriate for the company's fleet of more than 100 automobiles, other than the verification procedures generally applicable to all property and equipment.

14–10. Explain the use of a system of authorizations for additions to plant and equipment.

14–11. What is a principal objective of the auditors in analyzing a Maintenance and Repairs expense account?

14–12. In response to threats from a terrorist organization, Technology International installed protective measures consisting of chain-link fences, concrete road barriers, electronic gates, and underground parking at its manufacturing facilities. The costs of these installations were debited to the Land account. Indicate with reasons your approval or disapproval of this accounting treatment.

14–13. Gibson Manufacturing Company acquired new factory machinery this year and ceased using the old machinery. The old equipment was retained, however, and is capable of being used if the demand for the company's products warrants additional production. How should the old machinery be handled in the accounting records and on the financial statements?

14–14. What objections do some business executives have to the traditional practice of basing depreciation charges on original cost?

14–15. Explain how the existence of lease agreements may result in understated plant and equipment.

14–16. The auditors' verification of current assets such as cash, securities, and inventories emphasizes observation, inspection, and confirmation to determine the physical existence of these assets. Should the auditors take a similar approach to establish the existence of the recorded plant assets? Explain fully.

14–17. K–J Corporation has current assets of $5 million and approximately the same amount of plant and equipment. Should the two groups of assets require about the same amount of audit time? Give reasons.

14–18. You are making your first examination of Clarke Manufacturing Company. Plant and equipment represent a very substantial portion of the total assets. What verification, if any, will you make of the balances of the ledger accounts for Plant and Equipment as of the beginning of the period under audit?

14–19. Cite various substantive tests the auditors could employ that might detect unrecorded retirements of property, plant, and equipment.

(AICPA, adapted)

14–20. A part of the auditors' consideration of internal control is a *test of transactions*. Do the tests of transactions include depreciation expense? Explain.

14–21. Suggest several comparisons to be made as part of the auditors' analytical procedures for:
a. Plant and equipment.
b. Depreciation.

14–22. Should the auditors examine public records to determine the legal title of property apparently owned by the client?

**GROUP II:
QUESTIONS
REQUIRING
ANALYSIS**

14–23. Give the purposes of each of the following procedures that may be included in an internal control structure, and explain how each procedure contributes to strong internal control:
a. Forecasting of expenditures for property, plant, and equipment.
b. Maintaining a plant ledger for property, plant, and equipment.

(AICPA, adapted)

14–24. Kadex Corporation, a small manufacturing company, did not use the services of independent auditors during the first two years of its existence. Near the end of the third year, Kadex retained Jones & Scranton, CPAs, to perform an audit for the year ended December 31. Officials of the company requested that the CPA firm perform only the audit work necessary to provide an audit report on the financial statements for the current year.

During the first two years of its operation, Kadex had erroneously treated some material acquisitions of plant and equipment as revenue expenditures. No such errors occurred in the third year.
a. Under these circumstances, would Jones & Scranton, CPAs, be likely to learn of the transactions erroneously treated as revenue expenditures in Years 1 and 2? Explain.
b. Would the income statement and balance sheet prepared at the end of Year 3 be affected by the above accounting errors made in Years 1 and 2? If so, identify the specific items. Explain fully.

14–25. List and state the purpose of all audit procedures that might reasonably be applied by the auditors to determine that all property and equipment retirements have been recorded in the accounting records.   (AICPA)

14–26.   Your new client, Ross Products, Inc., completed its first fiscal year March 31, Year 10. During the course of your examination you discover the following entry in the general journal, dated April 1, Year 9.

Building.	2,400,000	
Mortgage Note Payable.		1,400,000
Common Stock.		1,000,000
To record (1) acquisition of building con-structed by J. A. Ross Construction Co. (a sole proprietorship); (2) assumption of Ross Construction Co. mortgage loan for construc-tion of the building; and (3) issuance of entire authorized common stock (10,000 shares, $100 par value) to J. A. Ross.		

Required:
Under these circumstances, what steps should the auditors take to verify the $2,400,000 recorded cost of the building? Explain fully.

14–27.   An executive of a manufacturing company informs you that no formal procedures have been followed to control the retirement of machinery and equipment. A physical inventory of plant assets has just been completed. It revealed that 25 percent of the assets carried in the ledger were not on hand and had presumably been scrapped. The accounting records have been adjusted to agree with the physical inventory. You are asked to outline internal control practices to govern future retirements.

14–28.   Allen Fraser was president of three corporations: Missouri Metals Corporation, Kansas Metals Corporation, and Iowa Metals Corporation. Each of the three corporations owned land and buildings acquired for approximately $500,000. An appraiser retained by Fraser in 198X estimated the current value of the land and buildings in each corporation at approximately $3,000,000. The appraisals were recorded in the accounts. A new corporation, called Midwest Corporation, was then formed, and Fraser became its president. The new corporation purchased the assets of the three predecessor corporations, making payment in capital stock. The balance sheet of Midwest Corporation shows land and buildings "valued at cost" in the amount of $9,000,000, the carrying values to the vendor companies at the time of transfer to Midwest Corporation. Do you consider this treatment acceptable? Explain.

14–29.   Shortly after you were retained to examine the financial statements of Case Corporation, you learned from a preliminary discussion with management that the corporation had recently acquired a competing business, the Mall Company. In your study of the terms of the acquisition, you find that the total purchase price was paid in cash and that the transaction was authorized by the board of directors and fully described in the minutes of the directors' meetings. The only aspect of the acquisition of the Mall Company that raises any doubts in your mind is the allocation of the total purchase price among the several kinds of assets acquired. The allocation, which had been specifically approved by the board of directors of Case Corporation, placed very high values on the tangible assets acquired and allowed nothing for goodwill.

You are inclined to believe that the allocation of the lump-sum price to the several types of assets was somewhat unreasonable because the total price for the business was as much or more than the current replacement cost of the tangible assets acquired. However, as an auditor, you do not claim to be an expert in property values. Would you question the propriety of the directors' allocation of the lump-sum purchase price? Explain fully.

14–30. Select the best answer for each of the questions below and explain fully the reason for your selection.

    a. With respect to an internal control measure that will assure accountability for fixed asset retirements, management should implement a system that includes:

        (1) Continuous analysis of miscellaneous revenue to locate any cash proceeds from sale of plant assets.

        (2) Periodic inquiry of plant executives by internal auditors as to whether any plant assets have been retired.

        (3) Utilization of serially numbered retirement work orders.

        (4) Periodic observation of plant assets by the internal auditors.

    b. The auditors may conclude that depreciation charges are insufficient by noting:

        (1) Insured values greatly in excess of book values.

        (2) Large amounts of fully depreciated assets.

        (3) Continuous trade-ins of relatively new assets.

        (4) Excessive recurring losses on assets retired.

    c. Which of the following is an internal control weakness related to factory equipment?

        (1) Checks issued in payment of purchases of equipment are not signed by the controller.

        (2) All purchases of factory equipment are required to be made by the department in need of the equipment.

        (3) Factory equipment replacements are generally made when estimated useful lives, as indicated in depreciation schedules, have expired.

        (4) Proceeds from sales of fully depreciated equipment are credited to other income.

    d. Which of the following accounts should be reviewed by the auditors to gain reasonable assurance that additions to property, plant, and equipment are *not* understated?

        (1) Depreciation.

        (2) Accounts payable.

        (3) Cash.

        (4) Repairs.

    e. The auditor is most likely to seek information from the plant manager with respect to the—

        (1) Adequacy of the provision for uncollectible accounts.

(2) Appropriateness of physical inventory observation procedures.

(3) Existence of obsolete machinery.

(4) Deferral of procurement of certain necessary insurance coverage.

f. Treetop Corporation acquired a building and arranged mortgage financing during the year. Verification of the related mortgage acquisition costs would be *least* likely to include an examination of the related:

(1) Deed.

(2) Canceled checks.

(3) Closing statement.

(4) Interest expense.   (AICPA, adapted)

GROUP III: PROBLEMS

14–31. The following are typical questions that might appear on an internal control questionnaire relating to plant and equipment.

1. Has a dollar minimum been established for expenditures to be capitalized?

2. Are subsidiary ledgers for plant and equipment regularly reconciled with general ledger controlling accounts?

Required:

a. State the purpose of each of the above internal control procedures.

b. Describe the manner in which each of the above procedures might be tested.

c. Assuming that the operating effectiveness of each of the above procedures is found to be inadequate, describe how the auditors might alter their substantive tests to compensate for the internal control weakness.

14–32. Chem-Lite, Inc. maintains its accounts on the basis of a fiscal year ending March 31. At March 31, 1991, the Equipment account in the general ledger appeared as shown below. The company uses straight-line depreciation, 10-year life, and 10 percent salvage value for all its equipment. It is the company's policy to take a full year's depreciation on all additions to equipment occurring during the fiscal year, and you may treat this policy as a satisfactory one for the purpose of this problem. The company has recorded depreciation for the fiscal year ended March 31, 1991.

Equipment		
4/1/90	Bal. forward	100,000
12/1/90		10,500
1/2/91		1,015
2/1/91		1,015
3/1/91		1,015

Upon further investigation, you find the following contract dated December 1, 1990, covering the acquisition of equipment:

List price	$30,000
5% sales tax	1,500
Total	31,500
Down payment	10,500
Balance	21,000
8% interest, 24 months	3,360
Contract amount	$24,360

Required:
Prepare in good form, including full explanations, the adjusting entry (entries) you would propose as auditor of Chem-Lite, Inc. with respect to the equipment and related depreciation accounts at March 31, 1991. (Assume that all amounts given are material.) (AICPA, adapted)

14–33. Nova Land Development Corporation is a closely held corporation engaged in purchasing large tracts of land, subdividing the tracts, and installing paved streets and utilities. The corporation does not construct buildings for the buyers of the land and does not have any affiliated construction companies. Undeveloped land usually is leased for farming until the corporation is ready to begin developing it.

The corporation finances its land acquisitions by mortgages; the mortgagees require audited financial statements. This is your first audit of the company, and you have now begun the examination of the financial statements for the year ended December 31.

Required:
The corporation has three tracts of land in various stages of development. List the audit procedures to be employed in the verification of the physical existence and title to the corporation's three landholdings.

(AICPA, adapted)

14–34. J. Barnes, CPA, has been retained to audit a manufacturing company with a balance sheet that includes the caption Property, Plant, and Equipment. Barnes has been asked by the company's management if audit adjustments or reclassifications are required for the following material items that have been included or excluded from Property, Plant, and Equipment.

1. A tract of land was acquired during the year. The land is the future site of the client's new headquarters, which will be constructed in the following year. Commissions were paid to the real estate agent used to acquire the land, and expenditures were made to relocate the previous owner's equipment. These commissions and expenditures were expensed and are excluded from Property, Plant, and Equipment.

2. Clearing costs were incurred to make the land ready for construction. These costs were included in Property, Plant, and Equipment.

3. During the land-clearing process, timber and gravel were recovered and sold. The proceeds from the sale were recorded as other income and are excluded from Property, Plant, and Equipment.

4. A group of machines was purchased under a royalty agreement, which provides royalty payments based on units of production from the machines. The cost of the machines, freight costs, unloading charges, and royalty payments were capitalized and are included in Property, Plant, and Equipment.

Required:

a. Describe the general characteristics of assets, such as land, buildings, improvements, machinery, equipment, and fixtures that should normally be classified as Property, Plant, and Equipment, and identify audit objectives (i.e., how an auditor can obtain audit satisfaction) in connection with the examination of Property, Plant, and Equipment. *Do not discuss specific audit procedures.*

b. Indicate whether each of the above items numbered 1 to 4 requires one or more audit adjustments or reclassifications, and explain why such adjustments or reclassifications are required or not required. Organize your answer as follows:

Item number	Is audit adjustment or reclassification required? Yes or no	Reasons audit adjustment or reclassification is required or not required

(AICPA, adapted)

14–35. You are engaged in the examination of the financial statements of Holman Corporation for the year ended December 31, 1991. The accompanying analyses of the Property, Plant, and Equipment, and related accumulated depreciation accounts have been prepared by the chief accountant of the client. You have traced the beginning balances to your prior year's audit working papers.

HOLMAN CORPORATION
Analysis of Property, Plant, and Equipment, and
Related Accumulated Depreciation Accounts
Year Ended December 31, 1991

Description	Final 12/31/90	Assets Additions	Assets Retirements	Per ledger 12/31/91
Land	$422,500	$ 5,000		$427,500
Buildings	120,000	17,500		137,500
Machinery and equipment	385,000	40,400	$26,000	399,400
	$927,500	$62,900	$26,000	$964,400

(Continued)

| | Final | Accumulated depreciation | | Per ledger |
Description	12/31/90	Additions*	Retirements	12/31/91
Buildings	$ 60,000	$ 5,150		$ 65,150
Machinery and equipment	173,250	39,220		212,470
	$233,250	$44,370		$277,620

* Depreciation expense for the year.

All plant assets are depreciated on the straight-line basis (no residual value taken into consideration) based on the following estimated service lives: building, 25 years; and all other items, 10 years. The company's policy is to take one half-year's depreciation on all asset additions and disposals during the year.

Your examination revealed the following information:

1. On April 1, the company entered into a 10-year lease contract for a die casting machine, with annual rentals of $5,000 payable in advance every April 1. The lease is cancelable by either party (60 days' written notice is required), and there is no option to renew the lease or buy the equipment at the end of the lease. The estimated service life of the machine is 10 years with no residual value. The company recorded the die casting machine in the Machinery and Equipment account at $40,400, the present value at the date of the lease, and $2,020 applicable to the machine has been included in depreciation expense for the year.

2. The company completed the construction of a wing on the plant building on June 30. The service life of the building was not extended by this addition. The lowest construction bid received was $17,500, the amount recorded in the Buildings account. Company personnel constructed the addition at a cost of $16,000 (materials, $7,500; labor, $5,500; and overhead, $3,000).

3. On August 18, $5,000 was paid for paving and fencing a portion of land owned by the company and used as a parking lot for employees. The expenditure was charged to the Land account.

4. The amount shown in the machinery and equipment asset retirement column represents cash received on September 5 upon disposal of a machine purchased in July 1987 for $48,000. The chief accountant recorded depreciation expense of $3,500 on this machine in 1991.

5. Harbor City donated land and building appraised at $100,000 and $400,000, respectively, to Holman Corporation for a plant. On September 1, the company began operating the plant. Since no costs were involved, the chief accountant made no entry for the above transaction.

Required:

Prepare the adjusting journal entries that you would propose at December 31, 1991, to adjust the accounts for the above transactions. Disregard income tax implications. The accounts have not been closed. Computations should be rounded off to the nearest dollar. Use a separate adjusting journal entry for each of the above five paragraphs.

(AICPA, adapted)

14-36. You are the senior accountant in the audit of Granger Grain Corporation, whose business primarily involves the purchase, storage, and sale of grain products. The corporation owns several elevators located along navigable water routes and transports its grain by barge and rail. Your staff assistant submitted the following working paper analysis for your review:

GRANGER GRAIN CORPORATION
Advances Paid on Barges under Construction—a/c 210
December 31, 1991

Advances made:

1/15/91—Ck. No. 3463—Jones Barge Construction Co.	$100,000*
4/13/91—Ck. No. 4129—Jones Barge Construction Co.	25,000*
6/19/91—Ck. No. 5396—Jones Barge Construction Co.	63,000*
Total payments	188,000
Deduct cash received 9/1/91 from City Life Insurance Co.	188,000†
Balance per general ledger—12/31/91	$ –0–

---

* Examined approved check request and paid check and traced to cash disbursements journal.
† Traced to cash receipts journal and to duplicate deposit ticket.

Required:

a. In what respects is this brief analysis incomplete for audit purposes? (Do not include any discussion of specific auditing procedures.)

b. What two different types of contractual arrangements may be inferred from your assistant's analysis?

c. What additional auditing procedures would you suggest that your staff assistant perform before you accept the working paper as being complete? (AICPA, adapted)

CHAPTER 15

Accounts payable and other liabilities

Chapter 15 study objectives

After studying this chapter, you should be able to:
— Describe the nature of accounts payable and other liabilities.
— Explain the fundamental necessary internal controls over purchase transactions and payables.
— Describe the auditors' objectives for the audit of accounts payable.
— Describe the nature of appropriate procedures to accomplish the auditors' objectives for the audit of accounts payable.
— Describe the nature of appropriate procedures for auditing other liabilities.

Now that the chapters dealing with the verification of assets have been completed, we are ready to consider the examination of liability accounts. In this chapter we discuss accounts payable and other current liabilities. Chapter 16 includes material on long-term debt (as well as equity capital and loss contingencies).

ACCOUNTS PAYABLE

Sources and nature of accounts payable

The term *accounts payable* (often referred to as *vouchers payable* for a voucher system) is used to describe short-term obligations arising from the purchase of goods and services in the ordinary course of business. Typical transactions creating accounts payable include the acquisition on credit of merchandise, raw materials, plant assets, and office supplies.

Other sources of accounts payable include the receipt of services, such as legal and accounting services, advertising, repairs, and utilities. Interest-bearing obligations should not be included in accounts payable but shown separately as bonds, notes, mortgages, or installment contracts.

Accounts payable arising from the purchase of goods or services and most *other liabilities* are usually evidenced by invoices and statements received from the suppliers. However, *accrued liabilities* (sometimes called accrued expenses) generally accumulate over time, and management must make accounting estimates of the year-end liability. Such estimates are often necessary for salaries, pensions, interest, rent, taxes, and similar items.

The auditors' approach in examination of accounts payable

The auditors' *objectives* in the examination of accounts payable are to determine that:

1. *Internal control* over accounts payable and the acquisition and payment cycle *is adequate.*
2. The recorded accounts payable are valid (*occurrence* and *obligations*).
3. All accounts payable are recorded (*completeness*).
4. Accounts payable schedules are mathematically correct and agree with general ledger accounts (*clerical accuracy*).
5. The *valuation* of accounts payable is proper.
6. The *presentation* and *disclosure* of payables is adequate.

Virtually all lawsuits against CPA firms allege that the auditors failed to detect an overstatement of earnings. Management, especially of publicly held firms, is often under some pressure to report increased earnings. In previous chapters, we discussed the auditors' concern about exaggeration of earnings that results from the overstatement of assets. In the audit of liabilities, the auditors are primarily concerned with the possibility of understatement, or omission, of liabilities. An *understatement of liabilities* will exaggerate financial strength of a company and conceal fraud just as effectively as *overstatement of assets.* Furthermore, the understatement of liabilities is usually accompanied by the understatement of expenses and an overstatement of net income. For example, delaying the recording of bills for December operating expenses until January overstates income while understating accounts payable. Therefore, audit procedures for liabilities should be designed to detect the *completeness* of recorded payables.

Audit procedures for detection of such understated liabilities differ from those used to detect overstated assets. Overstating an asset account usually requires an improper entry in the accounting records, as by the recording of a fictitious transaction. Such improper entries can be detected by the auditors through verification of the individual entries making up the balance of an asset account. Once a fictitious entry is detected, the individual responsible for the fraud has little alternative but to admit his acts. By way of contrast, understating a liability account is generally possible merely by *failing to make an entry* for a transaction creating a liability. The omission of an entry is less susceptible of detection than is a fictitious entry. If the omission is detected, there is at least a possibility of passing it off as an accidental error. Auditors have long recognized that the most difficult type of irregularity to detect is fraud based on the *nonrecording* of transactions.

When accounts payable entries have been recorded, the existence of a definite financial commitment makes accomplishment of the valuation audit objective less difficult than for assets (other than cash). The situation with accrued liabilities is different. As we suggested earlier, in many circumstances exact measurement of these accounts will be difficult; the CPAs must audit management's accounting estimates.

Internal control over accounts payable

In thinking about internal control for accounts payable, it is important to recognize that the accounts payable of one company are the accounts receivable of other companies. It follows that there is little danger of errors being overlooked permanently since the client's creditors will generally maintain complete records of their receivables and will inform the client if payment is not received. This feature also aids auditors in the discovery of irregularities, since the perpetrator must be able to obtain and respond to the demands for payment. Some companies, therefore, may choose to minimize their record keeping of liabilities and to rely on creditors to call attention to any delay in making payment. This viewpoint is not an endorsement of inaccurate or incomplete records of accounts payable, but merely a recognition that the self-interest of creditors constitutes a defective control in accounting for payables that is not present in the case of accounts receivable.

Discussions of internal control applicable to accounts payable may logically be extended to the entire purchase or acquisition cycle. In an effective purchasing system, a stores, or inventory control department will prepare and approve the issuance of a purchase requisition that will be sent to the purchasing department. A copy of the purchase requisition will be filed numerically and matched with the subsequently prepared purchase order and finally with a copy of the receiving report.

The purchasing department, upon receiving the purchase requisition, will (1) determine that the item should be ordered and (2) select the appropriate vendor, quality, and price. Then, a serially numbered purchase order is issued to order the goods. Copies of the purchase order should be sent to stores, receiving, and the accounts payable department. The copy sent to receiving is generally "blind" in that the quantities are not included so as to encourage receiving department counting of quantities. But the fact that a vendor's packing slip (with quantities) is almost always included when goods are received decreases the effectiveness of this control.

The receiving department should be independent of the purchasing department. When goods are received, they should be counted and inspected. Receiving reports should be prepared for all goods received. These documents should be serially numbered and prepared in a sufficient number of copies to permit prompt notification of the receipt of goods to the stores department, the purchasing department, and the accounts payable department. In smaller companies, vendors' packing slips often are utilized as receiving reports.

Within the accounts (vouchers) payable department, all forms should be stamped with the date received. Vouchers and other documents originating within the department can be controlled through the use of serial numbers. Each step in the verification of an invoice should be evidenced by entering a date and signature on the voucher. Comparison of the quantities listed on the invoice with those shown on the receiving report and purchase order will prevent the payment of charges for goods in excess of those ordered and received. Comparison of the prices, discounts, and terms of shipment as shown on the purchase order and on the vendor's invoice provides a safeguard against the payment of excessive prices.

The separation of the function of invoice verification and approval from the function of cash disbursement is another step that tends to prevent errors and irregularities. Before invoices are approved for payment, written evidence must be presented to show that all aspects of the transaction have been verified. The official who signs checks should stamp or perforate the voucher and supporting documents so that they cannot be presented to support payment a second time.

Another control procedure that the auditors may expect to find in a well-managed accounts payable department is the regular monthly balancing of the detailed records of accounts payable (or vouchers) to the general ledger controlling account. These trial balances should be preserved as evidence of the performance of this procedure and as an aid in locating any subsequent errors.

Monthly statements from vendors should be reconciled promptly with the accounts payable ledger or list of open vouchers, and any discrepancies fully investigated. In some industries, it is common practice to make advances to vendors, which are recovered by making percentage deductions from invoices. When such advances are in use, the auditors should ascertain that procedures are followed to assure that deductions from the invoices are made in accordance with the agreement.

The operation of a purchase or acquisition transaction cycle is illustrated in Figure 15–1.

Figure 15–1 Flowchart of a purchases system

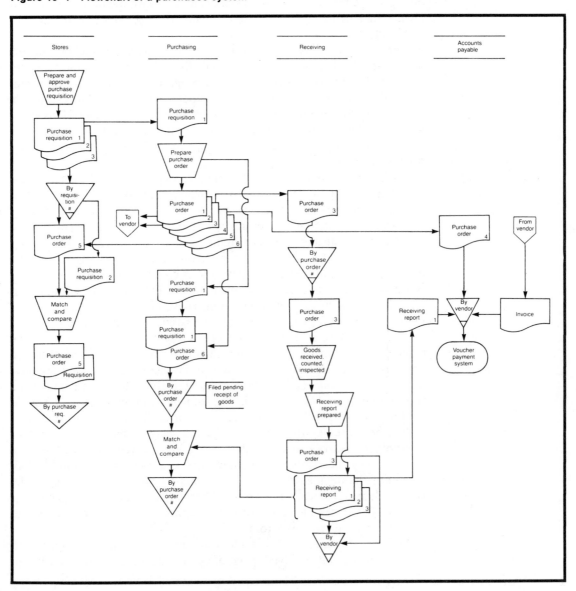

Internal control and the computer

Computer processing of purchase transactions can increase internal control. Purchase requisitions and purchase orders may be generated by a computer which maintains online perpetual inventory records. When goods are received, information may be keyed into the computer system with subsequent automated preparation of a receiving report and updating of inventory records. As indicated in Chapter 11, computer processing of both cash receipts and cash checks can provide management with a continually up-to-date cash record.

Audit working papers for accounts payable

The principal working papers are a lead schedule for accounts payable, trial balances of the various types of accounts payable at the balance sheet date, and confirmation requests for accounts payable. The trial balances are often in the form of computer printouts. In addition, the auditors may prepare a listing of *unrecorded* accounts payable discovered during the course of the audit, as illustrated in Figure 15–4.

AUDIT PROGRAM

The following procedures are typical of the work required in many engagements for the verification of accounts payable.

A. **Consider internal control for accounts payable**
1. *Obtain an understanding* of the internal control for accounts payable.
2. *Assess control risk* for each of the major financial statement assertions about accounts payable, *and design additional tests of controls.*
3. *Perform additional tests of controls* for those controls which the auditors plan to rely on to reduce their assessed level of control risk and, thus, the extent of substantive testing.
4. *Reassess control risk* for each of the major financial statement assertions about accounts payable based on the results of tests of controls, *and design substantive tests.*

B. **Substantive tests of accounts payable transactions and balances**
5. Obtain or prepare a trial balance of accounts payable as of the balance sheet date and reconcile with the general ledger.
6. Vouch balances payable to selected creditors by inspection of supporting documents.
7. Reconcile liabilities with monthly statements from creditors.
8. Confirm accounts payable by direct correspondence with vendors.
9. Perform analytical procedures for accounts payable and related accounts.
10. Search for unrecorded accounts payable.

11. Search for accounts payable to related parties.
12. Evaluate proper balance sheet presentation and disclosure of accounts payable.

Figure 15–2 relates the objectives of the major substantive tests of payables to the primary audit objectives.

Figure 15–2 Objectives of major substantive tests of accounts payable

Substantive tests	Primary audit objectives
Obtain trial balance of payables and reconcile with the ledgers	*Clerical accuracy*
Vouch balances payable to selected creditors to supporting documents Reconcile liabilities with creditors' monthly statements Confirm accounts payable Perform analytical procedures	*Completeness* *Validity (existence and obligations)*
Search for unrecorded accounts payable	*Completeness*
Search for accounts payable to related parties Evaluate financial statement presentation and disclosure	*Presentation and disclosure*

A. Consider internal control for accounts payable
1. Obtain an understanding of the internal control.

One approach used by auditors in becoming familiar with a client's system of internal control for accounts payable is to prepare a flowchart or to use flowcharts prepared by the client. In some engagements, the auditors may choose to prepare a narrative description covering such matters as the independence of the accounts payable department and the receiving department from the purchasing department. The auditors might also use a questionnaire to obtain a description of accounts payable controls. Typical of the questions are the following: Is an accounts payable trial balance prepared monthly and reconciled to the general ledger controlling account? Are monthly statements from vendors reconciled with accounts payable ledgers or unpaid vouchers? Are advance payments to vendors recorded as receivables and controlled in a manner that assures that they will be recovered by offset against vendors' invoices? Are debit memos issued to vendors for discrepancies in invoice prices, quantities, or computations? Are debit balances in vendors' accounts brought to the attention of the credit and purchasing departments?

2. Assess control risk and design additional tests of controls.

Control risk for a financial statement assertion may be assessed below the maximum only when tests indicate that related controls are designed and operating effectively. The auditors must decide which additional tests of controls will likely result in cost-justified restrictions of substantive tests.

3. Perform additional tests of controls.

A number of tests of controls relating to accounts payable have already been discussed in Chapters 11 and 13 on cash and inventories. In this chapter we briefly recap several tests.

a. Verify a sample of postings to the accounts payable controlling account.

The validity of the amount in the general ledger controlling account for accounts payable is established by tracing postings for one or more months to the voucher register and cash payments journal. Any postings to the controlling account from the general journal during this test period should also be traced. This work is performed before the balance sheet date as part of a general test of postings to all records. At the same time, the auditors should scrutinize all entries to the controlling account for the entire period under audit and should investigate any unusual entries.

b. Vouch to supporting documents a sample of postings in selected accounts of the accounts payable subsidiary ledger.

Testing the accuracy of the voucher register or the accounts payable ledgers by tracing specific items back through the cash payments journal, purchases journal, and other journals to original documents (such as purchase orders, receiving reports, invoices, and paid checks) is necessary to determine the adequacy of the internal control. If the functions of purchasing, receiving, invoice verification, and cash disbursement are delegated to separate departments and internal controls appear adequate, the tracing of individual items from the ledgers to the original records may be undertaken only to the extent necessary to determine that the control procedures are operating properly.

The auditors may also make tests by following the audit trail in the opposite direction. By tracing a representative sample of entries from the journals to the accounts payable ledger, the auditors can verify that journal entries have been posted consistently to the subsidiary ledger.

4. Reassess control risk and design substantive tests.

Completion of the above audit procedures enables the auditors to perform a final assessment of control risk for each of the major financial statement assertions about accounts payable. The internal control assessment provides the basis for selecting the necessary substantive tests for verification of accounts payable at the balance sheet date.

A rating of low control risk over accounts payable often means that the auditors have found that serially numbered receiving reports are prepared promptly by the client for all goods received, that serially numbered vouchers are promptly prepared and recorded in the voucher register, and that payments are made promptly on the due dates and immediately recorded in the cash payments journal and accounts payable subsidiary ledger. Finally, at the end of each month, an employee who does not participate in processing accounts payable compares the individual accounts in the accounts payable subsidiary ledger with vendors' statements, and also compares the total of the subsidiary record with the general ledger controlling account. This favorable picture of internal control would enable the auditors to minimize substantive testing of accounts payable.

On the other hand, a rating of high control risk over accounts payable often means that the auditors have found that the subsidiary record of accounts payable is not in agreement with the general ledger controlling account, that receiving reports and vouchers are not serially numbered and are used haphazardly, that purchase transactions often are not recorded until payment is made, and that many accounts payable are long past due. In this situation, the auditors must undertake extensive work if they are to determine that the balance sheet amount for accounts payable includes all liabilities in existence at the balance sheet date.

B.   Substantive tests

5.   Obtain or prepare a trial balance of accounts payable as of the balance sheet date and reconcile with the general ledger.

One purpose of this procedure is to prove that the liability figure appearing in the balance sheet is in agreement with the individual items comprising the detail records. A second purpose is to provide a starting point for substantive testing. The auditors will use the list of vouchers or accounts payable to select a representative group of items for careful examination.

The client company usually furnishes the auditors with a year-end trial balance. The auditors should verify the footing and the accuracy of individual amounts in the trial balance. If the schedule of individual items does not agree in total with the controlling account, the cause of the discrepancy must be investigated. In most situations, the auditors will arrange for the client's staff to locate such errors and make the necessary adjustments. Agreement of the controlling account and the list of individual account balances is not absolute proof of the total indebtedness; invoices received near the close of the period may not be reflected in either the controlling account or the subsidiary records, and other similar errors may exist without causing the accounts to be out of balance.

6.   Vouch balances payable to selected creditors by inspection of supporting documents.

Another substantive test of the validity of the client-prepared trial balance of accounts payable is the vouching of selected creditors' balances to supporting vouchers, invoices, purchase orders, and receiving reports.

For companies that use a voucher system, the verification of the individual vouchers is made most conveniently at the balance sheet date, when the vouchers will be together in the unpaid voucher file. The content of the unpaid voucher file changes daily; as vouchers are paid, they are removed from the file and filed alphabetically by vendor. Consequently, it is important that the client maintain a list of year-end unpaid vouchers. This listing should show the names of vendors, voucher numbers, dates, and amounts.

7. Reconcile liabilities with monthly statements from creditors.

In some companies, it is a regular practice each month to reconcile vendors' statements with the detailed records of payables. If the auditors find that this reconciliation is regularly performed by the client's staff, they may limit their review of vendors' statements to determining that the reconciliation work has been satisfactory.

If the client's staff has not reconciled vendors' statements and accounts payable, the auditors may do so. When internal control for accounts payable is weak, the auditors may control incoming mail to assure that all vendors' statements received by the client are made available to the auditors. Among the discrepancies often revealed by reconciliation of vendors' statements are charges by the vendor for shipments not yet received or recorded by the client. Although conceptually all goods on which title has passed should be included in inventory (thus items shipped FOB shipping point as of year-end and not yet received should be included), normal accounting procedures do not provide for recording invoices as liabilities until the merchandise has been received. In-transit shipments on which title has passed should be listed and a decision reached as to whether they are sufficiently material to warrant year-end adjustment.

A purpose of this audit procedure is to assure that an accurate year-end cutoff of accounts payable has been made. The cutoff of accounts payable is closely connected with the cutoff of purchase invoices in determining the year-end inventory. When observing the taking of a physical inventory on December 31, the auditors will make a record of the serial number of the last receiving report issued. This number should be identified with the corresponding vendor's invoice on the list of accounts payable at December 31. Any invoices corresponding to earlier receiving reports represent liabilities at December 31; any invoices associated with later receiving reports should not be part of the year-end amount for accounts payable. In other words, the year-end cutoff must assure that a liability is recorded for any goods received on the last day of the year *and included in the physical inventory.* Otherwise, net income would be overstated by the full amount of the omitted invoice.

If a shipment of merchandise arrives on December 31 after the physical inventory has been completed, income will not be affected if the goods are omitted from inventory and the related vendor's invoice is omitted from purchases and accounts payable. Although the omission is a cutoff error, it is far less *material* than if the goods had been included in inventory but the liability had not been recorded.

In more general terms, we can say that in judging the materiality of unrecorded liabilities, the auditors should consider the related unrecorded debits. If recording the transaction would mean adding an asset as well as a liability, the effect on the financial statements would be less significant than recording an invoice of like amount for which the debit belonged in an expense account. The auditors must be sure, however, that invoices have been recorded as liabilities for all goods received and included in the year-end physical inventory.

8.   Confirm accounts payable by direct correspondence with vendors.

Confirmation requests should be mailed to vendors from whom substantial purchases have been made during the year, regardless of the size of their accounts at the balance sheet date. An accounts payable confirmation request appears in Figure 15–3. Even accounts payable with zero balances at year-end should be confirmed if they represent major suppliers. These large suppliers can be identified by reference to the accounts payable subsidiary ledger or computer printouts of purchase volume for individual suppliers, or by inquiry of purchasing department personnel. Other accounts to be confirmed by the auditors include those for which monthly statements are not available, accounts reflecting unusual transactions, accounts with parent or subsidiary corporations, and accounts secured by pledged assets.

Confirmation of accounts payable is not a mandatory procedure as is the confirmation of receivables. One reason is that the greatest hazard in the verification of liabilities is the existence of unrecorded liabilities. To confirm the *recorded accounts payable* does not prove whether any *unrecorded accounts payable* exist. However, sending confirmation requests to suppliers whose accounts show *zero balances* at year-end is designed to disclose unrecorded liabilities. Another factor to be noted in comparing the confirmation of accounts receivable and accounts payable is that the auditors will find in the client's possession externally created evidence such as vendors' invoices and statements that substantiate the accounts payable. No such external evidence is on hand to support accounts receivable. Finally, many of the recorded liabilities as of the balance sheet date will be paid before the auditors complete their examination. The act of payment serves further to substantiate the authenticity of recorded liabilities. For all these reasons the audit procedure of confirmation is of less importance for accounts payable than for accounts receivable.

9.   Perform analytical procedures for accounts payable and related accounts.

To gain assurance as to the overall reasonableness of accounts payable, the auditor may compute ratios such as accounts payable divided by purchases, and accounts payable divided by total current liabilities. These ratios are compared with ratios for prior years to disclose trends that warrant investigation.

The list of amounts payable to individual vendors should be reviewed to identify any companies from which the client does not ordinarily acquire goods or services. The amounts owing to individual creditors should also be compared with balances in prior years. By studying yearly variations in purchases and other accounts closely related to accounts payable,

Figure 15–3

Packaging Systems, Inc.
9200 Channel Street
New Orleans, Louisiana 70128

January 2, 198X

Grayline Container, Inc.
4800 Madison Street
Dallas, Texas 75221

Dear Sirs:

Our independent auditors, Nelson & Gray, CPAs, are making an examination of our financial statements. For this reason, please inform them in the space provided below the amount, if any, owed to you by this company at December 31, 198X.

Please attach an itemized statement supporting any balance owed, showing all unpaid items. Your reply should be sent directly to Nelson & Gray, CPAs, 6500 Lane Avenue, New Orleans, Louisiana 70128. A stamped addressed envelope is enclosed for your reply. Thank you.

Sincerely,

Robert W. James

Robert W. James
Controller

Nelson & Gray, CAs

Our records show that the amount of $ 26,800 was owed to us by Packaging Systems, Inc., at December 31, 198X, as shown by the itemized statement attached.

Date: Jan. 6, 8X

Signature *Sharon Steele*

Title *Controller*

the auditors may become aware of errors in accounts payable. Finally, the portion of accounts payable which is past due at the year-end should be compared with corresponding data for previous years.

The auditors may test purchase discounts by computing the ratio of cash discounts earned to total purchases during the period and comparing this ratio from period to period. Any significant decrease in the ratio might indicate a change in terms of purchases, failure to take discounts, or fraudulent manipulation.

10. Search for unrecorded accounts payable.

Throughout the audit the auditors must be alert for any unrecorded payables. For example, the preceding three steps of this program, reconciliation, confirmation, and analytical procedures, may disclose unrecorded liabilities. In addition to normal trade payables that may be unrecorded, other examples include unrecorded liabilities related to customers' deposits recorded as credits to accounts receivable, obligations for securities purchased but not settled at the balance sheet date, unbilled contractor or architect fees for a building under construction at the audit date, and unpaid attorney or insurance broker fees.

In addition to the prior audit steps, when searching for unrecorded accounts payable the auditors will audit transactions that were recorded following year-end. A comparison of cash payments occurring after the balance sheet date with the accounts payable trial balance is an excellent means of disclosing unrecorded accounts payable. All liabilities must eventually be paid, and will, therefore, be reflected in the accounts at least by the time they are paid. Regular monthly expenses, such as rent and utilities, are often posted to the ledger accounts directly from the cash disbursements journal without any account payable or other liability having been set up. To help determine that they are aware of all payments after year-end, the auditors should account for the numerical sequence of all checks issued between the balance sheet date and the date of completion of field work.

The auditors should also consider sources of potential unrecorded payables such as the following:

1. Unmatched invoices and unbilled receivers. These documents are called work in process in a voucher system. The auditors should review such unprocessed documents at the balance sheet date to ascertain that the client has recorded an account payable where appropriate.
2. Vouchers payable entered in the voucher register subsequent to the balance sheet date. Inspection of these records may uncover an item that should have been recorded as of the balance sheet date.
3. Invoices received by the client after the balance sheet date. Not all vendors send invoices promptly when goods are shipped or services are rendered. Accordingly, the auditors' review of invoices received

by the client in the subsequent period may disclose unrecorded accounts payable as of the balance sheet date.

A form of audit working paper used to summarize unrecorded accounts payable discovered by the auditors is illustrated in Figure 15–4.

When unrecorded liabilities are discovered by the auditors, the next question is whether the omissions are sufficiently material to warrant proposing an adjusting entry. Will the adjustment cause a sufficient change in the financial statements to give a different impression of the company's current position or of its earning power? As previously indicated in the discussion of the reconciliation of vendors' statements with accounts payable, auditors seldom propose adjustments for the purpose of adding shipments in transit to the year-end inventory unless the shipments are unusually large.

As a further illustration of the factors to be considered in deciding upon the ***materiality*** of an unrecorded transaction, let us use as an example the December 31 annual audit of a small manufacturing company in good financial condition with total assets of $1 million and preadjustment net income of $100,000. The auditors' procedures bring to light the following unrecorded liabilities:

1. An invoice of $1,400, dated December 30 and bearing terms of FOB shipping point. The goods were shipped on December 30 but were not received until January 4. The invoice was also received and recorded on January 4.

    In considering the materiality of this omission, the first point is that net income is not affected. The adjusting entry, if made, would add equal amounts to current assets (inventories) and to current liabilities; hence it would not change the amount of working capital. The omission does affect the current ratio very slightly. The auditor would probably consider this transaction as not sufficiently material to warrant adjustment.

2. Another invoice for $4,000, dated December 30 and bearing terms of FOB shipping point. The goods arrived on December 31 and were included in the physical inventory taken that day. The invoice was not received until January 8 and was entered as a January transaction.

    This error should be corrected because the inclusion of the goods in the physical inventory without recognition of the liability has caused an error of $4,000 in pretax income for the year. Since the current liabilities are understated, both the amount of working capital and the current ratio are exaggerated. The owners' equity is also overstated. These facts point to the materiality of the omission and constitute strong arguments for an adjusting entry.

3. An invoice for $1,500, dated December 31, for a new office safe. The safe was installed on December 31, but the invoice was not recorded until paid on January 15.

Figure 15–4

The Palermo Company
Unrecorded Accounts Payable   M-1-1
December 31, 1991

Invoice Date	No.	Vendor and Description	Account Charged	Amount
Dec. 31,91	285	Hayes Mfg. Co.—invoice and shipment in transit	Inventories	10650 00
— —		Fox & Williams—unpaid legal fees—see M-4	Legal Expenses	1000 00
Dec. 28,91	428	Hart & Co.—machinery repairs (paid Jan. 1, 92)	Repairs Exp.	12600 00
Dec. 31,91	—	Allen Enterprises—Dec. 19 account sales for consigned goods	Sales	25680 00
— —		Grant Co.—shipment received Dec. 31, 91 per receiver no. 2907; invoice not yet received	Inventories	15820 00
— —		Arthur & Baker—earned but unpaid architects' fee for building under construction—see K-5	Construction in Progress	23370 00
				89120 00
				M-1
A.J.E. 8		131 Inventories	26470 00	
		156 Construction in Progress	23370 00	
		401 Sales	25680 00	
		518 Legal Expenses	1000 00	
		527 Repairs Expense	12600 00	
		203 Accounts Payable		89120 00
		To record unrecorded accounts payable at Dec. 31, 91		

Above payables were developed principally
in the audit of accounts payable. See audit program B-4 for procedures employed. In my opinion
the $89,120 adjustment includes all material un-
recorded accounts payable.

J.M.H.
Jan. 23,92

Since the transaction involved only asset and liability accounts, the omission of an entry did not affect net income. However, working capital and the current ratio are affected by the error since the debit affects a noncurrent asset and the credit affects a current liability. Most auditors would probably not propose an adjusting entry for this item.

4. An invoice for $3,000, dated December 31, for advertising services rendered during October, November, and December. The invoice was not recorded until paid on January 15.

The argument for treating this item as sufficiently material to warrant adjustment is based on the fact that net income is affected, as well as the amount of working capital and the current ratio. The adjusting entry should probably be recommended in these circumstances.

The preceding examples suggest that a decision as to the materiality of an unrecorded transaction hinges to an important extent on whether the transaction affects net income. Assuming that an omitted transaction does affect net income and there is doubt as to whether the dollar amount is large enough to warrant adjustment, the auditors should bear in mind that almost half of the effect of the error on net income may be eliminated by corporate income taxes. In other words, an adjusting entry to record an omitted expense item of $10,000 may reduce after-tax income by only $5,000. If the adjusting entry is not made, the only ultimate effect is a shift of $5,000 between the net income of two successive years. As a general rule, the auditors should avoid proposing adjusting entries for errors in the year-end cutoff of transactions unless the effect on the statements is clearly significant. However, it should be borne in mind that a number of insignificant individual errors may be material in their *cumulative* effect on the financial statements.

11. Search for accounts payable to related parties.

Payables to a corporation's officers, directors, stockholders, or affiliates require particular attention by the auditors since they are not the result of arm's-length bargaining by parties of opposing interests. Here the auditors should consider the possibility that these payables relate to purchases of inventory or other asset items for which there may be valuation questions.

The independent auditors must search for such payables. All material payables to related parties must be disclosed in the financial statements.

12. Evaluate proper balance sheet presentation and disclosure of accounts payable.

Proper balance sheet presentation of accounts payable requires that any material amounts payable to related parties (directors, principal stockholders, officers, and employees) be listed separately from amounts payable to trade creditors.

Debit balances of substantial amount sometimes occur in accounts payable because of such events as duplicate payments made in error, return of merchandise to vendors after payment has been made, and advances to suppliers. If these debit balances are material, a reclassification entry should be made in the audit working papers so that the debit balances will appear as assets in the balance sheet rather than being offset against other accounts payable with credit balances.

If the client company acts as a consignee of merchandise, it is possible that sales of consigned goods shortly before the year-end may not have been set up as a liability to the consignor. An accurate determination of any amounts owing to consignors at the balance sheet date is one step in proper balance sheet presentation of liabilities.

Accounts payable secured by pledged assets should be disclosed in the balance sheet or a note thereto, and cross-referenced to the pledged assets.

OTHER LIABILITIES

Notes payable are discussed in the next chapter. In addition to the accounts payable previously considered, other items classified as current liabilities include—

1. Amounts withheld from employees' pay.
2. Sales taxes payable.
3. Unclaimed wages.
4. Customers' deposits.
5. Accrued liabilities.

Amounts withheld from employees' pay

Payroll deductions are notoriously numerous; among the more important are social security taxes and individual income taxes. Although the federal and state governments do not specify the exact form of records to be maintained, they do require that records of amounts earned and withheld be adequate to permit a determination of compliance with tax laws.

Income taxes withheld from employees' pay and not remitted as of the balance sheet date constitute a liability to be verified by the auditors. Accrued employer payroll taxes may be audited at the same time. This verification usually consists of tracing the amounts withheld to the payroll summary sheets, testing computations of taxes withheld and accrued, determining that taxes have been deposited or paid in accordance with the federal and state laws and regulations, and reviewing quarterly tax returns.

Payroll deductions also are often made for union dues, charitable contributions, retirement plans, insurance, savings bonds, and other purposes. Besides verifying the liability for any such amounts withheld from employees and not remitted as of the balance sheet date, the auditors should review the adequacy of the withholding procedures and determine that payroll deductions have been properly authorized and accurately computed.

Sales taxes payable

In most sections of the country, business concerns are required to collect sales taxes imposed by state and local governments on retail sales. These taxes do not represent an expense to the business; the retailer merely acts as a collecting agent. Until the amounts collected from customers are remitted to the taxing authority, they constitute current liabilities of the business. The auditors' verification of this liability includes a review of the client's periodic tax returns. The reasonableness of the liability also is tested by a computation applying the tax rate to total taxable sales. In addition, the auditors should examine a number of sales invoices to ascertain that customers are being charged the correct amount of tax. Debits to the liability account for remittances to the taxing authority should be traced to copies of the tax returns and should be vouched to the paid checks.

Unclaimed wages

Unclaimed wages are, by their very nature, subject to misappropriation. The auditors, therefore, are particularly concerned with the adequacy of internal control over this item. A list of unpaid wages should be prepared after each payroll distribution. The payroll checks should not be left for more than a few days in the payroll department. Prompt deposit in a special bank account provides much improved control. The auditors will analyze the Unclaimed Wages account for the purpose of determining that (1) the credits represent all unclaimed wages after each payroll distribution and (2) the debits represent only authorized payments to employees, remittances to the state under unclaimed property laws, or transfers back to general cash funds through approved procedures.

Customers' deposits

Many companies require that customers make deposits on returnable containers. Public utilities and common carriers also may require deposits to guarantee payment of bills or to cover equipment on loan to the customer. A review of the procedures followed in accepting and returning deposits should be made by the auditors with a view to disclosing any shortcomings in internal control. In some instances, deposits shown by the records as refunded to customers may in fact have been abstracted by employees.

The verification should include obtaining a list of the individual deposits and a comparison of the total with the general ledger controlling account. If deposits are interest-bearing, the amount of accrued interest should also be verified. As a general rule, the auditors do not attempt to confirm deposits by direct communication with customers; but this procedure is desirable if the amounts involved are substantial or the internal control procedures are considered to be deficient.

Accrued liabilities

Most accrued liabilities represent obligations payable sometime during the succeeding period for services or privileges received before the balance sheet date. Examples include interest payable, accrued property taxes, accrued payrolls and payroll taxes, income taxes payable, and amounts accrued under service guarantees.

Because accrued items are based on client estimates of amounts which will subsequently become payable, subjective (as well as objective) factors may make it difficult to establish control over them. As a result, these estimates may be particularly susceptible to misstatement, especially in circumstances in which management is under pressure to show increased earnings.

The basic auditing steps for accrued liabilities are:

1. Examine any contracts or other documents on hand that provide the basis for the accrual.
2. Appraise the accuracy of the detailed accounting records maintained for this category of liability.
3. Identify and evaluate the reasonableness of the assumptions made that underlie the computation of the liability.
4. Test the computations made by the client in setting up the accrual.
5. Determine that accrued liabilities have been treated consistently at the beginning and end of the period.
6. Consider the need for accrual of other accrued liabilities not presently considered (that is, test completeness).

The following sections describe the nature of the audit of various accrued liabilities.

Accrued property taxes Property tax payments are usually few in number and substantial in amount. It is, therefore, feasible for the audit working papers to include an analysis showing all of the year's property tax transactions. Tax payments should be verified by inspection of the property tax bills issued by local government units and by reference to the related paid checks. If the tax accruals at the balance sheet date differ significantly from those of prior years, an explanation of the variation should be obtained. The auditors should verify that property tax bills have been received on all taxable property or that an estimated tax has been accrued.

Accrued payrolls   The examination of payrolls from the standpoint of appraising the adequacy of internal controls and substantiating the expenditures for the period under audit is considered in Chapter 17. The present consideration of payrolls is limited to the procedures required for the verification of accrued payrolls at the balance sheet date.

Accrued gross salaries and wages appear on the balance sheets of virtually all concerns. The correctness of the amount accrued is significant in the determination of total liabilities and also in the proper matching of costs and revenue. The verification procedure consists principally of comparing the amounts accrued to the actual payroll of the subsequent period and reviewing the method of allocation at the balance sheet date. Payments made at the first payroll dates of the subsequent period are reviewed to determine that no *unrecorded* payroll liability existed as of the balance sheet date.

Pension plan accruals   Auditing procedures for the accrued liability for pension costs may begin with a review of the copy of the pension plan in the auditors' permanent file. Then consideration should be given to the provisions of the Employee Retirement Income Security Act (ERISA). Other steps include confirmation of the client's pension cost for the year by direct correspondence with the client's actuary and analysis of the related liability account, including confirmation of any payments to the trustee. In obtaining evidence from the client's actuary, the auditors should comply with the requirements of *SAS 11* (AU 336), "Using the Work of a Specialist" (discussed in Chapter 7).

Accrued vacation pay   Closely related to accrued salaries and wages is the liability that may exist for accrued vacation pay. This type of liability arises from two situations: (1) an employee entitled by contract to a vacation during the past year may have been prevented from taking it by an emergency work schedule, and (2) an employee may be entitled to a future vacation of which part of the cost must be accrued to achieve a proper matching of costs and revenue.

The auditors' verification of accrued vacation pay may begin with a review of the permanent file copy of the employment contract or agreement stipulating vacation terms. The computation of the accrual should then be verified both as to arithmetical accuracy and for agreement with the terms of the company's vacation policy. The auditors should also ascertain whether the expense provision offsetting the vacation accrual qualifies as an income tax deduction. If not, income tax allocation will be required.

Service guarantees   The products of many companies are sold with a guarantee of free service or replacement during a rather extended warranty period. The costs of rendering such services should be recognized as expense in the year the product is sold rather than in a later year in which the replacement is made or repair service performed. If this policy is followed, the company will make an annual charge to expense and credit to a liability account based on the amount of the year's sales and the estimated future service or replacement. As repairs and replacements take place, the costs will be charged to the liability account.

The auditors should review the client's annual provision for estimated future expenditures and compute the percentage relationship between the amount in the liability account and the amount of the year's sales. If this relationship varies sharply from year to year, the client should be asked for an explanation. The auditors should also review the charges month by month to the liability account and be alert for the burial of other expenses in this account. Sudden variations in the monthly charges to the liability account require investigation. In general, the auditors should determine that the balance in the liability account for service guarantees moves in reasonable relationship with the trend of sales and is properly segregated into current and long-term portions in the balance sheet.

Current income tax laws prohibit the deduction of provisions for service guarantees; deductions are permitted only when actual expenditures are incurred. Accordingly, the auditors should ascertain that the client is properly allocating income taxes attributable to the nondeductible provisions.

Accrued commissions and bonuses Accrued commissions to sales representatives and bonuses payable to managerial personnel also require verification. The essential step in this case is reference to the authority for the commission or bonus. The basic contracts should be examined and traced to minutes of directors' meetings. If the bonus or commission is based on the total volume of sales or some other objective measure, the auditors should verify the computation of the accrual by applying the prescribed rate to the amount used as a base.

Income taxes payable Federal, state, and foreign income taxes on corporations represent a material factor in determining both net income and financial position. The auditors cannot express an opinion on either the balance sheet or income statement of a corporation without first obtaining evidence that the provision for income taxes has been properly computed. In the audit of small- and medium-size companies, it is customary for the audit engagement to include the preparation of the client's tax returns. If the income tax returns have been prepared by the client's staff or other persons, the auditors must nevertheless verify the reasonableness of the tax liability if they are to express an opinion on the fairness of the financial statements. In performing such a review of a tax return prepared by the client's staff or by others, the auditors may sometimes discover an opportunity for a tax saving that has been overlooked;

obviously such a discovery tends to enhance the client's appreciation of the services rendered by the auditors.

For businesses organized as single proprietorships or partnerships, no provision for income taxes appears on the income statement because taxes on the profits of these enterprises are payable by the individual owner or owners.

The tax expected to be paid by a corporation often differs from the actual tax paid due to temporary differences between taxable income and pretax accounting income. These differences result in the need to establish deferred tax liabilities or assets.

The auditors should analyze the Income Taxes Payable account and vouch all amounts to income tax returns, paid checks, or other supporting documents. The final balance in the Income Taxes Payable account will ordinarily equal the computed federal, state, and foreign taxes on the current year's income tax returns, less any payments thereon.

Besides reviewing the computation of the income tax liability for the current year, the auditors should determine the date to which income tax returns for prior years have been examined by IRS agents and the particulars of any disputes or additional assessments. Review of the reports of revenue agents is also an essential step. In the first audit of a new client, the auditors should review any prior years' income tax returns not yet examined by revenue agents to make sure that there has been no substantial underpayment of taxes that would warrant presentation as a liability.

Accrued professional fees   Fees of professional firms include charges for the services of attorneys, public accountants, consulting engineers, and other specialists who often render services of a continuing nature but present bills only at infrequent intervals. By inquiry of officers and by review of corporate minutes, the auditors may learn of professional services received for which no liability has yet been reflected in the accounts. Review of the expense account for legal fees is always essential because it may reveal damage suits, tax disputes, or other litigation warranting disclosure in the financial statements. Fees of public accountants for periodic audits are properly reflected in the accounts of the year subsequent to the period under audit. Accruals are desirable, however, for any other accounting services completed but unbilled as of the balance sheet date.

Balance sheet presentation

Accrued expenses—interest, taxes, rent, and wages—are included in the current liability section of the balance sheet and sometimes combined into one figure. Income taxes payable, however, may be sufficiently material to be listed as a separate item. Deferred federal income taxes resulting from tax allocations should be classified as current liabilities if they relate to current assets. Otherwise, deferred federal income taxes are classified as long term.

Deferred credits to revenue for such items as rent or interest collected in advance that will be taken into earnings in the succeeding period are customarily included in current liabilities. Deposits on contracts and similar advances from customers also are accorded the status of current liabilities because the receipt of an advance increases the current assets total and because the goods to be used in liquidating the advance are generally included in current assets.

Time of examination

The nature and amount of trade accounts payable may change greatly within a few weeks' time; consequently, the auditors' verification of these rapidly changing liabilities is most effective when performed immediately after the balance sheet date. As stressed at the beginning of this chapter, failure to record a liability will cause an overstatement of financial position. Audit work on accounts payable performed before the balance sheet date is of little value if the client fails to record important liabilities coming into existence during the remaining weeks of the year under audit. For this reason, many auditors believe that most of the audit work on accounts payable should be performed *after the balance sheet date.* Certainly, the auditors' search for unrecorded liabilities must be made after the balance sheet date because this search is concentrated on the transactions occurring during the first few weeks of the new year.

Some current liability accounts other than accounts payable are more suitable for preliminary audit work. The documents relating to accrued property taxes, for example, may be available in advance of the balance sheet date. Amounts withheld from employees' pay can be reviewed before the end of the year. The propriety of amounts withheld and of amounts remitted to the tax authorities during the year can be verified before the pressure of year-end work begins. The working papers relating to such liability accounts then may be completed very quickly after the end of the accounting period.

KEY TERMS INTRODUCED OR EMPHASIZED IN CHAPTER 15

Accrued liabilities (accrued expenses) Short-term obligations for services of a continuing nature that accumulate on a time basis. Examples include interest, taxes, rent, salaries, and pensions. Generally not evidenced by invoices or statements.

Confirmation Direct communication with vendors or suppliers to determine the amount of an account payable. Represents high quality evidence because it is a document created outside the client organization and transmitted directly to the auditors.

Consignment A transfer of goods from the owner to another person who acts as the sales agent of the owner.

Subsequent period The time extending from the balance sheet date to the date of the auditors' report.

Trade accounts payable Current liabilities arising from the purchase of goods and services from trade creditors, generally evidenced by invoices or statements received from the creditors.

Vendor's statement A monthly statement prepared by a vendor (supplier) showing the beginning balance, charges during the month for goods or services, amounts collected, and ending balance. This externally created document should correspond (except for timing differences) with an account in the client's accounts payable subsidiary ledger.

Voucher A document authorizing a cash disbursement. A voucher usually provides space for employees performing various approval functions to initial. The term ***voucher*** may also be applied to the group of supporting documents used as a basis for recording liabilities or for making cash disbursements.

Voucher register A special journal used in a voucher system to record liabilities requiring cash payment in the near future. Every liability recorded in a voucher register corresponds to a voucher authorizing future payment.

GROUP I: REVIEW QUESTIONS

15-1. If a corporation overstates its earnings, are its liabilities more likely to be overstated or understated? Explain.

15-2. Lawsuits against CPA firms are most likely to allege that the auditors were negligent in not detecting which of the following? (*a*) overstatement of liabilities and earnings, (*b*) understatement of assets and earnings, (*c*) overstatement of owners' equity. Explain the reasoning underlying your choice.

15-3. Assume that a highly placed employee has stolen company assets and is now planning to conceal the fraud by failing to make an accounting entry for a large transaction. Would the omission probably be for a transaction creating an asset or a liability? Explain.

15-4. Suggest two reasons why the adjustments proposed by independent auditors more often than not call for reducing recorded earnings.

15-5. Explain how the auditors coordinate the year-end cutoff of accounts payable with their observation of the year-end physical inventory.

15-6. Identify three audit procedures (other than "Search for unrecorded accounts payable") that are concerned directly or indirectly with disclosing unrecorded accounts payable.

15-7. What is the purpose of the auditors' review of cash payments subsequent to the balance sheet date?

15-8. The auditors usually find in the client's possession documentary evidence, such as invoices, supporting both accounts receivable and accounts payable. Is there any difference in the quality of such evidence for accounts receivable and for accounts payable? Explain.

15-9. Describe briefly an internal control procedure that would prevent a paid disbursement voucher from being presented for payment a second time.

15-10. Is the confirmation of accounts payable by direct communication with vendors as useful and important an audit procedure as is the confirmation of accounts receivable? Explain fully. (AICPA)

15-11. During the verification of the individual invoices comprising the total of accounts payable at the balance sheet date, the auditors discovered some receiving reports indicating that the merchandise covered by several of these invoices was not received until after the balance sheet date. What action should the auditors take?

15–12. What do you consider to be the most important single procedure in the auditors' search for unrecorded accounts payable? Explain.

15–13. Whitehall Company records its liabilities in accounts payable subsidiary ledgers. The auditors have decided to select some of the accounts for confirmation by direct communication with vendors. The largest volume of purchases during the year had been made from Ranchero Company, but at the balance sheet date this account had a zero balance. Under these circumstances should the auditors send a confirmation request to Ranchero Company, or would they accomplish more by limiting their confirmation program to accounts with large year-end balances?

15–14. Compare the auditors' approach to the verification of liabilities with their approach to the verification of assets.

15–15. Most auditors are interested in performing as many phases of an examination as possible in advance of the balance sheet date. The verification of accounts payable, however, generally is regarded as something to be done after the balance sheet date. What specific factors can you suggest that make the verification of accounts payable less suitable than many other accounts for interim work?

15–16. The operating procedures of a well-managed accounts payable department will provide for the verification of several specific points before a vendor's invoice is recorded as an approved liability. What are the points requiring verification?

15–17. List the major responsibilities of an accounts payable department.

15–18. In achieving adequate internal control over operations of the accounts payable department, a company should establish procedures that will ensure that extensions and footings are proved on all invoices and that the propriety of prices is reviewed. What is the most effective means of assuring consistent performance of these duties?

15–19. Which do you consider the more significant step in establishing strong internal control over accounts payable transactions: the approval of an invoice for payment, or the issuance of a check in payment of an invoice? Explain.

15–20. Outline a method by which the auditors may test the propriety of cash discounts taken on accounts payable.

15–21. For which documents relating to the accounts payable operation would you recommend the use of serial numbers as an internal control procedure?

15–22. What internal control procedure would you recommend to call attention to failure to pay invoices within the discount period?

15–23. As part of the investigation of accounts payable, auditors sometimes vouch entries in selected creditors' accounts back through the journals to original documents, such as purchase orders, receiving reports, invoices, and paid checks. What is the principal purpose of this procedure?

15–24. Vendors' statements and accounts payable confirmations are both forms of documentary evidence created outside the client organization and useful in audit work on accounts payable. Which of these two represents higher quality evidence? Why?

15–25. What documentary evidence created outside the client's organization is particularly important to the auditors in verifying accrued property taxes?

15–26. What differences should auditors expect to find in supporting evidence for accrued liabilities as contrasted with accounts payable?

GROUP II: QUESTIONS REQUIRING ANALYSIS

15–27. Early in your first audit of Star Corporation, you notice that sales and year-end inventory are almost unchanged from the prior year. However, cost of goods sold is less than in the preceding year, and accounts payable also are down substantially. Gross profit has increased, but this increase has not carried through to net income because of increased executive salaries. Management informs you that sales prices and purchase prices have not changed significantly during the past year, and there have been no changes in the product line. Star Corporation relies on the periodic inventory system. Your initial impression of internal control is that several weaknesses may exist.

You are to suggest a possible explanation for the trends described, especially the decrease in accounts payable while sales and inventory were constant and gross profit increased. Explain fully the relationships involved.

15–28. Compare the confirmation of accounts receivable with the confirmation of accounts payable under the following headings:

a. Generally accepted auditing procedures. (Justify the differences revealed by your comparison.)

b. Selection of accounts to be confirmed.   (AICPA, adapted)

15–29. In connection with their examination of the financial statements of Davis Company, the auditors reviewed the Federal Income Taxes Payable account.

Required:

a. Discuss reasons why the auditors should review the federal income tax returns for prior years and the reports of internal revenue agents.

b. What information will these reviews provide? (Do not discuss specific tax return items.)   (AICPA, adapted)

15–30. The *subsequent period* in an audit is the time extending from the balance sheet date to the date of the auditors' report.

Required:

Discuss the importance of the subsequent period in the audit of trade accounts payable.

15–31. During the course of any audit, the auditors are always alert for unrecorded accounts payable or other unrecorded liabilities.

Required:

For each of the following audit areas (1) describe an unrecorded liability that might be discovered and (2) state what auditing procedure(s) might bring it to light.

a. Construction in progress (property, plant, and equipment).

     b. Prepaid insurance.

     c. License authorizing the client to produce a product patented by another company.

     d. Minutes of directors' meetings.

15–32. Describe the audit steps that generally would be followed in establishing the propriety of the recorded liability for federal income taxes of a corporation you are auditing for the first time. Consideration should be given the status of (*a*) the liability for prior years and (*b*) the liability arising from the current year's taxable income. (AICPA)

15–33. In the course of your initial examination of the financial statements of Sylvan Company, you ascertain that of the substantial amount of accounts payable outstanding at the close of the period, approximately 75 percent is owed to six creditors. You have requested that you be permitted to confirm the balances owing to these six creditors by communicating with the creditors, but the president of the company is unwilling to approve your request on the grounds that correspondence in regard to the balances—all of which contain some overdue items—might give rise to demands on the part of the creditors for immediate payment of the overdue items and thereby embarrass Sylvan Company.

     In the circumstances, what alternative procedure would you adopt in an effort to satisfy yourself that the accounting records show the correct amounts payable to these creditors? (AICPA, adapted)

15–34. Select the best answer for each of the following and explain the reason for your selection.

     a. Which of the following procedures relating to the examination of accounts payable could the auditors delegate entirely to the client's employees?

        (1) Test footings in the accounts payable ledger.

        (2) Reconcile unpaid invoices to vendors' statements.

        (3) Prepare a schedule of accounts payable.

        (4) Mail confirmations for selected account balances.

     b. An examination of the balance in the accounts payable account is ordinarily *not* designed to:

        (1) Detect accounts payable that are substantially past due.

        (2) Verify that accounts payable were properly authorized.

        (3) Ascertain the reasonableness of recorded liabilities.

        (4) Determine that all existing liabilities at the balance sheet date have been recorded.

     c. Which of the following is the ***best*** audit procedure for determining the existence of unrecorded liabilities?

        (1) Examine confirmation requests returned by creditors whose accounts appear on a subsidiary trial balance of accounts payable.

        (2) Examine unusual relationships between monthly accounts payable balances and recorded purchases.

        (3) Examine a sample of invoices a few days prior to and subsequent to year-end to ascertain whether they have been properly recorded.

(4) Examine a sample of cash disbursements in the period subsequent to year-end.

d. Auditor confirmation of accounts payable balances at the balance sheet date may be **unnecessary** because:

(1) This is a duplication of cutoff tests.

(2) Accounts payable balances at the balance sheet date may **not** be paid before the audit is completed.

(3) Correspondence with the audit client's attorney will reveal all legal action by vendors for nonpayment.

(4) There is likely to be other reliable external evidence available to support the balances.

e. A client erroneously recorded a large purchase twice. Which of the following internal control measures would be most likely to detect this error in a timely and efficient manner?

(1) Footing the purchases journal.

(2) Reconciling vendors' monthly statements with subsidiary payable ledger accounts.

(3) Tracing totals from the purchases journal to the ledger accounts.

(4) Sending written quarterly confirmation to all vendors.

f. Review of professional fees is important because—

(1) The fees are always extremely material in amount.

(2) Such review may reveal a variety of possible contingent liabilities pertaining to legal matters.

(3) They often are a key determinant of cost of goods sold.

(4) Their proper balance sheet classification, current or noncurrent, must be determined. (AICPA, adapted)

GROUP III: PROBLEMS

15–35. The following are typical questions that might appear on an internal control questionnaire for accounts payable.

1. Are monthly statements from vendors reconciled with the accounts payable listing?

2. Are vendors' invoices matched with receiving reports before they are approved for payment?

Required:

a. Describe the purpose of each of the above internal control procedures.

b. Describe the manner in which each of the above procedures might be tested.

c. Assuming that the operating effectiveness of each of the above procedures is found to be inadequate, describe how the auditors might alter their substantive tests to compensate for the internal control weakness.

15–36. Taylor, CPA, is engaged in the audit of Rex Wholesaling for the year ended December 31. Taylor obtained an understanding of internal control relating to the purchasing, receiving, trade accounts payable, and cash disbursement cycles, and has decided not to proceed with tests of controls. Based upon analytical procedures, Taylor believes that the trade accounts payable on the balance sheet as of December 31 may be understated.

Taylor requested and obtained a client-prepared trade accounts payable schedule listing the total amount owed to each vendor.

Required:
What additional substantive audit procedures should Taylor apply in examining the trade accounts payable?

15–37. As part of your first examination of the financial statements of Marina del Rey, Inc., you have decided to confirm some of the accounts payable. You are now in the process of selecting the individual companies to whom you will send accounts payable confirmation requests. Among the accounts payable you are considering are the following:

Company	Amount payable at year-end	Total purchases from vendor during year
Dayco, Inc.	$ —	$1,980,000
Gearbox, Inc.	22,650	46,100
Landon Co.	65,000	75,000
Western Supply	190,000	2,123,000

Required:
a. Which two of the above four accounts payable would you select as the most important to confirm? Explain your choice in terms of the audit objectives in sending accounts payable confirmation requests.
b. Assume that you are selecting accounts receivable to be confirmed. Assume also that the four companies listed above are customers of your client rather than suppliers and that the dollar amounts are accounts receivable balances and total sales for the year. Which two companies would you select as the most important to confirm? Explain your choice.

15–38. James Rowe, CPA, is the independent auditor of Raleigh Corporation. Rowe is considering the audit work to be performed in the accounts payable area for the current year's engagement.

The prior year's working papers show that confirmation requests were mailed to 100 of Raleigh's 1,000 suppliers. The selected suppliers were based on Rowe's sample that was designed to select accounts with large dollar balances. A substantial number of hours was spent by Raleigh employees and by Rowe resolving relatively minor differences between the confirmation replies and Raleigh's accounting records. Alternative audit procedures were used for those suppliers that did not respond to the confirmation requests.

Required:
a. Identify the accounts payable audit objectives that Rowe must consider in determining the audit procedures to be followed.

b. Identify situations in which Rowe should use accounts payable confirmations and discuss whether Rowe is required to use them.

c. Discuss why the use of large dollar balances as the basis for selecting accounts payable for confirmation might not be the most efficient approach, and indicate what more efficient procedures could be followed when selecting accounts payable for confirmation.

(AICPA, adapted)

15–39. During the current year, your audit client, Video Corporation, was licensed to manufacture a patented type of television tube. The licensing agreement called for royalty payments of 50 cents for each tube manufactured by Video Corporation. What procedures would you follow in connection with your regular annual audit at December 31 to obtain evidence that the liability for royalties is correctly stated?

(AICPA, adapted)

15–40. Nancy Howe, your staff assistant on the April 30, 1992, audit of Wilcox Company, was transferred to another audit engagement before she could complete the audit of unrecorded accounts payable. Her working paper, which you have reviewed and are satisfied is complete, appears on page 570.

Required:
Prepare a proposed adjusting journal entry for the unrecorded accounts payable of Wilcox Company at April 30, 1992. The amounts are material. (Do not deal with income taxes.)

15–41. You were in the final stages of your examination of the financial statements of Scott Corporation for the year ended December 31, 1990, when you were consulted by the corporation's president, who believes there is no point to your examining the 1991 voucher register and testing data in support of 1990 entries. He stated that (1) bills pertaining to 1990 that were received too late to be included in the December voucher register were recorded as of the year-end by the corporation by journal entry, (2) the internal auditors made tests after the year-end, and (3) he would furnish you with a letter representing that there were no unrecorded liabilities.

Required:
a. Should the independent auditors' test for unrecorded liabilities be affected by the fact that the client made a journal entry to record 1990 bills that were received late? Explain.

b. Should the independent auditors' test for unrecorded liabilities be affected by the fact that a letter is obtained in which a responsible management official represents that to the best of his knowledge all liabilities have been recorded? Explain.

c. Should the independent auditors' test for unrecorded liabilities be eliminated or reduced because of the internal audit tests? Explain.

d. Assume that the client company, which handled some government contracts, had no internal auditors but that auditors for a federal agency spent three weeks auditing the records and were just completing their work at this time. How would the independent auditors'

Wilcox Company

Unrecorded Accounts Payable   AK-1-1

April 30, 1992

Invoice Date	Vendor and Description	Amount
	Hill & Harper—unpaid legal fees at Apr. 30, 92 (see lawyer's letter at AK-4)	1000 √
Apr. 1, 92	Drew Insurance Agency—unpaid premium on fire insurance for period Apr. 1, 92 – Mar. 31, 95 (see insurance broker letter at J-1-1)	1800 √
Apr. 30, 92	Mayo and Sage, Stockbrokers—advice for 100 shares of Madison Ltd. Common stock (settlement date May 7, 92)	2125 √
	Lane Company—shipment received Apr. 30, 92 per receiver no. 3361 and included in Apr. 30, 92 physical inventory; invoice not yet received (amount is per purchase order)	5863 √
		10 788 —

√ — Examined document described

In my opinion, the $10,788 adjustment includes all material unrecorded accounts payable.

N.A.H.
May 29, 92

unrecorded liability test be affected by the work of the auditors for a federal agency?

e. What sources in addition to the 1992 voucher register should the independent auditors consider to locate possible unrecorded liabilities? (AICPA, adapted)

Debt and equity capital; loss contingencies

Chapter 16 study objectives

After studying this chapter, you should be able to:

— Describe the nature of debt and equity capital.
— Explain the fundamental necessary internal controls over debt and equity capital.
— Describe the auditors' objectives for the audit of debt and equity capital.
— Describe the nature of appropriate procedures to accomplish the auditors' objectives for the audit of debt and equity capital.
— Describe the nature of accounting and auditing responsibilities for loss contingencies.

Business corporations obtain substantial amounts of their financial resources by incurring interest-bearing debt and by issuing capital stock. The acquisition and repayment of capital is sometimes referred to as the financing cycle. This transaction cycle includes the sequence of procedures for authorizing, executing, and recording transactions that involve bank loans, mortgages, bonds payable, and capital stock as well as the payment of interest and dividends. In this chapter we present material on the auditors' approach to both debt and equity capital accounts. In addition, we present information on loss contingencies. These contingencies involve situations in which there is possible impairment of assets, generally with a related possible existence of a liability.

INTEREST-BEARING DEBT

Sources and nature of interest-bearing debt

Nearly every business borrows. A business with an excellent credit reputation may find it possible to borrow from a bank on a simple unsecured note. A business of lesser financial standing may find that obtaining bank credit requires the pledging of specific assets as collateral or that it must agree to certain restrictive covenants, such as the suspension of dividends.

Long-term debt usually is substantial in amount and often extends for periods of 20 years or more. Debentures, secured bonds, and notes payable (sometimes secured by mortgages or trust deeds) are the principal types of long-term debt. Debentures are backed only by the general credit of the issuing corporation and not by liens on specific assets. Since in most respects debentures have the characteristics of other corporate bonds, we shall use the term *bonds* to include both debentures and secured bonds payable.

The formal document creating bonded indebtedness is called the *indenture* or *trust indenture.* When creditors supply capital on a long-term basis, they often insist upon placing certain restrictions on the borrowing company. For example, the indenture often provides that a company may not declare dividends unless the amount of working capital is maintained above a specified amount. The acquisition of plant and equipment, or the increasing of managerial salaries, may be permitted only if the current ratio is maintained at a specified level and if net income reaches a designated amount. Another device for protecting the long-term creditor is the requirement of a sinking fund or redemption fund to be held by a trustee. If these restrictions are violated, the indenture may provide that the entire debt is due on demand.

The auditors' approach in examination of interest-bearing debt

The auditors' *objectives* in the examination of interest-bearing debt are to determine that:

1. *Internal control* over interest-bearing debt *is adequate.*

2. The recorded interest-bearing debt is valid (*occurrence* and *obligations*).
3. All interest-bearing debt is recorded (*completeness*).
4. Interest-bearing debt schedules are mathematically correct and agree with general ledger accounts (*clerical accuracy*).
5. The *valuation* of interest-bearing debt is proper.
6. The *presentation* and *disclosure* of interest-bearing debt is adequate.

In conjunction with the audit of interest-bearing debt, the auditors will also obtain evidence about the adequate cutoff of cash receipts and disbursements related to debt, and the accounts of interest expense, interest payable, and bond discount and premium.

Many of the principles related to accounts payable also apply to the audit of interest-bearing debt. As is the case for accounts payable, the understatement of debt is considered to be a major potential audit problem. The standard bank confirmation serves as a potential aid in detection of unrecorded debt. Related to disclosure of interest-bearing debt, the auditors must determine that the company has met all requirements and restrictions imposed upon it by debt contracts.

Internal control over interest-bearing debt

Authorization by the board of directors Effective internal control over interest-bearing debt begins with the authorization to incur the debt. The bylaws of a corporation usually require that borrowing be approved by the board of directors. The treasurer of the corporation will prepare a report on any proposed financing, explaining the need for funds, the estimated effect of borrowing upon future earnings, the estimated financial position of the company in comparison with others in the industry both before and after the borrowing, and alternative methods of raising the amount desired. Authorization by the board of directors will include review and approval of such matters as the choice of a bank, the type of security, the choice of a trustee, registration with the SEC, agreements with investment bankers, compliance with requirements of the state of incorporation, and listing of bonds on a securities exchange. After the issuance of long-term debt, the board of directors should receive a report stating the net amount received and its disposition, as for example, acquisition of plant assets, addition to working capital, or other purposes.

Use of an independent trustee Bond issues are always for large amounts—usually many millions of dollars. Therefore, only relatively large companies issue bonds; small companies obtain long-term capital through mortgage loans or other sources. Any company large enough to issue bonds and able to find a ready market for the securities will almost always utilize the services of a large bank as an independent trustee.

The trustee is charged with the protection of the creditors' interests and must continually review the issuing company's compliance with the provisions of the indenture. Besides, the trustee maintains detailed records of the names and addresses of the registered owners of the bonds, cancels old bond certificates and issues new ones when bonds change ownership, follows procedures to prevent overissuance of bond certificates, distributes interest payments, and distributes principal payments when the bonds mature. Use of an independent trustee largely solves the problem of internal control over bonds payable. Internal control is strengthened by the fact that the trustee does not have access to the issuing company's assets or accounting records and the fact that the trustee is a large financial institution with legal responsibility for its actions.

Interest payments on bonds and notes payable   The auditors' appraisal of internal controls relating to bonds and notes payable must extend to the handling of interest payments. In the case of a note payable, there may be only one recipient of interest, and the disbursement may be controlled in the same manner as other cash payments.

Many corporations assign the entire task of paying interest to the trustee for either *bearer bonds* or *registered bonds*. Highly effective control is then achieved, since the company will issue a single check for the full amount of the semiannual interest payment on the entire bond issue. In the case of bearer bonds (coupon bonds), the trustee upon receipt of this check will make payment for coupons presented, cancel the coupons, and file them numerically. A second count of the coupons is made at a later date; the coupons then are destroyed and a cremation certificate delivered to the issuing company. The trustee does not attempt to maintain a list of the holders of coupon bonds, since these securities are transferable by the mere act of delivery. If certain coupons are not presented for payment, the trustee will hold the funds corresponding to such coupons for the length of time prescribed by statute. In the case of registered bonds, the trustee will maintain a current list of holders and will remit interest checks to them in the same manner as dividend checks are distributed to stockholders.

Audit working papers

A copy of the indenture relating to a bond issue should be placed in the auditors' permanent file. Analyses of ledger accounts for notes and bonds payable, and the related accounts for interest and discount or premium, should be obtained for the current working papers file or the permanent file. A lead schedule is seldom required for short-term notes payable or for long-term debt.

AUDIT PROGRAM FOR INTEREST-BEARING DEBT

This audit program does not provide for the usual distinction between substantive testing and internal control testing. This is because individual transactions will generally be examined for all large debt agreements. The auditors will usually prepare a written description and a flowchart, as well as an internal control questionnaire. Questions included on a typical questionnaire are the following: Are interest-bearing liabilities incurred only under authorization of the board of directors? Is an independent trustee retained to account for all bond issuances, cancellations, and interest payments? Has the board of directors specified banks from which loans may be obtained? Answers to these questions will help the auditors to determine the appropriate substantive tests.

Because transactions are few in number, but large in dollar amount, the auditors are generally able to substantiate the individual transactions. Therefore, testing of controls occurs through what actually amounts to dual-purpose transaction testing.

Audit procedures appropriate for the verification of interest-bearing debt include the following:

1. Obtain or prepare analyses of interest-bearing debt accounts and related interest, premium, and discount accounts.
2. Examine copies of notes payable and supporting documents.
3. Confirm interest-bearing debt with payees or appropriate third parties.
4. Vouch borrowing and repayment transactions to supporting documents.
5. Perform analytical procedures to determine the overall reasonableness of interest-bearing debt and interest expense.
6. Verify computation of interest expense, interest payable, and amortization of discount or premium.
7. Determine whether debt provisions have been met.
8. Trace authority for issuance of interest-bearing debt to the corporate minutes.
9. Review notes payable paid or renewed after the balance sheet date.
10. Search for notes payable to related parties.
11. Evaluate financial statement presentation and disclosure of interest bearing debt and related transactions.

Figure 16–1 relates these substantive tests to their primary audit objectives.

1. Obtain or prepare analyses of interest-bearing debt accounts and related interest, premium, and discount accounts.

A notes payable analysis shows the beginning balance, if any, of each individual note, additional notes issued and payments on notes during the year, and the ending balance of each note. In addition, the beginning balances of interest payable or prepaid interest, interest expense, interest paid, and ending balances of interest payable or prepaid interest may be presented in the analysis working paper.

An analysis of the Notes Payable account will serve a number of purposes: (a) the payment or other disposition of notes listed as outstanding

Figure 16–1 Objectives
of major substantive
tests of interest-bearing
debt transactions and
balances

Substantive tests	Primary audit objectives
Obtain analyses of interest-bearing debt and related accounts and reconcile to ledgers	Clerical accuracy
Examine copies of notes payable and supporting documents Confirm interest-bearing debt	Completeness Validity (existence and obligations)
Vouch borrowing and repayment transactions	Validity (existence and obligations)
Perform analytical procedures Verify computation of interest expense, interest payable, and amortization of discount and premium	Completeness Validity (existence and obligations) Valuation or allocation
Determine whether debt provisions have been met Trace authority for issuance of debt to corporate minutes Review notes payable paid or renewed after the balance sheet date Search for notes payable to related parties Evaluate financial statement presentation and disclosure	Presentation and disclosure

in the previous year's audit can be verified, (b) the propriety of individual debits and credits can be established, and (c) the validity of the year-end balance of the account is proved through the step-by-step verification of all changes in the account during the year.

In the first audit of a client, the auditors will analyze the ledger accounts for Bonds Payable, Bond Issue Costs, and Bond Discount (or Bond Premium) for the years since the bonds were issued. The working paper is placed in the auditors' permanent file; in later audits, any further entries in these accounts may be added to the analysis.

2. Examine copies of notes payable and supporting documents.

The auditors should examine the client's copies of notes payable and supporting documents such as mortgages and trust deeds. The original documents will be in the possession of the payees, but the auditors should make certain that the client has retained copies of the debt instruments and that their details correspond to the analyses described in the second procedure of this audit program.

3. Confirm interest-bearing debt with payees or appropriate third parties.

Notes payable to banks are confirmed as part of the confirmation of bank balances. The standard bank confirmation form illustrated in Chapter 11 includes a request that the bank prepare a list of all borrowings by the depositor. The primary objective of this inquiry is to bring to light any unrecorded notes. As mentioned previously in the discussion of bank accounts, confirmation requests should be sent to all banks with which the client has done business during the year. This step is necessary because a note payable to a bank may be outstanding long after a deposit account has been closed.

Confirmation requests for notes payable to payees other than banks should be drafted on the client's letterhead stationery, signed by the controller or other appropriate executive, and mailed by the auditors. Payees should be requested to confirm dates of origin, due dates, unpaid balances of notes, interest rates, dates to which interest has been paid, and collateral for the notes.

The auditors may also substantiate the existence and amount of a mortgage liability outstanding by direct confirmation with the mortgagee. The information received should be compared with the client's records and the audit working papers. When no change in the liability account has occurred in the period under audit, the only major procedure necessary will be this confirmation with the creditor. At the same time that the mortgagee is asked to confirm the debt, it may be asked for an opinion as to the company's compliance with the mortgage or trust deed agreement.

Bond transactions usually can be confirmed directly with the trustee. The trustee's reply should include an exact description of the bonds, including maturity dates and interest rates; bonds retired, purchased for the treasury, or converted into stock during the year; bonds outstanding at the balance sheet date; and sinking fund transactions and balances.

4. Vouch borrowing and repayment transactions to supporting documents.

The auditors must obtain evidence that transactions in interest-bearing debt accounts were valid. To accomplish this objective, the auditors trace the cash received from the issuance of notes, bonds, or mortgages to the validated copy of the bank deposit slip and to the bank statement. Any remittance advices supporting these cash receipts are also examined. The auditors can find further support for the net proceeds of a bond issue by referring to the underwriting contract and to the prospectus filed with the SEC.

Debits to a Notes Payable or a Mortgages Payable account generally represent payments in full or in installments. The auditors should examine paid checks for these payments; in so doing, they also will account for payments of accrued interest. The propriety of installment payments should be verified by reference to the repayment schedule set forth in the note or mortgage copy in the client's possession.

A comparison of canceled notes payable with the debit entries in the Notes Payable account provides further assurance that notes indicated as paid during the year have, in fact, been retired. The auditors' inspection of these notes should include a comparison of the maturity date of the note with the date of cash disbursement. Failure to pay notes promptly at maturity is suggestive of serious financial weakness.

There is seldom any justification for a paid note to be missing from the files; a receipt for payment from the payee of the note is not a satisfactory substitute. If, for any reason, a paid note is not available for inspection, the auditors should review the request for a check or other vouchers supporting the disbursement and should discuss the transaction with an appropriate official.

In examining the canceled notes, the auditors should also trace the disposition of any collateral used to secure these notes. A convenient opportunity for diversion of pledged securities or other assets to an unauthorized use may be created at the time these assets are regained from a secured creditor.

5. Perform analytical procedures to determine the overall reasonableness of interest-bearing debt and interest expense.

One of the most effective ways to verify the overall reasonableness of interest-bearing debt is to determine that the relationship between recorded interest expense and the principal amount of the debt is in line with the interest rate at which the client company should be able to borrow.

A second step is to compare the year-end amount of interest-bearing debt with the amount in the prior year's balance sheet. A similar comparison should be made of interest expense for the current year and the preceding year.

6. Verify computation of interest expense, interest payable, and amortization of discount or premium.

Interest expense is of special significance to auditors because it indicates the amount of outstanding liabilities. In other words, close study of interest payments is a means of bringing to light any unrecorded interest-bearing liabilities.

Verification of interest expense and interest payable for notes or mortgages is usually a simple matter. The auditors test the accuracy of the client's interest expense and interest payable computations. In addition, the auditors should examine paid checks supporting interest payments and review the confirmations received from the payees to verify the dates when interest on each note or mortgage has been paid.

The total bond interest expense for the period usually reflects not only the interest actually paid and accrued, but also amortization of bond premium or discount. The auditors will verify the amounts amortized by independent computations. The nominal interest on the bonds should be computed (interest rate times face value). Checks drawn in payment of interest are traced to the cash records. Any balance of interest expense that remains unpaid at the balance sheet date is traced to an accrued liability account. If the payment of interest to bondholders is handled through an independent trustee, a direct confirmation of the trustee's transactions should be obtained for the period under review.

7. Determine whether debt provisions have been met.

In the first audit of a client or upon the issuance of a new bond issue, the auditors will obtain a copy of the bond indenture for the permanent file. The indenture should be carefully studied, with particular attention to such points as the amount of bonds authorized, interest rates and dates, maturity dates, descriptions of property pledged as collateral, provisions for retirement or conversion, duties and responsibilities of the trustee, and any restrictions imposed on the borrowing company.

The indenture provisions frequently require maintenance of a sinking fund, maintenance of stipulated minimum levels of working capital, and insurance of pledged property. The indenture also may restrict dividends to a specified proportion of earnings, limit management compensation, and prohibit additional long-term borrowing, except under stipulated conditions. Adequate comments should appear in the audit working papers as to the company's compliance with the provisions of the indenture. If the company has not complied fully with the requirements, the auditors should inform both the client and the client's legal counsel of the violation. An explanation of the extent of noncompliance should also be included in the client's financial statements, and possibly in the audit report. In some cases of violation, the entire bond issue may become due and payable on demand, and hence a current liability. When the client is in violation of an indenture provision and the penalty is to make the debt become payable upon demand, the client usually will be able to obtain a waiver of compliance with the provision. In other words, creditors often choose not to enforce contract terms fully. To enable the liability to be presented as long term, the waiver must waive compliance for a period of one year from the balance sheet date.

Illustrative case

In the audit of a large construction company, the auditors found the client's working capital to be far below the minimum level stipulated in the indenture of long-term secured bonds payable. In addition to this, the client had allowed the required insurance coverage of pledged assets to lapse. These violations of the indenture were sufficient to cause the bond issue to become payable on demand.

Although the client agreed to reclassify the bond issue as a current liability, the auditors were unable to satisfy themselves that the client could meet the obligation if the bondholders demanded payment. Also, if the bondholders foreclosed on the pledged assets, the ability of the client to continue as a going concern would be questionable. Thus, even after the liability was reclassified as current, the auditors had to add an explanatory paragraph to their report referring to the uncertainty regarding the company's ability to meet its obligations and remain a going concern.

Auditors do not judge the legality of a bond issue; this is a problem for the client's attorneys. The auditors should be familiar, however, with the principal provisions of the federal Securities Act of 1933 and of the corporate blue-sky laws of the client's state of incorporation. They should ascertain that the client has obtained an attorney's opinion on the legality of the bond issuance. In doubtful cases, they should consult the client's legal counsel.

8. Trace authority for issuance of interest-bearing debt to the corporate minutes.

The authority to issue interest-bearing debt generally lies with the board of directors. To determine that the bonds outstanding were properly authorized, the auditors should read the passages in the minutes of directors' (and stockholders') meetings concerning the issuance of debt. The minutes usually will cite the applicable sections of the corporate bylaws permitting the issuance of debt instruments and may also contain reference to the opinion of the company's counsel concerning the legality of the issue. This information should be traced by the auditors to the original sources.

9. Review notes payable paid or renewed after the balance sheet date.

If any of the notes payable outstanding at the balance sheet date are paid before completion of the audit engagement, such cash payments will provide the auditors with additional evidence on the liability. Renewal of notes maturing shortly after the balance sheet date may alter the auditors' thinking as to the proper classification of these liabilities.

In the discussion of notes receivable in Chapter 12, emphasis was placed on the necessity of close scrutiny of loans to officers, directors, and affiliates because of the absence of arm's-length bargaining in these related-party transactions. Similar emphasis should be placed on the examination of notes payable to insiders or affiliates, although the opportunities for self-dealing are more limited than with receivables. The auditors should scan the notes payable records for the period between the balance sheet date and the completion of examination so that they may be aware of any unusual transactions, such as the reestablishment of an insider note that had been paid just prior to the balance sheet date.

10. Search for notes payable to related parties.

As has been the case in other portions of the audit, the auditors must make certain that any related party debt is properly disclosed. Note here that the lower number of transactions makes discovery of such transactions less difficult than in accounts with a large number of transactions such as accounts payable.

11. Evaluate proper financial statement presentation and disclosure of interest-bearing debt and related transactions.

Because of the interest of creditors in the current liability section of the balance sheet and the inferences that may be drawn from various uses of notes payable, adequate informative disclosure is extremely important. Classification of notes by types of payees, as well as by current or long-term maturity, is desirable. Separate listing is needed for notes payable to banks, notes payable to trade creditors, and notes payable to officers, directors, stockholders, and affiliates.

Secured liabilities and pledged assets should be cross-referenced to one another with an explanation in the footnotes to the financial statements. In the event of financial difficulties and dissolution, creditors expect to share in the assets in proportion to their respective claims; and if choice assets, such as current receivables, have been pledged to one creditor, the risk to unsecured creditors is increased. Current liabilities should include not only those notes maturing within a period of 12 months (or a longer operating cycle) but also any installments currently payable on long-term obligations such as mortgages.

The essential point in balance sheet presentation of long-term liabilities is that they be adequately described. Each category of long-term debt should be stated under a separate title, which describes the type of debt, amounts authorized and issued, interest rate, maturity date, and any conversion or subordination features.

Long-term debt payable in the current period   Long-term liabilities include all debts that will not be liquidated with the use of current assets. In other words, any bonds or notes falling due in the coming operating cycle that are to be paid from special funds or refinanced will be classified as long-term obligations regardless of maturity date. Before approving a long-term classification for maturing obligations, auditors must satisfy themselves that the client has both the *intent* and the *ability* to refinance the obligation on a long-term basis. Intent and ability to refinance are demonstrated by the client through either (1) refinancing the obligation on a long-term basis before the issuance of the audit report, or (2) entering into a financing agreement by that date, which clearly permits such refinancing. Any debt maturing currently and payable from current assets will be a current liability.

Restrictions imposed by long-term debt agreements   Most long-term debt agreements contain clauses limiting the borrowing company's right to pay dividends. Such a restriction is vitally significant to investors in common stocks. Consequently, the nature of the restriction should be clearly set forth in a footnote to the financial statement.

Unamortized bond premium or discount   Unamortized premium should be added to the face amount of the bonds or debentures in the liability section of the balance sheet. Similarly, unamortized discount should be deducted from the face amount of the debt.

Time of examination—interest-bearing debt

Analysis of the ledger accounts for interest-bearing debt and interest expense takes very little time in most audits because of the small number of entries. Consequently, most auditors prefer to wait until the end of the year before analyzing these accounts.

Audit procedures intended to bring to light any unrecorded liabilities cannot very well be performed in advance of the balance sheet date. Such steps as the confirmation of outstanding interest-bearing debt, the verification of accrued interest, and the investigation of notes paid or renewed shortly after the balance sheet date must necessarily await the close of the period being audited. We must conclude, therefore, that the opportunities for performing audit work in advance of the balance sheet date are much more limited in the case of interest-bearing debt than for most of the asset groups previously discussed.

EQUITY CAPITAL

Sources and nature of owners' equity

Most of this section is concerned with the audit of stockholders' equity accounts of corporate clients; the audit of owners' equity in partnerships and sole proprietorships is discussed briefly near the end of the chapter.

Owners' equity for corporate clients consists of capital stock accounts (preferred and common) and retained earnings. Balances in the capital stock accounts change when the corporation issues or repurchases stock. The account balances are not affected by transfer of ownership of shares from one shareholder to another. Retained earnings are normally increased by earnings and decreased by dividend payments. Additionally, a few journal entries (e.g., prior period adjustments) may directly affect retained earnings. Transactions in the owners' equity accounts are generally few in number, but material in amount. Often no change will occur during the year in the capital stock accounts, and perhaps only one or two entries will be made to the retained earnings account.

The auditors' approach in examination of owners' equity

The auditors' *objectives* in the examination of owners' equity are to determine that:

1. *Internal control* over owners' equity *is adequate.*
2. The recorded owners' equity is valid (*occurrence* and *obligations*).
3. All owners' equity transactions are recorded (*completeness*).
4. Owners' equity schedules are mathematically correct and agree with general ledger accounts (*clerical accuracy*).
5. The *valuation* of owners' equity is proper.
6. The *presentation* and *disclosure* of owners' equity is adequate.

In conjunction with the audit of owners' equity accounts, the auditors will also obtain evidence about the related accounts of dividends payable and capital stock discounts and premiums. Evidence is also gathered regarding the proper cutoff of cash receipts and disbursements relating to the equity accounts.

Because the transactions are few in number but material in amount, each requires careful attention. Additionally, to properly audit the owners' equity accounts, the auditors often need some familiarity with federal and state laws concerning securities as well as with rules and regulations of the Securities and Exchange Commission.

For a continuing client, the auditors will often find that audit time required will be small in relation to the dollar amounts in these accounts and much less than is required for assets, liabilities, revenue, or expense. Thus, while the capital stock account often has a larger balance than the cash account, the audit work required for capital stock is usually far less.

Internal control for owners' equity

There are three principal elements of strong internal control over capital stock and dividends. These three elements are: (1) the proper authorization of transactions by the board of directors and corporate officers; (2) the segregation of duties in handling these transactions (especially the use of independent agents for stock registration and transfer and for dividend payments); and (3) the maintenance of adequate records.

Control of capital stock transactions by the board of directors

All changes in capital stock accounts should receive formal advance approval by the board of directors. The substantive tests for verifying an entry in a Capital Stock account, therefore, should include tracing the entry to an authorization in the minutes of directors' meetings.

Let us consider for a moment some of the specific steps relating to capital stock transactions that require authorization by directors. The board of directors must determine the number of shares to be issued and the price per share; if an installment plan of payment is to be used, the terms must be prescribed by the board. If plant and equipment, services, or any consideration other than cash are to be accepted in payment for shares, the board of directors must set the valuation on the noncash assets received. Transfers from retained earnings to the Capital Stock and Paid-In Capital accounts, as in the case of stock dividends, are initiated by action of the board. Stock splits and changes in par or stated value of shares also require formal authorization by the board.

Authority for all dividend actions rests with the directors. The declaration of a dividend must specify not only the amount per share, but also the date of record and the date of payment.

If a corporation handles its own capital stock transactions rather than utilizing the services of an independent registrar and stock transfer agent, the board of directors should pass a resolution designating those officers who are authorized to (1) sign stock certificates, (2) maintain records of stockholders, (3) have custody of unissued certificates, and (4) sign dividend checks. The signatures of two officers are generally required on stock certificates.

Independent registrar and stock transfer agent

In appraising the adequacy of internal control over capital stock, the first question that the auditors consider is whether the corporation employs the services of an independent stock registrar and a stock transfer agent or handles its own capital stock transactions. Internal control is far stronger when the services of an independent stock registrar and a stock transfer agent are utilized because the banks or trust companies acting in these capacities will have the experience, the specialized facilities, and the trained personnel to perform the work in an expert manner. Moreover, by placing the responsibility for handling capital stock certificates in separate and independent organizations, the corporation achieves to the fullest extent the internal control concept of separation of duties. The New York Stock Exchange and most other exchanges require that listed corporations utilize the services of an independent registrar.

The primary responsibility of the stock registrar is to avoid any overissuance of stock. The danger of overissuance is illustrated by the old story of a promoter who sold a 25 percent interest in a new corporation to each of 10 investors. To prevent such irregularities, the registrar must verify that stock certificates are issued in accordance with the articles of incorporation and the formal authorizations by the board of directors. The registrar obtains copies of the documents authorizing the total shares to be issued and maintains records of total shares issued and canceled. Each new certificate must be presented to the registrar for examination and registration before it is issued to a stockholder. The dangers of fraud and accidental error relating to improper issuance of stock certificates are greatly reduced when an independent registrar is employed.

Corporations with actively traded securities also employ independent *stock transfer agents*. Although the stock transfer agent maintains a record of the total shares outstanding, its primary responsibility is maintaining detailed stockholder records (name and address of each stockholder) and carrying out transfers of stock ownership.

The stock certificate book

If the corporation does not utilize the services of an independent registrar and stock transfer agent, these functions usually are assigned by the board of directors to the secretary of the company. The stock certificates should be serially numbered by the printer; and from the time of delivery to the company until issuance, they should be in the exclusive custody of the designated officer.

The certificates often are prepared in bound books, with attached stubs similar to those in a checkbook. Each stub shows the certificate number and contains blank spaces for entering the number of shares represented by the certificate, the name of the stockholder, and the serial number of any previously issued certificate surrendered in exchange for the new one. Certificates should be issued in numerical sequence and not signed or countersigned until the time of issuance. When outstanding shares are transferred from one holder to another, the old certificate is surrendered to the company. The designated officer cancels the old certificate by perforating and attaching it to the corresponding stub in the certificate book.

The stockholders ledger

The stock certificate book is not in itself an adequate record of the capital stock outstanding. The certificates appear in the book in serial number order, and a single stockholder may own several certificates listed at various places in the certificate book.

A stockholders ledger provides a separate record for each stockholder, thus making it possible to determine at a glance the total number of shares owned by any one person. This record may be used in compiling the list of dividend checks or for any other communication with shareholders.

Internal control over dividends

The nature of internal control over the payment of dividends, as in the case of stock issuance, depends primarily upon whether the company performs the function of dividend payment itself or utilizes the services of an independent dividend-paying agent. If an independent dividend-paying agent is used, the corporation will provide the agent with a certified copy of the dividend declaration and with a check for the full amount of the dividend. The bank or trust company serving as stock transfer agent is usually appointed to distribute the dividend, since it maintains the detailed records of stockholders. The agent issues dividend checks to the individual stockholders and sends the corporation a list of the payments made. The use of an independent fiscal agent is to be recommended from the standpoint of internal control, for it materially reduces the possibility of fraud or error arising in connection with the distribution of dividends.

Audit working papers for owners' equity

In addition to the lead schedule for owners' equity accounts, an analysis of each equity account is prepared by the auditors for the permanent file. A detailed analysis is essential for all aspects of a stock option plan: options authorized, issued, and outstanding. For a closely held corporation not served by a transfer agent, the auditors will often prepare for the permanent file a list of shareholders and the number of shares owned by each.

AUDIT PROGRAM— CAPITAL STOCK

The following procedures are typical of the work required in many engagements for the verification of capital stock:

1. Obtain an understanding of internal control over capital stock transactions.
2. Review articles of incorporation, bylaws, and minutes for provisions relating to capital stock.
3. Obtain or prepare analyses of the capital stock accounts.
4. Account for all proceeds from stock issues.
5. Confirm shares outstanding with the independent registrar and stock transfer agent.
6. For a corporation acting as its own stock registrar and transfer agent, reconcile the stockholder records with the general ledger.
7. Determine compliance with stock option plans and with other restrictions and preferences pertaining to capital stock.

Capital stock transactions are usually few in number; consequently, the auditors usually substantiate all transactions rather than rely upon the client's internal control. In addition to the preceding steps, the auditors must determine the appropriate financial statement presentation of capital stock. This topic will be discussed later in this chapter, along with the financial statement presentation of other elements of owners' equity.

1. Obtain an understanding of internal control over capital stock transactions.

Even though the examination of capital stock consists primarily of substantive tests, the auditors must acquire an understanding of the client's procedures for authorizing, executing, and recording capital stock transactions. This may be achieved by preparing a written description or flowchart of the system, or by filling in an internal control questionnaire. If the questionnaire approach is employed, typical questions to be answered might include the following: Does the company utilize the services of an independent registrar and stock transfer agent? Are stockholder ledgers and transfer journals maintained? Are entries in owners' equity accounts reviewed periodically by the controller? These questions should be regarded as identifying the areas to be investigated, rather than as items requiring simple yes or no answers.

2. Review articles of incorporation, bylaws, and minutes for provisions relating to capital stock.

In a first audit, copies of the articles of incorporation, bylaws, and minutes of the meetings of directors and stockholders obtained for the permanent file should be read carefully. The information required by the auditors for each issue of capital stock includes the number of shares authorized and issued, the par or stated value if any, dividend rates, call and conversion provisions, stock splits, and stock options. By gathering evidence on these points, the auditors will have some assurance that capital stock transactions and dividend payments have been in accordance with legal requirements and specific authorizations by stockholders and directors. Also, they will be able to judge whether the balance sheet contains all necessary information to describe adequately the various stock issues and other elements of corporate capital.

3.   Obtain or prepare analyses of the capital stock accounts.

In an initial audit engagement, capital stock accounts should be analyzed from the beginning of the corporation to provide the auditors with a complete historical picture of corporate capital. Analysis of capital stock includes an appraisal of the nature of all changes and the vouching of these changes to the supporting documents and records. All changes in capital stock should bear the authorization of the board of directors.

The analyses of capital stock accounts may be prepared in a manner that permits additions during later audit engagements. After the initial audit, if the analyses are kept in the auditors' permanent file, all that will be necessary is to record the current period's increases and decreases and to vouch these transactions. The auditors then will have working papers showing all changes in capital stock from the inception of the corporation.

The auditors also should analyze the Treasury Stock account and prepare a list showing the number of shares of treasury stock on hand. All certificates on hand then may be inspected. If the certificates are not on hand, they should be confirmed directly with the custodian.

In their review of treasury stock transactions, the auditors should refer to permanent file copies of the minutes of directors' meetings to determine that (*a*) the acquisition or reissuance of treasury stock was authorized by directors and (*b*) the price paid or received was in accordance with prices specified by the board.

4.   Account for all proceeds from stock issues.

Closely related to the analyses of Capital Stock accounts is the audit procedure of accounting for the receipt and proper disposition of all funds derived from the issuance of capital stock. The proceeds should be traced to the cash records and bank statements. SEC registration statements and contracts with underwriters may also be available as evidence of the amounts received from stock issues.

When assets other than cash are received as consideration for the issuance of capital stock, the entire transaction requires careful study. Generally the value of assets and services received in exchange for capital shares is established by action of the board of directors. The auditors must determine that these accounting estimates made by the client result in a proper valuation.

5.   Confirm shares outstanding with the independent registrar and stock transfer agent.

The number of shares issued and outstanding on the balance sheet date may be confirmed by direct communication with the independent registrar and stock transfer agent. The confirmation request should be written by the client on the client's letterhead, but it should be mailed by the auditors. Confirmation replies should be sent directly to the auditors, not to the client. All information contained in these replies should be traced to the corporate records. It is essential that the general ledger controlling accounts agree with the amount of stock issued as reported by the independent registrar and stock transfer agent. Because of the strong internal controls usually maintained over stock certificates, it is not customary to communicate with individual stockholders in establishing the number of shares outstanding.

6. For a corporation acting as its own stock registrar and transfer agent, reconcile the stockholder records with the general ledger.

When a corporation acts as its own transfer agent and registrar, the auditors must adopt alternative procedures as nearly as possible equivalent to direct confirmation with outside parties. These procedures include (*a*) accounting for stock certificate numbers, (*b*) examining canceled certificates, and (*c*) reconciling the stockholder ledger and stock certificate book with the general ledger.

The audit working papers should include a record of the last certificate number issued during the year. Reference to the working papers for the preceding audit, combined with the verification of certificate numbers issued during the current period, will enable the auditors to account for all certificates by serial number.

A working paper prepared during the auditors' examination of the stock certificate book of a small closely held corporation is designed to be utilized during several audits; it may be retained in the permanent file or forwarded to successive current files. Additionally, it is desirable for the auditors to inspect the unissued certificates to determine that all certificates purported to be unissued are actually on hand and blank.

Adequate internal control for corporations not utilizing the services of an independent registrar and stock transfer agent requires that all canceled stock certificates be perforated or marked in a manner precluding the possibility of further use. Canceled certificates should be attached to the corresponding stubs in the stock certificate book and permanently preserved. If reacquired certificates are not canceled properly, the danger exists that they may be reissued fraudulently by officers or employees. Auditors, therefore, will examine all canceled stock certificates on hand, noting in particular that they have been voided.

The general ledger account for capital stock shows the total par value or stated value of all shares outstanding, plus any treasury shares. The subsidiary record for capital stock includes an account for each stockholder. The stock certificate book contains all canceled certificates, and also open stubs for outstanding certificates. These three records (general ledger controlling account, stockholder ledger, and stock certificate book) must be reconciled by the auditors to establish the amount of outstanding stock and to rule out the possibility of an overissuance of shares. If this verification were not made, it would be possible for a dishonest official to issue unlimited amounts of stock and to withhold the proceeds from such sales.

A trial balance of the subsidiary stockholder records may be obtained from the client or prepared by the auditors and compared with the general ledger controlling account. In conjunction with this procedure, the total shares outstanding, as shown by the stock certificate book stubs, should also be reconciled with the controlling account and with the subsidiary trial balance. These procedures assure the auditors of the accuracy of the ledger account balances for capital stock.

7.   Determine compliance with stock option plans and with other restrictions and preferences pertaining to capital stock.

Many corporations grant stock options to officers and key employees as an incentive-type compensation plan. When stock options are granted, a portion of the authorized but unissued stock must be held in reserve by the corporation so that it will be in a position to fulfill the option agreements. Similarly, corporations with convertible debentures or convertible preferred stocks outstanding must hold in reserve a sufficient number of common shares to meet the demands of preferred stockholders and debenture holders who may elect to convert their securities into common stock.

The auditors must become thoroughly familiar with the terms of any stock options and stock purchase plans and with the conversion features of debenture bonds and preferred stock, so that they can determine whether the financial statements make adequate disclosure of these agreements. The auditors must also verify the shares issued during the year through conversion or exercise of stock options and must ascertain that the number of shares held in reserve at the balance sheet date does not exceed the corporation's authorized but unissued stock.

RETAINED EARNINGS AND DIVIDENDS

Audit work on retained earnings and dividends includes two major steps: (1) the analysis of retained earnings and any appropriations of retained earnings, and (2) the review of dividend procedures for both cash and stock dividends.

The analysis of retained earnings and any appropriations of retained earnings should cover the entire history of these accounts. Such an analysis is prepared for the permanent file and is added to in each annual audit. Credits to the Retained Earnings account ordinarily represent amounts of net income transferred from the Income Summary account. Debits to the Retained Earnings account may include entries for net losses, cash, and stock dividends, and for the creation or enlargement of appropriated reserves. Appropriations of retained earnings require specific authorization by the board of directors. The only verification necessary for these entries is to ascertain that the dates and amounts correspond to the actions of the board.

In the verification of cash dividends, the auditors usually will perform the following steps:

1. Determine the dates and amounts of dividends authorized.
2. Verify the amounts paid.
3. Determine the amount of any preferred dividends in arrears.
4. Review the treatment of unclaimed dividend checks.

When reviewing minutes of the directors' meetings, the auditors should note the date and amount of each dividend declaration. This serves to establish the authority for dividend disbursements. The dividend payment may then be verified by multiplying the total number of shares as shown by the general ledger controlling account by the dividend per share.

The auditors' review of dividend declarations may reveal the existence of cash dividends declared but not paid. These declared but unpaid dividends must be shown as liabilities in the balance sheet. The auditors also may review the procedures for handling unclaimed dividends and ascertain that these items are recognized as liabilities. The amount of any accumulated dividends in arrears on preferred stock should be computed. If a closely held company has irregular dividend declarations or none at all, the auditors should consider whether the federal penalty surtax on unreasonably accumulated earnings might be assessed. In the verification of stock dividends, there is an additional responsibility of determining that the proper amounts have been transferred from retained earnings to capital stock and paid-in capital accounts for both large and small stock dividends.

Time of examination—stockholders' equity

The ledger accounts for capital stock, additional paid-in capital, and retained earnings ordinarily receive very few entries during the year. Consequently, most auditors agree that nothing can be gained by making a preliminary analysis of these accounts for a fraction of the year. It usually is more efficient to make the analysis in one step after the close of the period. Other audit procedures, such as the examination of the stock certificate book or the confirmation of outstanding shares with the independent registrar and stock transfer agent, also are performed at the year-end. In the first audit of a new client, some preliminary work can be done advantageously in obtaining and reviewing copies of the articles of incorporation and bylaws and in analyzing the capital accounts. For repeat engagements, however, there is usually little opportunity to perform audit work on owners' equity accounts before the end of the period.

Financial statement presentation of stockholders' equity

The presentation of capital stock in the balance sheet should include a complete description of each issue. Information to be disclosed includes the title of each issue; par or stated value; dividend rate if any; dividend preference; conversion and call provisions; number of shares authorized, issued, and in treasury; dividends in arrears if any; and shares reserved for stock options or for conversions.

Treasury stock preferably is shown in the stockholders' equity section, at cost, as a deduction from the combined total of paid-in capital and retained earnings. In many states, an amount of retained earnings equivalent to the cost of the treasury shares must be restricted. This restriction is disclosed by a footnote.

Changes in retained earnings during the year may be shown in a separate statement or combined with the income statement. The combined statement of income and retained earnings appears to be continuing in popularity. In this form of presentation, the amount of retained earnings at the beginning of the year is added to the net income figure, dividends paid are subtracted from the subtotal, and the final figure represents the new balance of retained earnings.

One of the most significant points to consider in determining the presentation of retained earnings in the balance sheet is the existence of any restriction on the use of this retained income. Agreements with banks, bondholders, and other creditors very commonly impose limitations on the payment of dividends. These restrictions must be fully disclosed in the notes to financial statements.

AUDIT OF SOLE PROPRIETORSHIPS AND PARTNERSHIPS

Perhaps the most common reason for a small business to arrange for an independent audit is the need for audited financial statements in order to obtain a bank loan. Often, a banker, when approached by the owner of a small business applying for a loan, will request audited financial statements as an aid to reaching a decision on the loan application.

It is natural for the owner of a business being audited for the first time to be concerned about the auditors' fee and to question whether all the procedures performed by the auditors are really necessary. The CPA retained to audit a small business, of course, will inquire as to the reason for the audit. If a bank loan is involved, the CPA may find it useful to arrange a joint meeting in which the owner, the banker, and the CPA discuss the objectives and scope of the examination. Such a meeting is helpful in making the small-business owner aware that the CPA must have unlimited access to all information about the business. The owner then is more likely to cooperate fully with respect to such audit procedures as confirmation of receivables and observation of inventories.

Procedures for audit of partners' accounts   A most significant document underlying the partnership form of organization is the partnership contract. The auditors are particularly interested in determining that the distribution of net income has been carried out in accordance with the profit-sharing provisions of the partnership contract. Maintenance of partners' capital accounts at prescribed levels and restriction of drawings by partners to specified amounts are other points often covered in the contract; compliance with these clauses should be verified by the auditors in determining the propriety of the year's entries in the capital accounts. Partners' loan accounts also require reference to the partnership contract to determine the treatment intended by the partners.

Occasionally auditors may find that a partnership is operating without any written agreement of partnership. This situation raises a question of whether profits have been divided in accordance with the understanding existing between the partners. The auditors may appropriately suggest that the firm develop a written partnership contract; for their own protection, the auditors may wish to obtain from each partner a written statement confirming the balance in his or her capital account and approval of the method used in dividing the year's earnings.

In general, the same principles described for the audit of corporate capital are applicable to the examination of the capital accounts and drawing accounts of a sole proprietorship or partnership. Analyses are made of all proprietorship accounts from the beginning of the business; the initial capital investment and any additions are traced to the cash and asset records; and the net income or loss for the period and any withdrawals are verified. In the case of a sole proprietorship, a common source of difficulty is the practice of intermingling business and personal transactions, making it necessary for the auditors to segregate personal net worth from business capital. Adjustments may also be required to transfer from expense accounts to the owner's drawing account any personal expenditures paid with company funds.

DISCLOSURE OF CONTINGENCIES

A *loss contingency* may be defined as a *possible* loss, stemming from past events, that will be resolved as to existence and amount by some future event. Central to the concept of a contingent loss is the idea of uncertainty—uncertainty both as to the amount of loss and whether, in fact, any loss has been incurred. This uncertainty is resolved when some future event occurs or fails to occur.

Most loss contingencies may also appropriately be called *contingent liabilities. Loss contingencies,* however, is a broader term, encompassing the possible impairment of assets as well as the possible existence of liabilities. The audit problem with respect to loss contingencies is twofold. First, the auditors must determine the existence of the loss contingencies. Because of the uncertainty factor, most loss contingencies do not appear in the accounting records, and a systematic search is required if the auditors are to have reasonable assurance that no important loss contingencies have been overlooked. Second, the auditors must appraise the probability that a loss has been incurred. This is made difficult both by the uncertainty factor and also by the tendency of the client management to maintain at least an outward appearance of optimism.

In *Statement No. 5* (AC section C59), the Financial Accounting Standards Board set forth the criteria for accounting for loss contingencies. Such losses should be reflected in the accounting records when both of the following conditions are met: (1) information available prior to the issuance of the financial statements indicates that it is *probable* that a loss had been sustained before the balance sheet date, *and* (2) the amount of the loss can be *reasonably estimated.* Recognition of the loss may involve either recognition of a liability or reduction of an asset. When a loss contingency has been accrued in the accounts, it is usually desirable to explain the nature of the contingency in a footnote to the financial statements and to disclose any exposure to loss in excess of the amount accrued.

Loss contingencies that do not meet both of the above criteria should still be disclosed when there is at least a *reasonable possibility* that a loss has been incurred. This disclosure should describe the nature of the contingency and, if possible, provide an estimate of the possible loss. If the amount of possible loss cannot be reasonably estimated, the disclosure should include either a range of loss or a statement that an estimate cannot be made.

Certain contingent liabilities traditionally have been disclosed in financial statements even though the possibility that a loss has occurred is remote. Such items include notes receivable discounted and guarantee endorsements. With the exception of those items for which disclosure is traditional, disclosure need not be made of loss contingencies when the possibility of loss is *remote.*

The procedures undertaken by auditors to ascertain the existence of loss contingencies and to assess the probability of loss vary with the nature of the contingent item. To illustrate these types of procedures, we will discuss several of the more frequent types of contingencies warranting financial statement disclosure.

1. Litigation.

Perhaps the most common loss contingency appearing in financial statements is that stemming from pending or threatened litigation. A *letter of inquiry* (or *lawyer's letter*) to the client's legal counsel is the auditors' primary means of obtaining evidence regarding pending and threatened litigation, as well as *unasserted claims* for which no potential claimant has yet demonstrated the intent to initiate legal action. In the past, many attorneys were reluctant to disclose information about such issues to auditors. They believed that such disclosure was a violation of their confidential relationship with their client and that it might adversely affect the outcome of the litigation. Auditors, on the other hand, thought that they could not issue an unqualified opinion on the financial statements of a client if they were not fully informed as to potential loss contingencies.

A joint effort by the AICPA and the American Bar Association was undertaken to resolve this conflict, and agreement was eventually reached between the professions. Later, the AICPA issued *SAS 12* (AU 337), "Inquiry of Client's Lawyer Concerning Litigation, Claims, and Assessments," to provide auditors with guidelines for this sensitive communication.

SAS 12 indicates that the auditors should generally obtain from management a list describing and evaluating threatened or pending litigation. The auditors then ask management to request the client's lawyers to comment on those areas where their views differ from those of management. The lawyers also are requested to identify any pending claims, litigation, and assessments that have been omitted from management's list. If management does not wish to prepare a list of pending litigation for review by the lawyers, the lawyers may be requested to provide an independent description of all pending claims, litigation, and assessments that they are handling.

Auditors must also inquire of the lawyers regarding the possibility of *unasserted claims,* on which individuals have not yet taken legal action. An unasserted claim should be disclosed if it is (1) *probable* that a claim will be asserted and (2) *reasonably possible* that a loss will result. If management prepares a list of matters for review by the lawyers, it should include such unasserted claims. The lawyers will provide any relevant additional information related to those listed unasserted claims. However, if management fails to disclose an unasserted claim, the lawyer is *not* required to describe the claim in the reply to the auditors; the lawyer is, however, generally required to inform the client of the omission and to consider resignation if the client fails to inform the auditors of the unasserted claim. For this reason, auditors must always consider carefully the reasons for any lawyer's resignation.

Illustration of disclosure The following footnote to the financial statements of an aircraft manufacturer illustrates the disclosure of the contingent liability associated with pending litigation:

> A number of suits are pending against the Company as the result of accidents in prior years involving airplanes manufactured by the Company. It is believed that insurance carried by the Company is sufficient to protect it against loss by reason of suits involving the lives of passengers and damage to aircraft. Other litigation pending against the Company involves no substantial amount or is covered by insurance.

The balance sheet of another large corporation contained the following note concerning such contingent liabilities:

> The Company has suits pending against it, some of which are for large amounts. The Company is advised by counsel that, while it is impossible to ascertain the ultimate legal and financial responsibility in respect to such litigation as of December 31, 1990, it is their opinion that the ultimate liability will not be materially important in relation to the total assets of the Company.

A refusal by a lawyer to furnish the information requested in the auditors' letter of inquiry would be a limitation of the scope of the auditors' examination and would necessitate qualification of the audit report. Even when all of the requested information is provided to the auditors and adequately disclosed in the financial statements, the uncertainty of the outcome of litigation may require the auditors to add an explanatory paragraph to their report referring to the uncertainty.

2. Income tax disputes.

The necessity of estimating the income tax liability applicable to the year under audit was discussed in Chapter 15. In addition to the taxes relating to the current year's income, uncertainty often exists concerning the amount ultimately payable for prior years. A lag of two or three years often exists between the filing of income tax returns and the final settlement after review by the Internal Revenue Service. Disputes between the taxpayer and the IRS may create contingent liabilities not settled for several more years. The auditors should determine whether internal revenue agents have examined any returns of the client since the preceding audit, and if so, whether any additional taxes have been assessed.

3. Accommodation endorsements and other guarantees of indebtedness.

The endorsement of notes of other concerns or individuals is very seldom recorded in the accounts, but may be reflected in the minutes of directors' meetings. The practice is more common among small concerns—particularly when one person has a proprietary interest in several companies. Officers, partners, and sole proprietors of small organizations should be questioned as to the existence of any contingent liability from this source. Inquiry should also be made as to whether any collateral has been received to protect the company. The auditors may suggest the desirability of maintaining a record of any accommodation endorsements by inclusion of a pair of memorandum accounts in the general ledger.

4. Accounts receivable sold or assigned with recourse.

When accounts receivable are sold or assigned *with recourse,* a guarantee of collectibility is given. Authorization of such a transaction should be revealed during the auditors' reading of the minutes, and a clue also may be found during the examination of transactions and correspondence with financial institutions. Confirmation by direct communication with the purchaser or assignee is necessary for any receivables sold or assigned.

Commitments

Closely related to contingent liabilities are obligations termed *commitments.* The auditors may discover during their examination many of the following commitments: inventory purchase commitments, commitments to sell merchandise at specified prices, contracts for the construction of plant and equipment, pension or profit-sharing plans, long-term operating leases of plant and equipment, employee stock option plans, and employment contracts with key officers. A common characteristic of these commitments is the contractual obligation to enter into transactions *in the future.*

To illustrate the relationship of a commitment to a loss contingency, assume that a manufacturer agrees to sell at a fixed price a substantial part of its output over the next three years. At the time of forming the agreement, the manufacturer, of course, believes the arrangement to be advantageous. However, it is possible that rising price levels could transform the fixed price sales agreement into an unprofitable one, requiring sales to be made at prices below manufacturing cost. Such circumstances could warrant recognition of a loss in the financial statements.

All classes of material commitments may be described in a single note to financial statements; or they may be included in a "Contingencies and Commitments" footnote.

General risk contingencies

In addition to loss contingencies and commitments, all businesses face the risk of loss from numerous factors called *general risk contingencies.* A general risk contingency represents a loss that *might occur in the future,* as opposed to a loss contingency that *might have occurred in the past.* Examples of general risk contingencies are threat of a strike or consumer boycott, risk of price increases in essential raw materials, and risk of a natural catastrophe.

General risk contingencies *should not be disclosed* in financial statements. Such disclosure would be confusing to investors, since the events that might produce a loss actually have not occurred, and since these risks are part of the general business environment. The lack of insurance coverage is a general risk contingency. Neither the adequacy nor the lack of insurance coverage need be presented in financial statements.

Audit procedures for loss contingencies

Although audit procedures vary with the individual type of loss contingency, the following steps are taken in most audits as a means of discovering these conditions:

1.   Review the minutes of directors' meetings to the date of completion of field work. Important contracts, lawsuits, and dealings with subsidiaries are typical of matters discussed in board meetings that may involve loss contingencies.
2.   Send a letter of inquiry to the client's legal counsel requesting:
     a.   A description (or evaluation of management's description) of the nature of pending and threatened litigation and of tax disputes.
     b.   An evaluation of the likelihood of an unfavorable outcome in the matters described.

   c. An estimate of the probable loss or range of loss, or a statement that an estimate cannot be made.

   d. An evaluation of management's description of any unasserted claims that, if asserted, have a reasonable possibility of an adverse outcome.

   e. A statement of the amount of any unbilled legal fees.

  3. Send a standard bank confirmation request to each bank with which the client has done business during the year. This standard form includes a request for information on any indirect or contingent liabilities of the client.

  4. Review correspondence with financial institutions for evidence of accommodation endorsements, guarantees of indebtedness, or sales or assignments of accounts receivable.

  5. Obtain a representations letter from the client indicating that all liabilities known to officers are recorded or disclosed.

Liability representations

Since contingent liabilities often are not entered in the accounting records, the officers of the company may be the only persons aware of the contingencies. It is therefore important that the auditors should ask the officers to disclose all liabilities and contingencies of which they have knowledge. To emphasize the importance of the request and to guard against any possible misunderstanding, the officers should be asked to sign a written liability representation, stating that all liabilities known to them are reflected in the accounts or otherwise disclosed in the financial statements.

Financial presentation of loss contingencies

Current practice utilizes supporting footnotes as a means of disclosure of loss contingencies. Presentation of information concerning loss contingencies should be limited to specific factual situations, such as accommodation endorsements, guarantees, and pending lawsuits. To fill the financial statements with vague generalities about the uncertainties of the future is more akin to fortune-telling than financial reporting.

KEY TERMS INTRODUCED OR EMPHASIZED IN CHAPTER 16

Additional paid-in capital Capital contributed by stockholders in excess of the par or stated value of the shares issued.

Commitment A contractual obligation to carry out a transaction at specified terms in the future. Material commitments should be disclosed in the financial statements.

Contingent liability A possible liability, stemming from past events, that will be resolved as to existence and amount by some future event.

Debenture bond An unsecured bond, dependent upon the general credit of the issuer.

General risk contingency   An element of the business environment that involves some risk of a future loss. Examples include the risk of accident, strike, price fluctuations, or natural catastrophe. General risk contingencies should not be disclosed in financial statements.

Indenture   The formal agreement between bondholders and the issuer as to the terms of the debt.

Lawyer's letter   A letter of inquiry sent by auditors to a client's legal counsel requesting a description and evaluation of pending or threatened litigation, unasserted claims, and other loss contingencies.

Liability representation   A written representation provided by key officers of the client that all liabilities and loss contingencies known to them are disclosed in the financial statements.

Loss contingency   A possible loss, stemming from past events, that will be resolved as to existence and amount by some future event. Loss contingencies should be disclosed in footnotes to the financial statements if there is a reasonable possibility that a loss has been incurred. When loss contingencies are considered probable and can be reasonably estimated, they should be accrued in the accounts.

Sinking fund   Cash or other assets set aside for the retirement of a debt.

Stock certificate book   A book of serially numbered certificates with attached stubs. Each stub shows the corresponding certificate number and provides space for entering the number of shares represented by the certificate, name of the shareholder, and serial number of the certificate surrendered in exchange for the new one. Surrendered certificates are canceled and replaced in the certificate book.

Stockholders ledger   A record showing the number of shares owned by each stockholder. This is the basic record used for preparing dividend payments and other communications with shareholders.

Stock option plan   A formal plan granting the right to buy a specified number of shares at a stipulated price during a specified time. Stock option plans are frequently used as a form of executive compensation. The terms of such plans should be disclosed in financial statements.

Stock registrar   An institution charged with responsibility for avoiding overissuance of a corporation's stock. Every new certificate must be presented to the registrar for examination and registration before it is issued to a stockholder.

Stock transfer agent   An institution responsible for maintaining detailed records of shareholders and handling transfers of stock ownership.

Treasury stock   Shares of its own stock acquired by a corporation for the purpose of being reissued at a later date.

Unasserted claim   A possible legal claim of which no potential claimant has exhibited an awareness.

GROUP I: REVIEW QUESTIONS

16–1.   Mansfield Corporation has outstanding an issue of 30-year bonds payable. There is no sinking fund for these bonds. Under what circumstances, if any, should this bond issue be classified as a current liability?

16–2.   What does the trust indenture used by a corporation in creating long-term bonded indebtedness have to do with the payment of dividends on common stock?

16–3. In addition to verifying the recorded liabilities of a company, the auditors must also give consideration to the possibility that other unrecorded liabilities exist. What specific steps may be taken by the auditors to determine that all of their client's interest-bearing liabilities are recorded?

16–4. Two assistant auditors were assigned by the auditor-in-charge to the verification of long-term liabilities. Some time later, they reported to the auditor-in-charge that they had determined that all long-term liabilities were properly recorded and that all recorded long-term liabilities were genuine obligations. Does this determination constitute a sufficient examination of long-term liabilities? Explain.

16–5. Palmer Company has issued a number of notes payable during the year, and several of these notes are outstanding at the balance sheet date. What sources of information should the auditors use in preparing a working paper analysis of the notes payable?

16–6. If the federal income tax returns for prior years have not as yet been reviewed by federal tax authorities, would you consider it necessary for the client to disclose this situation in footnotes to the financial statements? Explain.

16–7. What is the principal reason for verifying the Interest Expense account in conjunction with the verification of notes payable?

16–8. Is the confirmation of notes payable usually correlated with any other specific phase of the audit? Explain.

16–9. Audit programs for verification of accounts receivable and notes receivable often include investigation of selected transactions occurring after the balance sheet date as well as transactions during the year under audit. Are the auditors concerned with note payable transactions subsequent to the balance sheet date? Explain.

16–10. Most corporations with bonds payable outstanding utilize the services of a trustee. What relation, if any, does this practice have to the maintenance of adequate internal control?

16–11. "Auditors are not qualified to pass on the legality of a bond issue; this is a question for the company's attorneys. It is therefore unnecessary for the auditors to inspect the bond indenture." Criticize the quotation.

16–12. What is the meaning of the term *commitment?* Give examples. Do commitments appear in financial statements? Explain.

16–13. Long-term creditors often insist upon placing certain restrictions upon the borrowing company for the term of the loan. Give three examples of such restrictions, and indicate how each restriction protects the long-term creditor.

16–14. What information should be requested by the auditors from the trustee responsible for an issue of debentures payable?

16–15. What are *general risk contingencies?* Do such items require disclosure in the financial statements?

16–16. Compare the auditors' examination of owners' equity with their work on assets and current liabilities. Among other factors to be considered are the relative amounts of time involved and the character of the transactions to be reviewed.

16–17. What do you consider to be the most important internal control device a corporation can adopt with respect to capital stock transactions?

16–18. You have been retained to perform an audit of Valley Products, a small corporation which has not been audited during the previous 10 years of its existence. How will your work on the Capital Stock account in this initial audit differ from that required in a repeat engagement?

16–19. Comment on the desirability of audit work on the owners' equity accounts before the balance sheet date.

16–20. Name three situations that might place a restriction on retained earnings limiting or preventing dividend payments. Explain how the auditors might become aware of each such restricting factor.

16–21. Delta Company has issued stock options to four of its officers permitting them to purchase 5,000 shares each of common stock at a price of $25 per share at any time during the next five years. The president asks you what effect, if any, the granting of the options will have upon the balance sheet presentation of the stockholders' equity accounts.

16–22. Describe the significant features of a stock certificate book, its purpose, and the method of using it.

16–23. In the audit of a small corporation not using the services of an independent stock registrar and stock transfer agent, what use is made of the stock certificate book by the auditors?

16–24. What is the primary responsibility of an independent registrar with respect to capital stock?

16–25. What is the usual procedure followed by the CPA in obtaining evidence regarding pending and threatened litigation against the client?

16–26. What are *loss contingencies?* How are such items presented in the financial statements? Explain.

16–27. Explain how a loss contingency exists with respect to an *unasserted* claim. Should unasserted claims be disclosed in the financial statements?

16–28. What errors are commonly encountered by the auditors in their examination of the capital and drawing accounts of a sole proprietor?

16–29. Corporations sometimes issue their own capital stock in exchange for services and various assets other than cash. As an auditor, what evidence would you look for to determine the propriety of the values used in recording such transactions?

16–30. In your second annual examination of a corporate client, you find a new account in the general ledger, Treasury Stock, with a balance of $306,000. Describe the procedures you would follow to verify this item.

16–31. In examining the financial statements of Foster Company, you observe a debit entry for $200,000 labeled as Dividends in the Retained Earnings account. Explain in detail how you would verify this entry.

16–32. Your new client, Black Angus Valley Ranch, is a small corporation with less than 100 stockholders, and does not utilize the services of an independent stock registrar or transfer agent. For your first audit, you want to obtain or prepare a year-end list of stockholders showing the number of shares owned by each. From what source or record should this information be obtained? Explain.

16–33. The only long-term liability of Range Corporation is a note payable for $1 million secured by a mortgage on the company's plant and equipment. You have audited the company annually for three preceding years, during which time the principal amount of the note has remained unchanged. The maturity date is 10 years from the current balance sheet date. You are informed by the president of the company that all interest payments have been made promptly in accordance with the terms of the note. Under these circumstances, what audit work, if any, is necessary with respect to this long-term liability during your present year-end audit?

16–34. Current pronouncements of the FASB require that under certain circumstances loss contingencies *be accrued* in the financial statements. Under other circumstances, loss contingencies may require *disclosure only in notes* to the financial statements or may be *omitted entirely* from the financial statements and accompanying footnotes. You are to provide three separate examples of a loss contingency, one for each of these three categories.

16–35. During your annual audit of Walker Distributing Co., your assistant, Jane Williams, reports to you that although a number of entries were made during the year in the general ledger account, Notes Payable to Officers, she decided that it was not necessary to audit the account because it had a zero balance at year-end.

Required:

Do you agree with your assistant's decision? Discuss.   (AICPA)

16–36. In an audit of a corporation that has a bond issue outstanding, the trust indenture is reviewed and confirmation as to the issue is obtained from the trustee. List eight matters of importance to the auditors that might be found either in the indenture or in the confirmation obtained from the trustee. Explain briefly the reason for the auditors' interest in each of the items.   (AICPA)

16–37. You are retained by Columbia Corporation to make an examination of its financial statements for the fiscal year ended June 30, and you begin work on July 15. Your survey of internal control indicates a fairly satisfactory condition, although there are not enough employees to permit extensive subdivision of duties. The company is one of the smaller units in the industry, but has realized net income of about $500,000 in each of the last three years.

Near the end of your field work you overhear a telephone call received by the president of the company while you are discussing the audit with him. The telephone conversation indicates that on May 15 of the current year the Columbia Corporation made an accommodation endorsement of a 60-day, $430,000 note issued by a major customer, Brill Corporation, to its bank. The purpose of the telephone call from Brill was to inform your client that the note had been paid at the maturity date. You had not been aware of the existence of the note before overhearing the telephone call.

Required:

a. Do you think the auditors would be justified from an ethical standpoint in acting on information acquired in this manner?

b. Should the balance sheet as of June 30 disclose the contingent liability? Give reasons for your answer.

c. Prepare a list of auditing procedures that might have brought the contingency to light. Explain fully the likelihood of detection of the accommodation endorsement by each procedure listed.

16–38. You are the audit manager in the examination of the financial statements of Midwest Grain Storage, Inc., a new client. The company's records show that as of the balance sheet date, approximately 15 million bushels of various grains are in storage for the Commodity Credit Corporation, an agency of the U.S. government.

In your review of the audit senior's working papers, you ascertain the following facts:

1. All grain is stored under a Uniform Grain Storage Agreement, which holds Midwest responsible for the quantity and quality of the grain.
2. Losses due to shrinkage, spoilage, and so forth are inherent in the storage of grain. Midwest's losses, however, have been negligible due to the excellence of its storage facilities.
3. Midwest carries a warehouseman's bond covering approximately 20 percent of the value of the stored grain.

In the loss contingencies section of the working papers, the senior auditor has made the following notation: "I propose recommending to Midwest's controller that the contingent liability for grain spoilage and shrinkage be disclosed in a note to the financial statements."

Required:

Do you concur with the senior's proposal? Explain.

16–39. Linda Reeves, CPA, receives a telephone call from her client, Lane Company. The company's controller states that the board of directors of Lane has entered into two contractual arrangements with Ted Forbes, the company's former president, who has recently retired. Under one agreement, Lane Company will pay the ex-president $7,000 per month for five years if he does not compete with the company during that time in a rival business. Under the other agreement, the company will pay the ex-president $5,000 per month for five years for such advisory services as the company may request from the ex-president.

Lane's controller asks Reeves whether the balance sheet as of the date the two agreements were signed should show $144,000 in current liabilities and $576,000 in long-term liabilities, or whether the two agreements should be disclosed in a contingencies note to the financial statements.

Required:

How should Linda Reeves reply to the controller's questions? Explain.

16–40. You are engaged in the examination of the financial statements of Armada Corporation for the year ended August 31, 1991. The balance sheet, reflecting all of your audit adjustments accepted by the client to date, shows total current assets, $9,000,000; total current liabilities,

$7,500,000; and stockholders' equity, $1,500,000. Included in current liabilities are two unsecured notes payable—one payable to United National Bank in the amount of $900,000 due October 31, 1991; the other payable to First State Bank in the amount of $800,000 due September 30, 1991. On September 30, the last scheduled date for your audit field work, you learn that Armada Corporation is unable to pay the $832,000 maturity value of the First State Bank note, that Armada executives are negotiating with First State Bank for an extension of the due date of the note, and that nothing definite has been decided as to the extension.

Required:

a. Should this situation be disclosed in footnotes to Armada Corporation's August 31 financial statements?

b. After the question of financial statement disclosure has been resolved to the auditor's satisfaction, might this situation have any effect upon the audit report?

16–41. During an audit engagement, Robert Wong, CPA, has satisfactorily completed an examination of accounts payable and other liabilities and now plans to determine whether there are any loss contingencies arising from litigation, claims, or assessments.

Required:

What are the audit procedures Wong should follow with respect to the existence of loss contingencies arising from litigation, claims, or assessments? Do not discuss reporting requirements.

16–42. Valley Corporation has a stock option plan designed to provide extra incentive to its officers and key employees. A footnote to the financial statements includes a description of the plan and lists the number of options for shares that have been authorized, the number granted, the number exercised, and the number expired. The option price and the market price per share on the grant dates and the exercise dates are also shown.

Required:

a. In view of the fact that the information concerning the stock option plan appears in a footnote, rather than in the body of the financial statements, what responsibility, if any, do the independent auditors have for this information?

b. List the audit procedures, if any, that you believe should be applied to the stock option plan information.

16–43. Select the best answer choice for each of the following, and justify your selection in a brief statement.

a. The audit procedure of confirmation is *least* appropriate with respect to:

(1) The trustee of an issue of bonds payable.

(2) Holders of common stock.

(3) Holders of notes receivable.

(4) Holders of notes payable.

b. The performance of audit procedures prior to the balance sheet date is an efficient auditing approach for some items but not for others.

For which of the following is audit work prior to the balance sheet date most feasible?

(1) Capital stock.

(2) Unrecorded liabilities.

(3) Trade accounts payable.

(4) Plant and equipment.

c. In the audit of a manufacturing company of medium size, which of the following areas would you expect to require the least amount of audit time?

(1) Owners' equity.

(2) Revenue.

(3) Assets.

(4) Liabilities.

d. Small businesses often need audited financial statements to support an application for a bank loan. Prior to the audit of a small single proprietorship, a joint meeting of the owner, the banker, and the CPA for the purpose of discussing the audit and its objectives:

(1) Might be considered as impairing the objectivity of the CPA.

(2) Would provide an opportunity for developing a contingent fee arrangement for the audit.

(3) Could lead to the omission from the audit of any procedures that the banker did not consider necessary.

(4) Would often be helpful in convincing the business owner of the need to cooperate fully in making all information available to the auditors.

e. The auditors' program for the examination of long-term debt should include steps that require the—

(1) Verification of the existence of the bondholders.

(2) Examination of copies of debt agreements.

(3) Inspection of the accounts payable subsidiary ledger.

(4) Investigation of credits to the bond interest income account.

f. All corporate capital stock transactions should ultimately be traced to the—

(1) Minutes of the Board of Directors.

(2) Cash receipts journal.

(3) Cash disbursements journal.

(4) Numbered stock certificates. (AICPA, adapted)

GROUP III: PROBLEMS

16–44. In your first audit of Hydrafoil Company, a manufacturer of specially designed boats capable of transporting passengers over water at very high speeds, you find that sales are made to commercial transportation companies. The sales price per unit is $400,000, and with each unit sold, the client gives the purchasing company a certificate reading as follows:

> Hydrafoil Company promises to pay _____ the sum of $24,000 when the boat designated as Serial No. _____ is permanently retired from service and evidence of such retirement is submitted.

The president of Hydrafoil Company explains to you that the purpose of issuing the certificates is to ensure contact with customers when they are in the market for new equipment. You also learn that the company makes no journal entry to record a certificate when it is issued. Instead, the company charges an expense account and credits a liability account $200 per month for each outstanding certificate, based on the company's experience that its hydrafoil boats will be rendered obsolete by new, more efficient models in approximately 10 years from the date of sale.

Required:
Do you concur with Hydrafoil Company's accounting for the certificates? You may assume that the 10-year service life of the product (and therefore of the certificates) is an accurate determination. Explain your position clearly.

16–45. You have been retained to audit the financial statements of Midwest Products, Inc. for the year ended December 31. During the current year, Midwest had obtained a long-term loan from its bank in accordance with a financing agreement which provided that:
1. The loan was to be secured by the company's inventory and accounts receivable.
2. The company was to maintain a debt-to-equity ratio not to exceed two to one.
3. The company was not to pay dividends without permission from the bank.
4. Monthly installment payments were to commence July 1 of the next year.

In addition, during the current year, Midwest Products, Inc. borrowed, on a short-term basis, from its president, including substantial amounts just prior to the year-end.

Required:
a. For the purpose of your audit of the financial statements of Midwest Products, Inc., what procedures would you employ in examining the above described items? Do not discuss internal control.
b. What financial statement disclosures are appropriate with respect to the loans from the president? (AICPA, adapted)

16–46. The following covenants are extracted from the indenture of a bond issue of Case Company. The indenture provides that failure to comply with its terms in any respect automatically advances the due date of the loan to the date of noncompliance (the regular due date is 20 years hence). Give any audit procedures or reporting requirements you think should be taken or recognized in connection with each one of the following:
1. "The debtor company shall endeavor to maintain a working capital ratio of 2 to 1 at all times; and in any fiscal year following a failure to maintain said ratio, the company shall restrict compensation of officers to a total of $2,000,000. Officers for this purpose shall include chairman of the board of directors, president, all vice presidents, secretary, controller, and treasurer."
2. "The debtor company shall keep all property that is security for this debt insured against loss by fire to the extent of 100 percent of its

actual value. Policies of insurance comprising this protection shall be filed with the trustee.''

3. "The debtor company shall pay all taxes legally assessed against property that is security for this debt within the time provided by law for payment without penalty, and shall deposit receipted tax bills or equally acceptable evidence of payment of same with the trustee.''

4. "A sinking fund shall be deposited with the trustee by semiannual payments of $900,000, from which the trustee shall, in its discretion, purchase bonds of this issue." (AICPA, adapted)

16–47. You are engaged in the first audit of Microdent, Inc. The corporation has both a stock transfer agent and an independent registrar for its capital stock. The transfer agent maintains the record of stockholders, and the registrar determines that there is no overissue of stock. Signatures of both are required to validate stock certificates.

It has been proposed that confirmations be obtained from both the transfer agent and the registrar as to the stock outstanding at the balance sheet date. If such confirmations agree with the accounting records, no additional work is to be performed as to capital stock.

If you agree that obtaining the confirmations as suggested would be sufficient in this case, give the justification for your position. If you do not agree, state specifically all additional steps you would take and explain your reasons for taking them. (AICPA, adapted)

16–48. You are engaged in the audit of Phoenix Corp., a new client, at the close of its first fiscal year, April 30, 1991. The accounts had been closed before the time you began your year-end field work.

You review the following stockholders' equity accounts in the general ledger:

Capital Stock			
	5/1/90	CR1	500,000
	4/28/91	J12–5	50,000

Paid-In Capital in Excess of Stated Value			
	5/1/90	CR1	250,000
	2/2/91	CR10	2,500

Retained Earnings					
4/28/91	J12–5	50,000	4/30/91	J12–14	800,000

(Continued)

	Treasury Stock		
9/14/90 CP5	80,000	2/2/91 CR10	40,000

	Income Summary		
4/30/91 J12–13	5,200,000	4/30/91 J12–12	6,000,000
4/30/91 J12–14	800,000		

Other information in your working papers includes the following:
1. Phoenix's articles of incorporation filed April 17, 1990, authorized 100,000 shares of no-par-value capital stock.
2. Directors' minutes include the following resolutions:
   4/18/90   Established $50 per share stated value for capital stock.
   4/30/90   Authorized issue of 10,000 shares to an underwriting syndicate for $75 per share.
   9/13/90   Authorized acquisition of 1,000 shares from a dissident holder at $80 per share.
   2/1/91   Authorized reissue of 500 treasury shares at $85 per share.
   4/28/91   Declared 10 percent stock dividend, payable May 18, 1991, to stockholders of record May 4, 1991.
3. The following costs of the May 1, 1990, and February 2, 1991, stock issuances were charged to the named expense accounts: Printing Expense, $2,500; Legal Fees, $17,350; Accounting Fees, $12,000; and SEC Fees, $150.
4. Market values for Phoenix Corp. capital stock on various dates were:

9/13/90	$78.50
9/14/90	79.00
2/2/91	85.00
4/28/91	90.00

5. Phoenix Corp.'s combined federal and state income tax rates total 55 percent.

Required:
   a. Adjusting journal entries at April 30, 1991.
   b. Stockholders' equity section of Phoenix Corp.'s April 30, 1991, balance sheet.

16–49. Robert Hopkins was the senior office employee in Griffin Equipment Company and enjoyed the complete confidence of the owner, William Barton, who devoted most of his attention to sales, engineering, and production problems. All financial and accounting matters were entrusted to Hopkins, whose title was office manager. Hopkins had two assistants, but their only experience in accounting and financial work had been gained under Hopkins's supervision. Barton had informed Hopkins that it was his responsibility to keep him (Barton) informed on financial position and operating results of the company but not to bother him with details.

The company was short of working capital and would occasionally issue notes payable in settlement of past-due open accounts to suppliers. The situations warranting issuance of notes were decided upon by Hopkins, and the notes were drawn by him for signature by Barton. Hopkins was aware of the weakness in internal control and finally devised a scheme for defrauding the company through understating the amount of notes payable outstanding. He prepared a note in the amount of $24,000 payable to a supplier to whom several invoices were past due. After securing Barton's signature on the note and mailing it to the creditor, Hopkins entered the note in the Notes Payable account of the general ledger as $4,000, with an offsetting debit of $4,000 to Accounts Payable.

Several months later when the note matured, a check for $24,000 plus interest was issued and properly recorded, including a debit of $24,000 to the Notes Payable account. Hopkins then altered the original credit in the account by changing the figure from $4,000 to $24,000. He also changed the original debit to Accounts Payable from $4,000 to $24,000. This alteration caused the Notes Payable account to have a balance in agreement with the total of other notes outstanding. To complete the fraud, Hopkins called the supplier to whom the check had been sent and explained that the check should have been for only $4,000 plus interest.

Hopkins explained to the supplier that the note of $24,000 originally had been issued in settlement of a number of past-due invoices, but that while the note was outstanding, checks had been sent in payment of all the invoices. "In other words," said Hopkins over the telephone, "we made the mistake of giving you a note for those invoices and then going ahead and sending you checks for them as soon as our cash position had improved. Then we paid the note at maturity. So please excuse our mistakes and return the overpayment." After reviewing the record of invoices and checks received, the supplier agreed he had been overpaid by $20,000 plus interest and promptly sent a refund, which Hopkins abstracted without making any entry in the accounts.

Required:

a. Assuming that an audit by independent CPAs was made while the note was outstanding, do you think that the $20,000 understatement of the Notes Payable account would have been detected? Explain fully the reasoning underlying your answer.

b. If the irregularity was not discovered while the note was outstanding, do you think that an audit subsequent to the payment of the note would have disclosed the fraud? Explain.

c. What internal control procedures would you recommend for Griffin Equipment Company to avoid fraud of this type?

Further verification of revenue and expenses; completing the audit

Chapter 17 study objectives

After studying this chapter you should be able to:
— Describe the audit objectives for revenue and expense accounts.
— Describe appropriate audit procedures for the audit of revenue and expense accounts.
— Explain the fundamental necessary internal controls over payroll and be able to identify weaknesses.
— Describe the steps involved in completing the audit.

Throughout the previous chapters on balance sheet accounts we have discussed related procedures for income statement accounts. In this chapter we provide further information on the audit of revenues and expenses as well as present information on procedures involved with completing the audit.

Nature of revenue and expenses

Today, with greater emphasis being placed upon corporate earnings as an indicator of the health and well-being of corporations as well as of the overall economy, the income statement is of fundamental importance to management, stockholders, creditors, employees, and government. The relative level of corporate earnings is often a key factor in the determination of such issues as wage negotiations, income tax rates, subsidies, and government fiscal policies. In fact, accountants generally agree that the measurement of income is the most important single function of accounting.

Throughout Chapters 11 through 16, we have emphasized the relationships of revenues and expenses to the various balance sheet accounts. Put briefly, the principles used in making accounting decisions for balance sheet accounts often have a direct effect upon the measurement of income.

The auditors' approach in examination of revenues and expenses

The doctrine of conservatism is a powerful force influencing decisions on revenues and expenses. The concept remains important in large part due to the subjectivity involved with many accounting estimates (as for expected future credit losses on receivables, lives of assets, and the warranty of products sold). Conservatism in the valuation of assets means that when two (or more) reasonable alternative values are indicated, the accountant will choose the lower amount. For valuation of liabilities, the higher amount is chosen. Therefore, when applied to the income statement, the conservatism concept results in a low or "conservative" income figure.

Most auditors have a considerable respect for the doctrine of conservatism. In part, this attitude springs from the concept of legal liability to third parties. Financial statements that **understate** financial position and operating results almost never lead to legal action against the auditors involved. Nevertheless, auditors must recognize that overemphasis on conservatism in financial reporting is a narrow and shortsighted approach to meeting the needs of our society. To be of greatest value, financial statements should present fairly, rather than understate, financial position and operating results.

A fair, informative income statement is then surely as important as, if not more important than, the balance sheet. Nevertheless, audits continue to be organized in terms of balance sheet topics. The reasons for organizing audit work in this manner were discussed in Chapter 10.

As the significance of the income statement increased, auditors began to verify income statement accounts concurrently with related balance sheet accounts. Depreciation expense, for example, is most conveniently verified along with the plant and equipment accounts. Once the existence and cost of depreciable assets are established, the verification of depreciation expense is merely an additional step. On the other hand, to verify depreciation expense without first establishing the nature and amount of assets owned and subject to depreciation would obviously be a cart-be-fore-the-horse approach. The same line of reasoning tells us that the auditors' work on inventories, especially in determining that inventory transactions were accurately cut off at the end of the period, is a major step toward the verification of the income statement figures for sales and cost of goods sold. Much of the material in the preceding six chapters of this book has related to income statement accounts, although the sequence of topics has followed a balance sheet arrangement.

When the balance sheets at the beginning and end of an accounting period have been fully verified, the net income for the year is fairly well established, although considerable additional work remains to be done before the auditors can express a professional opinion that the income statement presents fairly the results of operations.

Let us emphasize the fact that the auditors' examination of revenue and expense transactions should be much more than an incidental by-product of the examination of assets and liabilities. They use a combination of cross-referencing, analytical procedures, and analysis of specific transactions to bring to light errors, omissions, and inconsistencies not disclosed in the examination of balance sheet accounts.

Specifically, the auditors' *objectives* in the examination of revenues and expenses are to determine that:

1. *Internal control* over revenues and expenses *is adequate.*
2. The recorded transactions for revenues and expenses are valid (*existence* and *rights*).
3. All revenue and expense transactions are recorded (*completeness*).
4. Revenue and expense schedules are mathematically correct and agree with general ledger accounts (*clerical accuracy*).
5. The *valuation* of revenue and expense accounts is proper.
6. The *presentation* and *disclosure* of revenue and expense accounts is adequate.

REVENUE

The auditors' review of sales activities was considered in connection with accounts receivable in Chapter 12. In this section we discuss (1) the relationship of revenue to balance sheet accounts and (2) the miscellaneous revenue account.

Relationship of revenue to balance sheet accounts

As pointed out previously, most revenue accounts are verified by the auditors in conjunction with the audit of a related asset or liability. The following list summarizes the revenue verified in this manner:

Balance sheet item	Revenue
Accounts receivable	Sales
Notes receivable	Interest
Securities and other investments	Interest, dividends, gains on sales, share of investee's income
Property, plant, and equipment	Rent, gains on sale
Intangible assets	Royalties

A common characteristic of the revenue items listed above is that most, if not all, are accounted for on the accrual basis. Accrual basis accounting for revenue results in strong internal control because it requires the recording of a receivable when the revenue is earned. Once the receivable is recorded, some follow-up is inevitable. Additional assurance is provided that attention will be drawn to any delay in the receipt of cash, or any failure to record a cash receipt. For example, if dividends earned are recorded as receivables by an accrual entry at the date of record, any failure to receive or to record dividend checks will be readily apparent.

Miscellaneous revenue

One category of revenue not included in the above listing, but of interest to the auditors, is miscellaneous revenue. Miscellaneous revenue, by its very nature, is a mixture of minor items, some nonrecurring and others likely to be received at irregular intervals. Consequently, many companies do not accrue such revenue, but merely debit Cash and credit Miscellaneous Revenue when cash is received. The weakness inherent in this procedure is not of particular significance if the amounts involved are minor and infrequent. However, the weakness can become serious if revenue of substantial amount is misclassified as Miscellaneous Revenue, a practice sometimes followed because of its convenience.

Illustrative case

An old story in public accounting circles concerns the auditors who inquired of a new client how extensive was the classification by the company of revenue and expenses. "Just two of each," was the reply, "general and miscellaneous."

For the reasons indicated above, the auditors should obtain an analysis of the Miscellaneous Revenue account. Among the items the auditors might find improperly included as miscellaneous revenue are the following:

1. Collections on previously written-off accounts or notes receivable. These collections should be credited to the allowance for doubtful accounts and notes receivable.
2. Write-offs of old outstanding checks or unclaimed wages. In many states, unclaimed properties revert to the state after statutory periods; in such circumstances, these write-offs should be credited to a liability account rather than to miscellaneous revenue.
3. Proceeds from sales of scrap. Scrap sale proceeds should generally be applied to reduce cost of goods sold, under by-product cost accounting principles.
4. Rebates or refunds of insurance premiums. These refunds should be offset against the related expense or unexpired insurance.
5. Proceeds from sales of plant assets. These proceeds should be accounted for in the determination of the gain or loss on the assets sold.

The auditors should propose adjusting journal entries to classify correctly any material items of the types described above that have been included in miscellaneous revenue by the client. Before concluding the work on revenue, the auditors should perform analytical procedures and investigate unusual fluctuations. Material amounts of unrecorded revenue may be discovered by these procedures, as well as significant misclassifications affecting revenue accounts.

EXPENSES

The auditors' work relating to purchases and cost of goods sold was covered, along with inventories, in Chapter 13. We are now concerned with audit procedures for other types of expenses.

Relationship of expenses to balance sheet accounts

Let us consider for a moment the number of expense accounts for which we have already outlined verification procedures in the chapters dealing with balance sheet topics:

Balance sheet item	Expenses (and costs)
Accounts and notes receivable	Uncollectible accounts and notes expense
Inventories	Purchases and cost of goods sold
Property, plant, and equipment	Depreciation, repairs and maintenance, and depletion
(Continued)	

Prepaid expenses and deferred charges	Various related expenses, such as rent, property taxes, advertising, postage, and others
Intangible assets	Amortization
Accrued liabilities	Commissions, fees, bonuses, product warranty expenses, and others
Interest-bearing debt	Interest

In the following sections, we shall complete our review of expenses by considering additional audit objectives and procedures for payrolls, for selling, and for general and administrative expenses, other than those listed above. The audit of payroll is presented as a unit without regard to the division of salaries and wages between manufacturing operations and other operations. Manufacturing salaries and wages are, of course, charged to inventories, either directly or by means of the allocation of factory overhead.

Audit program for selling, general, and administrative expenses

For other expenses not verified in the audit of balance sheet accounts, the following substantive tests are appropriate:

1. Perform analytical procedures related to the accounts.
    a. Develop an expectation of the account balance.
    b. Determine the amount of difference from the expectation that can be accepted without investigation.
    c. Compare the company's account balance with the expected account balance.
    d. Investigate significant deviations from the expected account balance.
2. Obtain or prepare analyses of selected expense accounts.
3. Obtain or prepare analyses of critical expenses in income tax returns.

1. Perform analytical procedures related to the accounts.
a. Develop an expectation of the account balance.

Auditors develop an expectation of the account balance by considering factors such as budgeted levels, the prior year audited balances, industry averages, relationships among financial data, and relevant nonfinancial data.

An effective budgeting program will reduce control risk since budgets provide management with information as to expected values. The existence of these expected values increases the likelihood that errors will be detected by management, since any significant discrepancy between budgeted and actual amounts receives timely attention.

The existence of a good budgeting program also helps the auditors in their audit of expense accounts. When the control over budgeting has been found to be effective, the budgeted amounts often provide the auditors with very good expected values for their analytical procedures.

One of the previously described audit objectives was to determine whether expenses had been correctly classified. The issue of classification is most important as between factory overhead costs, on the one hand, and selling, general, and administrative expenses on the other. Factory overhead costs may properly be carried forward as part of inventory cost, whereas the expenses of selling, general, and administrative functions usually are deducted from revenue in the period incurred. Consequently, an error in classification may cause an error in the net income of the period. The auditors' review of the propriety of classification of expenses can be linked conveniently with the comparison of monthly amounts of the various expenses. Comparison of yearly totals is accomplished by inclusion of amounts for the preceding year on the auditors' lead schedules or working trial balance, but this procedure should be supplemented by comparison of expenses on a month-by-month basis.

Comparison of expense (as well as revenue) accounts with industry and nonfinancial data is another means of bringing to light circumstances that require investigation. Deviations from industry averages should be investigated. Also, unusual relationships between financial and nonfinancial information, such as between production records stated in gallons or pounds and the dollar amounts of sales, should be investigated.

b.   Determine the amount of difference from the expectation that can be accepted without investigation.

The auditors use their estimates of materiality and tolerable error for the account to arrive at which differences are to be investigated and which might be expected to occur by chance.

c.   Compare the company's account balance with the expected account balance.

The expense accounts may be compared to the auditors' expected values developed in (a) above. For example, the current year's selling expenses as a percentage of sales may be compared with the percentage for the preceding year, with industry averages, or with budgeted percentages. Significant differences may then be identified. Figure 17–1 illustrates a working paper that compares major income statement categories for the year under audit with the prior year amounts and industry averages.

d.   Investigate significant deviations from the expected account balance.

The starting point for investigating significant variations in expenses is inquiry of management. The auditors substantiate management's explanations for significant variations by various means, including analyses of accounts. Analyses of expense accounts involves tracing entries in the accounts back to the voucher register or to the cash disbursements jour-

Figure 17–1

Cheviot Corporation
Comparative Income Statement
Year Ended December 31, 19X3
R-1-4

| | 19X2 | | 19X3 | | Industry Statistics |
	$	%	$	%	%
Sales	548784 –√	100	610740 –ᴎ▽	100	100
Cost of Goods Sold	374658 –√	68	403070 –ᴎ∅	66	65
Gross Profit	174126 –	32	207670 –∅	34	35
Selling Expenses	55484 –√	10	85654 –ᴎ△	14	15
General and Administrative Expenses	79634 –√	15	87557 –ᴎ∅	14	12
Income before Taxes	39008 –	7	34459 –∅	6	8
Taxes	12873 –√	2	6869 –ᴎ✗	1	3
Net Income	26135 –	5	27590 –∅	5	5
	∧		∧		

∧ Footed.

ᴎ Agreed to the general ledger.

√ Agreed to the prior year working papers.

∅ Amount appears reasonable in relation to prior year results and industry statistics.

▽ See audit procedures performed on Sales, R-1-2.

△ Large increase in Selling Expenses is due to the addition of a salesman to the sales staff. Based on a review of the payroll records the increase in the account appears reasonable.

✗ Decrease in tax rate is due to the realization of several thousand dollars in tax credits. See tax accrual working paper, O-3.

Conclusion:
The comparative analysis revealed no unusual fluctuations that could not be adequately explained.

J.M.H.
Jan. 15, X4   Conque C.M.
                     C.M.
                     Jan. 19, X4

nal. From these accounting records, reference may be made to invoices, receiving reports, purchase orders, or other supporting evidence.

2. Obtain or prepare analyses of selected expense accounts.

As a result of the above procedure, the auditors will have chosen certain expense accounts for further verification. The client should be requested to furnish analyses of the accounts selected, together with related vouchers and other supporting documents, for the auditors' review.

Which expense accounts are most likely to contain misstatements or indicate other audit problems and are most important for the auditors to analyze? The AICPA has suggested investigation of (1) advertising, (2) contributions, (3) legal expenses and other professional fees, (4) maintenance and repairs, (5) rents and royalties, and (6) taxes, licenses, and fees.[1]

The analyses of legal and other professional fees may disclose legal and audit fees properly chargeable to costs of issuing stock or debt instruments, or to costs of business combinations. Also, the analysis of professional fees expense furnishes the names of attorneys to whom letters should be sent requesting information as to pending litigation and other loss contingencies. Figure 17–2 illustrates an analysis of the professional fees expense account.

3. Obtain or prepare analyses of critical expenses in income tax returns.

Income tax returns generally require schedules for officers' salaries, taxes, travel and entertainment, contributions, and casualty losses. In addition to these, officers' expense account allowances are presented in the analysis of officers' salaries. Accordingly, the auditors should obtain or prepare analyses of any of these expenses that were not analyzed when performing other audit steps. The auditors should bear in mind that details of these expenses will probably be closely scrutinized when the state or federal revenue agents examine the client's tax returns.

THE AUDIT OF PAYROLL

The payroll in many companies is by far the largest operating cost, and, therefore, deserves the close attention of the auditors. In the past, payroll frauds were common and often substantial. Today, however, such frauds may be more difficult to conceal for several reasons: (1) extensive subdivision of duties relating to payroll; (2) use of computers, with proper controls, for preparation of payrolls; and (3) necessity of filing frequent reports to the government, listing employees' earnings and tax withholdings.

In addition to the objectives for expenses (and revenues) presented earlier in this chapter, the auditors have the following additional *objectives* relating to payroll:

---

[1] See AICPA, *Audit and Accounting Manual* (New York, 1986), par. AAM 6500.690.

Figure 17–2   Analysis of professional fees

Chevist Corporation
Acct. No. 547   Professional Fees Expense   R-3-7
Year Ended December 31, 198X

Date	Reference	Payee	Description	Amount	
Various	Various	Hale and Hale	Monthly retainer for legal services – 12 × $500u	6000 –	
Mar.5,8X	CD411	Jay + Wall, CPAs	Fee for the audit	7500 –	ц
May2,8X	CD602	Hale and Hale	Fee for legal services relating to acquisition of real property adjoining Vancouver plant	3000 –	ц
Sept.18,8X	CD1018	Hale and Hale	Fee for legal services relating to modification of instalment sales contract forms	400 –	ц
Dec.31,8X			Balance per ledger	16900 –	
Dec.31,8X	A.J.E. 41	To capitalize May 2, 8X disbursement as part of cost of land		K-1 (3000 –)	
Dec.31,8X			Adjusted balance	13900	ᴧ
				R-3	

A.J.E. 41
Land   3000 –
   Professional Fees   3000 –
To capitalize legal
fees re obtaining land.

Prepared by client
ᴧ – Footed and agreed to general ledger balance.
ц – Examined billing and copy of client's check in payment thereof.

Conclusion:
   Professional fees expense is fairly presented in the adjusted amount of $13,900.

J.M.H.
Jan. 9, 8X   J. Agee
                    C.M.
                    Jan. 21, 8X
                              C.M.
                              Jan. 19, 8X

1. To determine that the client has complied with government regulations concerning social security taxes, unemployment insurance, worker's compensation insurance, wages and hours, income tax withholding, and other federal, state, and local requirements concerning employment.
2. To determine that the company is complying with terms of union agreements as to wage rates, vacation pay, and similar items.

Internal control

The establishment of strong internal control over payrolls is particularly important for several reasons. Although payroll frauds are less frequent today, the possibility of large-scale payroll fraud still exists. Such frauds may involve listing fictitious persons on the payroll, overpaying employees, and continuing employees on the payroll after their separation from the company. A second reason for emphasizing internal control over payrolls is that a great mass of detailed information concerning hours worked and rates of pay must be processed quickly and accurately if workers are to be paid promptly and without error. Good employee relations demand that paychecks be ready on time and be free from error. As pointed out in previous chapters, internal control is a means of securing accuracy and dependability in accounting data as well as a means of preventing fraud.

Still another reason for emphasizing the importance of internal control over payrolls is the existence of various payroll tax laws and income tax laws, which require that certain payroll records be maintained and that payroll data be reported to the employee and to governmental agencies. Complete and accurate records of time worked are also necessary if a company is to protect itself against lawsuits under the Fair Labor Standards Act.

Methods of achieving internal control

Budgetary control of labor costs To control payroll costs means to avoid waste and to obtain the maximum production from the dollars expended for services of employees. As a means of establishing control over payroll costs, many companies delegate to department heads and other supervisors responsibility for the control of costs in their respective units of the business. The supervisor may be requested at the beginning of each year to submit for the budget an estimate of departmental labor costs for the coming period. As the year progresses and actual labor costs are compiled, the controller submits monthly reports to top management comparing the budgeted labor costs and the actual labor costs for each department. The effectiveness of this control device will depend largely upon the extent to which top management utilizes these reports and takes action upon variances from the budget.

Reports to governmental agencies Another important internal control over payroll lies in the necessity of preparing reports to government agencies showing the earnings and tax deductions for all employees. This type of control is not concerned with holding labor costs to a minimum, but is an effective means of preventing and detecting payroll fraud. In a few cases, falsified reports to government agencies have been prepared as part of a payroll fraud, but this involves such extensive scheming and falsification of records as to make fraud of this type rather unlikely.

Subdivision of duties Most important of all internal controls over payroll is the division of payroll work among several departments of the company. Payroll activities include the functions of employment, timekeeping, payroll preparation and record keeping, and the distribution of pay to employees. For strong internal control, each of these functions should be handled by a separate department of the company. Combination of these functions in a single department or under the authority of one person opens the door to payroll fraud. These several phases of payroll activities will now be considered individually.

The employment function

The first significant step in building strong internal control over payrolls is taken by the personnel department when a new employee is hired. At this point, the authorized rate of pay should be entered on a pay-rate record. The employee also should sign a payroll deduction authorization specifying any amounts to be withheld and a withholding tax exemption certificate. These records should be kept in the personnel department, but a notice of the hiring of the new employee, the rate of pay, and the payroll deductions should be sent to the payroll department. Notice of employment and of the authorized pay rate also is sent to the head of the department in which the employee is to work.

Under no circumstances is the payroll department justified in adding a name to the payroll without having received the formal authorization notice from the personnel department. When an employee's rate of pay is changed, the new rate will be entered on the pay-rate record that is maintained in the personnel department. An authorization for the new rate must be sent to the payroll department before the change can be made effective on the payroll. Upon the termination of an employee, notice of termination is sent from the personnel department to the payroll department. The work of the payroll department and the propriety of names and pay rates used in preparing the payroll, therefore, rest upon formal documents originating outside the payroll department.

Adequate internal control demands that the addition and removal of names from the company payroll, as well as rate changes and reclassification of employees, be evidenced by written approval of an executive in the personnel department and by the head of the operating department concerned. To permit the payroll department to initiate changes in pay rates, or to add names to the payroll without formal authorization from the personnel department, is to invite payroll fraud.

Timekeeping

The function of timekeeping consists of determining the number of hours (or units of production) for which each employee is to be paid. The use of electronic time-recording equipment is of considerable aid in establishing adequate internal control over the timekeeping function. Reports prepared by timekeepers who travel through the plant and contact an employee only once or twice during the day may be less dependable than time reports prepared by supervisors, whose duties keep them in continuous contact with a small group of employees.

Internal control can be improved by the practice of regular comparison of the time reports prepared by timekeepers or supervisors with time clock records showing arrival and departure times of employees. If pay is based on piecework, a comparison may be made between the reports of units produced and the quantities that are added to the perpetual inventory records.

Salaried employees receiving a fixed monthly or weekly salary may not be required to use time clocks. Some companies require salaried employees to fill out a weekly or semimonthly report indicating the time devoted to various activities. If a salaried employee is absent, the department head usually has authority to decide whether a pay reduction should be made.

Payroll records and payroll preparation

The payroll department has the responsibility of computing the amounts to be paid to employees and of preparing all payroll records. It is imperative that the payroll department should *not* perform the related functions of timekeeping, employment, or distribution of pay to employees. The output of the payroll department may be thought of as: (1) the payroll checks (or pay envelopes, if wages are paid in cash); (2) individual employee statements of earnings and deductions; (3) a payroll journal; (4) an employees' ledger, summarizing earnings and deductions for each employee; (5) a payroll distribution schedule, showing the allocation of payroll costs to direct labor, overhead, and various departmental expense accounts; and (6) quarterly and annual reports to the government showing employees' earnings and taxes withheld. If the client utilizes an electronic data processing installation, many of these functions may be delegated to the data processing department.

The computation of the payroll is made from the work hours reported by the timekeeping department, and from authorized pay rates and payroll deductions reported by the personnel department.

The auditors may find payroll records and procedures varying in complexity from a manual "write it once" system to the most sophisticated computerized techniques. However, they should expect the client's system to include such basic records as timecards, payroll journals, labor distributions, and employee earnings records.

Distributing paychecks or cash to employees

The distribution of paychecks or pay envelopes to employees is the task of the paymaster. If employees are paid in cash, a copy of the payroll register is forwarded from the payroll department, and the paymaster uses this record as a guide to filling the payroll envelopes. These envelopes preferably should be prepared by the payroll department. If employees are paid by check, the checks may be made ready for signature in the payroll department and forwarded to the treasurer for signature.

Under no circumstances should the signed payroll checks or pay envelopes containing cash be returned to the payroll department. Neither is it acceptable to turn paychecks or pay envelopes over to supervisors in the operating departments for distribution to employees. The function of distributing paychecks should be lodged exclusively with an employee who performs no other payroll activity. When delivering a check to an employee, the paymaster will require proof of identity by presentation of a badge or identification card. A check or pay envelope for an absent employee should be retained and never turned over to another employee for delivery. When the absentees later pick up their pay, they should be required to sign a receipt.

Most companies that pay employees by check use a special payroll bank account. A voucher for the entire amount of the weekly payroll may be prepared in the general accounting department based on the payroll summary prepared in the payroll department. This voucher is sent to the treasurer, who issues a check on the general bank account for the amount of the payroll. The check is deposited in the special payroll bank account, and checks to individual employees are drawn on this bank account. It also is the practice of some companies to have printed on the check a statement that this type of check is not valid if issued for an amount in excess of a specified dollar amount.

If wages are paid in cash, any unclaimed wages should be deposited in the bank and credited to a special liability account. Subsequent disbursement of these funds to employees then will be controlled by the necessity of drawing a check and preparing supporting documents. The auditors should investigate thoroughly all debits to the Unclaimed Wages account. The dangers inherent in permitting unclaimed pay envelopes to be retained by the paymaster, returned to the payroll clerk, or intermingled with petty cash are apparent.

Description of internal control for payroll

Typical of the questions to be answered by the auditors for the completion of an internal control questionnaire, a systems flowchart, or other record of payroll internal controls are the following: Are employees paid by check? Is a payroll bank account maintained on an imprest basis? Are the activities of timekeeping, payroll compilation, payroll check signing, and paycheck distribution performed by separate departments or employees? Are all operations involved in the preparation of payrolls subjected to independent verification before the paychecks are distributed? Are employee time reports approved by supervisors? Is the payroll bank account reconciled monthly by an employee having no other payroll duties?

Audit program for payrolls

The following audit procedures are representative of the work generally completed to establish the propriety of payments for salaries, wages, bonuses, and commissions:

1. Obtain an understanding of the internal control for payrolls.
2. Perform tests of controls over payroll transactions for selected pay periods, including the following specific procedures:
   a. Trace names and wage or salary rates to records maintained by the personnel department.
   b. Trace time shown on payroll to timecards and time reports approved by supervisors.
   c. If payroll is based on piecework rates rather than hourly rates, reconcile earnings with production records.
   d. Determine basis of deductions from payroll and compare with records of deductions authorized by employees.
   e. Test extensions and footings of payroll.
   f. Compare total of payroll with total of payroll checks issued.
   g. Compare total of payroll with total of labor cost summary prepared by cost accounting department.
   h. If wages are paid in cash, compare receipts obtained from employees with payroll.
   i. If wages are paid by check, compare paid checks with payroll and compare endorsements to signatures on withholding tax exemption certificates.
   j. Review subsequent payment of unclaimed wages, comparing receipts with payroll records, wage rates, and time reports.
3. Observe the use of time clocks by employees reporting for work, and investigate timecards not used.
4. Plan a surprise observation of one of the paycheck distributions, including control of payroll records and an accounting for all employees listed.

5. Determine that payrolls for the year do not exceed the number of weekly or monthly pay periods and that all payrolls have been properly approved.
6. Obtain or prepare a summary of compensation of officers for the year and trace to contracts, minutes of directors' meetings, or other authorization.
7. Investigate any extraordinary fluctuations in salaries, wages, and commissions.
8. Test computations of compensation earned under profit-sharing plans.
9. Test commission earnings by examination of contracts and detailed supporting records.
10. Test pension payments by reference to authorized pension plans and to supporting records.

The fourth procedure in the above list, calling for the auditors to plan a surprise observation of a regular distribution of paychecks to employees, deserves special consideration. The auditors' objective in observing the distribution of checks or cash to employees on a regular payday is to determine that every name on the company payroll is that of a bona fide employee presently on the job. This audit procedure is particularly desirable if the various phases of payroll work are not sufficiently segregated by departments to afford good internal control. The history of payroll frauds shows that permitting one person to have custody of employment records, timecards, paychecks, and employees' earnings records has often led to the entering of fictitious names on the payroll, and to other irregularities, such as use of excessive pay rates and continuance of pay after the termination of an employee.

The auditors first will determine that they have possession of all the checks or envelopes comprising the payroll. They will then accompany representatives of the client around the plant as all the checks or envelopes are distributed to employees. The whole procedure will be meaningless unless the auditors establish the identity of each employee receiving payment.

INCOME STATEMENT PRESENTATION

How much detail in the income statement?

One of the more interesting problems of statement presentation of revenue and expenses is the question of how much detailed operating information may be disclosed without causing the income statement to become unreasonably long and complex. As a minimum, the income statement should show the net sales revenue, cost of goods sold, selling expenses, general and administrative expenses, income taxes, and net income. Such special events as discontinued operations, extraordinary items, and the effects of accounting changes should be presented in the income statement in accordance with the requirements of the FASB.

Reporting earnings per share

FASB pronouncements require that companies with shares owned by the public present earnings per share on the face of the income statement. For these companies, per share figures should be reported for income from continuing operations, income before extraordinary items, cumulative effects of accounting changes, and net income. The computations should be based upon the weighted-average number of actual and *equivalent* common shares outstanding during the year. In addition to these *primary* earnings per share, companies with a complex capital structure may be required to report *fully diluted* earnings per share.

Reporting by diversified companies

The business combination movement in recent years has created many large conglomerate corporations by bringing together companies in quite unrelated industries. Although the word *conglomerate* is usually applied to a large family of corporations created by business combinations, other companies have achieved the same degree of diversification among unrelated industries through internal development and expansion. The term *diversified company* is therefore more appropriate for our use in considering the special financial reporting problems created by the emergence of this type of business entity.

For the diversified company carrying on operations in several unrelated industries, we may well question whether the traditional form of income statement constitutes a fair presentation. Would the income statement be more useful to financial analysts and others if it showed separately the revenue and operating results of the various industry segments comprising the diversified company? In the past, an investor or financial analyst easily could associate a given corporation with a specific industry. Since this is hardly possible for many large, diversified companies, a worthwhile analysis of the income statement may require disclosure of profitability of the several industry segments.

The Financial Accounting Standards Board requires companies with shares owned by the public to include certain business segments information in their annual financial statements. This disclosure includes information concerning the company's operations in different industries, its foreign operations, and its sales to major customers. Since the information is required for fair presentation of the financial statements in conformity with generally accepted accounting principles, it must be audited to provide a basis for an unqualified opinion on the financial statements. Accordingly, *SAS 21* (AU 435), "Segment Information," states that the auditors should perform the following procedures related to the business segment information:

1. Evaluate the reasonableness of management's methods of compiling the information.
2. Consider whether the information is presented in sufficient detail; apply analytical procedures to test its reasonableness.
3. Evaluate the reasonableness of methods used in allocating operating expenses among segments.

Examination of the statement of cash flows

The statement of cash flows is prepared from other financial statements and from analyses of increases and decreases in selected account balances. The amounts included in the statement of cash flows are audited in conjunction with the audit of balance sheet and income statement accounts. Thus, limited substantive testing is necessary. The auditors merely trace the amounts included in the statement of cash flows to other financial statement balances and amounts included in audit working papers.

Since receipts and payments must be classified in the statement of cash flows as to whether they are from operating, investing, or financing activities, the presentation and disclosure audit objective is especially important. The auditors must determine that the concept of cash or cash and cash equivalents analyzed in the statement agrees with an amount shown on the balance sheet. Finally, the auditors should ascertain that a statement of cash flows is presented for each year for which an income statement is presented.

COMPLETING THE AUDIT

The remainder of this chapter will review the audit procedures and other considerations involved in completing the audit engagement. These procedures and judgments are completed on, or near, the last day of field work, and they are important in determining the nature and content of the auditors' opinion.

Audit procedures

The auditors' opinion on the client's financial statements is based on all evidence gathered by the auditors up to the last day of field work, and any information that comes to their attention after that date. To be effective, certain audit procedures described in previous chapters cannot be completed before the end of audit field work. Among the procedures that must be performed at, or near, the last day of field work are the following.

Obtain the lawyer's letter The letter of inquiry from the client's legal counsel must be obtained near the end of field work. As discussed in

Chapter 16, the purpose of the lawyer's letter is to obtain information regarding pending or threatened litigation against the client. The lawyer's assessment of the probable outcome of significant litigation is important to the auditors' evaluation of the financial statement presentation of contingent liabilities.

Obtain the representations letter Chapter 7 included a general description of the letter of representations that the auditors must obtain from management. The primary purpose of the representations letter is to have the client's principal officers acknowledge that they are primarily responsible for the fairness of the financial statements. Since the financial statements must reflect all material subsequent events, the representations letter should be dated as of the last day of field work.

Perform other procedures to identify subsequent events Other audit procedures that are designed to identify significant subsequent events also must be completed near the end of the engagement. These audit procedures (described in Chapter 7) include review of the minutes of meetings of the stockholders and of the board of directors, inquiry of client officers, and review of interim accounting records and financial statements.

Perform overall review using analytical procedures The discussion of analytical procedures in Chapter 7 pointed out that they must be performed in planning as well as for overall review purposes at the completion of the audit. Analytical procedures performed as a part of the overall review assist the auditors in assessing the validity of the conclusions reached, including the opinion to be issued. This overall review may identify areas that need to be examined further as well as provide a consideration of the adequacy of data gathered in response to unusual or unexpected relationships identified during the audit.

Complete the search for unrecorded liabilities As discussed in Chapter 16, the search for unrecorded liabilities includes procedures performed through the last day of field work.

Review the working papers *SAS 22* (AU 311.11), "Planning and Supervision," states that "the work performed by each assistant should be reviewed to determine whether it was adequately performed and to evaluate whether the results are consistent with the conclusions to be presented in the auditors' report." This review of the work of the audit staff is primarily accomplished through a review of the audit working papers. The seniors on audit engagements typically perform their review of the audit working papers as the papers are completed. While audit partners and managers will generally communicate with seniors and other staff members throughout the audit, their review of the working papers generally is not performed until near (or after) completion of field work. The audit partner and manager will devote special attention to those accounts that have a higher risk of material misstatement, such as the significant accounting estimates of inventory obsolescence and warranty obligations. If a second partner review is required by the CPA firm's quality control policies, this review is usually performed just prior to issuance of the audit report.

Review the financial statement disclosures The recent proliferation of accounting standards makes it difficult for the auditors to evaluate the adequacy of financial statement disclosures. It is not effective to rely on the auditors' memories to evaluate the adequacy of disclosures, and it is not efficient for them to research the required disclosures each time they review a set of financial statements. Thus, many CPA firms have developed *disclosure checklists* that list all specific disclosures required by the FASB and the SEC. The auditors complete the checklist as a part of their review of the completed financial statements.

Evaluating audit findings

To issue an unqualified opinion, the auditors must conclude that there is a low level of audit risk of material misstatement of the financial statements. Therefore, in evaluating audit findings, the auditors must consider both quantitative and qualitative factors to make a final assessment of both materiality and audit risk. In evaluating the risk of material error in the financial statements, the auditors consider the errors that are *known to exist* in the statements, and also errors that they feel are *likely to exist,* based on the result of their audit procedures.

Known error in the financial statements During the course of the audit, the auditors will propose adjusting entries for all significant errors that they discover in the financial statements. Any *material* error that the auditors find must be corrected; otherwise, the auditors will be precluded from issuing an unqualified opinion on the financial statements.

Errors that are individually immaterial that have not been corrected by the client should also be considered. These immaterial errors could materially misstate the financial statements on an aggregate basis. Thus, the auditors accumulate the effects of all errors that are not corrected by the client to determine whether, in the aggregate, they result in a material misstatement of the financial statements.

Likely errors in the financial statements Many audit procedures, such as procedures that rely on audit sampling and analytical procedures, provide the auditors with an estimate of the error that is likely to exist in a financial statement account or balance. Recall that when audit sampling is used, this likely error is referred to as the *projected error,* as described in Chapter 8. By accumulating the likely errors and the known errors that have not been corrected, the auditors can obtain an estimate of the total error in the financial statements. Obviously, if the auditors estimate that there is a material error in the financial statements, they would not be in a position to issue an unqualified opinion on the financial statements.

Even if the total error in the financial statements is estimated to be somewhat less than material, the auditors still may decide not to issue an unqualified opinion. Recognizing that the actual error in the financial statements might be greater than their estimate, the auditors may conclude that the risk of material error in the financial statements is too high. If so, they will request management to adjust the financial statements for the known errors, or perform additional audit procedures to further reduce detection risk. The auditors should never issue an unqualified opinion on financial statements in which the risk of material misstatement is considered to be excessive.

Communication with the audit committee

SAS 60[2] and *SAS 61*[3] require the auditors to communicate certain matters to those who have responsibility for oversight of the financial reporting process, generally the client's audit committee. Recall from our discussion in Chapter 5 that the auditors must communicate to the audit committee any significant deficiencies in internal control, known as "reportable conditions." In addition, *SAS 61* requires the communication of certain other information on audits of SEC clients, as well as on audits of other entities with active audit committees or boards of directors. Auditing matters to be communicated to the audit committee include the auditors' responsibilities for the audit and other information included with the financial statements, and any significant audit adjustments proposed by the auditors.

Regarding accounting matters, the auditors are required to communicate information on the client's selection of significant accounting policies, as well as information on significant accounting estimates made by management. Finally, the auditors will discuss any disagreements with management or other difficulties encountered in performing the audit. If management contacted other auditors concerning an accounting or auditing matter, the auditors will present their viewpoint to the audit committee. The purpose of communicating these matters is to aid audit committees in their oversight role over senior management of the company.

---

[2] AICPA, *Statement on Auditing Standards 60,* "Communication of Internal Control Structure Related Matters Noted in an Audit" (New York, 1988).

[3] AICPA, *Statement on Auditing Standards 61,* "Communication with Audit Committees" (New York, 1988).

Responsibilities for other information in the financial report

Audited financial statements are often included in three types of reports: (1) annual reports to shareholders, (2) reports to the SEC, and (3) auditor-submitted financial reports. Included in these documents is a considerable amount of information in addition to the audited financial statements. In completing the audit engagement, the auditors also must fulfill certain responsibilities regarding this other information. The auditors' responsibility for specific information depends on the type of report and the nature of the information.

FASB and GASB-required supplementary information   As discussed in Chapter 13, the auditors have a responsibility to perform review procedures on supplementary information that is required by the FASB or the GASB. These procedures, as set forth in *SAS 27* (AU 553), include inquiries of management regarding the appropriate presentation of the supplementary information and comparisons of the information with audited and other data known to the auditors.[4] The AICPA has also issued statements that describe specific inquiries and comparisons to be performed regarding particular supplementary information. For example, *SAS 40* (AU 556), "Supplementary Mineral Reserve Information," establishes procedures to be applied to the mineral reserve information required by *FASB Statement No. 39.*

If required supplementary information is omitted or not appropriately presented, or the auditors are not able to complete their limited procedures, these facts should be described in an additional paragraph in the auditors' report. Since the information is not required for fair presentation of the financial statements, the inclusion of the additional paragraph does not constitute a qualification of the auditors' opinion.

Other information in client-prepared documents   Audit reports on the financial statements of large companies usually are included in an annual report to shareholders and in reports to the SEC. These annual reports contain information other than audited financial statements and required supplementary information, as, for example, a discussion of the company's plans and prospects for the future. In *SAS 8* (AU 550), "Other Information in Documents Containing Audited Financial Statements," the AICPA set forth guidelines for the independent auditors with respect to such information. The auditors should read the other information and consider whether it is materially inconsistent with information appearing in the audited financial statements or footnotes. If the other information is inconsistent and the auditors conclude that neither the audited financial

---

[4] AICPA, *Statement on Auditing Standards 27,* "Supplementary Information Required by the Financial Accounting Standards Board" (New York, 1979), AU 553.

statements nor the audit report requires revision, they should request the client to revise the other information. If the client refuses to do so, the auditors should consider such alternatives as (1) revising the audit report to describe the inconsistency, (2) withholding use of their audit report by the client, or (3) withdrawing from the engagement. The auditors should also be alert for, and discuss with the client, any other types of material misstatements included in the other information.

Information accompanying financial statements in auditor-submitted documents The auditors often type and reproduce financial reports for their clients, particularly for small companies with few shareholders. These documents may contain information in addition to the audited financial statements and the auditors' report. This *accompanying information* generally supplements or analyzes the basic financial statements, but is not necessary for the presentation of the statements in accordance with generally accepted accounting principles. When the auditors submit a document that contains audited financial statements and accompanying information to their clients or others, they should report on all the information. If the auditors have audited the information, they should express an opinion that it is fairly stated in all material respects in relation to the financial statements taken as a whole. Otherwise, the auditors should provide a disclaimer of opinion on the information.

**KEY TERMS
INTRODUCED OR
EMPHASIZED IN
CHAPTER 17**

Analytical procedures Evaluations of financial information made by a study of plausible relationships between financial and nonfinancial information.

Conservatism An accounting doctrine for asset valuation in which the lower of two alternative acceptable asset valuations is chosen.

Disclosure checklist A list of specific disclosures required by the FASB and the SEC that are used to evaluate the adequacy of the disclosures in a set of financial statements.

Extraordinary item An event or transaction that is distinguished by its unusual nature and by the infrequency of its occurrence.

Fully diluted earnings per share A pro forma presentation that reflects the dilution of earnings per share that would have occurred if all contingent issuances of common stock that individually would reduce earnings per share had taken place at the beginning of the period.

Likely errors in the financial statements Errors in the financial statements that are estimated by the auditors based on the results of audit procedures. For example, the projected error from an audit sample is an estimate of the likely error in the audit population.

Primary earnings per share A presentation of earnings per share based on outstanding common shares and those securities that are in substance equivalent to common shares and have a dilutive effect.

Public company A company whose securities are traded on an organized exchange or that is required to file financial statements with the SEC.

Segment A component of an entity whose activities represent a separate major line of business or class of customer.

17–1. Identify three revenue accounts that are verified during the audit of balance sheet accounts; also, identify the related balance sheet accounts.

17–2. Identify three expense accounts that are verified during the audit of balance sheet accounts; also, identify the related balance sheet accounts.

17–3. How are analytical procedures used in the verification of revenue?

17–4. Identify three items often misclassified as miscellaneous.

17–5. For which expense accounts should the auditors obtain or prepare analyses to be used in preparation of the client's income tax returns?

17–6. When you are first retained to examine the financial statements of Wabash Company, you inquire whether a budget is used to control costs and expenses. The controller, James Lowe, replies that he personally prepares such a budget each year, but that he regards it as a highly confidential document. He states that you may refer to it if necessary, but he wants you to make sure that no employee of the firm sees any of the budget data. Comment on this use of a budget.

17–7. What division of duties among independent departments is desirable to achieve maximum internal control over payrolls?

17–8. What specific procedures are suggested by the phrase "test of controls over payroll transactions"?

17–9. What safeguards should be employed when the inaccessibility of banking facilities makes it desirable to pay employees in cash?

17–10. You are asked by a client to outline the procedures you would recommend for disposing of unclaimed wages. What procedures do you recommend?

17–11. Why does the auditors' examination of the statement cash flows usually not involve a substantiation of the statement amounts?

17–12. What auditing procedure can you suggest for determining the reasonableness of selling, general, and administrative expenses?

17–13. Describe how the auditors use analytical procedures in the examination of selling, general, and administrative expenses.

17–14. What standards did the FASB enact for disclosures of operating details on the income statements of diversified companies?

17–15. How should the independent auditors advise the client to present discontinued operations in the income statement?

17–16. List the audit procedures that must be completed near the end of audit field work.

17–17. Describe a disclosure checklist. What is its purpose?

17–18. During an initial audit, you observe that the client is not complying with federal regulations concerning wages and hours. Would you (*a*) report the violation to regulatory authorities, (*b*) discuss the matter with the client, (*c*) ignore the matter completely, (*d*) withdraw from the engagement, or (*e*) follow some other course of action? Explain.

17–19. Describe the manner in which the auditors evaluate their audit findings.

17–20. What is the independent auditors' obligation with respect to information in client-prepared annual reports to shareholders, other than the audited financial statements?

17–21. When auditors submit documents to their clients that contain audited financial statements, what are their responsibilities concerning information that accompanies the financial statements?

17–22. In a properly planned examination of financial statements, the auditors coordinate their reviews of specific balance sheet and income statement accounts.

Required:
Why should the auditors coordinate their examinations of balance sheet accounts and income statement accounts? Discuss and illustrate by examples. (AICPA, adapted)

17–23. Your new audit client, Coin-O-Mat Company, leases coin-operated laundry equipment to military bases. Usage of the equipment requires the insertion of coins into metered receptacles, which record expired time of equipment operation. How can you determine whether all revenue earned by Coin-O-Mat Company has been recorded in the accounting records?

17–24. In your first examination of the financial statements of Willman Company, you discover that the company has included in the Miscellaneous Revenue account a $10,000 commission from Bradley Realtors, Inc. Your investigation discloses that Bradley negotiated Willman's purchase for $500,000 of a tract of land from Payne Company, and that Payne had paid Bradley's commission of $50,000 on the sale.

Required:
Would you take exception to Willman Company's accounting for the commission received from Bradley Realtors, Inc.? Explain.

17–25. During your regular audit of Payton Company, you discover that the company signed a 10-year lease on a building at the beginning of the company's fiscal year. The lease, which is an operating lease, requires monthly rental payments of $1,000 per month for the last nine years of the lease only. Nancy James, controller of Payton Company, explains that the lessor waived the first year's rent because the building had remained vacant for a long period. James states that, in her view, Payton Company had incurred no rent expense for the fiscal year your audit covers. Do you agree? Explain.

17–26. The Wickerson Corporation is a public company with diversified operations, including several foreign subsidiaries. The management of the company has prepared Wickerson's financial statements, including disclosure of the business segment information required by *FASB Statement No. 14*.

Required:
List the procedures that the auditors should perform to audit the business segment information.

17–27. Bowden Company owed property taxes of $5,972. Through error, Morton Bryant, who served the company as office manager, cashier, and accountant, paid the tax bill twice. Realizing his error after having mailed the second check, he wrote to the county officials requesting a refund.

When the refund was received some weeks later, Bryant substituted the check from the city for cash receipts and abstracted $5,972 in currency.

Would this error and theft probably be discovered in an audit by independent public accountants? Indicate what auditing procedure, if any, would disclose the facts.

17–28. Barton Company is a highly diversified public company with segments that manufacture and sell antibiotics, dairy products, hospital supplies, toiletries, and chemicals. In what form should the income statement of Barton Company be prepared?

17–29. Select the best answer for each of the following, and explain fully the reason for your selection.

a. As a result of analytical procedures, the independent auditors determine that the gross profit percentage has declined from 30 percent in the preceding year to 20 percent in the current year. The auditors should—
   (1) Express an opinion that is qualified due to the inability of the client company to continue as a going concern.
   (2) Evaluate management's performance in causing this decline.
   (3) Require footnote disclosure.
   (4) Consider the possibility of an error in the financial statements.

b. Which of the following is the *best* way for the auditors to determine that every name on a company's payroll is that of a bona fide employee presently on the job?
   (1) Examine personnel records for accuracy and completeness.
   (2) Examine employees' names listed on payroll tax returns for agreement with payroll accounting records.
   (3) Make a surprise observation of the company's regular distribution of paychecks.
   (4) Visit the working areas and confirm with employees their badge or identification numbers.

c. Which of the following *best* describes the independent auditors' approach to obtaining satisfaction concerning depreciation expense in the income statement?
   (1) Verify the mathematical accuracy of the amounts charged to income as a result of depreciation expense.
   (2) Determine the method for computing depreciation expense, and ascertain that it is in accordance with generally accepted accounting principles.
   (3) Reconcile the amount of depreciation expense to those amounts credited to accumulated depreciation accounts.
   (4) Establish the basis for depreciable assets and verify the depreciation expense.

d. Proper internal control over the cash payroll function would mandate which of the following?
   (1) The payroll clerk should fill the envelopes with cash and a computation of the net wages.
   (2) Unclaimed pay envelopes should be retained by the paymaster.
   (3) Each employee should be asked to sign a receipt.
   (4) A separate checking account for payroll should be maintained.

    e. The auditor's performance of analytical procedures will be facilitated if the client—
        (1) Uses a standard cost system that produces variance reports.
        (2) Segregates obsolete inventory before the physical inventory count.
        (3) Corrects material weaknesses in internal control before the beginning of the audit.
        (4) Reduces inventory balances to the lower of cost or market.
    f. An auditor accepted an engagement to audit the 19X8 financial statements of EFG Corporation and began the field work on September 30, 19X8. EFG gave the auditor the 19X8 financial statements on January 17, 19X9. The auditor completed the field work on February 10, 19X9, and delivered the report on February 16, 19X9. The client's representations letter normally would be dated—
        (1) December 31, 19X8.
        (2) January 17, 19X9.
        (3) February 10, 19X9.
        (4) February 16, 19X9.   (AICPA, adapted)

GROUP III: PROBLEMS

17–30. The following are typical questions that might appear on an internal control questionnaire for payroll procedures:
    1. Is there adequate separation of duties between employees who maintain personnel records and employees who approve payroll disbursements?
    2. Is there adequate separation of duties between personnel who maintain timekeeping or attendance records for employees and employees who distribute payroll checks?

Required:
    a. Describe the purpose of each of the above internal control procedures.
    b. Describe the manner in which each of the above procedures might be tested.
    c. Assuming that the operating effectiveness of each of the above procedures is found to be inadequate, describe how the auditors might alter their substantive tests to compensate for the internal control weakness.

17–31. In connection with an examination of the financial statements of Olympia Company, the auditors are reviewing procedures for accumulating direct labor-hours. They learn that all production is by job order and that all employees are paid hourly wages, with time and a half for overtime hours.

Olympia's direct labor-hour input process for payroll and job-cost determination is summarized in the flowchart shown on page 637. Steps A and C are performed in timekeeping, step B in the factory operating departments, step D in payroll audit and control, step E in data preparation (keypunch), and step F in computer operations.

Required:
For each input processing step A through F—
    a. List the possible errors or discrepancies that may occur.

b. Cite the corresponding control procedure that should be in effect for each error or discrepancy.

Note: Your discussion of Olympia's procedures should be limited to the input for direct labor-hours, as shown in steps A through F in the flow-chart. Do not discuss personnel procedures for hiring, promotion, termination, and pay-rate authorization. In step F do not discuss equipment, computer program, and general computer operational controls.

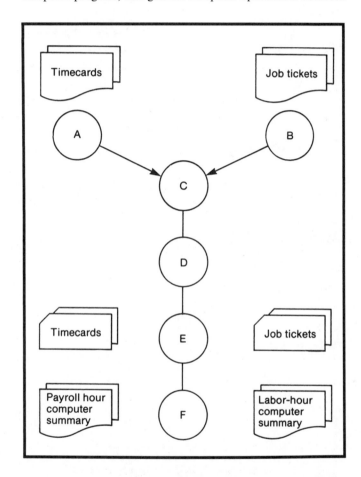

Organize your answer for each input-processing step as follows:

Step	Possible errors or discrepancies	Control procedures
A		

(AICPA, adapted)

17–32. Rita King, your staff assistant on the April 30, 19X2, audit of Maxwell Company, was transferred to another assignment before she could prepare a proposed adjusting journal entry for Maxwell's Miscellaneous

Revenue account, which she had analyzed per the working paper below. You have reviewed the working paper and are satisfied with King's procedures. You are convinced that all the Miscellaneous Revenue items should be transferred to other accounts. Maxwell Company's state of incorporation has an Unclaimed Properties Law.

	Maxwell Company			
Acct. No. 430	Miscellaneous Revenue			Q-2
	Year Ended April 30, 19X2			
			C. M. May 19, X2	
Date	Description		Reference	Amount
May 8, X1 thru April 7, X2	Proceeds of sale of scrap from manufacturing process (total of 12 monthly sales)		Various CR	5843 ✓
July 18, X1	Write-off of old outstanding checks; nos. 118 - $500; 214 - $400; 407 - $200		GJ 7-4	1100 ✓
Sept. 22, X1	Recovery of previously written-off account receivable from Wilson Company.		CR 9-1	4381 ✓
Feb. 6, X2	Cash proceeds from sale of machine. Cost of $10,000 and accumulated depreciation of $8,000 as of Feb. 6, X2 not removed from accounts.		CR 2-1	3500 ✓
April 28, X2	Refund of premium overcharge on fire insurance policy no. 1856, for period April 1, X2 - Mar. 31, X3		CR 4-1	600 ✓
April 30, X2	Balance per ledger			15424
	✓ - Traced to cash receipts journal or general journal; vouched to appropriate supporting documents.			
			R. A. K. May 18, X2	

Required:

Draft a proposed adjusting journal entry at April 30, 19X2, for Maxwell Company's Miscellaneous Revenue account.

17–33. Rowe Manufacturing Company has about 50 production employees and uses the following payroll procedures.

The factory supervisor interviews applicants and on the basis of the interview either hires or rejects the applicants. After being employed, the applicant prepares a W-4 form (Employee's Withholding Exemption Certificate) and gives it to the supervisor. The supervisor writes the hourly rate of pay for the new employee in the corner of the W-4 form and then gives the form to a payroll clerk as notice that the applicant has been employed. The supervisor verbally advises the payroll department of pay rate adjustments.

A supply of blank timecards is kept in a box near the entrance to the factory. Each employee takes a timecard on Monday morning, signs it, and notes in pencil on the timecard the daily arrival and departure times. At the end of the week, the employees drop the timecards in a box near the door to the factory.

The completed timecards are taken from the box on Monday morning by a payroll clerk. Two payroll clerks divide the cards alphabetically between them, one taking the A to L section of the payroll, and the other taking the M to Z section. Each clerk is fully responsible for one section of the payroll. The payroll clerks compute the gross pay, deductions, and net pay; post the details to the employees' earnings records; and prepare and number the payroll checks. Employees are automatically removed from the payroll when they fail to turn in a timecard.

The payroll checks are manually signed by the chief accountant and given to the supervisor, who distributes the checks to the employees in the factory and arranges for the delivery of the checks to the employees who are absent. The payroll bank account is reconciled by the chief accountant, who also prepares the various quarterly and annual payroll tax reports.

Required:
List your suggestions for improving Rowe Manufacturing Company's system of internal control for factory hiring practices *and* payroll procedures. (AICPA, adapted)

17–34. Your client is a shopping center with 30 store tenants. All leases with the store tenants provide for a fixed rent plus a percentage of sales, net of sales taxes, in excess of a fixed dollar amount computed on an annual basis. Each lease also provides that the lessor may engage CPAs to audit all records of the tenant for assurance that sales are being properly reported to the lessor.

You have been requested by your client to audit the records of Traders Restaurant to determine that the sales totaling $390,000 for the year ended December 31, 198X, have been properly reported to the lessor. The restaurant and the shopping center entered into a five-year lease on January 1, 198X. Traders Restaurant offers only table service; no liquor is served. During meal times there are four or five waitresses in attendance who prepare handwritten prenumbered restaurant checks for the customers. Payment is made at a cash register, operated by the proprietor, as the customer leaves. All sales are for cash. The proprietor also is the accountant. Complete files are kept of restaurant checks and cash register tapes. A daily sales journal and general ledger are also maintained.

Required:
List the auditing procedures that you would employ to verify the total annual sales of Traders Restaurant.   (AICPA, adapted)

17–35. City Loan Company has 100 branch loan offices. Each office has a manager and four or five employees who are hired by the manager. Branch managers prepare the weekly payroll, including their own salaries, and pay employees from cash on hand. The employees sign the payroll sheet signifying receipt of their salary. Hours worked by hourly personnel are inserted in the payroll sheet from time reports prepared by the employees and approved by the manager.

The weekly payroll sheets are sent to the home office, along with other accounting statements and reports. The home office compiles employee earnings records and prepares all federal and state payroll tax returns from the weekly payroll sheets.

Salaries are established by home office job-evaluation schedules. Salary adjustments, promotions, and transfers of full-time employees are approved by a home office salary committee based upon the recommendations of branch managers and area supervisors. Branch managers advise the salary committee of new full-time employees and terminations. Part-time and temporary employees are hired without referral to the salary committee.

Required:
a.   How might funds for payroll be diverted in the above system?
b.   Prepare a payroll internal audit program to be used in the home office to audit the branch office payrolls of City Loan Company.

                                                                                        (AICPA, adapted)

Auditors' reports

Chapter 18 study objectives

After studying this chapter, you should be able to:

— Describe the auditors' standard audit report.

— Explain the circumstances that result in inclusion of additional explanatory language to an unqualified audit report.

— Discuss how materiality affects the consideration of the type of audit report to be issued.

— Identify the circumstances that may result in qualified opinions, adverse opinions, and disclaimers of opinion.

Expressing an independent and expert opinion on the fairness of financial statements is the most important and valuable service rendered by the public accounting profession. The fourth standard of reporting states:

> The [auditor's] report shall either contain an **expression of opinion** regarding the financial statements, taken as a whole, or an assertion to the effect that an opinion cannot be expressed. When an overall opinion cannot be expressed, the reasons therefore should be stated. In all cases where an auditor's name is associated with financial statements, the report should contain a clear-cut indication of the **character of the auditor's examination,** if any, and the **degree of responsibility he is taking.** [Emphasis added.]

In Chapter 1, we saw that the auditors' standard report meets this standard by (*a*) stating that the auditors' examination was performed in conformity with generally accepted auditing standards and (*b*) expressing an opinion that the client's financial statements are presented fairly in conformity with generally accepted accounting principles. However, if there are deficiencies in the client's financial statements or limitations in the auditors' examination, or if there are other unusual conditions about which the readers of the financial statements should be informed, auditors *cannot* issue the standard report. Instead, they must carefully modify their report to make these problems or conditions known to users of the audited financial statements.

In this chapter, we shall discuss the different types of reports that auditors may issue in order to indicate clearly the character of their examination and the degree of responsibility they are taking for the client's financial statements.

Financial statements

The reporting phase of an auditing engagement begins when the independent auditors have completed their field work and their proposed adjustments have been accepted and recorded by the client. Before writing their report, the auditors must review the client-prepared financial statements for form and content, or draft the financial statements on behalf of the client.

The financial statements on which the independent auditors customarily report are the balance sheet, the income statement, the statement of retained earnings, and the statement of cash flows. Often, the statement of retained earnings is combined with the income statement. In some cases, the retained earnings statement may be expanded to a statement of stockholders' equity. Financial statements generally are presented in comparative form for the current year and the preceding year and are accompanied by explanatory footnotes. The financial statements for a parent corporation usually are consolidated with those of the subsidiaries.

Financial statement disclosures

The purpose of notes to financial statements is to achieve adequate disclosure when information in the financial statements proper is insufficient to attain this objective. Although the notes, like the financial statements themselves, are representations of the client, the independent auditors generally assist in drafting the notes. The writing of notes to financial statements is a challenging task because complex issues must be summarized in a clear and concise manner. Adequate disclosure in the footnotes to the financial statements is necessary for the auditors to issue an unqualified opinion on the financial statements.

In addition to footnote disclosures, many clients are required by the FASB, the GASB, or the SEC to present *supplementary information.* Such information is not a required part of the basic financial statements, but is presented in unaudited supplementary schedules accompanying the financial statements.

Recent pronouncements by the Financial Accounting Standards Board and the Securities and Exchange Commission have required extensive additions to disclosures in financial statements. Listed below are a few of the many items for which supplementary disclosures are now mandatory. For each of the sample items listed, reference is made to the FASB *Statement of Financial Accounting Standards (SFAS)*, or to the AICPA *Accounting Principles Board Opinion (APBO)*, or to the SEC *Accounting Series Release (ASR)*, which mandates the disclosure.

1. Footnote disclosure of significant accounting policies, such as principles of consolidation, and the basis of valuation and amortization of assets (*APBO 22*).
2. Footnote disclosure of accounting changes (*APBO 20*).
3. Footnote disclosure of loss contingencies (*SFAS 5*).
4. Supplementary disclosure of selected interim financial data (*ASR 177,* now incorporated in Financial Reporting Release No. 1).

In drafting financial reporting disclosures, the auditors should keep in mind that disclosures are meant to supplement the information in the financial statements and not to *correct* improper financial statement presentation. Thus, a footnote or supplementary schedule, no matter how skillfully drafted, does not compensate for the erroneous presentation of an item in the financial statements.

The auditors' standard report

For convenient reference, the auditors' standard unqualified report, which was introduced and discussed in Chapter 1, is presented again:

Independent Auditors' Report

To the Board of Directors and Stockholders
XYZ Company:

We have audited the accompanying balance sheet of XYZ Company as of December 31, 19—, and the related statements of income, retained

(Continued)

earnings, and cash flows for the year then ended. These financial statements are the responsibility of the Company's management. Our responsibility is to express an opinion on these financial statements based on our audit.

We conducted our audit in accordance with generally accepted auditing standards. Those standards require that we plan and perform the audit to obtain reasonable assurance about whether the financial statements are free of material misstatement. An audit includes examining, on a test basis, evidence supporting the amounts and disclosures in the financial statements. An audit also includes assessing the accounting principles used and significant estimates made by management, as well as evaluating the overall financial statement presentation. We believe that our audit provides a reasonable basis for our opinion.

In our opinion, the financial statements referred to above present fairly, in all material respects, the financial position of XYZ Company as of December 31, 19—, and the results of its operations and its cash flows for the year then ended in conformity with generally accepted accounting principles.

Los Angeles, Calif.

Blue, Gray + Company

Certified Public Accountants
February 26, 19XX

Before continuing, let us mention a few details about this report. Recall that it was adopted in 1988 by the Auditing Standards Board. Unlike standard reports of the past, the report has a title, "Independent Auditors' Report," and has three, rather than two, paragraphs. The first paragraph is referred to as the *introductory paragraph*. It clearly indicates that (1) the financial statements have been audited, (2) the financial statements are the responsibility of management, and (3) the auditors' responsibility is to express an opinion on them. The second paragraph, which describes the nature of an audit, is called the *scope paragraph*. The final paragraph, the *opinion paragraph,* presents the auditors' opinion on whether the financial statements are in conformity with generally accepted accounting principles.

Notice that the report is signed with the name of the CPA *firm,* not the name of an individual partner in the firm. This signature stresses that it is the *firm,* not an individual, that takes responsibility for the auditors' report. If the CPA performing the audit is an individual practitioner, the report will be signed with the CPA's personal signature. In addition, a sole practitioner should use the word *I* instead of *we* in the auditors' report.

Also notice the date under the signature. This date is normally the *last day of field work*—that is, the date upon which the auditors conclude their investigative procedures. Recall from Chapter 7 that this date is quite significant in determining the auditors' responsibility for disclosure of information discovered after the balance sheet date.

The standard unqualified auditors' report may be issued only when the following conditions have been met:

1. The financial statements are presented in conformity with **generally accepted accounting principles,** including adequate disclosure, applied on a basis consistent with that of the preceding period.
2. The auditors' examination was performed in accordance with generally accepted auditing standards, and there were no significant **scope limitations** preventing them from gathering the evidence necessary to support their opinion.
3. The effects of any existing substantial **uncertainties** which could have a material impact on the financial statements can be reasonably estimated.

When considered material, the existence of any of these conditions results in a situation in which modification of the audit report is required. Additionally, when certain other conditions exist, the auditors may voluntarily choose to express an **unqualified opinion,** but still modify the report.

Modification of the report may involve modifying the opinion or the description of the scope of the audit, and/or adding other explanatory language to the report. The nature of the explanatory language, if any, depends upon the circumstances and the type of opinion being expressed.

EXPRESSION OF AN OPINION

The auditors' alternatives when expressing an opinion on financial statements may be summarized as follows:

1. **An unqualified opinion.** An unqualified opinion may be either the standard form (presented earlier) or a modified form to reflect certain circumstances pertaining to the audit. Examples of such circumstances are those in which other auditors have performed a portion of the audit, or when major uncertainties exist with respect to the company being audited.
2. **A qualified opinion.** A qualified opinion is basically a positive opinion. It asserts that the financial statements, viewed as a whole, are not misleading. Qualified reports are issued when the financial statements depart materially from generally accepted accounting principles, or limitations are placed on the scope of the auditors' procedures. The problems, while material, **must not overshadow the overall fairness of the statements.**
3. **An adverse opinion.** This is a **negative opinion,** asserting that the financial statements **are not** a fair presentation. Auditors will issue an adverse opinion when the deficiencies in the financial statements are **so significant** that the financial statements taken as a whole are mis-

leading. All significant reasons for the issuance of an adverse opinion should be set forth in explanatory paragraphs.

4. **A disclaimer of opinion.** A disclaimer of opinion means that due to significant scope restrictions (or to major uncertainties), the auditors *were unable to form an opinion* on the fairness of the financial statements. A disclaimer is neither a positive nor a negative opinion—it simply means that the auditors do not have an adequate basis for expressing an opinion.

Materiality

Auditors must qualify their report whenever there are *material* deficiencies in the client's financial statements. However, they may issue an unqualified report if the only deficiencies are *immaterial.* The term *material* may be defined as "sufficiently important to influence decisions made by reasonable users of financial statements."

For example, many companies follow a policy of charging all purchases of office supplies directly to expense accounts and making no effort to record as an asset the small quantities of office supplies remaining on hand at year-end. In most instances, this "deficiency" would not cause any material distortion in the financial statements. Auditors would not qualify their report over such an insignificant issue; in fact, they probably would not even propose an adjusting entry to correct this "error." The concept of materiality also allows auditors to "pass over" such conceptual accounting "errors" as:

1. Charging low-cost items such as small tools or desk-top calculators directly to expense accounts.
2. Rounding financial statement amounts. For small clients, the valuation of items listed in the financial statements may be rounded to the nearest hundred or nearest thousand dollars. Amounts shown in the financial statements of large companies usually are rounded to the nearest million.
3. The policy of not accruing liabilities for payroll taxes when the period ends between payroll dates. Many companies follow this policy in order to keep their accounting records consistent with the deductibility of payroll taxes for income tax purposes.

In addition, auditors should design their audit procedures so as to not waste time searching for immaterial errors that cannot affect the auditors' report. For example, some auditors do not investigate the client's accounting for prepaid insurance, on the premise that *any* error in this account *cannot be material* in relation to the financial statements.

The auditors need to carefully consider whether the results of any client estimates such as the above are likely to depart materially from generally accepted accounting principles. Such estimates are not acceptable simply because the client's management says the amounts involved are immaterial or because the amounts involved were considered immaterial in the past. The auditors need to determine that all of management's estimates are reasonable and that they are not likely to depart materially from amounts arrived at by following generally accepted accounting principles.

Illustrative case

For many years a company had maintained its small tools as a set amount in a "tools inventory" asset account. Tools were expensed as purchased based on the assumption that annual purchases approximated annual "depreciation." Consistent with this, no inventory of tools was taken annually.

The auditors had agreed with the above accounting approach for several years. However, when the company began to grow, the client agreed with the auditors' request for a year-end count of the inventory of tools on hand. The asset account was subsequently written up approximately 80 percent based on the count.

"Very material" distortions in financial statements Notice that auditors are required to issue an adverse opinion when the deficiencies in financial statements are "*so significant* that a qualified opinion would be inappropriate." A qualified opinion is considered *insufficient* when the deficiencies in financial statements are so material that they *overshadow the fairness of the financial statements viewed as a whole*. For example, misstatements that make an insolvent business appear to be solvent would be considered sufficiently material as to overshadow the fairness of the statements viewed as a whole.

The distinction between problems that are material but do not overshadow the fairness of the statements and those problems that do overshadow the fairness of the statements is again a matter of professional judgment. In our following discussions, it will not be practicable to present sufficient detail for readers to make these judgments. Therefore, we will use the term *material* to describe problems sufficient to require qualification of the auditors' report, but which do not overshadow the fairness of the statements. Problems overshadowing the fairness of the statements will be described as *"very material"* or as causing the statements to be *"substantially misleading."*

The unqualified report

Auditors express an unqualified opinion on the client's financial statements when they have no material exceptions as to the fairness of the application of accounting principles, and there have been no unresolved restrictions on the scope of their engagement. The unqualified opinion is, of course, the most desirable report from the client's point of view. The client usually will make any necessary adjustments to the statements to enable the auditors to issue this type of opinion. The wording of an unqualified opinion usually parallels that of the auditors' standard report illustrated on pages 644–45.

Explanatory language added to the unqualified opinion

Under certain circumstances auditors add explanatory language to the standard report, even when issuing an unqualified opinion. Adding the additional language *is not regarded as a qualification* because it does *not lessen* the auditors' reporting responsibility for the financial statements. Rather, the language merely *draws attention* to a significant situation. Auditors add explanatory language to an unqualified opinion to indicate a division of responsibility with another CPA firm, to refer to an uncertainty that could have a material impact on the financial statements, to indicate an inconsistency in the application of accounting principles, to emphasize a matter, and to justify a departure from officially recognized accounting principles. The auditors may also add an explanatory paragraph to their report to refer to problems regarding supplementary or other information included with the audited financial statements; these circumstances were discussed in Chapter 17.

Reliance upon other auditors   On occasion it may be necessary for the principal auditors of a company to rely upon another CPA firm to perform a portion of the audit work. The most common situation in which CPAs rely upon the work of other auditors is in the audit of consolidated entities. If certain subsidiaries have been audited by other CPA firms, the auditors of the parent company may decide to rely upon the work of these other CPAs rather than conduct another examination of the subsidiaries. In other situations, the auditors of a multibranch client may even retain another CPA firm to perform audit procedures at a specific branch location.

When more than one CPA firm participates in an engagement, the auditors' report is issued by the *principal auditors*—that is, by the CPA firm that did the majority of the audit work. The principal auditors have three basic alternatives in wording their report:

1. Make no reference to the other auditors.   If the principal auditors *make no reference* in their report to the portions of the engagement performed by other CPAs, the principal auditors *assume full responsibility* for the other auditors' work. This approach is usually followed when the other CPA firm is well known, or when the principal auditors hired the other auditors. When no reference is made, the principal auditors should consider visiting the other auditors, reviewing the other auditors' audit programs and working papers, or performing additional audit procedures. If the principal auditors elect to make no reference, they may issue the standard auditors' report with no additional wording.

2. Make reference to the other auditors. Making reference to the work done by other auditors *divides* the responsibility for the engagement *among the participating CPA firms.* This type of report is called a *shared responsibility opinion,* even though it is signed only by the principal auditors. A shared responsibility opinion is usually issued when the other auditors were engaged by the client, rather than by the principal auditors.

A shared responsibility opinion should indicate the portion of the engagement performed by the other auditors. A typical shared responsibility opinion is illustrated below, with emphasis on the special wording added to the standard report:

Independent Auditors' Report

To the Board of Directors and Stockholders
XYZ Company:

We have audited the consolidated balance sheet of XYZ Company as of December 31, 19__, and the related statements of income, retained earnings, and cash flows for the year then ended. These financial statements are the responsibility of the Company's management. Our responsibility is to express an opinion on these financial statements based on our audit. *We did not audit the financial statements of Sub Company, a wholly owned subsidiary, which statements reflect total assets of $____ as of December 31, 19__ and total revenues of $____ for the year then ended. These statements were audited by other auditors whose report has been furnished to us and our opinion, insofar as it relates to the amounts included for Sub Company, is based solely on the report of the other auditors.*

We conducted our audit in accordance with generally accepted auditing standards. Those standards require that we plan and perform the audit to obtain reasonable assurance about whether the financial statements are free of material misstatement. An audit includes examining, on a test basis, evidence supporting the amounts and disclosures in the financial statements. An audit also includes assessing the accounting principles used and significant estimates made by management, as well as evaluating the overall financial statement presentation. We believe that our audit *and the report of other auditors* provide a reasonable basis for our opinion.

In our opinion, *based on our audit and the report of other auditors,* the consolidated financial statements referred to above present fairly, in all material respects, the financial position of XYZ Company as of December 31, 19__, and the results of its operations and its cash flows for the

(Continued)

---

year then ended in conformity with generally accepted accounting principles.

Los Angeles, Calif.   *Blue, Gray + Company*

Certified Public Accountants
February 26, 19XX

The additional wording found in a shared responsibility opinion is not a
qualification, as it does not lessen the auditors' collective responsibility
for the fairness of the statements. Rather, the report merely divides this
responsibility between two or more CPA firms.

What if the other auditors qualify their report on a particular subsidiary? The principal auditors **do not necessarily have to qualify their shared
responsibility report.** The shared responsibility report focuses upon the
consolidated entity, which may involve a very different level of materiality than does the subsidiary examined by the other auditors.

Whether or not the principal auditors plan to make reference to the
work of the other auditor, they should make inquiries concerning the
other auditors' **professional reputation and independence.** Inquiries concerning the other auditors' reputation might be made of the AICPA, other
practitioners, or bankers. A letter should also be obtained from the other
auditors stating that they are aware of the use of their report and that they
meet the AICPA's standards of independence.

3. Qualify their report.   Principal auditors are never *forced* to rely on
the work of other auditors. Instead, they may insist upon *personally* auditing any aspect of the client's operations. If the client refuses to permit
them to do so, the auditors may regard this action as a *scope limitation*
and, depending upon materiality, issue a qualified report or a disclaimer of
opinion. For practical purposes, qualified opinions are seldom issued for
this reason. Satisfactory arrangements as to who will audit the various
aspects of a client's business normally will be worked out before the audit
begins.

Uncertainties   If substantial uncertainty exists as to the outcome of an
important contingency affecting the client's financial statements, auditors
should add an explanatory paragraph to their audit report to indicate the
existence of the uncertainty. The term uncertainty does not include contingencies whose outcome is merely difficult to estimate. In accordance
with FASB *Statement No. 5,* contingencies that are probable and can be
reasonably estimated should be accrued in the financial statements. Failure to do so would be a departure from generally accepted accounting
principles that lead to a qualified or an adverse opinion by the auditors. It
is when the contingency is not *susceptible of reasonable estimation* that

the auditors should consider adding an explanatory paragraph to their unqualified opinion based on the materiality of the contingency and the probability of unfavorable outcome. When a material loss is probable, but management is unable to estimate it, the auditors should add an explanatory paragraph to their unqualified report. When the loss is reasonably possible, the auditors *should consider* the need for an explanatory paragraph; as the magnitude of the amount of the loss and the likelihood of its occurrence increase, the auditors are more likely to add such a paragraph. No explanatory paragraph is required for a loss with a remote likelihood of occurrence.

Illustrative case

The auditors of a company that produced asbestos-containing products modified their report for the uncertainty pertaining to claims arising due to products sold 10 (and more) years earlier. The uncertainty pertained to (1) the future outcome of legal proceedings currently filed and expected to be filed in the future against the company in numerous courts, and (2) uncertainty relating to the results of the company's suits against its insurers who have disputed liability under various company insurance policies. The company's financial statements suggested that many years may pass before the problems are finally resolved and their impact, "if any," on the company's financial position, can be determined.

The standard report modified for uncertainty includes a fourth paragraph following the opinion paragraph that describes the uncertainty. The following is an example of such a paragraph:

As discussed in Note X to the financial statements, the Company is currently a defendant in a number of legal proceedings and may in the future be a defendant in additional, related proceedings expected to be filed alleging damages due to products sold in the past. The Company has filed a legal action against its insurers who have disputed liability under various company insurance policies. The ultimate outcome of the current and expected future lawsuits cannot presently be determined. Accordingly, no provision for any liability that may result upon adjudication has been made in the accompanying financial statements.

Historically, uncertainties have resulted in "subject to" qualified reports. Currently, the reports contain explanatory paragraphs, but they are unqualified.

Question about a company's continued existence   A special type of significant uncertainty concerns the ability of a client company to continue as a going concern. Under generally accepted accounting principles, both assets and liabilities are recorded and classified on the assumption that the company will continue to operate. Assets, for example, may be presented at amounts that are significantly greater than their liquidation values.

The auditors must evaluate whether there is substantial doubt about the entity's ability to continue as a going concern. Conditions that may challenge the applicability of the going-concern assumption include negative cash flows from operations, defaults on loan agreements, adverse financial ratios, work stoppages, and legal proceedings. When such conditions are identified, the auditors should gather clarifying information about the conditions and events and consider whether there appears to be substantial doubt about the entity's ability to continue as a going concern. The auditors also should consider whether management's plans for dealing with the conditions and events are likely to negate the problem. If, after evaluating management's plans a substantial doubt still exists, the auditors should modify their report for uncertainty, with an additional last paragraph such as the following:

> The accompanying financial statements have been prepared assuming that Company XYZ will continue as a going concern. As discussed in Note X to the financial statements, Company XYZ has suffered recurring losses from operations and has a net capital deficiency that raises substantial doubt about the entity's ability to continue as a going concern. Management's plans in regard to these matters are also described in Note X. The financial statements do not include any adjustments that might result from the outcome of this uncertainty.

GAAP not consistently applied   If a client company makes a change in accounting principle (including a change in the reporting entity), the nature of, justification for, and effect of the change are reported in a note to the financial statements for the period in which the change was made. Any such change having a material effect upon the financial statements will also require modification of the auditors' report, even though the auditors are in full agreement with the change. Changes in accounting estimates need not be reported in the auditors' report.

Changes from one generally accepted accounting principle to another generally accepted accounting principle do not result in qualification of the auditors' report. The report is merely modified to highlight the lack of consistent application of acceptable accounting principles. Of course, if the client elects to change to an unacceptable accounting principle, the auditors should qualify their report for lack of conformity with generally accepted accounting principles, or issue an adverse opinion. A report modified for a change to an acceptable accounting principle includes a fourth paragraph following the opinion paragraph, such as the one illustrated below:

> As discussed in Note 2 to the financial statements, XYZ Company changed its method of computing depreciation in 19X2.

In the preceding example, Note 2 to the financial statements would describe the nature and justification for the change in method of computing depreciation.

Emphasis of a matter   Auditors also may issue an unqualified opinion that departs from the wording of the standard report in order to emphasize some element within the client's financial statements. For example, the auditors may add an additional paragraph to their unqualified opinion calling attention to a significant related party transaction described in a note to the financial statements. The paragraph may either precede or follow the opinion paragraph.

Justified departures from officially recognized accounting principles   FASB *Statements,* GASB *Statements,* and APB *Opinions* have the status of officially recognized accounting principles. On rare occasions, however, auditors may consider it appropriate to depart from these official principles in order to achieve the more important objective of a fair presentation. In such cases, the CPAs may still issue an unqualified report, but they must disclose the departure in an explanatory paragraph, either before or after the opinion paragraph. Such reports are sometimes called "203 reports," because Rule 203 of the AICPA *Code of Professional* officially recognized standards. The *Code of Professional Conduct* was discussed in Chapter 2.

Qualified opinions

A qualified opinion restricts the auditors' responsibility for fair presentation in some areas of the financial statements. The opinion states that *except for* the effects of some deficiency in the financial statements, or some limitation in the scope of the auditors' examination, *the financial statements are presented fairly.* The auditors' reports for all qualified opinions should have a *separate explanatory paragraph* before the opinion paragraph disclosing the reasons for the qualification. The opinion paragraph of a qualified report includes the appropriate qualifying language and a reference to the explanatory paragraph.

The materiality of the exception governs the use of the qualified opinion. The exception must be sufficiently significant to warrant mentioning in the auditors' report, but it must not be so significant as to necessitate a disclaimer of opinion or an adverse opinion. Consequently, the propriety of a qualified opinion in the event of a significant exception is a matter for careful professional judgment by the auditors.

Qualifications as to accounting principles The auditors sometimes must qualify their opinion because they do not agree with the accounting principles used in preparing the statements. Usually when the auditors' objections are carefully examined, the client will agree to change the statements in an acceptable manner. If the client does not agree to make the suggested changes, the auditors will be forced to qualify their opinion (or if the exception is sufficiently material, to issue an adverse opinion). When the report is modified, the introductory and scope paragraphs of the standard report are unaffected. The modification involves adding an explanatory paragraph following the scope paragraph and qualifying the opinion paragraph. The qualifying language used in the report always begins with the term *except for*. Following is an example of the explanatory and opinion paragraphs of an audit report qualified as to accounting principles.

The Company has excluded from property and debt in the accompanying balance sheet certain lease obligations that, in our opinion, should be capitalized in order to conform with generally accepted accounting principles. If these lease obligations were capitalized, property would be increased by $____, long-term debt by $____, and retained earnings by $____ as of December 31, 198X, and net income and earnings per share would be increased (decreased) by $____ and $____, respectively, for the year then ended.

In our opinion, *except for the effects of not capitalizing lease obligations, as discussed in the preceding paragraph,* the financial statements referred to above present fairly, in all material respects, the financial position of XYZ Company as of December 31, 19XX, and the results of its operations and its cash flows for the year then ended in conformity with generally accepted accounting principles.

The third standard of reporting addresses a particular type of departure from generally accepted accounting principles, inadequate disclosures, and states that:

Informative disclosures in the financial statements are to be regarded as reasonably adequate unless otherwise stated in the [auditors'] report.

Thus, auditors may need to issue a qualified or an adverse opinion if they consider the disclosure in the client's financial statements to be inadequate.

SAS 32 (AU 431), "Adequacy of Disclosure in Financial Statements," requires auditors to make the omitted disclosure in an additional paragraph of their auditors' report, if it is practicable to do so. The word *practicable* in this context means that the information can reasonably be obtained and that its inclusion in the report would not cast the auditors in the role of the preparer of the information. For example, the omission by the client of a statement of cash flows would not cause the auditors to include such a statement in their report.

Obviously a client who is reluctant to make a particular disclosure would rather make the disclosure in a footnote than to have it highlighted in the auditors' report. Therefore, very few auditors' reports actually are qualified because of inadequate disclosure. Instead, the requirements of *SAS 32* usually convince the client to include the necessary disclosure among the notes to the financial statements.

Scope limitations Limitations in the scope of the auditors' examination arise when the auditors are unable to perform a usual audit procedure. Limitations may be due either to circumstances surrounding the audit (for example, the auditors were engaged too late in the year to observe the client's beginning inventory[1]) or due to the client (for example, the client refuses to allow the auditors to send confirmations).

When a circumstance-imposed scope limitation is involved, the auditors attempt to perform alternate procedures to gather sufficient competent evidential matter. If such evidential matter is collected and the auditors believe that it is sufficient, an unqualified opinion may be issued. In situations in which alternate procedures do not provide sufficient evidence, the auditors will either qualify the opinion to reflect the scope limitation or disclaim an opinion. The qualifying language and the explanatory paragraph that distinguish the qualified report from the auditors' standard report are emphasized below.

Except as discussed in the following paragraph, we conducted our audit in accordance with generally accepted auditing standards. Those standards require that we plan and perform the audit to obtain reasonable assurance about whether the financial statements are free of material misstatement. An audit includes examining, on a test basis, evidence supporting the amounts and disclosures in the financial statements. An audit also includes assessing the accounting principles used and significant estimates made by management, as well as evaluating the overall financial

(Continued)

---

[1] Note that even though this may be the "fault" of the client, it is considered a circumstance-imposed limitation because the client is not refusing to allow the auditor to perform a procedure which is possible to perform.

statement presentation. We believe that our audit provides a reasonable basis for our opinion.

We were unable to obtain audited financial statements supporting the Company's investment in a foreign affiliate stated at $___, or its equity in earnings of that affiliate of $___, which is included in net income, as described in Note 8 to the financial statements; nor were we able to satisfy ourselves as to the carrying value of the investment in the foreign affiliate or the equity in earnings by other auditing procedures.

In our opinion, *except for the effects of such adjustments, if any, as might have been determined to be necessary had we been able to examine evidence regarding the foreign affiliate investment and earnings,* the financial statements referred to above present fairly, in all material respects, the financial position of XYZ Company as of December 31, 19__, and the results of its operations and its cash flows for the year then ended in conformity with generally accepted accounting principles.

If a circumstance-imposed scope limitation affects a "very material" portion of the financial statements or if a client imposes the limitation, a qualified opinion would be considered inappropriate, and the auditors should issue a disclaimer of opinion.

Two or more qualifications

An auditors' report may be qualified for two or more reasons. For example, the report may be qualified because of both a scope limitation and a separate problem involving accounting principles. The wording of such a report would include the appropriate qualifying language and explanatory paragraphs from both types of qualifications.

When there are several reasons for qualifying an opinion, the auditors should consider the cumulative effects of these problems. If the effect of the problems is to overshadow the fairness of the statements viewed as a whole or to prevent the auditors from forming an overall opinion, a qualified opinion would be inappropriate. In such cases, the auditors should issue either an adverse opinion or a disclaimer of opinion, depending upon the circumstances.

Adverse opinions

An adverse opinion is the opposite of an unqualified opinion; it is an opinion that the financial statements *do not* present fairly the financial position, results of operations, and cash flows of the client, in conformity with generally accepted accounting principles. When the auditors express an adverse opinion, they must have accumulated sufficient evidence to support their unfavorable opinion.

The auditors should express an adverse opinion if the statements are so lacking in fairness that a qualified opinion would not be warning enough. Whenever the auditors issue an adverse opinion, they should disclose in a separate paragraph of their report the reasons for the adverse opinion and the principal effects of the adverse opinion on the client company's financial position and operating results.

Thus, an audit report that includes an adverse opinion generally includes standard introductory and scope paragraphs, one or more explanatory paragraphs preceding the opinion paragraph and describing the reasons for the adverse opinion, and an opinion paragraph. Because the reasons for an adverse opinion are usually lengthy and complex, we illustrate only the opinion paragraph below:

> In our opinion, because of the effects of the matters discussed in the preceding paragraph, the financial statements referred to above do not present fairly, in conformity with generally accepted accounting principles, the financial position of XYZ Company as of December 31, 19XX, or the results of its operations or its cash flows for the year then ended.

Adverse opinions are rare because most clients follow the recommendations of the independent auditors with respect to fair presentation in financial statements. One possible source of adverse opinions is the actions of regulatory agencies that require organizations to use accounting practices not in accordance with generally accepted accounting principles.

Disclaimer of opinion

A disclaimer of opinion is *no opinion.* In an audit engagement, a disclaimer is required when substantial scope restrictions or other conditions preclude the auditors' compliance with generally accepted auditing standards.

Substantial circumstance-imposed scope restrictions If a scope restriction is so severe that a qualified opinion is inappropriate, the auditors should issue a disclaimer of opinion. This might happen, for example, if the auditors were engaged after year-end or if the client had not taken a physical inventory. A disclaimer issued because of a scope limitation will omit the scope paragraph of the standard report and will include an explanatory paragraph describing the scope limitation in its place. The wording of the opinion paragraph will change considerably, because the auditors are *not expressing an opinion*—rather, they are saying that *they have no opinion.* A disclaimer of opinion is illustrated below:

> We were engaged to audit the accompanying balance sheet of XYZ Company as of December 31, 198X, and the related statements of income, retained earnings, and cash flow for the year then ended. These financial statements are the responsibility of the Company's management.
>
> The Company did not take a physical inventory, stated in the accompanying financial statements at $____ as of December 31, 198X, and at $____ as of December 31, 198Y. Further, evidence supporting the cost of property and equipment acquired prior to December 31, 198X, is no longer available. The Company's records do not permit the application of other auditing procedures to inventories or property and equipment.
>
> Since the Company did not take physical inventories and we were not able to apply other auditing procedures to satisfy ourselves as to inventory quantities and the cost of property and equipment, the scope of our work was not sufficient to enable us to express, and we do not express, an opinion on these financial statements.

Disclaimers of opinion because of scope restrictions are relatively rare. The auditors should be able to foresee these types of problems in early planning stages of their engagement. The client usually will not want to incur the cost of an audit if it is apparent from the start that the auditors must issue a disclaimer of opinion.

Scope restrictions imposed by the client   The professional standards state that when client-imposed restrictions significantly limit the scope of the audit, the auditor generally should disclaim an opinion on the financial statements. Two reasons exist for this requirement. First, a disclaimer is relatively useless to the client. Therefore, the fact that the auditors may have to issue a disclaimer is a substantial deterrent to the client imposing any scope restrictions in the first place. Second, a client who imposes scope restrictions upon the auditors apparently has something to hide. An audit must be undertaken with an atmosphere of trust and cooperation. If the client is attempting to conceal information, no audit can provide assurance that all of the problems have been brought to light.

Disclaimer because of uncertainty   An unqualified opinion with an explanatory paragraph is generally appropriate for a material uncertainty that is described adequately in notes to the client's financial statements. However, the standards do not rule out the issuance of a *disclaimer of opinion* because of major uncertainty. If a disclaimer because of uncertainty is issued by the auditors, it should be in the same format as the disclaimer of opinion illustrated above.

Other disclaimers issued by CPAs   In this section, we have discussed only disclaimers of opinion issued in *audit* engagements. CPA firms issue disclaimers of opinion in many other types of engagements; these disclaimers are dealt with in Chapter 19.

Disclaimers are not alternatives to adverse opinions A disclaimer can *only* be issued when the auditors do not have sufficient information to form an opinion on the financial statements. If the auditors have *already formed a negative opinion,* the disclaimer *cannot* be used as a "way out" to avoid expressing an adverse opinion. In fact, even when auditors issue a disclaimer of opinion, they should express in explanatory paragraphs in their report *any reservations* they have concerning the financial statements. These reservations include exceptions as to generally accepted accounting principles, including disclosure. In short, the issuance of a disclaimer *can never be used to avoid warning financial statement users about problems that the auditors know to exist in the financial statements.*

Summary of auditors' reports

Figure 18–1 summarizes the types of auditors' reports that should be issued under different conditions. Figure 18–2, on the following page, summarizes the format and the modifying language found in each of the different reports.

Figure 18–1 Summary of appropriate auditors' reports

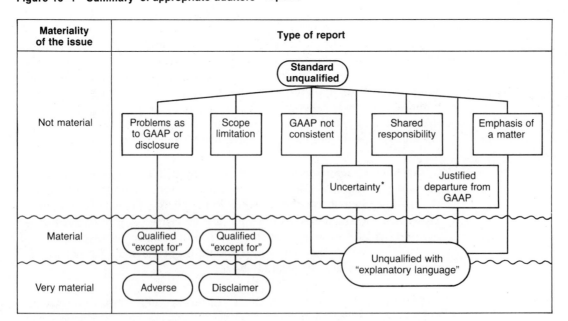

* The auditors are not precluded from issuing a disclaimer when the client is faced with a material uncertainty.

Figure 18–2

Type of report	Modifications required in the auditors' report:		
	Introductory or scope paragraph	Explanatory paragraph	Opinion paragraph
Unqualified reports:			
Shared responsibility opinions	Describe work of other auditors	None	". . . based on our audit and the report of other auditors . . ."
Uncertainty*	None	Describe uncertainty	None
GAAP not consistently applied	None	Describe change in accounting principle	None
Emphasis of a matter	None	Describe matter	None
Justified departure from official GAAP	None	Describe departure	None
Qualified opinions:			
Exception as to GAAP, including disclosure	None	Describe departure or make disclosure	". . . except for (the problem) the financial statements present fairly . . ."
Scope restriction	"Except as explained in the following paragraph . . ."	Describe scope restriction	". . . except for the effects of such adjustments . . . the financial statements present fairly . . ."
Adverse opinion:			
Very material exception as to GAAP	None	Describe substantial reasons for adverse opinion	". . . the financial statements do not present fairly . . ."
Disclaimer of opinion:			
Scope restriction (client imposed or very material)	"Except as explained in the following paragraph . . ."	Describe scope restriction and any reservations	". . . we do not express an opinion on the financial statements"

* The auditors may decide to issue a disclaimer in this situation.

Different opinions on different statements

The fourth standard of reporting states that the auditors shall express an opinion on the financial statements "taken as a whole." This phrase may apply to an entire set of financial statements, or to an individual financial statement, such as a balance sheet. Thus, it is acceptable for the auditors to express an unqualified opinion on one of the financial statements while expressing a qualified, adverse, or disclaimer of opinion on the others.

This situation is unusual, but occurs when the auditors are retained *after* the client has taken its *beginning* inventory. In this case, the auditors can satisfy themselves as to the amounts in the year-end balance sheet, but not as to the statements of income, retained earnings, and cash flows. Therefore, the auditors may be able to perform a useful service by issuing an unqualified opinion on the balance sheet and a disclaimer of opinion on the other statements.

Comparative financial statements in audit reports

The AICPA has long supported the presentation of comparative financial statements for a series of accounting periods in annual or interim reports to shareholders. Comparative statements show changes and trends in the financial position and operating results of a company over an extended period, and thus are more useful to investors and creditors than are financial statements for a single period.

When comparative financial statements are presented by the client company, the auditors should report upon the statements of prior periods if their firm has examined them. Publicly owned companies include in their annual reports the balance sheets for each of the last two years, and the related statements of income, retained earnings, and cash flows for each of the last three years. The auditors report on all of these statements. In the scope paragraph, the auditors should specify both the statements and the periods covered. An unqualified report on comparative financial statements is illustrated below:

Independent Auditors' Report

To the Board of Directors and Stockholders
XYZ Company:

We have audited the accompanying balance sheets of XYZ Company as of December 31, 1991, and 1990, and the related statements of income, retained earnings, and cash flows for the two years then ended. These financial statements are the responsibility of the Company's management.

(Continued)

> Our responsibility is to express an opinion on these financial statements based on our audits.
>
> We conducted our audits in accordance with generally accepted auditing standards. Those standards require that we plan and perform the audit to obtain reasonable assurance about whether the financial statements are free of material misstatement. An audit includes examining, on a test basis, evidence supporting the amounts and disclosures in the financial statements. An audit also includes assessing the accounting principles used and significant estimates made by management, as well as evaluating the overall financial statement presentation. We believe that our audits provide a reasonable basis for our opinion.
>
> In our opinion, the financial statements referred to above present fairly, in all material respects, the financial position of XYZ Company as of December 31, 1991, and 1990, and the results of its operations and its cash flows for the years then ended in conformity with generally accepted accounting principles.

The auditors may express different opinions on the financial statements of different years. In addition, auditors should update their reports for all prior periods presented by the client. *Updating* the report means either to re-express the same opinion or, depending upon the circumstances, to issue a different opinion from that originally issued. New information may come to light that causes the auditors to alter their original opinion. For example, the client may revise previously issued financial statements to correct a deficiency, indicating that a qualified opinion is no longer needed.

If the financial statements of prior comparative periods were unaudited or were examined by another CPA firm whose report is not presented, these facts should be disclosed in the applicable financial statements or in the current auditors' report. Any significant exceptions to the prior year's statements should be disclosed by the auditors in their current report.

An example of the introductory paragraph of a report in which another CPA firm's report on the prior year was qualified but not presented in the current year is illustrated below, with the explanatory language emphasized.

> We have audited the balance sheet of XYZ Company as of December 31, 1991, and the related statements of income, retained earnings, and cash flows for the year then ended. These financial statements are the responsibility of the Company's management. Our responsibility is to express an opinion based on our audit. *The financial statements of XYZ Company for the year ended December 31, 1990, were examined by*
>
> *(Continued)*

> *other auditors whose opinion, dated March 1, 1991, on those state-ments was qualified as being presented fairly except for the effects on the 1990 statements of the adjustments pertaining to the valuation of inventory, as discussed in Note X to the financial statements.*

Reports to the SEC

Most publicly owned corporations are subject to the financial reporting requirements of the federal securities laws, administered by the Securities and Exchange Commission (SEC). Many of the reports, or *forms,* filed with the SEC include audited financial statements for one or more years. Among the most important of these forms are the following:

1. **Forms S-1 through S-18.** These forms are the "registration state-ments" for clients planning to issue securities to the public. They are accompanied by an audited balance sheet and three years' statements of income and cash flows.
2. **Form 8-K.** This is a "current report" filed for any month in which significant events occur for a company subject to the Securities Acts. If the significant event is a business combination, audited financial statements of the acquired company often are required in the current report.
3. **Form 10-Q.** This form is filed quarterly with the SEC by publicly owned companies. It contains unaudited financial information. The companies' auditors do perform reviews of this data, but their work is substantially less in scope than an audit.
4. **Form 10-K.** This report is filed annually with the SEC by publicly owned companies. The report includes audited financial statements and other detailed financial information.

A great many audit clients are under SEC jurisdiction. Thus, any CPA firm that does an extensive amount of auditing will find itself practicing before the SEC. The preceding points represent only a brief summary of the complex reporting requirements of the SEC. Auditors dealing with these reports should be well versed on the requirements of each form, as well as in the provisions of the SEC's Regulation S-X, which governs the form and content of financial statements filed with the various forms.

The SEC has the power to enforce a high quality of audit work on financial statements submitted to it. The federal securities laws provide both civil and criminal penalties for any person, including auditors, re-sponsible for misrepresentations of fact in audited statements filed with the SEC. The auditors' legal liability under the federal securities acts was discussed in Chapter 3.

**KEY TERMS
INTRODUCED OR
EMPHASIZED IN
CHAPTER 18**

Accounting change   A change in an accounting principle, in an accounting estimate, or in the reporting entity.

Adverse opinion   An opinion that the financial statements *do not* present fairly financial position, results of operations, and cash flows, in conformity with generally accepted accounting principles.

Disclaimer of opinion   A form of report in which the auditors state that they do not express an opinion on the financial statements.

Explanatory paragraph   A paragraph inserted in an auditors' report to emphasize a matter or to explain the reasons for giving something other than an unqualified opinion.

Introductory paragraph   The paragraph of the auditors' report in which the auditors indicate that they have audited the financial statements and that the financial statements are the responsibility of management.

Last day of field work   The day upon which the auditors conclude their investigative procedures on a particular audit.

Material   Being of substantial importance. Significant enough to affect evaluations or decisions by users of financial statements. Information that should be disclosed in order that financial statements constitute a fair presentation. Involves both quantitative and qualitative criteria.

Modifying language   Language inserted in the audit report clarifying the responsibility taken by the auditors for the client's financial statements.

Opinion paragraph   The paragraph of an auditors' report that communicates the degree of responsibility that the auditors are taking for the financial statements.

Principal auditors   Auditors who use the work and reports of other independent CPAs who have examined the financial statements of one or more subsidiaries, branches, or other segments of the principal auditors' client.

Qualified opinion   A modification of the auditors' standard report, employing an *except for* clause to limit the auditors' opinion on the financial statements. A qualified opinion indicates that except for some limitation on the scope of the examination or some departure from generally accepted accounting principles, the financial statements are fairly presented.

Qualifying language   Language inserted in the opinion paragraph, and sometimes in the scope paragraph, to lessen the responsibility taken by the auditors for the client's financial statements.

Scope limitation   Something that prevents the auditors from being able to apply all of the audit procedures that they consider necessary under the circumstances. Scope limitations may be client imposed, may stem from cost considerations, or may be imposed by other circumstances.

Scope paragraph   The paragraph of an auditors' report in which the auditors describe the character of their examination.

Shared responsibility opinion   An auditors' report in which the principal auditors decide to share responsibility with other auditors who audited some segment of the client's business. The sharing of responsibility is done by making reference to the other auditors. Making reference is not, in itself, a qualification of the auditors' report.

Standard report The "standard wording" of an unqualified auditors' report, not including such modifications as emphasis of a matter, a material uncertainty, a change in accounting principle, departures from official GAAP, or a shared responsibility opinion.

Unqualified opinion An opinion that the financial statements present fairly financial position, results of operations, and cash flows, in conformity with generally accepted accounting principles.

GROUP I: REVIEW QUESTIONS

18–1. Identify the four basic types of opinions that an auditor may issue and explain when each is appropriate.

18–2. Howard Green is a partner with Cary, Loeb, & Co. On February 20, Green completed the audit of Baker Manufacturing for the year ended last December 31. It is now March 1, and Green is about to sign the auditors' report. How should Green sign and date the report?

18–3. What is meant by the term *qualifying language* in an auditors' report?

18–4. What basic conditions must be met before auditors can issue the standard auditors' report?

18–5. What is the function of notes to financial statements?

18–6. Criticize the following statement: "For all aspects of this audit we will define a 'material amount' as $500,000."

18–7. Is a shared responsibility opinion a qualified opinion? Explain.

18–8. Explain three situations in which the wording of an *unqualified* opinion might depart from the auditors' standard report.

18–9. The auditors do not believe that certain lease obligations have been reflected in conformity with generally accepted accounting principles in the client's financial statements. What type of opinion should the auditors issue if they decide that the exceptions are immaterial? Material? Very material?

18–10. Can the client change a set of financial statements to receive an unqualified opinion instead of an opinion qualified as to disclosure? Can the client change the financial statements to avoid a report modified because of uncertainty? Explain.

18–11. Why are adverse opinions rare?

18–12. What type of report should auditors issue when the client has imposed significant scope limitations?

18–13. The auditors know that the client's accounting for deferred income taxes is not in accordance with generally accepted accounting principles, but they have not been able to form an opinion on the financial statements taken as a whole. What type of report should they issue?

18–14. Only one type of qualified opinion has qualifying language in both the scope paragraph and the opinion paragraph. What is the reason for this type of qualification?

18–15. Assume that CPAs are attesting to comparative financial statements. Can the CPAs express differing opinions on the financial statements of two successive years?

18–16. Assume that CPAs are attesting to comparative financial statements. Can the CPAs change their report on the prior year's statements?

18–17. Wade Corporation has been your audit client for several years. At the beginning of the current year, the company changed its method of inventory valuation from average cost to LIFO. The change, which had been under consideration for some time, was in your opinion a logical and proper step for the company to take. What effect, if any, will this situation have on your audit report for the current year?

18–18. Describe the reports containing audited financial statements customarily filed by a company subject to the reporting requirements of the SEC.

GROUP II:
QUESTIONS
REQUIRING
ANALYSIS

18–19. Lando Corporation is a domestic company with two wholly owned domestic subsidiaries. Michaels, CPA, has been engaged to audit the financial statements of the parent company and one of the subsidiaries and to act as the principal auditor. Thomas, CPA, has audited the financial statements of the other subsidiary whose operations are material in relation to the consolidated financial statements.

The work performed by Michaels is sufficient for Michaels to serve as the principal auditor and to report as such on the financial statements. Michaels has not yet decided whether to make reference to the audit made by Thomas.

Required:
a. There are certain required audit procedures that Michaels should perform with respect to the audit made by Thomas, whether or not Michaels decides to make reference to Thomas in Michaels' auditors' report. What are these audit procedures?
b. What are the reporting requirements with which Michaels must comply if Michaels decides to make reference to the audit of Thomas? (AICPA, adapted)

18–20. The following statement is representative of attitudes and opinions sometimes encountered by CPAs in their professional practices: "It is important to read the footnotes to financial statements, even though they often are presented in technical language and are incomprehensible. The auditors may reduce their exposure to third-party liability by stating something in the footnotes that contradicts completely what they have presented in the balance sheet or income statement."

Required:
Evaluate the above statement and indicate—
a. Areas of agreement with the statement, if any.
b. Areas of misconception, incompleteness, or fallacious reasoning included in the statement, if any. (AICPA, adapted)

18–21. Rowe & Myers are the principal auditors of Dunbar Electronics. During the audit, Rowe & Myers engaged Jones & Abbot, a Canadian public accounting firm, to audit Dunbar's wholly owned Canadian subsidiary.

Required:
a. Must Rowe & Myers make reference to the other auditors in their audit report? Explain.
b. Assume that Jones & Abbot issued a qualified report on the Canadian subsidiary. Must Rowe & Myers include the same qualification in their report on Dunbar Electronics?

18–22. Criticize the following audit report:

Mr. Richard Dillon
Dillon Enterprises

    We have audited the accounts and records of Dillon Enterprises (a sole proprietorship) at April 30, 1991, and present herewith a statement of financial position as at April 30, 1991, and the related statement of income for the year then ended.
    Our examination included such tests as we considered necessary to generally satisfy ourselves as to the reasonableness of the aforementioned statements. However, we did not perform all tests required by statute so that we might issue an independent accountants' opinion.

Farley, Jackson & Co., CPAs
June 2, 1991

18–23. What type of audit report (unqualified opinion, qualified opinion, adverse opinion, disclaimer of opinion) should the auditors *generally* issue in each of the following situations? Explain.

    a. Client-imposed restrictions limit significantly the scope of the auditors' procedures.

    b. The auditors decide to make reference to the report of another CPA firm as a basis, in part, for the auditors' opinion.

    c. The auditors believe that the financial statements have been stated in conformity with generally accepted accounting principles in all respects other than those contingent on the outcome of a material uncertainty.

18–24. While performing your audit of Williams Paper Company, you discover evidence that indicates that Williams may not have the ability to continue as a going concern.

Required:

    a. Discuss the types of information that may indicate a going-concern problem.

    b. Explain the auditors' reporting obligation in such situations.

18–25. Select the best answer for each of the following and explain fully the reason for your selection:

    a. Once auditors have determined that an exception is material enough to warrant qualification on their auditors' report, they must determine if the exception is sufficiently material to negate an overall opinion. If the auditors are applying this decision process to an exception based on a departure from generally accepted accounting principles, they are deciding:

        (1) Whether to issue an adverse opinion rather than a disclaimer of opinion.

      (2) Whether to issue a disclaimer of opinion rather than an "except for" opinion.

      (3) Whether to issue an adverse opinion rather than an "except for" opinion.

      (4) Nothing, because this decision process is not applicable to this type of exception.

b. The auditors' report should be dated as of the date on which the:

      (1) Report is delivered to the client.

      (2) Field work is completed.

      (3) Fiscal period under audit ends.

      (4) Review of the working papers is completed.

c. In the report of the principal auditor, reference to the fact that part of the examination was made by another auditor is:

      (1) Not to be construed as a qualification, but rather as a division of responsibility between the two CPA firms.

      (2) Not in accordance with generally accepted auditing standards.

      (3) A qualification that lessens the collective responsibility of both CPA firms.

      (4) An example of a dual opinion requiring the signatures of both auditors.

d. Assume that the opinion paragraph of an auditor's report begins as follows: "With the explanation given in footnote 1, the financial statements referred to above present fairly. . . ." This is:

      (1) An unqualified opinion.

      (2) A disclaimer of opinion.

      (3) An "except for" opinion.

      (4) An improper type of reporting.

e. The auditor who wishes to point out that the entity has significant transactions with related parties should disclose this fact in:

      (1) An explanatory paragraph to the auditors' report.

      (2) An explanatory footnote to the financial statements.

      (3) The body of the financial statements.

      (4) The "summary of significant accounting policies" section of the financial statements.

f. When restrictions that significantly limit the scope of the audit are imposed by the client, the auditor should normally issue which of the following opinions?

      (1) Qualified.

      (2) Disclaimer.

      (3) Adverse.

      (4) Unqualified.   (AICPA, adapted)

GROUP III: PROBLEMS

18–26. Sturdy Corporation owns and operates a large office building in a desirable section of New York City's financial center. For many years, the management of Sturdy Corporation has modified the presentation of their financial statements by:

1. Reflecting a write-up to appraisal values in the building accounts.

2. Accounting for depreciation expense on the basis of such valuations.

Wyley, CPA, was asked to examine the financial statements of Sturdy Corporation for the year ended December 31, 1990. After completing the examination, Wyley concluded that, consistent with prior years, an adverse opinion would have to be expressed because of the materiality of the deviation from the historical cost principle.

Required:
a. Describe in detail the appropriate content of the explanatory paragraph of the auditor's report on the financial statements of Sturdy Corporation for the year ended December 31, 1990. ***Do not discuss deferred taxes.***
b. Write a draft of the opinion paragraph of the auditor's report on the financial statements of Sturdy Corporation for the year ended December 31, 1990.

18–27. What type of auditors' report would be issued in each of the following cases? Justify your choice.
a. Bowles Company is engaged in a hazardous trade and cannot obtain insurance coverage from any source. A material portion of the company's assets could be destroyed by a serious accident.
b. Draves Company owns substantial properties, which have appreciated significantly in value since the date of purchase. The properties were appraised and are reported in the balance sheet at the appraised values with full disclosure. The CPA firm believes that the values reported in the balance sheet are reasonable.
c. The CPA firm is examining the financial statements that are to be included in the annual report to the stockholders of Eagle Company, a regulated company. Eagle's financial statements are prepared as prescribed by a regulatory agency of the U.S. government, and some items are not presented in accordance with generally accepted accounting principles. The amounts involved are somewhat material and are adequately disclosed in footnotes to the financial statements.
d. London Company has material investments in stocks of subsidiary companies. Stocks of the subsidiary companies are not actively traded in the market, and the CPA firm's engagement does not extend to any subsidiary company. The CPA firm is able to determine that all investments are carried at original cost, and the auditors have no reason to suspect that the amounts are not stated fairly.
e. Slade Company has material investments in stocks of subsidiary companies. Stocks of the subsidiary companies are actively traded in the market, but the CPA firm's engagement does not extend to any subsidiary company. Management insists that all investments shall be carried at original costs, and the CPA firm is satisfied that the original costs are accurate. The CPA firm believes that the client will never ultimately realize a substantial portion of the investments, and the client has fully disclosed the facts in footnotes to the financial statements.   (AICPA, adapted)

18–28. Your client, Quaid Company, requests your assistance in rewriting the footnote presented below, to make it clearer and more concise.

> *Note 6.* The indenture relating to the long-term debt contains certain provisions regarding the maintenance of working capital, the payment of dividends, and the purchase of the company's capital stock. The most restrictive of these provisions requires that: (a) working capital will be maintained at not less than $4,500,000; (b) the company cannot pay cash dividends or purchase its capital stock, if after it has done so, working capital is less than $5,000,000; and (c) cash dividends paid since January 1, 1989, plus the excess of capital stock purchased over the proceeds of stock sold during the same period, cannot exceed 70 percent of net earnings (since January 1, 1989) plus $250,000. At December 31, 1992, $2,441,291 of retained earnings were available for the payment of dividends under this last provision, as follows:
>
> | | |
> |---|---:|
> | Net earnings since January 1, 1989 | $5,478,127 |
> | 70 percent of above | $3,834,688 |
> | Additional amount available under indenture | 250,000 |
> | | 4,084,688 |
> | Cash dividends paid since January 1, 1989 | 1,643,397 |
> | Retained earnings available | $2,441,291 |

Required:

Rewrite the footnote in accordance with your client's instructions.

18–29. On September 30, 1991, White & Co., CPAs, was engaged to audit the consolidated financial statements of National Motors, Inc. for the year ended December 31, 1991. The consolidated financial statements of National had not been audited the prior year. National's inadequate inventory records precluded White from forming an opinion as to the proper or consistent application of generally accepted accounting principles to inventory balances on January 1, 1991. Therefore, White decided not to express an opinion on the results of operations for the year ended December 31, 1991. National decided not to present comparative financial statements.

Rapid Parts Company, a consolidated subsidiary of National, was audited for the year ended December 31, 1991, by Green & Co., CPAs. Green completed its field work on February 28, 1992, and submitted an unqualified opinion on Rapid's financial statements on March 7, 1992. Rapid's statements reflect total assets and revenues of $7,000,000 and $8,000,000, respectively, of the consolidated totals of National. White decided not to assume responsibility for the work of Green. Green's report on Rapid does not accompany National's consolidated statements.

White completed its field work on March 28, 1992, and submitted its auditors' report to National on April 4, 1992.

Required:

Prepare White & Company's auditors' report on the consolidated financial statements of National Motors, Inc.

18-30. Roscoe and Jones, CPAs, have completed the examination of the financial statements of Excelsior Corporation as of and for the year ended December 31, 1991. Roscoe also examined and reported on the Excelsior financial statements for the prior year. Roscoe drafted the following report for 1991:

We have audited the accompanying balance sheet of Excelsior Corporation Inc. as of December 31, 1991, and the related statements of income and retained earnings for the year then ended. These financial statements are the responsibility of the Company's management. Our responsibility is to express an opinion on these financial statements based on our audit.

We conducted our audit in accordance with generally accepted auditing standards. Those standards require that we plan and perform the audit to obtain reasonable assurance about whether the financial statements are free of material misstatement. An audit includes examining, on a test basis, evidence supporting the amounts and disclosures in the financial statements. An audit also includes assessing the accounting principles used and significant estimates made by management, as well as evaluating the overall financial statement presentation. We believe that our audit provides a reasonable basis for our opinion.

In our opinion, the financial statements referred to above present fairly, in all material respects, the financial position of Excelsior Corporation as of December 31, 1991, and the results of its operations for the year then ended in conformity with generally accepted accounting principles, applied on a basis consistent with that of the preceding year.

Roscoe & Jones, CPAs
March 15, 1992

Other information:

(1) Excelsior is presenting comparative financial statements.
(2) Excelsior does not wish to present a statement of cash flows for either year.
(3) During 1991, Excelsior changed its method of accounting for long-term construction contracts and properly reflected the effect of the change in the current year's financial statements and restated the prior year's statements. Roscoe is satisfied with Excelsior's justification for making the change. The change is discussed in footnote 12.
(4) Roscoe was unable to perform normal accounts receivable confirmation procedures, but alternate procedures were used to satisfy Roscoe as to the validity of the receivables.
(5) Excelsior Corporation is the defendant in litigation, the outcome of which is highly uncertain. If the case is settled in favor of the plaintiff, Excelsior will be required to pay a substantial amount of cash that might require the sale of certain fixed assets. The litigation and the possible effects have been properly disclosed in footnote 11.
(6) Excelsior issued debentures on January 31, 1990, in the amount of

$10 million. The funds obtained from the issuance were used to finance the expansion of plant facilities. The debenture agreement restricts the payment of future cash dividends to earnings after December 31, 1990. Excelsior declined to disclose this essential data in the footnotes to the financial statements.

Required:

Consider all facts given, and rewrite the auditors' report in acceptable and complete format, incorporating any necessary departures from the standard report.

Do not discuss the draft of Roscoe's report, but identify and explain any items included in *"Other information"* that need not be part of the auditors' report. (AICPA, adapted)

18–31. Various types of accounting changes can affect the second reporting standard of the generally accepted auditing standards. This standard addresses whether accounting principles have been consistently observed in the current period in relation to the preceding period.

Assume that the following list describes changes that have a material effect on a client's financial statements for the current year.

(1) A change from the completed-contract method to the percentage-of-completion method of accounting for long-term construction-type contracts.

(2) A change in the estimated service lives of previously recorded plant assets based on newly acquired information.

(3) Correction of a mathematical error in inventory pricing made in a prior period.

(4) A change from prime costing to full absorption costing for inventory valuation.

(5) A change from presentation of financial statements of individual companies to presentation of consolidated financial statements.

(6) A change from deferring and amortizing preproduction costs to recording such costs as an expense when incurred because future benefits of the costs have become doubtful. The new accounting method was adopted in recognition of the change in estimated future benefits.

(7) A change to including the employer share of FICA taxes as "Retirement benefits" on the income statement from including it with "Other taxes."

(8) A change from the FIFO method of inventory pricing to the LIFO method of inventory pricing.

Required:

Identify the type of change that is described in each item above; state whether any modification is required in the auditors' report as it relates to the second standard of reporting; and state whether the prior year's financial statements should be restated when presented in comparative form with the current year's statements. Organize your answer sheet as shown on the following page.

For example, a change from the LIFO method of inventory pricing to FIFO method of inventory pricing would appear as shown.

Item no.	Type of change	Should auditors' report be modified?	Should prior year's statements be restated?
Example	An accounting change from one generally accepted accounting principle to another generally accepted accounting principle.	Yes	Yes

(AICPA, adapted)

18–32. Brown & Brown, CPAs, was engaged by the board of directors of Cook Industries, Inc. to audit Cook's calendar year 19X8 financial statements. The following report was drafted by an audit assistant at the completion of the engagement. It was submitted to Brown, the partner with client responsibility for review on March 7, 19X9, the date of the completion of field work. Brown has reviewed matters thoroughly and properly concluded that an adverse opinion was appropriate.

Brown also became aware of a March 14, 19X9 subsequent event which the client has properly disclosed in the notes to the financial statements. Brown wants responsibility for subsequent events to be limited to the specific event referred to in the applicable note to the client's financial statements.

The financial statements of Cook Industries, Inc. for the calendar year 19X7 were examined by predecessor auditors who also expressed an adverse opinion and have not reissued their report. The financial statements for 19X7 and 19X8 are presented in comparative form.

> To the President of Cook Industries, Inc.:
>
> We have audited the accompanying balance sheet of Cook Industries, Inc. as of December 31, 19X8, and the related statements of income, retained earnings, and cash flows for the year then ended. These financial statements are the responsibility of the Company's management. Our responsibility is to express an opinion on these financial statements based on our audit. As discussed in Note K to the financial statements, the Company has properly disclosed a subsequent event dated March 14, 19X9.
>
> We conducted our audit in accordance with generally accepted auditing standards. Those standards require that we plan and perform the audit to obtain reasonable assurance about whether the financial statements are free of material misstatement. An audit includes examining, on a test basis, evidence supporting the amounts and disclosures in the financial statements. An audit also includes assessing the accounting principles used and significant estimates made by management, as well as evaluat-
>
> *(Continued)*

ing the overall financial statement presentation. We believe that our audit provides a reasonable basis for our opinion.

In our opinion, except for the matters discussed in the first and the final paragraphs of this report, the financial statements referred to above present fairly, in all material respects, the financial position of Cook Industries, Inc. as of December 31, 19X8, and the results of its operations and its cash flows for the year then ended in conformity with generally accepted accounting principles applied on a basis consistent with that of the preceding year.

As discussed in Note G to the financial statements, the Company carries its property and equipment at appraisal values, and provides depreciation on the basis of such values. Further, the company does not provide for income taxes with respect to differences between financial income and taxable income arising because of the use, for income tax purposes, of the installment method of reporting gross profit from certain types of sales. We believe that these appraisal values are reasonable.

Brown & Brown, CPAs
March 7, 19X9

Required:

Identify the deficiencies in the draft of the proposed report. Do **not** redraft the report or discuss corrections.   (AICPA, adapted)

GROUP IV: RESEARCH AND DISCUSSION CASE

18–33. Your firm audits Metropolitan Power Supply (MPS). The issue under consideration is the treatment in the company's financial statements of $700 million in capitalized construction costs relating to Eagle Mountain, a partially completed nuclear power plant.

Seven years ago, MPS began construction of Eagle Mountain, with an original cost estimate of $400 million and completion expected within five years. Cost overruns were enormous, and construction has been repeatedly delayed by litigation initiated by the antinuclear lobby. At present, the project is little more than 50 percent complete, and construction has been halted because MPS does not have the funds to continue.

If Eagle Mountain is ultimately completed, the state utilities commission will determine the extent to which MPS may recover its construction costs through its rate structure. The commission's rulings are difficult to predict, but it is quite possible that the commission will not allow MPS to include all of the Eagle Mountain construction costs in its "rate base." If Eagle Mountain were abandoned today, none of the construction costs would be recoverable. The related write-off would amount to over 70 percent of MPS's stockholders' equity, but the company would survive.

MPS's management, however, remains committed to the completion of the Eagle Mountain facility. Management has obtained authorization from the company's stockholders to issue $500 million in bonds and additional shares of common stock to finance completion of the project. If MPS incurs this additional debt and is still not able to make Eagle

Mountain fully operational, it is doubtful that the company can avoid bankruptcy. In short, management has elected to gamble—all of its chips are riding on Eagle Mountain.

Required:

a. Discuss the arguments for and against the auditors insisting that MPS begin expensing some portion of the construction costs rather than continuing to accumulate an ever-increasing asset. Indicate the position you would take as the auditor.

b. Discuss whether the auditors should modify their report because of uncertainty as to whether or not MPS can remain a going concern. Indicate the type of opinion that you would issue. (You need not limit yourself to a "going-concern" modification.)

Suggested references:

Part a:

FASB Statement No. 19, "Financial Accounting and Reporting by Oil and Gas Producing Companies," paragraphs 15, 28.

FASB Statement No. 5, "Accounting for Contingencies," paragraph 31.
Part b:

Statement on Auditing Standards No. 59, "The Auditor's Consideration of an Entity's Ability to Continue as a Going Concern" (AU 341).

Statement on Auditing Standards No. 58, "The Auditor's Standard Report" (AU 508).

Other attestation and accounting services

Chapter 19 study objectives

After studying this chapter you should be able to:

— Distinguish between attestation and accounting services.

— Identify the types of special reports that auditors issue.

— Distinguish between accounting and review services.

— Discuss the issuance of letters for underwriters.

— Describe the nature of accountants' reports on prospective financial information and internal accounting control.

— Describe operational auditing.

In the preceding chapters, we have emphasized the CPAs' principal type of attestation engagement—audits of a company's financial statements prepared in accordance with generally accepted accounting principles. However, CPAs perform numerous other types of attestation and accounting services.

How do attestation and accounting services differ? When performing attestation engagements, the CPAs' role is one of ***providing assurance*** as to whether information is presented in accordance with the appropriate criteria. In addition to audits of historical financial statements, the attest function is currently applied to information as diverse as prospective financial information, internal control, evaluation of controls in software, and evaluation of corporate codes of conduct.[1]

---

[1] For the performance of these services, the AICPA has issued *Statement on Standards for Attestation Engagements* (New York, 1986), AU 2010.

Illustrative case

The United States' major defense contractors have made a commitment to adopt and implement a number of principles of business ethics and conduct. One requirement is that each firm annually complete the defense industry *Questionnaire on Business Ethics and Conduct.* Included are questions such as whether the corporation's Code of Ethics addresses standards that govern employee conduct in their dealings with suppliers, consultants, and customers.

The contractors agreed that each company would have its independent CPAs or a similar independent organization report upon the questionnaire. As a result the public accounting profession developed standards for association with such information. The opinion paragraph of a report on the examination of the information appears below:

In our opinion, the affirmative responses in the Questionnaire accompanying the *Statement of Responses to the Defense Industry Questionnaire on Business Ethics and Conduct for the period from January 1, 19X1 to December 31, 19X1* referred to above are appropriately presented in conformity with the criteria set forth in the *Defense Industry Initiatives on Business Ethics and Conduct,* including the Questionnaire.

In performing accounting services, CPAs provide *no explicit assurance* as to whether the information follows the appropriate criteria. The role is one of assisting the client, and not one of providing assurance to third parties about the information. An example of an accounting service is assisting the client in preparing or *compiling* its financial statements.

At this point it is helpful to distinguish between the manner in which the terms auditor and accountant are used. The term *auditor* is most frequently used when discussing a CPA's role of attesting to the annual historical financial statements and to a lesser extent the role of performing operational auditing. The term *accountant,* on the other hand, refers to CPAs when they are performing other attestation services and accounting services.

This chapter describes other attestation and accounting services. Our discussion of attestation services first presents an overall discussion and then is divided into two sections—historical financial information and other information. In the final section of the chapter we discuss various accounting services.

THE ATTESTATION FUNCTION

The generally accepted auditing standards were passed by the accounting profession to provide guidance for the performance of audits of annual historical financial statements. The expansion of the attestation function has led the accounting profession to develop more general attestation standards. These attestation standards, presented as Figure 19–1, are meant to serve as a general framework for and set boundaries for the attest function. The standards thus do not supersede other professional standards. The relationship of the attestation standards to other professional standards is illustrated in Figure 19–2.

Figure 19–1 AICPA attestation standards

General standards

1. The engagement shall be performed by a practitioner or practitioners with adequate technical training and proficiency in the attest function.
2. The engagement shall be performed by a practitioner or practitioners having adequate knowledge in the subject matter of the assertion.
3. The practitioner shall perform an engagement only if he or she has reason to believe that the following two conditions exist:
    a. The assertion is capable of evaluation against reasonable criteria that either have been established by a recognized body or are stated in the presentation of the assertion in a sufficiently clear and comprehensive manner for a knowledgeable reader to be able to understand them.
    b. The assertion is capable of reasonably consistent estimation or measurement using such criteria.
4. In all matters relating to the engagement, an independence in mental attitude shall be maintained by the practitioner or practitioners.
5. Due professional care shall be exercised in the performance of the engagement.

Standards of field work

1. The work shall be adequately planned and assistants, if any, shall be properly supervised.
2. Sufficient evidence shall be obtained to provide a reasonable basis for the conclusion that is expressed in the report.

Standards of reporting

1. The report shall identify the assertion being reported on and state the character of the engagement.
2. The report shall state the practitioner's conclusion about whether the assertion is presented in conformity with the established or stated criteria against which it was measured.
3. The report shall state all of the practitioner's significant reservations about the engagement and the presentation of the assertion.
4. The report on an engagement to evaluate an assertion that has been prepared in conformity with agreed-upon criteria or on an engagement to apply agreed-upon procedures should contain a statement limiting its use to the parties who have agreed upon such criteria or procedures.

**Figure 19–2
Relationship of
attestation standards to
other professional
standards**

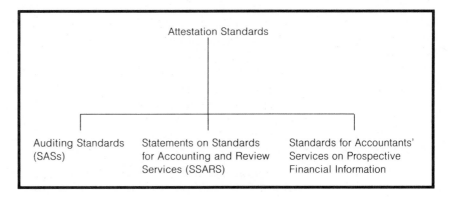

The attestation function requires both the existence of accepted criteria (such as generally accepted accounting principles) and an assertion that the information follows the criteria.

Currently, attestation standards establish three types of engagements—*examinations, reviews,* and *agreed-upon procedures.* These engagements all result in reports which provide some level of assurance with respect to whether the information being presented is in accordance with the specified criteria.

Examinations, referred to as audits when historical financial statements are involved, are designed to provide the highest level of assurance. When performing an examination, accountants select from all available procedures to gather evidence to allow the issuance of a report with a positive opinion on whether the information follows the established or stated criteria.

Reviews consist of procedures generally limited to inquiries and analytical procedures. The resulting report provides only limited assurance. Limited assurance is also referred to as negative assurance because the accountants' report disclaims an opinion on the reviewed information but includes statements such as "we are not aware of any material modifications that should be made" in order for the information to be in conformity with the appropriate criteria. Of course, when uncorrected departures are noted, the report must so indicate.

Finally, companies and specific users of the information may engage accountants to perform agreed-upon procedures. In this situation, the accountants perform those procedures requested by the user. Because the nature of these procedures has been determined by a specific party, these engagements result in reports that are restricted to use by only that party. Agreed-upon procedure reports are referred to as "limited use" (limited distribution) reports, as contrasted to "general use" reports such as reports on examinations and reviews which are made available to any third parties.

ATTESTATION
ENGAGEMENTS—
HISTORICAL
FINANCIAL
INFORMATION

Although we have thoroughly discussed audits of a company's annual financial statements in detail throughout the text, independent accountants are also associated with a variety of other types of historical financial information. In this section, we discuss special reports, audits of financial statements prepared for use in other countries, audits of personal financial statements, reviews of historical information, and "comfort letters."

Special reports

Auditors use the term *special reports* (or special-purpose reports) to describe auditors' reports issued on any of the following:[2]

1. Financial statements prepared in accordance with a comprehensive basis of accounting *other than* generally accepted accounting principles. (Example: cash-basis statements.)
2. Specific elements, accounts, or items of financial statements. (Example: amount of net sales or of working capital.)
3. Compliance with aspects of contractual agreements or regulatory requirements *related to audited financial statements.* (Example: client's compliance with a bond indenture contract.)
4. Audited financial information presented in prescribed forms or schedules that require a prescribed form of auditors' report. (Example: filings with a regulatory agency.)

Although the term *special reports* seems general, its use is restricted to those four listed above. *SAS 14* (AU 621) provides guidance to auditors in the issuance of special reports. In all such reports, the auditors must describe the scope of their engagements and clearly report their findings.

1. Other comprehensive bases of accounting Auditors are sometimes requested to audit financial statements that are prepared on a comprehensive basis of accounting *other than* generally accepted accounting principles. Auditors may accept such engagements, but they must modify their report in several ways. Most importantly, the report must describe the basis of accounting being used or refer to a footnote that provides such a description. Next, consider the first generally accepted auditing standard of reporting. Notice that this standard does not require that financial statements *be* presented in accordance with GAAP. Rather, it requires auditors to state in their report *whether* the financial statements are presented in accordance with GAAP. Thus, if the statements are prepared on some other comprehensive basis of accounting, the auditors' report must specifically state that they are *not presented in accordance with GAAP.*

---

[2] AICPA, *Statement on Auditing Standards 14,* "Special Reports" (New York, 1976), AU 621.

Finally, the auditors should be cautious about the names given to the financial statements. Names such as "balance sheet," "income statement," and "statement of cash flows" are generally associated with financial statements presented in accordance with GAAP. Consequently, the auditors should insist on more descriptive titles for statements that are presented on some other basis. For example, a cash-basis "balance sheet" is more appropriately titled, "statement of assets and liabilities arising from cash transactions." Perhaps the most common type of financial statements prepared on a basis other than GAAP is cash-basis statements. An unqualified special report on cash-basis statements is shown below. The distinctive wording has been emphasized.

We have audited the accompanying **statement of assets and liabilities arising from cash transactions** of XYZ Company as of December 31, 19X1, and the related statement of revenue collected and expenses paid for the year then ended. These financial statements are the responsibility of the Company's management. Our responsibility is to express an opinion on these financial statements based on our audit.

We conducted our audit in accordance with generally accepted auditing standards. Those standards require that we plan and perform the audit to obtain reasonable assurance about whether the financial statements are free of material misstatement. An audit includes examining, on a test basis, evidence supporting the amounts and disclosures in the financial statements. An audit also includes assessing the accounting principles used and significant estimates made by management, as well as evaluating the overall financial statement presentation. We believe that our audit provides a reasonable basis for our opinion.

As described in Note 1, these financial statements were prepared on the **basis of cash receipts and disbursements** and **are not intended to be a presentation in conformity with generally accepted accounting principles.**

In our opinion, the financial statements referred to above present fairly, in all material respects, the **assets and liabilities arising from cash transactions** of XYZ Company as of December 31, 19X1, and the **revenue collected and expenses paid** during the year then ended, **on the basis of accounting described in Note 1.**

The essence of this special report is the expression of an opinion as to whether the statements fairly present what they purport to present. The wording of the footnote mentioned in the report will vary from case to case in order to give an accurate indication of the content of the statements.

2. Specified elements, accounts, or items of financial statements Auditors may be engaged to attest to specified elements, accounts, or items in a financial statement. For example, auditors may be requested by a lessee to provide reports based solely on the company's revenue. Such reports are commonly required by the provisions of lease agreements and may be relied upon to compute lease payments that are contingent on the lessee's revenue. These engagements may involve expressing an opinion on the elements or reporting the results of agreed-upon procedures.

When the CPAs are engaged to *express an opinion* on specified elements or accounts, they modify their report to indicate the information examined, the basis of accounting used, and whether the information is presented fairly on that basis. It should be noted that materiality for such engagements is determined *in relation to the information presented;* it is generally *less* than would be used in an audit of the complete financial statements.

On occasion, the CPAs' client may request that they *not* apply the procedures necessary to express an opinion, but perform only limited *agreed-upon procedures* in substantiating elements of financial statements. For example, the landlord of a shopping center may request that the CPAs substantiate the revenue reported by tenants merely by agreeing the figures with the tenants' internal financial statements and state sales tax returns. The reason for limiting the CPAs' investigation procedures usually is to reduce the cost of the investigation.

SAS 35 (AU 622) provides guidance to CPAs who are engaged to report on the application of agreed-upon procedures to specified elements of financial statements.[3] CPAs may accept such engagements if (*a*) the parties involved have a clear understanding of the procedures to be performed and (*b*) distribution of the report is limited to those informed parties.

The accountants' report disclaims an opinion on the information but does provide *negative assurance* when the accountants' procedures do not reveal the need for any adjustments. Overall, the accountants' report should (1) indicate the information to which the procedures were applied, (2) indicate the intended limited distribution of the report, (3) enumerate the procedures performed, (4) state the accountants' findings, (5) disclaim an opinion on the information, and (6) state that the report does not extend to the financial statements viewed as a whole. Following is an example of the final paragraph of such a report in which the accountants state their findings, disclaim an opinion, and indicate that the report does not extend to the financial statements as a whole. The language of the report which provides the negative assurance has been emphasized.

---

[3] AICPA, *Statement on Auditing Standards 35,* "Special Reports—Apply Agreed-Upon Procedures to Specified Elements, Accounts, or Items of a Financial Statement" (New York, 1981), AU 622.

> Because the above procedures do not constitute an examination made in accordance with generally accepted auditing standards, we do not express an opinion on the revenues balance for the year ended December 31, 19X1. In connection with the procedures referred to above, **no matters came to our attention** that caused us to believe that the revenues balance might require adjustment. Had we performed additional procedures or had we made an examination of the financial statements in accordance with generally accepted auditing standards, other matters might have come to our attention that would have been reported to you. This report relates only to the account specified above and does not extend to any financial statements of XYZ Company, taken as a whole.

3. Compliance reports Regulatory requirements and debt agreements often require companies to provide compliance reports prepared by their independent auditors, the third type of special report. A common example of such reports is that prepared for bond trustees as evidence of the company's compliance with restrictions contained in the bond indenture. The maintenance of certain financial ratios and restrictions on the payment of dividends are provisions that are commonly contained in such documents.

Auditors may issue a compliance report *only if they have first performed an audit* of the related financial statements. The compliance report provides negative assurance as to the client's compliance with the requirements of the agreement.

> In connection with our examination, nothing came to our attention that caused us to believe that the Company was not in compliance with any of the terms, covenants, provisions, or conditions of Sections 8 to 15, inclusive, of the Indenture dated July 21, 19X1, with AAA Bank. However, it should be noted that our examination was not directed primarily toward obtaining knowledge of such noncompliance.

4. Financial information presented in prescribed forms or schedules Auditors may attest to the fairness of information supplied on prescribed forms, such as loan applications or filings with regulatory agencies. However, the language of some forms may call for the auditors to make reporting assertions that are not consistent with their function or responsibilities. In such cases, the auditors should reword the form or issue a separate report that is then attached to the form. This is the last form of special reports.

Financial statements prepared for use in other countries

A U.S.-based organization may prepare financial statements for use in other countries. For example, the organization may have a subsidiary in Germany and may prepare financial statements for that subsidiary as part of an effort to raise German capital. *SAS 51* addresses the auditors' responsibility in this situation.[4] The auditors need to be familiar with both the accounting and auditing standards used in the foreign country. They also need to obtain the client's written representations concerning the purpose and use of the statements.

When auditing the information, the auditors should follow general and field work standards of the AICPA to the extent the standards are appropriate. In addition, if so requested, the auditors may also apply the other country's auditing standards and indicate so in their report.

The report issued depends upon whether it is for use primarily outside the United States (most frequently the case) or within the United States. If it is for use outside the United States the auditors may issue (1) a U.S. report, modified as appropriate to reflect the principles of the other country, or (2) the report form of the other country, if the auditors are certain they understand the responsibilities relating to issuance of that report. In circumstances in which the report is for general use in the United States, the auditors should use the U.S. standard report, modifying it for any departures from generally accepted accounting principles. Frequently, two sets of financial statements and audit reports are prepared—one following generally accepted accounting principles for distribution in the United States, and the other following the principles of the foreign country for distribution outside the United States.

Audits of personal financial statements

In recent years, a number of politicians have had their personal financial statements audited and made public. Audited personal financial statements also may be required with large loan applications, or when an individual seeks to purchase a business using his or her personal credit.

Personal financial statements are unique in several respects. For example, the generally accepted accounting principles used in these statements are quite different from those applicable to business entities. In personal financial statements, assets are shown at their *estimated current values.* Thus, auditors must apply audit procedures that will substantiate these estimates, rather than substantiating historical costs. On occasion, the auditors may need to rely upon appraisers, following the guidelines set forth in *SAS 11* (AU 336), "Using the Work of a Specialist."

The "balance sheet" for an individual is termed a *statement of financial condition.* This statement shows the individual's *net worth* in lieu of

---

[4] AICPA, *SAS 51,* "Reporting on Financial Statements Prepared for Use in Other Countries" (New York, 1987), AU 534.

"owners' equity" and includes a liability for income taxes on the differences between the estimated current values of assets and their income tax bases. The "income statement" for an individual is called the ***statement of changes in net worth.*** In addition to showing revenue and expenses, this statement includes the changes in the estimated current values of assets and in the estimated amounts of liabilities during the period.

The accounting principles for personal financial statements are described in *Statement of Position 82-1,* issued by the Accounting Standards Division of the AICPA.[5] In addition, the AICPA has issued the *Guide for Prospective Financial Statements* to provide auditors with guidelines in auditing personal financial statements.[6] The reports issued on personal financial statements are standard in form, modified only for the change in financial statement names.

Completeness—a special problem in personal financial statements

One of the assertions that a client makes regarding its financial statements is that the statements are complete—that is, that they reflect all of the client's assets, liabilities, and transactions for the period. Determining the completeness of financial statements may be especially difficult in the audit of personal financial statements for several reasons. First, there is generally poor internal control—all aspects of each transaction usually are under the control of the individual. Second, some individuals may seek to omit assets and income from their personal financial statements. The motivation to conceal earnings or assets may stem from income tax or estate tax considerations, anticipation of a divorce, or illegal sources of income.

The omission of assets and income from financial statements is far more difficult for auditors to detect than is the overstatement of assets and income. Thus, auditors should assess the risk that an individual may be concealing assets in deciding whether to accept a personal financial statements audit engagement. If auditors conclude during an engagement that the individual is concealing assets, it is doubtful that they can ever develop confidence that their audit procedures have located all of the concealed assets. Therefore, they should withdraw from the engagement.

Illustrative case

The fact that hidden assets are difficult to substantiate can be demonstrated by the court-ordered investigation in the spectacular bankruptcy of

(Continued)

---

[5] AICPA, *Statement of Position 82-1,* "Accounting and Financial Reporting for Personal Financial Statements" (New York, 1982).

[6] AICPA, *Guide for Prospective Financial Statements* (New York, 1986).

J. David & Co., a company specializing in trading foreign currencies. When the company was forced into bankruptcy, it was suspected that over $100 million in investors' money was on deposit in various foreign banks. The bankruptcy court engaged a "Big Eight" CPA firm to track down the money. After several months of investigation, the CPA firm had only been able to locate $1 million or $2 million and was uncertain whether any additional deposits actually existed. As of this writing, the search for the $100 million is still going on.

Most engagements involving personal financial statements are **not** audits of statements presented in accordance with generally accepted accounting principles. If an individual prepares personal financial statements using a comprehensive basis of accounting **other than** GAAP, an audit might be performed for the purpose of issuing a **special report**. Comprehensive bases of accounting other than GAAP which might be used in personal financial statements include cash basis, income tax basis, and historical cost. Also, the approaches described for reviews and compilations later in the chapter are appropriate for financial statements of individuals.

Review reports on interim statements of public companies

In *Accounting Series Release No. 177,* now incorporated in *Financial Reporting Release No. 1,* the SEC requires disclosure of selected interim (quarterly financial data) in a note to the annual financial statements of public companies. The Commission permits the required note to be labeled unaudited, even though it is a part of the notes to audited financial statements. Also, the SEC urges companies it supervises to have independent CPAs *review* the unaudited interim financial data reported in Form 10-Q, which is filed with the Commission within 45 days following the end of each of a company's first three fiscal quarters.

Guidance for CPAs engaged to review interim financial data is contained in *SAS 36* (AU 722), "Review of Interim Financial Information." The objective of a review is to provide **limited** assurance that the information contained in the interim statements is in accordance with the generally accepted accounting principles. This assurance is necessarily limited, as a review consists of only limited investigatory procedures. These limited procedures do not guarantee that the CPAs will become aware of all of the significant matters that would be disclosed by an audit.

The procedures applied in a review of interim information consist primarily of inquiries and of analytical procedures. These procedures include inquiries of client management concerning the operation of the accounting system and any changes in internal control; analytical procedures applied to the interim financial data by reference to prior interim information, budgets, and other data; reading minutes of meetings of stockholders, the board of directors, and committees of the board; and obtaining written representations from management regarding the presentation and completeness of the interim data. If the accountant encounters no departures from GAAP that should be disclosed, *SAS 36* recommends the following format for reporting the results of the review (emphasis added):

We have made a ***review*** of the balance sheet and related statements of income, retained earnings, and cash flows of ABC Company and consolidated subsidiaries as of September 30, 19X1, and for the three-month and nine-month periods then ended, in accordance with ***standards established by the American Institute of Certified Public Accountants.***

A review of interim financial information consists principally of ***obtaining an understanding of the system*** for the preparation of interim financial information, ***applying analytical procedures*** to financial data, ***and making inquiries*** of persons responsible for financial and accounting matters. ***It is substantially less in scope than an examination in accordance with generally accepted auditing standards,*** the objective of which is the expression of an opinion regarding the financial statements taken as a whole. ***Accordingly, we do not express such an opinion.***

Based on our review, ***we are not aware of any material modifications*** that should be made to the accompanying financial statements for them to be in conformity with generally accepted accounting principles.

A review is *not sufficient to enable the accountants to express an opinion on the fairness of the financial statements.* Therefore, the middle paragraph of the accountants' report concludes with a disclaimer of opinion. The report would be modified, however, to describe any *departures* from generally accepted accounting principles that come to light during the review. Each page of the interim financial data should be clearly marked as "unaudited," and the report date should be the date of completion of the review.

To perform a review, the accountants must possess a high level of knowledge of the client's accounting and financial reporting practices. This knowledge provides the basis for intelligent inquiry and for interpreting the results of the analytical procedures. The accountants usually possess this knowledge as a result of having audited the client's financial statements for the prior year. If the accountants have not previously audited the client, this knowledge must be obtained prior to performing a review. Accountants performing a review must be independent of the client in accordance with the AICPA *Code of Professional Conduct.*

Review services for nonpublic companies

Audits are clearly cost justified for publicly owned corporations (public companies). The two major factors accounting for this are: (1) the separation of ownership from management in such companies and (2) economies of scale in auditing—as the size of the company increases, the cost of auditing does not increase on a pro rata basis.

For smaller companies, however, the cost of an audit may exceed the benefits derived. Consider, for example, a small company applying for a $20,000 bank loan. If the bank were to require the company to supply annual audited financial statements as a condition of the loan, the company's annual audit fees might well exceed its annual interest expense for the loan. Audits should not be performed unless the benefits are expected to exceed the cost. Therefore, companies that do not offer their securities for sale to the public (nonpublic companies) are not required to have annual audits. These companies are free to engage CPAs only for those services that the company wants and can afford.

The needs of nonpublic companies may differ significantly from those of public companies. Whereas public companies have large accounting departments that can prepare financial statements internally, a small nonpublic company might not even employ a full-time accountant. Therefore, the nonpublic company may turn to a CPA firm for the preparation of its financial statements. Whereas public companies need annual audits and quarterly reviews, nonpublic companies may only occasionally need CPAs to add credibility to their financial statements. On these occasions, a *review* may meet the company's needs at a far lower cost than an audit.

Serving the needs of small business represents a sizable part of the practice of most CPA firms. For smaller firms, especially those with only a single office, nonpublic clients may represent the firm's entire practice. To provide CPAs with guidance in meeting the accounting needs of these nonpublic clients, the AICPA has established the Accounting and Review Services Committee. This committee was given authority to set professional standards for CPAs associated with the **unaudited** financial statements of nonpublic companies. These standards are published in a sequentially numbered series called *Statements on Standards for Accounting and Review Services,* or *SSARS.*

Rule 202 of the AICPA *Code of Professional Conduct* requires members to comply with the standards set forth in the *SSARS.* Thus, the Accounting and Review Services Committee has authority comparable to that of the Auditing Standards Board and the FASB.

SSARS 1 established standards for two types of engagements involving unaudited financial statements of nonpublic companies: (1) **compilations,** which involve the preparation of financial statements with no attempt to verify the fairness of the presentation, and (2) **reviews,** which are limited investigations, far less in scope than an audit, for the purpose of providing limited assurance that the statements are presented in accordance with

GAAP.[7] The following considerations regarding screening of clients and engagement letters apply to both compilation and review services. Compilation services are accounting services that will be described in detail in the final section of this chapter.

Screening clients   One of the basic elements of quality control in a CPA firm relates to the acceptance and continuance of clients. The purpose of policies and procedures in this area is to minimize the risk of association with a client whose management lacks integrity. One means of acquiring information about a prospective client is to contact the client's predecessor CPAs.

SSARS 4 provides guidelines for accountants making certain inquiries of the predecessor accountants before accepting a compilation or review engagement.[8] These inquiries should include questions regarding the integrity of management, disagreements over accounting principles, the willingness of management to provide or to revise information, and the reasons for the change in accountants. The decision of whether or not to contact the predecessor accountants is left to the judgment of the successor CPAs. However, if inquiries are made with the client's consent, the predecessor accountants are generally required to respond.

Engagement letters for compilation and review services   Compilations and reviews are quite different from audits. The need to establish a clear understanding with the client concerning the nature of such services was dramatically illustrated in the *1136 Tenants' Corporation* case discussed in Chapter 3. CPAs must avoid the implication that they are performing audits when they are engaged to perform other services. Accordingly, it is very important that the CPAs prepare an ***engagement letter*** clearly specifying the nature of the services to be provided and the degree of responsibility the CPAs are assuming. This letter should include a discussion of the limitations of the services and a description of the accountants' report to be issued.

Review procedures   The nature of the procedures of a review for a nonpublic company parallel those for interim reviews of financial statements of public companies. A review does ***not involve a consideration of internal control*** or the obtaining of sufficient evidential matter to enable the accountants to express an opinion on the financial statements.

To evaluate the responses to their inquiries and the results of other review procedures, the independent accountants should develop a knowledge of the accounting principles and practices in the client's industry and

---

[7] AICPA, *Statements on Standards for Accounting and Review Services 1*, "Compilation and Review of Financial Statements" (New York, 1978), AR 100.

[8] AICPA, *Statement on Standards for Accounting and Review Services 4*, "Communication between Predecessor and Successor Accountants" (New York, 1981), AR 400.

a thorough understanding of the client's business. The CPAs' understanding of the client's business should include a general understanding of the company's organization, its methods of operations, and the nature of its financial statement accounts.

The procedures for a review of the financial statements of nonpublic companies include inquiries of officers and other executives; analytical procedures applied to the financial data by reference to prior financial statements, budgets, and other operating data; and inquiries concerning the actions taken in meetings of stockholders, the board of directors, and committees of the board. The CPAs' inquiries should focus on whether the financial statements are in accordance with generally accepted accounting principles consistently applied, and also on changes in business activities and significant subsequent events. Additional procedures should be performed if the accountants become aware that information may be incorrect, incomplete, or otherwise unsatisfactory. The CPAs should perform these procedures to the extent considered necessary to provide limited assurance that there are no material modifications that should be made to the statements.

Review reports A review provides the accountants with a basis for expressing *limited assurance* that they are not aware of any required material modifications to the financial statements. This limited assurance is appropriate because of the limited scope of procedures. The accountant's standard report on a review of a company's financial statements reads as follows (emphasis added):

> We have **reviewed** the accompanying balance sheet of XYZ Company as of December 31, 19XX, and the related statements of income, retained earnings, and cash flows for the year then ended, in accordance with **standards established by the American Institute of Certified Public Accountants.** All information included in these financial statements is the representation of the management of XYZ Company.
>
> A review consists principally of **inquiries** of company personnel **and analytical procedures** applied to financial data. **It is substantially less in scope than an examination in accordance with generally accepted auditing standards,** the objective of which is the expression of an opinion regarding the financial statements taken as a whole. **Accordingly, we do not express such an opinion.**
>
> Based on our review, **we are not aware of any material modifications** that should be made to the accompanying financial statements in order for them to be in conformity with generally accepted accounting principles.

The date of completion of the review procedures should be used as the date of the report, and each page of the financial statements should be labeled "See Accountants' Review Report."

Providing outsiders with *any degree* of assurance requires that the CPAs be independent. Thus, the accountants performing a review must be independent of the client.

Departures from generally accepted accounting principles Review reports are not altered in cases involving a lack of consistent application of generally accepted accounting principles or the existence of major uncertainties. However, a modification of the report is required when the accountants are aware of a material departure from generally accepted accounting principles. The departure and its effects on the financial statements, if known, is described in a separate paragraph of the review report. The following is an example of a report paragraph that discusses a departure from generally accepted accounting principles:

> As disclosed in Note 5 to the financial statements, generally accepted accounting principles require that land be stated at cost. Management has informed us that the Company has stated its land at appraised value and that, if generally accepted accounting principles had been followed, the land account and stockholders' equity would have been decreased by $500,000.

Accountants' reports on comparative statements

As with audited financial statements, accountants who have reviewed comparative statements are obliged to report on these statements. *SSARS 2* provides guidelines for writing accountants' reports on comparative financial statements.[9] In many cases, the accountants write one report covering the current year's financial statement and the financial statements presented for comparative purposes. However, if the accountants are compiling the current year's financial statements, they should not update a review report on prior financial statements. To do so would imply that the CPAs have applied review procedures up to the date of the current report. Such situations call for the accountants to reissue their prior report carrying its original date with an indication that review procedures were not extended beyond that date or to include the following reference to the prior report in the current report:

> The accompanying 19X1 financial statements of XYZ Company were previously reviewed by us and our report dated March 1, 19X2, stated that we were not aware of any material modifications that should be made to
>
> *(Continued)*

---

[9] AICPA, *Statement on Standards for Accounting and Review Services 2,* "Reporting on Comparative Financial Statements" (New York, 1979), AR 200.

> those statements in order for them to be in conformity with generally accepted accounting principles. We have not performed any procedures in connection with that review engagement after the date of our report on the 19X1 financial statements.

A reference similar to the one above should also be included in the current report when another CPA firm, whose report is not presented, reviewed the comparative financial statements.

Letters for underwriters

Investment banking firms that underwrite a securities issue often request independent auditors who examined the financial statements and schedules in the registration statement to issue a letter for the underwriters. This letter, commonly called a *comfort letter,* usually covers the following:

1. A statement as to the auditors' independence.
2. An opinion as to whether the audited financial statements and schedules in the registration statement comply in all material respects with the applicable requirements of the Securities Act of 1933 and related rules of the SEC.
3. Negative assurance as to whether any *unaudited* financial statements or condensed financial statements included in the registration statement comply with the 1933 Act and SEC pronouncements, and are presented on a basis consistent with the *audited* financial statements.
4. Negative assurances as to whether during a specified period following the date of the latest financial statements in the registration statement there has been any change in long-term debt or capital stock, or any decrease in other specified financial statement items.

Comfort letters help the underwriters in fulfilling their obligation to perform a reasonable investigation of the securities registration statement. No definitive criteria exist for the underwriters' "reasonable investigation." Therefore, the underwriters should approve the adequacy of the CPAs' procedures serving as a basis for the comfort letter. The independent auditors engaged in writing these letters should consult *SAS 49* (AU 634), "Letters for Underwriters," which contains guidelines and illustrations of typical letters.

ATTESTATION ENGAGEMENTS— OTHER INFORMATION

As the needs of society have changed over the years, CPAs have been asked to attest to a variety of information other than historical financial statements. In this section we describe three of these types of attestation engagements involving prospective financial information, internal accounting control, and operational performance.

Prospective financial statements

Securities analysts and loan officers are giving increased attention to prospective financial statements. Although such statements may be presented in various forms, accountants most frequently are involved with *financial forecasts* and *financial projections.* A financial forecast presents information about the entity's *expected* financial position, results of operations, and cash flows. On the other hand, a financial projection presents expected results, given one or more hypothetical assumptions. For example, a projection might present expected results assuming the company expanded its plant. While a forecast may be issued for general distribution, a projection's distribution should be limited to the party for whom it was prepared, for example, a bank considering loaning funds to the company to expand the plant. Both forecasts and projections must include certain minimum prospective financial statement items, background information, and a list of the major assumptions and accounting policies.[10]

Users of forecasts and projections are requesting assurances that this forward-looking information is properly presented and based upon reasonable assumptions. To provide such assurances, CPAs may be engaged to examine prospective statements, or they may get a request to perform certain agreed-upon procedures.[11]

Examinations In an examination of prospective financial statements, the accountants gather evidence relating to the client's procedures for preparation of the statements, evaluate the underlying assumptions, obtain a written representation letter from the client, and evaluate whether the statements are presented in conformity with AICPA guidelines. The report issued states whether, in the accountants' opinion, the statements are presented in conformity with AICPA guidelines and whether the underlying assumptions provide a reasonable basis for the statements. In no circumstance is an accountants' report to vouch for the achievability of the forecast or projection.

Following is an example of an unqualified forecast examination report:

> We have **examined** the accompanying forecasted balance sheet, statements of income, retained earnings, and cash flows of XYZ Company as of December 31, 1991, and for the year then ending. Our **examination was made in accordance with standards for an examination of a forecast**
>
> *(Continued)*

---

[10] Details of required disclosures are presented in the AICPA's *Guide for Prospective Financial Statements* (New York, 1986).

[11] Standards for providing these services are contained in the AICPA's *Statement on Standards for Accountants' Services on Prospective Financial Information* (New York, 1986).

> **established by the American Institute of Certified Public Accountants** and, accordingly, included such procedures as we considered necessary to evaluate both the assumptions used by management and the preparation and presentation of the forecast.
>
> In our opinion, the accompanying forecast is **presented in conformity with guidelines for presentation of a forecast established by the American Institute of Certified Public Accountants,** and **the underlying assumptions provide a reasonable basis for management's forecast.** However, there will usually be differences between the forecasted and actual results, because events and circumstances frequently do not occur as expected, and those differences may be material. We have no responsibility to update this report for events and circumstances occurring after the date of this report.

A projection report is similar, but a paragraph is added prior to the opinion paragraph indicating that the use of the report should be limited to the specified user, and the opinion paragraph explicitly states the hypothetical assumption that has been assumed.

Agreed-upon procedures   Specific users may request the accountants to perform certain agreed-upon procedures on prospective financial statements. In such circumstances the accountants may perform the procedures and provide negative assurance on the statements. For example, the report might state that "no matters came to our attention that caused us to believe that the statements should be adjusted or that the forecast is mathematically incorrect." As is the case with all engagements involving agreed-upon procedures, the report should indicate that its use is restricted to the specific users.

Reports on internal accounting control

Another special type of accountants' report is a report on the adequacy of a client's system of internal accounting control. Guidance for the issuance of such reports is provided in *SAS 30* (AU 642), "Reports on Internal Accounting Control." This type of report may be based either upon a special study or solely upon the consideration of internal control performed during an audit of the client's financial statements. In either case, the CPAs issuing the report must be independent of the client.

A report on internal accounting control differs from a *management letter* in that it is intended for distribution to others. A management letter, on the other hand, is designed exclusively for use by management and does not require the formal precautionary language used in reports to outsiders. Outsiders interested in the adequacy of a company's system of internal control are most likely to be regulatory agencies or customers who are contracting with the company on a "cost-plus" basis.

Accountants may be engaged to report on the system of internal accounting control in several ways. They may be engaged to:

1. Express an opinion on the system based upon the results of a special study. No restrictions need be placed upon the distribution of this type of report.
2. Issue a report based solely upon the auditors' consideration of internal control performed during an audit of the client's financial statements. This type of report is limited to use by management, the audit committee, and other specified outside parties.
3. Report on all or part of the system, based upon criteria established by a regulatory agency. This report is limited to use by management and the specified regulatory agency.
4. Issue a special report on all or part of the system based upon criteria described in the report. This report also is limited to use by management and specified third parties.

Expressing an opinion on internal accounting control The objectives of internal accounting control are to provide management with reasonable assurance that assets are safeguarded and financial records are reliable for the preparation of financial statements. The CPAs' opinion on internal accounting control expresses the CPAs' assurance as to whether the client's existing controls are sufficient to meet these objectives. If the CPAs' examination discloses material weaknesses in the system, those weaknesses should be described in the report.

When examining a system of internal accounting control for the purpose of expressing an opinion on the system, the CPAs should (1) plan the scope of the engagement, (2) review the system design, (3) test the operating effectiveness of prescribed procedures, and (4) evaluate the test results. These steps are similar to those used in the auditors' consideration of internal control for audit purposes, but the scope of the study differs. Tests of the system for audit purposes are not comprehensive. Consequently, the auditors' consideration of internal accounting control for audit purposes generally is not adequate to express an opinion on the system taken as a whole.

An unqualified opinion on a company's system of internal accounting control should be expressed as follows (certain precautionary language has been emphasized):

We have made a study and evaluation of the system of internal accounting control of XYZ Company and subsidiaries in effect at April 1, 198X. Our study and evaluation was conducted in accordance with standards established by the American Institute of Certified Public Accountants.

The management of XYZ Company is responsible for establishing and maintaining a system of internal accounting control. In fulfilling this re-

(Continued)

sponsibility, estimates and judgments by management are required to assess the expected benefits and related costs of control procedures. The objectives of a system are to provide management with **reasonable, but not absolute,** assurance that assets are safeguarded against loss from unauthorized use or disposition and that transactions are executed in accordance with management's authorization and recorded properly to permit the preparation of financial statements in accordance with generally accepted accounting principles.

Because of inherent limitations in any system of internal accounting control, *errors or irregularities may occur and not be detected.* Also, *projection of any evaluation of the system to future periods is subject to the risk that procedures may become inadequate* because of changes in conditions or that the degree of compliance with the procedures may deteriorate.

In our opinion, the system of internal accounting control of XYZ Company and subsidiaries in effect at April 1, 198X, taken as a whole, *was sufficient* to meet the objectives stated above insofar as those objectives pertain to the prevention or detection of errors or irregularities in amounts that would be *material in relation to the consolidated financial statements.*

The opinion should be modified if material weaknesses are disclosed by the study and evaluation, or if the scope of the study is restricted.

The CPAs' opinion should not extend to an indication that the company is in compliance with the accounting provisions of the Foreign Corrupt Practices Act. This is a legal determination rather than one made by accountants.

Restricted use reports on internal accounting control CPAs may prepare reports covering only limited areas of the client's system of internal accounting control. Such limited reports may be prepared for the exclusive use of management or some specified third party, such as a regulatory agency. These reports should describe the limited purpose of the consideration of internal control and indicate that distribution of the report is limited. The CPAs should indicate clearly that they are *not expressing an opinion* on the system taken as a whole and that weaknesses may exist that did not come to their attention.

A report on internal control based solely upon the auditors' consideration of internal control conducted during an audit of the financial statements was presented in Chapter 5.

Operational audits

The term *operational audit* refers to a comprehensive examination of an operating unit of an organization to evaluate its performance measured by the objectives set by management. A *financial audit* focuses on the measurement of financial position and results of operations, whereas an operational audit focuses on the efficiency and effectiveness of specific operating units within an organization. The operational auditor appraises the administrative controls over such varied activities as purchasing, receiving, shipping, office services, advertising, and engineering.

The major users of an operational audit report are managers at various levels. Top management needs assurance that every component of the organization is working to attain the organization's goals. For example, management needs the following:

1. Assurance that its plans (as set forth in statements of objectives, programs, budgets, and directives) are comprehensive, consistent, and understood at the operating levels.
2. Objective information on how well its plans and policies are being carried out in all areas of operations.
3. Reassurance that all operating reports can be relied on as a basis for action.
4. Information on weaknesses in administrative controls, particularly as to possible sources of waste.
5. Aid in measuring the efficiency of operations by feedback of information on the quality and cost of the work and adherence to schedule.

In attempting to meet these managerial needs, operational auditors sample the work performed to see whether it is in accordance with approved procedures. They verify the accuracy and consistency of the information contained in operating reports, and they study the format of these reports to determine whether the information is presented in a meaningful form.

Above all, the operational auditors are alert for indications of, and opportunities for, improvement. The auditors' traditional protective responsibility for seeing that the company's assets are safeguarded against fraud is expanded to a responsibility to provide protection against all kinds of waste. A company may have such strong internal control over its cash, inventories, and other personal property that it will never suffer a serious loss from fraud or theft, yet will lose substantial amounts of its assets through hidden waste.

Waste comes in many guises—for example, the waste of materials by poor planning of purchases or inadequate storage protection; waste of personnel by overstaffing or poor scheduling; waste of equipment by improper planning of requirements; waste of capital by failure to bill and collect receivables properly or maintenance of excessive inventories; improper investments or failure to use idle funds productively; and countless others. Not the least of the sources of potential waste for which the operational auditors must be alert is the temptation to recommend the imposition of too costly administrative control measures that cannot be justified by the safeguards or results achieved.

The operational audit report is issued to top management of the organization and summarizes the auditors' findings. The report generally includes suggested improvements in the internal administrative controls of the organization and a list of situations in which compliance with administrative controls is less than adequate.

Currently, economic pressures are forcing companies and government at all levels to economize, resulting in an increased demand for the information provided by operational audits. The demand has been so pronounced that operational auditing has become an extension of the internal audit function of most large companies. Also, governmental auditors engage extensively in evaluating the cost and effectiveness of various government programs. The not-for-profit nature of governmental units makes them especially suited to operational audits. To a lesser extent, the management advisory services departments of many CPA firms perform operational audits for both profit and not-for-profit enterprises. It is desirable that operational auditors have a high degree of *objectivity* with respect to the organization unit that they are auditing. However, they need not be *independent* in the sense that CPAs use this term.

ACCOUNTING SERVICES

Because CPAs are experts in accounting as well as attestation matters, many clients request CPAs to perform accounting services either in addition to, or instead of, attestation services. Reports resulting from accounting services provide *no explicit assurance* that the information constitutes a fair presentation. Because no explicit assurance is provided, accountants performing such services need *not* be independent of their client, although a lack of independence must be indicated in the accountants' report. In this section we will discuss compilations of financial statements of nonpublic companies, other "association" with the financial statements of public companies, and compilations of prospective financial information.

Compilation engagements for financial statements of nonpublic companies

A *compilation* involves the *preparation* of financial statements from the accounting records and other representations of the client. The purpose of a compilation is to organize the client's representations into the format of financial statements.

Prior to performing a compilation, *SSARS 1* requires the accountants to have knowledge of the accounting principles and practices used within the client's industry and a general understanding of the client's business transactions and accounting records. The CPAs must evaluate the client's representations in light of this knowledge.

At a minimum, the accountants should read the compiled statements for appropriate format and obvious material error. CPAs performing a compilation must not accept patently unreasonable information! If the client's information appears to be incorrect, incomplete, or otherwise unsatisfactory, the CPAs should insist upon revised information. If the client refuses to provide revised information, the CPAs should withdraw from the engagement. Beyond these basic requirements, CPAs have *no responsibility to perform any investigative procedures to substantiate the client's representations.*

Since a compilation does not enable the CPAs to form an opinion as to the fairness of the statements, their *accountants' report* should include a disclaimer of opinion. The recommended wording for an accountants' report on the compilation of financial statements is shown below (emphasis added):

We have **compiled** the accompanying balance sheet of XYZ Company as of December 31, 198X, and the related statements of income, retained earnings, and cash flows for the year then ended, in accordance with **standards established by the American Institute of Certified Public Accountants.**

A compilation is limited to presenting in the form of financial statements information **that is the representation of management. We have not audited or reviewed the accompanying financial statements and, accordingly, do not express an opinion or any other form of assurance on them.**

Each page of the unaudited financial statements should be marked "See Accountants' Compilation Report," and the accountants' report should be dated as of the completion of the compilation.

Accountants may issue a compilation report on one or more financial statements, without compiling a complete set of statements. Also, financial statements may be compiled on a comprehensive basis of accounting *other than* generally accepted accounting principles. In this case, the basis of accounting used must be disclosed either in the statements or in the accountants' report.

Departures from generally accepted accounting principles Treatment of departures from generally accepted accounting principles parallels that for reviews of financial statements. A departure from generally accepted accounting principles requires the accountants to discuss the departure in a separate paragraph in the compilation report. A lack of consistency of application of generally accepted accounting principles or the existence of major uncertainties does not lead to modification of the report.

Compilations that omit substantially all disclosures The numerous disclosures required by generally accepted accounting principles may not be particularly useful in the financial statements of a nonpublic business, especially when the statements are intended for internal use. Therefore, a nonpublic client may request CPAs to compile financial statements that omit substantially all of the disclosures required by GAAP. CPAs may compile such statements, provided that the omission is clearly indicated in the accountants' report. In such situations, the accountants should add the following last paragraph to their report:

> Management has elected to omit substantially all of the disclosures (and the statement of cash flows) required by generally accepted accounting principles. If the omitted disclosures were included in the financial statements, they might influence the user's conclusions about the company's financial position, results of operations, and in cash flows. Accordingly, these financial statements are not designed for those who are not informed about such matters.

If the client wishes to include only some of the disclosures required by GAAP, these disclosures should be labeled "Selected Information—Substantially All Disclosures Required by Generally Accepted Accounting Principles Are Not Included."

Compilations of information in prescribed forms   Prescribed forms refer to standard, preprinted forms designed or adopted by the agency to which the form is to be submitted. An example is a bank loan application. CPAs may compile financial statement information in the format required by prescribed forms. Often, the prescribed form requires that information be presented on a basis other than generally accepted accounting principles. There is a presumption that the information requested by a prescribed form meets the needs of the agency that designed the form. Therefore, the CPAs need not advise the agency of the specific departures from GAAP. *SSARS 3* suggests the following modification of the compilation report when a prescribed form calls for departures from GAAP:

> We have compiled the (identification of financial statements, including period covered and name of entity) included in the accompanying prescribed form in accordance with standards established by the American Institute of Certified Public Accountants.
>
> Our compilation was limited to presenting in the form prescribed by (name of body) information that is the representation of management. We have not audited or reviewed the financial statements referred to above and, accordingly, do not express an opinion or any other form of assurance on them.
>
> These financial statements (including related disclosures) are presented in accordance with the requirements of (name of body), which differ
>
> *(Continued)*

> from generally accepted accounting principles. Accordingly, these finan-
> cial statements are not designed for those who are not informed about
> such differences.[12]

Compilations when the CPAs are not independent Since compilations
are accounting and not attestation services, CPAs may perform them
even when they are not independent of the client. The accountants should
indicate their lack of independence by adding the following last paragraph
to their compilation report:

> We are not independent with respect to XYZ Company.

Other "association" with the financial statements of public companies

CPAs also may become "associated" with the financial statements of a
public company by assisting the company in preparing those statements,
or submitting the statements to the client or another third party. In such
cases, the CPAs have no responsibility for performing investigative procedures, except to read the statements for obvious material errors. When
CPAs are associated with the statements of a public company, but have
neither audited nor reviewed these statements, they should mark each
page of the statements as "unaudited" and issue the following disclaimer
of opinion:

> The accompanying balance sheet of XYZ Corporation as of December
> 31, 198X, and the related statements of income, retained earnings, and
> cash flows for the year then ended were not audited by us and, accord-
> ingly, we do not express an opinion on them.

If the CPAs know that unaudited financial statements are not in accordance with generally accepted accounting principles, or do not contain
adequate informative disclosures, they should insist upon appropriate
revision or should state their reservations in the disclaimer of opinion. If
necessary, the CPAs should withdraw from the engagement and refuse to
be associated with the financial statements.

CPA firm not independent Although a CPA firm that is not independent of its client cannot perform an audit or a review, it may be associated

---

[12] AICPA, *Statement on Standards for Accounting and Review Services 3,* "Compilation
Reports on Financial Statements Included in Certain Prescribed Forms" (New York, 1981),
AR 300.03.

with *unaudited* financial statements of that client. In such cases, the CPAs must issue a special disclaimer of opinion, which discloses the lack of independence. The AICPA has suggested the following language for the independence disclaimer.

> We are not independent with respect to XYZ Company, and the accompanying balance sheet as of December 31, 19X1, and the related statements of income, retained earnings, and cash flows for the year then ended were not audited by us and, accordingly, we do not express an opinion on them.

Notice that the accountant's report does not explain *why* the CPA firm is not independent of the client. The Auditing Standards Board believes it would be confusing to users of the report if these reasons were spelled out.

Compilations of prospective financial statements

In addition to examining prospective statements, accountants may assist their clients in compiling the forward-looking data. A compilation

Figure 19–3 Services performed by CPAs

	Compilation	Agreed-upon procedures	Review	Examination
Type of service	Accounting	Attest	Attest	Attest
Explicit assurance	None	Limited (negative)	Limited (negative)	Opinion
Distribution of report	Not limited	Limited to parties involved	Not limited	Not limited
Minimum procedures	Read statements	Agreed-upon	Inquiry and analytical procedures	Collection of sufficient evidence to support opinion
Comments	Referred to as "unaudited statements" for public companies		Available only for historical financial information	Referred to as "audits" for financial statements

consists of assembling, to the extent necessary, the prospective financial information, performing various inquiry procedures, considering whether there are obvious inconsistencies in assumptions or mathematical errors, and obtaining a representations letter from the client. Because this is an accounting and not an attestation service, the report issued provides no explicit assurance with respect to the presentation of the statements or the reasonableness of the underlying assumptions.

SUMMARY OF REPORTING

At this point you might feel overwhelmed by what might seem to be a bewildering array of services performed by CPAs. The role of accountants has changed significantly over the years to meet society's demands for new types of services. Future modifications of accountant responsibility might be expected to be built around the compilation, agreed-upon procedures, review, and examination distinctions discussed in this chapter. Figure 19–3 (opposite page), summarizes the key aspects of each of these forms of services.

KEY TERMS INTRODUCED OR EMPHASIZED IN CHAPTER 19

Attestation   To provide assurance as to whether information is presented in accordance with appropriate criteria. That is, to bear witness as to its reliability and fairness.

Comfort letter   A letter issued by the independent auditors to the underwriters of securities registered with the SEC under the Securities Act of 1933. Comfort letters deal with such matters as the auditors' independence and the compliance of unaudited data with requirements of the SEC.

Compilation   An accounting service that involves the preparation of information from client records. No assurance is provided in a compilation.

Financial forecast   Prospective financial statements that present an entity's expected financial position, results of operations, and cash flows for one or more future periods.

Financial projection   Prospective financial statements that present expected results, given one or more hypothetical assumptions.

Limited assurance (negative assurance)   Assurance provided by CPAs who have performed an attestation service of a lesser scope than an audit. Substantially less assurance than is provided by an audit.

Management letter   A report to management containing the auditors' recommendations for correcting any deficiencies disclosed by their consideration of internal control. In addition to providing management with useful information, a management letter may also help limit auditor liability in the event that an internal control weakness subsequently results in a loss by the client. See also, report on internal control.

Negative assurance   An assertion by CPAs that after applying limited investigative techniques to certain information, they are not aware of the need to modify the presentation of the information. Equivalent to limited assurance.

Nonpublic company   A company other than one whose securities are traded on a public market or that makes a filing with a regulatory agency in preparation for sale of securities on a public market.

Prospective financial statements   Either financial forecasts or financial projections, including the summaries of significant assumptions and accounting policies.

Public company   A company whose stock is traded on a public market or a company in the process of registering its stock for public sale.

Report on internal control   This type of report may be based either upon a special study of internal control or based solely upon the auditors' consideration of internal control performed during an audit of the client's financial statements.

Review   A form of attestation, using primarily analytical and inquiry procedures for the purpose of expressing limited assurance that information is presented in accordance with appropriate criteria.

Special report   An auditors' report issued on any of the following: (1) financial statements prepared on a comprehensive basis of accounting other than GAAP, (2) elements of financial statements, (3) compliance with terms of an agreement, or (4) audited information presented in prescribed forms.

GROUP I: REVIEW QUESTIONS

19–1. Evaluate this statement: Auditors perform attestation services and accountants perform accounting services.

19–2. When the auditors are performing an audit of financial statements, do the attestation standards apply? Explain.

19–3. Distinguish among forms of attestation that are for ''general'' versus ''limited'' use or distribution.

19–4. Evaluate this statement: ''All companies should be audited annually.''

19–5. Can auditors express an unqualified opinion on financial statements that are not presented in accordance with generally accepted accounting principles? Explain.

19–6. In communications with clients, should CPAs refer to themselves as auditors or as accountants? Explain.

19–7. Does the issuance of a special report based on agreed-upon procedures indicate an audit engagement or an accounting service? Why?

19–8. Jane Wilson has prepared personal financial statements in which her assets are valued at her historical cost, less appropriate depreciation. Is this presentation in conformity with generally accepted accounting principles? Can a CPA firm audit these statements and issue an unqualified opinion?

19–9. What are the procedures performed during a review of the quarterly financial statements of a public company?

19–10. Discuss the possible forms of audit reports for a U.S.-based client that is issuing a report for use primarily outside the U.S.

19–11. What types of services may be performed by CPAs with respect to the financial statements of nonpublic companies?

19–12. How does a review of the financial statements of a nonpublic company differ from an audit?

19–13. What are the types of procedures performed during the review of the financial statements of a nonpublic company?

19–14. Are engagement letters needed for accounting and review services? Explain.

19–15. Can the CPAs report on a nonpublic client's financial statements that omit substantially all disclosures required by generally accepted accounting principles? Explain.

19–16. What should the accountants do if they discover that the financial statements they are compiling contain a material departure from generally accepted accounting principles?

19–17. What is the purpose of a comfort letter? Discuss.

19–18. What is the objective of an examination of a financial forecast?

19–19. Can CPAs issue an opinion on internal control as the result of their consideration of internal control performed during an audit? Explain.

19–20. List the steps involved in expressing an opinion on a system of internal accounting control.

19–21. What is an operational audit?

19–22. Who is the major user of operational audit reports? Discuss.

19–23. List two types of engagements discussed in this chapter that may be performed by a CPA who is not independent of the client.

GROUP II: QUESTIONS REQUIRING ANALYSIS

19–24. Rose & Co., CPAs, has satisfactorily completed the examination of the financial statements of Dale, Booster & Co., a partnership, for the year ended December 31, 198X. The financial statements that were prepared on the entity's income tax (cash) basis include footnotes that indicate that the partnership was involved in continuing litigation of material amounts relating to alleged infringement of a competitor's patent. The amount of damages, if any, resulting from this litigation could not be determined at the time of completion of the engagement. The prior years' financial statements were not presented.

Required:
Prepare an auditors' unqualified special report on the financial statements of Dale, Booster & Co. Your report should include two "explanatory paragraphs": one to describe the basis of accounting used, and another to emphasize the matter of the pending litigation. Address your report to Dale, Booster & Co. (AICPA, adapted)

19–25. "When performing accounting services, accountants provide no assurance in their reports. These reports may therefore be considered "special reports."

Required:
a. Do you agree or disagree with the above statement? Explain.
b. Discuss the major types of special reports.
c. Provide an example of an accounting service.

19–26. The attestation standards present three basic forms of association with information.
a. List these three types of association.
b. Discuss the type of assurance provided by each of these forms of association.

19–27. An accountants' report was appended to the financial statements of Worthmore, Inc., a public company. The statements consisted of a balance sheet as of November 30 and statements of income and retained earnings for the year then ended. The first three paragraphs of the report contained the wording of the standard unqualified report, and a fourth paragraph read as follows:

> The wives of two partners of our firm owned a material investment in the outstanding common stock of Worthmore, Inc. during the fiscal year ending November 30. The aforementioned individuals disposed of their holdings of Worthmore, Inc. on December 3 in a transaction that did not result in a profit or a loss. This information is included in our report in order to comply with certain disclosure requirements of the *Code of Professional Conduct* of the American Institute of Certified Public Accountants.
>
> Bell & Davis
> Certified Public Accountants

Required:
a. Was the CPA firm of Bell & Davis independent with respect to the examination of Worthmore, Inc.'s financial statements? Explain.
b. Do you find Bell & Davis' report satisfactory? Explain.

(AICPA, adapted)

19–28. Many CPA firms are engaged to report on specified elements, accounts, and items of financial statements.

Required:
a. Discuss the two types of reports that may be provided for specified elements, accounts, and items of financial statements.
b. Why should reports on the application of agreed-upon procedures to information be restricted as to their distribution?

19–29. You have been engaged by the management of Pippin, Inc., a nonpublic company, to review the company's financial statements for the year ended December 31, 198X. To prepare for the engagement you consult the *Statements on Standards for Accounting and Review Services.*

Required:
a. Discuss the procedures required for the performance of a review of financial statements.
b. Explain the content of the report on a review of financial statements.
c. Discuss your responsibilities if you find that the financial statements contain a material departure from generally accepted accounting principles.

19–30. You have been asked by Ambassador Hardware Co., a small nonpublic company, to submit a proposal for the audit of the company. After performing an investigation of the company, including its management and accounting system, you advise the president of Ambassador that the audit fee will be approximately $10,000. Ambassador's president was somewhat surprised at the fee, and after discussions with members of the board of directors, he concluded that the company could not afford an audit at this time.

Required:

a. Discuss management's alternatives to having their financial statements audited in accordance with generally accepted auditing standards.

b. What should Ambassador's management consider when selecting the type of service that you should provide? Explain.

19–31. Andrew Wilson, CPA, has assembled the financial statements of Texas Mirror Co., a small public company. He had not performed an audit of the financial statements in accordance with generally accepted auditing standards. Wilson is confused about the standards applicable to this type of engagement.

Required:

a. Explain where Wilson should look for guidance concerning this engagement.

b. Discuss the concept of association with financial statements.

c. Explain Wilson's responsibilities with respect to a preparation of unaudited financial statements.

19–32. You are a CPA retained by the manager of a cooperative retirement village to do write-up work. You are expected to compile unaudited financial statements accompanied by a standard compilation report. In performing the work you discover that there are no invoices to support $25,000 of the manager's claimed disbursements. The manager informs you that all the disbursements are proper.

Required:

Explain the steps that you should take in this situation.

(AICPA, adapted)

19–33. In connection with a public offering of first-mortgage bonds by Guizzetti Corporation, the bond underwriter has asked Guizzetti's CPAs to furnish them with a comfort letter giving as much assurance as possible on Guizzetti's unaudited financial statements for the three months ended March 31. The CPAs had expressed an unqualified opinion on Guizzetti's financial statements for the year ended December 31, the preceding year; they also performed a review of Guizzetti's financial statements for the three months ended March 31. Nothing has come to their attention that would indicate that the March 31 statements are not properly presented.

Required:

a. Explain what can be stated about the unaudited financial statements in the letter.

b. Discuss other matters that are typically included in comfort letters.

19–34. The management of Williams Co. is considering issuing corporate debentures. To enhance the marketability of the bond issue, management has decided to include a financial forecast in the prospectus. Williams management has requested that your CPA firm examine the financial forecast to add credibility to the prospective information.

Required:

a. Explain what is involved in an examination of a financial forecast.

b. Discuss the content of the report on an examination of a financial forecast. (Do not write a report.)

19–35. You have been performing a financial audit for Wallace Shoe Co. for several years. The president of Wallace Shoe Co. has recently read an article on the benefits of operational auditing and has come to you with several questions about such audits.

Required:

a. Explain the difference between a financial audit and an operational audit.

b. Discuss the major users of operational audit reports.

c. Discuss the types of auditors that perform operational audits.

19–36. Select the best answer for each of the following and explain fully the reason for your selection.

a. When an auditor issues an unqualified opinion on an entity's system of internal accounting control, it is implied that the—

(1) Possibility of management or employee fraud is remote.

(2) The entity has not violated the provisions of the Foreign Corrupt Practices Act.

(3) The entity's financial statements have been audited.

(4) Financial records are sufficiently reliable to permit the preparation of financial statements.

b. Special reports are appropriate for—

(1) Limited reviews of interim statements.

(2) Compliance with regulatory requirements related to audited financial statements.

(3) Forecasts.

(4) Feasibility studies.

c. Which of the following procedures is *not* included in a review engagement of a nonpublic entity?

(1) Inquiries of management.

(2) Inquiries regarding events subsequent to the balance sheet date.

(3) Any procedures designed to identify relationships among data that appear to be unusual.

(4) A consideration of internal control.

d. Which of the following best describes the operational audit?

(1) It requires constant review by internal auditors of the administrative controls as they relate to the operations of the company.

(2) It concentrates on implementing financial and accounting control in a newly organized company.

(3) It concentrates on seeking out aspects of operations in which waste would be reduced by the introduction of controls.

(4) It attempts and is designed to verify the fair presentation of a company's results of operations.

e. In which of the following reports should a CPA *not* express negative or limited assurance?

(1) A standard compilation report on financial statements of a nonpublic entity.

(2) A standard review report on financial statements of a nonpublic entity.

(3) A standard review report on interim financial statements of a public entity.

(4) A standard comfort letter on financial information included in a registration statement of a public entity.

f. Comfort letters are ordinarily signed by the:

(1) Independent auditor.

(2) Client.

(3) Client's lawyer.

(4) Internal auditor. (AICPA, adapted)

GROUP III: PROBLEMS

19–37. On March 12, 19X5, Brown & Brown, CPAs, completed the audit engagement of the financial statements of Modern Museum, Inc. for the year ended December 31, 19X4. Modern Museum presents comparative financial statements on a modified cash basis. Assets, liabilities, fund balances, support, revenues, and expenses are recognized when cash is received or disbursed, except that Modern includes a provision for depreciation of buildings and equipment. Brown & Brown believes that Modern's three financial statements, prepared in accordance with a comprehensive basis of accounting other than generally accepted accounting principles, are adequate for Modern's needs and wishes to issue an auditors' special report on the financial statements. Brown & Brown has gathered sufficient competent evidential matter in order to be satisfied that the financial statements are fairly presented according to the modified cash basis. Brown & Brown audited Modern's 19X3 financial statements and issued the auditors' special report expressing an unqualified opinion.

Required:

Draft the auditors' report to accompany Modern's comparative financial statements. (AICPA, adapted)

19–38. Jiffy Clerical Services is a company that furnishes temporary office help to its customers. The company maintains its accounting records on a basis of cash receipts and cash disbursements. You have audited the company for the year ended December 31, 198X, and have concluded that the company's financial statements represent a fair presentation on the basis of accounting described above.

Required:

a. Draft the unqualified auditors' report you would issue covering the financial statements (a statement of assets and liabilities and the related statement of revenue collected and expenses paid) for the year ended December 31, 198X.

b. Briefly discuss and justify your modifications of the conventional standard auditors' report on accrual-basis statements.

19–39. Norman Lewis, an inexperienced member of your staff, has compiled the financial statements of Williams Grocery. He has submitted the following report for your review:

> The accompanying financial statements have been compiled by us. A compilation is an accounting service, but we also applied certain analytical procedures to the financial data.
>
> As explained in Note 3, the Company changed accounting principles accounting for its inventories. We have not audited or reviewed the accompanying financial statements, but nothing came to our attention to indicate that they are in error.

Required:

Describe the deficiencies in the report, give reasons why they are deficiencies, and briefly discuss how the report should be corrected. Do not discuss the addressee, signature, and date. Organize your answer sheet as follows:

Deficiency	Reason	Correction

19–40. Upon completion of their consideration of internal control for the audit of the financial statements of Weaver Corporation, the following opinion on internal control was issued by Milburn and Jones, CPAs:

> To the Board of Directors of Weaver Corporation:
>
> We have obtained an understanding of the system of internal control of Weaver Corporation. Our consideration of internal control was conducted as a part of our audit of Weaver Corporation.
>
> Our management advisory division established Weaver Corporation's system of internal control, and we take responsibility for maintaining the system.
>
> In our opinion, the system of internal control of Weaver Corporation is sufficient to prevent or detect all errors and irregularities. We also believe that the system is adequate to assure that Weaver Corporation is not in violation of the internal accounting control provisions of the Foreign Corrupt Practices Act.
>
> Milburn and Jones, CPAs
> April 23, 1990

Required:

List and explain the deficiencies and omissions in the opinion and explain how it might be corrected. Organize your answer as follows:

Deficiency or omission	Correction

19–41. The financial statements of Tiber Company have never been audited by independent CPAs. Recently Tiber's management asked Anthony Burns, CPA, to provide an opinion on Tiber's internal control; this management advisory services engagement will not include an examination of Tiber's financial statements. Following completion of his consideration of internal control, Burns plans to prepare a report that is consistent with the requirements of *SAS 30* (AU 642) dealing with reports on internal control.

Required:

a. Describe the inherent limitations that should be recognized in considering the potential effectiveness of any system of internal control.

b. Explain and contrast the consideration of internal control that Burns might make as part of an examination of financial statements with his study and evaluation to express an opinion on the system, covering each of the following:

(1) Objectives of review or study.

(2) Scope of review or study.

(3) Nature and content of reports.

Organize your answer for part (b) as follows:

Examination of financial statements	Opinion on internal accounting control
1. Objective	1. Objective
2. Scope	2. Scope
3. Report	3. Report

(AICPA, adapted)

19–42. The limitations on the CPAs' professional responsibilities when they are associated with unaudited financial statements are often misunderstood. These misunderstandings can be substantially reduced if the CPAs follow professional pronouncements in the course of their work, and take other appropriate measures.

Required:

The following list describes seven situations CPAs may encounter, or contentions they may have to deal with in their association with and preparation of **unaudited** financial statements. Briefly discuss the extent of the CPAs' responsibilities and, if appropriate, the actions they should take to minimize any misunderstandings. Number your answers to correspond with the numbering in the following list.

1. The CPAs were engaged by telephone to perform write-up work including the compilation of financial statements. The client believes that the CPAs have been engaged to audit the financial statements and examine the records accordingly.

2. A group of investors who own a farm that is managed by an indepen-

dent agent engage CPAs to compile quarterly unaudited financial statements for them. The CPAs prepare the financial statements from information given to them by the independent agent. Subsequently, the investors find the statements were inaccurate because their independent agent was embezzling funds. They refuse to pay the CPAs' fee and blame them for allowing the situation to go undetected, contending that they should not have relied on representations from the independent agent.

3. In comparing the trial balance with the general ledger, the CPAs find an account labeled Audit Fees in which the client has accumulated the CPAs' quarterly billings for accounting services including the compilation of quarterly unaudited financial statements.

4. Unaudited financial statements for a public company were accompanied by the following letter of transmittal from the CPAs:

> We are enclosing your company's balance sheet as of June 30, 19X9, and the related statements of income and retained earnings and changes in financial position for the six months then ended to which we have performed certain auditing procedures.

5. To determine appropriate account classification, the CPAs examined a number of the client's invoices. They noted in their working papers that some invoices were missing, but did nothing further because it was felt that the invoices did not affect the unaudited financial statements they were compiling. When the client subsequently discovered that invoices were missing, he contended that the CPAs should not have ignored the missing invoices when compiling the financial statements and had a responsibility to at least inform him that they were missing.

6. The CPAs compiled a draft of unaudited financial statements from the client's records. While reviewing this draft with their client, the CPAs learned that the land and building were recorded at appraisal value.

7. The CPAs are engaged to compile the financial statements of a non-public company. During the engagement, the CPAs learn of several items that by generally accepted accounting principles would require adjustments of the statements and footnote disclosure. The controller agrees to make the recommended adjustments to the statements, but says that she is not going to add the footnotes because the statements are unaudited.

(AICPA, adapted)

19–43. Loman, CPA, who has examined the financial statements of the Broadwall Corporation, a publicly held company, for the year ended December 31, 19X6, was asked to perform a review of the financial statements of Broadwall Corporation for the period ending March 31, 19X7. The engagement letter stated that a review does not provide a basis for the expression of an opinion.

Required:

a. Explain why Loman's review will **not** provide a basis for the expression of an opinion.

b. What are the review procedures Loman should perform, and what is the purpose of each procedure? Structure your response as follows:

Procedure	Purpose of procedure

(AICPA, adapted)

19–44. Brown, CPA, received a telephone call from Calhoun, the sole owner and manager of a small corporation. Calhoun asked Brown to compile the financial statements for the corporation and emphasized that the statements were needed in two weeks for external financing purposes. Calhoun was vague when Brown inquired about the intended use of the statements. Brown was convinced that Calhoun thought Brown's work would constitute an audit. To avoid confusion, Brown decided not to explain to Calhoun that the engagement would only be to compile the financial statements. Brown, with the understanding that a substantial fee would be paid if the work was completed in two weeks, accepted the engagement and started the work at once.

During the course of the work, Brown discovered an accrued expense account labeled Professional Fees and learned that the balance in the account represented an accrual for the cost of Brown's services. Brown suggested to Calhoun's bookkeeper that the account name be changed to Fees for Limited Audit Engagement. Brown also reviewed several invoices to determine whether accounts were being properly classified. Some of the invoices were missing. Brown listed the missing invoice numbers in the working papers with a note indicating that there should be a followup on the next engagement. Brown also discovered that the available records included the fixed asset values at estimated current replacement costs. Based on the records available, Brown compiled a balance sheet, income statement, and statement of stockholders' equity. In addition, Brown drafted the footnotes, but he decided that any mention of the replacement costs would only mislead the readers. Brown suggested to Calhoun that readers of the financial statements would be better informed if they received a separate letter from Calhoun explaining the meaning and effect of the estimated replacement costs of the fixed assets. Brown mailed the financial statements and footnotes to Calhoun with the following note included on each page:

> The accompanying financial statements are submitted to you without complete audit verification.

Required:

Identify the inappropriate actions of Brown, and indicate what Brown should have done to avoid each inappropriate action.

Organize your answer sheet as follows:

Inappropriate action	What Brown should have done to avoid inappropriate action

(AICPA, adapted)

GROUP IV: RESEARCH AND DISCUSSION CASE

19–45. You are a young CPA just starting your own practice in Hollywood, California, after five years' experience with a "Big Eight" firm. You have several connections in the entertainment industry and hope to develop a practice rendering income tax, auditing, and accounting services to celebrities and other wealthy clients.

One of your first engagements is arranged by John Forbes, a long-established business manager for a number of celebrities and a personal friend of yours. You are engaged to audit the personal statement of financial condition (balance sheet) of Dallas McBain, one of Forbes' clients. McBain is a popular rock star, with a net worth of approximately $10 million. However, the star also has a reputation as an extreme recluse who is never seen in public except at performances.

Forbes handles all of McBain's business affairs, and all of your communications with McBain are through Forbes. You have never met McBain personally and have no means of contacting the star directly. All of McBain's business records are maintained at Forbes' office. Forbes also issues checks for many of McBain's personal expenses, using a check-signing machine and a facsimile plate of McBain's signature.

During the audit, you notice that during the year numerous checks totaling approximately $240,000 have been issued payable to Cash. In addition, the proceeds of a $125,000 sale of marketable securities was never deposited in any of McBain's bank accounts. In the accounting records, all of these amounts have been charged to the account entitled "Personal Living Expenses." There is no further documentation of these disbursements.

When you bring these items to Forbes' attention, he explains that celebrities such as McBain often spend a lot of cash supporting various "hangers-on," whom they don't want identified by name. He also states, "Off the record, some of these people also have some very expensive habits." He points out, however, that you are auditing only the statement of assets and liabilities, not McBain's revenue or expenses. Furthermore, the amount of these transactions is not material in relation to McBain's net worth.

Required:

a. Discuss whether or not the undocumented disbursements and the missing securities' proceeds should be of concern to you in a balance sheet only audit.

    b. Identify the various courses of action that you might at least consider under these circumstances. Explain briefly the arguments supporting each course of action.

    c. Explain what you would do and justify your decision.

    d. Assume that you are a long-established CPA, independently wealthy, and that the McBain account represents less than 5 percent of the annual revenue of your practice. Would this change in circumstances affect your conclusion in part (*c*)? Discuss.

Suggested references:

This textbook, discussion of *1136 Tenants Corporation* case, pages 95–97; "Audit of Sole Proprietorships and Partnerships," pages 592–93; and "Audits of Personal Financial Statements," pages 686–88.

AICPA, *Personal Financial Statements Guide* (New York, 1983), pages 12–13 and 25–26.

Statement on Auditing Standards 60, "Communication of Internal Control Structure Related Matters Noted in an Audit" (AU 325).

Index

Index